Rick Steves®

EUROPE
THROUGH THE
BACK DOOR

CONTENTS

Rick Steves®

EUROPE
THROUGH THE
BACK DOOR

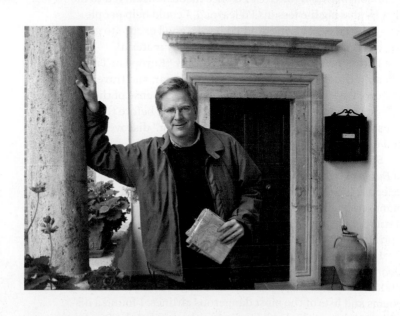

Preface

This guidebook, based on lessons learned from more than 30 years of exploring Europe, is your handbook for traveling smart. With the tips and advice I've assembled here, you can plan, create, and enjoy a trip that will live up to your dreams.

My first five trips to Europe were purely for kicks. I made my share of blunders—I missed train connections, wasted money on dreary hotels and bad restaurants, and showed up at sights after they had closed. But each new trip became smoother than the last. It was clear: I was learning from my mistakes.

While traveling, I saw others making the same costly and time-consuming errors that I'd once made. It occurred to me that by sharing the lessons I'd learned, I could help people enjoy better, easier trips. And I'd have a good excuse to go back to Europe every summer to update my material.

Throughout the late 1970s I taught my "European Travel Cheap" class in Seattle during the school year, and traveled to Europe every summer. I developed a good sense of the fears and apprehensions that troubled people before their trips, and I gathered lots of great "Back Door" discoveries and experiences throughout Europe.

So, in 1980, with all that material, writing the first edition of *Europe Through the Back Door* was easy. I rented an IBM Selectric typewriter, sweet-talked my girlfriend into typing the manuscript, and cajoled my roommate into sketching the illustrations. I gingerly delivered that precious first pile of pages to a printer, and, on my 25th birthday, picked up 2,500 copies.

I sold all those first editions of *Europe Through the Back Door* through my travel classes. With the second edition, in 1981, I got a bit more professional, taking out my personal poems and lists of the most dangerous airlines. I found a distributor who got the book into stores throughout the Pacific Northwest. The third edition, although it was typeset, still looked so simple and amateurish that reviewers repeatedly mistook it for a "prepublication" edition.

All this time I was supporting myself as a piano teacher. But my recital hall was gradually becoming a travel lecture classroom, and I needed to choose what I would teach: Europe or music. I chose Europe, let my piano students go, and began building my travel business. At the same time, an actual publisher agreed to bring out the fourth edition of *Europe Through the Back Door.* Happily, I could now focus on researching and writing rather than publishing.

Since then I've kept to the same teaching mission— although now this mission is amplified by 100 workmates at my company in Edmonds, Washington, and by technology I never could have dreamed of back when I started. Working together, we've developed a wide-ranging program of travel material—guidebooks, guided bus tours, a public television series, a weekly public-radio program, information-packed apps, personally designed gear, a generous website, and more. Everything we do is designed to inform and inspire American tourists to turn their travel dreams into smooth and afford-able reality—and this book is the foundation of our work.

My favorite part of this job remains my on-the-ground research. I spend four months every year in Europe: April and May in the Mediterranean, July and August north of the Alps. I use some of that time to film my TV series, but for the majority of it, I'm alone, eyes and ears open: exploring new places, revisiting old favorites, tracking down leads, collect-ing experiences, and updating my guidebooks. When I get home, I can't wait to splice the lessons I've learned from my most recent travels into the book you're about to read.

I still make mistakes with gusto—and take careful notes. Working up a big thirst after a long day of sightseeing in Naples, I come back to the hotel, order a "margarita"...and get a pizza. Sometimes I pretend to screw up, just to see what'll happen. When I get ripped off, I celebrate—the scammer doesn't know who he just ripped off. I'll learn that scam, and pack that lesson—with all the others—into this book.

You can be your own top-notch tour guide—simply equip yourself with the best information. Expect to travel smart... and you will.

Happy travels!

Rick Steves

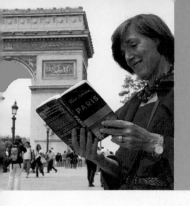

Introduction

Why do I find Europe so endlessly fun and entertaining? Because I know where to look. And I know how to experience more by spending less.

Europe is my beat. For more than three decades, it's been my second home. Sure, I love the biggies...from the Eiffel Tower to "Mad" King Ludwig's castles to Michelangelo's *David*. But even more than the must-see sights, I value the Back Door experiences that Europe has to offer: meeting pilgrims at Santiago, sampling stinky cheese in a Czech town, pondering an ancient stone circle in Dartmoor, and cheering for a high-school soccer team with new friends in Turkey. Looking back on my European travels, having spent much of my adult life living out of a carry-on-sized bag, I'm thankful that, for me, Europe never gets old. When I first started traveling, I wanted to "feel the fjords and caress the castles"... and I still do. My curiosity will always take me back to that wonderful continent.

But many American travelers miss the real Europe because they enter through its grand front door. This Europe greets you with cash registers cocked, $8 cups of coffee, high-rise hotels, and service with a purchased smile. Instead, you can give your trip an extra, more real dimension by coming with me through the back door, where a warm, relaxed, personable Europe welcomes us as friends. Rather than being just part of the economy, we become part of the party.

Sure, Europe is expensive. Prices are high for locals—and even steeper for travelers. But the Back Door style of travel is better because of—not in spite of—your budget. Spending money has little to do with enjoying your trip. In fact, as we can learn from Europeans, even those who don't have much money can manage plenty of *la dolce vita*.

When I reread my trip journals, I'm reminded that the less I spend, the richer the experience I have. Often the best travel memories have cost little or nothing. If you see dancers in Barcelona celebrating their Catalan heritage in the *sardana* circle dance, join in. In Rome, climb up the Scala Santa Holy Stairs on your knees to learn what it feels like to be a pilgrim. Watch tourists run for their lives from the bulls in Pamplona. Talk with a Muslim in Turkey about the separation between mosque and state. At a French produce market, gather a gourmet picnic to enjoy in the garden of a Loire château...or perched in a Provençal hill town amid fields of lavender. Even in London (Europe's most expensive city), you can have a world-class experience by soaking up its many free museums: Visiting the Tate Gallery, British Museum, and National Gallery won't cost you a pence.

Participate in sports and games, and everyone wins. Join the Scotsman who runs your B&B in a game of lawn bowling, the Frenchman who runs your *chambre d'hôte* in a game of *pétanque,* or the Greek who runs your *dhomatia* for backgammon. Even if you don't know the rules, you'll end up with a memory that's easy to pack and costs nothing.

ABOUT THIS BOOK

The first half of this book covers the practical skills of Back Door European travel: how to plan a smart itinerary, pack light, take public transportation, find good-value accommodations, eat cheaply but well, stay healthy, use technology wisely, avoid theft and scams, save money and time—and best of all, connect with locals. Even more important than saving you money, my travel tips (which apply whether you're traveling on your own or with a tour group) will steer you toward matchless experiences that become indelible memories. These are the kind of souvenirs you'll enjoy for a lifetime.

The second half of the book gives you a vivid sampling of the experiences that await you in each country or region of Europe. With limited vacation time, it's important to understand what each place has to offer. These country introductions will help you sort through the many options so you can come up with a terrific trip, immersing yourself in the Europe of *your* dreams.

STOKE YOUR TRAVEL DREAMS

Kicking off your European adventure can be a matter of simple logistics (you've got 10 days off in April) or the fulfillment of a lifetime dream (you've always wanted to see where your French grandmother was born). Whether your trip is fueled by practicality or inspiration, the planning part can be instrumental in its success and an enjoyable part of the experience itself. Start by finding out all you can about the destinations you'd like to visit. Many resources are standing by to help inform and inspire your planning. For in-depth itinerary-planning advice, see "Creating an Itinerary" on page 42.

Find inspiration from other travelers. Firsthand, fresh information can be good stuff—whether you're at home or in Europe. Travelers love to share the tips and lessons they've learned. Take advantage of every opportunity to confer with fellow travelers who've been to where you want to go. Solicit tips and ideas from your Facebook friends, ogle images of places you might want to visit, read travel blogs, and talk to travelers in online forums.

Keep in mind, however, that all assessments of a place's touristic merit are a product of that person's personality and experiences there. Maybe it was raining, or the crowds were out of control that particular weekend, or that person got sick in "that lousy, overrated city." Every year, I find travelers hell-bent on following bad advice from friends at home. Treat opinions as opinions (except, of course, those found in this book).

Look through travel books and magazines. Spend a couple of hours in the travel section of a bookstore, thumbing through guidebooks. (Make it a date with your travel partner.) Page through coffee-table books with eye-candy pictures of the places you're thinking of visiting. Your hometown library has a lifetime of valuable reading on European culture. Navigate toward nonfiction: Dewey gave Europe the numbers 914 and 940. (For reading recommendations by country, check the "Explore Europe" pages at RickSteves.com.)

Pick up a few glitzy travel magazines loaded with images of enticing destinations. Try the visually stunning *National Geographic Traveler* (travel advice, trip ideas, and money-saving tips), *Travel & Leisure,* and *Smithsonian* (combines beautiful photography with scholarly articles, often on travel-related topics).

Feast on videos. My public television series, *Rick Steves' Europe,* captures the best of Europe in 100 half-hour

Free Travel Resources from Rick Steves

This book is just the tip of a flying wedge of information I've produced and designed to make your trip smooth, efficient, and affordable. By tapping into the resources listed below, you'll have access to the collective travel experience of my 100-person staff and legions of smart travelers.

RickSteves.com

My mobile-friendly website is *the* place to explore Europe. You'll find thousands of fun articles, videos, photos, and radio interviews organized by country, a wealth of money-saving tips

My goal is to inspire, inform, and equip Americans to have European trips that are fun, affordable, and culturally broadening.

for planning your dream trip, monthly travel news dispatches, a video library of my travel talks, my travel blog, and my latest guidebook updates.

Our Travel Forum is an immense yet well-groomed collection of message boards, where our travel-savvy community answers questions and shares their personal travel experiences. Learn, ask questions, and share your own opinions as you browse topics on each country, other travelers' tips, and reviews of restaurants and hotels. You can even ask one of our well-traveled staff to chime in with an answer.

You'll also find information on our small-group European bus tours, rail passes for independent travelers, and a wide array of guidebooks, luggage, and accessories for sale.

episodes (www.ricksteves.com/tv), getting you up-close with awe-inspiring art, centuries-old churches, colorful markets, romantically cobbled streets, pristine lakes, and peaceful vineyards.

Watching movies, television series, and documentaries set in Europe can also stoke your wanderlust. The Tuscan picnic scene in *A Room with a View* will have you packing your bags for Italy. *Downton Abbey* makes English manors and manners enthralling. *The Sound of Music* sends fans singing into the streets of Salzburg, and *Midnight in Paris* will inspire you to stay out after dark in the City of Light.

Documentaries can be equally compelling: *The Rape of Europa*, telling the fascinating story of the rescue of Europe's great art from Nazi plunderers, adds an extra dimension to your museum going. *The Singing Revolution* gives you stirring background on how the people of Estonia literally—and courageously—sang their way to freedom. (For more TV and

Rick Steves' Europe on Public Television

My public television series covers my favorite continent in 100 half-hour episodes, and we're working on new shows every year. For more about my television series, see the sidebar on page 506. To watch episodes online, or for transcripts and other details, see www.ricksteves.com/tv.

Travel with Rick Steves on Public Radio

My one-hour weekly radio show airs on 400 public radio stations across the US. I talk with experts and everyday travelers about the places, people, and ideas we encounter as we explore our world. You can also listen to it as a podcast on iTunes, iHeartRadio, Stitcher, Tune In, and other platforms. Excerpts from the weekly broadcast are featured in my free Rick Steves Audio Europe app. A list of local broadcast times, and on-demand archives of the show, are at www.ricksteves.com/radio.

Rick Steves Audio Europe™

My free app includes dozens of self-guided audio tours of Europe's top neighborhoods, museums, and sights, and hundreds of my radio interviews, all organized into handy geographic playlists. You can download the app from Apple's App Store or Google Play, and with one click, you'll have me as your tour guide anytime. For more information, see www.ricksteves.com/audioeurope.

Our free audio tours cover the top sights in London, Paris, Rome, Florence, Venice, Vienna, Athens, and other locales.

film suggestions by country, check the "Explore Europe" pages at RickSteves.com.)

Take classes. Understanding a subject makes it interesting. To avoid getting "cathedraled" or "museumed" out, take an art history class, especially if you're going to Italy or Greece. A European history class will bring "dull" museums to life, while a conversational language class can be fun and practical. My travel talks, available on my website, range from lectures on countries and travel skills to lessons in art history (www.ricksteves.com/travel-talks).

Study this book. I've been teaching Americans how to travel smart in Europe on a budget for more than three decades, and the tips in this book are tried and tested on the ground every year. The feedback from my readers makes it clear: Enjoying Europe through the back door can be done—by you.

MAKING THE MOST OF YOUR TRIP

On the road, I get out of my comfort zone and meet people I'd never encounter at home. In Europe, I'm immersed in a place where people do things—and see things—differently. That's what distinguishes cultures, and it's what makes travel interesting. By being open to differences and staying flexible, I have a better time in Europe—and so will you. Be mentally braced for some surprises, good and bad. Much of the success of your trip will depend on the attitude you pack.

Don't be a creative worrier. Some travelers actively cultivate pretrip anxiety, coming up with all kinds of reasons to be stressed. Every year there are air-traffic-controller strikes, train wrecks, terrorist threats, small problems turning into large problems, and old problems becoming new again...and yet the world keeps turning. Don't sweat stuff that hasn't yet happened (and is very unlikely to happen) to you. And don't underestimate yourself. Think you're too old to travel? I've learned that age only matters if you're a cheese: If you want to travel with a youthful spirit, you certainly can.

Expect problems, **and tackle them creatively.** Travel is exciting and rewarding because it requires you to ad-lib, to be imaginative and spontaneous while conquering surprise challenges. Make an art out of taking the unexpected in stride. Relax—you're on the other side of the world playing games in a continental backyard. Be a good sport, enjoy the uncertainty, and frolic in the pits.

No trip is without its disappointments: If your must-see cathedral isn't covered with scaffolding, or your must-visit museum isn't closed for restoration, then your favorite artist's masterpiece will be out on loan—probably to the US.

Many of my readers' richest travel experiences have been the result of seemingly terrible mishaps: the lost passport in Slovenia, having to find a doctor in Ireland, the blowout in Portugal, or the moped accident on Corfu.

When I see a bunch of cute guys on a bench, I ask 'em to scoot over... and 30 years later, I'm still one of the gang.

Most of the time, the worst result is a missed museum or two, and maybe a blown budget for the week. But you may well make some friends and stack up some fond memories. This is the essence of travel that you'll enjoy long after your journal is shelved and your photos are archived in your mind.

KISS: "Keep it simple, stupid!" Don't complicate your trip. Simplify! Travelers can get stressed and clutter their minds over the silliest things, which, in their niggling ways, can suffocate a happy holiday: standing in

If people stare... sing cowboy songs.

a long line at the post office on a sunny day in the Alps, worrying about the correct answers to meaningless bureaucratic forms, having a picnic in pants that make you worry about grass stains. Concerns like these are outlawed in my travels.

People can complicate their trips with clunky camera gear, special tickets for free entry to all the sights they won't see in England, inflatable hangers, immersion heaters, instant coffee, and 65 Handi-Wipes. They ask for a toilet in 17 words and use a calculator to convert currencies to the third digit. Travel more like Gandhi—with simple clothes, open eyes, and an uncluttered mind.

Head off screwups before they happen. You make a rental-car reservation six weeks early, have everything in careful order, show up to pick up your car...and it's not there. The rental agency's fault? Sure. But if you'd called a day ahead to confirm, you'd have avoided an annoying hiccup in your travel plans. Double-checking things along the way minimizes the chances of having your trip marred by other people's mistakes.

Don't be penny wise, pound foolish. Smart travelers will spend a little extra to polish off the rough edges of a trip. Take a taxi instead of a bus when catching an early morning flight at the airport. Enjoy a touristy town without the crowds by spending the night there. If you're traveling solo and feeling lonely, just hire a guide and you've got a buddy to hang out with who really knows the local culture.

Be militantly humble—Attila had a lousy trip. All summer long I'm pushing for a bargain, often for groups. It's the hottest, toughest time of year. Tourists and locals clash—often due to misunderstandings compounded by linguistic and cultural differences. Many tourists leave needlessly soured.

Don't let an unpleasant interaction ruin your travel day. When I catch a Spanish merchant shortchanging me, I correct the bill, smile, and say *"Adiós."* When a French hotel owner blows up at me for no legitimate reason, I wait, smile, and try again. Usually the irate ranter comes to his senses, and we work things out.

"Turn the other cheek" applies perfectly to those riding Europe's magic carousel. If you slap back, the ride is over. The militantly humble and hopelessly optimistic can happily spin forever.

Ask questions. If you are too proud to ask questions, your dignity will stay nicely intact...until you hop the wrong train, order the dish you didn't want, or lead your travel partner in circles. Many tourists are too timid to ask questions, even to prevent mistakes that can cost precious time and money. Locals are a wealth of information: Use them. Most people are happy to help a traveler. Hurdle the language barrier. Use a paper and pencil, charades, or whatever it takes to be understood. Don't be afraid to butcher the language.

Ask questions—or be lost. If you are lost, get help. Perceive friendliness and you'll find it.

Make yourself an extrovert, even if you're not. The meek may inherit the earth, but they make lousy travelers. Be a catalyst for adventure and excitement. Meet people. Don't wait for cultural experiences—reach out and make them happen. The American casual-and-friendly social style is charming to Europeans who are raised to respect social formalities. While our slap-on-the-back friendliness can be overplayed and obnoxious, it can also be a great asset for the American interested in meeting Europeans. Consider that cultural trait a plus. Enjoy it. Take advantage of it.

Every town in Europe has an amazing open-air market place. If you're like me, you might feel a little awkward—you don't speak the language, you're not good with the metric system, you just want to buy one apple and two carrots, the coins are new to you, and there's a long line of local people. Hold your ground. You're not a gawky tourist who is out of his league, you're one in a thousand-year-long line of hungry travelers. You're legit. Stop looking at it as if you were on a stage, get out there, and risk making mistakes. Connect.

Accept that today's Europe is changing. Europe is a complex, mixed bag of the very old, the very new, and everything in between. Among its palaces, quaint folk dancers,

Extroverts Have More Fun

I'm not naturally a wild-and-crazy kind of guy. But when I'm shy and quiet, things don't happen, and that's a bad rut to travel in. So when I'm on the road I make myself an extrovert...and everything changes. Let me describe the same evening twice—first with the mild-and-lazy me, then with the wild-and-crazy me.

The traffic held me up, so by the time I got to that great museum I'd always wanted to see, it was 12 minutes before closing. No one was allowed to enter. Disappointed, I walked to a restaurant and couldn't make heads or tails out of the menu. I recognized "steak-frites" and settled for a meat patty and French fries. On the way home I looked into a pub but it seemed dark, so I walked on. A couple waved at me from their balcony, but I didn't know what to say, so I ignored them. I returned to my room and did some laundry.

That's not a night to be proud of. An extrovert's journal would read like this:

I got to the museum only 12 minutes before closing. The guard said no one could enter, but I pleaded with him, saying I'd traveled all the way to see this place. I assured him that I'd be out by closing time, and he gave me a glorious 12 minutes in a hall slathered with Renaissance frescoes. At a restaurant that the guard recommended, I couldn't make heads or tails out of the menu. Inviting myself into the kitchen, I met the cooks and got a firsthand look at what was cookin'. What I chose was delizioso! On the way home, I passed a pub, and, while it seemed uninviting, I stepped in anyway, and was greeted by a guy who spoke broken English. He proudly befriended me, and we shared stories about our kids (he had pictures...and so did I)—while treating me to his favorite brew. As I headed home, a couple waved at me from their balcony, and I waved back, saying "Buon giorno!" I knew it didn't mean "Good evening," but they understood. They invited me up to their apartment. We joked around—not understanding a lot of what we were saying to each other—and had fun. What a lucky break to be welcomed into a local home! And to think that I could've been back in my room doing laundry!

Pledge every morning to do something entirely different that day. Meet people and create adventure—or bring home a boring journal.

and dusty museums, you'll find a living civilization grasping for its future while we romantic tourists grope for its past.

This presents us with a sometimes-painful dose of truth. Europe can be crowded, tense, seedy, polluted, industrialized, and increasingly hamburgerized. Hans Christian Andersen's statue has four-letter words scrawled across its base. Amsterdam's sex shops and McDonald's share the same streetlamp. In Paris, armies of Sudanese salesmen bait tourists with ivory bracelets and crocodile purses. Drunk punks do their best to repulse you as you climb to St. Patrick's grave in Ireland, and Greek ferryboats dump mountains of trash into their dying Aegean Sea. A 12-year-old boy in Denmark smokes a cigarette like he was born with it in his mouth. On town squares, tattooed violinists play Vivaldi while statue-mime Napoleons jerk into action at the drop of a coin.

Cherish the cultural diversity—your Dublin B&B host is as likely to be Polish as he is Irish. Europe is a society of 400 million people just like us, sorting through social challenges and dealing with them in a creative, productive, and positive way. Contemporary Europe is alive and in motion. Keep up!

Savor the differences. Europeans' eating habits can be an adjustment. They may have next to nothing for breakfast, mud for coffee, mussels in Brussels, snails in Paris, and dinner at 10 p.m. in Spain. Beer is room-temperature here and flat there, coffee isn't served with dinner, and ice cubes are only a dream.

Germans wait patiently—in the rain—for the traffic light before they cross an empty street, while Roman cars stay in their lanes like rocks in an avalanche. Trains are speedy but rail strikes are routine.

Locals are more attracted to sidewalk cafés and modern malls than medieval cathedrals. The latest government tax or protest march has everyone talking. Today's problems will fill tomorrow's museums. Feel privileged to walk the vibrant streets of Europe as a student—not as a judge. Be open-minded. Absorb, accept, and learn.

If you can think positively, travel smartly, adapt well, and connect with the culture, you'll have a truly rich European trip. So raise your travel dreams to their upright and locked positions, and let this book fly you away.

Rick Steves' Back Door Travel Philosophy

Travel is intensified living—maximum thrills per minute and one of the last great sources of legal adventure. Travel is freedom. It's recess, and we need it.

Affording travel is a matter of priorities. (Make do with the old car.) You can eat and sleep—simply, safely, and enjoyably—anywhere in Europe for $100 a day plus transportation costs. In many ways, spending more money only builds a thicker wall between you and what you traveled so far to see. Europe is a cultural carnival, and time after time, you'll find that its best acts are free and the best seats are the cheap ones.

Experiencing the real Europe requires catching it by surprise, going casual..."through the Back Door." A tight budget forces you to travel close to the ground, meeting and communicating with the people. Never sacrifice sleep, nutrition, safety, or cleanliness to save money. Simply enjoy the local-style alternatives to expensive hotels and restaurants.

Connecting with people carbonates your experience. Extroverts have more fun. If your trip is low on magic moments, kick yourself and make things happen. If you don't enjoy a place, maybe you don't know enough about it. Seek the truth. Recognize tourist traps. Give a culture the benefit of your open mind. See things as different, but not better or worse. Any culture has plenty to share. When an opportunity presents itself, make it a habit to say "yes."

Of course, travel, like the world, is a series of hills and valleys. Be fanatically positive and militantly optimistic. If something's not to your liking, change your liking.

Our Earth is home to seven billion equally precious people. It's humbling to travel and find that other people don't have the "American Dream"—they have their own dreams. Europeans like us, but with all due respect, they wouldn't trade passports.

Can travel be a political act? Yes. Travelers learn that the world is basically a good place, and that caring for our environment and finding international solutions can be a win-win rather than a win-lose. In the Industrial Age (RIP), the adage was, "What's good for GM is good for America." But now we live in a global age, and we can't make that go away by denying facts and building walls. A new maxim might be, "What's good for the world is good for America."

Thoughtful travel engages us with the world. It reminds us what is important and teaches new ways to measure quality of life. I believe that if Americans were required to travel before they could vote, the US would be safer, stronger, and happier. That's why, rather than saying, "Have a safe trip," I say, "Keep on travelin'."

Globetrotting destroys ethnocentricity, and helps us understand and appreciate other cultures. Rather than fear the diversity on this planet, celebrate it. Among your most prized souvenirs will be the strands of different cultures you choose to knit into your own character. The world is a cultural yarn shop, and Back Door travelers are weaving the ultimate tapestry. Join in!

Travel Skills

In Europe, life's very good—even if you're on a budget.

Budgeting & Planning

The best travelers aren't those with the fattest wallets, but those who take the planning process seriously. Jack might jet off to Europe as a free spirit, without much planning and no real itinerary—and return home with a backpack full of complaints about how expensive and stressful it all was. Jill, who enjoys planning and insists on traveling with good information, maps out a detailed day-to-day plan—and returns home with rich stories of spontaneous European adventures. It's the classic paradox of good travel: Structure rewards a traveler with freedom, and "winging it" can become a ball-and-chain of too many decisions, too little information, and precious little time to relax.

In this chapter, I'll help you create a budget for your trip, guide you through the best resources for researching and planning, give you the scoop on Europe's travel "seasons," and walk you through creating a smart itinerary.

AFFORDING YOUR TRIP

Anticipating costs, knowing your options, and living within your budget are fundamental to a good trip.

Budget Breakdown

Start penciling out your European budget by getting a handle on your biggest expenses. Five components make up your trip costs: airfare, transportation within Europe, room and board, sightseeing and entertainment, and shopping and miscellany.

Airfare: The same round-trip flight between the US and Europe can cost anywhere from $1,000 to $2,000, depending on the time of year, where you are flying from, and the various fees (such as airport taxes, fuel surcharges, and baggage fees). Traveling outside of peak season alone can save you several hundred dollars per ticket. Understand all of your alternatives (maybe with the help of a good travel agent) in order to make the best choice.

Transportation Within Europe: This can be reasonable if you use Europe's excellent public transportation system (taking advantage of the best deals) or split a car rental among several people. And cheap flights—about $100 one-way between most major European cities—can save time and money on long journeys. Within cities, figure about $2-3 for each bus or subway ride. Transportation expenses are generally fixed, but your budget shouldn't dictate how freely you travel in Europe. If you want to go somewhere, do it, making the most of whatever money-saving options you can. You came to travel.

Room and Board: The areas that will make or break your budget—over which you have the most control—are your eating and sleeping expenses. Smart travelers can thrive on $125 a day for room and board: $75 per person in a $150 hotel double with breakfast, $15 apiece for lunch, and $30 for dinner. That leaves you $5 for cappuccino or gelato. Remember that these prices are averages— Scandinavia, Britain, and Italy are more expensive, while Spain, Portugal, Greece, and Eastern Europe are cheaper. Also, as a general rule, you'll pay less in the countryside and more in big cities.

If $125 per day is too steep for your budget, that's no reason to stay home—you can picnic more and stay at simpler accommodations to get by on less. Make your trip match your budget (rather than vice versa). The key is consuming only what you want to consume. If you want real tablecloths and

Trip Costs

You can travel comfortably for a month for $5,750 (not including your airfare). If you have extra money, it's more fun to spend it in Europe.

Allow approximately (per person):

$1,000	long-distance transportation (trains, car rental, and short-haul flights)
800	sightseeing and entertainment
200	shopping and miscellany
+3,750	room and board ($125/day)
$5,750	

Students or rock-bottom budget travelers can enjoy a month of Europe for about 40 percent less–$3,200 plus airfare.

Allow approximately (per person):

$800	one-month youth rail pass
500	sightseeing and entertainment
100	shopping and miscellany
+1,800	room and board ($60/day)
$3,200	

Go with a Group or on Your Own?

Putting together a dream trip requires time and skills. As with any do-it-yourself project, at the outset it's wise to honestly assess whether you want to handle your endeavor (in this case, exploring Europe) on your own. Some people are not inclined to figure things out on a trip, and that's OK. They make their living figuring things out 50 weeks a year, and that's not their idea of a good vacation. These people should travel with a tour...or a spouse.

Tours and cruises are an easy way to see Europe and can make a lot of sense for people with limited time. You don't have to waste any mental energy on where to sleep or how to get to the next town. With a good tour company, you'll enjoy the insights of local guides who'll bring Roman life alive in Pompeii or help you recall recent history in Berlin. And cruises offer the undeniable efficiency of sleeping while you travel to your next destination, allowing you to tour six dynamically different destinations in a single week—provided you're OK with experiencing Europe as day trips in port rather than as a 24/7 immersion course.

Some tours and cruises can also end up being cheaper than independent travel. Large tour companies get deals on hotels and restaurants, and using your cruise ship as a floating hotel can be cheaper than paying separately for hotels and city-to-city transportation (provided you don't get sucked into buying lots of extras; for tips on taking tours and cruises smartly, see the Bus Tours & Cruises chapter).

On a bus tour or cruise, you dip into Europe here and there. But these options can tend to show you a veneered version of Europe. If you really want to have an intimate challenge, an educational, experiential time, and a break from being surrounded by a bunch of other Americans, you'll get the most satisfaction from traveling independently. Just as someone trying to learn a language will do better by actually experiencing that culture rather than sitting in a classroom for a few hours, I believe that travelers in search of engaging, enlightening experiences should eat, sleep, and live Europe.

black-tie waiters, your tomato salad will cost 20 times what it costs in the market. If you want a suite with fancy room service and chocolate on your pillow, you'll pay in a day for accommodations what many travelers pay in a week.

Sightseeing and Entertainment: Admissions to major attractions are roughly $8-20; smaller sights usually charge $2-5. Concerts, plays, and bus tours cost about $30. Don't skimp here. This category powers most of the experiences that all of the other expenses are designed to make possible. And fortunately, some of the best sights are free.

Shopping and Miscellany: Shopping can vary in cost from nearly nothing to a small fortune. Good budget travelers find that this category has little to do with assembling a trip full of lifelong and wonderful memories.

Budget Tips

I traveled every summer for years on a part-time piano teacher's income (and, boy, was she upset). My idea of "cheap" is simple, not sleazy. I'm not talking about begging and groveling around Europe. I'm talking about enjoying a one-star hotel rather than a three-star hotel ($100 saved), ordering a carafe of house wine at an atmospheric hole-in-the wall rather than a bottle of fine wine in a classy restaurant ($40 saved), and taking the shuttle bus in from the airport rather than a taxi ($50 saved). There are plenty of ways to keep your expenses in check without compromising your travel experience. In many ways, the less you spend, the more engaged you are with the culture around you, and the more you actually experience life as a temporary European.

Sleep in cheap hotels. I go for safe, central, friendly, local-style hotels, shunning swimming pools, people in uniforms, and transplanted American niceties. Hotels are pricey just about everywhere in Europe. But, equipped with good information, you can land some fine deals—which often come with the most memories, to boot. In Dubrovnik, for example, I pick a centrally located room in a private home over a pricey resort hotel on a distant beach.

Find deals at local institutions. Rome has many convents that rent out rooms—the beds are twins and English is often in short supply, but the price is right. In London, you don't need to be a student to stay at colleges (such as the London School of Economics), which have openings in their dorms from July through September.

Try inexpensive, unique alternatives to standard accommodations. On recent visits, I slept well in a former medieval watchtower along Germany's Rhine River (Hotel Kranenturm, $90 double), a room in a private home on the Italian Riviera (Camere Fontana Vecchia in Vernazza, $120 double), and a welcoming guesthouse in Dubrovnik's old town (Villa Ragusa, $100 double). If you're willing to rough it, you'll save even more. Consider a renovated jail in Ljubljana (Hostel Celica, $30 for a bunk in a 12-bed dorm) or a summer-only circus tent in Munich ($10 per foam mattress).

Delve into the "sharing economy." Staying in locals' houses is interesting and affordable, whether through pay-for-stay arrangements like Airbnb, home exchanges, or organizations that emphasize intercultural exchange such as Couchsurfing and Servas.

Patronize family-run restaurants with a local following. The best values are not in the places with glossy menus in six languages out front. I look for family-run restaurants away from the high-rent squares, filled with enthusiastic locals and offering a small, handwritten menu in the local language only. You'll get more for your money at mom-and-pop places; they pay less in labor (family members) and care more about their customers.

Look for daily deals. You can eat well for less nearly anywhere in Europe by taking advantage of daily specials, lunch deals, and early-bird dinners. In Britain, the Loch Fyne seafood chain has a "set menu" offering a three-course deal before 7 p.m. In Stockholm, eat your main meal at lunch, when cafés and restaurants have daily special plates called *dagens rätt*.

Economize where it's expensive and splurge where it's cheap. The priciest parts of Europe (Scandinavia, Britain, and much of Italy) can be twice as expensive as Europe's cheapest corners (Spain, Portugal, Greece, and Eastern Europe). Exercise budget alternatives where they'll save you the most money. A hostel may save you $10 in Crete but $50 in Finland. In Scandinavia I picnic, walk, and sleep on trains, but I live like a king in Portugal or Poland, where my splurge dollars go the farthest. Those on a tight budget manage better by traveling more quickly through the expensive countries and lingering in the cheap ones.

Eastern European hotels are nearly as pricey as in the West, but other items are a relative steal. A mug of Czech beer costs $2 (versus $6 in Britain or Ireland, or $9 in Oslo). A ticket for Mozart in a sumptuous Budapest opera house runs

LEFT Lunch for $10, *no problema*

RIGHT When young Norwegians "eat out," they drop by the grocery store for a disposable "one-time grill" and head for the park.

Comparing *Apfels* to *Pommes:* Relative Prices in Europe's Top Cities

Budget alone should not determine where you go in Europe. People on a shoestring budget can have a blast in Europe's most expensive countries...if they travel smart. But knowing roughly what you'll pay in various destinations can help you craft a more wallet-friendly itinerary. This chart attempts to compare apples to apples by showing rough costs in US dollars for basic tourist expenses in several of Europe's major cities (and, by way of comparison, my hometown in the USA). Prices are based on midrange hotels and restaurants, second-class trains, and first-class museums.

	Double Room	Main Dish at Dinner	One-Hour Train Ride to a Nearby Town	Museum Entry Fee
Amsterdam	$165	$22	$15	$18
Athens	$115	$15	$5	$17
Budapest, Kraków	$120	$15	$5	$8
Copenhagen, Oslo	$160	$25	$21	$15
London	$200	$20	$39	$25
Madrid, Lisbon	$130	$16	$14	$15
Munich	$125	$21	$28	$10
Paris	$190	$25	$19	$15
Prague	$170	$12	$6	$12
Rome	$210	$15	$13	$17
Vienna	$145	$21	$21	$15
Zürich	$195	$28	$25	$10
Seattle	$175	$15	$14	$15

$20 (versus $65 in Vienna). And your own private Slovenian guide is $100 for a half-day (versus $200 in London).

Learn from the locals. When you're in Europe's priciest places, take the high cost of living gracefully in stride by following the lead of people who live there. Instead of paying dearly for dinner at a restaurant, Norwegians "eat out" in the parks, barbecuing their groceries on disposable "one-time grills" ($4 in supermarkets). The last time I was in a restaurant in Oslo, 16 of 20 diners were drinking only tap water. While you'll see crowds of young people drinking beer along Copenhagen's canals, that doesn't mean alcohol consumption is higher in Denmark—it's just that many young adults can't afford to drink in the bars, so they pick up their beer at the grocery store and party al fresco. Why not drop by the local equivalent of a 7-Eleven and do the same?

Swallow pride and save money. This is a personal matter, depending largely on how much pride and money you have. Many people cringe every time I use the word "cheap"; others appreciate the directness. Find out the complete price before ordering anything, and say "no thanks" if the price isn't right. Expect equal and fair treatment as a tourist. When appropriate, fight the price, set a limit, and search on. If the tech store at Heathrow airport wants to charge you $30 for a mobile phone SIM card, wait until you're in central London and buy it at a newsstand for half the price. If you act like a rich fool, you're likely to be treated as one.

Spend money to save time. When you travel, time really is money. (Divide the complete cost of your trip by your waking hours in Europe, and you'll see what I mean. My cost: $20 per hour.) Don't waste your valuable time in lines. In Europe's most crowded cities (especially Paris, Rome, and Florence), easy-to-make reservations and museum passes let you skirt the long ticket-buying lines. If it costs $1 to use your mobile phone to confirm museum times, but it saves you trekking across town to discover the sight is closed, that's a buck very well spent.

Go communal. If you're traveling with a buddy or small group of friends, pool your money for everyday expenses. Separate checks and long lists of petty IOUs are a pain. Plus, combining costs can save you money; for instance, a group of four often travels more cheaply in a shared taxi or rental car than by subway, bus, or train. Note how much each person contributes, and just assume everything equals out in the long run. Keep track of major individual expenses, but don't worry about who got an extra postcard or cappuccino. Enjoy treating each other to taxis and dinners out of your "kitty," and after the trip, divvy up the remains. If one person consumed $50 or $60 more, that's a small price to pay for the convenience and economy of communal money.

Don't take budget tips too far. The true "value" of a trip isn't just a function of how cheaply you travel, but how much you enjoy it. If everyone says, "Portugal is cheap," but your travel dreams feature the Swiss Alps, then *your* best value is in Switzerland.

RESEARCHING YOUR TRIP

Europe is always changing, and it's essential to plan and travel with the most up-to-date information. Study before you go. Guidebooks, maps, and travel apps and websites are all key resources in getting started.

While information is what keeps you afloat, too much can

sink the ship. So winnow down your resources to what best suits your travel needs and interests. WWII buffs research battle sites, wine lovers brainstorm a wish list of wineries, and MacGregors locate their clan's castles in Scotland.

A word of warning as you hatch your plans: Understand what shapes the information that shapes your travel dreams. Information you seek out yourself is likely to be impartial, whereas information that comes at you is propelled by business (see the sidebar). Many publications and websites are supported by advertisers who have products and services to sell; their information is often useful, but it's not necessarily unbiased. Don't believe everything you read. Many sources are peppered with information that is flat-out wrong. (Incredibly enough, even this book may have an error.) Some "writers" succumb to the temptation to write travelogues based on hearsay, travel brochures, other books, public-relations junkets, and wishful thinking. A writer met at the airport by an official from the national tourist board learns tips that are handy only for others who are met at the airport by an official from the national tourist board.

Understanding the Travel Industry

When sorting through all of the options for your trip, you need to understand that we travelers are consumers—and the travel industry is all about selling us things.

Travel media—TV shows, magazines, newspaper articles, and websites—are careful not to offend advertisers. Just like big business lobbies our government, big travel lobbies the travel media. There's a huge appetite these days in travel journalism for lists. "The Top Ten This" and "Top Twenty That" are what the typical tourist is gobbling up. Plenty of factors that aren't in your interest shape these reports.

The industry in general is geared toward filling resorts, cruise ships, big tour buses, and fancy hotels. There's very little money to be made from independent travel. Consequently, there's little reason to sing its praises in the glossy media that shape many people's travel dreams.

As it's expensive to promote things, attractions and activities that are free or unprofitable are rarely marketed. It's important to be smart about which information you use to determine your itinerary. Don't be too led on by the attractions promoted by leaflets in your hotel lobby, by advertising disguised as tourist information, or by the recommendations of your commission-hungry concierge.

Enjoy the highly publicized attractions—many of them are popular for a reason. But don't let the promotion lead you away from the wonderful world of travel experiences that are most likely to put you in touch with the people, nature, and culture of Europe. These dimensions, which no big business is pushing with slick publicity, are most likely to be the highlights of your trip.

LEFT Never underestimate the value of an up-to-date guidebook.

RIGHT My planning maps highlight what you want to see...not just the biggest cities.

Guidebooks and Planning Maps

I am amazed by the many otherwise smart people who base the trip of a lifetime on a borrowed copy of a three-year-old guidebook. The money they save in the bookstore is wasted the first day of their trip, searching for buses that no longer run and restaurants that have long since closed. Guidebooks are $25 tools for $4,000 experiences. As a writer—and user— of guidebooks, I am a big believer in their worth. When I visit somewhere as a rank beginner, I equip myself with a good, up-to-date guidebook. I travel like an old pro, not because I'm a super traveler, but because I have reliable information and I use it.

Guidebooks: With a good guidebook, you can come into Paris for your first time, go anywhere in town for less than $2 on the subway, enjoy a memorable bistro lunch for $25, and pay $150 for a double room in a friendly hotel on a pedestrian-only street a few blocks from the Eiffel Tower—so French that when you step outside in the morning, you feel you must have been a poodle in a previous life.

Before buying any guidebook, check the publication date. If it's last year's edition, find out when the new version is due out. Most guidebooks get an update every three or four years. Only a handful of titles (including my most popular books) are actually updated in person with regularity. When I'm choosing between guidebooks for a certain destination, the publication date (often on the copyright page) is usually the deciding factor.

Planning Maps: When you pick up your guidebook, choose a map or two for planning purposes. The *Michelin Map Europe 705* provides an excellent overall view of Europe. Many guidebook publishers (including Rough Guides, Lonely Planet, and my series) make maps or combination map-guidebooks. While there are many online mapping tools that are excellent for help in planning the finer points of your itinerary (especially if you're driving), there's nothing quite like laying out a large map on the table to get a sense of relative locations and distances, then inking in your intended route.

Ebooks: Many guidebook series, including most of my titles, are available as ebooks. While I still consider myself a paper guy, there are advantages to going digital. You can carry multiple ebooks without adding weight to your bag (great for long, multidestination trips), and you can buy books on the go (convenient for spur-of-the-moment detours). Someday ebooks may offer more benefits than traditional paper books, but for now they have limitations. It can be difficult to find the information you're looking for; flipping from page to page is awkward; and maps—often designed to run across two pages—don't always appear correctly. Until the perfect digital solution arrives, I believe a printed guidebook remains the most practical format.

Rick Steves Guidebooks

The book you're holding is the foundation of a series of books—written and refined over the last three decades—that work together to help smooth your travels and broaden your cultural experiences. With the help of my research partners, I update my guidebooks lovingly and in person. In order to experience the same Europe that most of my readers do, I insist on doing my research in the peak tourist season—from April through September. And I'm stubbornly selective, writing about fewer destinations than other guidebooks. For example, Italy has dozens of hill towns, but my Italy book zooms in on the handful that are truly worth the trip. I base my depth of coverage on a place's worthiness, rather than its population or fame. For the titles in my guidebook series, see the sidebar.

A trio of my books is best read before your trip. This book, *Europe Through the Back Door,* teaches you the nuts and bolts of how to travel affordably and efficiently, with maximum opportunities to connect to the culture. *Europe 101: History and Art for the Traveler* (co-authored with Gene Openshaw) will help you achieve a deeper understanding of the story of Europe. (It's for smart people who slept through their art history classes

Rick Steves Guidebook Series

My take-along guidebooks create a blueprint for your trip, weaving my favorite sights, accommodations, and restaurants into strategies designed to make the most out of every mile, minute, and dollar. I focus on helping you explore and enjoy Europe's big cities, small towns, and regions, mixing must-see sights with intimate Back Door nooks and offbeat crannies.

Rick Steves City, Regional, and Country Guidebooks

These comprehensive guidebooks cut through the superlatives to give you the best possible plan for your trip, with all the info and tips you need to tour Europe's top destinations and sights.

Amsterdam & the Netherlands
Barcelona
Belgium: Bruges, Brussels, Antwerp & Ghent
Berlin
Budapest
Croatia & Slovenia
Eastern Europe
England
Florence & Tuscany
France
Germany
Great Britain
Greece: Athens & the Peloponnese
Ireland
Istanbul
Italy
London
Paris
Portugal
Prague & the Czech Republic
Provence & the French Riviera
Rome
Scandinavia
Scotland
Spain
Switzerland
Venice
Vienna, Salzburg & Tirol

Rick Steves "Best Of" Guidesbooks

This series covers Europe's best destinations in condensed form. Full-color and easy-to-scan, they focus on the top cities and sights in England, France, Germany, Ireland, Italy, and Spain, plus a roundup of my all-time favorites across Europe.

Rick Steves Pocket Guidebooks

For travelers taking short, focused trips, my colorful Pocket guidebooks slip right into your pocket. They cover some of Europe's major destinations–including Amsterdam,

before they knew they were going to Europe...and now wish they knew who the Etruscans were.) The next step, **Travel as a Political Act,** illustrates how Americans who travel with an open mind and a curious spirit can have the time of their lives and come home smarter—with a keener appreciation for the interconnectedness of the world around them.

This trilogy forms a pyramid—similar to Abraham Maslow's "hierarchy of needs"—for the thinking traveler. You start off with the basics: Pack light, stay safe, catch the train, and eat and sleep well. When those needs are met, you can enjoy the art, history, and culture. Finally you reach the pinnacle of travel: gaining a deeper understanding of our place on this delightful planet.

Athens, Barcelona, the Cinque Terre, Florence, London, Munich, Paris, Prague, Rome, Venice, and Vienna.

Rick Steves Snapshot Guidebooks
Excerpted from my bigger country guidebooks, these slim titles zoom in on many of my favorite destinations, including Lisbon, Normandy, Edinburgh, and the Hill Towns of Central Italy.

Rick Steves Cruise Guidebooks
My *Mediterranean Cruise Ports* and *Northern European Cruise Ports* help you choose and book a cruise, enjoy your time on board, and make the most of your time in port.

Rick Steves Phrase Books
Fun and practical, these guides will help you get along in French, Italian, German, Spanish, and Portuguese.

More Rick Steves Titles
Europe 101: History and Art for the Traveler
European Christmas
European Easter
Travel as a Political Act

Andy Steves' Europe
My son Andy has written *Andy Steves' Europe: City-Hopping on a Budget*, sharing his experiences for travelers on a shoestring budget. Covering 13 of Europe's best cities, he gives down-to-earth advice for today's students, backpackers, and weekend adventurers.

Other Guidebook Series
Every guidebook series has an area of specialization: Some are great for hotels, but fall down on restaurants. Other series can't be beat for history and culture. Some guidebooks (like mine) are more opinionated and selective, choosing only the most worthwhile destinations in each country and covering them in depth. Others seek to cover every possible destination you might find yourself in. When I travel in Europe and beyond—to areas I don't cover in my books—I routinely use guidebooks from these publishers, and find them helpful.

Lonely Planet: The worldwide standard for a solid guidebook, Lonely Planet covers most countries in Europe,

Asia, Africa, and the Americas. The Lonely Planet series offers comprehensive, no-nonsense facts, low- and mid-budget listings, and helpful on-the-ground travel tips.

Frommer's Guides: The granddaddy of travel publishing, Arthur Frommer has reinvented his series to be leaner and more focused on the budget traveler. These books are especially well attuned to the needs of older travelers, but some readers may feel like they're being handled with unnecessary kid gloves.

Fodor's Travel: A stalwart of travel publishing, Fodor's has been producing good basic European guidebooks for American travelers since the 1930s. Their coverage is more encyclopedic than inspiring.

A good guide-book allows you to play "tour guide" and brings Europe's museums to life.

DK Eyewitness Travel: These gorgeous visual guides offer appealing color photos and illustrations (like cutaway cross-sections of important castles and churches). They are great for trip planning and visual learners, but the written information is scant—I don't travel with them.

National Geographic Traveler: These guides are well-produced, with beautiful maps and sharp photos. They're highly selective and a bit stingy with information, but great for trip planning and dreaming.

Rough Guides: This British series is written by Europeans who understand the contemporary social scene better than most American writers. While their hotel listings can be skimpy and uninspired, the historical and sightseeing information tends to offer greater depth than others.

Michelin Green Guides: From a French publisher, these tall, green books are packed with color maps and photos, plus small but encyclopedic chapters on history, lifestyles, art, culture, and customs. Recent editions also list hotels and restaurants. The **Michelin Red Guides** are the hotel and restaurant connoisseur's bibles.

Bradt Travel Guides: This British series, specializing in off-the-beaten-track destinations throughout Europe (and the world), offers plenty of cultural insights in addition to solid nitty-gritty details.

Blue Guides: Known for a dry and scholarly approach, these guides are ideal if you want a deep dive into history, art, architecture, and culture. With the Blue Guide to Greece, I had all the information I needed about every sight

Guidebooks: Small, Handy, and Hidden

I often buy several guidebooks for each country I visit, rip them up, and staple the pertinent chapters together into my own personalized hybrid guidebook. On the road, I bring only the applicable pages—there's no point in carrying 100 pages of information on Madrid to dinner in Barcelona.

As I travel in Europe, I've met lots of people with clever book treatments. One couple was proud of the job they did in the name of packing light: cutting out only the pages they'd be using and putting them into a spiral binding. Another couple put their guidebook in a brown-paper-bag book cover so they wouldn't look so touristy (a smart move, I'll admit).

I love the ritual of customizing the guidebooks I'll be using: I fold the pages back until the spine breaks, neatly slice out the sections I want with a box cutter or utility knife, then pull them out with the gummy edge intact. I use a monster stapler to "rebind" the sections I'm keeping, then finish it off with some clear, heavy-duty packing tape to smooth and reinforce the spine. Another option is to tear out the chapters you don't need and bring the rest in the original binding. To make things even easier, I've created a line of slide-on laminated covers to corral your pages (for details see www.ricksteves.com/shop).

and never needed to hire a guide. Scholarly types actually find a faint but endearing personality hiding between the sheets of their Blue Guides.

Online Resources

The Internet has taken much of the mystery and uncertainty out of European travel. Wondering where a certain hotel is in Barcelona? Map it with Google Maps, then check "street view" to get the neighborhood vibe (though be aware that you might be looking at an early morning or evening photo taken when the area is not as bustling as usual). Thinking about visiting the Eiffel Tower, but worried about getting stuck in a long line? Order advance tickets online. Want to eat at the latest hot spot in Berlin? Get the inside scoop from a local blog.

Start your Web research with the professionals: Every guidebook publisher has a website, as do travel magazines and major newspapers with good travel sections. But don't overlook homegrown talent and opinions from other travelers. Here are some sources to consider:

Tourist Information Office Websites

Just about every European city has a centrally located tourist information office loaded with maps and advice. This is my essential first stop upon arrival in any town, but you don't need to wait until you get to Europe to access their information. Each European country has its own official tourism website—often a great place to begin researching your trip. Many of these sites are packed with practical information, suggested itineraries, city guides, interactive maps, colorful photos, and free downloadable brochures describing walking tours and more. In addition, nearly every European country has a national tourism board, often with an office in the US that you can email with specific questions.

Local Websites

I'm a big fan of local websites and blogs loaded with insider tips. Not only do they fill you in on the latest happenings and hot spots, but they help you feel like a native in no time.

Any major city has a host of online resources dedicated to arts, culture, food, and drink. For instance, AOK is a great city guide to Copenhagen, with helpful information on restaurants, nightlife, and neighborhoods (www.aok.dk). Serious foodies looking for Paris restaurants and specialty shops should consult the always appetizing ParisByMouth.com. The Local (www. thelocal.de) has websites devoted to Germany and eight other countries and is the largest English-language news network in Europe.

One of my favorite resources is Matt Barrett's Athens Survival Guide (www.athensguide.com). Matt, who splits his time between North Carolina and Greece, splashes through his adopted hometown like a kid in a wading pool, enthusiastically sharing his discoveries and observations on his generous site. Matt covers emerging neighborhoods that few visitors venture into, and offers offbeat angles on the city and recommendations for vibrant, untouristy restaurants.

Resources for Trip Planning

Travel.state.gov: US State Department's official travel site, with foreign entry requirements, travel warnings, and more

TripAdvisor, Booking.com: Prices, availability, and traveler reviews

Stay.com, VisitaCity.com: Itinerary planning, budgeting, and sharing

ViaMichelin.com: Maps and route planner

Bahn.com: German rail website listing schedules for trains all over Europe

Rome2Rio.com: Compiles different transportation options from one destination to another

WeatherPlanner.com: Weather prediction site that uses historical data

RickSteves.com: Destination info, trip-planning advice, festival and holiday dates, travel forum, and a trove of Rick's TV shows, radio interviews, articles, and travel-skills talks

TripIt app: All-in one travel organizer

Traveler Reviews

To plan a trip, I once relied on travel agents, other travel writers, and the word-of-mouth advice of friends. Those sources are still valid—but my circle of "friends" has increased exponentially. With the advent of user-review sites and apps such as Yelp, Booking.com, and TripAdvisor, the opinions of everyday travelers are changing the way we approach trip planning.

User reviews can be helpful as you plan, allowing you to browse destinations and get a consensus of traveler opinions about everything from hotels and restaurants to sights and nightlife. But these reviews also have their drawbacks.

When I started traveling, there wasn't enough information. Now there's too much, and it's uncurated. Those enamored with crowd-sourcing might plan an entire trip based solely on user reviews. But it's risky: Your reviewer may be someone who visited once and had a bad day; a company in India that's being paid to say good (or bad) things about European businesses; a couple who promised to write a good review of a B&B in exchange for a free breakfast; or a guy who goes to Paris to eat Tex-Mex. My hunch is that a significant percentage of user reviews aren't legit (it's estimated that one-third to one-half of the travel reviews you see on the Internet are fake).

Review sites can also become an echo chamber, where one or two well-located, flashy businesses camp out atop the ratings. Travelers rave about these already-popular places, creating a self-perpetuating cycle of positive reviews. Meanwhile, a better, more affordable, and more authentic alternative may sit ignored, tucked down a side street. Or a hotel can pay a website to be a "preferred property" and get its listing bumped to a high spot—even if the reviews are mediocre. And hotels or B&Bs who refuse to pay a commission won't be listed at all.

As a guidebook writer, my sense is that there is a big difference between this uncurated information and a guidebook. A user review is based on the experience of one person, who likely stayed at one hotel and ate at a few restaurants, and doesn't have much of a basis for comparison. A guidebook is the work of a trained researcher who, year after year, visits many alternatives to assess their relative value.

The most helpful crowd-sourced ideas for travelers usually come from the categories for tours, sightseeing experiences, and entertainment. If I'm coming into Amsterdam and I want to know what's new, I might look at TripAdvisor: It lists every food tour, every bike tour, every zipline, and every goofy goblin tour. You can sort through all of those options and decide what you want to do with your time.

But also keep in mind that guidebook writers have already done that for you. I see review sites as a useful complement to a thoughtfully updated guidebook. If something is well-reviewed in a guidebook, and also gets good ratings on one of these sites, it's likely a winner.

CREATING AN ITINERARY

Each spring through my college years, I'd first determine how much time I could get away for, then I'd buy the cheapest plane ticket to Europe—then I'd figure out where I'd actually go. Filling in the blanks between the flight out and the flight home is one of the more pleasurable parts of trip planning. It's armchair travel that turns into real travel.

I never start a trip without having every day planned out. Your reaction to an itinerary may be, "Hey, won't my spontaneity and freedom suffer?" Not necessarily. Even with my well-thought-out plan, I maintain my flexibility and make changes as needed, using my itinerary to see the consequences of any on-the-fly revisions I make. With the help of an itinerary, you can lay out your goals, maximize their potential, and avoid regrettable changes.

Your itinerary depends on several factors, including weather, crowds, geography, timeline, and travel style. (Are you antsy to see as much as you can, or do you like settling into a place for a few days?) Take the following considerations into account as you build your European itinerary.

Europe by (Tourist) Season

Some people have flexible enough jobs and lifestyles to cherry-pick when to take their vacations, but many others have less choice. Fortunately, Europe welcomes visitors 365 days a year—and each season offers a different ambience and experience.

In travel-industry jargon, the year is divided into three seasons: peak season (roughly mid-June through August), shoulder season (April through mid-June and September through October), and off-season (November through March). Each has its pros and cons. Regardless of when you go, if your objective is to "meet the people," you'll find Europe filled with them any time of year.

Peak Season

Summer is a great time to travel—except for the crowds and high temperatures. Sunny weather, long days, and exuberant nightlife turn Europe into a powerful magnet. I haven't missed a peak season in 30 years. Families with school-age children are usually locked into peak-season travel. Here are a few tips to help you keep your cool:

Arrange your trip with crowd control in mind. Go to the busy places as early or late in peak season as you can. Consider, for instance, a six-week European trip beginning June 1, half with a rail pass to see famous sights in Italy and Austria, and half visiting relatives in Scotland. It would be wise to do the rail pass section first, enjoying fewer crowds, then spend time with the family during the last half of your vacation, when Florence and Salzburg are teeming with tourists. Salzburg on June 10 and Salzburg on July 10 are two very different experiences.

Spend the night. Popular day-trip destinations near big cities and resorts such as Toledo (near Madrid), San Marino (near huge Italian beach resorts), and San Gimignano (near Florence) take on a more peaceful and enjoyable atmosphere at night, when the legions of day-trippers retreat to the predictable plumbing of their big-city or beach-resort hotels. Small towns normally lack hotels big enough for tour groups and are often inaccessible to large buses. So, at worst, they experience midday crowds. Likewise, popular cruise-ship destinations, such as Venice and Dubrovnik, are hellishly packed during the day—but more bearable at night, when the cruise crowds sail off.

Prepare for intense heat. Europeans swear that it gets hotter every year. Even restaurants in cooler climates (like Munich or Amsterdam) now tend to have ample al fresco seating to take advantage of the ever longer outdoor-dining season. Throughout Europe in July and August, expect

In peak season, sunbathers are packed like sardines on Europe's beaches. In shoulder season, the beaches are wide open.

St. Mark's Square in July—no wonder Venice is sinking...but any time of the year, walk a few blocks away and it's just you and Venice.

high temperatures—even sweltering heat—particularly in the south.

Don't discount July and August. Although Europe's tourist crowds can generally be plotted on a bell-shaped curve that peaks in July and August, there are exceptions. For instance, Paris is relatively empty in July and August but packed full in June and September for conventions and trade shows. Business-class hotels in Scandinavia are cheapest in the summer, when business travel there is down.

In much of Europe (especially Italy and France), cities are partially shut down in July and August, when local urbanites take their beach breaks. You'll hear that these are terrible times to travel, but it's really no big deal. You can't get a dentist, and many launderettes may be closed, but tourists are basically unaffected by Europe's mass holidays. Just don't get caught on the wrong road on the first or fifteenth of the month (when vacations often start or finish, causing huge traffic jams), or try to compete with all of Europe for a piece of French Riviera beach in August.

Some places are best experienced in peak season. Travel in the peak season in Scandinavia, Britain, and Ireland, where you want the best weather and longest days possible, where the horrible crowds of other destinations are rare, and where sights are sleepy or even closed in shoulder season. Scandinavia has an extremely brief tourist season—basically from mid-June to late August; I'd avoid it outside this window.

Shoulder Season

"Shoulder season"—generally April through mid-June, and September through October—combines the advantages of both peak- and off-season travel. In shoulder season, you'll enjoy decent weather, long-enough daylight, fewer crowds, and a local tourist industry still ready to please and entertain.

Shoulder season varies by destination. Because fall and spring bring cooler temperatures in Mediterranean Europe, shoulder season in much of Italy, southern France, Spain, Croatia, and Greece can actually come with near peak-season crowds and prices. For example, except for beach resorts, Italy's peak season is May, June, September, and October—not July and August. As mentioned earlier, Paris is surprisingly quiet in July and August.

Spring or fall? If debating the merits of traveling before or after summer, consider your destination. Both weather and crowds are about the same in spring or fall. Mediterranean Europe is generally green in spring, but parched in fall. For hikers, the Alps are better in early fall, because many good hiking trails are still covered with snow through the late spring.

On a budget note, keep in mind that round-trip airfares are determined by your departure date. Therefore, if you fly over during peak season and return late in the fall (shoulder season), you may still pay peak-season round-trip fares.

Off-Season

Every summer, Europe greets a stampede of sightseers. Before jumping into the peak-season pig pile, consider a trip during the off-season—generally November through March.

Expect to pay less (most of the time). Off-season airfares are often hundreds of dollars cheaper. With fewer crowds in Europe, you may find you can sleep for less: Many fine hotels drop their prices, and budget hotels will have plenty of vacancies. And while some smaller or rural accommodations may be closed, those still open are usually empty and, therefore, more comfortable. The opposite is true of big-city business centers (especially Berlin, Brussels, and the Scandinavian capitals), which are busiest with corporate travelers and most expensive off-season.

Enjoy having Europe to yourself. Off-season adventurers loiter undisturbed in Leonardo da Vinci's home, ponder Rome's Forum all alone, kick up sand on lonely Adriatic beaches, and chat with laid-back guards by log fires in French châteaux. In wintertime Venice, you can be by yourself atop St. Mark's bell tower, watching the clouds of your breath roll over the church's Byzantine domes to a horizon of cut-glass Alps. Below, on St. Mark's Square, pigeons fidget and wonder, "Where are the tourists?"

European Weather

Make sure to consider weather conditions when you make your travel plans. Europe and North America share the same latitudes and a similar climate. This map shows Europe superimposed over North America (shaded) with latitude lines. Use the map as a general weather guide. For example, London and Vancouver, Canada are located at a similar latitude and are both near the sea, so you can assume their climates are nearly the same. But you can't go by latitude alone. Rome and New York City should have similar weather, but Rome is hotter because it's surrounded by the warm Mediterranean. Inland areas have colder winters, so Prague can get as chilly as Minneapolis. Elevation affects climate as well. For average temperatures, check www.wunderground.com.

Off-season adventurers enjoy step-right-up service at shops and tourist offices, and experience a more European Europe. Although many popular tourist-oriented parks, shows, and tours will be closed, off-season is in-season for high culture: In Vienna, for example, the Boys' Choir, opera, and Lipizzaner stallions are in all their crowd-pleasing glory.

Be prepared for any kind of weather. Because much of Europe is at Canadian latitudes, the winter days are short. It's dark by 5 p.m. The weather can be miserable—cold, windy, and drizzly—and then turn worse.

Pack for the cold and wet—layers of clothing, rainproof parka, gloves, wool hat, long johns, waterproof shoes, and an umbrella. Dress warmly. Cold weather is colder when you're outdoors trying to enjoy yourself all day long, and cheap hotels can be cool and drafty in the off-season. But just as summer can be wet and gray, winter can be crisp and blue, and even into mid-November, hillsides blaze with colorful leaves.

LEFT In the north, darkness falls early in the winter. This is Oslo at 3:30 p.m.

RIGHT Italy's Cinque Terre villages are empty in the winter...and the good restaurants close for a much-needed holiday.

Beware of shorter hours. Make the most out of your limited daylight hours. Some sights close down entirely in the off-season, and most operate on shorter hours, with sunset often determining the closing time. Winter sightseeing is fine in big cities, which bustle year-round, but it's more frustrating in small tourist towns, which can be boringly quiet, with many sights and restaurants closed down. In December, most beach resorts shut up as tight as canned hams. While Europe's wonderful outdoor evening ambience survives all year in the south, wintertime streets are empty in the north after dark. English-language tours, common in the summer, are rarer off-season, when most visitors are natives. Tourist information offices normally stay open year-round, but have shorter hours in winter.

Itinerary Considerations

When planning your trip itinerary, deal thoughtfully with issues such as weather, culture shock, health maintenance, fatigue, and festivals—and you'll travel happier.

Establish a logical flight plan. Avoid needless travel time and expense by flying into one airport and out from another. You usually pay just half the round-trip fare for each airport. Even if this type of flight plan is more expensive than the cheapest round-trip fare, it often saves you lots of time and money when surface connections are figured in. For example, you could fly into London, travel east through whatever interests you in Europe, and fly home from Athens. This eliminates the costly, time-consuming, and needless return to London.

I used to fly into Amsterdam, travel to Rome, then ride one full day by train back to Amsterdam to fly home because

I thought it was "too expensive" to pay $200 extra to fly out of Rome. Now I understand the real economy—in time and money—in breaking out of the round-trip mold.

Plug various cities into flight websites and check the fares. For more on choosing flights, see page 98.

See countries in order of cultural hairiness. If you plan to see Britain, the Alps, Greece, and Turkey, do it in that order so you'll grow steadily into the more intense and crazy travel. If you've never been out of the US, flying directly into Istanbul can be overwhelming. Even if you did survive Turkey, everything after that would be anticlimactic. Start mild—that means England. England, compared to any place but the United States, is pretty dull. Don't get me wrong—it's a wonderful place to travel. But go there first, when cream teas and roundabouts will be exotic. You're more likely to enjoy Turkey, Naples, or Sarajevo if you gradually work your way south and east.

Match your destination to your interests. If you're passionate about Renaissance art, Florence is a must. England's Cotswolds beckon to those who fantasize about thatched cottages, time-passed villages, and sheep lazing on green hillsides. For World War II buffs, there's no more stirring experience than a visit to Normandy. Beer connoisseurs make pilgrimages to Belgium. If you like big cities, you'll enjoy London, Paris, Rome, and Madrid. Want to get off the beaten path? Nothing rearranges your mental furniture like a trip to Bosnia's Mostar or Morocco's Tangier.

If you have European roots, a fun part of travel is to discover a kinship with people from the land of your ancestors. I can't tell you how many American Murphys, Kellys, and O'Somethings I meet in Ireland, in search of their roots and a good beer. I'm Norwegian, and anywhere in Scandinavia, I feel like I'm among cousins, but when I cross the border into Norway, it's like I'm among brothers and sisters.

Seek out places with no promotional budgets. Keep in mind that accessibility and promotional budgets may determine a place's fame and popularity just as much as its worthiness as a tourist attraction. Places that are heavily promoted sometimes get attention not out of love for travel, beauty, and art, but out of love for your money.

Don't let well-advertised tourist traps trump more worthwhile sights.

The beaches of Greece's Peloponnesian Peninsula enjoy the same weather and water as the highly promoted isles of Santorini and Ios but are out of the way, underpromoted, and wonderfully deserted. In England, you can find yourself all alone at your own private little stone circle, and even though it's not as grandiose as Stonehenge, there's more magic there. If you're traveling by car, take advantage of your mobility by leaving the well-worn tourist routes. Europe away from the train tracks is less expensive and feels more peaceful and relaxed. Overlooked by the rail pass mobs, it's one step behind the modern parade.

Moderate the weather conditions you'll encounter. Over my many years of travels, my routine has been spring in the Mediterranean area and summer north of the Alps. Match the coolest month of your trip with the warmest area, and vice versa. For a spring and early-summer trip, enjoy comfortable temperatures throughout by starting in the southern countries and working your way north. If possible, avoid the midsummer Mediterranean heat and crowds of Italy and southern France. Spend those weeks in Scandinavia, Britain, Ireland, or the Alps (which may also increase your odds of sun in places prone to miserable weather).

Alternate intense big cities with villages and coun-tryside. For example, break a tour of Venice, Florence, and Rome with an easygoing time in Italy's hill towns or on the Italian Riviera. Judging Italy by Rome alone is like judging America by New York City.

Join the celebration. If you like parties, hit as many festivals, national holidays, and arts seasons as you can (or, if you hate crowds, learn the dates to avoid). An effort to visit the right places at the right times will drape your trip with festive tinsel. This takes some planning. One of the best places to start is with the list of major holidays and festivals, organized by country, at www.ricksteves.com/festivals. Remember that event dates can change, so be sure to verify them on each festival's website or with a local tourist infor-mation office (and book your room well in advance).

Train or plane within Europe? Do a cost and time analy-sis to help you decide the best mode of transportation for your trip. Not too long ago, I'd piece together a trip based on which towns could be connected by train. Today, there are fewer night trains, and it's relatively cheap and easy to com-bine, say, Portugal, Poland, and Palermo on a single itinerary by air (for more on cheap flights, see page 112).

Numbers and Stumblers

Europeans convey numerical information differently than we do, from measurements to schedules and even dates. Knowing the differences will save needless confusion when planning itineraries or making reservations.

Time and Date

The 24-hour clock (military time) is used in any official timetable. This includes bus, train, and tour schedules. Learn to use it quickly and easily. Everything is the same until 12:00. Then, the Europeans keep on going—13:00, 14:00, and so on. For any time after noon, subtract 12 and add p.m. (18:00 is 6 p.m.).

To figure out the time back home, remember that European time is generally six/nine hours ahead of the East/West Coasts of the US. (These are the major exceptions: British, Irish, and Portuguese time is five/eight hours ahead; Greece and Turkey are seven/ten hours ahead.) Europe observes Daylight Saving Time (called "Summer Time" in the UK), but on a slightly different schedule than the US: Europe "springs forward" on the last Sunday in March (three weeks after most of North America) and "falls back" the last Sunday in October (one week before North America). For a handy online time converter, try www.timeanddate.com/worldclock.

When it comes to dates, remember—especially when making reservations—that European date order is written day/month/year. Christmas 2019, for example, is 25/12/19 instead of 12/25/19, as we would write it. Also, European wall calendars tend to start on a Monday, not Sunday.

Written Numbers

A European's handwritten numbers look different from ours. The number 1 has an upswing (∕). The number 4 often looks like a short lightning bolt (∮). If you don't

A train ride itself may take longer than a flight, but for most train journeys you just hop aboard (no lengthy check-in), and most trains arrive right in the heart of town. For a flight, you'll need to add in the time it takes to get to and from the airport, as well as how early you'll need to arrive for check-in.

Minimize one-night stands. Even the speediest itinerary should be a series of two-night stands. I'd stretch every other day with long hours on the road or train and hurried sightseeing along the way in order to enjoy the sanity of two nights in the same bed. Minimizing hotel changes saves time and money, and gives you the sensation of actually being comfortable in a town on the second night.

Leave some slack in your itinerary. Don't schedule yourself too tightly (a common tendency). Everyday chores, small business matters, transportation problems, constipation, and planning mistakes deserve about one day of slack per week in your itinerary. For long trips, schedule a "vacation from your vacation" in the middle of it. Most people need several days in a place where they couldn't see a museum or cross your 7 ($\mathcal{7}$), it may be mistaken as a sloppy 1, and you could miss your train. Don't use "#" for "number"—it's not common in Europe.

On the continent, commas are decimal points and decimals are commas, so a euro and a half is €1,50 and there are 5.280 feet in a mile. (Britain and Ireland use commas and decimal points like North America.)

Metric Conversion

Expect to confront the metric system in your European travels. Here are some easy ways to guesstimate metric conversions: Since a meter is 39 inches, just consider a meter roughly equivalent to a yard. A kilometer is a bit more than a half-mile (1 kilometer = 0.62 mile). A liter is nearly the same as a quart (1.056 quarts, to be exact)—about four to a gallon. A centimeter is about half the distance across a penny (1 inch = 2.54 centimeters), while a millimeter is about the thickness of a penny (1 inch = 25 millimeters). In markets, it's handy to know that 1 ounce = 28 grams, and 2.2 pounds = 1 kilogram.

Converting Temperatures

Europeans measure temperatures in degrees Celsius (zero degrees C = 32 degrees F). To convert Celsius to Fahrenheit, divide C by 5, multiply by 9, and add 32 to get F. If that's too scary, it's easier and nearly as accurate to double the Celsius temperature and add 30. So if it's 27° C, double to 54 and add 30 to get 84° F (it's actually 81° F, but that's close enough for me). To convert Fahrenheit to Celsius, subtract 32, divide by 9, then multiply by 5; or take the easy route—just subtract 30 and divide by 2. A memory aid: 28° C = 82° F—balmy summer weather.

take a tour even if they wanted to. A stop in the mountains or on an island, in a friendly rural town, or at the home of a relative is a great way to revitalize your tourist spirit.

Assume you will return. This "General MacArthur" approach is a key to touristic happiness. You can't cover all of Europe in one trip—don't even try. Enjoy what you're seeing. Forget what you won't get to on this trip. If you worry about things that are just out of reach, you won't appreciate what's in your hand. I've taken dozens of European trips, and I still need more time. I'm happy about what I can't get to. It's a blessing that we can never see all of Europe.

Your Best Itinerary in Eight Steps

Trying to narrow your choices among European destinations is a bit like being a kid in a candy shop. The options are endless and everything looks delicious (and consuming too much isn't good for you). Start by listing every place you'd like to visit, then turn that list into a smart itinerary by following these steps.

1. Decide on the places you want to see. Start by writing out your wish list ("Places I want to see—London, Alps, Bavaria, Florence, Amsterdam, Paris, the Rhine, Rome, Venice, Greece"). Then make sure you have a reason for every stop. Don't visit Casablanca because you liked the movie. Just because George Clooney bought a villa on Lake Como doesn't mean you should go there, too.

2. Establish a route and timeline. Circle your destinations on a map, then figure out a logical geographical order and length for your trip. Pin down any places that you have to be on a certain date (and ask yourself if it's really worth stifling your flexibility). Once you've settled on a list, be satisfied with your efficient plan, and focus any more study and preparation only on places that fall along your proposed route.

Sample Itinerary

NT   Night Train
•   Overnight
.... Rhine Cruise

3. Decide on the cities you'll fly in and out of. Flying into one city and out of another is usually more efficient than booking a round-trip flight. Think carefully about which cities make the most sense as a first stop or a finale. If you'll be renting a car, remember that a one-way drop-off fee can add to your costs, especially if you are crossing country borders.

4. Determine the mode of transportation. Base this not solely on cost, but by what's best for the trip you envision. Study the ins and outs of the many ways of getting from point A to point B—whether flying, riding the rails, driving, biking, or hiking.

For example, if you're traveling alone, traversing a huge area, and spending the majority of your time in big cities, it makes more sense to go by train with a rail pass than to mess with a car.

5. Make a rough itinerary. Sketch out an itinerary, writing in the number of days you'd like to stay in each place (knowing you'll probably have to trim it later). Take advantage of weekends to stretch your time and minimize lost workdays.

Carefully consider travel time. Estimate how long various journeys will take by rail (www.bahn.com), air (www.

Planning an Itinerary

SEPTEMBER

SUN.	MON.	TUE.	WED.	THUR.	FRI.	SAT.
		1	2 Mom's Birthday! ··	3	4 Fly USA	5 Arrive London L
6 London L	7 London L	8 London, eve. train to Paris P	9 Paris P	10 Paris P	11 S.T. Versailles P	12 Train to Alps A
13 Alps A	Uffizi Closed 14 Train to Florence F	15 Florence, see museums F	Early 16 train to Rome R	17 Rome R	Early 18 train to Venice V	19 Venice N.T.
Oktober-Fest! 20 ·· Munich M	Dachau Closed 21 S.T. Neusch. Castle M	22 S.T. Salzburg M	To 23 Romantic Road, Rothenburg ROT	Train to 24 Rhine, River Cruise RH	25 To Amst. A	26 Amsterdam A
Fly 27 Arrive USA	Back to 28 Work ‿	29	30			

Use abbreviations in the bottom right of each calendar day to indicate where you'll spend the night (for example, L = London).
N.T. = Night Train; S.T. = Side Trip.

skyscanner.com), or by car (www.viamichelin.com). Rome2Rio.com provides an overview of transportation options from Point A to Point B, including by plane, train, bus, car, or boat. Consider night trains or overnight boats to save time and money.

My rough itinerary, with desired number of days:

3 *London*
5 *Paris*
3 *Alps*
2 *Florence*
3 *Rome (flight or train)*
7 *Greece (flight or train + night boat)*
1 *Bologna*
2 *Venice (night train)*
3 *Munich/Bavaria*
3 *Romantic Road/Rhine Cruise*
3 *Berlin*
4 *Amsterdam*

39 TOTAL DAYS

6. Adjust by cutting, streamlining, or adding to fit your timeline or budget. If your rough itinerary exceeds your available time or money, look for ways to save on travel time and/or cost. If two destinations are equally important to you but you don't have time for both, cut the place that takes the most time, hassle, or expense to reach. For example, my rough itinerary (on previous page) is too long: I have only 22 days for my trip. Based on time saved, I cut Greece, and even though I'd like to see both Amsterdam and Berlin, I drop Berlin because it takes longer to get to.

Then I minimize clutter. A so-so destination (Bologna) breaking up a relatively short train ride (Rome-Venice) is clutter.

Next, eliminate repetition. On a quick trip, focus on only one part of the Romantic Road (my favorite stop is Rothenburg). The Rhine Valley is chock-a-block with castles. Choose one (Rheinfels, above the town of St. Goar).

Finally, I trim time from each stop. Five days in Paris would be grand, but I can see the high points in four. There's a slope of diminishing return for each day that you stay in a town. Day number five in a great city is not as good as day number one in a secondary city.

It can also help to consider economizing on car rental or a rail pass. For instance, a 22-day trip can be managed with a 15-day train pass by seeing London, Paris, and Amsterdam before or after using the pass.

My final itinerary, with number of days adjusted to time limitations:

3	London
4	Paris
2	Alps
2	Florence
2	Rome
2	Venice
3	Munich/Bavaria
2	Romantic Road/Rhine Cruise
2	Amsterdam
22	TOTAL DAYS

7. Fine-tune your itinerary. Study your guidebook. Take advantage of online tools and apps that allow you to browse destinations, map itineraries, and even get advice from friends or fellow travelers. Be sure crucial sights are open the day you'll be in town. Remember that most major tourist attractions close for one day during the week (usually Monday). It would be a shame to be in Paris only on a Monday, when the Orsay is *fermé*. Write out a day-by-day itinerary that takes into account any can't-miss sights, festivals, or markets. Note that when flying from the United States, you'll most likely arrive in Europe on the next day. When returning, you arrive home the same day (or so you hope).

8. Organize and share your itinerary. Whether you want to meet up with friends along the way, let family members know where you'll be, or just corral all your travel details in one place—an itinerary chart saved in a Word document or Excel chart makes it easy to share your plans. Tools such as TripIt can also help; using your confirmation emails, the app creates an itinerary—with maps, directions, and recommendations—that you can access from your smartphone and share.

The Home-Base Strategy

Staying longer in one spot can be a good way to make your trip itinerary smoother, simpler, and more efficient. Set yourself up in a central location and use that place as a base for day trips to nearby attractions.

The home-base approach minimizes set-up time. Changing hotels frequently can be exhausting, frustrating, and time-consuming. Many hotels give a better price, or at least more smiles, for longer stays. Some B&Bs don't accept those staying only one night.

You are freed from your luggage. Being able to leave your luggage in the hotel lets you travel freely and with the peace of mind that you are set for the night. Bags are less likely to be lost or stolen in your hotel than en route.

You feel "at home" in your home-base town. This comfortable feeling takes more than a day to get, and when you're changing locations every day or two, you may never enjoy this important sense of rootedness. Home-basing allows you to become attuned to the rhythm of daily life.

Day-trip to a village, enjoy the nightlife in a city. The home-base approach lets you spend the evening in a city, where there is more exciting nightlife. Most small countryside towns die after 9 p.m. If you're not dead by 9 p.m., you'll enjoy the action in a larger city.

Transportation is a snap. Europe's generally frequent and punctual train and bus systems (many of which operate out of

Tracking Your Itinerary

Once I've fine-tuned my itinerary, I put everything into a chart like this one. This system keeps me organized, since I can collect all my reservations, train times, and other trip notes in one place. As I travel, I can see at a glance where I'll be sleeping a week from now, or what time the train leaves on Saturday. Even if you're not a detail person, it pays to be disciplined about this. And it's handy to give to family, friends, and coworkers who are curious about where you'll be.

Once you've created the chart, use it to keep track of your progress as you systematically set up your trip. Work your way through your list and request rooms, slogging away until the entire trip is confirmed. Make any advance train or sightseeing reservations you'll need (for this itinerary, I'd reserve the Eurostar and overnight trains ahead of time, as well as tickets for the Eiffel Tower). For the biggest discounts, buy train tickets up to three months ahead (but keep in mind these tickets are nonrefundable and nonchangeable). Then…travel, enjoying a well-planned trip.

Date	Travel	Sleep/Notes
Fri, Sept 4	Fly to London after work (depart 6 p.m.)	Plane
Sat, Sept 5	Arrive London at 11:45 a.m., check in at hotel, take orientation bus tour	Luna Simone Hotel, London Original London Sightseeing Bus Tour is discounted with guidebook
Sun, Sept 6	Sightsee London (Tower of London, Shakespeare's Globe tour, Tate Modern)	Luna Simone Hotel, London Many sights closed today; Speaker's Corner open today only
Mon, Sept 7	See more London (Westminster Abbey, National Gallery, evening play)	Luna Simone Hotel, London Parliament open late; check for discount theater tickets at Leicester Square

a hub anyway) make this home-base strategy practical. With a train pass, trips are "free"; otherwise, the transportation is reasonable, sometimes with reductions offered for round-trip tickets (especially for "same-day return").

Good Home-Base Cities

Here are some of my favorite places to call home, along with the best day trips from each.

Madrid: Toledo, Segovia, El Escorial, and even Sevilla and Córdoba with the AVE bullet trains

Amsterdam: Most of the Netherlands, particularly Alkmaar, Enkhuizen's Zuiderzee Museum, Arnhem's Netherlands Open-Air Museum and Kröller-Müller Museum, Delft, The Hague, Scheveningen, and Edam

Date	Travel	Sleep/Notes
Tue, Sept 8	Wrap up London (St. Paul's/ The City, British Museum); take evening train to Paris (6-9:20 p.m.)	Grand Hôtel Lévêque, Paris Confirm Paris hotel before leaving London
Wed, Sept 9	Sightsee Paris (historic core, incl. Notre-Dame, Sainte-Chapelle; also Louvre, Eiffel Tower at night)	Grand Hôtel Lévêque, Paris Museums crowded today; Louvre open late
Thu, Sept 10	Sightsee Paris (Champs-Elysées, Rodin Museum, Orsay)	Grand Hôtel Lévêque, Paris Orsay open late
Fri, Sept 11	Side-trip to Versailles	Grand Hôtel Lévêque, Paris
Sat, Sept 12	Take morning train (7 a.m.-2 p.m) to Interlaken, Swiss Alps; maybe hike in late afternoon	Olle and Maria's B&B, Gimmelwald
Sun, Sept 13	Sightsee Alps (breakfast at the Schilthorn, Männlichen-Kleine Scheidegg hike)	Olle and Maria's B&B, Gimmelwald If rainy, visit Bern
Mon, Sept 14	Short morning hike and/ or visit Trümmelbach Falls, afternoon train to Florence (from Interlaken 1:30-7 p.m.)	Hotel Centrale, Florence If rainy, take morning train to Florence (from Interlaken 7:30 a.m.-1 p.m.); on arrival, do walking tour since most museums closed

and so on...

Copenhagen: Frederiksborg Castle, Roskilde, Helsingør, Odense, and over the bridge to Malmö (Sweden)

Paris: Versailles, Chartres, Vaux-le-Vicomte, Fontainebleau, Chantilly, Giverny, Reims

London: Bath, Stonehenge, Cambridge, York, and many others; even Paris is less than three hours away by train

Arles: Pont du Gard, Nîmes, Avignon, and the rest of Provence

Florence: Siena, Pisa, San Gimignano, and many other hill towns

Venice: Padua, Vicenza, Verona, and Ravenna

Munich: Salzburg, "Mad" King Ludwig's castles (Neuschwanstein and Linderhof), the Wieskirche, Oberammergau, and other small Bavarian towns

Sorrento: Naples, Pompeii, Herculaneum, Mount Vesuvius, Amalfi Coast, Paestum, and Capri

High-Speed Town-Hopping

When I tell people that I saw three or four towns in one day, many think, "Insane! Nobody can really see several towns in a day!" Of course, it's folly to go too fast, but many stop-worthy towns take only an hour or two to cover. Don't let feelings of guilt tell you to slow down and stay longer if you really are finished with a town. There's so much more to enjoy in the rest of Europe. Going too slow is as bad as going too fast.

If you're efficient and use the high-speed town-hopping method, you'll amaze yourself with what you can see in a day. Let me explain with an example:

You wake up early in A-ville. Checking out of your hotel, you have one sight to see before your 10 a.m. train. (You checked the train schedule the night before.) After the sightseeing and before getting to the station, you visit the open-air market and buy the ingredients for your brunch, and pick up a B-burg map and tourist brochure at A-ville's tourist office.

From 10 to 11 a.m. you travel by train to B-burg. During that hour you have a restful brunch, enjoy the passing scenery, and prepare for B-burg by reading your literature and deciding what you want to see. Just before your arrival, put the items you need (camera, jacket, tourist information) into your small daypack. Then, as soon as you get there, check the rest of your luggage in a locker. (Most stations have storage lockers or a baggage-check desk.)

Before leaving B-burg's station, write down the departure times of the next few trains to C-town. Now you can sightsee as much or as little as you want and still know when to comfortably catch your train.

B-burg is great, so you stay a little longer than anticipated. After a snack in the park, you catch the train at 2:30 p.m. By 3 p.m. you're in C-town, where you repeat the same procedure you followed in B-burg. C-town just isn't what it was cracked up to be, so after a walk along the waterfront and a look at the church, you catch the next train out at 5 p.m.

You arrive in D-dorf, the last town on the day's agenda, by 5:30 p.m. A man in the station directs you to a good budget pension two blocks down the street. You're checked in and unpacked in no time, and, after a few horizontal moments, it's time to find a good restaurant and eat dinner. After a meal and an evening stroll, you're ready to call it a day. As you write in your journal, it occurs to you: This was a great sightseeing day. You spent it high-speed town-hopping.

PRIORITIZING YOUR TIME

So much to see, so little time. How to choose? It depends on your interest and your tastes. One person's Barcelona is another person's Bucharest.

The Best and Worst of Europe (with No Apologies)

Good travel writers should make hard choices and give the reader solid opinions. Just so nobody will accuse me of gutlessness, I've assembled a pile of spunky opinions. Chances are that you have too many stops on your trip wish list and not enough time. To make your planning a little easier, heed these warnings. These are just my personal feelings after more than 100 months of European travel. And if you disagree with any of them, you obviously haven't been there.

Let's start with the dullest corner of the British Isles, southern Scotland. It's so boring the Romans decided to block it off with Hadrian's Wall. However, like Venice's St. Mark's Square at midnight and Napoleon's tomb in Paris, Hadrian's Wall itself covers history buffs with goose bumps.

London, York, Bath, and Edinburgh are the most interesting cities in Britain. Belfast, Liverpool, and

LEFT Geneva's newspaper objects to my "denigrating" its dull city on the Internet.

RIGHT In Switzerland, special scenic trains give you front row seats and the Alps in your lap.

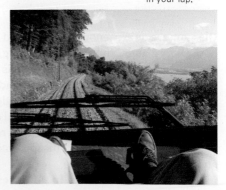

Itinerary Priorities, Country by Country

Use this chart to get ideas on how speedy travelers can prioritize limited sightseeing time in various countries. Add places from left to right as you build plans for the best of that country in 3, 5, 7, 10, or 14 days. (These suggestions take geographical proximity into account.) So, according to this chart, the best week in Britain would be spread between London, Bath, the Cotswolds, and York.

3 Days	5 Days	7 Days	10 Days	14 Days
EUROPE				
Forget it	London, Paris	Amsterdam	Rhineland, Swiss Alps	Rome, Venice
BRITAIN				
London	Bath, Cotswolds	York	Stratford, Edinburgh	North Wales, Wells, Glastonbury, Avebury
IRELAND				
Dublin	Dingle Peninsula	Galway, Aran Islands	County Clare/ Burren, Kilkenny/ Cashel	Belfast, Antrim Coast, Kinsale, Kenmare/Ring of Kerry
FRANCE				
Paris, Versailles	Normandy	Loire	Dordogne, Carcassonne	Provence, Riviera
GERMANY				
Munich, Bavarian castles	Rhine Valley, Rothenburg	More Bavaria, Salzburg (Austria)	Berlin	Baden-Baden, Black Forest, Dresden
AUSTRIA				
Vienna	Salzburg	Hallstatt	Danube Valley, Tirol, Bavaria (Germany)	Innsbruck, Hall, Bratislava (Slovakia)

Glasgow are quirky enough to be called interesting. I enjoy both Oxford and Cambridge, but seeing one university town is enough. Stratford-upon-Avon is little more than Shakespeare's house—and that's as dead as he is.

The west coast of Ireland (the Dingle Peninsula), Wales' Snowdonia National Park, and England's Windermere Lake District are the most beautiful natural regions of the British Isles. The North York Moors disappoint most creatures great and small.

Extra caution is merited in southwest England, a

3 Days	5 Days	7 Days	10 Days	14 Days
SWITZERLAND				
Berner Oberland	Luzern and Central Switzerland	Bern, Lake Geneva area, Golden Pass scenic rail	Zermatt, Appenzell, Glacier Express train	Lugano and Pontresina area, Bernina Express and Gotthard Panorama Express trains
ITALY				
Florence, Venice	Rome	Cinque Terre	Civita di Bagnoregio, Siena	Sorrento, Naples, Pompeii, Amalfi Coast, Paestum
SCANDINAVIA				
Copenhagen, side-trips	Stockholm	Oslo, "Norway in a Nutshell" train trip	Bergen, Helsinki	Ærø, Odense, Roskilde, Frederiksborg
SPAIN				
Madrid, Toledo	Barcelona	Sevilla, Granada	Andalucía, Morocco	Salamanca, Segovia
PORTUGAL				
Lisbon, Sintra	Algarve	Évora, Nazaré	Sights near Nazaré, Coimbra	Porto, Douro Valley
EASTERN EUROPE				
Prague	Budapest	Kraków and Auschwitz	Slovenia, Český Krumlov	Ljubljana, Lake Bled, Vienna
CROATIA & SLOVENIA				
Dubrovnik	Mostar, Split	Korčula/Hvar, Montenegro, or Sarajevo	Lake Bled, Plitvice Lakes, Julian Alps	Ljubljana, Istria
GREECE				
Athens	Hydra	Delphi	Nafplio, Epidavros, Mycenae	Olympia, Monemvasia, Kardamyli and the Mani Peninsula

minefield of tourist traps. The British are masters at milking every conceivable tourist attraction for all it's worth. Here are some booby traps: the Devil's Toenail (a rock that looks just like a...toenail), Land's End (pay, pay, pay), and cloying Clovelly (a one-street town lined with knickknack shops selling the same goodies—like "clotted cream that you can mail home"). While Tintagel's castle, famous as the legendary birthplace of King Arthur, offers thrilling windswept and wave-beaten ruins, the town of Tintagel does everything in its little power to exploit the profitable Arthurian legend. There's even a pub in town called the Excali Bar.

Germany's Heidelberg, Ireland's Blarney Stone (slobbered on by countless tourists to get the "gift of gab"), Spain's Costa del Sol, and the French Riviera in July and August are among Europe's most overrated spots. The tackiest souvenirs are found next to Pisa's leaning tower and in Lourdes.

Sognefjord is Norway's most spectacular fjord. The Geirangerfjord, while famous as a cruise-ship stop, is a disappointment. The most boring countryside is Sweden's (yes, I'm Norwegian), although Scandinavia's best medieval castle is in the Swedish town of Kalmar.

Norway's Stavanger, famous for nearby fjords and its status as an oil boomtown, is a large port that's about as exciting as...well, put it this way: Emigrants left it in droves to move to the wilds of Minnesota. Time in western Norway is better spent in and around Bergen.

Geneva, one of Switzerland's largest and most sterile cities, gets the "nice place to live but I wouldn't want to visit" award. It's pleasantly situated on a lake—just like Buffalo, New York. While it's famous, name familiarity is a rotten reason to go somewhere. If you want a Swiss city, see Bern or Luzern. However, it's almost criminal to spend a sunny Swiss day in a city if you haven't yet been high in the Alps.

Bordeaux must mean "boredom" in some ancient language. If I were offered a free trip to that town, I'd stay home and clean the fridge. Connoisseurs visit for the wine, but Bordeaux wine country and Bordeaux city are as different as night and night soil. There's a wine-tourism information bureau in Bordeaux that, for a price, will bus

LEFT Kissing the Blarney Stone: Slathered with spit and lipstick, it's a standard stop for typical big-bus tours in Ireland.

RIGHT England's Land's End... pay, pay, pay.

you out of town into the more interesting wine country nearby.

Andorra, a small country in the Pyrenees between France and Spain, is as scenic as any other chunk of those mountains. People from all over Europe flock to Andorra to take advantage of its famous duty-free shopping. As far as Americans are concerned, Andorra is just a big Spanish-speaking outlet mall. There are no bargains here that you can't get at home. Enjoy the Pyrenees elsewhere, with less traffic. Among Europe's other "little countries," San Marino and Liechtenstein are also not worth the trouble.

Germany's famous Black Forest disappoints more people than it excites. If it were all Germany offered, it would be worth seeing. For Europeans, any large forest is understandably a popular attraction. But I'd say the average American visitor who's seen more than three trees in one place would prefer Germany's Romantic Road and Bavaria to the east, the Rhine and Mosel country to the north, the Swiss Alps to the south, and France's Alsace region to the west—all high points that cut the Black Forest down to stumps.

Kraków (Poland) and Budapest (Hungary) are, after Prague, Eastern Europe's best cities. Bucharest, Romania's capital, has little to offer. Its top-selling postcard is of the InterContinental Hotel. If you're heading from Eastern Europe to Greece, skip Thessaloniki, which deserves its place in the Bible but doesn't belong in travel guidebooks.

Europe's most scenic train ride is the Glacier Express, across southern Switzerland from Chur to Zermatt. The most scenic boat ride is from Stockholm to Helsinki—countless islands and blondes. Europe's most underrated sight is Rome's ancient seaport, Ostia Antica, and its most misunderstood wine is Portugal's *vinho verde* (green wine).

The best French château is Vaux-le-Vicomte, near Paris. The best Gothic interior is found in Paris' Sainte-Chapelle

Varenna, on Italy's beautiful Lake Como, whispers *lune di miele* (honeymoon).

church. The top two medieval castle interiors are Germany's Burg Eltz on the Mosel River, and northern Italy's Reifenstein, near the Brenner Pass. Lisbon, Oslo, Stockholm, Brussels, and Budapest are the most underrated big cities.

To honeymoon (or convalesce), try these tiny towns: Beilstein on Germany's Mosel River; Hallstatt on Austria's Lake Hallstatt; Varenna on Italy's Lake Como; Ærøskøbing on an island in south Denmark; and Gimmelwald, high in the Swiss Alps. Have fun (or get well)!

Paper Chase

Someday, perhaps, travel will be completely paperless. But we're not there yet, so you'll need to be equipped with the necessary documents, identification, and insurance coverage. Here's how to stay ahead in the inevitable paper chase.

TRAVEL DOCUMENTS

Your trip won't get off the ground if you don't prepare your documents well before your departure date. Give yourself plenty of lead time.

Passports

In much of Europe, the only document a US or Canadian citizen needs is a passport. (The US Passport Card works only for those driving or cruising to Canada, Mexico, Bermuda, and the Caribbean.) And for most American travelers, the only time any customs official looks at you seriously is at the airport as you re-enter the United States.

Getting or Renewing Your Passport: US passports, good for 10 years, cost $135 ($110 to renew). The fee for minors under 16 (including infants) is $105 for a passport good for five years—kids under 16 must apply in person with at least one parent and the other parent's notarized permission. (See page 454 for other document needs when traveling abroad with children.)

You can apply at some courthouses and post offices, as well as municipal buildings, such as your City Hall. For details and the location of the nearest passport-acceptance facility, see Travel.state.gov or call 877-487-2778. Processing time varies; the current wait is posted on the State Department website. During busier periods, a six-week wait is common. Five to seven days after you apply, you can check online for the status of your application and your passport's estimated arrival date.

If you need your passport in less than six weeks, tack on an additional $60 expediting fee (plus overnight shipping both ways), and you'll get it by mail within three weeks. In a last-minute emergency, call the above number and speak to a customer-service representative. If you can prove that you must travel within two weeks (by showing evidence of a purchased airline ticket or a letter from work requiring you to go overseas on short notice), you may be able to receive a passport in 24-72 hours. Make an appointment to go in person to the nearest US Passport Agency and pay the additional $60 fee.

Your passport is your most important travel document.

Keep an eye on your passport's expiration date. Many European countries require that your passport be valid for at least six months *after* your ticketed date of return to the United States. This means that even if your passport doesn't expire for a few months, you may be denied entry to a country. Check your destination country's requirements, and if necessary, get your passport renewed well before you go.

Some countries can have surprising entry requirements. For example, the Czech Republic and Poland technically require visitors to carry proof of medical insurance (your health insurance card usually suffices). For requirements per country, check with the US Department of State at Travel.state.gov.

If you're a frequent international traveler, consider the US Customs' Global Entry Program, which lets you bypass passport control at major US airports ($100 fee, www.globalentry.gov).

Any US citizen can use the free Mobile Passport app (www.mobilepassport.us), which lets you use an express lane to pass through customs. Download it before you leave, enter your individual flight info when you return to the US, then scan your phone at a Mobile Passport express lane.

Canadian citizens can refer to the government of Canada's travel site at Travel.gc.ca for passport information.

Traveling with Your Passport: Take good care of your passport. Keep it in your money belt, and if you're asked to show it, put it back in your money belt right away. For tips on keeping your money belt—and its contents safe—see page 377.

Replacing Your Passport: If you need to replace a lost or stolen passport in Europe, it's much easier to do if you have a photocopy of it and a couple of passport-type photos, either brought from home or taken in Europe. For details on getting a replacement, see page 385. For tips on preparing and protecting key documents while traveling, see page 69.

Visas

A visa is a stamp placed in your passport by a foreign government, allowing you to enter that country. Visas are not required for Americans or Canadians traveling in Western Europe and most of the East (including the Czech Republic, Slovakia, Poland, Hungary, Slovenia, Croatia, Bosnia-Herzegovina, Montenegro, and the Baltic states). Visas *are* required to visit Turkey and Russia. For travel beyond Europe, get information on visa requirements from your travel agent or the US Department of State.

No Visa Required: When you enter a country without a visa you're officially on "short stay visitor" status. Within the Schengen area (see sidebar), that means you can stay up to 90 days within a 180-day period; most non-Schengen countries in Europe also have a 90-day limit (one big exception is the UK, which allows you to stay up to six months within a 12-month period). If your trip will extend beyond the three-month mark, you'll need to get creative with your travel plans (for example, spend the requisite amount of time outside the Schengen area before re-entering) or look into a long-stay visa.

Turkey: Both Canadians and Americans must obtain a visa before entering Turkey. You can get your "e-visa" online (www.evisa.gov.tr), or

European Borders (or Not)

Thanks to a series of treaties known as the Schengen Agreement, today there are virtually no border checks between 26 of Europe's countries: Austria, Belgium, the Czech Republic, Denmark, Estonia, Finland, France, Germany, Greece, Hungary, Iceland, Italy, Latvia, Liechtenstein, Lithuania, Luxembourg, Malta, the Netherlands, Norway, Poland, Portugal, Slovakia, Slovenia, Spain, Sweden, and Switzerland. Of the current European Union countries, only the United Kingdom and the Republic of Ireland are holdouts when it comes to passport control.

So what does Schengen mean for you? Schengen or no, you always need to show your passport at your first point of entry into Europe, when you exit Europe, and to re-enter the US. When traveling between participating countries, you usually won't have to stop or show a passport: You'll simply blow past abandoned border posts on the superhighway or high-speed train. Non-Schengen countries still have border checks—but the border crossing is generally just a quick wave-through for US citizens.

Be aware that the policy of free movement within the Schengen area is constantly changing in the wake of terrorist attacks and the migrant crisis. You may face internal border checks in some countries. These measures aren't aimed at leisure travelers, but don't be surprised if you encounter an ID check within the EU at an airport, train station, or highway border crossing.

visit a Turkish consulate or embassy. US residents pay $20; Canadians pay $60—that's US dollars, not Canadian. However, cruise-line passengers don't need a visa if they visit Turkey by day but spend nights aboard their ship. On the other hand, cruise passengers arriving in Turkey to start their cruise, or staying on Turkish soil for more than 72 hours, must get a visa before their arrival in Turkey. For more information, see the websites Washington.emb.mfa.gov.tr (Turkey's embassy in the US) or Ottava.be.mfa.gov.tr (Turkey's embassy in Canada).

Your passport will be stamped when you enter your first European country.

Russia: Travelers to Russia also need visas. The process can be expensive, and you should begin at least 60 days before your departure. Before applying for a visa, you must first get an official document called a "visa invitation" or a "visa support letter" (generally from a hotel or visa agency). You'll also need to fill out an electronic visa application. The Russian embassy does not accept visa applications by mail, so it's smart to use an agency that specializes in steering your application through the process. Passport Visas Express is one of many such vendors (www.passportvisasexpress.com). The costs add up; figure around $325 total per person to cover the visa, visa invitation, service fee, and secure shipping. For more details, go to www.ricksteves.com/russianvisa or see RussianEmbassy.org (which lists Russian consulate locations in New York, San Francisco, Seattle, Houston, and Washington, DC). If you live near one of these consulates, you can save some money (but go through a lot of steps) by applying for your visa in person at the consulate.

Student Cards

Students in high school or college should always carry their school ID cards when traveling. In general, people under 26 years of age are eligible for many discounts in Europe: Show your student ID at ticket counters, museums, and bus and train stations, and you'll be surprised at the number of discounts you'll receive.

Some young travelers like to carry the International Student Identity Card (ISIC), an internationally recognized student ID card that provides discounts on transportation and sightseeing throughout Europe, and includes some basic trip insurance. Cards cost $25 and are good for one year from the date of issue (you must be a full-time student). They're

available on the ISIC website (www.myisic.com), through
STA Travel (www.statravel.com), or from your university
foreign-study office.

Rail Passes and Car Documents

Most rail passes are not sold in Europe and must be purchased before you leave home (for more on rail passes, see
the Trains, Buses & Boats chapter). If you're renting a car,
be aware that an International Driving Permit is required in
Austria, Bosnia-Herzegovina, Croatia, Greece, Hungary, Italy,
Poland, Romania, Slovakia, Slovenia, and Spain ($20 plus tax,
get it at AAA before your departure). Even if you aren't renting a car in Europe, bring along your driver's license—it can
come in handy if you need to leave a piece of ID to rent a bike
or audioguide and you don't want to part with your passport.
For specifics, see the Driving & Navigating chapter.

Copying Key Documents

Before your trip, make photocopies and/or take photos of
your documents (front and back) to pack along or leave with
someone at home in case of an emergency. It's smart to make
copies of the following:

- Passport
- Rail pass
- Car-rental voucher
- Prescriptions for eyewear and medicine

Don't photocopy a debit or credit card—instead, keep just
the number in a retrievable place. Consider bringing a couple
of extra passport-type pictures, which can expedite the
replacement process for a lost or stolen passport (to replace a
passport, see page 386). If you're traveling with a companion,
carry photocopies of each other's passports and other important documents. Guard your photocopies as carefully as you
would the originals. I hide mine in a pouch clipped into the
bottom of my luggage (don't tell anyone).

Some people scan their documents and email them
to their account, or store them on a cloud service such as
Dropbox for easy access from the road (see page 433 for more
about online storage). If you're concerned about electronic
copies of your key documents floating around in cyberspace,
you could save them to a USB flash drive and tuck it into your
money belt.

It's also smart to have a backup physical or digital copy of
your itinerary, including hotel and car-rental confirmations
and sight reservations. An itinerary-storage website, such

as TripIt.com, is handy; you can also store a list of contacts, including your hotels—printed as small as you can read on a slip of paper—in your money belt.

TRAVEL INSURANCE

Travel insurance can minimize the considerable financial risks of traveling: accidents, illness, missed flights, canceled tours, lost baggage, theft, terrorism, travel-company bankruptcies, emergency evacuation, and getting your body home if you die. Each traveler's potential loss varies, depending on how much of your trip is prepaid, the refundability of the air ticket you purchased, your state of health, the value of your luggage, where you're traveling, the financial health of your tour company and airline, and what coverage you already have (through your medical insurance, homeowners or renters insurance, and/or credit card).

For some travelers, insurance is a good deal; for others, it's not. What are the chances you'll need it? How willing are you to take risks? How much is peace of mind worth to you? Take these considerations into account, understand your options, and make an informed decision for your trip.

Insurance Basics

The insurance menu includes five main courses: trip cancellation and interruption, medical, evacuation, baggage, and flight insurance. Supplemental policies can be added to cover specific concerns, such as identity theft or political evacuation. The various types are generally sold in some combination—rather than buying only baggage, medical, or cancellation insurance, you'll usually purchase a package that includes most or all of them. "Comprehensive insurance" covers all of the above (plus expenses incurred if your trip is delayed, if you miss your flight, or if your tour company changes your itinerary).

Companies such as Travelex and Travel Guard offer comprehensive packages that serve as your primary coverage; they'll take care of your expenses regardless of what other insurance you might have (for instance, if you have health insurance through your job). That means they pay first and don't ask questions about your other insurance. This can be a real plus if you want to avoid out-of-pocket expenses.

Insurance prices can vary widely, with most packages costing between 5 and 12 percent of the total trip. Age is one of the biggest factors affecting the price: Rates go up dramatically for every decade over 50, while coverage is generally inexpensive or even free for children 17 and under.

Travel agents recommend that you get travel insurance (because they get a commission when you buy it, and because they can be held liable for your losses if they don't explain insurance options to you). While travel agents can give you information and advice, they are not insurance agents—always direct any specific questions to the insurance provider (for a list, see the sidebar).

The policies available vary by state, and not all insurance companies are licensed in every state. If you have to make a claim and encounter problems with a company that isn't licensed in your state, you don't have a case.

Note that some travel insurance, especially trip-cancellation coverage, is reimbursement-only: You'll pay out-of-pocket for your expenses, then submit the paperwork to your insurer to recoup your money. With medical coverage, you may be able to arrange to have expensive hospital or doctor bills paid directly. Either way, if you have a problem, it's wise to contact your insurance company immediately to ask them how to proceed. Many major insurance companies are accessible by phone 24 hours a day—handy if you have problems in Europe.

Travel Insurance Providers

For extensive travel insurance coverage, go with a big-name company. Avoid buying insurance from a no-name company you found online. Consider the package deals sold by:

- **Betins** (Betins.com, tel. 866-552-8834)
- **Allianz** (AllianzTravelInsurance.com, tel. 866-884-3556)
- **Travelex** (TravelexInsurance.com, tel. 800-228-9792)
- **Travel Guard** (TravelGuard.com, tel. 800-826-4919)
- **Travel Insured International** (TravelInsured.com, tel. 800-243-3174)

You can compare insurance policies and costs among various providers at InsureMyTrip.com (they also sell insurance; tel. 800-487-4722).

Types of Coverage

For each type of insurance, I've outlined some of the key legalese. But be warned—these are only guidelines. Policies can differ, even within the same company. Certain companies and policies have different levels of coverage based on whether you purchase the car rental, hotel, or flight directly or through a travel agent. Ask a lot of questions, and always read the fine print to see what's covered (e.g., how they define "travel partner" or "family member"—your great-aunt might not qualify).

Trip-Cancellation or Interruption Insurance

For me, this is the most usable and worthwhile kind of insurance. It's expensive to cancel or interrupt any prepaid travel, and for a fraction of the trip cost, you can alleviate the risk of losing money if something unforeseen gets in the way.

Trip-cancellation insurance can be worthwhile if your travel plans go haywire.

The rugged, healthy, unattached, and gung-ho traveler will probably forego trip-cancellation or interruption coverage. I have skipped it many times, and my number has yet to come up. If it turns out that I need to cancel or interrupt, I'll just have to take my financial lumps—I played the odds and lost. But in some cases it's probably a good idea to get this coverage—for instance, if you're paying a lot of up-front money for an organized tour or short-term accommodation rental (both of which are expensive to cancel), if you or your travel partner have questionable health, or if you have a loved one at home in poor health.

Before purchasing trip-cancellation or interruption coverage, check with your credit-card issuer; yours may offer limited coverage for flights or tours purchased with the card.

A standard trip-cancellation or interruption insurance policy covers the nonrefundable financial penalties or losses you incur when you cancel a prepaid tour or flight for an acceptable reason, such as:

- You, your travel partner, or a family member cannot travel because of sickness, death, layoff, or a list of other acceptable reasons.
- Your tour company or airline goes out of business or can't perform as promised.
- A family member at home gets sick (check the fine print to see how a family member's preexisting condition might affect coverage).
- You miss a flight or need an emergency flight for a reason outside your control (such as a car accident, inclement weather, or a strike).

So, if you or your travel partner accidentally break a leg a few days before your trip, you can both bail out (if you both have this insurance) without losing all the money you paid for the trip. Or, if you're on a tour and have an accident on your first day, you'll be reimbursed for the portion of the tour you were unable to use.

This type of insurance can be used whether you're on an organized tour or cruise, or traveling independently (in which case, only the prepaid expenses—such as your flight and any nonrefundable hotel reservations—are covered). Note the difference: Trip *cancellation* is when you don't go on your trip at all. Trip *interruption* is when you begin a journey but have to cut it short; in this case, you'll be reimbursed only for the portion of the trip that you didn't complete. If you're taking a tour, it may already come with some cancellation insurance—ask.

Some insurers won't cover certain airlines or tour operators. Many are obvious—such as companies under bankruptcy protection—but others can be surprising (including major airlines). Make sure your carrier is covered.

Buy your insurance policy within a week of the date you make the first payment on your trip. Policies purchased later than a designated cutoff date—generally 7 to 21 days, as determined by the insurance company—are less likely to cover tour company or air carrier bankruptcies, preexisting medical conditions (yours or those of family members at home), or terrorist incidents. Mental-health concerns are generally not covered.

Jittery travelers are fretful about two big unknowns: terrorist attacks and natural disasters. Ask your company for details. A terrorist attack or natural disaster in your hometown may or may not be covered. You'll likely be covered only if your departure city or a destination on your itinerary becomes the target of a terrorist incident within 30 days of your trip. Even then, if your tour operator offers a substitute itinerary, your coverage may become void. As for natural disasters, you're covered only if your destination is uninhabitable (for example, your hotel is flooded or the airport is gone). War or outbreaks of disease generally aren't covered.

You can avoid the question of what is and what isn't covered by buying a costly "any reason" policy. These offer at least partial reimbursement (generally 75 percent) no matter why you cancel the trip. But the premiums are so hefty that these policies appeal mostly to deep-pocketed nervous Nellies.

Medical Insurance

Before buying a special medical insurance policy for your trip, check with your medical insurer—you might already be covered by your existing health plan. While many US insurers cover you overseas, Medicare does not. Also, be aware of any policy exclusions such as preauthorization requirements.

Even if your health plan does cover you internationally, you may want to consider buying a special medical travel policy. Much of the additional coverage available is supplemental (or "secondary"), so it covers whatever expenses your health plan doesn't, such as deductibles. But you can also purchase primary coverage, which will take care of your costs up to a certain amount. In emergency situations involving costly procedures or overnight stays, the hospital will typically work directly with your travel-insurance carrier on billing (but not with your regular health insurance company; you'll likely have to pay up front to the hospital or clinic, then get reimbursed by your stateside insurer later). For routine care, a visit to a doctor will likely be an out-of-pocket expense (you'll bring home documentation to be reimbursed). Whatever the circumstances, it's smart to contact your insurer from the road to let them know that you've sought medical help.

Many preexisting conditions are covered by medical and trip-cancellation coverage, depending on when you buy the coverage and how recently you've been treated for the condition. If you travel frequently to Europe, multitrip annual policies can save you money. Check with your agent or insurer before you commit.

The US State Department periodically issues warnings about traveling to at-risk countries—see Travel.state.gov. If you're visiting one of these countries, your cancellation and medical insurance will likely not be honored, unless you buy supplemental coverage.

For travelers over 70 years old, buying travel medical insurance can be expensive. Compare the cost of a stand-alone travel medical plan with comprehensive insurance (described earlier), which comes with good medical and evacuation coverage. A travel-insurance company can help you sort out the options. Certain Medigap plans cover some emergency care outside the US; call the issuer of your supplemental policy for the details.

Other Insurance
Evacuation insurance covers the cost of getting you to a place where you can receive appropriate medical treatment in the event of an emergency. (In a worst-case scenario, this can mean a medically equipped—and incredibly expensive—private jet.) This is usually not covered by your regular medical-insurance plan back home. Sometimes this coverage can get you home after an accident, but more often, it'll

Theft Protection

Theft is especially worrisome when you consider the dollar value of the items we pack along. Laptops, tablets, cameras, smartphones, and ebook readers are all expensive to replace.

One way to protect your investment is to purchase travel insurance from a specialized company such as Travel Guard, which offers a variety of options that include coverage for theft. Before buying a policy, ask how they determine the value of the stolen objects and about any maximum reimbursement limits for jewelry, electronics, or cameras.

Thieves rifled through this backpack before dumping it—minus any valuables— on the street in Rome.

It's also smart to check with your homeowners or renters insurance company. Under most policies, your personal property is already protected against theft anywhere in the world—but your insurance deductible still applies. If you have a $1,000 deductible and your $700 tablet is stolen, you'll have to pay to replace it. Rather than buying separate insurance, it may make more sense to add a rider to your existing policy to cover expensive items while you travel.

Before you leave, it's a good idea to take an inventory of all the high-value items you're bringing. Make a list of serial numbers, makes, and models of your electronics, and take photos that can serve as records. If anything is stolen, this information is helpful to both your insurance company and the police. If you plan to file an insurance claim, you'll need to get a police report in Europe. (If dealing with the police is intimidating, ask your hotelier for help.) For tips on avoiding theft while traveling, see the Theft & Scams chapter.

just get you as far as the nearest major hospital—so it may be worth buying if you're planning an adventure in a remote area. "Medical repatriation"—that is, getting you all the way home—is likely to be covered only if it's considered medically necessary. Before purchasing a policy, ask your insurer to explain exactly what's covered before *and after* you get to the hospital.

Keep in mind that medical and evacuation insurance may not cover you if you're participating in an activity your insurer considers to be dangerous (such as skydiving, mountain climbing, bungee jumping, scuba diving, or even skiing). Some companies sell supplementary adventure-sports coverage.

Baggage insurance—for luggage that is lost, delayed,

or damaged—is included in most comprehensive policies, but it's rare to buy it separately, and there's a strict cap on reimbursement for such items as jewelry, eyewear, electronics, and camera equipment. If you check your baggage for a flight, it's already covered by the airline (ask your airline about its luggage liability limit; if you have particularly valuable luggage, you can buy supplemental "excess valuation" insurance directly from the airline). Homeowners or renters insurance typically covers your possessions anywhere you travel; the baggage insurance covers the deductibles and items excluded from your homeowners policy. Double-check the particulars with your agent. If your policy doesn't cover expensive rail passes, consider Rail Europe's Rail Protection Plan, which must be purchased when you buy your pass; it covers loss and theft of the pass—but doesn't cover trip interruptions.

Flight insurance ("crash coverage") is a statistical rip-off that heirs love. It's basically a life insurance policy that covers you when you're on the airplane. Since plane crashes are so rare, there's little sense in spending money on this insurance.

Collision coverage, an important type of insurance for rental cars, is covered on page 165. Collision insurance may be included in some comprehensive travel-insurance plans or available as an upgrade on others.

BEFORE YOU GO

You'll have a smoother trip if you tackle a few things ahead of time. I've collected my suggestions here, with references for where to find more detailed information elsewhere in the book.

❏ Get a proper **guidebook** (see page 34). If traveling with one of mine, check for recent changes in your destination at www.ricksteves.com/update.

❏ Make sure your **passport** is valid. If it's due to expire within six months of your ticketed date of return, renew it. Allow up to six weeks to renew or get a passport (see page 65).

❏ Book your **international flights** (see page 98).

❏ Figure out your main form of **transportation** for your trip: Get a rail pass (see page 125), rent a car (see page 156), or take a cheap flight (see page 111). You can generally buy rail tickets as you travel (see page 120), but it can be smart to reserve seats on certain trains before you leave (see page 133).

❑ If you'll be **renting a car,** bring your driver's license. An International Driving Permit is required in some countries (see page 163).

❑ Make **reservations** well in advance, especially during peak season, for accommodations (see page 208), popular restaurants, major sights (see page 325), and local guides.

❑ Do your homework if you want to buy **travel insurance.** Check whether your existing insurance (health, homeowners, or renters) covers you and your possessions overseas (see page 70).

❑ Call your bank. Alert them that you'll be using your **debit and credit-cards** in Europe, ask about fees, and get the PIN for your credit card (see sidebar on page 189). Note your bank's emergency phone number in the US (but not its 800 number) to call collect if you have a problem

❑ If you're bringing the **kids,** make sure you have the right paperwork, including passports, and, if applicable, a letter of consent to travel without both parents and documentation for adopted children (see page 454).

❑ Make backup **copies of important travel documents,** including your itinerary (see page 69).

❑ **Students** should carry a valid school-issued ID (or consider an International Student Identity Card) to take advantage of discounts throughout Europe.

❑ Get smart about your **smartphone.** Consider signing up for an international plan to reduce your costs, or plan to rely on Wi-Fi (see page 290). Follow common sense safety precautions to protect your phone and its data (see page 298).

❑ Download any **apps** you'll use on the road (maps, translators, transit schedules, and Rick Steves Audio Europe— with free audio tours of major sights and hours of travel interviews; see page 16). Also download any videos (TV shows or movies) you want to watch, as you probably won't be able to use streaming services overseas (see page 295).

❑ Enroll in the State Department's **Smart Traveler Enrollment Program** to get safety updates about your destination and to help loved ones get in touch with you in case of emergency (http://step.state.gov).

❑ Take care of any **medical needs.** Visit your doctor for a checkup, and see your dentist if you have work that needs to be done. If you use prescription drugs, stock up before your trip (see page 408), and pack a copy of the prescription, plus one for contact lenses or glasses if you wear them.

❑ Attend to **household needs.** Cancel your newspapers, hold your mail delivery, and prepay your bills.

❑ Make a **list of valuables** that you're bringing (such as electronics). Include serial numbers, makes, and models, and take photos of your items to serve as a record for the police and your insurance company should anything be stolen.

❑ Check **airline carry-on restrictions.** The Transportation Security Administration's website (www.tsa.gov) has an up-to-date list of what you can bring on the plane with you...and what you must check.

Pack Light

The importance of packing light cannot be overemphasized, but, for your good, I'll try. You'll never meet a traveler who, after five trips, brags: "Every year I pack heavier." You can't travel heavy, happy, and cheap. Pick two.

ONE BAG—THAT'S IT

My self-imposed limit is 20 pounds in a 9" × 21" × 14" carry-on-size bag (it'll fit in an airplane's overhead bin, at least on your transatlantic flight; many European airlines restrict hand luggage to even smaller specs). At my company, we've taken tens of thousands of people of all ages and styles on tours through Europe. We allow only one carry-on bag. For many, this is a radical concept: 9" × 21" × 14"? That's my cosmetics kit! But they manage, and they're glad they did. After you enjoy that sweet mobility and freedom, you'll never go any other way.

No matter your age, you can travel like college kids: light, mobile, and wearing your convertible suitcase/backpack.

You'll walk with your luggage more than you think you will. Before flying to Europe, give yourself a test. Pack up completely and walk around your house or block. Or practice being a tourist in your hometown for an hour. Fully loaded, you should enjoy window-shopping. If you can't, stagger home and thin things out.

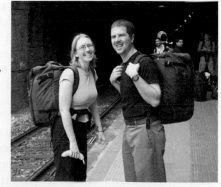

When you carry your own luggage, it's less likely to get lost, broken, or stolen. Quick, last-minute flight changes become simpler. A small bag sits on your lap on the bus or taxi and stashes easily overhead on an airplane. You don't have to worry about it, and, when you arrive, you can hit the ground running. It's a good feeling. When I land in London, I'm on my way downtown while everyone else stares anxiously at the luggage carousel. When I fly home, I'm the first guy the dog sniffs.

These days, you can also save money by bringing less. While it's still free to check one bag on most overseas trips, you'd likely pay a fee to check a second bag. If you're taking a separate flight within Europe, expect to be charged to check even just one bag (see "Baggage Restrictions," later).

Pack light. You won't have a mule to haul your bags around. (If you do, you're taking advantage of your spouse.)

It can be a drag, dragging your bag through airports, and even I sometimes wonder why I followed my own advice to bring only a carry-on. But then I'm reminded of the joy of having everything with you—like the time I avoided a long layover by hopping on an earlier flight from Copenhagen to Bergen. After getting to my hotel two hours before planned, I enjoyed a jumpstart on my Norway time with a lovely evening in a salty port town, where summer's "magic hour" lasts until 11 p.m.

Packing light isn't just about saving time or money—it's about your traveling lifestyle. Too much luggage marks you as a typical tourist. It slams the Back Door shut. Serendipity suffers. Changing locations becomes a major operation. Con artists figure you're helpless. Porters are a problem only to those who need them. With only one bag, you're mobile and in control. Take this advice seriously.

Choosing a Bag

A fundamental packing decision is your luggage. When shopping for a bag, consider these factors:

External Dimensions: Is the bag small enough to work as a carry-on? (If not, are you willing to put up with the likely delays and extra fees that come with checking your bag?)

Comfort and Mobility: Consider whether you want a bag with wheels or without, and remember you'll need to maneuver it not just through airport terminals but also along uneven surfaces (cobblestones, gravel) and stairs. If picking a bag without wheels, consider how easily you can carry 20–25 pounds on your back.

Efficiency of Space: Look for the most (usable) capacity.

Expandability: A nice option, especially for the trip home.

Quality: Go with a well-established and/or well-reviewed brand. As for cost, it's easy to spend a fortune on your luggage, but you don't need to. If your bag costs more than $250, you're probably paying more for a brand name than quality. Just make sure your bag is made well enough to withstand at least a few trips' worth of wear and tear; a product guarantee is a good sign. Sturdy stitching, front and/or side pockets, padded shoulder straps (for backpacks), and a low-profile color are virtues.

Bag Breakdown

Here's my personal take on your main options. Note that I only consider carry-on-size luggage.

Soft Backpacks: To me, this kind of bag (see photo on page 79) makes the most sense. These bags hang on your shoulders and work fine for getting from the train station to the hotel. They're also well-suited as carry-ons, since they can squish down to fit in virtually any overhead bin. And I really appreciate the mobility and practicality of having both hands free while en route—I can eat a sandwich or buy a bus ticket and hop on board without breaking my stride. I live out of my backpack for four months each year—and I absolutely love it. The day will come when I'll be rolling my bag through Europe with the rest of the gang. But as long as I'm hardy enough to carry my gear on my back, I will.

A 9" × 21" × 14" carry-on bag (with or without wheels) is the ideal size.

Internal-Frame Backpacks: An internal-frame backpack is the most comfortable bag to wear, as the frame and hip belt keep the weight off your shoulders and balanced over your hips. However, these bags can be expensive, they're often "taller" than carry-on size, and I don't think the comfort is worth the trade-off. If you pack light, a soft backpack won't cause too much strain (and shorter carry-on-size framed backpacks force you to limit your stuff).

Rolling Bags: If carrying a pack on your back isn't for you, wheels are the way to go. A rolling bag frees your back for a smaller day bag, or you can set your smaller bag on top and roll it along. The drawbacks: Bags with wheels usually cost more, weigh more, and offer a little less capacity than backpacks of similar dimensions (since wheel wells and the retractable handle cut into the internal space).

Unless you're traveling with your own butler, remember that you'll need to lift and lug your wheeled bag from time to time—up stairs, into and out of overhead compartments, on and off transit, over muddy footpaths, etc. Wheeled bags are great in airports, but can be cumbersome when negotiating narrow B&B staircases, crowded subways, and villages with stepped or cobbled lanes.

Look for a rolling bag that's as roomy as possible while still being small and light enough to lift and fit in a plane's overhead bin. Plenty of wheeled bags are well-designed—most of my staffers prefer to roll with one. Just don't let wheels delude you into packing heavier.

Rolling Backpacks: Having both wheels and backpack straps seems like the best of both worlds—but the wheels and retractable handle eat up interior space. Many travelers tell me that, while they appreciate having flexibility, they end up using their rolling backpack almost exclusively as a wheeled bag. Personally, I'd go with one or the other.

You can see a comparison chart of my backpacks and rolling bags—and purchase them—at RickSteves.com.

Baggage Restrictions

Pack light...and pack smart. You can't bring anything potentially dangerous—such as knives, lighters, or large quantities of liquids or gels—in your carry-on bag. (This list can change—for details, see "What Can't I Carry On?" on page 107.) These days I leave my Swiss Army knife at home, bring smaller bottles of toiletries, and carry on my bag as usual.

Be aware that some airlines, particularly Europe's budget carriers, have more stringent carry-on regulations than what we're used to in the US: Confirm policies before your flight. (When in doubt, for flights within Europe—especially on cheapo airlines like Ryanair or EasyJet—opt to check your bag when booking the flight, as on-the-spot baggage-check fees can easily top the cost of the flight itself.) Even if you play by the rules, airline personnel may still ask you to check your bag if bin capacity is limited (though gate-checking your bag at the airline's request is free as long as your bag complies with the airline's policies).

When you carry your bag onto the plane, all liquids, gels, creams, and aerosols must be in 3.4-ounce or smaller containers, all of which must fit into one clear, quart (or liter)-size, plastic zip-top bag. You can also find sturdier, TSA-approved toiletry bags. Exceptions are made for certain prescription and over-the-counter medicines, as well as contact-lens solution (see www.tsa.gov for details), but European airports don't always hew to the same guidelines.

If you check your bag, you can pack all the liquids you want (but I wouldn't). Before checking, mark your bag inside and out with your name, address, and emergency phone number. If you have a lock on your bag, you may be asked to remove it to accommodate a security check, or it may be opened or even cut off so the bag can be inspected (even a TSA-approved lock may be cut by European inspectors). An alternative is to use a heavy-duty wire or nylon cable tie—but be sure you have a tool to cut it off (such as a nail clipper). I've never locked my bag and have never had a problem. Still, just in case, don't pack anything valuable (such as cash, a camera, or jewelry) in checked luggage.

PACKING 101

How do you fit a whole trip's worth of luggage into a small backpack or suitcase? The answer is simple: Bring very little.

Spread out everything you think you might need on the living-room floor. Scrutinize each item. Ask yourself, "Will I really use my snorkel and fins enough to justify carrying them around all summer?" Not "Will I use them?" but "Will I use them enough to feel good about hauling them over the Swiss Alps?" Frugal as I may be, I'd buy a set in Greece and give them away before I'd carry that extra weight over the Alps.

Don't pack for the worst-case scenario. Pack for the best-case scenario and buy yourself out of any jams. Bring layers rather than a heavy coat. Think in terms of what you can do without—not what will be handy on your trip. When in doubt, leave it out. I've seen people pack a whole summer's supply of deodorant or razors, thinking they can't get them in Europe. The world is small: You can buy Dial soap, Colgate toothpaste, Nivea cream, and Gillette razors in Sicily and Slovakia. Tourist shops in major international hotels are a sure bet whenever you have difficulty finding a personal item. If you can't find one of your essentials, ask yourself how half a billion Europeans can live without it. Rather than carry a whole trip's supply of toiletries, take enough to get started and look forward to running out of toothpaste in Bulgaria. Then you have the perfect excuse to go into a Bulgarian department store, shop around, and pick up something you think might be toothpaste.

When getting way off the beaten path—like this traveler, who's staying at a tiny guesthouse in Italy's Civita di Bagnoregio—you'll be glad you're packing light.

One Carry-on Bag

Here's what I travel with for two months (photos taken naked in a Copenhagen hotel room): 9" × 21" × 14" soft back-pack; lightweight nylon day bag; ripped-up sections of several of my guide-books, notes, maps, journal, tiny pocket notepad; money belt (with debit card, credit card, driver's license, passport, rail pass, cash reserve, sheet of phone numbers and addresses); second money belt clipped inside my bag for "semi-precious" items and documents (flash drive for back-ups, house key, left-over foreign currency, advance tickets and documentation of hotel reserva-tions, car rental, flights, etc.); toiletries stuff bag (with squeeze bottle of sham-poo, soap in a plastic container, shaver, toothbrush and paste, comb, nail clip-

pers, squeeze bottle of liquid soap for clothes); bag with electronic gear (travel alarm clock, laptop power cord, plug adapters); miscellaneous bag (with family photos, business cards, back-up toiletries, first aid kit, tiny odds and ends); light rain jacket, long khaki cotton pants (button pockets) in summer or dark jeans off-season, super-light long pants, shorts, five pairs of socks and underwear, two long-sleeved shirts, two short-sleeved shirts, two T-shirts; stuff bag with sweater and plastic laundry bag; light pair of shoes; and mobile phone and charger, light-weight laptop, camera, and noise-canceling headphones.

Whether you're traveling for three weeks or three months, pack exactly the same. To keep your clothes tightly packed and well organized, zip them up in packing cubes. To really maximize bag space, consider airless baggies or a clothes compressor (look for heavy-duty ones made to withstand everyday use). I also like specially-designed fold-ing boards (such as Eagle Creek's Pack-It Folder) to fold and carry clothes with minimal wrinkling. Mesh bags also come in handy. I use one for underwear and socks, another for miscellaneous stuff such as a first-aid kit, earplugs, clothes-line, sewing kit, and gadgets. (Note that I sell many of these organizational type items, including packing cubes and com-pression packs, on my website.)

Pack your bag only two-thirds full to leave room for sou-venirs, or bring along an empty featherweight nylon bag to use as a carry-on for your return flight, then check your main bag through (this is when expandable compartments really come in handy).

Go casual, simple, and very light. Remember, in your travels you'll meet two kinds of tourists—those who pack light and those who wish they had. Say it out loud: "PACK LIGHT PACK LIGHT PACK LIGHT."

What to Pack

I've broken the contents of your bag into five major categories: clothing, travel documents (including money), toiletries, electronics, and miscellaneous extras. My core packing recommendations are all included on my Packing Checklist (see page 87). At the end of this chapter, I've also included a list of optional bring-alongs. Throughout, an asterisk (*) indicates an item you can purchase at RickSteves.com.

Resources for Packing Light

TSA.gov: Official list of what you can and cannot carry on

Europa.eu/youreurope/citizens/ travel: EU version of TSA website

OneBag.com: More tips on traveling light

www.ricksteves.com/packing: Rick's packing list and more

www.ricksteves.com/travel-talks: Rick's travel skills talks, including one on packing

Pack the Bag, Packing Pro, TripList apps: Customizable packing lists with reminders

Clothing Basics

The bulk of your luggage is filled with clothing. Minimize by bringing less. Experienced travelers bring only things that will be worn repeatedly, complement other items, and have multiple uses (for example, I don't swim much, so I let my shorts double as a swimsuit). Pack with color coordination in mind. Neutral colors (black, navy, khaki) dress up easily and can be extremely versatile.

To extend your wardrobe, plan to spend 10 minutes doing a little wash every few nights, or consider a visit to a local launderette, which is in itself a Back Door experience (for details on doing laundry in Europe, see page 419). Choose fabrics that resist wrinkling or look good wrinkled. If you wring with gusto, lightweight clothing should dry overnight in your hotel room. Do a test wash before your trip and pick items that hand-wash well.

Many travelers are concerned about appropriate dress. During tourist season, even Europe's concert halls go casual. I have never felt out of place at symphonies, operas, or plays wearing a decent pair of slacks and a good-looking sweater or collared shirt. Some cultural events require more formal attire, particularly outside of high season, but the casual tourist rarely encounters these. Women who don't pack a

dress or skirt will do just fine with a pair of
nice pants.

While Europeans—especially younger
people—do wear casual clothing, their definition of casual is a bit dressier than ours. Shorts
are uncommon on older women and in big
cities, and the cutoff temperature for "hot
enough for shorts" is much higher than in the
US. Especially in southern Europe, women
can blend in with the locals by wearing capri
pants or a skirt instead; men can pack a pair of
as-light-as-possible pants.

Shorts, tank tops, and other skimpy summer attire can put a crimp in your sightseeing
plans. Some churches, mostly in southern Europe, have
modest-dress requirements for men, women, and children:
no shorts or bare shoulders. Except at the strict St. Peter's
Basilica (in Rome) and St. Mark's (in Venice), the dress code
is often loosely enforced. If necessary, it's usually easy to
improvise some modesty (buy a cheap souvenir T-shirt to
cover your shoulders, or carry a wide scarf to wear like a kilt
over your legs). At some heavily touristed churches in southern Europe, people hand out sheets of tissue paper you can
wrap around yourself like a shawl or skirt.

In Britain, they say there's no bad weather...only inappropriate clothing.

It can be worth splurging a little to get just the right
clothes for your trip. For durable, lightweight travel clothes,
consider ExOfficio, TravelSmith, Tilley, Eddie Bauer, and REI.

But ultimately—as long as you don't wear something
that's outrageous or offensive—it's important to dress in a
way that makes you comfortable. And no matter how carefully you dress, your clothes will probably mark you as an
American. And so what? Europeans will know anyway. To
blend in and be culturally sensitive, I watch my manners, not
the cut of my clothes.

Here's a rundown of what should go in your suitcase:

Shirts: Bring five or six short-sleeved or long-sleeved
shirts or blouses (how many of each depends on the season).
Shirts with long sleeves that roll up easily can double as
short-sleeved. Look for a wrinkle-camouflaging pattern or
fabrics that show a minimum of wrinkles. Synthetic-blend
fabrics (such as Coolmax or microfiber) often dry overnight.
Lightweight, light-colored clothes are more comfortable in
very hot weather.

Pants/Shorts/Skirts: Bring two pairs of pants. I suggest one lightweight cotton and another super-lightweight

Packing Checklist

Clothing

- ☐ 5-6 shirts: long- & short-sleeve
- ☐ 2 pairs pants (or skirts/capris)
- ☐ 1 pair shorts
- ☐ 5 pairs underwear & socks
- ☐ 1 pair walking shoes
- ☐ Sweater or warm layer
- ☐ Rainproof jacket with hood
- ☐ Tie, scarf, belt, and/or hat
- ☐ Swimsuit
- ☐ Sleepwear/loungewear

Money

- ☐ Debit card(s)
- ☐ Credit card(s)
- ☐ Hard cash ($100-200 in US dollars)
- ☐ Money belt

Documents

- ☐ Passport
- ☐ Tickets & confirmations: flights, hotels, trains, rail pass, car rental, sight entries
- ☐ Driver's license
- ☐ Student ID, etc.
- ☐ Photocopies of important documents
- ☐ Insurance details
- ☐ Guidebooks & maps
- ☐ Notepad & pen
- ☐ Journal

Toiletries Kit

- ☐ Basics: soap, shampoo, toothbrush, toothpaste, floss, deodorant, sunscreen, brush/comb, etc.
- ☐ Medicines & vitamins
- ☐ First-aid kit
- ☐ Glasses/contacts/sunglasses
- ☐ Sewing kit
- ☐ Packet of tissues (for WC)
- ☐ Earplugs

Electronics

- ☐ Mobile phone
- ☐ Camera & related gear
- ☐ Tablet/ebook reader
- ☐ Laptop & flash drive
- ☐ Headphones
- ☐ Chargers & batteries
- ☐ Smartphone car charger & mount (or GPS device)
- ☐ Plug adapters

Miscellaneous

- ☐ Daypack
- ☐ Sealable plastic baggies
- ☐ Laundry supplies: soap, laundry bag, clothesline, spot remover
- ☐ Small umbrella
- ☐ Travel alarm/watch

Optional Extras

- ☐ Second pair of shoes (flip-flops, sandals, tennis shoes, boots)
- ☐ Travel hairdryer
- ☐ Picnic supplies
- ☐ Water bottle
- ☐ Fold-up tote bag
- ☐ Small flashlight
- ☐ Mini binoculars
- ☐ Small towel or washcloth
- ☐ Inflatable pillow/neck rest
- ☐ Tiny lock
- ☐ Address list (to mail postcards)
- ☐ Extra passport photos
- ☐ Good book
- ☐ Duct tape
- ☐ Insect repellent
- ☐ Office supplies
- ☐ Hostel sheet

pair (or a skirt) for hot and muggy big cities. If you prefer jeans, choose the lightest-weight pair you have (heavy denim can be too hot for summer travel and is slow to dry). Some travelers like convertible pants/shorts with zip-off legs. While not particularly stylish, they're especially functional in Italy, where you can use them to cover up inside churches while still beating the heat outside. Button-down wallet pockets are safest (though still not nearly as thief-proof as a money belt). If you bring shorts, one pair is probably enough. Shorts can double as a swimsuit when swimming in lakes or the sea.

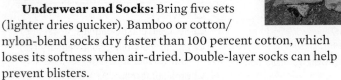

Underwear and Socks: Bring five sets (lighter dries quicker). Bamboo or cotton/nylon-blend socks dry faster than 100 percent cotton, which loses its softness when air-dried. Double-layer socks can help prevent blisters.

Shoes: Bring one pair of comfortable walking shoes with good traction. Mephisto, Ecco, and Rieker look dressier than sneakers, but are still comfortable. Sturdy, low-profile tennis shoes with a good tread are fine, too. If you bring a second pair, consider sandals in summer or waterproof shoes in winter or rainy weather. Flip-flops are handy if you'll be using bathrooms down the hall. Whichever shoes you bring, make sure they're well broken in before you leave home.

Sweater or Warm Layer: Warm and dark is best—for layering, dressing up, and not showing dirt. Consider a cashmere sweater or a lightweight fleece.

Jacket: Bring a light and water-resistant windbreaker with a hood. A hooded jacket of Gore-Tex or other waterproof material is good if you expect rain. (For summer travel, I wing it without rain gear—but always pack for rain in Britain and Ireland.) For travel to cooler climes, come prepared to add an insulating layer, or consider a super lightweight puffer coat that can squish compactly.

Swimsuit: To use public pools, you'll need a swimsuit (men can't just wear shorts; and in France, men need to wear Speedo-type swimsuits—not swim trunks).

Sleepwear/Loungewear: Comfy streetwear—such as shorts, leggings, T-shirts, tank tops, yoga pants, and other lightweight athletic gear—can be used as pajamas, post-dinner loungewear, and a modest cover-up to get you to the bathroom down the hall.

Packing Tips for Women

Thanks to our tour guide Joan Robinson for the following tips.

Skirts: Skirts (knee-length is appropriate for churches) are as cool and breathable as shorts, but dressier, and have a key advantage over dresses: They can be worn with a money belt. A lightweight skirt made with a blended fabric packs compactly. Make sure it has a comfy waistband. Skirts can easily be mixed and matched, and can be dressed up with a pair of tights with flats or boots.

Underwear and Swimwear: Silk, microfiber, or stretch lace underwear dries faster than cotton, but breathes more than nylon. Bring at least two bras (what if you leave one hanging over your shower rail by accident?). A sports bra can double as a hiking/sunning top. You don't need a bikini to sunbathe topless on European beaches—local women with one-piece bathing suits just roll down the top.

Toiletries: Before cramming in every facial cleanser, lotion, hair gel, and cosmetic item you think you might use, ask yourself what toiletries you can live without for a short time. But do estimate how many tampons and pads you might need and bring them with you (unless you're taking a very long trip). Even though many of the same brands are sold throughout Europe, it's best to have them when you need them, and it's easier than having to buy a too-small or too-large box in Europe. (For more on women's health and medication, see page 412.)

Accessories: Scarves give your limited wardrobe just the color it needs. They dress up your outfit, are lightweight and easy to pack, and if purchased in Europe, make a great souvenir. Some women bring a shawl-size scarf or pashmina to function as a sweater substitute, head wrap, skirt at a church, or even a blanket on a train. Functional, cheap, but beautiful imitation pashminas can be found all over Europe. Vests and cardigans can be mixed-and-matched to give you several different looks as well as layers for cold weather. Leave valuable or flashy jewelry at home. Bring a few pieces you can live with losing, or buy some interesting artisan jewelry in Europe.

Accessories: For instant respectability, bring a **tie** or **scarf,** which can break the monotony and make you look snazzy. Consider a light, crushable, wide-brimmed **hat** for sunny days, especially if you're prone to sunburn. Don't forget a **belt** if you need one.

Winter Travel: Even if traveling in winter, you can pack just about as light. Wear heavier, warmer, waterproof shoes. Add a coat, long underwear (super-light silk or other quick-drying fabric), scarf, gloves, hat, and an extra pair of socks and underwear, since things dry more slowly. Layer your clothing for warmth, and assume you'll be outside in the cold for hours at a time.

Documents, Money, and Travel Info

Organizing your possessions, travel documents, money, guidebooks, and maps is just as important as assembling your wardrobe.

*Money Belt: This flat, hidden, zippered pouch—worn around your waist and tucked under your clothes—is essential for the peace of mind it brings. You could lose everything except your money belt, and the trip could still go on. Get a lightweight one with a low-profile color (I like beige). A ***neck wallet** or ***hidden pocket** (which attaches to your belt and tucks into your pants) are other alternatives. For more about money belts, see page 377.

Money: Bring your preferred mix of a debit card, a credit card, and an emergency stash of hard US cash. For detailed recommendations, see page 184.

Documents: Bring your **passport, driver's license,** and any other useful cards (**student ID** and so on). In your luggage, pack a record of **all reservations,** including flights, hotels, trains, rental cars, and tickets for sights. Bring any necessary health or travel **insurance** contact info. Photocopies of **key documents** and a couple of **passport-type photos** can help you get replacements more quickly if the originals are lost or stolen (for more information on the travel documents you need and what to photocopy, see page 65).

Guidebooks and Maps: Pack the travel info you'll need on the ground, whether in paper or electronic form. I like to rip out appropriate chapters from guidebooks and staple them together (see page 39 for a how-to), or use a special slide-on ***page binder.**

Notepad and Pen: A small notepad in your back pocket or daypack is a great organizer, reminder, and communication aid.

*Journal: An empty book to be filled with the experiences of your trip will be your most treasured souvenir (for more on journaling, see page 438). Attach your itinerary. Use a hardbound type designed to last a lifetime, rather than a floppy spiral notebook. My custom-designed Rick Steves Travel Journals are rugged, simple blank books. Another great brand, with a cult following among travel writers, is Moleskine (www.moleskine.com).

Toiletries and Personal Items

Even if you check your suitcase on the flight, always carry on essential toiletries, including any prescription medications (don't let the time

With a hangable toiletries kit, you know the hairs on the toothbrush are yours.

difference trick you into forgetting a dose). Because sinks in many hotels come with meager countertop space, I prefer a *toiletries kit that can hang on a hook or a towel bar (there are also TSA-approved toiletry bags for carrying on liquids in case you don't want to use a plastic baggie). In-flight pressure changes can cause bottles to leak, making it a good idea to seal all squeeze bottles in plastic baggies, whether you carry on or check your bag.

Basics: Unless you plan on using the hotel bathroom "itsy-bitsies," pack your own **soap** and small bottle of **shampoo** (and **conditioner** if needed). Other items include a toothbrush, toothpaste, floss, sunscreen, deodorant, hairbrush/comb, razors, and nail clipper.

Medicine and Vitamins: Keep medicine in original containers, if possible, with legible prescriptions. For a list of items to pack in a **first-aid kit,** see the sidebar. For advice on handling prescriptions in Europe, see pages 408 and 418.

Glasses/Contacts/Sunglasses: Contact-lens solutions are widely available in Europe. Carry your lens prescription, as well as extra glasses, in a hard protective case. If it's a sunny season, bring your sunglasses.

***Small Towel/Washcloth:** You'll find bath towels at all fancy and moderately priced hotels, and most cheap ones. Some people bring a thin hand towel for the occasional need. Washcloths are rare in Europe, so you might want to pack a *quick-drying microfiber cloth.** Disposable washcloths that pack dry but lather up when wet (such as Olay 4-in-1 Daily Facial Cloths) are another option; cut them in half to make them last longer.

***Sewing Kit:** Clothes age rapidly while traveling. Add a few safety pins and extra buttons.

Packet of Tissues: Stick one of these in your daypack, in case you wind up at a bathroom with no toilet paper.

Earplugs: If night noises bother you, you'll love a good

Traveler's First-Aid Kit

You can buy virtually anything you need in Europe. But if you'd rather stick with a specific name-brand medication, bring it from home (see page 414 for addressing first-aid needs in Europe). It's also handy to pack:

- Band-Aids
- hand sanitizer
- antibiotic cream (in Europe, you may need a prescription to buy skin ointments with antibiotics)
- moleskin (to cover blisters)
- tweezers
- over-the-counter pain reliever
- thermometer (if traveling with kids)
- any medication you may need, including for colds, diarrhea, constipation, motion sickness, allergies, and sleep (if possible, bring nonliquids)
- prescription medications (preferably in labeled, original containers)

Packing Tips from Rick's Readers

Rick's readers—his Road Scholars—have a wealth of travel information to share. To read many more hot-out-of-the-rucksack tips on travel topics (and to contribute your own), visit our Travel Forum at www.ricksteves.com/travel-forum.

Pencil Pouch: I use a cloth one with a plastic window to corral my passport, itinerary, emergency contact papers, and other important information. I use one of the holes along the edge to clip it inside my bag for extra security.

Inflatable Beach Ball: Partially inflated, it works as an in-flight inflatable footrest and doubles as an armrest, pillow, or padding.

Backpack Cinch: I "cinch-tied" the opening of my backpack to make it less accessible for would-be thieves (punched holes in the band at the top of the bag and ran an extendable cable lock through the holes, pulled it tight, and locked it).

Dental Floss or **Fishing Line:** Strong, versatile, waterproof, nearly weightless. Tied backpack together when it broke, doubled as a shoelace, etc.

White Noise Machine: In noisy hotel rooms, its various soothing sounds are a true godsend.

Pillowcase: To put your backpack/travel bag in while you sleep on it on an overnight train. It's another obstacle thieves must overcome.

S-Shaped Double Carabiner: I use two cheap carabiners to clip a pouch with small essentials to the top edge of my seatback pocket.

set of expandable foam plugs. They're handy for snoozing on trains and flights, too.

Miscellaneous

Consider the following:

Small Daypack: A lightweight pack is great for carrying a sweater, camera, guidebook, and picnic goodies while you leave your large bag (with most of your belongings) at the hotel. Don't use a fanny pack—they're magnets for pickpockets.

Laundry Supplies: Bring a bag for dirty laundry (such as a *mesh bag or a plastic baggie). Travel-size packets of detergent or a squeeze bottle of concentrated, multipurpose, biodegradable *liquid soap is handy for laundry. I find hotel shampoo works fine as laundry soap when I'm doing my wash in the sink (for tips on doing laundry in Europe, see page 419). For a spot remover, bring a few Shout wipes or a dab of Goop grease remover in a small plastic container. A small *clothesline lets you hang laundry in your hotel room (the twisted-rubber type needs no clothespins).

Small Umbrella: Consider bringing a collapsible umbrella or plan to buy one in Europe. Umbrella vendors, like worms, appear with the rain.

Travel Alarm: Make sure you have an alarm to wake

Cotton Bandanas: Use them as hand towels, washcloths, picnic blankets, emergency seat covers, and even towels (use two to dry your entire body). Tie a bandana on your luggage so you can quickly identify it. Although it marks me as American, I'll wear one as a headband or hair scarf, too.

Comfy Slippers: If your feet aren't happy, YOU aren't happy. Pamper them!

Inflatable Hangers: Clothes dry faster.

Wrinkle Wiz: Sprays out the wrinkles after I've unpacked my clothes—no more travel iron!

Binder Clips: I always take a few small, medium, and large binder clips to hang clothes to dry, keep window curtains together, weigh down shower curtains, and keep plastic bags shut.

Disposable Plastic Utensils: Great for taking on an impromptu picnic, or when clean utensils aren't available, a set of plastic silverware is a must to take anywhere.

Travel Blanket: Look for a "parachute blanket" that rolls up into its own nylon bag and has four corner pockets—it can be used for beaches, picnics, and shade in a sunny area. It also serves as an extra blanket at night and even as a pillow when rolled up.

Mailing Tube: To collect prints and posters (cut tube to fit your luggage).

Large, Strong Rubber Bands: Use them to keep shoes compactly fitted together in your luggage.

yourself up (your smartphone, a little clock, etc.). At budget hotels, wake-up calls are particularly unreliable.

Sealable Plastic Baggies: In addition to holding carry-on liquids, these are ideal for packing leftover picnic food, containing wet clothes, and bagging potential leaks before they happen. The two-gallon jumbo size can be used to pack (and compress) clothing or do laundry. Bring a variety of sizes, and extras for the flight home.

Electronics

Go light with your electronic gear—you want to experience Europe, not interface with it. Consider insuring particularly high-ticket items (see page 75).

Mobile Phone: Bring your smartphone to snap photos, keep in touch with folks back home, and access email, travel apps, and GPS on the road. For more on using phones in Europe, see the Staying Connected chapter.

Camera: If you bring a separate camera, take along an extra memory card and battery, and don't forget the charger (and a cable if you plan to download images). For a list of camera gear, see page 430.

Tablet/Ebook Reader: Download apps, ebooks, videos, and music before you leave home.

LEFT When traveling with a smartphone, it's cheaper to use Wi-Fi to surf the Web.

RIGHT Wireless hotspots allow you to get online from a park bench.

Laptop: If you're traveling with a laptop, consider bringing a **flash drive** for backing up files and photos (in case the Internet connection is too spotty to access cloud storage—see page 433.

Headphones/Earbuds: These are a must for listening to music, tuning in to audio tours, or simply drowning out whiny kids on the plane. (I never travel without my noise-canceling Bose headphones.) Bring a Y-jack so you and a partner can listen together.

Chargers/Batteries: Bring each device's charger, or consider a charger capable of charging multiple devices at once.

Car Phone Charger and Mount (or GPS Device): If you'll be doing a lot of driving and plan to use mapping apps on your smartphone, remember a car charger and car mount. Or bring your GPS device (preloaded with Europe maps). For details on both, see page 171.

*__Plug Adapters:__ You'll need several adapters so you can plug your various devices into European outlets (see sidebar).

Optional Bring-Alongs

I don't advocate bringing everything listed here. Choose the items that fit with your travel style and needs.

Hairdryer: These are generally provided in $100-plus rooms or are available from your hotel's reception desk. If you can't risk a bad-hair day, buy a cheap, compact hairdryer in Europe or bring a travel-friendly one from home.

Picnic Supplies: Bring a plastic plate (handy for dinner in your hotel room), cup, spoon, fork, and maybe salt and pepper. Fozzils dishware folds completely flat (see www.

Adapters and Converters

Europe's electrical system is different from ours in two ways: the voltage of the current and the shape of the plug.

American appliances run on 110 volts, while European appliances are 220 volts. Today's gadgets are "dual voltage," which means they work on both American and European current. If you see a range of voltages printed on the item or its plug (such as "110-220"), you're OK in Europe. Some older appliances have a voltage switch marked 110 (US) and 220 (Europe)—switch it to 220 as you pack.

Even older devices (and some handheld gaming systems) aren't equipped to deal with the voltage difference—you'll need a separate, bulky **converter.** Consider replacing your appliance instead.

A small ***adapter** allows American-style plugs (two flat prongs) to fit into British or Irish outlets (which take three rectangular prongs) or continental European outlets (which take two round prongs). I bring a handful of both continental and British adapters (handy for long layovers at Heathrow Airport). Secure your adapter to your device's plug with electrical or duct tape; otherwise it can easily get left behind in the outlet (hotels or B&Bs sometimes have a box of abandoned adapters—ask). Many sockets in Europe are recessed into the wall; your adapter should be small enough so that the prongs seat properly in the socket. Although you can get universal adapters that work Europewide (or even worldwide), these tend to be large and more expensive.

In Europe, two kinds of adapters fit virtually all outlets: two little round prongs for the Continent, three big rectangular ones for Britain and Ireland.

Sockets in Switzerland and Italy only accept plugs with slimmer prongs: three slim round prongs arranged in a triangular shape. If you're going to these countries, don't buy an adapter with the thicker ("Schuko" style) prongs—it won't work. If, for some reason, your adapter doesn't work in your hotel, just ask at the desk for assistance; hotels with unusual sockets will invariably have the right adapter to loan you.

Some budget hotel rooms have only one electrical outlet, occupied by the lamp. Hardware stores in Europe sell cheap three-way plug adapters that let you keep the lamp on while you charge your camera battery and smartphone.

fozzils.com). Buy a Swiss Army-type knife with a corkscrew and can opener in Europe (or bring one from home if you're checking your luggage on the plane).

*Water Bottle: The plastic half-liter mineral water bottles sold throughout Europe are reusable and work great. If you bring one from home, make sure it's empty before you go through airport security.

*Fold-up Tote Bag: A large-capacity tote bag that rolls up into a pocket-size pouch is useful for laundry, picnics, and those extra souvenirs you want to take back home.

*Small Flashlight: Handy for reading under the sheets after "lights out" in the hostel, late-night trips down the hall, exploring castle dungeons, and hypnotizing street thieves. Tiny-but-powerful LED flashlights—about the size of your little finger—are extremely bright, compact, and lightweight. Camping-type headlamps also do the trick.

*Small binoculars: For scenery or church interiors.

*Inflatable Pillow/Neck Rest: These are great for snoozing in planes, trains, and automobiles. Some travelers also swear by an ***eye mask** for blocking out early-rising or late-setting sun.

Duct Tape: A small roll of duct tape can work miracles as a temporary fix—mending a punctured bag, solving an emergency shoe problem, and so on. Conserve space by spooling only as much as you might need (less than a foot) around a short pencil or dowel.

Insect Repellent: Bring some along if you're prone to bites and are going somewhere especially buggy.

*Tiny Lock. Use it to lock your backpack zippers shut. Note that if you check your bag on a flight, the lock may be broken to allow the bag to be inspected. Improve the odds of your lock's survival by buying one approved by the Transportation Security Administration—security agents can open the lock with a special master key. Or use zip-ties or ***flight locks** to secure zippers—be sure to pack nail clippers or TSA-approved scissors so you can open them when you arrive.

Office Supplies: Bring paper, pens, and sticky notes (such as Post-Its) to keep your place in your guidebook.

Address List: If you plan to mail postcards, you could print your mailing list onto a sheet of adhesive address labels before you leave. You'll know exactly whom you've written to, and the labels will be perfectly legible.

Reading Material: There's plenty of empty time on a trip to either be bored or enjoy a good book. Popular English-language paperbacks are often available in European airports and major train stations (usually costing more than at home). An ebook reader carries lots of books without the additional weight (and you can easily buy more as you go).

Gifts: If you'll be the guest of local hosts, show your appreciation with small, unique souvenirs from your hometown.

Universal Drain Stopper: Some hotel sinks and tubs have no stoppers. This flat, flexible plastic disc—which works with any size drain—allows you to wash your clothes or take a bath.

Hostel Sheet: Sheets are usually included in the price of a hostel, but if they aren't, you can rent one for about $5 per stay. Still, you might want to bring your own sheet (silk is lighter and smaller, cotton is cheaper), which can double as a beach/picnic blanket and cover you up on overnight train rides. See page 244 for hosteling tips.

A Guilty Pleasure: It's worth sacrificing space to bring something that makes you happy. My guilty pleasure is my Bose noise-canceling headphones. I love these things. When I'm on a plane or train, I can slip these on my head and relax with my music or movie without hearing the rumble and noise around me.

Flying

Before you can enjoy Europe, you have to get there. And unless you're a romantic who's signing up to crew on a tramp steamer, you'll be riding on a jet plane. This chapter will help you figure out how to get the lowest fare, both for transatlantic and intra-European flights, and also provides tips for flying comfortably and navigating European airports smartly.

BOOKING YOUR FLIGHT

Your plane ticket to Europe will likely be your biggest trip expense. It pays to be on your toes to get the best deal.

Using Flight Search Websites

If you're not using a travel agent, your first step is to research your options. Rather than checking each airline's website, I begin my search with a site that compiles my choices.

Flight search websites compare fares available at multiple airlines, online travel agencies, or both, then sort them by price. I've tested a number of them on a variety of journeys, both transatlantic and within Europe. Overall, **Kayak** has the best results for both intercontinental and intra-European flights on a combination of mainstream and budget carriers. An alternative is **Google Flights,** which has an easy-to-use system to track prices and lets you see how much you'd save by departing a day earlier or later.

A couple of sites are better for flights *to* Europe than flights *within* Europe, and some nice features make their results easier to navigate. **Expedia** is easy to use and consistent at finding good fares. **CheapoAir** offers pricing tables for mixed-airline flights to and from Europe. **Vayama** specializes in international flights, with cheaper fares that might not show up elsewhere—but beware that its customer service doesn't have a stellar reputation for handling cancellations and changes. (For cheap flights *within* Europe, I prefer **Skyscanner**—see page 113.)

Flight-Search Tips

Here are some things to keep in mind when looking for flights.

Look around. No single flight search engine includes every possible airline—and some airlines deliberately limit where their airfares appear. It's always smart to check more than one website, and to look directly on airlines' websites as well.

Think flexibly about airports and dates. If you are flying into a city with several airports, select either "all airports" or simply the city name ("LON" for London) rather than a specific airport name ("LHR" for London Heathrow). If offered, select "include nearby airports"—doing so will return more flight options (for example, Pisa for Florence or Bratislava for Vienna). Choosing "flexible dates" lets you see what you might save by flying a few days before or after your ideal time frame.

Consider flying into one city and out of another. Since it rarely makes sense to spend time and money returning to your starting point, this strategy can be very efficient (see page 52). For most "multicity" flights, the fare is figured simply by taking half of the round-trip cost for each of those ports, though you'll likely save money by using the same airline for each segment.

Delete your cookies and history. When searching for fares, it may help to regularly delete your Internet cookies and search history if you repeatedly search for the same itinerary. Cookies remember what you've searched in the past. So if you're looking again and again for the same flights on the same website, the site becomes aware of your search habits...and increases the prices. To delete your cookies, look under "content settings" or "browsing data" in your browser's privacy settings.

Multiple-City Flights

FROM NORTH AMERICA

TO NORTH AMERICA

OSLO

EXPLORE...

LISBON

Buying Tickets

While it's possible to book your flights on most search sites (they certainly hope you will, to garner their commission),

I use these sites only as a first step. Once I've zeroed in on which airline has the best deal for my trip, I check the airline's own site to compare fares. You can often avoid added costs by booking direct (the commissions are charged either as higher prices or in the form of fees for booking through a third party). And airlines may offer bonuses (such as extra frequent-flier miles) to those who book direct.

Search sites occasionally beat the fares on the airline's official site, sometimes by using "mix and match" journeys to connect the legs of a single trip on multiple airlines. (However, these trips can be difficult to rebook in case of a delay or missed leg—review the schedule carefully, watching out for very tight connections or extremely long layovers.)

For maximum peace of mind, it's usually best to book directly with the airline, which can more easily address unexpected problems or deal with rescheduled flights. If you do buy tickets through a third-party site, make sure you carry their phone number with you—you'll need to speak to a person if you have a problem.

Flight-Booking Tips

There's no such thing as a free lunch in the airline industry. (In fact, there's usually no lunch at all.) Before grabbing the cheapest ticket you can find, make sure it meets your travel needs with the best combination of schedule, economy, and convenience.

Buy your tickets at the right time (to the extent possible). Airfares flex like crazy, but in general it's wise to start looking for international flights at least four to six months before your trip, especially for travel in spring, summer, or fall. Good deals on winter travel (November through March) can usually be purchased a month or so in advance, with the exception of winter breaks and holidays, which require even earlier booking. Year-round, it's generally cheaper to book midweek.

All that said, knowing the best time to buy is still a guessing game, though you can improve your chances by taking advantage of Google's Flight Explorer (www.google.com/flights/explore), which shows the best prices to your destination in an easy-to-read graph and can be tailored to your time frame. And several search sites, including Kayak and Expedia, offer price-trend graphs.

Be ready to buy. Given how erratic airline pricing can be, be ready to pounce on a good fare when you see it. Waiting to talk with your travel partner could cost you a good fare. As you delay, dates sell out and prices generally go up. Figure out in advance what constitutes a good fare, then grab it when you find it. A few airlines will let you pay a small fee to hold a fare for three days. US Department of Transportation regulations state that you're entitled to cancel or change a flight within 24 hours of purchase without a fee, but if you're changing flights, you may have to pay the fare difference. Airlines find sneaky ways around these rules, so call before buying if you think you'll need to cancel.

Be sure of your dates before you book. Changing or canceling your ticket can be very expensive, as airlines can be aggressive about change fees, with most charging around $250 per ticket per change. Unexpected circumstances can happen to anyone, so understand your ticket's change policies before you buy. (While nonrefundable tickets are cheaper and the most restrictive, even certain types of business and first-class tickets have penalties for changes.)

If you need to alter your return date in Europe, call your airline's European office. If you absolutely must get home early, go to the airport and talk to your airline's representatives at the ticket desk: If you're standing at the airport two days before your ticket says you can go home, and seats are available, they may just let you fly.

Pick a seat as early as possible. Most airlines let you choose your seat when you book, and most charge extra for roomier seats. If your first choice is not open, select another seat and try to change it later. If seat assignments aren't available at booking, ask about the earliest possible date that you can request your seat (for example,

Resources for Air Travel

Kayak.com: Top site (and app) for flight options to and within Europe

Google.com/flights: Another good search site with easy tracking and price alerts

Skyscanner.com: Best search engine for cheap flights within Europe

Expedia.com, CheapoAir.com, Vayama.com: Alternative search engines for flights to Europe

WhichAirline.com, Momondo.com, Dohop.com: Alternative search engines for intra-European flights

AirfareWatchdog.com, FareCompare.com: Low-fare alerts and deals, but clunky user interface

Fly.com, TravelZoo.com, Priceline.com, Hotwire.com: Search engines and deals tailored to those with flexible itineraries

Google.com/flights/explore: Graphs the best prices to your destination

SeatGuru.com: Airplane-seat maps and advice

FlyerTalk.com: Travel forum site with tips on frequent flyer miles

TSA.gov: Latest US flight rules and regulations

www.ricksteves.com/hub-airports: Advice for passing through Europe's hub airports

www.ricksteves.com/travel-talks: Rick's travel skills talks, including one on transportation

TripIt app: Itinerary organizer with flight-change alerts

FlightAware app: Live flight tracker

LoungeBuddy app: Airport-lounge locator that lets you book access instantaneously

90 or 30 days before your flight)—and put it on your calendar. A week before your flight, airlines will sometimes release extra seats or change equipment: Check to see if you can get a better seat. And try to check in online exactly 24 hours before your flight, when even more seats may be released— including bulkhead and exit-row seats.

Larger or taller travelers may find it worth the extra cost for the extra legroom afforded by "Economy Plus" seats (or whatever your airline calls their intermediate class between Economy and Business). For pointers on which seats are best on specific airplanes, see SeatGuru.com.

Review your ticket information carefully when you book. Double-check your dates, times, destinations, baggage allowance, and exact spelling of your name. Confirm that the name on your reservation exactly matches the one on your passport; this can be an expensive hassle to correct later. Decline extras that you don't want (for example, premium seating—with an extra fee). On each page of the transaction, be sure that no boxes are checked unless you want them to be.

Money-Saving Tips

Here are some additional ideas for finding low fares.

Comparison-shop "air plus hotel" promotional deals. Some airfare aggregators and airlines offer "getaway" deals. For one low price, you get a round-trip flight to a European city as well as a few nights' lodging. Given Europe's high accommodation costs—especially in big cities—these can be a good value, though you can expect to be put up in a soulless business hotel.

Sign up for low-fare alerts. Many airfare search sites— as well as the official airline sites—will email and tweet automated updates about low fares for specific routes. Or check out the website AirfareWatchdog, a free service that does a particularly good job of finding the cheapest fares across multiple airlines (including those that don't show up on most search sites), and limits their alerts to flights that actually have seats available. A similar site called FareCompare tweets alerts specific to your home airport.

Consider budget European airlines. A few of Europe's low-cost carriers have flights between the US and Europe; these don't normally show up in the search results of most US-based airfare comparison sites. Check the list on page 113 for carriers with hubs near your European destination, then find out if they fly to any US airports. Be forewarned that passenger reviews of these budget carriers' trans-Atlantic flights are mixed regarding their legroom, onboard services, and overall comfort—all of which are more important on a long overseas flight than a quick intra-European hop. Do your homework before committing to a lengthy flight.

Use any scheduling flexibility to your advantage. At certain times—for instance, when shoulder season turns into peak season (and vice versa) for your destination—shifting your flight by one day could save you hundreds of dollars. And consider that fares are generally a bit cheaper for travel Monday through Thursday than for weekends.

If your travel dates aren't set, you may be able to score a great deal—try sites like AirfareWatchdog and TravelZoo, both of which keep track of the latest deals, or Fly.com, which displays an up-to-date list of cheap deals from your city to various destinations.

Some sites offer the option to purchase a discounted ticket without knowing full details about your airline and flight times. For example, Priceline allows you to suggest a price for your itinerary if you're flexible about your airline and flight schedule. Hotwire offers discount "hot rates" that provide details of your airline and flight time after you have purchased the ticket. Just keep in mind that you're just as likely to stumble upon deals on the airlines' own websites—particularly if you sign up for their email alerts.

Frequent-Flier Miles

Personally, I don't collect frequent-flier miles. (It's my own quirky hang-up, but I view frequent-flier programs as a cynical way for airlines to produce nothing while prodding their customers to jump through needless hoops and compromise flexibility.) However, for a traveler who's willing to play the game, frequent-flier miles can be a useful budget tool. Here are some strategies for getting the most travel out of your miles. For more tips, check out FlyerTalk.com.

Book as far ahead as possible. Airlines reserve only a handful of "award seats" on each flight—and they go fast. Book months in advance—or even close to a year for peak travel season.

Maximize the miles you earn. Booking direct with the airline, rather than on a third-party booking site, might earn you bonus miles. Many credit cards allow you to accrue miles with each purchase you make, flight-related or not.

Know about alliances. Most major airlines belong to one of three gigantic frequent-flier collectives: Star Alliance, SkyTeam, or OneWorld, all of which cover North American airlines as well as European carriers. Before booking, check the latest on which airlines belong to which group (these partnerships are as slippery as political alliances). If you have miles on one airline in the alliance, you can redeem them on any of the others.

Redeem miles online if possible. Check if the flight you want is available on the airline's website. If not, try speaking directly with an airline agent. While this can come with a small additional fee, it may be worth it to talk with a live person who has all your options at his or her fingertips—especially if you...

Research and know your options. If you try to redeem miles over the phone, the agent might say you're out of luck just because the most straightforward route is sold out. Before you call, make a list (in order of preference) of the connections that would work for your trip, or ask the agent to try a less convenient alternate route.

If you're a little short on miles, get creative. Look into buying miles from the airline or paying a fee to transfer them from someone else (such as a family member). Many airlines also allow you to "pay" for one leg of the ticket with miles and the other in cash.

Watch the expiration date. Miles generally expire at a certain point after you accrue them. It's a good idea to note these expiration dates in your calendar, with a reminder several months ahead. Typically the miles must be redeemed for a ticket before the expiration date, but the flight can occur anytime—even months later. If you've got miles but aren't ready to redeem them, you can usually extend their life by doing some online shopping through your airline's website (send a bouquet of flowers to your mom).

Expect to pay fees. Even if your ticket is "free," you'll likely pay taxes and booking fees (sometimes hundreds of dollars; British Airways even has a fuel surcharge). The amount depends on the airline, class of service, and destination.

Using a Travel Agent

While travel agents may seem like an antiquated notion—or perhaps only the purview of business travelers and wealthy jetsetters—even the Web-savviest budget traveler shouldn't be too quick to rule out using the services of a living, breathing agent. A good travel agent will almost certainly save you time, may also save you money, and can be a vital ally should you or your trip run into problems. Like many of my readers, I value the personal touch and expertise that only an experienced agent can provide.

Most agents charge a $35-150 fee per ticket. In the long run, paying a modest fee could be a worthwhile expense—think of it as a reasonable charge for the hassle of tracking down flight options, and/or a consulting cost for your travel agent's expertise. I enjoy the convenience of explaining my travel plans to my agent, getting a briefing on my options, and choosing the best flight.

Travel agents not only save you the time of looking up your own flights, but sometimes have access to cheaper fares. A good travel agent—especially one who specializes in the region you're traveling to—offers both regular airline fares and discounted consolidator fares. (Consolidators are wholesalers who negotiate with airlines to get deeply discounted fares, then sell those tickets cheaply but with a markup; check cancellation policies and other restrictions carefully.)

Using an agent can be beneficial if you are booking a complicated trip (whether coordinating a group and/or a complex, multileg itinerary), need to obtain visas, or if you're taking a cruise (most cruise lines prefer that you book through an agent).

An agent can also be helpful in smoothing any bumps in the road. Once, just after boarding my plane in the US and settling in for my flight to London, the flight crew announced that a fire had shut down Heathrow. Back in the terminal, you can imagine the chaotic scene as everyone from my flight scrambled to sort out their plans. But I simply called my agent and asked her to get me to my end destination, Berlin, any way but through London. With little fuss, I was rebooked on a flight early the next morning via Amsterdam, and made it to Berlin before noon.

While I often use an agent for my plane ticket, car rental, advice on visas, and possibly travel insurance, I turn to a good guidebook for everything else (such as hotel advice). Although an agent may be able to give you tips on Irish B&Bs or sporadic advice on biking in Holland, it's safe to assume you'll get more helpful information from your guidebook. For intra-Europe flights, do your own search, as a travel agent's reservations networks don't include most cheap, no-frills European airlines (see "Flying Within Europe," page 111).

If you're seeking a good travel agent, recommendations from other travelers provide excellent leads. But the right agency doesn't guarantee the right agent. You need someone whose definition of "good travel" matches yours. When you contact an agency, ask for their "independent Europe specialist."

FLYING TO EUROPE

I love a nonstop Seattle-to-Europe trip. Just about ten hours (five hours of work, one hour for dinner, then pop a quarter-tab of Ambien to get four hours of sleep, happy to wake learning I missed breakfast, eat my clean-the-cupboard peanut butter sandwich from home as we touch down)...and I'm in Europe.

Your flight and arrival are part of the adventure—here's how to make them go efficiently and enjoyably.

Checking In

Most carriers allow you to check in and print your boarding pass 24 hours before departure. This can save a lot of time and hassle at the airport. Even if you check in beforehand, plan to arrive at the airport at least two hours in advance (some airlines recommend three hours).

If your flight includes a connection to a different carrier, you may not be able to check in online (even if they're partnered—for example, the first leg on United and the second leg on Lufthansa). First try checking in on the website of the company from which you bought the ticket; if that doesn't work, try the other carrier's site. Otherwise, you'll have to check in for the entire journey at the airport; in rare cases, you may have to wait until your layover to check in for your connecting flight. Don't dawdle—check in as early as possible.

If checking in online, you may have the option to skip a printed boarding pass and instead have it sent to your mobile phone. If you chose this option, be sure that your phone is adequately charged before you head to the airport. (It's also important to charge your electronic devices before you board because security checks may require you to turn them on.)

Keep your passport with you (not in a checked bag), as you'll be required to show it at airport security checkpoints. It's always smart to have your flight confirmation on hand (either printed or easily accessed on your phone) in case you run into complications.

Making the Most of Your Flight

Flying economy class doesn't have to be miserable. I've never paid for anything more than coach—and many times I've ended up on a full flight, spending ten hours in a middle seat. These aren't ideal conditions for a good night's sleep, but I make it work. Here are my tricks for a comfortable flight in cattle-car "luxury":

Dress for comfort and relaxation. I dress warm and loose, taking off my shoes and belt, and cuddling up with a sweater and scarf. Next, I slip on my noise-canceling headphones, which both mute the rumble of the engines and the mind-numbing chatter of people around me. With headphones on, I get into conversations only if I want to, which makes the flight much more restful.

Come prepared to stay busy. I board the plane with a fully charged laptop, ebook reader, or tablet—and lots of reading or writing to do. This provides me with a mental escape and an opportunity to prepare for my upcoming travels, and it helps the time race by. Some airlines offer charging ports on long-haul flights—even in coach—but I wouldn't count on it. Some flights also include Wi-Fi, though access isn't fast enough for streaming video (either download videos or use the in-flight entertainment).

Get some rest. For me, just a quarter-tablet of Ambien (*zolpidem*) is good for a couple of blissful hours of sleep. And a neck rest can do wonders. When I wake up, I'm thankful for the shut-eye. It enables me to function much better on my first day in Europe (for more on how to handle jet lag, see page 408). I also believe that good health on your trip starts with the flight over—see my tips on page 410.

What Can't I Carry On?

The list of prohibited carry-on items can change without notice—especially just after a terrorist threat. And while most security rules are similar on either side of the Atlantic, carry-on restrictions can differ between the US and Europe, as well as between any two European countries. Don't assume you know what's allowed. Shortly before your flight, check www.TSA.gov/travel, as well as the websites for your airline and any airports you're flying through. (This is an especially good idea if you're flying through London, which often enforces tighter restrictions than other European hubs; see www.gov.uk/hand-luggage-restrictions.)

Tempted to pick up some duty-free booze or perfume on your way back home? It's no problem if you have a nonstop flight. Passengers with a connection are permitted to carry liquids (or oil- or liquid-packed foods) in excess of 3.4 ounces if they were purchased in a duty-free shop and are packaged in a "STEB"—a secure, tamper-evident bag. Your STEB sack will be screened when you transfer to your connecting flight. But stay away from liquids in opaque, ceramic, or metallic containers, which usually cannot be successfully screened (STEB or no STEB); place these products in your checked baggage or forfeit them. For more tips, see "Hauling Home Heavenly Wines" on page 372.

Use your layovers well. If your flight requires a connection and layover, use the time to charge your mobile devices and handle routine tasks (e.g., if it's your first stop in Europe, get cash at an ATM if your layover shares a currency with your destination). With a really long layover, consider a brief excursion downtown—most of Europe's airports are connected to the city center by fast, frequent, and affordable public transit. For key details on Europe's hub airports (London, Amsterdam, Frankfurt, and Paris), see www.ricksteves.com/hub-airports.

Dealing with Delays

Even the best-planned travel arrangements can run into snags. Planes have mechanical problems, hurricanes and blizzards blow through, and flight delays cause missed connections. Planning ahead is the key to diminishing the downside of delays.

Sign up for alerts from your airline via text, email, or app. You can also get info about flight changes from third-party apps such as TripIt or FlightAware.

If your flight is canceled, your airline is likely to rebook you on the next flight that has available seats, or offer you a refund. Consider calling the airline as you wait in line to get rebooked; you may reach someone by phone before you make it to the counter. Remember that jumping on another flight—especially if it's leaving soon—is much easier to do if you haven't checked any bags (another good reason to pack light and carry on).

It's important to know your rights as a passenger in case you get grounded by a long delay. The Department of Transportation requires that US airlines give passengers waiting inside the plane food, water, and bathroom access by the time the delay reaches two hours. After waiting for three hours on the tarmac, passengers must be allowed to leave the plane.

For longer delays, you may need to figure out where in the airport to while away several hours...or make plans to spend the night. Some airports have hotels right in the terminal (for instance, Heathrow's Yotel or CitizenM inside Amsterdam's Schiphol). If you need a place to sleep, ask if the airline can arrange a discount for you at a local hotel. Cheapskates can find tips at SleepingInAirports.net.

In the US, don't expect much help from your airline, such as hotel reimbursement or food vouchers, especially in the case of delays or cancellations caused by weather. Each

The Fear of Flying

I can understand why many people are afraid to fly. It's easy to think of the little rubber wheels splashing down on a rain-soaked runway and then hydroplaning out of control. Or the spindly landing gear crumbling. Or, if not that, then the plane tilting just a tad, catching a wing tip, and flipping over and bursting into flames.

I overcome these concerns with simple logic. The chances of being in an airplane crash are minuscule. I remind myself that worldwide, only one passenger plane is involved in a fatal accident for every 4,125,000 flights that take to the sky. That means that I could catch a flight each day for an average of 123,000 years before dying in a plane crash. There's a good reason that the pilot and crew don't seem terrified, even though they fly daily. For more than 30 years, my company has had countless tour-group members fly over to meet us—20,000 tourists a year these days—and, as far as I know, never has one of our travelers even picked up a scratch while flying.

Consider this: The odds of dying in a commercial airplane accident are 1 in 11 million. Worldwide, more than a million people die each year in road accidents— about the same as if a fully loaded 747 crashed every four hours. If you worry about safety, the real time to panic is during the drive to the airport.

I comfort my nervousness with the knowledge that flying is a matter of physics and aerodynamics. Air has mass, and the plane maneuvers itself through that mass. I can understand a boat coming into a dock—maneuvering through the water. That doesn't scare me. So I tell myself that a plane's a boat with an extra dimension to navigate, and its "water" (air) is a lot thinner. Also, the pilot, who's still "flying" the plane after it lands, is as much in control on the ground as in the air. Only when he's good and ready does he allow gravity to take over.

Turbulence scares me, too. But a United pilot once told me that he'd have bruises from his seat belt before turbulence really bothered him. Still, every time the plane comes in for a landing, I say a prayer, close my eyes, and take my pen out of my shirt pocket so it won't impale me if something goes wrong. And every time I stick my pen back in my shirt pocket, I feel thankful.

airline's "conditions of carriage" details what passengers are entitled to receive when flights are canceled. Many major carriers have contracts that remove liability for problems related to weather.

If you are flying in the European Union, you have much stronger passenger rights; see the "EU Passenger Rights" sidebar on page 115.

If you don't need a full night's sleep, consider purchasing a one-time pass for an airport lounge (about $50). You can rest, freshen up, have a drink and a snack, charge your devices, and do a little work. The LoungeBuddy app can help you locate and book access to lounges in airports across North America and Europe. Be aware that many lounges are closed after midnight or limit how long you can stay—check the hours before you buy a pass.

Navigating European Airports

Most European airports are slick, modern, and well-connected to the city center, but they still can be a jumble of tired travelers, torn-up terminals, and tardy taxis. Channel your inner Boy Scout and be prepared to navigate the airport smartly once you arrive.

Utilize airport services. You may be jet-lagged and just want to get to your hotel, but take advantage of airport services before you leave. Stop by the tourist information office for maps, museum passes, subway tickets, and advice (usually they're less crowded than the downtown office). If you need a SIM card for your mobile phone (see page 294), you should be able to find one in an airport convenience store. I've also found that free Wi-Fi at executive lounges in airports often leaks into the main hall. Sitting nearby, I can get online for free.

Just say no to exchange booths. At airport exchange booths, you lose around 15 percent when you change dollars to euros or other currency. To get local cash, find an airport ATM (for more on withdrawing cash in Europe, see page 191).

Know where you're going. Some airlines offer apps that provide airport maps and tips for navigating them upon arrival. Google has started mapping airport interiors with its Street View program. Lower-tech travelers can visit the website for their arrival airport in advance and print out a floor plan. Also have on hand instructions for getting to your hotel so you'll know which train, shuttle bus, or taxi stand to look for.

Don't get lost in translation. Nearly everything is labeled in English at European airports, but you still need to pay careful attention. For example, the shuttle train between terminals at Paris' Charles de Gaulle Airport is called the CDGVAL—you have to look carefully to see that it is also marked "Airport Shuttle" in smaller letters.

LEFT European airports are modern, efficient, and filled with tired travelers.

RIGHT Helpful airport staff can point you in the right direction.

If taking public transit, consider buying a transit pass at the airport. Airport buses and trains are usually part of a city's larger transport network, which means you can often include the ride on whichever transit card you'll be using while you're in town. For example, when I fly into London Heathrow, I buy the one-week public transit pass covering the Tube and city buses, and pay a small airport supplement. I get to my hotel from the airport and I get the whole week of travel covered for what I would spend if I took a taxi from the airport to my hotel.

Ensure happy returns. Before you leave the airport upon your arrival, note which terminal you'll use for your departure (assuming you're flying out from the same airport). Don't count on the taxi driver or shuttle bus driver knowing where you should be dropped off when you come back for your flight home. At some airports, terminals are very far apart, and arriving at the wrong one will mean wasted time riding around the airport on a shuttle bus.

FLYING WITHIN EUROPE

When I started traveling, no one spending their own money bought one-way airline tickets within Europe. It simply wasn't affordable. But today that kind of thinking is so 20th century. Before buying any long-distance train or bus ticket, it's smart to first check the cost of a flight—you might be surprised.

The proliferation of extremely competitive discount carriers has revolutionized European-itinerary planning and turned vagabonds into jetsetters. You can hop just about anywhere on the Continent for less than $250 a flight, making deciding where to go mostly just a question of following your travel dreams. You're no longer limited to places within a convenient train ride or reasonable drive from each other (though those are still perfectly fine ways to travel—it's smart to run through all of your options). It's now entirely feasible to lace together a far-flung trip from Ireland to Portugal to Sicily, if you please.

Using Budget Airlines

After Europe deregulated its airways in the 1990s, a flock of budget-conscious, no-frills airlines took flight. Some established ones (such as EasyJet and Ryanair) have route maps that rival their mainstream competitors. Meanwhile, dozens of smaller, niche airlines stick to a more limited flight plan. For a partial list, see the sidebar on page 113.

Budget airlines typically offer flights between major European cities for $50-250. These days, you can also fly within Europe on major airlines affordably—and without all the aggressive restrictions. You can even find some remarkable, it-must-be-a-typo deals if your timing is right (for

example, Ryanair routinely flies from London to any one of dozens of European cities for less than $30). Even after adding taxes and a boatload of fees, these flights can still be a good value. To get the lowest fares, book long in advance. The cheapest seats sell out fast (aside from occasional surprise sales), leaving pricier fares for latecomers. Of course, it's important to consider the downsides of flying budget airlines (described later).

Europe's no-frills, smaller airlines offer cut-rate fares and scaled-down services.

One-way flights on low-cost airlines are generally just as affordable as round-trips. Consider linking a couple of cheap flights, either with the same or different airlines, to reach your destination. But leave plenty of time for connections—you're on your own if a delay on one airline causes you to miss your next flight on a different airline. Pay attention to which terminal your flights use, as low-cost carriers are often in a different terminal than traditional carriers, and you'll need extra time to get between them. If you're using a budget carrier to connect to your US-bound flight, allow enough of a layover to absorb delays—maybe even an overnight.

Smart travelers use low-cost airlines to creatively connect the dots on their itinerary. If there's no direct cheap flight to Florence, maybe there's an alternative that goes to Pisa (1.5 hours away by train); remember that many flight-search websites have a "nearby airports" option that broadens your search. Even adding the cost of the train ticket from Pisa to Florence, the total could be well below the price of a long overland journey, not to mention several hours faster.

Booking Cheap Flights Within Europe

Most budget airlines focus on particular hubs. When looking for cheap flights, first check airlines that use either your starting point or your ending point as a hub. For example, for a trip from Berlin to Oslo, I'd look at Air Berlin (with a hub in Berlin) and at Norwegian (which has a hub in Oslo). Be

Budget Airlines in Europe

These are some of the budget airlines crisscrossing the European skies, along with their main hubs. To discover more, check out Skyscanner.com, or search online for "cheap flights" plus the cities you're interested in flying to/from. New airlines appear—and old ones go out of business—all the time.

Airline	Main Hubs
Aer Lingus	Dublin, Shannon
AirBaltic	Riga
Air Berlin	Berlin, Düsseldorf
Blue Air	Bucharest
CityJet	London (London City)
Condor	Frankfurt
EasyJet	London (Gatwick, Stansted, Luton), Milan, Berlin, Paris (Charles de Gaulle, Orly), and more
Flybe	Birmingham, Manchester
Eurowings	Cologne, Düsseldorf, Hamburg
Icelandair	Reykjavik
Meridiana	Milan, Cagliari
Monarch Airlines	London (Gatwick, Luton), Birmingham, Manchester
Niki	Vienna
Norwegian	Oslo, London (Gatwick)
Pegasus Airlines	Istanbul
Ryanair	London (Stansted), Dublin, and many other European cities
SmartWings	Prague
Transavia	Amsterdam, Paris (Orly)
Vueling	Barcelona, Rome
Widerøe	Oslo, Bergen
Wizz Air	Budapest

aware that some airlines forego this "hub-and-spoke" model for a less predictable "point-to-point" schedule. Some major European airlines, faced with competition from budget carriers, have even joined the discount-airfare game.

My first stop when seeking budget flights online is **Skyscanner;** this straightforward website specializes in European budget airlines, and gives an overview of all of my options. Skyscanner also includes major nonbudget carriers.

Several other websites, including the all-purpose **Kayak,** are worth a look. **WhichAirline** does a good job of searching budget carriers, and specializes in creative options for getting rock-bottom fares. The visually engaging **Momondo** automatically includes nearby airports in search results (be clear on which airport it's using). **Dohop** has a clean interface and generally good results.

What's the Catch?

With cheaper airfares come potential pitfalls. Budget tickets are usually nonrefundable and nonchangeable. Many airlines take only online bookings, so it can be hard to reach a customer service representative if problems arise. (Read all the fine print carefully, so you know what you're getting into.) Flights are often tightly scheduled to squeeze more flying time out of each plane, which can exaggerate the effects of delays. Deadlines are strictly enforced: If they tell you to arrive at the check-in desk an hour before the flight, and you show up with 50 minutes to spare, you've just missed your plane. Also, it's not uncommon for budget carriers to unexpectedly go out of business or cancel a slow-selling route—leaving you scrambling to find an alternative.

Since budget airlines aren't making much money on your ticket, they look for other ways to pad their profits—bombarding you with ads every step of the way (as you book, via email after you've bought your ticket, on board the plane), selling you overpriced food and drinks on board (nothing's included), and gouging you with fees. For instance, you may get dinged for paying with a credit card (even though there's no option for paying cash), checking in and printing your boarding pass at the airport (instead of online), "priority boarding" ahead of the pack, reserving a seat, carrying an infant on board, and—of course—checking bags. The initial fare you see on the website can be misleadingly low: Once you begin the purchasing process, each step seems to come with another charge.

If you plan to check a bag, pay the fee when you purchase your ticket—on many budget airlines, the price per bag gets progressively higher the closer you get to your departure. Be aware that you may have to pay extra to check a bag if it's over a certain (relatively low) weight limit. Don't assume your bag qualifies as carry-on in Europe; many budget airlines use smaller dimensions than other carriers. To avoid

Even if the name of your budget airline (such as Wizz Air) doesn't exactly inspire confidence, these carriers can get you to many destinations cheaper and a whole lot faster than the train.

unpleasant surprises, read the baggage policy carefully before you book.

Ryanair, one of the biggest budget carriers, is as famous for its low fares as it is for the creative ways it's devised to nickel-and-dime passengers. For instance, their complicated checked-luggage price schedule varies depending on how many bags you have, how heavy they are, what time of the year you're flying, and whether you prebook online—ranging from about $20 for a small bag prebooked off-season to $180 for a bigger bag booked at the airport in peak season, plus about $12 per extra kilogram over 20 kilos (44 pounds).

Another potential headache: Budget airlines sometimes use obscure airports. For example, one of Ryanair's London hubs is Stansted Airport, one of the farthest airports from London's city center. Ryanair's flights to "Frankfurt" actually take you to Hahn, 75 miles away. You may even wind up in a different (though nearby) country: For example, a flight advertised as going to Copenhagen, Denmark, might go to Malmö, Sweden, or a flight bound for Vienna, Austria, might land in Bratislava, Slovakia. These are still safe and legal airstrips, but it can take money and time to reach your final destination by public transportation. On the other hand, the money you save often more than pays for the difference.

EU Passenger Rights

You don't have to be European to benefit from the EU's consumer-protection laws, which are particularly robust when it comes to air travel. The most important one to know: If your European airline is at fault for a sudden cancellation or significant delay—say, if your plane has a mechanical problem—you're entitled to compensation for hotel and food costs you incurred while in air-travel limbo. Reimbursement depends not only on the length of your delay but on the length of your flight, with an upper limit of €600 per traveler. (Weather-related changes are exempt.)

This law applies to any last-minute change of plans, including being moved to an earlier flight. Even US-based carriers are bound by this law for any flights departing *from* the EU.

Not surprisingly, airlines don't automatically fork over these reimbursements—but gate agents or customer-service reps must inform affected passengers about their rights (they have printed handouts). And all airlines that serve Europe must list the details on their websites (usually under "passenger rights" or "claims," albeit in fine-print legalese). For details, see www.europa.eu/youreurope and choose "Passengers Rights" under "Travel."

If you need to seek reimbursement, the websites Refund.me and AirHelp explain what you're entitled to and how to request it. (And for a 25 percent commission, these companies will handle the whole process for you.)

Trains, Buses & Boats

In Europe, public transportation works. Over the years, Europeans have invested hugely in their public transit, and it's generally fast and effective. Of course, digging the English Channel Tunnel, building a bridge between Denmark and Sweden, and adding bullet trains all cost money, and train travel is not cheap like it once was. But savvy travelers can still get around on a tight budget.

Europe's commitment to public transportation is not just limited to populated areas—it's nearly everywhere. For example, in Scotland's Highlands—way up north—if the population is too sparse to justify a public bus service, citizens needing to get to a remote farmstead are welcome to ride with the postman for the cost of a bus ticket. In Europe, I use this rule of thumb: If there are people here and people there, there's a way to get between them by public transit. I can't think of a popular European sight that you can't reach by bus, boat, or train.

This chapter pays special attention to the pros and cons of buying rail passes and point-to-point train tickets, figuring out train schedules, and navigating Europe's train stations. Travel by bus and ferry is covered at the end of the chapter; for information on subways, city buses, and taxis, see the chapter on Getting Around in Cities. For information on flying within Europe, see page 111.

The Benefits of Train Travel

The European train system shrinks what is already a small continent, making the budget whirlwind or far-reaching tour a reasonable and exciting possibility for anyone. The system works great for locals and travelers alike, with well-signed stations, easily accessed schedules, and efficient connections between popular destinations. First-time train travelers get the hang of it faster than they expect. Generally, European trains go where you need them to go and are fast, frequent, and affordable. Lace this network together to create the trip of your dreams.

For many travelers, the pleasure of journeying along Europe's rails really is as good as the destination. As Americans, we're accustomed to being shoehorned into a cramped passenger car or an economy-class airline seat. On the train, you can walk around, spread out in comparatively wide seats, and easily retrieve an extra sweater from your luggage. It's also quite time-efficient, especially with Europe's ever-growing network of super-fast trains. With night trains, you can easily have dinner in Paris, sleep on the train, and have breakfast in Venice. And (with the exception of the Eurostar, which goes under the English Channel and connects London with Paris and Brussels) you don't need to show up early. As long as you're on board when the train leaves, you're on time.

When to Choose Train Travel

So how does train travel compare to driving or flying? Though not as flexible as having a rental car, trains can be less stressful. On a train, you can forget about parking hassles, confusing road signs, speed limits, bathroom stops, and Italian drivers. You can watch the scenery instead of fixing your eyes on the road, and maybe even enjoy a glass of the local wine (for more guidance on choosing between trains and cars, see page 157).

Although flying can save both time and money when making long journeys in Europe, that's not always the case. For instance, taking the Eurostar from London to Paris can be faster than flying when you consider the train zips you directly from downtown to downtown. And if you're focusing on a single country or region and connecting nearby destinations, the train is generally more practical than flying.

Trains connect big cities, but also small towns—such as Manarola—in Italy's Cinque Terre.

Compared to flying, both trains and cars keep you close to the scenery, to Europe, and to Europeans. Ground transportation is also less likely to be disrupted by bad weather, mechanical problems, or scheduling delays, and it allows for more spontaneity. If a town looks too cute to miss, just jump off the train (or stop the car).

For me, trains remain the quintessentially European way to go, and the best option for romantics. Driving to the Austrian lakeside hamlet of Hallstatt is easy, but arriving by train is magical: Hop off at the hut-sized station across the lake, catch the waiting boat, and watch the town's shingled roofs and church spires grow bigger as the mist lifts off the water.

TRAIN TICKETS AND PASSES

A train traveler's biggest pretrip decision is whether to get a rail pass or stick with point-to-point tickets (or use a mix of both). Many travelers make a costly mistake by skipping over the details of this decision, as rail passes are no longer the sure bet they once were. It pays to know your options and choo-choose what's best for your trip.

Tickets or Passes?

Point-to-point tickets are just that: tickets bought individually to get you from Point A to Point B. It's simplest to buy these in train stations as you travel, but they're becoming easier to purchase online (especially handy if you need to secure an advance reservation for a certain train). By contrast, a **rail pass** covers train travel in one or more countries for a certain number of days (either a continuous span of days or a number of days spread over a wider window of time). Most rail passes available to non-Europeans can only be bought outside Europe, so you'll need to decide whether to get one before your trip.

Major Considerations

To figure out whether you want to buy a rail pass or go with

Train Travel Tips at RickSteves.com

While this chapter provides a good start in planning your train travel, the Trains & Rail Passes section of my website has even more details and one-stop shopping for rail passes, seat reservations, and point-to-point tickets.

At www.ricksteves.com/rail you'll find clear, concise advice for figuring out the smartest options for your train trip. Our goal: To create smart consumers (and sell a few rail passes) by providing all the information you need to make the best rail pass decision for your trip. For each European country I cover, you'll get my frank opinion on which passes are a good value, handy region-specific ticket-price maps, and tips for saving money on point-to-point tickets.

point-to-point tickets, sketch out your itinerary, then answer the following questions:

How many days do you expect to ride the train? If you'll be on the train for just one or two days, you almost certainly won't benefit from a pass. The more time you expect to spend on the train, the more likely you'll want a pass.

How many countries will you be visiting by train? The more countries you plan to visit, the more probable it is that you'll save money with a pass. If you're planning a whirlwind trip all around the continent, a pass (or passes) is almost certainly the way to go.

Roughly how much would point-to-point tickets cost? You don't have to laboriously look up exact train fares—to get a rough idea of what you'd pay for bigger journeys, check the map on page 122. If you're traveling in just one or two countries, you can check the more detailed regional maps at www.ricksteves.com/cost-maps. Connect the dots and add up the fares to get an approximate cost for your tickets. Don't worry if some of your destinations aren't shown: Ticket prices are mostly based on distance, so you can estimate fares. For example, if you're going to Italy's Orvieto, about halfway between Florence and Rome, it's safe to assume the train fare to Orvieto from either Florence or Rome is roughly half the total shown for the whole Florence-Rome stretch.

How does your point-to-point ticket cost compare to the price of a pass? Look up the cost of a pass that covers the region you'll be in and the number of days you'll be on the train (see "Choosing Among Passes" on page 126). Several countries, mostly in southern and eastern Europe, have train fares so low that rail passes rarely beat out point-to-point tickets. If you're sticking to moderate distances in Italy, for example, it's unlikely a pass will save you money. If you're traveling in Germany, however, a pass is likely a smart move.

Resources for Trains, Buses & Boats

Bahn.com: User-friendly, Europe-wide timetable

Nationalrail.co.uk: Britain-specific train-schedule and ticket-booking site

RailFanEurope.net: Compendium of other national railway websites (click on "Links")

Seat61.com: Rail-travel advice, including route details, ticket-buying help, and particularly useful night-train info

www.ricksteves.com/travel-talks: Rick's travel skills talks, including one on transportation

DB Navigator app: Schedules for trains throughout Europe

Reading

Europe by Rail: The Definitive Guide for Independent Travellers (Nicky Gardner and Susanne Kries, 2016): Details on major train routes, from planning and ticketing advice to colorful descriptions

Other Factors

If your price comparison doesn't produce an obvious winner, take a closer look at factors that could tilt your decision one way or another, such as:

Sparse Rail Coverage: In some areas, such as southern Spain, coastal Croatia, much of Scotland, and all of Greece and Ireland, rail passes make little sense because trains don't reach many of the places you're planning to go. (To learn whether your destinations are served by train, check online train schedules, described on page 130.)

Pricey Fast-Train Supplements: Passes lose their luster when fees are tacked on. In some countries, pass holders are required to pay extra for each trip on a high-speed train. In Italy, for instance, it costs about an additional $12 per ride for mandatory fast-train reservations on most convenient connections between major cities. On the Thalys train that monopolizes direct service from Paris to Brussels or Amsterdam, pass holders pay extra fees of up to $25 in second class and $45 in first class. (For more on reservations, see page 133.)

First-Class-Only Passes: A few rail passes don't offer a second-class option for adult travelers. If a first-class pass costs about the same as traveling with second-class tickets, go with the pass for comfort. (For more on the differences between classes, see the sidebar on the next page.)

Advance-Purchase Discounts: If you don't mind forgoing some spontaneity, you'll probably be able to save money with advance-purchase discounts on point-to-point tickets. But what you save in dollars you will lose in flexibility, as these discounts are usually valid only for nonrefundable, nonchangeable reserved tickets.

Convenience: In countries or regions where reservations usually aren't required, a pass allows you to hop on and off trains without fussing with buying multiple tickets; if all other things are equal, a pass can make sense for ease of travel.

Point-to-Point Tickets

Unlike rail passes, which must be purchased before you get to Europe, it's generally easiest to buy point-to-point train tickets at the station. But it can be smart to buy in advance for certain trains and destinations, especially if your dates are set and you don't want to risk a specific train journey selling out, or if you're hoping to land an advance-purchase discount.

With a valid rail pass, you just hop on any covered train that doesn't require reservations. But even unreserved

First or Second Class?

First class is plusher and roomier, but second class is where you'll make friends.

Nearly every European train has both first- and second-class cars (and some newer fast trains even have one or two extra rungs of "premier" or "executive" fanciness), all going at precisely the same speed. Yet on most trains in most countries, tickets in second class cost about a third less than those in first class.

Many Americans, familiar with the huge difference between first- and coach-class seating on airplanes, are surprised to see just how small the difference is on European trains. Second class is plenty comfortable; it's generally a no-brainer for anyone on a budget. It can also be more fun. Many first-class travelers are businesspeople looking to get work done; you'll have an easier time striking up a conversation in second class. Most Europeans don't travel in first class unless someone else is paying for it.

First class is often less crowded—a significant plus on popular routes at peak times, when it can be hard to find a seat in second class. First class also has wider seats and aisles, and is more likely to have amenities such as air-conditioning and power outlets (though outlets are still rare on Europe's trains, in any class). While first class is less conducive to conversation, it's more conducive to napping.

With some rail passes, anyone age 28 or older must buy a first-class pass. But youth passes (for those under age 26 or 28), always have a second-class option. First-class pass holders can travel in second-class compartments, although the conductor may give you a puzzled look. Those with second-class passes can pay the difference in ticket price to upgrade to first (except in Britain).

point-to-point tickets have some flexibility, since you can still make any number of stops and connections along the most direct route between the starting and ending stations printed on your ticket. Within a single country your trip usually has to be completed within the same calendar day (or within a few hours in Italy); for many international point-to-point tickets you have four days to complete the journey.

Where to Get Train Tickets

You have three main options for buying point-to-point tickets: through a US-based retailer before leaving home (such as www.ricksteves.com/rail), through the website of one of

Point-to-Point Train Tickets: Cost & Time

— RAIL   --- BUS   ••• BOAT
● CITY COVERED BY EURAIL GLOBAL PASS   ○ CITY NOT COVERED BY EURAIL GLOBAL PASS

This chart shows the approximate cost of second-class train tickets. Connect the dots for your itinerary, then add up the cost to see which is better for your trip: point-to-point tickets or a rail pass.

The first number between cities is the **cost** for a one-way, second-class ticket. (For first-class fares, add 33 percent.) The second number is the trip duration in **hours**.

The fares shown here are for the fastest trains on a given route. Actual prices may vary (and may be cheaper with advance purchase). For more detailed regional maps, see www.ricksteves.com/cost-maps.

Europe's national railways, and in person at Europe's train stations (and at some European travel agencies). For big discounts, buy tickets up to three months ahead (these tickets are nonrefundable and nonchangeable).

US Retailer: You may pay a little more to purchase your ticket through a US retailer than if you were to buy that same ticket in person at a European train station—but for a can't-miss train, the extra cost can be worth it for the peace of mind. (And rail-pass holders who still need tickets and/ or seat reservations on certain trains—most notably the Eurostar, Thalys, and any TGV—are smart to get their pass holder-fare tickets through a US-based site, as these fares sell out quite far in advance and aren't available elsewhere online.)

National Railway Websites: Many European national rail companies allow customers to buy tickets online at the going European price (usually for faster classes of trains for which reservations are required, or at least recommended). If you're looking for the cheapest possible ticket between A and B—especially if A and B are in the same country—this is the way to go. Advance tickets can be an especially smart buy for popular high-speed trains (such as France's TGV trains, which frequently sell out).

Not all national-railway sites are created equal. While many are fairly easy to navigate (including the German, Austrian, British, French, Irish, Italian, Swedish, and Swiss railway sites), some are difficult for foreigners to use, and some won't accept your credit card (notably the Spanish railway site; PayPal solves some credit card issues).

Your "ticket" may be a barcode on your mobile phone, an emailed confirmation code redeemable at the station (in the same country that operates the website you bought it on), or a print-at-home document. Online tickets are valid for a specific date and time and have strict refund restrictions, so read the fine print carefully.

In Europe: Once in Europe, you can buy tickets at the station, usually without much fuss, either on your day of travel or in advance (for tips, see page 137). This is the best option if you'd prefer to keep your itinerary more spontaneous. You can even get tickets for trains in another country: For example, if your trip starts in Paris, you can buy your Berlin-to-Prague ticket at any Parisian train station (as any Parisian would). Tickets bought at train-station windows tend to be easier to change (or have refunded) than tickets bought online.

In some cities you can avoid trekking to the train station by visiting a neighborhood travel agency or branch office of the national railroad. This convenience may come with a fee, but if the agency is easier for you to get to than the train station, buying tickets there can save lots of time and hassle (and travel agents may have more time and English-language skills than the people behind the train-station counter).

Train Fares and Discounts

European train fares are based primarily on the distance traveled. Each country has its own "euros per kilometer" formula, though the type of train also affects the price (logically, slower trains are usually cheaper than faster ones). For faster classes of trains, however, many European rail companies have moved to a dynamic pricing system—similar to how airfares work—in which a fare can vary depending on demand, restrictions, and how early you purchase.

The cost-estimate map on page 122 gives a rough idea of what you'd pay for any given train trip in Europe. If you're buying point-to-point tickets, be aware of the ways you can qualify for a discount (whether buying through a national railway website or in person):

Advance purchase (a week to three months in advance) can save you money in many countries (most notably Austria, Britain, Finland, France, Germany, Italy, Spain, and Sweden), especially for faster or longer rides. In some areas (such as Switzerland and most eastern countries), advance-purchase deals either don't exist or aren't worth the hassle. In most places, for regional or medium-speed trains, tickets cost the same whether they're bought two months or two minutes before the train leaves.

Round-trip tickets can be cheaper than two one-way tickets in some countries (Britain, Ireland, and Spain; sometimes in combination with advance purchase). In Britain, a "day return" ticket (round-trip in a single day) can be only a little bit more expensive than a single one-way ticket.

Children get ticket discounts in most of Europe (typically about 50 percent off for ages 4-11, sometimes free with an adult). And most rail passes now offer one or two free kids with each adult. Whether you're traveling with tickets or a rail pass, kids under 4 always travel free on your lap (though if there's an empty seat, feel free to use it).

Youths ages 12-25 can buy discount cards in Austria, Belgium, Britain, France, Germany, and Italy.

Seniors can find a few ticket deals, most of which require a discount card purchased in Europe (discounts start between ages 60 and 67; see page 472).

Off-peak travel (such as midday or midweek) can be cheaper than peak-time journeys (mainly in Britain and France).

Rail Passes

For independent travelers armed with a rail pass, Europe is a playground. You can travel virtually anywhere, anytime, often without any seat reservations. Just step on the right train, sit in an unreserved seat, and when the uniformed conductor comes, flash your pass. High-speed, international, or overnight trains are more likely to require reservations, but despite that chore, a rail pass is still a joy.

Do You Speak Rail Pass?

When shopping for a rail pass, you're likely to come across some unfamiliar terms. Here's what they mean in plain English.

Global Pass: The classic "Eurail" pass, letting you travel freely throughout most of continental Europe, from Portugal to Finland to Greece.

Select Pass: Covers two, three, or four neighboring countries in continental Europe.

Eurail: Brand name under which many European rail passes are sold (though more commonly used as a generic term for any European rail pass).

Continuous Pass: Gives you unlimited train travel for the duration of the pass.

Flexipass: Lets you pay for just a certain number of train travel days within a specified window of time (for example, any 10 days within a two-month period).

Saverpass: Discounted pass for groups of two to five people traveling together.

Youth Pass: Discounted pass for travelers ages 12-27 (or for ages 16-25 on BritRail and Swiss passes).

Rail-Pass Bonuses: Boat, bus, and non-train trips that are either covered or discounted with a rail pass.

Benelux: Belgium, the Netherlands, and Luxembourg—collectively treated as one country by rail passes.

Activation: Step required before using your pass for the first time—have it stamped by someone behind a station counter.

Reservation: Paid seat assignment (required for pass holders on many faster trains), or *couchette* or sleeper assignment on a night train.

Point-to-Point Ticket: Covers travel from Point A to Point B (an option when you're outside your rail pass coverage area or choose not to use it).

Couchette (koo-shet): A night-train bunk bed in a compartment (with a blanket, pillow, clean linen, and up to five compartment mates).

Sleeper: Compartment with more privacy than a *couchette*, with one, two, or three beds.

All rail passes work in more or less the same way: Every pass covers a specific geographical area (one or more countries), has a fixed number of travel days, and is either good for a continuous block of time (a "continuous pass") or selected days in a window of time (a "flexipass"). Most passes offer "saverpass" deals to people traveling together.

Choosing Among Passes

Carefully compare passes to find the best fit for your itinerary and style of travel. The range of options may seem intimidating, but mostly it's a matter of simply knowing which countries you intend to travel in and for how many days.

Where To? First find the pass that best matches the area you'll be traveling in. If you're planning on covering a lot of ground by train, you probably want a multicountry pass, as it generally makes little sense to cobble together several single-country passes.

A **Global Pass,** covering the widest area, gives you most of Europe by the tail, buying you unlimited travel on all public railways in most of Europe (Britain is the big exception). If you've got a whirlwind trip planned, the Global Pass is probably the best way to go. (You need to essentially travel from Amsterdam to Rome to Madrid and back to Amsterdam to justify the purchase of a one-month Global Pass.)

For a less ambitious multicountry trip, consider a **Select Pass,** which lets you preselect two, three, or four adjoining countries. If you're traveling just a tad beyond four main countries, consider whether buying one or two extra point-to-point tickets might be cheaper than bumping up to a Global Pass. If a certain **multicountry regional pass,** such as for Scandinavia, happens to fit your plans, it can be cheaper than a Select Pass.

Virtually every European country has its own **single-country pass.** These are especially worth considering for Britain (which does not participate in the Global Pass or Select Pass) and for Switzerland (where its pass covers more than just trains). The relative value of a single-country pass over individual tickets really varies across Europe, so price it out before buying one.

A Global Pass covers most of Europe except Great Britain and some nations in Eastern Europe. A Select Pass lets you narrow the scope to a few adjacent countries.

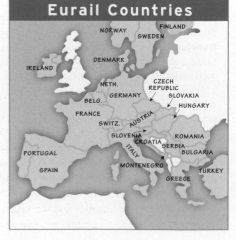

Eurail Countries

Flexipass or Continuous? If you plan to linger for a few days at most of your destinations, a **flexipass** makes the most sense, as it lets you pay only for the days on which you actually travel. Most rail passes are of this type. You don't have to decide beforehand which days you'll travel on, but you do have a certain window in which you must use up your train days (usually two months after you start using the pass). You can take as many trips as you like within each travel day, which runs from midnight to midnight (though most direct overnight rides can count as only one travel day on a flexipass—see page 125).

A **continuous pass** can save you money if you plan to travel nearly daily and cover a lot of ground. Global, BritRail, French, German, and Swiss passes offer this option. If you have a 15-day continuous pass, you can ride the trains as many times as you like for 15 days. The number of days you can travel with a one-month continuous pass depends on the month you start traveling: If you set off on any day in February, the pass is only good for the next 28 days; if you start in July, it's good for 31 days.

For those with open-ended plans, continuous passes can provide an extra sense of flexibility. Let's say you're planning a three-week trip and choosing between two versions of a Global Pass: a 21-day continuous pass and a cheaper 10-days-in-two-months flexipass. For not much more money, the continuous pass gives you the freedom to take any train without calculating whether a particular trip justifies the use of a travel day.

Getting the Most Out of a Rail Pass

Many people spend more on their rail pass than they have to. Consider the following tips before purchasing one:

Stretch a flexipass by paying out of pocket for shorter trips. If you plan to ride the train on, say, eight different days, but two of those days have very short trips, you may save money by getting a six-day pass and buying point-to-point tickets for your short-haul days. Use your flexipass only for those travel days that involve long hauls or several trips. To determine whether a trip is a good use of a travel day, divide the cost of your pass by the number of travel days (or look at what it costs to add a day onto the pass's base price). If the pass you're considering costs about $60 per travel day, it makes no sense to use one of your days for a trip that would otherwise cost $10.

One rail pass is usually better than two. To cover a multicountry trip, it's almost always cheaper to buy one

Select Pass or Global Pass with lots of travel days than to buy several country passes with a few high-cost travel days per pass. If you travel over a border (such as Germany to Switzerland) using separate country rail passes, you'll use up a day of each pass.

Understand your bonuses. Some boat, bus, and other non-train rides—called "bonuses"—may be either included or discounted with any rail pass that covers that country (for example, some Swiss lake boats and Italy-Greece ferry crossings). A bonus trip is no different from a train trip: To use your flexipass to cover the cost of a bonus boat or bus, you must fill in a travel day on your pass (you can take multiple trips, whether train or non-train, on that travel day). Trips offered only at a discount (rather than those that are completely covered by the pass) usually don't cost you a flexipass travel day, but you must use the discount within your pass's validity period (the flexi version of the Swiss Travel Pass is an exception).

With careful juggling, a shorter pass can cover a longer trip. For example, for a one-month trip, you don't necessarily need a one-month pass. You may be able to get by with a 21-day continuous pass by starting and/or ending your trip in a city where you'd like to stay for several days or in a country not covered by your pass. On a one-month London-Vienna trip, you could spend a few days in London, pay separately for travel to Paris on the Eurostar train (for which it's not always cost-effective to use a Eurail pass), sightsee in Paris for several days, then activate your rail pass as you head to Vienna. Plan for your pass to expire in Vienna, where you can easily spend a few days without the use of a rail pass.

It can make sense to buy a longer pass for a shorter trip. One long, expensive train ride at the end of a 25-day trip can justify jumping from a 21-consecutive-day rail pass to a one-month pass.

Using Your Rail Pass

Rail passes are straightforward but come with a lot of fine print (worth reading). It's important to understand at least the basics before your first day of train travel.

Activate your pass before your first use. You must officially activate your rail pass, in person at a European train station, for it to be valid for train travel. Your pass comes printed with an issue date (usually the day you bought it) and must be activated within six months (for single-country Swiss passes and the European East pass) or 11 months

Sample Select Pass

Don't write anything on your rail pass before it's activated. When you're ready to use it, the ticket agent will fill in validity dates and your passport number, and stamp the activation box on the far right. Each day when you take your seat on the train, write down the date in ink (day first, then month) before the conductor comes around.

(for most passes: all Eurail-brand passes, plus BritRail and single-country German passes). For example, if May 24 is stamped on your Eurail-brand pass as the issue date, you must start the pass by April 23. Never write anything on your rail pass before it's been activated.

Activation is easy: At any European train station, present your rail pass and passport to a railway official at a ticket or information window. The ticket agent (not you) writes in your passport number, and the first and last dates of your travel period, and stamps the activation box on the far right. For example, a two-month validity period starting May 15 will end at midnight on July 14.

Agents will assume that you intend to use the pass on the same day you present it, so if you're activating it a few days beforehand, write your desired dates (European style, e.g., 15/05/19 - 14/07/19) on a slip of paper to show the agent before handing over the pass (only Swiss passes and a few special offers come preactivated for a specific travel period). All train trips and non-train bonuses (covered or discounted boats and buses) must be started and finished within the valid life of your rail pass. If you have a saverpass, all group members must be present when the rail pass is activated.

You may activate your rail pass before arriving in the (first) country it covers. Let's say you're in Copenhagen with a German rail pass, you're heading to Berlin, and you want the German portion of your route to be covered by your rail pass. At the Copenhagen train station, buy a ticket to the German border and have the agent activate your rail pass at the same time.

Don't get caught with a pass that hasn't been activated: If you forget to do it before boarding, approach the conductor right away to have it done on board (you may be charged a fee of $5-30).

Fill in travel days (for flexipasses) and trip details. With a continuous rail pass, nobody counts how many days you travel during the validated period. But if you're using a flexipass, you must fill in your travel days as you go. On your flexipass, you'll see a string of blank boxes, one for each travel day available to you. Either just before or after boarding, fill in that day's date in ink in one of the blank boxes on your pass before the conductor reaches you. (Don't fill out any dates in advance, in case your plans change.)

Note that a travel day is a calendar day, running from midnight to midnight. You can take as many trips as you like within each travel day that you've marked on your pass. A nice bonus is the "7 p.m. rule" for night trains: A direct overnight train uses up only one flexipass travel day (not two), as long as you board after 7 p.m. and don't change trains before 4 a.m. (you just write the arrival date on your flexipass).

Some passes (continuous or flexi) also require you to fill in your trip destinations on the foldout sheets of your pass cover.

Show your pass if asked. After the train starts, the conductor heads down the aisle, asking for tickets and passes, and checking that they are dated correctly. You may be asked to present your passport, too.

Keep your pass in your money belt. Your rail pass is a valuable slip of paper—if you lose it, it's gone. (Even if you bought the "Rail Protection Plan" when you got your pass, a lost or stolen pass presents a logistical headache.) While some national railways are slowly moving toward paperless ticketing, most rail passes are still only available in old-fashioned hard-copy form. Guard yours carefully.

Looking Up Train Schedules

Online timetables are user-friendly, providing you with the fastest connections, frequency, and length of a train trip (and whether reservations are required). Schedules can also be essential to basic itinerary planning, as they tell you where trains do and don't go.

No matter where you're traveling in Europe, Germany's Deutsche Bahn website at www.bahn.com should be your

City Name Variations

English Name	European Name
Athens, Greece	Athina (Greek), Athenes (German)
Basel, Switzerland	Bâle (French)
Bolzano, Italy	Bozen (German)
Bratislava, Slovakia	Pressburg (German), Pozsony (Hungarian)
Basel, Switzerland	Bâle (French)
Brussels, Belgium	Bruxelles (French)
Carlsbad, Czech Republic	Karlovy Vary (Czech), Karlsbad (German)
Cologne, Germany	Köln or Koeln
Copenhagen, Denmark	København
Cracow, Poland	Kraków
Dubrovnik, Croatia	Ragusa (Italian and German)
Florence, Italy	Firenze
Gdańsk, Poland	Danzig (German)
Geneva, Switzerland	Genève (French), Genf (German)
Genoa, Italy	Genova
Gothenburg, Sweden	Göteborg
The Hague, Netherlands	Den Haag, 'S Gravenhage
Helsinki, Finland	Helsingfors (Swedish)
Liège, Belgium	Luik (Flemish/Dutch), Lüttich (German)
Lisbon, Portugal	Lisboa
London, England	Londres (French)
Lucerne, Switzerland	Luzern (German), Lucerna (Italian)
Milan, Italy	Milano (Italian), Mailand (German)
Munich, Germany	München or Muenchen (German), Monaco di Baviera (Italian)
Naples, Italy	Napoli (Italian), Neapel (German)
Nice, France	Nizza (Italian)
Nuremberg, Germany	Nürnberg or Nuernberg
Padua, Italy	Padova
Pamplona, Spain	Iruña (Euskara)
Paris, France	Parigi (Italian)
Prague, Czech Republic	Praha
Rome, Italy	Roma
San Sebastián, Spain	Donostia (Euskara)
Tralee, Ireland	Trá Lí
Venice, Italy	Venezia (Italian), Venedig (German)
Vienna, Austria	Wien (German), Bécs (Hungarian), Dunaj (Slovene), Vídeň (Czech), Viedeň (Slovak)
Warsaw, Poland	Warszawa (Polish), Warschau (German)

first stop for timetable information. (While each country's national rail company has its own website with schedules, the German site has schedules for virtually all of Europe.) I use this site, along with their DB Navigator app, to plan my connections for almost every trip in Europe.

Finding Schedules on the Deutsche Bahn Site

The German railway's online schedule is an invaluable tool for any European train traveler. Here's how to use it:

1. Start with a station-to-station search. Enter just the city name, unless you know the name of the specific station you want. Since many cities have several stations, you'll then need to specify one from the drop-down menu. To avoid accidentally selecting a bus stop instead of the train station, select the option with just the city name (if available). To choose the main station, look for the words "central," "terminus," or "Hbf," which stands for *Hauptbahnhof* (you can also try re-entering it with "main station" after the city's name). Sometimes the search results show a city name in all capital letters; selecting that option will look up the best connections for that city, regardless of the station.

2. Enter the date and time. Make your best guess about when you might travel (using the 24-hour clock). Don't worry about the exact date and time of your train trips, as schedules for most trains don't vary much (except for Sundays and holidays, when trains are less frequent). Though many schedules aren't available more than three months out, you can still get a good idea of trip length and frequency by trying a closer date on the same day of the week you'll be traveling.

3. Skip the extra search fields. If you're just looking up schedules, there's no need to fill in any fields beyond the stations, date, and time—just skip right to "Search." (If you're then prompted to select from a drop-down list of stations, see #1, above.)

4. Review your options. The results will show three possibilities for your journey; use the "Earlier" and "Later" buttons to see more. Each result shows the start and end points (with stations specified), departure and arrival times, trip duration, number of changes, types of trains, and train category (indicated by a set of acronyms). Results may show local names for cities (for example, "Praha" instead of "Prague").

A circled "R" indicates that the train requires a reservation. (Note: The site often does not show reliable reservation information for Italy's fastest trains. Assume that any "Eurostar Italia" trains do require seat reservations.)

5. Check the details. Clicking "show details" for a journey will give you more information, including transfer points. Select "show intermediate stops" to see every stop on your route or the train number to see the entire route, including stops before and/or after your stations.

The Deutsche Bahn site doesn't display fares for most trains outside Germany and Austria. For full-fare estimates for other countries, use the map on page 122. You can also check ticket prices on each country's own national railway site (useful if you're looking for advance-purchase discounts).

If your destination isn't listed on the Deutsche Bahn site, it likely doesn't have train service. But before giving up—especially for train travel in Spain and Italy—double-check their national railway sites.

For even more tips on using the Deutsche Bahn website, head to www.ricksteves.com/schedules.

Seat Reservations

Some kinds of trains require all passengers to have reservations (which guarantee you a specific seat), and sometimes it's smart to reserve even when it's not compulsory. But many trains don't require reservations, and the vast majority of trains usually have more than enough seating—so don't make the mistake of over-reserving. Many American travelers waste money and surrender their flexibility after being swayed by US-based agents who profit from exaggerating the need for reservations.

Do I Need Reservations?

Your best resource for identifying trains that truly require a reservation is the Deutsche Bahn online schedule—it's objective, complete, and easy to use.

Though relatively few train types require reservations, those that do are among the most popular. They include a few privately run international trains, such as the Eurostar, the Brussels-based Thalys, and a handful of special just-for-tourists trains (such as several of Switzerland's specially-designated scenic trains).

Aside from these, many countries have at least one category of high-speed train that always requires reservations—most notably France, Italy, Spain, and Sweden. Some countries have a few long-distance must-reserve routes. And you'll need to book ahead (or at least pay a little extra) for a spot on nearly all overnight trains.

In many cases, required reservations aren't so much a

matter of space constrictions, but a surcharge for the privilege of riding the fastest (or fanciest) train. But on certain routes, seats can sell out quickly (see "How Far Ahead?" later).

Reservations can sometimes be a good idea on trains that don't require them. For example, it's wise to reserve at least several days ahead if you are traveling during a peak time (summer, weekends, holidays), on a route with infrequent service, if you need several seats together (a family with children), or for a train you simply cannot afford to miss.

Otherwise, I wouldn't recommend reserving a seat if you don't have to; most slower regional trains don't even give you the option. Most of the time, trains have plenty of seating for everyone, and even if you wind up on a crowded train, the worst-case scenario is that you'll stand a while before a seat frees up.

How to Reserve

For trains that don't need to be booked very far in advance, it's best to simply make all your reservations at one time at any staffed station in Europe.

If you need to lock in your reservations before your train trip, book them ahead of time from home through a US-based retailer (such as www.ricksteves.com/rail) or Euraide (www.euraide.com), a European-based vendor whose prices can be a good value for those who need to book multiple seat reservations.

Key Train Vocabulary

English	French	Italian	German	Spanish
train	train	treno	Zug	tren
ticket	billet	biglietto	Fahrkarte	billete
station	gare	stazione	Bahnhof	estación
main station	gare centrale	stazione centrale	Hauptbahnhof	estación principal
platform/track	quai/voie	binario	Bahnsteig/ Gleis	andén/vía
timetable	horaire	orario	Fahrplan	horario
supplement	supplément	supplemento	Zuschlag	suplemento
delay	retard	ritardare	Verspätung	retraso
strike	grève	sciopero	Streik	huelga
reservation	réservation	prenotazione	Reservierung	reserva
berth/couchette	couchette	cuccetta	Liegeplatz	litera

Typical Train Ticket

❶ Point of Departure
❷ Destination
❸ Type of Train (IC = Intercity)
❹ Kilometers Traveled
❺ Class (1 = First; 2 = Second)
❻ Via These Towns
❼ Ticket Valid Until This Date
❽ Number of Passengers
❾ Validation Stamp
❿ Date Ticket Purchased
⓫ Place Ticket Purchased
⓬ Ticket Cost

Seat reservations typically range from $5 to $35 (except in Britain, where they're free). In some cases, the fee may be higher, depending on the kind of train, whom you're buying from, and possibly which rail pass you have. This cost is included in the price of a point-to-point ticket for any train that requires reservations (dates, times, and seat assignments are built in, just like with an airline ticket), but on trains for which reservations are optional, it's an extra fee.

For more information on pass holder reservation fees for popular trains, check the country-specific rail pages at www.ricksteves.com/rail.

How Far Ahead?

Whether you're traveling with a rail pass or just buying tickets as you go, you can purchase seat (or overnight berth) reservations anywhere from an hour to several months in advance.

How far in advance to reserve any given train depends on the rigidity of your schedule (do you have hotel reservations or a flight to catch?), how many departures in a day could get you there on time (2 or 20?), the likelihood of seats (or at least reservations) selling out, and other factors mentioned above.

Be aware that trains with compulsory reservations may have a limited number of seats available to pass holders, and may place restrictions on when pass holders can reserve those seats (most notoriously France's TGV trains, for which pass holders are at times prohibited from booking seat reservations in the three days before departure). Along some of the most popular routes, such as between Paris and Italy, direct trains run only a few times per day; these can sell out weeks ahead (and overnight Paris-Italy trains don't accept rail passes at all).

No matter when you're going, I'd recommend booking as far ahead as possible for the following trains:

- Eurostar (London-Paris/Brussels)
- TGV (France's high-speed trains)
- Any direct train between Paris and Italy
- Thalys (high-speed Brussels-based trains)
- Nightjet (international night trains, including the popular Munich-Venice route)

TRAIN STATIONS

Great European train stations stir my wanderlust. Stepping off a train in Munich, I stand under the station's towering steel and glass rooftop and study the big, black schedule board crowned by the station clock. It lists two-dozen departures. Every few minutes, the letters and numbers on each line spin and tumble as one by one cities and departure times work their way to the top and flutter away.

Surrounded by Germany on the move, I notice businessmen in tight neckties, giddy teenage girls, and a Karl-Marx-like bum leaning on a *Bierstube* counter. The fast and the slow, the young and the old, we're all in this together—working our way up life's departure board.

There's plenty of romance here, but the hustle and bustle at train stations can also be confusing. Here are some tips on navigating Europe's temples of transportation.

Whether old or new, bustling European train stations are temples of travel. Just pick a platform...and explore Europe.

Buying Tickets at the Station

Nearly every station has at least a few old-fashioned ticket windows staffed by human beings, usually marked by long lines; avoid them by using ticket machines, which almost always offer instructions in English.

Be aware that some ticket machines won't take American credit cards (even if they claim to), or accept them only if you key in your card's PIN (for more on using credit cards in Europe, see page 188). If the machines won't cooperate with your card, try cash (most machines are labeled according to the kind of payment they accept), or head for the ticket window.

If you opt for a ticket window, find the appropriate line— larger stations may have different windows for domestic, international, sleeper cars, or immediate departures. When buying tickets, you can most clearly communicate your intentions by writing what you need and showing it to the ticket agent: destination, date, time, how many people, first or second class.

It's often possible to buy tickets aboard the train, but you should expect to pay an additional fee for the convenience. Be sure that you have enough cash in case the conductor can't use your American credit card. If you're buying a ticket on board, find the conductor before he finds you; otherwise, your "fee" could turn into a much heftier "fine" for traveling without a valid ticket. Be aware that on most local trains (especially commuter lines), all trains in Switzerland, and many others around Europe, you can be fined for traveling without a ticket, no matter what the circumstances are. Look for warning signs on train doors.

LEFT Savvy travelers save time by using ticket machines: Choose English, then follow the instructions.

RIGHT Bridge communication gaps by writing out your plan: departure and destination, date, time (if you want a reservation and/or a printout of your departure options), how many people, first or second class.

Schedule Information

Even if you've looked up your train schedules in advance, always confirm your plans at the station. Every station has some kind of schedule information available, whether it's posted in printed or electronic form, or at information counters staffed by people eager (or at least able) to help you. All European timetables use the 24-hour clock (see page 50).

Learning to decipher printed schedules makes life easier on Europe's rails. Posters list all trains that arrive at and depart from a particular station each day. This information is clearly shown in two separate listings: Departures are usually in yellow, and arrivals in white. In some stations, you'll find free schedule booklets listing all their daily departures.

Familiarize yourself with the symbols in schedules that indicate exceptions: Crossed hammers, for instance, mean the train goes only on workdays (daily except Sundays and holidays); a cross signifies that it runs only on Sundays and holidays. Most other symbols are easy enough to guess—for instance, a little bed means the train has sleeping compartments, and crossed silverware indicates a dining car.

Many stations also have either video screens or big flippy boards that list the next several departures. These often befuddle travelers who don't realize that all over the world, the same five easy-to-identify columns are listed: destination, major stops along the way, type of train, track number, and departure time. I don't care what language they're in; without much effort you can accurately guess which column is which.

Stations may also have self-service computer terminals—many of which are ticket machines—where you can look up schedule information. These computers are almost always multilingual and can be real time-savers. Use them to

LEFT Posted train schedules show departure times, destinations, arrival times, and track numbers.

RIGHT In Munich's train station, easy-to-read electronic boards list departures and arrivals. Railroad staff is standing by to answer questions.

understand all your options. Many even print out a schedule tailored to your trip.

Of course, your best authority is the person at the train station information window. Uniformed employees on the platforms and on board the trains can also help.

Other Services

Besides offering travel-related services, most stations are great places to take care of your basic to-do list, with ATMs, grocery stores (usually with longer hours than you'll find in the town center), restaurants, bike-rental kiosks, and shops selling mobile-phone SIM cards.

Baggage Check: Most major stations have storage lockers and/or a luggage-checking service where, for about $3-8 a day, you can leave your bags. People traveling light can fit two bags into one locker, cutting their storage costs in half. Some train stations have removed lockers due to security concerns; in this case travelers can check bags at a luggage-deposit desk—often after going through an airport-type security check. You'll pay $5 to $15 per bag. Lock your bag and don't leave valuables inside—both for your own security and because some luggage desks won't accept unlocked bags. They may not take laptops, so be prepared to haul yours. Allow plenty of time to retrieve your bag before boarding your train. Bag-check desks come with lines, can close for lunch in smaller stations, and usually aren't open all night— confirm opening and closing times before storing your bag. If the station doesn't offer a place to leave your bag, head to a nearby tourist-information office, hotel, or gift shop: Ask nicely, offer your most charming smile (or a small fee), and you'll likely find someone willing to keep an eye on your things for a few hours.

Train stations often have good, long-hours grocery stores. This one in Vienna is open every day, 5:30 a.m.-11:00 p.m.

Wi-Fi: You'll find Wi-Fi hotspots at major train stations throughout most of Europe, sometimes for a fee. Wi-Fi is typically free in the first-class lounge. Finding Wi-Fi onboard is more serendipitous than reliable, with the exception of high-speed trains on some common business routes.

Tourist Information: Many stations have a tourist information office either in the station or very nearby. Pick up a map, find out about local transit, and double-check the hours of your must-see sights (for more on these offices, see page 315).

Waiting Rooms: Most stations have comfortable waiting rooms, and travelers with fancy tickets often enjoy fancy business or VIP lounges. Before you spend hours idling in one of these rooms, take advantage of the station's services (look up schedules for the next leg of your trip, get groceries) or explore the area around the station. You may well find yourself within a short walk of something really cool. For example, if you're changing trains in Cologne, even on a tight schedule you can easily pop outside for a jaw-dropping look at its cathedral, just across the square. Waiting rooms can be decent last-ditch sleeping options (but guard your valuables).

Transit Connections: Train stations are also major transit hubs, so connections from train to bus, subway, or tram are generally no more difficult than crossing the street. If an airport is nearby, you'll find airport-train or transit services (usually well marked) at the train station.

Buses connect from the station to nearby towns that lack train service. If you have a bus to catch, be quick, since many are intended for commuters and are scheduled to connect with the train and leave promptly.

Getting on the (Right) Train

For many Americans, Europe presents their first experience with a bustling train station, and the task of navigating the system and finding the right train can sound daunting. But anyone who's managed to find their way in a sprawling American airport will find Europe's train stations a snap. As you head for your train, ticket or pass in hand, keep these pointers in mind.

Get yourself to the right station. Many cities have more than one train station: Paris has six, Brussels has three, and even Switzerland's little Interlaken has two. Be sure you know whether your train is leaving from Interlaken East or Interlaken West, even if that means asking what might seem like a stupid question.

Find your track. A few countries publish track numbers in their train schedules, but in most places you'll need to look for your platform information once you get to the station. Upcoming departures are displayed on computer screens or mechanical boards; track information is usually posted about a half-hour before the train departs.

Ask for help. I always ask someone on the platform if the

train is going where I think it is. Uniformed train personnel can answer any question you can communicate. Speak
slowly, clearly, and with caveman simplicity. Resist the urge
to ask, "Pardon me, would you be able to tell me if this train
is going to Rome?" Just point to the train or track and say,
"Roma?"

Be observant. If the loudspeaker comes on while you're
waiting for your train at track 7, gauge by the reaction of
those around you whether the announcement affects you.
If everyone dashes over to track 15, assume your train is no
longer leaving from track 7, and follow the pack.

**Allow yourself sufficient time to navigate the
station.** Stations are generally laid out logically, with
numbered tracks lined up in a row. But the biggest stations
are so extensive they can take time to navigate. Some large
stations have entirely separate sections for local and long-
distance trains. For example, Madrid's Atocha station is
divided into sections for *cercanías* (local trains) and AVE
(high-speed, long-distance trains). A Paris train station
might have some tracks devoted to Grandes Lignes ("grand
lines" to other cities), and others for Transilien (local milk-
run trains). At the Frankfurt airport, regional trains depart
from the *Regionalbahnhof,* while long-distance trains use
the *Fernbahnhof.* Many large stations also have vast sections
devoted to subway trains or regional buses.

Be on guard for pickpockets. With travelers already
distracted by announcements and luggage, a busy train station is an ideal work environment for thieves. Wear your
money belt, keep your bags in hand, and be very wary of

The train on
track 5 will stop
at Olten, Bern,
Thun, and Spiez
en route to
Interlaken's East
Station. But
it's two hours
late *(später).*

"helpful" locals hanging around ticket machines. For more tips, see the Theft & Scams chapter.

Where required, validate your ticket and/or seat reservation before boarding. In France and Italy, most point-to-point tickets and seat reservations aren't valid until you've date-stamped them by inserting them into a machine near the platform (if you've printed tickets at home, they don't need validating). If you have multiple parts to your ticket (for example, a ticket and a reservation), each one must be validated. Watch (or ask) others, and imitate—but don't assume that you can skip this step just because others have, as locals with commuter passes don't need to date-stamp them. Rail passes, however, always need to be activated in person at a ticket window before using them for the first time (with the exception of the Swiss Travel Pass).

Expect no-hassle boarding. For the vast majority of Europe's trains, you stroll (or dash) right to your boarding platform, ticket or pass in hand, without any check-in formalities. The main exception is the Eurostar, which has a check-in deadline (30 minutes before departure) and an airline-style security procedure. You may encounter pre-boarding security or ticket checks in a few other places. In Spain, for instance, your tickets will be checked and luggage scanned before you access the platform to board fast AVE trains. Many stations in Britain now require you to slide your paper ticket or tap your barcode on a turnstile reader both to enter and exit the boarding areas (if you're traveling with a rail pass, just show it to the attendants at these gates), and train doors close 30 seconds before departure. The Netherlands' OV-chipkaart and TripKey cards must be scanned at the card reader both when entering and exiting the station.

Scope out the train ahead of time. The configuration of many major trains is charted in display cases on the platform. As you wait, study the display to note where the first-class, second-class, restaurant, and sleeping cars are, and which cars are going where. First-class cars are always marked with a big "1" on the outside, second-class cars with a "2." Some train schedules will say, in the fine print, "Munich-bound cars in the front, Vienna-bound cars in the rear." Knowing which cars you're eligible

Train cars are usually labeled. This non-smoking second-class car has video surveillance and room for wheelchairs but not bikes. The eye (top left) means you'll be fined if a ticket patroller catches you without a valid ticket or pass.

Know Where to Stand

For some high-speed or long-distance trains, a handy diagram showing your train configuration can help you decide where to stand while waiting to board. (The letters indicate the platform section at which each car will arrive.) Understanding this can make the difference between snagging a great seat...or scrambling for what's left.

for can be especially handy if you'll be competing with a mob for a seat. When expecting a real scramble, I stand on a bench at the far end of the track and study each car as the train rolls by, looking in the windows to note where the empty places are. If there are several departures within an hour and the first train looks hopeless, I'll wait for the next.

Never assume the entire train is going where you are. For long hauls, each car is labeled separately, because cars are usually added and dropped here and there along the journey. I'll never forget one hot afternoon in the center of Spain. My train stopped in the middle of nowhere. There was some mechanical rattling. Then the train pulled away, leaving me alone in my car—in La Mancha. Ten minutes later, another train came along, picked up my car, and I was on my way. To survive all this juggling without any panic, be sure that the city on your car's nameplate is your destination. The nameplate lists the final stop and some (but not all) of the stops in between.

ON THE TRAIN

Once you're on board, it's time to sit back and enjoy the journey.

Find a seat. If you have a seat assignment, locate it and plop yourself down. If you're traveling without a seat reservation, you can claim any unreserved seat. If these are in short supply, take a closer look at the reservation tags posted above the seats or on compartment doors. Each tag shows which stretch of the journey that seat is reserved for. You may well be getting off the train before the seat owner even boards. For example, if you're headed from Luzern to Lugano, and you see a seat that's only reserved from Lugano to Milan, it's all yours.

Stow your luggage. In more than 30 years of train travel, I've never checked a bag. Simply carry it on and heave it up onto the rack above the seat or wedge it into the triangular space between back-to-back seats. I've seen Turkish families moving all their worldly goods from Germany back to Turkey without checking a thing. People complain about the porters in the European train stations. I think they're great—I've never used one.

Be savvy with your bags. I assume every train has a thief planning to grab a bag. Store your luggage within sight, rather than at the far end of the train car. Before leaving my luggage in a compartment, I establish a relationship with everyone there. I'm safe leaving it among mutual guards. I don't lock my bag, but to be safe, I often clip my rucksack straps to the luggage rack. When a thief makes his move in the darkness of a train tunnel, and the bag doesn't give, he's not going to ask, "*Scusi,* how is your luggage attached?"

Use train time wisely. The time you spend on long train rides can be an opportunity to get organized or make plans for your next destination. Read ahead in your guidebook, write journal entries, delete yesterday's bad photos, double-check your connection information with the conductor, organize your daypack, or update your trip's blog. If the train has power outlets (rare but becoming more common), charge your gadgets. Don't, however, get so immersed in chores that you forget to keep an eye out the window for beautiful scenery around the next bend.

Use WCs—they're free. To save time and money, use the toilets on the train rather than those in the station (which can cost money, and are often less clean). Toilets on first-class cars are a cut above second-class toilets. I "go" first class even with a second-class ticket. Train toilets are located on the ends of cars, where it's most jiggly. A trip to the train's john always reminds me of the rodeo. Some toilets empty directly on the tracks, so never use a train's WC while stopped in a station (unless you didn't like that particular town). A train's WC cleanliness deteriorates as the journey progresses.

Follow local train etiquette. Pay attention to the noise level in your car. If everyone else is speaking in hushed tones, follow suit. Watch for signs indicating that you're sitting in a designated quiet car, where businesspeople come to work and others to nap. No matter where I'm sitting, I make an effort not to be the loudest person in earshot (easily done on the average Italian train, but takes extra awareness in, say,

Strikes

Some travelers worry about getting stranded because of a strike. But in general, they're nothing to stress about.

Strikes can affect rail service anywhere in Europe (especially in Italy). They're usually announced long in advance in stations and online. Most last a day, or even just several hours. Anticipate strikes–ask your hotelier, talk to locals, look for signs, check online–but don't feel bullied by them. In theory, train service shuts down, but in reality, sporadic trains lumber down main-line tracks during most strikes (preserving "essential service").

If a strike occurs on your travel day, check the national railway website–special strike schedules are generally posted. Otherwise, head to the station, where the few remaining station personnel can tell you the expected schedule. You'll likely find a workable train to your destination, though it may involve a wait. While it's usually possible to get a refund for reservations affected by a strike, there are no refunds for partially used rail passes.

Know the local word for "strike": *sciopero* (Italian), *grève* (French), *apergia* (Greek), and so on. They're a nuisance but, in many countries, a normal part of life.

For the Back Door traveler, strikes can be a cultural experience. On a visit to Marseille, I was surrounded by thousands of strikers marching through the streets. It was a festive occasion. The museums were closed, so I explored the markets and enjoyed photographing striking parents–children rode on their shoulders and learned firsthand what labor action is all about.

Germany). Resting your feet on the seat across from you without taking your shoes off is perhaps an even graver faux pas.

Talk to locals or other travelers. There is so much to be learned. Europeans are often less open and forward than Americans. You could sit across from a silent but fascinating and friendly European for an entire train ride, or you could break the ice by asking a question, quietly offering some candy, or showing your Hometown, USA postcards. This can start the conversation flowing and a friendship growing.

Pack a picnic. For the best dining value and variety, stock up at a local deli, bakery, supermarket, or wine cellar before you board; most train stations offer at least one of these. Food sold on the train costs more, with options ranging from a basic coffee and sandwich cart to a more extensive bar car or sit-down dining car (noted on most schedules when available). A few trains offer a "complimentary" meal, in first class only, usually covered by a higher seat-reservation fee.

Strategize your arrival. Use your guidebook to study up on your destination city while you're still on board—it's far more time-efficient and less overwhelming to arrive in a station already knowing how to reach the city center (or your hotel). If you're trying to make a tight connection, it's good to know which platform your next train leaves from.

If you don't already have that information, flag down a conductor, who either knows the answer or can find out for you.

As you approach your destination, have a game plan ready for when you get off the train. Know what you need to accomplish in the station before heading out—e.g., looking up the schedule (and perhaps making seat reservations) for the next leg of your train trip, picking up a map from a trackside information office, hitting an ATM, buying a transit pass, or grabbing provisions from a grocery store (especially if you're arriving late, after most city-center shops and restaurants have closed). If you'll depart from the same station later, pay attention to the layout.

Know where to get off. In Dresden, I twice got off my train too early—at two different suburban stations—before arriving at the central station. Know which station you need before you arrive, and be patient. When arriving in a city (especially on a commuter train), you may stop at several suburban stations with signs indicating your destination's name and the neighborhood (e.g., Madrid Vallecas, Roma Ostiense, or Dresden Neustadt). Don't jump out until you've reached the central station (Madrid Chamartín, Roma Termini, or Dresden Hauptbahnhof)—ask fellow passengers or check your guidebook to find out which name to look for. Learn the local word for "main station."

Be aware that some trains (especially express trains) stop only at a major city's suburban station—if you stay on board, expecting to get off in the center a few minutes later, you'll bypass your destination city altogether. For instance, several trains to "Venice" leave you at Venice's suburban station (Venezia Mestre), where you'll be stranded without a glimpse of a gondola. (You'll have to catch another train to reach the main Venezia Santa Lucia station, on the Grand Canal.) On the other hand, it can be handy to hop out at a

Europe's trains are so fast, they pull into stations with squashed birds on their windshields. You'd wait all your life to see a bird squashed onto the windshield of a train back home. I guess with Europe's impressive transportation infrastructure, "DB" stands for "dead bird."

suburban station if it's closer to your hotel than the main station. Many trains headed for Barcelona's big Sants station also stop at the Plaça de Catalunya subway station, which is near many recommended accommodations. If you do find yourself at the wrong station, don't despair: It's a safe bet that a city's stations are connected by frequent trains, and probably subway or buses as well. If all else fails, you can link by taxi.

Sleeping on Trains

The economy of night travel is tremendous. Sleeping while rolling down the tracks saves time and money: For every night you spend on the train, you gain a day for sightseeing and avoid the cost of a hotel.

The first concern about night travel is usually, "Aren't you missing a lot of beautiful scenery? You just slept through half of Sweden!" The real question should be, "Did the missed scenery matter, since you gained an extra day for hiking the Alps or biking through tulips?" The answer: No. Maximize night trips.

Your overnight options may look slim, at least at first—as daytime trains speed up and flights within Europe become cheaper, night-train service is being reduced. When you're checking schedules for night trains, pay attention to the details. A connection doesn't have to be direct to be a workable overnight option—it all depends on the timing. If you need to change trains a half hour after boarding, you'll still get some sleep (though rail-pass holders should be aware of the "7 p.m. rule"—see page 130). But if the connection involves getting off at 2:00 a.m...and waiting until 5:30 a.m. for the next leg, that's not a night train, it's a nightmare.

Book your night-train reservation at least a few days in advance. On some popular routes, particularly between Paris and Italy, reservations can sell out weeks in advance, making it worthwhile to commit before you even leave for Europe. For advice on making reservations, see page 133.

Some train travelers are ripped off while they sleep—they're usually the ones who haven't safely stashed their money and valuables in a money belt. And while you may hear stories of entire train cars being gassed and robbed in Italy, Spain, and countries farther east, it's extremely rare and I wouldn't lose sleep over it.

Types of Compartments

Most overnight trains offer one or two different ways to

sleep; the more comfortably you sleep, the more you pay. For much more on night trains in Europe, go to www.seat61. com/sleepers.htm.

Couchettes: To ensure a safer and uninterrupted night's sleep, you can reserve a sleeping berth known as a *couchette* (koo-shet). For a surcharge of about $35, you'll get sheets, a pillow, and blankets on a bunk bed in a compartment with up to five other people—and, hopefully, a good night's sleep.

Most *couchettes* are the same in first and second class. However, some trains have more spacious four-berth *couchette* compartments (two sets of doubles rather than triple bunks for about $50 apiece). These may be considered second-class options, but occasionally require a first-class ticket or pass.

When booking your *couchette*, you can request the top, middle, or bottom berth. While the top bunk gives you more privacy and luggage space, it can be hotter and stuffier than lower bunks and a couple of inches shorter (a concern if you're six feet or taller). Compartments may be co-ed or single gender, depending on the route.

As you board, you'll give your *couchette* voucher and rail pass or ticket to the attendant. This is the person who deals with the conductors and keeps out the thieves so you can sleep uninterrupted. In case of a border check (unlikely in most of Europe these days), you'll either be woken up to show your passport, or your attendant will ask for your passport in advance and handle this task for you.

Private Sleepers: These sleeper compartments are more comfortable but pricier than *couchettes*. Compartments with two or three beds range from about $40 to $150 per person. Single-sleeper surcharges range from $70 to $190.

Sleeping Free

Shoestring travelers just sack out for free, draping their tired bodies over as many unoccupied seats as possible. But trust me: Trying to sleep overnight without a bed can be more lumpy than dreamy. And even free seat "sleeping" isn't always an option, since not all night trains offer standard seats—and many that do require a paid seat reservation. One night of endless head-bobbing, very swollen toes, glaring overhead lighting, a screaming tailbone, sitting up straight in an eternity of steel wheels crashing along rails, trying doggedly—yet hopelessly—to get comfortable, will teach you the importance of finding a spot to stretch out for the night. (If you decide you want a *couchette* after all, seek out a conductor—provided there's a *couchette* available, you can book one onboard.)

Some older trains have seats that you can pull out to make a bed—assuming your compartment isn't too full. Skilled shoestring travelers know to look for traditional train cars: the kind that have about 10 compartments, each with six or eight seats (three or four facing three or four). Some have seats that pull out and armrests that lift, turning your compartment into a bed on wheels. These cars make sleeping free quite manageable, but they're increasingly rare.

LEFT You can rent a *couchette* (bunk bed) on your overnight train. Top bunks give you a bit more room and safety—but B.Y.O.B. & B.

RIGHT They didn't rent a *couchette*.

BUSES

In most countries, trains are faster, more comfortable, and have more extensive schedules than long-distance buses. But in some places—especially Greece, Turkey, Ireland, Croatia, and Portugal, along with parts of the Czech Republic, Spain, and Morocco—buses are often the better (or only) option. Bus trips are usually less expensive than trains—especially in the British Isles—and are occasionally included on your rail pass (where buses are operated by train companies, as many are in Germany, Switzerland, and Belgium). Note that in Great Britain and Ireland, a long-distance bus is called a "coach," while a "bus" provides only in-city transit.

I use buses mainly to pick up where Europe's great train system leaves off. Buses fan out from the smallest train stations to places trains can't get to. For towns with train stations far from the center (such as Italian hill towns), buses are often scheduled to meet each arrival and shuttle passengers to the main square (often at no extra cost—show your train ticket to the bus driver and see what happens). Many bus connections to nearby towns not served by train are timed to depart just after the train arrives. Miss that connection in a remote place and you'll wait with the ghosts in an empty station until the next train arrives.

Schedules

In general, bus service can be less frequent on holidays, Saturdays, and especially Sundays.

In most countries, bus routes are operated by multiple companies, each with its own timetables and fares. Finding a unified source for schedule and price information can be next to impossible. If you're lucky, the city you're traveling from will have one main bus station that can offer consolidated timetables online. But it's more likely that you'll have to check several websites, run by the various companies that serve the cities you're connecting. If you're going from a small town (with no online timetable) to a big city, try checking the "arrivals" schedules on the big city's website instead. Always confirm the schedule in person.

Learn the code words for deciphering local schedules. For example, in Spain, *pista* or *autopista* means the bus takes the freeway—the fastest option. Buses that are *directa* (direct) are faster than those labeled *semidirecta* or *ruta* (roundabout journeys with several stops en route). Posted schedules list many, but not all, stops on each route. If your intended destination isn't listed, ask at the ticket/information window.

If your trip involves a connection at an intermediate station, don't be surprised if it's difficult to get schedule details for your onward journey. Try calling the tourist information office or bus station in the transfer town (or at your final destination) for details.

Stations and Tickets

It's common for a big city to have a number of smaller bus stations serving different regions, rather than one terminal for all bus traffic. Sometimes a bus "station" can just be an open parking lot with lots of stalls and a tiny ticket kiosk. Your hotel or the local tourist information office can usually point you in the right direction. Larger bus stations have an information desk (and, often, a telephone number) with timetables. In smaller stations, check the

Buses can help you reach places trains don't go.

destinations and schedules posted on the window of each company's office. Bus-station staffers are less likely to speak English than their train-station counterparts. Bus stations have WCs (often without toilet paper) and cafés that offer quick, forgettable, overpriced food.

For popular routes during peak season, ensure you'll get a seat by dropping by the station to buy your ticket a few hours in advance. If you're downtown, need a ticket, and the bus station isn't central, save time by asking at the tourist information office about travel agencies that sell bus tickets. If you arrive in a city by bus, and plan to leave by bus, it can be convenient to buy your outbound ticket when you arrive.

Riding the Bus

Before you get on a bus, ask the ticket seller and the conductor if you'll need to transfer. If so, pay attention (and maybe even follow the route on a map) to be sure you don't miss your change. When you transfer, look for a bus with the same name/logo as the company you bought the ticket from.

For long trips, your ticket might include an assigned seat. If your bag doesn't fit in the overhead storage space, you may be required to check it under the bus (sometimes for a small fee). Your ride likely will come with a soundtrack: recorded pop music, radio, sports games, movies, or TV shows. Earplugs and/or headphones can go a long way toward preserving your sanity. In most of Europe, smoking is not allowed on buses.

Drivers may not speak English. Buses generally lack toilets, but they stop every two hours or so for a short break. Drivers announce how long the stop will be, but if in doubt, ask the driver so you know if you have time to get out. Listen for the bus horn as a final call before departure.

Budget Bus Lines

Cheap long-haul buses are a good option for the very budget-conscious. For example, Eurolines' priciest one-way bus fare from Amsterdam to Paris is $70 (compared to $175 second class by train); from Barcelona to Madrid, it's $45 or less (often as much as $165 by train). Megabus operates throughout Great Britain and has some service on the Continent, too. In Germany, privately owned bus lines such as FlixBus are giving the national rail system some tough competition—for example, a full-fare (second-class) train ticket between Munich and Nürnberg costs about $60, while a bus ticket for this route can cost $20 or less (as low as $5 if you're willing to buy a few days ahead and aren't picky about departure times). FlixBus' €99 InterFlix Pass covers up to five trips within three months among 20 European countries. Hippie-type "magic bus" companies such as Busabout offer hop-on, hop-off connections all around Europe—something like a rail pass for buses.

Crossing the English Channel by bus and ferry takes more than twice as long as the Eurostar train, but costs a small fraction of the price (London to Paris by Eurolines bus: about $25-60 one-way for economy fares booked at least three days in advance).

Package Bus Excursions

One-day bus tours from big cities into the countryside are designed for sightseeing, but can also serve as useful trans-portation. For example, rather than buy a train ticket from London to Bath (about $55), consider taking a one-day bus tour from London (about $130) that visits Salisbury, Stone-henge, and Bath. Bring your luggage and leave the tour in Bath before it returns to London, having enjoyed a day of transportation, unforgettable stops, and a live guide bubbling with information. It can be well worth the extra cost, and it's more efficient and faster than lacing together the stops on your own, using a combination of trains and public buses. If you do look into taking a bus tour as transportation, confirm the order of stops with the company (will they be stopping at your end destination last?), and let them know your plans.

FERRIES

Boats can be a romantic mode of European travel. They're particularly useful for Greek or Croatian island-hopping, for day-tripping from Spain to Morocco, for Norwegian fjord gawking, or for connecting Scandinavian destinations over-night—saving both time and the expense of a pricey hotel room. But for any ferry ride of more than a couple of hours, it's smart to compare the cost of the ferry trip with the cost of a budget-airline flight.

Ferries rarely bunny-hop along the coastline of any one country, though Norway's Hurtigruten ferries still do. Instead, ferries primarily serve islands or connect two coun-tries. For instance, rather than the Eurostar train, you can take a Portsmouth-Normandy ferry to travel between Great Britain and France.

Most ferries are either big and slow, or small and fast (catamarans). The hulking, slow-moving ferries usually carry cars as well as passengers, run in almost any weather, and tend to be cheaper than catamarans. They have virtually unlimited deck space for walk-on passengers, though their space for cars is limited. On many islands, big car ferries arrive at a different point (usually farther from the main town) than smaller catamarans (which may drop you right in the town center).

The sleek, speedy passenger-only catamarans generally cost more, but save time. However, keep in mind that they have to slow down (or sometimes can't run at all) in high winds or other inclement weather. Catamarans have limited seating that can sell out. They're also the less-romantic option, as most require you to stay inside the boat while en route (for safety's sake—they're that fast). Instead of watching the coastline lazily slide by, as you do on slower boats, on fast boats you'll sit inside and peer out through saltwater-spattered windows.

Schedules

Some countries have a national ferry company (such as Croatia's Jadrolinija), but in most places, routes are operated by a variety of smaller companies. You can usually find schedules online; however, particularly in Mediterranean countries, they may not be posted more than a few days before the season starts, making it challenging to plan your midsummer trip in the springtime. It's a good idea to confirm the boat's sailing time at least one day ahead—the boat you found online two months ago might run earlier, later, or less frequently than you'd expected. Service to the smaller

Mediterranean islands is particularly seasonal: Routes that run once daily in summer may drop to four days per week in shoulder season and two days per week in winter. Small, tourist-oriented boats along Italy's Cinque Terre and Amalfi Coast run roughly from Easter through October.

To search for schedules, check the websites AFerry.co.uk for most of Europe; Danae.gr, GreekFerries.gr, and Gtp.gr for Greek island services; VisitNorway.com for Norwegian fjord boats; and Jadrolinija.hr, Krilo.hr, and GV-Line.hr for Croatian boat service.

You can also search for the name of the company (if you know it) that operates a particular route.

Getting Tickets

You can buy most ferry tickets online, and some offer advance-purchase discounts (such as those to or from the UK). In person, either visit a local travel agency or ticket office—or in some cases, simply show up at the ticket window an hour before departure (most tickets cost the same whether you buy them in advance or at the last minute). During peak times in popular destinations (July-August, Croatia's Dalmatian Coast, and Greece's more famous islands), get advice from your hotelier, the local tourist information office, or a local travel agency about how far ahead you should book your ticket.

If you'll be setting sail very soon after your arrival in Europe, do your research from home, and book a ticket in advance. Otherwise, the ferry could sell out and you'll be stranded on a castaway isle—or unable to reach it—for longer than you intended. This is particularly important if you're driving a car onto a ferry—in which case you may need to line up hours in advance. (If it's possible to book a space in advance, do so.)

Some international ferry routes are covered or discounted with a rail pass (such as Ancona or Bari, Italy, to Patra, Greece; and Sweden to Germany or Denmark). Swiss lake boats are integrated into that country's comprehensive public transportation system (and rail pass).

If you're taking an overnight ferry, consider your sleeping options. A basic passenger ticket is "deck class," meaning you'll simply have to camp out wherever you can find room. You can pay a little more for a seat. A "berth" (bed) costs more, similar to a night train. The more private your lodgings, the more you'll pay, especially if a toilet and shower are included in the compartment. You usually can (and should) reserve overnight accommodations in advance. Some Greek island ferries allow you to reserve beds only upon boarding.

On Board

While many ferry companies tell foot passengers to be at the dock 30 minutes before the boat leaves, there's usually no need to show up that far ahead, especially for short-haul day-time boats. One advantage to turning up early is the chance to grab a better seat, which does make a difference if your ferry has open seating.

On the ferry, you may be able to stow your luggage on a public rack on the boarding level; otherwise you'll haul it up several flights of stairs to the passenger decks. You can buy food and drinks on board most boats. It's not too expensive, but it's usually not top quality, either. Bring your own snacks or a picnic instead. Dining is a featured attraction on a few ferries, such as the *smörgåsbord* service on Scandinavian overnight cruises. Ferries of all sizes typically have bathrooms on board. Some ferries offer Wi-Fi (generally for a fee), but don't count on it being reliable.

For information about taking a cruise in Europe, see page 488.

Driving & Navigating

While many European travel dreams come with a clickety-clack "rhythm of the rails" soundtrack—and most first trips are best by train—you should consider the convenience of driving. Behind the wheel you're totally free, going where you want, when you want. Start your engine!

Driving is ideal for countryside-focused trips—and places accessible only by car typically have fewer tourists and more locals. If you glimpse a cute hill town out the window, you can easily stop and linger. If you're exploring the lochs of Scotland, you're going to be glad you've got a car.

The mobility of a car lets you find cheaper accommodations in small towns and away from the train lines. You can also play it riskier in peak season, arriving in a town with no reservation—if the hotels are full, simply drive to the next town. And driving is a godsend for those who don't believe in packing light—you can even rent a trailer. As train prices go up, car rental becomes a better option for budget travelers in Europe. Three or four people sharing a rented car will usually travel for less than they would by train.

Small car, big scenery

RENTING A CAR

Renting a car in Europe isn't much more complicated than in the US, except for some byzantine insurance options. Making informed choices can help you avoid hassles and save money. Once you're free and easy behind the wheel of a European car, it's all worth it.

Car-Rental Costs

Basic rental rates vary from company to company, month to month, and country to country.

The cheapest company for rental in one country might be the most expensive in the next. Comparison-shop to figure out which one is best for your trip (see "Booking a Car," later).

The basic rates you'll see quoted nearly always include unlimited mileage, value-added tax, and (legally required) third-party liability insurance. When getting estimates, be sure to include any extras (second driver, child seat, automatic transmission).

Here are some components of your car-rental rate:

Taxes: Value-added tax (VAT) generally runs 18-25 percent (each country sets its rate). Other non-negotiable fees, such as a "road tax" or "eco tax," also differ per country (road tax is usually less than $5 per day; expect about $5-10 per day for environmental fees). Taxes are typically included in any price quote, but it's smart to double-check. If it's not clear whether these taxes are included in a price, ask.

Insurance: Your biggest potential extra cost when renting a car is insurance. Your credit card may already cover the extra insurance you need—check in advance. If you buy insurance from the rental company, figure on paying roughly 30-40 percent extra, or about $15-30 a day, for a collision damage waiver supplement (described on page 165).

Theft Protection: This charge, about $15-20/day, is required in Italy; most companies include this in their advertised rates for Italy.

Extra Driver(s): Expect to pay about $5-25/day to add another driver. This is worthwhile if you plan to share the driving duties; if you let an unlisted driver take the wheel and an accident occurs, your insurance won't cover it.

Child-Safety Seats: Every country has different requirements for child-safety seats; it's good to check the rules before you travel. Expect to pay about $50-70 to add a child-safety seat to your rental (if you're not bringing a child seat from home).

Automatics and Other Add-Ons: You'll pay extra for a car with automatic transmission (about 50 percent more than the same car with stick shift), GPS (about $100 per week, though often included in more expensive models),

Car or Train?

Consider these variables:
- Geographical range (trains cover broad areas more easily)
- Rail coverage (for example, Switzerland is crisscrossed by an extensive train network, whereas Ireland's trains are sparse)
- Urban vs. rural (a car is a hassle in big cities, but helpful in the countryside)
- Number of travelers (a car can be cheaper when shared by more than 2 people)
- Luggage (a car is better if you're bad at packing light)
- Kids in tow (car travel is more flexible; trains allow room to roam)

winter tires (required in snowy conditions by some countries; often included in basic rental rates), and ski racks. Emergency roadside assistance is usually included in the cost of your rental to cover mechanical failure, but be sure to clarify this. Roadside service for a flat tire may or may not incur a charge; if you aren't comfortable changing a tire, ask about an extra protection plan.

From sleek German autobahns to windy, cliffside Irish lanes, driving is a fun part of European travel.

Pickup and Drop-Off Fees: In some countries, you'll pay 10-25 percent more to pick up a car at the airport or train station than in the town center. To drop the car in a different country, it will generally cost an extra $100-300, though you'll find exceptions—some happy (free) and some outrageous ($1,000+). The farther the distance between your start and end points, the higher the fee. For tips on choosing a pickup and drop-off location, see page 160.

Other Fees: Rental companies usually charge extra if you plan to drive the car to certain points in eastern Europe (a line that generally follows old Iron Curtain borders). Wintertime driving can carry extra costs beyond the required snow tires. Some fees are easily avoided: Return your car on time to avoid late drop-off fees (don't assume you've got a grace period), fill 'er up shortly before returning to avoid refueling fees (see page 181), and return your car in good shape to sidestep a cleaning fee.

Other Driving Costs

When budgeting for your trip, remember that renting a car involves some significant costs beyond what you'll pay for the car itself.

Fuel: Paying about $100-150 a week will get you roughly 840 miles in a car that gets 40 miles to the gallon; most rental agencies offer hybrid or diesel cars with better fuel efficiency—ask. (For tips on buying gas in Europe, see page 181).

Tolls: You'll pay tolls figured on the distance you drive (about 12 cents per mile) for expressways in certain places (especially the Mediterranean countries). Some countries, mostly in central Europe, require drivers to buy a sticker ("vignette") for their car window ($10-20). And in a few countries, freeways really are free (such as Germany's autobahn system). For more on tolls and vignettes, see page 177.

Parking: Estimate $35 a day in big cities (more like $40-55/day in London and Paris—don't park there); otherwise it's usually free, or at least fairly cheap.

Booking a Car

For the best deal on long-term rentals, book in advance from home. If you decide to rent a car while in Europe, drop by or call a local car-rental agency, or book through a travel agency. You'll need to decide from whom to rent, what kind of car to get, and where to pick it up and drop it off.

Which Rental Company?

Most of us start our search on a travel-booking site such as Kayak, Expedia, or AAA. Of course, if you have a favorite car-rental agency at home, consider using the same company in Europe.

When shopping around, don't stop at comparing initial price quotes. You'll want to determine which company's offer involves the best combination of rates (including all fees and any extras you want), service, and pickup/drop-off locations (with workable office hours) for your trip.

It's generally an advantage to go with a larger company, with a wider choice of pickup and drop-off locations. Most of the big US rental agencies have offices throughout Europe, as do the two major Europe-based agencies, Europcar and Sixt. With these companies, if you get into car trouble, a replacement car is likely to be close at hand.

It's also worth considering a consolidator, such as Auto Europe (my favorite) or Europe by Car. These companies compare rates among various companies (including many of the big-name firms), find the best deal, and—because they're wholesalers –pass the savings on to you. You pay the consolidator, and they issue you a voucher to pick up your car in Europe. Auto Europe's European website (www.autoeurope. eu) may have better deals (and a wider selection) than the US version (www.autoeurope.com)—check both and compare.

With a consolidator as a middleman, it's especially important to ask ahead of time about add-on fees and restrictions; otherwise you might not learn this critical information

---

Ballpark Cost of Renting a Car

This rough estimate is for a one-week rental of a compact car with unlimited mileage. Base prices for car rentals can flex dramatically with demand, length of trip, location, additional services, and fees.

Compact Rental: $250/week (including tax)
CDW Insurance: $120/week
Fuel: $150/week ($7/gallon, 40 mpg, 120 miles/day)
Parking: $90 ($70 for 2 days in big cities, $20 for 4 days in small towns)
Freeway Tolls: $10 (about 90 miles on toll roads)
Ballpark Total: $620/week

until you pick up the car. If any dispute arises when you show up at the rental desk, call the consolidator to try to resolve the issue (the consolidator should provide a toll-free number that works in your rental country). Once you sign off on something with the vendor, it's difficult for the consolidator (or anyone else) to reverse what you've agreed to. If you have a problem with the rental agency, the consolidator may not be able to intervene to your satisfaction, but at least you'll have someone in your corner.

No matter whom you rent through, be sure to hang onto all your paperwork (including the checklist used by the company to check the car's condition when you turn it in) for a few months after the rental period, in case a billing dispute arises.

Choosing a Car

Expect some differences between your typical American rental car and what you'll likely get in Europe, where mid-range cars have less passenger room, vast trunk space is unheard of, and manual transmissions are the norm. Automatics are more expensive (usually about 50 percent more) and may only be available if you upgrade to a bigger, pricier car. (Some Americans find automatics worthwhile in Great Britain and Ireland, where it can be enough of a challenge just to drive on the left.) Since supplies are limited, you'll need to book an automatic further in advance than a manual-transmission car. You'll find a better selection of automatics in big cities and airports.

When checking out options for budget rentals, you'll see some familiar makes (Ford, VW)—though not always familiar models—as well as some less familiar ones, most commonly Opel, Fiat, Citroën, Peugeot, Renault, Škoda, and Seat. Don't waste time carefully choosing among models, since you're not guaranteed to get the exact car you signed up for, just a "similar" model.

I normally rent the smallest, least-expensive model with a stick shift—not just to save money, but because larger cars are not as maneuverable on Europe's narrow, winding roads. If more than two adults are traveling, it can be worth it to move up to a larger class of car.

Choosing a Pickup (and Drop-Off) Place and Time

It's best and less stressful to begin your driving experience away from big cities, so try picking up your car away from major destinations. A pleasant scenario for a trip to England would be to start out (*sans* car) in the smaller city of Bath,

When Booking a Rental Car

Keep These Factors in Mind
- What the car company's basic insurance covers
- Office locations and hours (consider the most efficient pickup and drop-off points)
- Age limitations (under age 25 or over age 69)
- Geographic restrictions (such as eastern European countries)

Nail Down Extra Costs
- CDW insurance (or zero-deductible "super CDW")
- Theft insurance (required in Italy)
- Adding another driver
- One-way rental (returning the car to a different location/country)
- Airport, train station, city center pickup—or hotel delivery
- Extras such as automatic transmission, child-safety seats, and GPS
- Mandatory road taxes or winter-tire fees
- Cancellations or changes to drop-off location or time

rent a car when leaving Bath, explore Britain at your driving leisure, then drop off the car in York and take the train into London, where you can rely on the excellent public transportation system. That way you'd enjoy the three major city stops on your England itinerary—where the last thing you'd want is a car—without paying for one.

That said, beware the possible inconveniences of picking up your car in a small town—a tiny regional office almost certainly has a smaller fleet on hand. Don't plan to pick up or drop off your car in a small town on a Saturday afternoon, Sunday, or holiday, when offices are likely to be closed (except for train station and airport locations).

Picking up a car at an airport or city train station usually costs more than picking it up downtown. (Airport/train-station fees apply only to your pickup, not drop off.) If you don't need a car immediately after your arrival, look into a cheaper rental with a downtown pickup price. But airport or train-station pickup may still be worth it; many in-town rental locations have shorter hours (and may close at midday) or are buried in a maze of narrow streets. Also consider traffic—it may be easier to drive away from an airport or train station than a parking garage in the heart of the city. Before choosing a rental location, find it on a map. Some rental agencies will drop the car off at your hotel—for a fee.

European cars are rented in 24-hour periods, so select your pickup and drop-off times carefully—if you pick up the car at 10 a.m. on the first day and drop it off at noon on the last day, you'll be charged a whole day's rental for just those two hours. Don't book your pickup time for earlier than you really need the car. Book a drop-off time that falls within that location's office hours (or make sure the drop-off location has an after-hours drop box).

Sometimes it can make a lot of sense to start and end your car rental in different cities. One-way rentals are often free within the same country, but dropping off in another country will likely cost extra. Expect fees of $100-300, but if the start and end points are quite far apart, or if the drop-off point is an out-of-the-way location, this cost can top $1,000. Certain places seem to be especially expensive for one-way cross-border trips (Italy, Spain, Scandinavia, and far eastern Europe). The extra cost of a one-way rental can still be worth it if it saves you a very long drive back to your first country. But if the last leg of your trip isn't too far from the border of the country you started in, a small tweak to your rental plans can save you plenty. Let's say you're renting a car in France for a trip that ends in Barcelona. By dropping the car off within France (as close to the border as possible) and hopping a train to Barcelona (roughly $40 per person), you could save hundreds in drop-off fees.

When booking, also ask about your options (and the costs involved) in case you change your plans en route and want to drop off your car at an office in another city or on a different date.

More Tips for Renting a Car
Get quotes for weekly rentals. Typically, the longer you rent, the less it'll cost per day. You may find that renting for a full seven days costs the same as, or even less than, five or six days.

Double-check currency conversions when comparing prices. Some foreign-based rental-company sites use fudged conversion rates that make the price in dollars look cheaper than the price that'll actually show up on your credit-card bill. Convert prices yourself on a conversion site such as Oanda.com.

Pay up front. If your itinerary is set, it's almost always smarter to pay for a rental car when you book, rather than at the agency counter in Europe. Not only are you likely to get a discount, but, assuming that your quote was in dollars, you'll know you're paying the exact amount you were quoted. You'll also avoid paying an international transaction fee on your credit card. If you're purchasing a collision damage waiver from the rental company, that'll likely also be cheaper when paid up front. But beware cancellation fees: Don't pay if your itinerary may change, and be clear on the company's cancellation policy.

Read the fine print. Carefully read your entire reservation voucher before you leave home. By asking about fees in advance and double-checking the charges at pickup, you can avoid unpleasant surprises.

Reconfirm your plans. It's a good idea to confirm your reservation a day or two in advance. When filming my public-television show in Ireland, I took a minute to call Avis in England to reconfirm my car pickup the next day at the ferry dock in North Wales. The man at Avis said, "Right-tee-o, Mr. Steves, we'll have your car waiting for you, noon tomorrow, at Heathrow Airport." No, in North Wales! "Oh, sorry, Mr. Steves. It's good you called ahead."

Red Tape and Restrictions

Every country has its own take on who can rent/drive a car. Follow these tips to make sure you'll be able to take the wheel at your destination.

Passports, Driver's Licenses, and International Driving Permits: Whether you're American or Canadian, your passport and driver's license are all you need in most European countries. However, some countries also require an International Driving Permit (IDP). An IDP is an official translation of your US license (making it easier for the cop to write out a ticket). You can get an IDP at your local American Automobile Association or Canadian Automobile Association office ($20 plus the cost of two passport-type photos—OK to bring your own; doesn't require AAA membership). AAA is authorized by the US State Department to issue permits; avoid scam artists peddling overpriced, fake international licenses.

You may hear contradictory information on exactly where you need an IDP. People who sell them say you should have them almost everywhere. People who rent cars say you need them almost nowhere. People who drive rental cars say the IDP is overrated, but can come in handy as a complement to your passport and driver's license. It's a good idea to get one if you'll be driving in Austria, Bosnia-Herzegovina, Croatia, Greece, Hungary, Italy, Poland, Romania, Slovenia, Slovakia, or Spain—countries where you're technically required to carry a permit. If all goes well, you'll likely never be asked to show it—but the permit is a must if you end up dealing with the police. That said, I've never been asked to show one.

Age Limits: Minimum and maximum age limits for renting a car vary by country, type of car, and rental company. Younger renters can get stuck with extra costs, such as being required to buy extra insurance or pay a surcharge of $15-40 per day (fortunately, there are usually maximum surcharge limits). Many companies will not rent a car to someone under age 21 (with some exceptions, depending on the country and type of car), but those who are at least 25 years old should have no problem.

In the mountainous northwest corner of Slovenia, you're just a few miles' drive from both Austria and Italy.

Drivers over age 70 may have trouble renting in the Czech Republic, Great Britain, Greece, Northern Ireland, Poland, Slovakia, Slovenia, and Turkey; drivers over 80 may have trouble in Denmark. If you're over 69, you may be required to pay extra to rent a car in the Republic of Ireland, where the official age limit is 75 (although some rental companies will rent to those ages 76-79 if they provide extensive proof of good health and safe driving). If you're considered too young or too old, look into leasing (explained on page 167), which has less stringent age restrictions.

Crossing Borders: Your car comes with the paperwork you need to drive wherever you like throughout most of Europe (always check when booking). But if you're heading to a country in far eastern or southeastern Europe—especially one that has closed borders (such as Croatia, Bosnia-Herzegovina, or Montenegro), you may need to pay extra—for the rental itself and/or for additional insurance. State your travel plans up front to the rental company when you book. Some companies may have limits on eastward excursions because of the higher incidence of car thefts (for example, you can only take cheaper cars, and you may have to pay extra insurance fees). When you cross these borders, you may be asked to show proof of insurance (called a "green card"). Ask your car-rental company if you need any other documentation for crossing the borders on your itinerary. It's a bad idea to take your rental car anywhere that's prohibited by your contract, as doing so voids any insurance coverage.

If you want to drive on the Continent as well as in Britain and/or Ireland, it's probably cheaper to rent separate cars, thanks to the high cost of taking cars on ferries or the Eurotunnel car train. Some companies allow you to take a rental car from Britain to the Continent or to Ireland, but be prepared to pay high surcharges and extra drop-off fees.

Insurance and the Collision Damage Waiver

When you rent a car, you can be liable for a very high deductible, sometimes equal to the entire value of the car. Fortunately, there's usually more than one way to limit your financial risk in case of an accident.

Baseline rates for European rentals nearly always include liability coverage—for accident-related damage to anyone or anything outside the car. (The company may offer additional liability insurance, but I wouldn't buy this without some extenuating reason.)

It's (usually) up to you, however, to decide how to cover the risk of damage to or theft of the car itself. You have three main options: Buy a "collision damage waiver" (CDW) through the car-rental company (easiest but most expensive), use your credit card's coverage (cheapest), or get collision insurance as part of a larger travel-insurance policy.

If you're renting in either Ireland or Italy, you'll have little choice but to buy the company's CDW. If you need a car for at least three weeks, you're probably better off leasing (described later), which includes zero-deductible collision and theft insurance (and is tax-free to boot). Note that theft insurance covers just the loss of the car itself, not anything stolen from inside it.

Car-Rental Company CDW

The simplest solution is to buy a CDW supplement from the car-rental company. This coverage technically isn't insurance—it's a waiver: The car-rental company waives its right to collect a high deductible from you in the event the car is damaged. Note that this "waiver" doesn't actually eliminate the deductible, but just reduces it. CDW covers most of the car if you're in a collision, but usually excludes the undercarriage, roof, tires, windshield, windows, interior, and side mirrors.

CDW generally costs $15-30 a day (figure roughly 30-40 percent extra). Sometimes the CDW charge itself is a little less when combined with theft/loss insurance as part of an inclusive rental rate—and it's often cheaper to pay for this kind of coverage when you book than when you pick up the car.

When purchasing CDW, the deductibles can still be substantial, with most hovering at about $1,000-1,500 (or more, depending on the car type). Most rental companies also offer a second tier of coverage, called "super CDW" or "zero-deductible coverage" to buy down the deductible to zero or near zero (if you didn't opt for this when booking from home, expect to hear a sales pitch from the counter agent). This is pricey—figure an additional $10-30 per day—but, for some travelers, the peace of mind is worth it. There's a huge comfort in knowing you can bring your car back in an unrecognizable shamble and say, "Sorry, I'm new in this country."

When comparing rental options online, beware that some European rental agencies quote "basic" rates that include CDW/theft coverage. (In this case, it's not an optional extra, so you can't decline it.) If these CDW-inclusive rates seem too good to be true, they probably are: The unwaived deductible is almost certainly high (expect $2,000-3,000), so you'll have to spend extra to buy the "super CDW" anyway to get the deductible down to a reasonable level.

Given these costs, the alternatives to paying for the rental company's CDW are worth considering: credit-card coverage or collision coverage through your travel-insurance provider.

Credit-Card Coverage

Car-company CDW surcharges can seem like a racket when you consider that most American credit cards already include collision coverage. By paying with the right credit card, you get zero-deductible collision coverage (comparable to "super" CDW)...likely for free. In other words, if your car is damaged or stolen, your credit card will cover whatever costs you're liable for. The only major downside: If you do end up in an accident, dealing with credit-card coverage can be more of a hassle than what you'd encounter with the car-company CDW. But if a potential headache seems like a worthwhile trade-off for certain—and significant—cost savings, look into this option.

To make this work, first double-check that your credit card does indeed offer this coverage (Visa, MasterCard, and American Express usually do—but not Discover). Remember that restrictions apply and coverage varies between issuers: Get a complete description of the coverage offered by your credit-card company. Ask in which countries it is applicable, which parts of the car (if any) are excluded, the types of vehicles that are eligible, whether it covers theft/loss, the maximum reimbursement allowed (if it's less than the price of the car, the rental company may require you to buy their CDW), and the maximum number of rental days covered (often 30 or 31 days; if your rental period exceeds that

Alternatives to Renting

For longer car trips, leasing a car can be more affordable than renting; for short jaunts, consider a car-share program. Neither is as widely available as rentals. For a cheap lift, consider ride sharing.

Leasing: Leasing gets around many tax and insurance costs, and is a great deal for three weeks or more. Leases are available for periods of up to five and a half months. Prices include all taxes, as well as zero-deductible theft and collision insurance valid all over Europe, including eastern countries. You won't pay extra for additional drivers or for venturing too far east, and you get a shiny new car. Leased cars can most easily be picked up and returned in France, but for an additional fee you can lease in the Netherlands, Belgium, Germany, Spain, Portugal, Italy, and Great Britain. Auto Europe, for example, leases no-frills Peugeot 208s for as few as 21 days for about $700—about $33 per day. Europe by Car, which invented leasing more than 50 years ago, and Renault Eurodrive offer similar deals. In general, the longer you lease the car, the lower the price.

Car Sharing: Car sharing makes the most sense for day trips. Car-sharing providers place cars throughout a city, let users rent them for just a few hours or days, and charge no enrollment or annual fees. You book your car online, pick it up at a set location, and return it to the nearest location when you're done. The fee includes insurance, fuel, and GPS. There's no extra fee for drivers ages 21-24, and prices are relatively reasonable—in London a Ford Fiesta costs about $15 per hour or $75 per day. Europe's main car-sharing provider is Hertz 24/7 (www.hertz247.com), currently available in Britain, France, Germany, Italy, Spain, Belgium, and the Netherlands. Zipcar operates in Austria, Great Britain, France, Spain, and Turkey. Car2go, which rents the smallest Smart model, operates mostly in Germany.

Ride Sharing: BlaBlaCar (www.blablacar.com), operating throughout Europe, connects passengers with drivers who are making long-distance trips. Riders pay a low fare (called a "cost contribution") that is often cheaper than public transit. The fee is paid through the website, and drivers can't profit off the service (fees cover fuel, tolls, maintenance, insurance, and other car-related costs). The website allows passengers and drivers to rate each other, and for drivers to indicate how chatty they are (from one to three "bla's").

number, your card won't cover any of the rental). Have them explain the worst-case scenario to you. It can be smart to ask for a "Letter of Coverage"—take a hard copy of it with you to the rental counter in Europe.

Once you've confirmed your credit card's coverage, be sure to decline the CDW offered by your car-rental company. If you accept any coverage offered by the rental agency, you automatically forego your credit-card coverage. (In other words, if you buy CDW that comes with a $1,000 deductible, your credit card will not cover that deductible.) This may also be the case if you book and prepay for a rental that already includes CDW and/or theft coverage—don't sign any rental contract until you're sure that by doing so you're not accidentally accepting the rental company's coverage.

A credit card's collision coverage applies even if the damage happens while the car is being driven by someone else, as long as that other driver, and the cardholder, are both listed as drivers on the rental contract. Remember to use that same card not only to reserve the car, but also to pay for it and any other related fees, whether when booking at home, or when picking up or dropping off the car in Europe—switching cards can invalidate the coverage.

If you get in an accident, the rental company will charge your credit card for the value of the damage (up to the deductible amount) or, if the vehicle is stolen, the value of the deductible associated with theft. It's then up to you to seek reimbursement for these charges from your credit-card company when you get home. You'll need to submit the police report and the car-rental company's accident report. (When deciding between rental companies, consider that American-based rental companies can be easier to work with if you have a claim to resolve.)

Be warned that, as far as some rental companies are concerned, by declining their CDW offer, you're technically liable for the full deductible (which can equal the cost of the car). Because of this, the car-rental company may put a hold on your credit card for the full value of the car. This is bad news if your credit limit is low—particularly if you plan on using that card for other purchases during your trip. (Consider bringing two credit cards—one for the rental car, the other for everything else.) If you don't have enough credit on your card to cover the car's value, the rental company may require you to purchase their CDW.

Since most credit card companies don't offer collision insurance to European cardholders, counter agents—especially those unaccustomed to American clients—may be skeptical that declining their CDW is a prudent move (all the more reason to have hard-copy proof of your credit-card coverage on hand). Don't be surprised if you hear a warning about how credit cards provide only "secondary" coverage—that's moot as long as you've declined the rental company's coverage. By clearly understanding the coverage from your credit-card company, you can ward off a hard sell on the rental-company CDW.

Collision Coverage Through Your Travel-Insurance Provider

If you're already purchasing a travel-insurance policy for your trip, adding collision coverage is an option. Travel Guard, for example, sells affordable renter's collision insurance as an add-on to its other policies. It's valid everywhere in Europe except the Republic of Ireland, and some Italian car-rental companies refuse to honor it.

If you do go with an insurer's comprehensive travel coverage, be sure to add the insurance company's name to your rental agreement when you pick up the car. For more on travel insurance, see page 70.

Picking Up Your Car

When you arrive at the rental counter, ask for a copy of the contract in English if it's not provided as a matter of course. If you haven't already paid for the car, know what your quote is in the local currency. Be sure to decline any offer of "dynamic currency conversion" (explained on page 196).

If you can, avoid prepaying for your first tank of gas (although some offices won't let you out of this). Prepaying for fuel is virtually always a rip-off, since agencies charge far more per gallon than the going rate. The only upside is that you can return the car with a nearly empty tank.

Be sure to check the entire vehicle for scratches or dents. Rental agencies in Europe are very strict when it comes to charging for even minor damage, so be sure to mark everything on the checklist. Some travelers photograph all dings and scratches, even the tiniest ones (be sure the date/time stamp is on). If any damage is not already noted on the rental agreement, return to the counter to make adjustments.

Before you drive off, get to know your car. Try out all the features and gadgets: Run the front and rear windshield wipers and sprayers, figure out whether the headlights come on automatically with the engine, switch the headlights to high-beam, get comfortable with the gearshift—including shifting into reverse, check if you have a locked fuel cap, and so on.

This is also a good time to quiz the rental agent on a few things, including:

- grace period for drop-off, if any
- how to use features such as the alarm system, lights, radio, GPS, etc.
- what type of fuel the car takes (diesel vs. unleaded), the local term for that fuel, and how to release the gas cap

- location of insurance "green card" and other paperwork
- whether your car has a valid toll-highway vignette (if needed)
- info on making repairs and any included emergency roadside services
- location of spare tire and directions for using it (don't accept a car without a spare)
- location of breath-testing kit for measuring alcohol levels (required in France, included with rental or available at counter for small fee)

Before leaving, make sure the tank is full and get instructions for driving to your next stop (or at least to the expressway). Then drive around the parking lot for a few minutes to test rearview mirrors, the gearshift and clutch, backing up, and the lights and signals.

When you leave the lot, don't be surprised if your engine seems to "die" at the first stop. Many European cars now have "stop-start" technology, where the engine automatically switches off when you're stopped—and then starts up again when you step on the gas or release the clutch.

Dropping Off Your Car

Be on time to drop off your car—you could be charged an extra day's rent if you show up a little late. Most companies allow only a 30-minute grace period, and once that's up you'll be liable for another full day's rental. If you know you'll be late, notify the rental company in advance.

Unless you've already prepaid for a tank of gas, top up your car before returning it—otherwise you may end up paying more than double the going rate, plus an additional "refueling fee." To avoid last-minute hassles, I check online in advance for gas stations close to my drop-off point. Save your final gas receipt as proof that you filled the tank, and don't toss it until you've seen your credit-card bill.

Once you're at the rental office, inspect the car with the attendant to be sure there are no new problems. Some drivers take pictures of the returned vehicle as proof of its condition (an especially good idea at unstaffed after-hours drop-off points).

A car works best for exploring rural areas that are often not well served by public transportation.

Ask for a copy of the final condition report and keep it until you've seen your credit-card statement. Unexpected charges that show up on your credit-card statement are easier to dispute if you have good documentation on hand.

If you're relying on your credit card's collision coverage and you have a balance to pay at the returns desk, remember to use that same card—using a different card could invalidate your coverage.

BEHIND THE EUROPEAN WHEEL

Horror stories about European traffic abound. They're fun to tell, but driving is really only a problem for those who make it one. The most dangerous creature on the road is the panicked foreign visitor. Drive defensively, observe, fit in, avoid big-city driving when you can, have a good map on hand, and wear your seat belt.

Some places are easier to handle than others. The British Isles are good for driving—reasonable rentals, no language barrier, exciting rural areas, and fine roads...and after one near head-on collision scares the bloody heck out of you, you'll have no trouble remembering which side of the road to drive on.

Other good driving areas are Scandinavia (hug the lip of a majestic fjord as you meander from village to village); Belgium and the Netherlands (yield to bikes—you're outnumbered); Spain and Portugal (explore out-of-the-way villages and hill towns); Germany (zip along wonderfully engineered freeways much loved by wannabe race-car drivers); Switzerland and Austria (drive down sunny alpine valleys with yodeling on the stereo for auto ecstasy); and Slovenia (enjoy its many diverse, picturesque sights that are hard to reach by public transit).

Once you're behind the wheel, you may curse the traffic jams, narrow roads, and macho habits, but it's all part of the experience. Driving at home is mundane; driving in Europe is memorable.

Maps and GPS

Online or on paper, a good map is a must-have on any European road trip. Don't rely blindly on your phone's mapping app or a GPS device for directions; always have at least a vague sense of your route, keep a paper map handy, and pay attention to road signs so you can consider alternatives if you feel the GPS route is Getting Pretty Screwy.

One time, driving from St. Moritz to Lugano via Italy's Lake Como, I realized that my GPS had just directed me right past the Lugano turnoff. Hitting the brakes and checking my paper map, I figured out that the GPS was aiming to send me on the freeway, then on a ferry across the lake. I stuck with the "slower" roads on the correct side of the lake—and arrived an hour earlier.

Your Mobile Device: The mapping app on your mobile phone works fine for navigation in Europe. The downside is that to get real-time turn-by-turn directions and traffic updates, you'll need Internet access (a concern abroad, where you are likely paying more for data; see the Staying Connected chapter).

Unless data roaming isn't an issue, the best option for travelers can be an app that works offline: Google Maps, Here WeGo, and Navmii will give you turn-by-turn voice directions without a data connection—and if you make a wrong turn, will recalibrate and send you on the right way. They're basically a GPS system on your smartphone, for free.

Download your map before you head out—it's smart to select a large region. Then turn off your cellular connection so you're not charged for data roaming. Call up the map, enter your destination, and you're on your way. For the best performance in Google Maps, use standard view (not satellite view) to limit data demands. Be aware that Google Maps' traffic setting does not work offline, so check traffic before you hit the road or use data roaming for a brief period to get current conditions.

Bring a car charger for your device, since mapping apps, even offline, gobble up battery life. It's also smart to bring a car mount for your phone that works for lots of vehicles.

As of this printing, other navigation apps—such as Apple Maps and Waze—do not offer turn-by-turn directions offline. GPS apps from TomTom, Garmin, CoPilot, and others do work offline but tend to be very expensive.

GPS Devices: If you'll be traveling without a

Resources for Driving & Navigating

ViaMichelin.com, Maps.Google.com: Reliable route planners with estimated driving times and distances

TheAA.com: Country-by-country driving tips and local road laws

www.ricksteves.com/travel-talks: Rick's travel skills talks, including one on transportation

Google Maps, Here WeGo, Navmii: Apps with turn-by-turn driving directions that work offline

Waze: Crowd-sourced app with navigation and traffic info, including cheapest nearby gas

smartphone, or want the convenience
of a dedicated GPS, consider renting
a GPS device with your car ($10-30
per day). You'll get real-time turn-by-
turn directions and traffic without
the data limitations of a phone app.
Note that the unit may come loaded
only with maps for its home country;
if you need additional maps, ask. Also
make sure the device is set to English
before you drive off.

Like most goats, I appreciate a good, old-fashioned map.

The other option is to bring a GPS from home. You'll likely
need to buy and download European maps before your trip
(check that the maps available through the manufacturer are
detailed enough for the areas you're visiting.) Remember to
bring your unit's car charger and a portable car mount.

Maps and Atlases: Even when navigating primarily
with a phone app or GPS, I always have a paper map on hand.
It's invaluable for getting the big picture, understanding
alternate routes, and filling in when my phone runs out of
juice. The free maps you get from your car-rental company
usually don't have enough detail. Better maps and atlases
are sold at European gas stations, bookshops, newsstands,
and tourist shops. Michelin offers good individual regional
maps and road atlases for each country (with good city maps
and detailed indexes). Though they can be heavy, atlases are
compact, a good value, and easier for drivers to use than big
foldout maps.

Sometimes the best regional road maps are available
locally. For example, if you're exploring your roots in the
Norwegian fjord country, Cappelens 1:200,000 maps are
detailed enough to help you find Grandpa Ole's farm. Other
quality European brands include Hallwag, Freytag Berndt,
Marco Polo, Berndtson & Berndtson, AA (Britain's AAA-type
automobile club), Road Editions (for Greece), and Kod & Kam
(for Croatia and Slovenia).

Study the map legend; most maps include navigational as
well as sightseeing information, such as types of roads, scenic
routes and towns, ruined castles, hostels, mountain huts, viewpoints, and so on. Good maps even include such specific details
as tolls and opening schedules of remote mountain roads.

Tips for the Road

The mechanics of driving in Europe aren't all that different
from home, but the first day or two can be an adjustment.

Below are my top tips for driving safely, and enjoyably, on European roads. (For an A-to-Z index of European-country driving tips, see the website of the British Automobile Association—www.theaa.com/motoring-advice—and look for "Driving Abroad.")

Road Rules

Driving in Europe tends to be more aggressive than in the US, and some Europeans, particularly Italians and Greeks, seem to make up their own rules of the road. In Rome, for instance, red lights are considered discretionary. On one trip, my cabbie went through three red lights. White-knuckled, I asked, "*Scusi*, do you see red lights?" He said, "When I come to light, I look. If no cars come, red light *stupido*, I go through. If policeman sees no cars—*no problema*. He agree—red light *stupido*." Here are some tips for sharing the roads with European drivers.

Passing: When you pass other drivers, be bold but careful. On winding, narrow roads, the slower car ahead of you may use turn-signal sign language to indicate when it's OK to pass. This is used inconsistently—and don't rely on it blindly. Be sure you understand the lane markings—in France a single, solid, white line in the middle of the road means no passing in either direction; in Germany it's a double white line. After a few minutes on the autobahn, you'll learn that you don't linger in the passing lane. For passing, use the left-hand lane on the Continent and the right-hand lane in Britain and Ireland. In some countries (such as France, Germany, and the Netherlands), it's illegal to use the slower lane for passing. In Greece, slower drivers don't pull over, but drift as far right as possible to let cars pass.

Roundabouts: In roundabouts, traffic continually flows in a circle around a center island. While you'll see them sporadically throughout continental Europe (where vehicles move counterclockwise), roundabouts are everywhere in the British Isles (where traffic flows clockwise). These work wonderfully if you follow the golden rule: Traffic in a roundabout always has the right-of-way, while entering vehicles yield. For many, roundabouts are high-pressure circles that require a snap decision about something you don't completely understand: your exit. To replace the stress with giggles,

A roundabout: Take a spin... or two.

How to Navigate a UK Roundabout

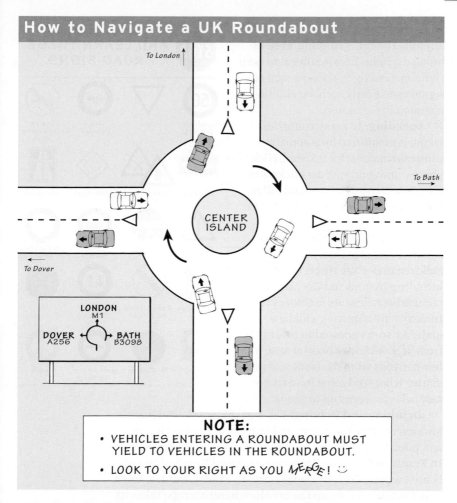

NOTE:
- VEHICLES ENTERING A ROUNDABOUT MUST YIELD TO VEHICLES IN THE ROUNDABOUT.
- LOOK TO YOUR RIGHT AS YOU MERGE! ☺

make it standard operating procedure to take a 360-degree case-out-your-options exploratory circuit. Discuss the exits with your navigator, go around again if necessary, then confidently wing off to the exit of your choice. (Don't worry. No other cars will know you've been in there enough times to get dizzy.) When approaching an especially complex roundabout, you'll first pass a diagram showing the layout and the various exits. And in many cases, the pavement is painted with the name of the road or town to which the lane leads.

Signs: All of Europe uses the same simple set of road symbols (see graphic on next page). It takes just a few minutes to learn them. Many superhighway rest stops have local driving almanacs (or cheap maps) that explain such signs, roadside facilities, and exits.

Signals and Lights: Many European countries require

you to have your headlights on anytime the car is running, even in broad daylight. It's also illegal to turn right on a red light, unless a sign or signal specifically authorizes it (most common in Germany).

Speeding: In many countries, traffic is monitored by automatic cameras that check car speed, click photos, and send speeders tickets by mail. It's smart to know—and follow—the area speed limit. See page 182 for more on tickets.

Driving with Children: Most countries require safety seats for children under age three, and a few—including Ireland and Germany—require booster seats for older kids. In nearly all countries, children under 12 aren't allowed to ride in the front seat without a booster seat; a few ban kids from the front seat no matter what, and some have front-seat rules for teens up to age 18.

Drinking and Driving: The legal blood-alcohol limit is lower across the Continent and in Ireland than in the US, and punishment ranges from steep fines to imprisonment. In France, all cars need to have an unused Breathalyzer on board (supplied if your rental starts in France, but ask about this if you're picking up the car elsewhere). Europe takes its DUI laws seriously, and so should you.

Other Rules: Nearly all countries forbid talking on a mobile phone without a hands-free headset. Many countries require each car to carry a reflective safety vest or kit with a reflecting triangle (typically supplied by the rental company). In many cities, cars must meet a certain emission standard to enter the city limits. Your car-rental company should be aware of these rules—just ask. Or you can research them on the US State Department's travel website (www.travel. state.gov, search for your country in the "Learn about your destination" box, then click "Travel and Transportation").

Smart Navigation

Your trip will go more smoothly if you familiarize yourself with the quirks of navigating in Europe. Note that Europeans have the same rush hours we do, especially in the north. Mediterranean resort areas are extremely congested on summer weekends.

Metric: European countries (except the UK) use kilometers instead of miles. One kilometer is six-tenths of a mile. To convert kilometers to miles, cut the kilometers in half and add 10 percent of the original number (360 km = 180 + 36 = 216 miles; 90 km/hour = 45 + 9 = 54 mph—not very fast in Europe). Some people prefer to drop the last digit and multiply by 6 (if 80 km, multiply 8 × 6 = 48 miles), though this can be challenging with large numbers (340 km × 6 = ?). Choose whichever formula works for you.

When estimating how long a drive will take, figure you'll average 100 kilometers per hour on expressways (about the same as going 60 mph back home). Determining how much ground you can cover off the freeway is a crapshoot. I use a trick an Irish bus driver taught me: Figure a minute for every kilometer (covering 90 km will take you about an hour and a half). Double that for slow, curvy roads, such as in Italy's Dolomites or Amalfi Coast.

Navigating by Road and Town Names: Study the roads and major interchanges you'll be using before you set out. If you're headed for a small or midsize town, know which big city is nearby (and most likely to be signposted) to keep you headed in the right direction.

In some countries, road numbers can help you find your way: For example, take road A-1 to London, then B-23 to Bristol, then C-456 to Bath. Normally, the more digits the road number has, the smaller it is; so in Britain, M-1 is a freeway, A-34 is a major road, and B-4081 is a secondary road. In other countries, local signs ignore the road numbers (which can change along the way), so it's necessary to navigate by town name. Signs are often color-coded: yellow for most roads, green or blue for expressways, and brown for sightseeing attractions.

Most international European expressways are designated with an "E" (similar to the "I" designation on American freeways), but they may also be labeled on maps and signs with their national letters (for example, the main route between Paris and Lyon is known as both A-6 and E-15).

Tolls and Expressways: The shortest distance between any two European points is the *Autobahn/strada/route/cesta*. Some prefer the more scenic national highway systems. These small roads can be a breeze, or they can be dreadfully jammed up.

It's free to drive on expressways in some countries, such as nearly all highways in Great Britain and Germany's famous autobahn. But on major expressways in much of Mediterranean Europe—including Italy, France, Spain, Portugal, Greece, and Croatia—you'll encounter toll booths; fees are based on the distance you drive (about 12 cents/mile). Some countries are introducing automatic, cashless toll systems (such as Portugal)—but there is typically a toll-booth option to pay with cash or a card. Other countries require drivers who are using expressways to buy a permit sticker (called a "vignette") to display in their windshields (Austria, Bulgaria, Czech Republic, Hungary, Romania, Slovakia, Switzerland, and Slovenia). You'll pay about $40 for the decal in Switzerland (good for a year); everyplace else offers a short-term permit (7-10 days) for $10-20. Your rental car may already have an unexpired sticker; if not, you can usually buy one at border crossings, gas stations, and post offices. If you don't have a sticker, you'll soon meet your first local...in uniform. Fines start at around $150.

Although tolls can add up (for example, it's about $70 to get from Paris to the French Riviera, and about $20 from Rome to Naples), the fuel and time saved on European expressways justifies the expense. Note that in any country, if you're skipping the expressways and sticking to secondary roads, you don't need to buy a toll sticker or otherwise pay for road use.

Driving in Towns and Cities: You can drive in and out of strange towns fairly smoothly by following a few basic signs. Most European towns have signs directing you to the "old town" or the center (such as *centrum, centro, centar, centre-ville, Zentrum, Stadtmitte*). Most tourist offices, normally right downtown, are clearly signposted (*i, turismo, VVV,* or various abbreviations that you'll learn in each country). The tallest spire often marks the center of the old town. Park in

LEFT As you approach a tollbooth, check the signs. Here the lanes on the right take credit cards while those on the left require a special pass.

RIGHT Urban driving can involve some tight squeezes.

its shadow and look for the tourist information office. When leaving a city, look for "all directions" signs (*toutes directions*, *alle Richtungen*, etc.) pointing you out of town.

If visiting big cities, it's best to park your car on the outskirts and use public transportation or taxis (see "Parking," below). Cities across Europe have taken measures to discourage urban driving. For example, to drive anywhere in downtown London or Stockholm, you'll pay a "congestion charge." You'll pay a toll to drive into Oslo and Bergen—but because of their automated systems, you may not know it until you get a bill two months later.

Car traffic is banned altogether in many Italian city centers, including Rome, Naples, Florence, Pisa, Lucca, Siena, San Gimignano, Orvieto, and Verona. Don't drive or park anywhere you see signs reading *Zona Traffico Limitato* (ZTL, often shown above a red circle). If you do, even briefly by accident, your license plate will be photographed, usually without your knowledge, and a hefty ticket—or tickets, if you did it multiple times—will be waiting for you at home (for advice on handling tickets, see page 182).

When you reserve your hotel room, ask your hotelier for detailed directions on how to reach the place and where to park. If possible, figure out your arrival route before you enter the city limits. While some small towns helpfully post signs directing you to individual hotels, in many cases you're on your own. If your hotel is within a restricted driving area, ask your hotelier to register your car ahead of your arrival or direct you to legal parking.

Parking

The best advice for avoiding parking hassles in Europe: Use common sense, and if you're unclear on the rules, ask locals. Park carefully—Europe's narrow streets are responsible for more than their fair share of insurance claims.

Street Parking: Learn what the pavement markings mean (different curb colors can mean free parking—or no parking), look for signs indicating where and when you can't park, and double-check with a local that your car's parked legally. Don't assume that an absence of meters means you can leave your car there: You may need to get a timed ticket from a nearby pay-and-display machine, or display a parking-clock disc that allows you to use free, time-limited spots (see photo).

Parking Clocks

Dashboard "parking clocks" *(left)* are used in some areas instead of parking meters. Common in Germanic countries, these clocks *(Parkscheibe)* come with rental cars or can be bought cheaply at gas stations, newsstands, or tobacco shops. Park, set the clock to indicate the time you arrived, and leave it on your dash. The street sign *(right)* tells you the hours when free parking is allowed (here parking is limited to *2 Stunden*—2 hours).

Lots and Garages: "Parking" is the European word for a parking lot or garage, universally marked with a blue *P* sign. In midsize towns, I generally just pull into the most central and handy lot I can find. In bigger cities, I avoid the center (often an unpleasant grid of one-way streets) and head straight to a parking lot outside the core. In an effort to make well-touristed places more pedestrian-friendly, many cities have stopped providing any parking at all in the city center. Look for huge government-sponsored park-and-rides on the outskirts of town, where local transit will zip you easily into the center— commonly, the affordable parking fee includes a transit ticket (or the transit is cheap and the parking itself is free).

Parking Prices: Just like at home, the bigger the city, the more you'll pay for parking. Small towns don't usually charge more than $10 per day (and are likely to have free limited-time spots), whereas in bigger cites you'll pay upwards of $35-55 per day. Street parking can be cheaper than parking in a lot or garage, but often comes with a time limit too short for sightseeing. In smaller towns, you may find a cheaper hourly rate by parking farther away from the big-name sight. Parking machines on the street or at unstaffed garages might not accept your American credit card, and many don't give change, so keep plenty of coins and bills on hand. Don't spend a lot of time cruising around looking for a free spot. I get as close as I can to the city center and pay. You'll save time and have a safer place to leave your car.

Overnight Stops: If parking overnight, it's crucial to choose a safe, well-traveled, and well-lit spot for your car. Ask your hotelier about parking options (and rules governing overnight parking); the hotel may offer a permit or free spot, whether in their own lot or through an agreement with a neighbor. For advice on theft-proofing your car, see page 380.

Filling the Tank

The cost of fuel in Europe (about $7 a gallon) sounds worse than it is. Distances are short, petite cars get great mileage, and, when compared to costly train tickets (for the price of a two-hour train ride, you can fill your tank), expensive gas is less of a factor. You'll be impressed by how few miles you need to travel to enjoy Europe's diversity.

Pumping gas in Europe is easy—the English word "self-service" is universal. Paying, however, may be more complicated (observe other customers and follow suit). At some stations, you pump the gas first and then pay the cashier (your pump may be "frozen" until the previous customer pays his or her bill). At others, you pay at a central kiosk and then select your pump number. Some places offer full service.

Other stations are like the ones in the US, where you pay at the pump. But most of these machines (especially those in the UK, France, the Low Countries, and Scandinavia) won't accept magnetic-stripe credit cards, and even if your US credit card has a chip, it might not work at the offline terminals common at gas pumps (be sure you know your card's PIN in case you need to enter it; for details on chip and PIN, see the Money chapter). If your card doesn't work, pay the cashier (with cash; in some cases they might be able to swipe your card). Note that gas stations can be unattended: For instance, if you're traveling on rural highways, automated gas stations—which don't take cash—may be the only ones open on Sundays, holidays, and late at night. It's best to fill up ahead of time.

Fuel prices are listed by the liter (about a quart, four to a gallon). As in the US, most cars take unleaded, but diesel is widely in use. In Europe, regular gas is marked "95" while super or premium gasoline is usually designated "97" or "98." Unleaded gas is called *essence, petrol,* or *benzine,* while diesel is known as *gasoil, gasol, gaz-oil, gasolio, gasóleo, dieselolie, mazot, motorina, nafta,* or just plain *diesel* (ask about the proper local term when you rent your car). Pay extra attention in Spain, where gasoline is *gasolina* and diesel is sometimes called *gasóleo.* Be aware that in some countries there's no size or color difference between the nozzles for diesel and gasoline, so make sure you're not putting the wrong fuel in your car.

Freeway gas stations are more expensive than those in towns, but sometimes (e.g., during the lunchtime siesta) only freeway stations are open. Giant suburban supermarkets often offer the cheapest gas.

If Something Goes Wrong

Some travelers obsess about the possibility of a car accident while driving in Europe. Most come back bragging about their road skills and missing the freedom of the autobahn. Those who do have a mishap usually tell me it was the result of a tight squeeze in a parking garage. Still, it's good to know what to do if you hit a bump in the road. Figure out where to find your rental company's emergency service number *before* you need it (it's likely on a windshield sticker, your keychain, and the rental paperwork).

Traffic Accidents: If there's major damage to your vehicle, call your rental company's 24-hour roadside assistance line. If the accident involves another car, you'll need to show your driver's license and insurance "green card" to the other driver and/or the police. Fill out the European Accident Report form that the agency includes with your rental documents. If you're going to submit an insurance claim, notify your insurer as soon as possible, and file a police report—and get copies of that report—even if no other cars are involved. Both steps must happen within your policy's time limit. If the police refuse to write up a report ("it's only a scrape"), ask your hotelier to help you type up a report, take it to the police station, and ask them to stamp it. It's a good idea to take photos of the damage to your car and the license plate of any other vehicles involved.

Flat Tires and Mechanical Problems: Rental companies typically include roadside assistance or a towing service in the event your car becomes undrivable (sometimes for a fee). Ask about this possibility when you pick up the car. If your car has a serious issue, in theory, you should be able to swap it out for a replacement car at the rental company's nearest office. In reality, it may not be so convenient, especially if you break down in the middle of nowhere. If that happens, call your 24/7 roadside assistance number right away...then expect a wait for the tow truck. (If you rented through a consolidator, they may be of some help in speeding things up—but call roadside assistance first.) The repair will be covered by the rental company as long as it's clear it was the car's fault, not yours. It's worth noting that burnt clutches account for the vast majority of breakdowns experienced (and paid for) by American drivers in Europe—go easy on the transmission.

Traffic Tickets: Just because there was no police car in sight when you ran a red light (or ignored the speed limit, drove into a restricted zone, or even tailgated too closely) doesn't mean you weren't caught—Europe's traffic cameras are everywhere. Quite likely, you won't know about the infraction until months later, when a letter arrives in your mail and/or a charge shows up on your credit card.

You likely won't get a chance to dispute a fine. Europe doesn't have traffic courts—you're simply expected to pay up. In some cases, the fine may be automatically billed to your credit card. In other cases, the rental agency may charge you $50 just for providing your address to local authorities.

Of course, many renters just ignore any notices that show up months after their trip. It's understandable—paying the fine may not be all that straightforward, and it's not as if Interpol's on your tail. But be aware that fees go up the longer you delay, an unpaid ticket can follow you for years, and you'll likely be forced to pay it the next time you rent a car in Europe (especially if it's in the same country).

Roadside assistance may be slow to arrive if you break down on a Tuscan country road, but at least the view is nice!

Money

Let's face it: Any international trip is going to put a strain on your wallet—but savvy spenders know how to keep expenses in check. Being aware of banking pitfalls is one of the easiest ways to keep your trip from costing more than it has to. When it comes to money, it's all about maximizing ease, minimizing fees, and keeping it safe.

At the end of this chapter, we cover another money topic on every traveler's mind: tipping.

MONEY STRATEGIES

Money-wise, Europe's never been easier. Thanks to the ubiquity of cash machines, gone are the days of having to go to your hometown bank for travelers' checks or foreign cash, of lining up at AmEx offices overseas, or getting fleeced at exchange bureaus at every border. And these days, I'm enjoying thinking of the euro as being worth a buck—whether or not that's the official exchange rate.

Here's my basic strategy for handling money in Europe:
- Upon arrival, head for an ATM at the airport and load up on local currency, using a debit card with low international transaction fees.
- Withdraw large amounts at each transaction (to limit fees) and keep cash safe in a money belt.
- Pay for most items with cash.
- Pay for larger purchases with a credit card with low (or no) international fees.
- Smile and enjoy your trip, feeling very clever for avoiding unnecessary hassle and expense.

Plastic Versus Cash

Even though credit cards are widely accepted in Europe, day-to-day spending is generally more cash-based than in the US. I find cash is the easiest—and sometimes only—way to pay for cheap food, bus fare, taxis, tips, and local guides.

Even if you don't keep cash in your wallet at home, there are several reasons to carry cash in Europe. Some businesses (especially smaller ones, such as B&Bs and mom-and-pop cafés and shops) may charge you extra for using a credit card—or might not accept credit cards at all. Having cash on hand helps you out of a jam if your card randomly doesn't work. And paying in cash can save you from racking up international credit-card fees (explained later). Minimizing card use also guards against fraud or theft: The less you use your card, the less likely your information will be stolen.

I use my credit card to book hotel reservations, to buy advance tickets for events or sights, and to cover major expenses (such as car rentals or plane tickets). It can also be smart to use plastic near the end of your trip, to avoid another visit to the ATM. If you'll be shopping a lot or settling bills at pricey business-class hotels, you might use your credit card more than I do—but you'll still be better off using cash for smaller purchases. (A major exception is Sweden, with its preference for electronic payments.)

A dependence on plastic can reshape the Europe you experience. Pedro's Pension, the friendly guide at the cathedral, and most merchants in the market don't take credit cards. Going through the Back Door often means using hard local cash.

Resources for Money
FTC.gov/idtheft: Advice on bank-card theft and more
Oanda.com: Currency conversion tool
NerdWallet.com: Objective advice on debit- and credit-card options for overseas trips
Bankrate.com: Compares bank-card fees
www.ricksteves.com/travel-talks: Rick's travel skills talks, including one on money
Currency Converter, XE Currency apps: Real-time currency conversion
AroundMe app: Locates nearby ATMs and banks (and restaurants, pharmacies, etc.)

What to Bring

I pack the following and keep it all safe in my money belt.

Debit Card: Use this at cash machines (ATMs) to withdraw local cash, which you'll use to pay for most purchases.

Credit Card: Use this to pay for larger items (generally accepted at hotels, larger shops and restaurants, travel agencies, car-rental agencies, and so on). Although Europe's card readers use a chip-and-PIN system that differs from the one used in the US, it shouldn't cause much hassle (explained below, under "Will My Cards Work?").

Backup Card: Some travelers carry a third card (debit or credit; ideally from a different bank), in case one gets lost, demagnetized, eaten by a temperamental machine, or simply doesn't work.

Welcome to €uroland

The 21 countries labeled on this map use the euro, including 19 European Union countries along with Montenegro and Kosovo (not in the EU). Nine EU countries use their own currency.

Major EU holdouts are Denmark and Sweden; the United Kingdom, which also uses its own currency, is preparing to leave the EU (Norway and Switzerland also have their own currency, but aren't EU members).

Several EU members in Eastern Europe (Czech Republic, Poland, Hungary, Croatia, Romania, and Bulgaria) are committed to adopting the euro sometime in the future. For now, these countries still use their traditional currencies (see the sidebar on page 195).

EU countries that use the euro
EU countries that do not use the euro
Non-EU countries that use the euro

FINLAND
ESTONIA
LATVIA
LITHUANIA
IRELAND
NETHER-LANDS
GERMANY
BELGIUM
LUX.
FRANCE
SLOVAKIA
AUSTRIA
SLOVENIA
MONTENEGRO
ITALY
KOSOVO
PORTUGAL
SPAIN
GREECE
MALTA
CYPRUS

For information about using traveler's checks...see the 1995 edition of this book.

While debit cards can make decent backup credit cards (provided your card has a Visa or MasterCard logo), credit cards make rotten backup ATM cards because of their sky-high withdrawal fees and cash-advance interest rates. I'd only use a credit card at an ATM as a last resort. (Note that an extra credit card can be helpful if you rent a car and use your card to cover a collision damage waiver—see page 165).

US Dollars: I carry $100-200 as a backup. While you won't use it for day-to-day purchases, American cash in your money belt comes in handy for emergencies, such as when banks go on strike or your ATM card stops working. I've been in Greece and Ireland when every bank went on strike, shutting down without warning. But hard cash is hard cash. People always know roughly what a dollar is worth. (For details on exchanging money, see page 194.)

What NOT to Bring: Don't bother with traveler's checks. They're a waste of time (long lines at slow banks) and money (fees to get them, fees to cash them).

Also, resist the urge to buy foreign currency before your trip. Some tourists feel like they just have to have euros or British pounds in their pockets when they step off the airplane, but they pay the price in bad stateside exchange rates. Wait until you arrive to withdraw money. I've yet to see a European airport that didn't have plenty of ATMs.

BEFORE YOU GO

Before you travel, alert your bank as to when and where you're headed. Studious travelers will want to dig a little deeper to find out about fees and hidden charges. If fees are exorbitant, it may be worthwhile to apply for a new card.

Will My Cards Work?

The short answer is, yes. Debit cards from any major US bank will work in any standard European bank's ATM (ideally, use a debit card with a Visa or MasterCard logo). As for credit cards, Visa and MasterCard are universal, American Express is less common, and Discover is unknown in Europe.

Today's credit and debit cards are equipped with chips that authenticate and secure transactions (called EMV or chip cards). Chip cards in the US differ from those used overseas. In Europe, the cardholder inserts the card into the payment machine slot, then enters a PIN; the embedded chip authorizes the transaction (a signature is not necessary). In the US, instead of a PIN, you provide a signature to verify your identity.

Any American card, whether with a chip or an old-fashioned magnetic stripe, will work at Europe's hotels, restaurants, and shops—as long as there's a cashier. And while I've been inconvenienced a few times by self-service payment machines that wouldn't accept my card, it's never caused me any serious trouble. For more on using your US chip card in Europe—including tips on what to do if your card doesn't work—see page 190.

If you're concerned, ask if your bank offers a true chip-and-PIN card. Cards with low fees and chip-and-PIN technology include those from Andrews Federal Credit Union (www.andrewsfcu.org) and the State Department Federal Credit Union (www.sdfcu.org). Some banks may also offer true chip-and-PIN cards for travelers—ask.

Pretrip Checklist

Before you leave on your trip, you'll need to sort out a few details to ensure smooth use of your debit and credit cards.

Check your cards' expiration dates. If your card will expire during or soon after your trip, get a new one.

Report your travel dates. Let your bank(s) know that you'll be using your debit and credit cards in Europe. Banks will want to know the countries you're visiting and the dates you'll be gone. Though some banks may tell you this step is

Ask Your Bank

When you alert your bank to your travel plans, it's smart to also ask these questions:

- What fees do you charge for withdrawals or purchases made in Europe (percentage, flat fee, or both)?
- Are other currency conversion or foreign transaction fees tacked on?
- If my credit/debit card is lost or stolen, what is my liability?
- What phone number should I call in an emergency?

For Debit Cards:

- What is my daily limit for ATM withdrawals in Europe? (You may need to change it.)
- Do you have partner banks in Europe whose ATMs I can use without a fee?
- What transaction fees will I be charged for making a purchase with my debit card (as opposed to a cash withdrawal)?

For Credit Cards:

- What's my PIN? (Request one if you don't have one, as it may be required for purchases in Europe. Allow time for it to be mailed to you.)

unnecessary, it's best to alert them so they don't freeze your card if they detect unusual activity.

Know your PIN. Make sure you know the four-digit PIN for all of your cards, both debit and credit. Request it if you don't have one, as it may be required for purchases in Europe. It's important to contact your bank well before your trip to request a PIN (if your bank says the PIN is only for cash withdrawals, ask for it anyway); allow time to receive this information by mail. Memorize your PIN by number rather than by letter, since you may encounter a keypad with only digits.

Adjust your ATM withdrawal limit. Find out how much you can take out daily and ask for a higher daily withdrawal limit if you want to get more cash at once. If your bank charges a flat fee per transaction (explained below), you'll save money by withdrawing larger amounts. I prefer a higher limit that allows me to take out more cash at each ATM stop; some travelers prefer to set a lower limit as a security measure, in case their card is stolen.

Note that European ATMs will withdraw funds only from checking accounts. You are unlikely to be able to dip into your savings account or transfer funds between accounts from a European ATM, so make sure your checking account balance is healthy before you go.

Ask about fees. American travelers often discover they paid more for their trip than they thought they had, thanks to banks charging high fees for overseas transactions. For any purchase or withdrawal made with a card, you may be charged any or all of the following fees:

1) A currency conversion fee (usually 1-3 percent of the whole amount)

2) A Visa or MasterCard international transaction fee (1 percent; a few banks absorb this fee for you)

3) For debit cards, a flat $2-5 transaction fee each time you use a foreign ATM (note that some major US banks partner with European bank chains, allowing you to use those ATMs with no fees at all—ask)

While these fees are legal, they're basically a slimy way for banks to wring a few more dollars out of their customers. So before you travel, ask your bank how much you'll pay in fees for debit-card cash withdrawals and credit-card charges (for a list of questions to ask your bank, see page 189; to see how fees add up, read the sidebar on page 191).

If you're getting a bad deal, consider getting a new debit or credit card. Shop around. Some companies offer lower international fees than others—and some don't charge any at all. Reputable no-fee cards include those from Capital One, as well as Charles Schwab debit cards. Most credit unions and some airline loyalty cards have low-to-no international transaction fees. Bankrate.com has a good "Currency Conversion Costs" chart that compares major credit cards and their currency-conversion fees.

IN EUROPE

Once you're on the ground, you'll navigate the world of foreign currencies, unfamiliar ATMs, exchange desks, European chip card readers, and a cryptic thing called dynamic currency conversion.

Avid coin collectors have the joy of filling in coin books with the eight denominations of euro coins from 19 different countries (plus the tiny nations of Vatican City, Monaco, and San Marino). Europhiles can buy these books in Europe and chart their travels by gradually completing the collection.

Transaction Fees Add Up

If you're considering switching banks, or opening a special account for your travels, it pays to shop around for the best rates, both for debit-card ATM withdrawals and credit-card transactions. See NerdWallet.com and Bankrate.com for a helpful comparison of issuers' rates. Consider these examples and you'll see how fees can add up over the length of your trip.

$300 ATM withdrawal (with debit card)

	Bank A	Bank B	Bank C
International ATM fee*	$5 (flat)	$3 (1%)	$5 (flat)
Currency conversion fee	$6 (2%)	$1 (.33%)	$0 (0%)
Visa/MC international fee	$3 (1%)	$3 (1%)	$0 (0%)
Total fees	**$14**	**$7**	**$5**

$300 credit-card purchase

	Bank A	Bank B	Bank C
Currency conversion fee	$6 (2%)	$0 (0%)	$0 (0%)
Visa/MC international fee	$3 (1%)	$3 (1%)	$0 (0%)
Total fees	**$9**	**$3**	**$0**

Note that most banks charge a 1-3 percent (but no flat per-transaction fee) for debit-card purchases, as opposed to cash withdrawals.

Getting Cash

ATMs are the easiest and smartest way for travelers to get cash. You'll pay withdrawal fees, but you'll still get a better rate than you would exchanging dollars for local cash at a currency exchange booth (terrible rates). If you do need to exchange money, you'll find advice later in this section.

Finding Cash Machines

In most places, cash machines are easy to locate—ask for a *distributeur* in France, a "cashpoint" in the UK, and a *Bankomat* just about everywhere else. Small towns may have a limited number of or even no ATMs. Consider stocking up on cash before heading to a small-town or rural destination, to avoid getting into a bind.

How to use a European cash machine: Insert card, pull out cash.

When possible, withdraw cash from bank-run ATMs located just outside that bank. Ideally use them during the bank's opening hours; if your card is munched by the machine, you can go inside for help. Bank ATMs usually do not charge usage fees and are generally more secure, as a thief is less likely to target a cash machine near surveillance cameras (see "Card Security Tips," page 197). Many European banks place their ATMs in a small entry lobby, which protects users from snoopers and bad weather. To get in, look for a credit-card-size slot next to the door and insert your card.

Avoid "independent" ATMs, such as Travelex, Euronet, Moneybox, Cardpoint, and Cashzone. These have high fees and may try to trick users with "dynamic currency conversion" (see page 196). Note that these "independent" ATMs are often found next to bank ATMs in the hope that travelers will be too confused to notice the difference.

Withdrawing Cash

Cash machines are easy to use. They always have English-language instructions and work just like they do at home—except they spit out foreign cash instead of dollars, calculated at the day's standard bank-to-bank rate.

Debit Card Help

If your debit card doesn't work...
- Try a lower amount; your request may have exceeded your withdrawal limit, or the ATM's limit.
- Try a different ATM.
- Come back later. Your card's 24-hour withdrawal maximum is based on US time, or your bank's network may be temporarily down.

If all else fails, and you can't get your debit card to work at all...
- Use the emergency dollars stashed in your money belt.
- Use your credit card to get a cash advance (you'll need your credit-card PIN for the ATM, and you'll pay a sizeable cash-advance fee).
- Have a friend or relative wire you money via Western Union (see page 388).
- Contact the nearest American embassy/consulate; they can help arrange a wire transfer.

It's best to use a debit card that charges low fees for international ATM transactions (explained earlier). To further reduce fees, limit the number of withdrawals you make by taking out larger sums.

Remember that you're withdrawing cash in the local currency. If your daily limit is $300 in US dollars, you may be able to withdraw just €270 or so (depending on the exchange rate). Many frustrated travelers get an "insufficient funds" message and walk away from ATMs thinking their cards were rejected, when actually they were asking for more cash in euros than their daily limit allowed.

Be aware that ATMs themselves have withdrawal limits. If the ATM won't let you withdraw your daily maximum, try several smaller withdrawals to get the total amount you want. (Or, to avoid excessive per-transaction fees, try another cash machine—maximum withdrawals vary by bank and location.) Note that few ATM receipts list the exchange rate, and some machines don't dispense receipts at all.

Anatomy of a Euro Coin

The first euro coins and notes were introduced in 2002 and today are used in 19 countries, meaning more than 300 million Europeans have the same coins jangling in their pockets. It also means that the design of these coins has to make as much sense to the crêpe vendor in Paris as it does to the fisherman in Santorini. Despite the fact that each country issues its own money, euro coins have several standard features, and using them is remarkably easy (compare that to American coins—for instance, where on a dime does it say that it's worth 10 cents?).

Size and Look: There are eight euro coins. Each has its numeric value prominently displayed on one side. Generally, the bigger the coin, the greater the value. The bronze 1-, 2-, and 5-cent coins are the smallest of the bunch. The 10-, 20-, and 50-cent coins are gold. While the 10- and 50-cent coins are ridged (like a quarter), the 20-cent euro is distinguished by its "Spanish flower" shape. The two-toned €1 coin is mostly silver with a gold border, whereas the €2 coin—the largest of the bunch—is mostly gold with a silver border. There are no €1 or €2 bills, only coins. So that handful of change that you might toss in the tip jar at home can actually pay for your lunch in Europe.

The common, or "European," side of the euro coin shows its value and is identical throughout Europe.

Common, or "European" Side: Each coin denomination shares a universal design on one side, no matter which country it's issued in. The common side displays its value, an image of the European continent, the 12 stars of the EU flag, and the small initials "LL" for its Belgian designer, Luc Luycx.

National Side: Akin to the different state quarter designs, the reverse side of each euro coin varies from country to country. The only common requirements are the designer's initials, the year of issue, and an outer ring featuring the 12 stars of the EU. The national side can be the same for all eight denominations—Ireland's Celtic harp, a traditional symbol of that country, appears on all of its coins. Or each coin can have a unique national design. For example, each of Italy's eight coins pictures a national masterpiece, from Botticelli's *Birth of Venus* (10-cent coin) to the equestrian statue of Marcus Aurelius (50-cent coin) to Raphael's portrait of Dante Alighieri (€2 coin).

The reverse side of the euro coin shows traditional symbols of the issuing country. For instance, each coin from Italy features a famous building or piece of art.

In some countries (especially east of the eurozone), an ATM may give you high-denomination bills, which can be difficult to break. My strategy: Request an odd amount (such as 2,800 Czech *koruna* instead of 3,000), and/or head right inside a bank to exchange your withdrawal for smaller bills.

Exchanging Cash

In general, I avoid exchanging money in Europe; it's a big rip-off. On average, at a bank you lose about 8 percent when you change dollars to euros or another foreign currency. When you use an airport currency exchange booth such as Forex or Travelex, the hit can be as much as 15 percent.

But exchanging money can make sense in certain situations, including emergencies (if your card—or the only ATM in town—doesn't work), or when crossing into a country that uses a different currency. For instance, if you have a few Czech korunas in your pocket when you cross the border into Poland, an exchange booth can convert them into złotys.

If you do need to exchange money, look for places that don't charge a commission. Note the difference between the rates for buying (the bank buys foreign currency from you to exchange into local cash) and selling (the bank sells foreign currency to you). A good rule of thumb: The difference between the buy and sell rates should be less than 10 percent.

Transactions are based on the local currency. For example, if you exchange money in England on your way to France, the bank would "sell" you euros in exchange for your pounds. If you're returning to the US from Spain, the desk at the Madrid airport would "buy" your euros in exchange for dollars.

Note that banks in some countries don't exchange money for non-customers. In a pinch you can always find exchange desks at major train stations or airports—convenient but with crummy rates. You can also try a post office: In some countries, the post office runs its own bank, and usually has the best rates.

The small gap between the buying and selling rates suggests this Polish exchange bureau is a good deal.

Using Credit Cards

European cards use chip-and-PIN technology, while most cards issued in the US use a chip-and-signature system. Despite the differences, there's little to worry about: US credit cards (Visa and MasterCard) generally work fine.

Most European card readers can

Non-Euro Currencies

Country	Currency	Abbreviation
Bosnia and Herzegovina	Convertible Mark (Konvertibilna Marka)	KM/BAM
Bulgaria	Lev	Лв/BGN
Croatia	Kuna	kn/HRK
Czech Republic	Koruna	Kč/CZK
Denmark	Krone	Kr/DKK
Hungary	Forint	Ft/HUF
Iceland	Króna	kr/ISK
Norway	Krone	kr/NOK
Poland	Złoty	zł/PLN
Romania	Leu	lei/RON
Russia	Ruble	руб/RUB
Sweden	Krona	kr/SEK
Switzerland	Swiss Franc	SF/CHF
Turkey	Turkish Lira	₺/TL/TRY
United Kingdom	Pound Sterling	£/GBP

automatically generate a receipt for you to sign, just as you would at home. If a cashier is present, you should have no issues. Some payment machines will instead prompt you to enter your PIN, so it's important to know the code for each of your cards, including your credit card (see "Pretrip Checklist," earlier).

At self-service machines (transit-ticket kiosks, parking, etc.), results are mixed, as US chip-and-signature cards are not configured for some unattended transactions. Your US cards should work in many kiosks, including those in the London Underground and Amsterdam's Metro, but not in others, such as the Paris Métro (though it's always worth a try, as the situation is constantly changing).

Drivers Beware: Drivers in particular need to be aware of potential problems using a credit card to fill up at an unattended gas station, enter a parking garage, or exit a toll road. Be prepared to move on to the next gas station if necessary (don't let your tank get too low, especially if driving at night or on Sundays).

When Europeans buy something with their chip-and-PIN card, they insert the card in a machine like this one, then type in their PIN.

When approaching a toll plaza, err on the easier (if slower) side by using the "cash" lane.

What to Do if Your Credit Card Won't Work

If you don't know your credit-card PIN, try the following:

- Press the "Continue" button without entering any numbers; you may be able to skip the PIN step.
- Use your debit card, as most people have that PIN memorized.

If a payment machine won't accept your card—even with a PIN code—you'll have to find an alternative way to pay.

- Look for a cashier who can process your card manually. For this reason, it's a good idea to allow a little extra time at train stations and the like, as staffed service windows almost always have longer lines than ticket machines.
- Pay in cash. Since most payment machines take coins (and possibly small bills), it's smart to keep spare change handy (especially for highway toll booths, parking garages, luggage lockers, bike-rental kiosks, etc.).
- In a pinch, you could ask a local if you can pay them cash to run a transaction on their card.

If your card is rejected by a card reader manned by a cashier, you'll likely need to contact your bank—you may have forgotten to authorize the card for use overseas.

Dynamic Currency Conversion: Just Say No

Some European merchants and hoteliers—capitalizing on the fact that some Americans are intimidated by unusual currencies—cheerfully charge you for converting your purchase price into dollars. If it's offered, refuse this "service" (called dynamic currency conversion, or DCC). You'll pay extra for the expensive convenience of seeing your charge in dollars. The price is usually based on a lousy exchange rate set by the merchant—and even though you're paying in "dollars," your credit-card issuer may still levy its standard foreign-transaction fee.

DCC charges are common in Ireland, Spain, and Portugal, and also pop up in large department stores in cities such as London and Paris. If you're handed a receipt with two totals—one in the local currency and the other in US dollars—circle the amount in the local currency before you sign.

According to Visa and MasterCard, consumers have the right to decline DCC service: If your receipt shows the total in dollars only, ask that it be rung up again in the local currency. If the merchant refuses to run the charge again, pay in cash, or mark the receipt "local currency not offered" and warn the clerk that you will be disputing the charges with your bank.

Some ATM machines also offer DCC, often in purposefully confusing or misleading terms. If an ATM offers to "lock in" or "guarantee" your conversion rate, choose "proceed without conversion." Other prompts might state, "You can be charged in dollars: Press YES for dollars, NO for euros." Always choose the local currency.

Card Security Tips

While you're not at any more risk for bank fraud when on the road than at home, the hassle involved is greater. Here are some tips for protecting your debit and credit cards on the road.

At Cash Machines

Be vigilant, and look out for various ATM scams.

Safeguard your PIN code. Memorize your PIN; you'd be surprised how many people foolishly write it on their card. (If you don't trust your memory, you can keep a clue to your code in your money belt and/or your phone—just be sure that your reminder is utterly inscrutable to a thief.) "Shoulder surfing"—a thief watching you as you type your PIN into a keypad—is worth being aware of. When entering your PIN, block other people's view of the keypad by covering it with your free hand.

Inspect the ATM for card skimmers. Before inserting your card into a cash machine, inspect the front (especially if it's not inside a bank). If anything looks crooked, loose, or damaged—or if the entry to the card slot bulges out dramatically—it could be a sign of a card-skimming device (which captures your keystrokes as you enter your PIN).

Beware of stuck cards. Keep an eye out for anything in the card slot that could trap your card (or in the cash dispenser that could trap the cash). If your debit card gets stuck in an ATM, don't re-enter your PIN. Thieves have been known to insert a thin loop of tape cleverly designed to trap your card in the slot, then promptly arrive on the scene posing as a Good Samaritan. They'll either tell you that you can retrieve it by retyping your PIN, or point to a sign recommending that you enter your PIN twice if there's trouble. Either way, someone is nearby watching you enter your code. Once you give up on getting your card to eject and leave the scene, the criminals collect it and use it.

If your card or cash does get stuck, try to avoid leaving

the machine. If you're traveling with a partner, have one person go inside the bank while the other one stands by the machine—if your card or cash has indeed been trapped, the thieves won't wait long to retrieve it.

Don't trust "helpful" strangers. Honest strangers willing to lend a hand abound in Europe, as they do here at home—but when it comes to troubles with your bank card, politely decline any offers of help.

Also, pay attention to strangers loitering near a cash machine, especially if they're in pairs (most commonly, the first one distracts you; the second one grabs your cash). Remember that you're most vulnerable just after you have entered your PIN and the withdrawal amount. Be savvy about the many clever ruses used to distract ATM-goers. The scammer may pretend to sell you a newspaper, place a €5 bill at your feet and tell you that you dropped some money, or ask you for a charitable donation. Sometimes the scammers are children.

General Security

Here are a few other tips for protecting your cards.

Bring fewer cards and keep tabs on them. Take to Europe only the credit and debit cards that you expect to use, plus a backup, and keep them in your money belt. Upon returning home, verify the balance and charges on your debit and credit cards. Some travelers monitor balances as they travel (see page 300 for hints on doing so safely). For tips on money belts and foiling pickpockets, see page 376.

Don't use a debit card for purchases. Because a debit card pulls funds directly out of your bank account, potential charges incurred by a thief are scary—it's *your* money that's gone, and it will stay gone until the fraudulent use is investigated by your bank. For that reason, I limit my debit card use to cash-machine withdrawals. To make purchases, I pay with cash or a credit card.

Act quickly if your card is lost or stolen. Report it immediately by making a collect call to your credit-card company (see the sidebar on page 387 for details), as your liability can be linked to timely reporting. You'll likely be on the hook for only $50, but you should still act quickly.

Cash and Currency Tips

With the following tips, you'll make the most of every cent you spend.

Don't bother with prepaid cards. It's possible to buy prepaid "cash cards" before you leave, then use them like any other credit or debit card, but they come with high fees and aren't worth considering for most trips.

Use local cash. Many Americans are thrilled to find a store advertising "We accept dollars." But the happy sales clerk doesn't tell you that your purchase is costing about 20 percent more because of the store's terrible exchange rate. Without knowing it, you're changing money—at a lousy rate—every time you buy something with dollars.

Likewise, in some non-eurozone countries, the euro is commonly accepted, but usually a bad deal. For example, in Switzerland, which officially uses Swiss francs, some ATMs give euros, prices in touristy areas are listed in both curren-cies, and travelers can get by with euro cash. But if you pay in euros, you'll get a rotten exchange rate. Ideally, if you're in a non-euro country for more than a few hours, head to the ATM and use local currency instead.

Use your credit card to get cash only in emergencies. If you lose your debit card, you can use your credit card at an ATM to get a cash advance—but you need to know your PIN, and you'll pay a sizeable cash-advance fee.

Don't stress over currency conversions. Local cur-rencies are all logical. Each system is decimalized just like ours. There are a hundred "little ones" (cents, pence, groszy, stotinki) in every "big one" (euro, pound, złoty, lev). Only the names have been changed—to confuse the tourist. Examine the coins in your pocket soon after you arrive, and in two minutes you'll be comfortable with the nickels, dimes, and quarters of each new currency.

You don't need to constantly consult a currency converter. While you can do real-time conversion with an app, I've never bothered. You just need to know the rough exchange rates. I see no need to have it figured to the third decimal.

Very roughly determine what the unit of currency (euros, kroner, Swiss francs, or whatever) is worth in American dol-lars. For example, let's say the exchange rate is €1 = $1.10. If a strudel costs €5, then it costs five times $1.10, or $5.50. Ten euros is about $11, and €250 = $275 (figure 250 plus about one-tenth more). With the euro so close to the dollar right now, that difference might not be worth computing—but for, say, the British pound (worth roughly $1.30), it's more important to mentally adjust the numbers. Make a game out of quizzing yourself or your travel partner, and soon it'll be second nature. Survival on a budget is easier when you're comfortable with the local currency.

Assume you'll be shortchanged. In banks, restaurants,

at ticket booths, everywhere—expect to be shortchanged if you don't do your own figuring. Some people who spend their lives sitting in booths for eight hours a day taking money from strangers have no problem stealing from clueless tourists who don't know the local currency. For 10 minutes I observed a man in the Rome subway shortchanging half of the tourists who went through his turnstile. Half of his victims caught him and got their correct change with apologies. Overall, about 25 percent didn't notice and probably went home saying, "*Mamma mia*, Italy is really expensive."

Plan your cash withdrawals wisely. Avoid having a lot of unused currency left over when you cross borders between countries that use different currencies.

Coins become worthless when you leave a country. Since big-value coins are common in Europe, exporting a pocketful of change can be an expensive mistake. Spend them (on knickknacks or snacks), change them into bills, or give them away. Otherwise, you've just bought a bunch of round, flat souvenirs. Note, however, that while euro coins each have a national side (indicating where they were minted—see the sidebar on page 193), they are perfectly good in any country that uses the euro currency.

Consider getting back to dollars at the end of your trip. If you have foreign cash left at the end of your trip, and some time to spare, you can change it into dollars or simply spend it at the airport before you fly home. Although you might get a few more dollars from your hometown bank for that last smattering of foreign bills, to me it feels clean and convenient to simply fly home with nothing but dollars in my pocket.

TIPPING

Here's a tip: Don't stress over tipping.

While tips are appreciated no matter where you travel, tipping in Europe isn't as automatic and generous as it is in the US, and in many countries, tips aren't expected at all. The proper amount depends not only on the country you're in, but, just as in the US, on your resources, tipping philosophy, and the circumstances. Still, some general guidelines apply.

Restaurants: You don't need to tip if you order your food at a counter. At restaurants that have a wait staff, check the menu to see if service is included in the prices—in some countries, you don't need to tip extra; in others, it's common to round up 5-10 percent (since the service charge may go to the owner, not the wait staff). If a service charge is not included, you're generally safe in tipping about 10 percent after a good meal (for a rundown of restaurant tipping recommendations by country, see pages 270-271).

Taxis: For a typical ride, round up your fare a bit (for instance, if your fare is €4.70, pay €5; for more advice, see page 313).

Local Guides: Guides who give talks at public sights or on bus or boat tours sometimes hold out their hands for tips after they give their spiel. If I've already paid for the tour or admission to the sight, I don't tip extra (but if you want to tip, a euro or two is enough for a job well done).

If taking a group tour—for instance, a two-hour city walking tour—a tip of €2-5 per person is appropriate, depending on the size of the group (the higher tip is for small groups). For a couple of hours with a private guide, a tip of €10-20 for the group is fine (more if the guide goes above and beyond, such as booking advance tickets or arranging for a driver for you).

Other Services: At hotels with porters, give a euro for each bag they carry. It's nice (but optional) to leave a small tip in your room for the housekeeping staff when you depart. In general, if someone in the service industry does a super job for you, a small tip of a euro or two is appropriate...but not required.

When in doubt, ask. The French and British generally tip hairdressers, the Dutch and Swedish usually don't. If you're not sure whether (or how much) to tip for a service, ask a local for advice; they'll fill you in on how it's done on their turf.

Sleeping

After airfare, lodging is typically the expense that can take the biggest bite out of a vacation budget. Fortunately, I've found that, in many cases, the less you spend, the more you experience. The key is to seek out good information and consider your options thoroughly. When chosen properly, your lodging can connect you with Europe's culture and its people, making your overnight stays a beautiful part of the trip itself.

Europe offers a wide variety of accommodations: homey guesthouses, traditional old hotels, impersonal business-class chains, chic boutiques, and rustic farm stays—plus hostels, apartments and other short-term rentals, and a slew of other options.

Wherever possible, I opt for a family-run guesthouse—a pension or B&B that offers a good price to stay with welcoming locals in a characteristic old home. A close second is a small, friendly, independently owned hotel in a central location. But don't rule out other types of accommodations. While B&Bs and small hotels are a specialty in some destinations, they aren't as easy to find in other places, where a business-class or chain hotel may be the best option. For families, it can make sense to rent an apartment or a house. Budget travelers should consider hostels or room rentals.

My favorite European hotels are well-located, small, friendly, charming, and moderately priced.

Independent Traveler Seeks Good-Value Accommodations

People often ask me how I choose which accommodations to list in my guidebooks. There's no secret trick to it: I collect recommendations, do online searches, and then explore the neighborhoods of my choice in person. By the end of the day, the best-value options stand out.

I seek places that are centrally located and family run. I love the thrill of being immersed in local culture, with hosts who take pride in offering a good value. In Paris, I go for the two-star hotel on a pedestrian-only street in a vibrant neighborhood: There's a market outside in the morning, it's just seven blocks from the Eiffel Tower, and $150 for my double room. Europe is filled with these types of characteristic places to sleep. Although they may be small and lack comforts like fluffy robes and room service, they offer a warmth and intimacy that you won't find in larger establishments—and they won't break the bank.

After visiting and evaluating countless accommodations across Europe, it's still striking to me how little correlation there is between what you pay and what you get. I recently spent a day in Amsterdam, scaling the stairs and checking out the rooms of 20 different places, all offering double rooms. I found that you are just as likely to spend $150 for a big, impersonal hotel on a noisy highway as you are to spend the same or less for a charming, family-run guesthouse on a bikes-only stretch of canal.

The bottom line: If you do your homework, you can sleep in an authentically local hotel at a fair price.

There's certain to be a perfect home-away-from-home for you. In this chapter we'll first cover the basics of finding and reserving a room. Then we'll take a spin through the various types of lodging.

Value for Your Money

Expensive hotels can rip through a tight travel budget like a grenade through a dollhouse. I've overheard people complaining about that "$300 double in Frankfurt" or the "$400-a-night room in London." True, you can spend $400 for a double, but I never have. That's three days' accommodations budget for me.

As far as I'm concerned, spending more for your room often just builds a bigger wall between you and what you traveled so far to see. Consider the typical, amenity-laden, high-rise intercontinental hotel. The experience is the same everywhere you go—designed for people who, deep-down inside, wish they weren't traveling, people spending someone else's money, people who need a strip of paper over the toilet promising them no one's sat there yet. It's uniform sterility, a lobby full of stay-press Americans, English menus, and lamps bolted to tables. It may be spacious and comfortable, but you won't know where you are.

One of my joys as a guidebook writer is connecting my readers with the small-hotel owners I've come to know over the years. Even if you're willing to spend more, you'll have a far richer trip if you stay in places with a strong sense of local character. Europe's small guesthouses and midrange hotels may not have fancy bars and turn-down service, but their staffs are more interested in seeing pictures of your children and helping you have a great time than in thinning out your wallet. And that's something you can't put a price on.

FINDING AND RESERVING ROOMS

You could spend days sorting through information on Europe's lodging options. But with the right resources and focus, finding a room that fits your budget and needs should be fairly painless.

Resources

Most people use several resources to research their accommodation options.

Guidebook Listings: A trusted guidebook remains the best place to start your search for a great hotel. It offers a curated list of recommendations, organized by price and

---

Resources for Accommodations

TripAdvisor, Booking.com: Prices, availability, and traveler reviews

Expedia, Orbitz, Venere: Good sites for hotel research

Trivago, HotelsCombined, Kayak: Search engines for comparing rates at multiple hotel sites

Priceline, GetARoom: Booking sites with deep discounts for flexible travelers

EuroCheapo: Curated online listings of budget hotels

HotelTonight: Last-minute hotel deals in about 100 European cities

Hipmunk: Booking site with good mapping feature; shows Airbnb and HomeAway rentals as well as hotels

www.ricksteves.com/travel-talks: Rick's travel skills talks, including one on sleeping in Europe neighborhood, and selected with a certain quality standard. Most important, the opinions in a guidebook come from professionals who take their jobs seriously and know what they're talking about. Guidebook writers tramp in and out of a good share of a town's rooms to get a sense of what each has to offer and how they compare. Guidebook writers have been to—and likely stayed in—many of the places they recommend; the best guidebooks offer insights and tips that you can't find anywhere else.

Guidebook listings for B&Bs will lead you to friendly hosts eager to invite you into their homes.

Find and use at least one guidebook whose travel philosophy matches yours. (For a rundown of various guidebook series, see page 37.) Even if you don't go with one of the recommended listings, a guidebook can give you a good idea of reasonable rates and desirable neighborhoods.

User-Review and Booking Sites: TripAdvisor, Booking.com, and other aggregator websites are a good resource for those who know how to use them effectively. You can pore over loads of listings and consumer reviews; though these evaluations may not be objective, they can still be helpful. The reviews at Booking.com are generally more reliable than TripAdvisor, since it limits reviews to those who have actually stayed at a property (for the pros and cons of user-review sites, see page 41).

These sites are most useful for comparison shopping. To winnow down a seemingly endless list of options to a reasonable size, filter listings by price range, number of beds, location (say, in a certain neighborhood or close to the train station), must-have amenities, and so on. Plug in your travel dates to screen out any places that are already full (although be aware that even if a hotel appears booked on one of these sites, it may have a few rooms available for direct booking).

I avoid booking rooms through these big sites (they take a commission on each booking they make). Instead, I use them to narrow down my options, but then contact the place where I want to stay to reserve. By booking direct, you'll establish a relationship with your host, get more complete information, and you may save money.

Hotel and Guesthouse Websites: A hotel or guesthouse's own website is an essential last stop on your quest. Here you'll find additional details, photos of rooms, exact prices, special offers, and contact information. Use the hotel's booking form or send an email to inquire about a room (see "Reserving Rooms," later).

Hotel Star Ratings: Europe's hotel-rating system varies quite a bit from country to country. In general, you can make these basic assumptions: In a well-chosen one-star place, budget travelers can usually sleep well and safely in simple no-frills rooms. Two-star hotels generally offer a balance of price and comfort—still basic but with good beds, an attached bathroom, and often small but appreciated elevators. Three-star hotels can be a decent value, but you'll pay for extras like a lounge and room service. Four- and five-star places bring luxury that I generally find not worth the price.

Rates and Deals

Room prices can fluctuate significantly with demand and amenities. At guesthouses and smaller hotels, rates generally change depending upon the season. So a standard double at a Santorini guesthouse may be €150 in peak season, €130 in shoulder season, and €70 in the off-season. At popular weekend getaways, rates may be higher for Friday and Saturday night stays. Other factors that affect prices are room size and class (i.e., standard versus superior double), special features (view, balcony, bathtub, etc.), and length of stay (possibly cheaper if you stay longer). Taxes, which can vary from place to place, are generally insignificant (a dollar or two per person, per night).

Room rates are especially volatile at larger hotels and chains that use dynamic pricing to respond to demand: If reservations are thin, rates drop, but if rooms are filling fast, prices rise. Rates can skyrocket during festivals and conventions, while business hotels can have deep discounts on weekends when demand plummets.

Family-run hotels offer the warmest welcome and the best value.

As a result, it's difficult to say which hotel will be the better value on a given day—until you do your homework. Once your dates are set, confirm the specific price at several hotels. You can do this by comparing prices online on the hotel websites, or by emailing several hotels directly and asking for their best rate. Even if you start your search at TripAdvisor or Booking.com, you'll usually find the lowest rates through a hotel's own website.

Additionally, many hotels offer

a discount if you pay cash, pay in advance, stay longer than three nights, or mention your Rick Steves guidebook. To cut costs further, try asking for a cheaper room (for example, with a shared bathroom or no window) or offer to skip breakfast. For more ideas on how to save money on accommodations, see "Booking Tips for the Budget-Minded," later.

1977: It slowly dawns on Rick that cheap beds aren't always good beds.

When establishing prices, confirm if the charge is per person or per room (if a price is too good to be true, it's probably per person).

Comparing Your Options

The place you temporarily call home can color your travel experience. Landing in the right room in the right neighborhood merits a little research.

Consider your priorities; this is especially important if you're traveling with others. For many, price is the primary concern. For others (including me), location is the most important factor; character also counts. I'm more impressed by a convenient locale—near the sights and public transportation—and a fun-loving philosophy than flat-screen TVs and a fancy gym.

When evaluating rooms, I look for places that are clean, centrally located, relatively quiet at night, reasonably priced, friendly, small enough to have a hands-on owner and stable staff, and run with a respect for local traditions. I can tolerate dingy wallpaper, stairs, and a bathroom down the hall, but I won't compromise when it comes to safety and being able to get a decent night's sleep. Most places I recommend in my guidebooks fall short of perfection. But if I can find a place with most of these features, it's a keeper. And, if I save a few dollars on a room, that's money better spent on a good meal or a local tour.

As you select accommodations, consider these factors:

Location: I love being steps away from the action—not only to feel at home in an atmospheric neighborhood, but to avoid wasting time getting to and from major sightseeing and good restaurants. In bigger cities, being near a transit stop is almost as good as being in the middle of town.

Room Needs: If **air-conditioning** is important, make sure the hotel has it. Air-conditioning is not as ubiquitous in

Europe as in the US. It's common to find hotels in northern Europe that lack air-conditioning, and even some places in southern Europe don't have it. I don't sweat this when booking rooms north of the Alps—I'm OK with the risk of suffering through an uncomfortably hot day now and then. But for a summer visit in southern Europe, air-con's a must.

Likewise, **elevators** are not a given in European accommodations. I prefer a place in the center without an elevator over one a long walk away with an elevator. But an elevator—or at least minimal stairs—can be a welcome feature for those with mobility challenges.

Some rooms come with **kitchenette** facilities, which can help save on food costs. Even with just a minifridge, you'll be able to stock snacks or breakfast items and save money on eating out.

If you're planning a relaxing vacation to a Greek island or the French Riviera, consider whether it's worth seeking out and paying for **other amenities,** such as extra space, a view, or a balcony. If you're a go-go sightseer staying for a night or two, you're unlikely to be in the room long enough to make such features worth a splurge: Any affordable, reasonably appealing room with a convenient location will do the trick. Remember, all hotels look the same when you're asleep.

Extras: When comparing prices, pay attention to whether **breakfast** is included in the rate. If it's extra, this per-person charge can add up, particularly for families. While hotels hope you'll buy their breakfast, it's optional unless otherwise noted.

Consider any other costs that aren't included in the basic room rate. For example, if you'll be traveling by car, ask about **parking.** If two nearly identical, neighboring hotels have similar room rates—but one charges $20 a night to park while the other has a spot for free, you know where you're staying.

Cancellation Policy: Take this into account, especially if there's anything uncertain about your itinerary. If all other things are equal, opt for the place with the most forgiving fine print.

Reserving Rooms

Booking a place to stay in Europe is not too different from booking a place in the US. But there are a few things to be aware of.

When to Book

I used to travel with absolutely no reservations. Europe at

that time was relatively ramshackle, things were cheaper, and fewer people could afford to travel for fun, so there was less competition for budget rooms. I could make itinerary decisions on the go, show up in a new town, browse a handful of lodging choices, and take my pick of affordable, perfectly acceptable rooms.

European innkeepers at small hotels offer friendly advice.

These days Europe's best-value rooms are generally found by booking ahead. If flexibility isn't a concern, book your rooms as soon as your itinerary is set. When I want to be certain to get my first choice, I reserve weeks or even months in advance (lately I've been getting aced out by my own readers at my favorite accommodations).

It's especially important to make reservations as early as possible for stays that fall on national holidays and during big festivals (for a rundown, see www.ricksteves.com/festivals). I also book far in advance for stays during peak season and in big, popular cities, such as London, Paris, Madrid, or Venice.

Book Direct

My best tip for booking rooms: Skip the middleman. While third-party sites and room-booking services may seem convenient, booking directly with a hotel or guesthouse can often save you money and puts you in direct contact with your host.

Booking sites and most local room-booking services

Sample Room Request

From:	rick@ricksteves.com
Sent:	Today
To:	info@hotelcentral.com
Subject:	Reservation request for 19-22 July

Dear Hotel Central,
I would like to stay at your hotel. Please let me know if you have a room available and the price for:
• 2 people
• Double bed and en suite bathroom in a quiet room
• Arriving 19 July, departing 22 July (3 nights)

Thank you!
Rick Steves

extract a commission—up to a whopping 20 percent—from the hotel. Personally, I prefer that my hardworking hosts pocket all of my money. Logically, booking through a third-party service closes the door on any special deal you might negotiate if you book directly with the hotel. In addition, plenty of hotels, especially big chains, offer special rates only to guests who book direct.

Booking directly also increases the chances that the hotelier will be able to accommodate any special needs or requests, especially if they involve shifting or canceling your reservation. Going through a middleman makes it more difficult for the hotel to adjust your booking.

If you find a special or promotional discount on a booking site that's lower than the hotel's price, it's worth asking the hotel to match it. If at first you don't succeed, try (politely) asking for the owner or manager. If a hotel can't match the price, go ahead and reserve through the booking site—but first be aware of any restrictions, such as a tighter cancellation policy.

Requesting a Reservation

It's usually easiest to book your room through the guest-house or hotel's website. If the website doesn't have a built-in reservation form—or if you have a complicated request—send a short email. Most hotels on the Continent are accustomed to guests who speak only English, but it helps to keep your email short and simple. Skip the pleasantries and stick to the facts the hotelier wants to know:

- type of room(s) you need and size of your party
- number of nights you'll stay
- arrival and departure dates, written European style as day/month/year
- special requests (see below)
- applicable discounts (such as a Rick Steves reader discount, cash discount, or promotional rate)

When making reservations, communicate your needs clearly to your hotelier.

Special Requests: When you request a reservation, let the hotel know about any special requests or preferences. These can include room features (air-conditioning, balcony, quiet, view, ground floor, fewer stairs, wheelchair accessibility, and so on), bathroom style (for a private bathroom connected to your room, use the European term "en

Types of Rooms

When requesting rooms, be specific about your needs. If you're particularly tall, let them know: They'll try to avoid putting you in the attic or the short bed with a footboard.

Double Rooms: These can have either a double bed or two twins. Double-bedded rooms are usually cheaper; twin-bedded rooms tend to be larger. If you request a "double," the hotelier may assume you'll only take a double bed. To keep your options open, ask for "a room for two people." If you do want a double bed, it can help to specify "one big bed for two people." Most hoteliers understand "double bed" in English, but here's some local lingo: *französische Bett* (German), *un grand lit* (French), *matrimoniale* (Italian), and *matrimonial* (Spanish).

Single Rooms: If you're traveling on your own, it's worth seeking out a true single room, as these are generally a better deal than paying the single-occupancy rate for a double room. True singles are much smaller and sometimes more basic than a hotel's doubles, and usually lack a view.

True single rooms can offer the perfect fit—and price—for a solo traveler.

Triples and Quads: A triple comes with a double or queen-size bed plus a sliver-sized single; sometimes it has three singles. Quad rooms usually have two double beds.

Family Rooms: A three- or four-bed family room is much cheaper than two smaller rooms. Generally, kids sleep for free or a small fee, and teenagers are charged as adults. If you need a small extra bed or a crib, let the hotelier know. Always be upfront about the size of your entourage: Hotels cannot legally allow more people to sleep in the room than what's shown on their official price list.

A triple room works well for small families.

suite"), and bed types (twin beds vs. double bed). If you wait to mention these requests until you arrive, the hotelier may not be able to accommodate you.

Nonsmoking Rooms: Nearly all of Europe's hotels are completely non-smoking. In a few countries (such as Germany, Spain, Ireland, and Britain), some hotels still have a floor or two of designated rooms where guests are allowed to smoke, though lobbies, halls, and breakfast rooms are required to be smoke-free. It's been years since I noticed smokiness in a hotel room. But if you don't want a room that may have been occupied by a smoker, let the hotelier know when you make your reservation.

Confirming a Reservation

Once a guesthouse or hotel replies to your emailed room request citing availability and rates, you must write back to say you want the room.

Most places request a credit-card number to hold your room. If the hotel's website doesn't have a secure form where you can enter the number directly, it's best to share that confidential info via a phone call. Email is far less secure—I mitigate the risk by sending the info in two emails (splitting my number between them).

This is also a good time to read the fine print of the hotel's cancellation policy, especially if your itinerary is at all iffy.

A deposit generally isn't required at smaller guesthouses, especially those that don't take credit cards—but every now and then I come across ones that ask guests to put money down to hold a room (usually possible via PayPal).

Once you receive a final confirmation, keep the email: It can come in handy on the off chance the hotel loses track of your reservation (or the details of your room request). Some travelers like to bring along a printed copy of each confirmation.

Reconfirming While You Travel

Always email or call to reconfirm your room reservation a few days in advance. This gives you time to improvise in the unlikely event that something has gone wrong with your reservation. For B&Bs or small hotels, I also call on my day of arrival to tell my host what time I expect to get there (especially important if you expect to arrive late—after 5 p.m.). If you end up running behind on your arrival day, it's helpful to follow-up to assure the front-desk staff that you're coming.

Cancellations

If you must cancel your reservation, it's good karma—and smart—to do so with as much notice as possible, especially for smaller family-run places. Request confirmation of your cancellation in case you are accidentally billed.

Be warned that cancellation policies can be strict—if you cancel on short notice, you could lose your deposit or be billed for one night...or even your entire stay. Many discount deals come with a substantial financial risk: They require prepayment, with no refunds for cancellations.

Booking Tips for the Budget-Minded

If your accommodation costs are adding up, there are ways to scale back. These tricks work for me.

Don't consume above your needs. A three-star hotel is not necessarily a bad value, but if I stay in a three-star hotel, I've spent $50 extra for things I probably don't need. Amenities such as air-conditioning, elevators, room service, a 24-hour reception desk, and staff in uniforms each add about $10 to your per-night rate.

Stick with smaller places. Larger hotels are often pricier than small hotels and guesthouses, partly because of taxes (for example, in Britain, once a B&B exceeds a certain revenue level, it's required to pay an extra 20 percent tax). Hoteliers who pay high taxes pass their costs on to you.

Hotels that cater to the expense-account crowd can be especially bad values. For example, while small hotels generally offer free Wi-Fi, expensive business-class places tend to charge heartily for it. One exception: In many northern European capitals, you can sometimes land a deeply discounted room in an upscale business-class hotel if you're there when the corporate crowd is not (summer and weekends year-round).

Ask for the best price and cheapest room. Room prices can vary within a hotel according to facilities provided. If you're looking for the cheapest possible room, scour the hotel's website for pricing details. You may find that a room with a shower costs less than one with a bathtub, or a double bed is cheaper than twins. If you would be happy with either, let the hotelier know when you book.

Don't dismiss bathrooms down the hall. While demand has (sadly) pushed many hoteliers to cram a tiny bathroom into the corner of every room, some older places— especially guesthouses—may have one or two rooms that lack an en suite bathroom. Instead, the room has a "private bathroom," which means that it's not attached, but it's for your use only. If you'd happily cross the hall for a shower or toilet to save about $20 a night, say so when you book (many hoteliers will say they're full rather than offer this type of room to Americans, because they assume we'll find it unacceptable).

Try to wrangle a discount. Prices can soften if you stay three nights or longer (fewer bedding changes), pay in cash (saves the hotelier credit-card fees), pay in full in advance (be careful, though, as these deals are almost always nonrefundable), or visit in low season (when prices are discounted anyway). It doesn't hurt to ask. Outside of high season (July and August in much of Europe, though this can vary by region), try haggling: If the place is too expensive, tell them your limit; they might meet it.

Skip the hotel's breakfast. Check to see if room rates include breakfast; if so, ask what you'd save by skipping it. Especially in northern Europe, hotel breakfasts can be a great value and a fun chance to sample some regional treats (see page 254). But in countries where the hotel breakfast is skimpy—or if you're not a big breakfast person—ask for the rate without breakfast when you book. You can buy a thriftier breakfast at the supermarket or corner bakery.

If you're a small group, put more people in a room. Many doubles come with a small double bed and a tiny single, so a third person pays very little (usually about $30 extra). If there's room for a cot, they'll cram it in for you. Family suites are common; the ones with two private bedrooms are a fine option for two couples who don't mind sharing a bathroom, as it's much cheaper than paying for two separate doubles.

Avoid room-and-board deals. Some hotels offer room rates that include dinner in their dining room (called "half-board" or "half-pension"); a few places (often resorts) even require it, especially in peak season. While it might not be that expensive, it does limits when and where you eat. I prefer the freedom to explore and sample local restaurants or shop for picnics. On the other hand, if half-pension is required, but the charge is less per meal than you'd pay for an average restaurant meal, it can be worth considering— especially if the chef is good or if you're in a village with no convenient alternatives.

Check out discount-hunting search engines. Sites such as HotelsCombined and Trivago compile prices from travel agencies, consolidators, and hotel websites, while EuroCheapo specializes in budget hotels. (If you find a deal you like, still go to the hotel's website to book it.) If your travel dates are flexible, consider the deep discounts available on sites such as Priceline and GetaRoom. It's also worth checking out the cost of "air plus hotel" packages available on Kayak, Expedia, and similar sites. Just keep in mind that what you save in dollars you'll likely lose in customer service.

Finding Rooms on the Fly

Thinking back on my vagabonding days reminds me of the fun of tossing the schedule and living in the moment. There's nothing more liberating than stepping onto a platform, realizing the train on track 6 is going to Hamburg and the train on track 7 is Copenhagen-bound...and you're free to go where the spirit moves you. Or to be tired of the rain in Munich, hop on a train, and a couple of hours later be on the other side of the Alps in hot and sunny Italy.

LEFT In smaller towns, guesthouse owners meet travelers arriving by train or bus.

RIGHT Ask today's hotel to call tomorrow's hotel to make a reservation for you in the native language.

To leave room for this kind of spontaneity, book your lodging as you go. This works best when there's relatively little demand for rooms (outside high season, or in less-crowded destinations).

To ease your entry into Europe, I advise booking in advance for the first few nights, as finding a room when jet-lagged can be stressful. After that, you can book your next hotel once you know where you're going and when you'll arrive. Nail down a place in the morning so you know where you'll sleep that night; you'll spend your day sightseeing and traveling relaxed, knowing a room is waiting for you. (One tactic that can work well for longer stays: Book just the first night or two before arriving, then use some of your first day to explore lodging options for the rest of your visit.)

Besides the usual channels for finding a room, some booking sites—such as HotelTonight—specialize in last-minute rooms. You can also ask your current hosts to recommend accommodations at your next destination. They may even be willing to call around to see what's available. A good time to contact the next hotel is around 9 or 10 a.m., when the receptionist knows who'll be checking out and which rooms will be available.

If you show up in a new town with no reservations, your approach to room-finding will be determined by whether it's a buyer's or seller's market. These trends can be obvious (a beach resort will be crowded in summer, empty in winter).

Sometimes you can arrive late, be selective, and even talk down the price. Other times you'll happily accept anything with a pillow and a blanket.

I'll never forget struggling off the plane on my arrival on a Greek island. Fifteen women were begging me to spend the night. Thrilled, I made a snap decision and followed the most attractive offer to a very nice budget accommodation.

If you do find yourself in a new place without a reservation, keep the following advice in mind.

Shop around. It's worth 20 minutes of poking your head into a few different hotels to see which of your options feels like the best value. Never judge a hotel by its exterior or lobby: Lavish interiors with shabby exteriors are a cultural trait of Europe.

Consider hotel runners. As you step off the train (or bus, or ferry), you may be met by guesthouse runners wielding pictures of their rooms for rent. If you like the look of what they're promising, agree to see the room—you're under no obligation to take it. But establish the location very clearly (some otherwise-good options can be miserably far from the center).

View a room before accepting it. Think about heat, noise, and general comfort level. If you don't like what you see, ask to see another room. Or point out any negative attributes—the price may come down. If the room's no good, just leave.

Use room-finding services as a last resort. Popular tourist cities usually have a room-finding service at the train station or tourist information office. For a small fee, they can probably get you a room in the price range and neighborhood of your choice. These services normally make no judgments about hotel quality or value, so what you get is potluck. They'll recommend places that have paid for the service, but fail to mention cheaper options.

Ask hoteliers to help. Nobody knows the hotel scene better than hotel managers do. If one place doesn't have a vacant room, ask for tips on where else to look. They're usually happy to phone a friend's place for you. The priciest hotels have English-speaking staff willing to help out the polite traveler in search of a cheap room.

Follow taxi tips. One way to find a place in a tough situation is to let a cabbie take you to his favorite hotel.

If all else fails, leave the trouble zone. If you simply cannot find a vacancy, head away from the trouble zone. An hour by car, train, or bus from the most miserable hotel situation anywhere in Europe is a town—Dullsdorf or Nothingston—with the Dullsdorf Gasthaus or the

Nothingston Inn just across the street from the station or right off the main square. It's not full—never has been, never will be. There's a guy sleeping behind the reception desk. Drop in at 11 p.m., ask for a bed, and he'll say, "Head to the third floor—the keys are in the doors." The rooms are dingy, and probably not a great value...but you've got a bed. It always works. Oktoberfest, Cannes Film Festival, St-Tropez Running of the Girls, Easter at Lourdes—your bed awaits in nearby Dullsdorf.

GUESTHOUSES AND HOTELS

"Guesthouse" is a catch-all term for the small, warm, family-run accommodations that thrive across Europe—from prim British B&Bs, to cozy German pensions, to a set of keys and a basic bed in the spare room of a Croatian grandma's house. They have different names from country to country, but all give you the privacy of a hotel and the comforts of home—at a price you can afford.

While a guesthouse is my go-to when I'm looking for a place to stay, a small hotel is a close runner-up (usually family-run but much like a guesthouse). Both are described in this section.

Guesthouses

Guesthouses offer double the cultural intimacy for less money than most hotel rooms of comparable comfort. While you may lose some of the conveniences hotels offer—such as lounges, in-room phones, daily towel changes, and credit-card payments—I happily make the trade-off. For instance, I love it when Kathleen in western Ireland runs out after me because she's noticed I've left for the day without an umbrella, hands me hers...and reminds me to be back by 8 o'clock that night, when her brother's playing folk music in the pub around the corner. It's a bit like having your own temporary mother while you travel.

You'll find guesthouses in every European country, though they're more popular in certain regions. In general, you're more likely to find guesthouses in the countryside and smaller towns. They're an especially smart choice in regions where budget hotels are hard to come by. In Scandinavia, for example, guesthouse rooms are often good quality and surprisingly cheap compared to nearby hotels. And in Croatia—where mass tourism and overpriced resort hotels reign—rooms in private homes provide a safe, comfortable place for value-minded independent travelers.

Guesthouses don't work for every type of traveler. For instance, some places don't allow kids, or require them to be over a certain age (often around 8-12). If mobility is a challenge, you're probably better off at a hotel with an elevator, as guesthouses commonly have rooms tucked away in attics or perched at the top of

Staying at a guesthouse can come with a good workout.

several flights of stairs (inquire about a ground-floor room before ruling a place out). En suite bathrooms aren't a given, nor are the usual hotel trappings (such as air-conditioning, TV, or a staff that's reliably fluent in English). Many guest-house owners are also pet owners. If you're allergic, ask about resident pets when you reserve. Absentee management—where the proprietors live off-site (or even in another town)—is becoming more common.

It's not uncommon for guesthouses to require a two-night stay, especially in popular vacation areas and in private homes. Some guesthouses give a discount for longer stays, while others levy a surcharge for single-night stays. In popular weekend-getaway spots, you may have a hard time finding a guesthouse willing to take you for Saturday night only.

Finding and booking a guesthouse is no different than reserving a hotel. Even most smaller places are listed on hotel-booking sites—but a direct booking is especially appreciated at mom-and-pop places, and will likely net you a better price.

B&Bs

Bed-and-breakfasts are my favorite way to sleep cheap—or at least reasonably affordably—in Britain and Ireland. (True B&Bs are somewhat rare on the Continent, though there are some in the Low Countries, Scandinavia, and elsewhere.) Across the British Isles, small towns and villages are littered with charming, older B&Bs with three to eight lovingly tended guest rooms. Don't confuse these with their frilly, fancy cousins in America. In a European B&B, rather than seven pillows and a basket of jams, you get a warm welcome and a good price.

Never judge a B&B by its name.

Guesthouse Etiquette

Pensions, B&Bs, and other guesthouse-style accommodations come with their own etiquette and quirks. Keep the following in mind.

Let your host know if you're coming or going at odd times. Owners' daily schedules can be built around the whim of their guests. If you're getting up early, so are they; if you check in late, they must wait up for you. Be considerate.

Be careful around the house. Treat these lovingly-maintained homes as you would a friend's house. Be gentle when maneuvering your bag up narrow staircases with fragile walls and banisters. Use the suitcase rack rather than setting your bag on the bedspread. A charming, inexpensive room only stays that way through the care of its owner, who counts on having thoughtful guests like you. (It's one of the reasons so many guesthouses offer discounts for my readers— you're well known as some of the best guests in the biz.)

Be eco-conscious. Because many regions depend on expensive imported fuel, you'll endear yourself to your hosts if you turn off lights and air-conditioning when you leave and avoid excessively long showers.

Keep the noise level down. Guesthouses tend to come with thin walls and creaky floorboards that can make for a noisy night. If you're a light sleeper, bring earplugs. And please be quiet in the halls and in your rooms at night (talk softly, and keep the TV volume low)...those of us getting up early will thank you for it.

Join in—if you want. The "part of the family" element of a guesthouse stay is usually your choice. Chatty friendliness is not forced on guests. Depending on my mood and workload, I often keep to myself during my stays—hosts are hardly offended. But when I have the time and opportunity, I join the children in the barn for the sheep-shearing fun or grandma at the TV for tea and cookies.

B&Bs are typically run by a charming couple or family who call their guesthouse home. Hosts tend to be gregarious and genuinely invested in your visit (it's hard work—those who don't love meeting their guests don't tend to stick with it).

B&B travelers scramble at the breakfast table.

Some places have a common room that you're free to use for reading or hanging out. Free Wi-Fi and a well-stocked tea table are standard in your room. Your hosts may offer to make you a simple dinner for a good price, and if you have time to chat, you might get in on an evening social hour.

Of course, breakfast comes with the bed (something to remember when comparing prices against hotels)—and in the British Isles, this is no ordinary breakfast (for details, see page 621). Because your host is often also the cook, breakfast hours are usually relatively short: It's bad form to show up at the very end of the breakfast period and expect the whole shebang.

While you are finishing your tea, your host may present you with her guest book, inviting you to make an entry and pointing out others from your home state who have stayed in her house. When you bid your hosts farewell in the morning and thank them for the good sleep and full stomach, it can be difficult to get away: Determined to fill you with as much information as food, your hosts want you to have the best day of sightseeing possible.

LEFT A special bonus when enjoying Britain's great B&Bs: You get your own temporary mother.

RIGHT In most British towns, B&Bs line up along the same street–find one, and you've found a dozen.

Pensions

Continental Europe's equivalent to the B&B is the pension. Typically located in charming older buildings, with 10 or fewer rooms, most pensions are relatively inexpensive, cozy, and friendly. Most hosts—though generally not as chatty as B&B owners in Ireland and Britain—have at least some basic English skills. Rooms are reasonably simple, but usually well cared for.

In many countries the name for this kind of guesthouse is a variant of the French word *pension*. They may also go

Family-run pensions provide a welcoming place to call home.

by local names, such as *Gasthaus* and *Gasthof* in German; *albergo* and *locanda* in Italian; or *fonda, casas de huespedes,* and *hostal* in Spanish (not to be confused with "hostel"—two very different things).

Breakfast isn't always included (even at places that have appended "B&B" to their name in hopes of attracting English-speaking guests). When it is offered, a pension's breakfast rarely approaches the magnificence of the full British or Irish version. Quality and quantity depend mostly on what's considered standard in each country. For instance, a cheap place in Austria will likely serve up a heartier spread than a fancier pension in Sicily (for more on what to expect for breakfast in various countries, see page 254).

The lines separating a charming small hotel from a larger pension are pretty blurry—but on the whole hotels are more formal, more regulated, and more expensive. Legally, Italy's *albergo, locanda,* and *pensione* all technically belong to a nationwide hotel-rating system—but places boasting these traditional names tend to be synonymous with family-run enterprises offering simple, budget beds.

Rooms in Private Homes

The cheapest guesthouse is a (mostly) private residence that runs a business regularly renting out a room or two to travelers. For about $20-40 per person you get your own room, a bathroom down the hall, and an even more intimate peek into small-town Europe (like other guesthouses, these kinds of rooms are most common outside big cities).

Staying in one of these places is not too different from being in a small pension. You'll likely have your own entrance, with a clear separation between your space and the owner's residence. One-night stays are discouraged in the smallest operations (in Croatia, for example, most charge extra for guests staying less than three nights).

Rooms like this are often listed on Airbnb and similar sites, and at the tourist information office. If you're scouting for a place, keep your eye out for posted signs with the local word for "rooms": *Zimmer* in Germany and Austria, but also commonly used across eastern Europe, *chambres (d'hôte)* in France (often abbreviated "CH"), *(affitta) camere* in Italy, *sobe* in Croatia and Slovenia, *pokoje* in

Rooms in private homes, like this cozy *sobe* in Croatia, offer affordable accommodation.

Poland, *dhomatia* in Greece, *(hus) rum* in Sweden, *rom* in Norway, *værelser* in Denmark, and *quartos* in Portugal. In Spain, look for *camas* (beds), *habitación*, or *casa particular.*

In more remote but touristy locales, hardworking entrepreneurial hosts await the arrival of trains and buses at any hour, eager to whisk backpackers away to see their rooms. Along the Croatian coast, *soba* skimmers meet every arriving ferry. If you don't see any promising prospects on arrival, ask around town. Italy's small-town bars are plugged into the *affittacamere* grapevine. In Greek villages with no hotels, ask for *dhomatia* at the town *taverna*.

Expect some personal attention from your host (but no more than you'd like), simple, stripped-down rooms, and little or nothing in the way of public spaces. Your bathroom may be across the hall, but at most you'll share it with just one other set of guests. You probably won't have a TV or air-conditioning, and breakfast may or may not be included. In southwestern Europe (France, Italy, Spain, and Portugal), hosts may not speak more than a handful of English words, but they're almost always enthusiastic and welcoming.

Rural Guesthouses

A stay in the European countryside is an unforgettable experience—ideal for travelers more interested in being on vacation than being caught up in a sightseeing whirlwind.

Rural guesthouses tend to clump in areas famous for their pastoral charm. For instance, Italy's *agriturismi* (farmhouse accommodations) are especially abundant in Tuscany and Umbria (technically a true *agriturismo* must generate more money from its farm activities than from tourism—insuring that the land is worked and preserved.) You'll find *quintas* (countryside inns) in Portugal's Douro

Valley region, haciendas (country estates) in Spain's Andalucía, *agroturizams* (farm stays) in Croatia's Istrian peninsula, and *turistične kmetije* (family-run farms) in the Slovenian countryside. In Britain, farmhouse B&Bs in the Lake District and other bucolic settings get you close to the land (and sheep).

Rural accommodations are generally family-run and often rent by the week. They can span the amenity scale: Some properties are simple and rustic, while others offer luxuries such as swimming pools and riding stables (but don't expect daily maid service). Most have clean and comfortable rooms for rent, often with a kitchen, a living room, and a bathroom or two. Some travelers with romantic dreams of *agriturismi* are turned off when they arrive to actual farm smells and sounds. These folks would be happier at a countryside B&B or villa that offers more upscale comfort. Another option is to rent out an entire farmhouse or cottage (described later, under "Short-Term Rentals"). You'll likely need a car to fully enjoy—or even reach—a rural guesthouse.

At some places, a half-pension rate—including a home-cooked lunch or dinner—may be an option (or built into the price, whether you want it or not). Most places serve tasty homegrown food, often organic; and many are gourmet.

To stay in the countryside, try a website that specializes in rural accommodations (see the "Resources for Rural Guesthouses" sidebar), or do an online search for the country-specific terms mentioned earlier. You can also try

> ### Resources for Rural Guesthouses
>
> **AgriturismoItaly.it:** Farm stays in Italy
> **Gite.com, Gites-de-France.com:** Countryside rental homes in France
> **EcoTurismoRural.com, MiCasaRural.co.uk:** Rural rentals in Spain and Portugal
> **FarmStay.co.uk, NationalTrust-Holidays.org.uk, CottageHolidays.co.uk:** Countryside rental homes in Britain

Stay on a working farm (*agriturismo*) for an authentic slice of rural Italy.

vacation rental resources such as Airbnb. Since location is a big part of the draw, glean as much objective information about the setting as you can—a place that looks secluded on its website may actually be set right next to the local garage.

Hotels

In any European city you can find big, Old World-elegant hotels with modern amenities, as well as familiar-feeling business-class hotels that are no different from what you experience at home. But you'll also find hotels that are more uniquely European.

Classic Splurges

When I want to spend a little extra money for a special experience, I put my dollars toward a stay in a small, elegant hotel in the charming center. Throughout Europe, boutique hotels in the old town offer tradition and class for the price of sleek, transplanted American niceties in a newer international-class hotel.

In Florence, for example, I sometimes stay in a stately former convent, crisp with elegance and history. Yes, it's a splurge—but it stokes Medici fantasies like you can't imagine. There's a creaky freestanding armoire, and a heavy wood-beamed ceiling fifteen feet overhead. Looking out the window, I've got a view of the first Renaissance building—designed by Brunelleschi. You don't get that at the Sheraton.

A few splurges on an extended trip can just feel nice (and romantic). If it's in your budget, pick a Parisian room with a view of the Eiffel Tower, a canalside room in Venice, or a Swiss guesthouse tucked into a mountainside. Many such hotels have been in the same friendly family for generations; have unique amenities such as wine cellars, reading rooms, or roof terraces; and enjoy great locations in the most appealing parts of town.

Old-Fashioned Budget Hotels

Europe has a class of budget hotels that's all but unknown in the US: Friendly, no-nonsense, quirky little places—usually family-run—offering good-enough-for-the-European, good-enough-for-me beds for an average of $100 a night (less in southern Europe, more in big cities north of the Alps). While these older, traditional hotels are becoming something of an endangered species, they're certainly out there, and not too hard to find, particularly in southern Europe (Italy, France, Spain, Portugal, and Greece).

The best of these places offer comfort and character at affordable prices in smartly renovated older buildings that still retain their Old World feel. You'll climb lots of stairs, as a hotel's lack of an elevator is often the only reason it can't raise its prices. And you'll be given a front-door key because the desk is not staffed all night.

A typical budget hotel room: tidy, small, affordable.

At the very low-end range, you'll likely get a simple bed, a rickety old chair and table, a free-standing closet, a small window, and a view of another similar room across a tall, thin interior courtyard. In the cheapest places, you might have a TV, but likely not a telephone, and you'll share the toilet and shower or tub down the hall with a handful of other rooms (saving you a bundle of money).

This is hard-core Europe: fun, cheap, and characteristic. The hotel I'm describing may be appalling to many Americans; to others, it's charming, colorful, or funky. To me, "funky" means spirited and full of character(s): a caged bird in the TV room, grandchildren in the backyard, a dog sleeping in the hall, no uniforms, singing maids, a handwritten neighborhood history lesson on the wall, different furniture in each room, and a willingness to buck the system when the tourist board starts requiring shoeshine machines in the hallways. An extra $40-50 per night will buy you cheerier wallpaper and less funkiness.

As Europe becomes more affluent, its big cities are gentrifying, and Europeans are coming to expect what were once considered "American" standards of plumbing and comfort. Centrally located, old-school hotels are being bought out, gutted, and turned into pricier modern places. But you can still find good values at the remaining budget hotel that structurally can't fit showers in every room or an elevator up its spiral staircase. Prices are regulated, and regardless of how comfy and charming it is, with no elevator and a lousy shower-to-room ratio, it is—and will remain—a cheap hotel.

Europe's cheap, no-character hotels cater to business travelers interested in going home with some of their per diem still in their pockets.

Modern Chain Hotels

Difficult as it is for me to admit, soulless chain hotels can sometimes be a good option. You'll give up the charm and warmth of a family-run establishment, and breakfast probably won't be included, but the price may be right. They're never my first choice, but when more traditional accommodation pickings are slim—in peak season, or any time of year in pricey places like London—modern chain hotels can make up for a lack of character with reasonable rates and convenient locations.

Chains provide predictable comfort and amenities (elevators, 24-hour reception), and can be an especially good choice for families who need triple or quad rooms. And they can offer some of the best prices in town, especially if you snag an advance-booking discount or a last-minute deal. When demand is extra low, even fancier business-class chains (such as NH, Sorat, and Barceló) may offer prices far below their peak-season rates.

Here's a run-down of some of Europe's affordable hotel chains, roughly from bare bones to the plusher end of the budget range:

Hotel F1 (France): Stark, cheap rooms with bathrooms down the hall—like hosteling with privacy; often located on major roads outside city centers

EasyHotel: Tiny, super-efficient, no-frills rooms that feel popped out of a plastic mold, with low base rates and steep add-on charges; mostly located in big cities

B&B Hotel (Germany): Basic, playfully colorful rooms with a slightly institutional feel

Ibis: Reliable, good-value, colorful, modern rooms; "Ibis Budget" subset is basic but a step above F1 and EasyHotel

Travelodge (Britain, Ireland): Plain, serviceable rooms often at great prices

Premier Inn (Britain, Ireland): Nice-enough, family-friendly rooms; most are conveniently located and operated with industrial-strength efficiency

Motel One (Germany, Austria, Britain): Small but surprisingly chic rooms, usually in great locations; prices generally fluctuate between two levels (normal and peak) but are always affordable

Jurys Inn (Britain, Ireland): Reasonably priced, usually spacious rooms with American-hotel feel

Best Western: Rooms of varied cushiness and personality, but always with standard amenities; often located in older buildings with character

Holiday Inn: Corporate-feeling rooms akin to their US cousins; good family option

Mercure: Stylish and cushy business-class rooms

Novotel: Often large (but characterless) rooms with Mercure-level quality but more amenities

What to Expect at Guesthouses and Hotels

Whether staying at a characteristic European hotel or three-room guesthouse, be prepared for some quirkiness.

Arrival and Check-In

In European cities, hotels and B&Bs (and their reception desks) are sometimes located on the higher floors of multi-purpose buildings. You may arrive to find the ground-floor entrance is locked; if so, look for the hotel's name on the buzzer plate. Someone at the front desk will buzz you in when you ring the bell.

At check-in, you'll likely be asked to fill out a short form and possibly show your passport. (While once customary for front desk staff to take your passport for the night to register you with the police, nowadays this paperwork is usually handled on the spot—but don't be alarmed if they ask to keep your passport for a bit. Having a photocopy ready can be handy.)

Check-in is a good time to reconfirm the complete and final price of your room, including any discounts. Know what's included in the price and what taxes and other charges (breakfast, Wi-Fi, etc.) will be added. Once when checking out, I was given a bill that was double what I expected. (Dinners were required, and I was billed whether I ate them or not, or so I was told—in very clear Italian.) Avoid such mishaps by going over everything at check-in.

Before leaving the front desk, request the Wi-Fi network name and password. Find out when and where breakfast is served. And pick up the hotel's business card, which likely comes with a handy little "you are here" map. If you get lost while out sightseeing, armed with the hotel's card, you can hop into a cab and be home in minutes. Most hotels also give out free city maps.

Check-in is a good time to clarify details, such as what time breakfast is served.

The 🔑 to Keys

The following "keys" will help you unlock the mystery of European hotel-room doors.

Like in the US, many European hotels use a **key-card system.** If there's no slot in which to insert the card, try touching it to your door's keypad. If it doesn't work, try flipping the card or holding it against the keypad longer. Once inside the room, you'll probably need to insert your

card into a slot near the door to turn on the lights. (This "green" measure prevents guests from leaving the lights on when they're not in the room).

At places that have yet to switch to key cards, you may fumble with old **skeleton keys** in rickety hotel doors. The haphazard, nothing-square construction of old hotels means the lock may need babying: Always turn the key away from the doorframe to open it. Some locks take two key revolutions to open. If the key doesn't work at first, don't push it in all the way. Lift the door in or up. Try a little in, quarter turn, and farther in for full turn.

When leaving the hotel for the first time, ask the hotelier if you should take the key with you or drop it off at the desk (bulky keychains are generally an indication that a key is meant to be left behind, but it's good to check). It can be handy to leave the key behind, as you can split up with your travel partner without worrying about who will get back to the room first. Before you drop your key and walk out, confirm when reception closes. In some smaller places, you're expected to keep the key to the outside door with you, so you can get back in after hours.

If you're arriving in the morning, your room probably won't be ready. Check your bag safely at the hotel and dive right into sightseeing.

Getting to Your Room

In general, European accommodations have more stairs and fewer elevators than we're used to. When climbing to your room, think of the exercise you're getting, and be glad you've packed light. Remember that the floors of buildings are numbered differently in Europe. The bottom floor is called the ground floor, and what we call the second floor is a European's first floor. So if your room is on the second floor (European), bad news—you're on the third floor (American). On the bright side, higher floors generally have better views and less street noise than lower ones.

Hotel elevators in Europe tend to be minuscule. Sometimes only one person with a backpack can fit at one time (couples can split up, sending bags up separately for the other person to retrieve). In the elevator, push whatever's below "1" to return to the ground floor.

In Your Room

As European hotels are likely to be in small, centuries-old buildings, be prepared for some idiosyncrasies. (For details on hotel-room bathrooms, see page 423.)

Beds: At many hotels—especially in northern and eastern Europe—a "double bed" is two twin beds pushed together, and each one gets its own twin-sized comforter. If you asked for separate beds and arrive to find one big one, check to see if it's actually two twins that you can pull apart.

Expect regional differences in bedding. In France, some beds have irregular pillows (shaped like a wedge or a log). In alpine areas and in northern Europe, many hotels use covered duvets instead of a top sheet; don't be confused if your top sheet is "missing." In warm climates, you may only have a sheet, and no comforter. To get an American-style pillow or extra blankets, look in the closet or ask at the desk.

Air-Conditioning and Heat: While not universal, air-conditioning is becoming more common in European hotels. Most units come with a remote control with a fan icon (for toggling through wind power), louver icon (for steady air flow or waves), sunshine and snowflake icons (cool in summer, heat in winter), two clock settings (to preset when the unit will turn on or off), and temperature control (20 degrees Celsius is comfortable). It's good form to turn off the air-conditioning when you leave your room for the day.

Be aware that local regulations may prohibit turning on the air-conditioning between October and May—if it's important to you, confirm that air-conditioning will be available during your stay (most hotels without air-conditioning provide fans upon request). Similarly, some hotels and guesthouses in warmer regions don't run their central heat before

LEFT A remote lets you cool off the room without getting out of bed.

RIGHT French hotels sometimes come with Lincoln Log pillows.

November and after March unless it's unusually cold—prepare for cool evenings if you travel in spring and fall.

Windows: Much of northern Europe favors clever "turn-tilt" windows that you operate by turning an L-shaped handle in one of three positions: Down is closed, horizontal allows you to swing the entire window wide open at its vertical hinges, and up lets you tilt it outward on top—perfect for airing out the room without letting in rain.

Safes: Many hotel rooms come with safes, but I've never bothered using one. (Years of tour guiding have taught me that the risk of accidentally leaving behind valuables stashed in a safe is far greater than the chance of theft.) But it's always smart to keep your most tempting items—cash, jewelry, electronics, cameras—out of sight (as maids may leave the doors open for long stretches during the day). In the rare case that something is stolen from your room, report your loss to the hotelier right away.

Wi-Fi: Don't be surprised if the Wi-Fi signal is less than robust in your room. The quirky configurations and often thick stone walls of older buildings can be too much of a hurdle for some routers. Try logging on near the front desk—or wait until late in the evening (or midday), when fewer guests are competing for bandwidth.

Televisions: Hotel rooms generally have TVs, while many guesthouse rooms don't—but this varies. European TVs differ from US ones only in that they usually take an extra button press to turn on (possibly on the TV itself). Once the power's on, press any channel number (or the channel-up or channel-down button) on the remote to bring the TV to life.

Hairdryers: All but the very cheapest hotels and guesthouses tend to provide hairdryers—if you don't see one on the bathroom wall or under the sink, ask at reception; they likely have one to lend.

Hotelier Help

Front-desk clerks can be a great help and source of advice. Hoteliers and guesthouse hosts know their city well, and can assist you with everything from public transit and airport connections to finding a good restaurant, the nearest launderette, or a late-night pharmacy. Staff at any full-service hotel will happily call a taxi

Hoteliers can offer valuable advice about visiting their city.

for you, make restaurant reservations, telephone your next hotel, or give you driving instructions for your departure. Guesthouse hosts might not have as much time to field these sorts of requests, but asking nicely usually does the trick.

Many hoteliers can book bus tours and evening entertainment for you—just be wary that their recommendations may be biased, as they usually get a commission for these bookings. In general, it's a good idea to seek objective sightseeing advice and handle your own entertainment plans: You'll be less likely to find yourself in a tourist herd, and you may even save a little money.

For especially critical or cumbersome sightseeing tasks, however, hoteliers can be a huge help. For instance, in Florence, hoteliers can make time-saving museum reservations for the Uffizi Gallery and for Michelangelo's *David*.

Hotel Hassles

As at any hotel anywhere, the room you're assigned might not be exactly what you expected. Since it's easier to change rooms before you've settled in, consider potential headaches and report any problem with the room as soon as possible (noisy, too small, broken fixtures, moldy shower, etc.)—fixing it may be as simple as handing you the keys to a different room.

Disappointing Rooms: I always take a few minutes upon arrival to tweak my room to my tastes. If the furniture's arranged in a way that doesn't work for me, I move it (carefully). If the mattress has one of those protective rubber mats that causes me to sweat through the night, I take it off. If my weird pillow has "neck cramps" written all over it, I look in the closet for a different one—or ask at the front desk. Being proactive can make a huge difference.

That said, it's important to have a sense of what's normal—but not actually problematic—about your average budget European hotel room. A hotel charging €50 per night may not have the money to regularly repaint scuffed walls. European hotel bathrooms—especially showers—are often teeny by our standards, and the capacity of the hot-water tank is limited (for more on hotel bathrooms, see page 423).

It can be especially disappointing to arrive at a hotel and find that your room is in a less-desirable annex or in a partner hotel. If you feel the hotel has misrepresented its offer, it can help to show the front desk a copy of their confirmation email and press them to change your room (if they don't accommodate you, you don't need to stay).

Noise: Europe seems to excel in thin-walled rooms,

narrow streets that amplify traffic noise, and people who party until the wee hours in formerly romantic piazzas. If you suspect night noise will be a problem, ask for a room in the back or on an upper floor.

Mechanical Issues: These are a reality for any building—sinks leak, hot water turns cold, toilets may gurgle or smell, the Wi-Fi goes out, or the air-conditioning dies when you need it most. After you've (calmly) reported your concerns at the front desk, be patient. Don't expect instant results, especially if it's right after breakfast (when the staff is busy checking out other guests) or in a family-run place with a small staff.

Phones: If you're trying to dial out from your room but the phone won't work, check with the reception desk. They might have to open up an outside line for you on the switchboard, or you may need to first dial an access number.

Bugs: Now and then travelers encounter bedbugs, even at fine hotels. Make it a habit to check mattress seams for specks of blood before you unpack. Otherwise your first sign of trouble will be small, itchy welts (similar to mosquito bites), which may not show up until a day or two after you've been bitten. These critters are a nuisance, but they don't spread disease. If you find evidence of bedbugs, it doesn't necessarily mean the hotel is overrun with them. Report the problem, and see how it's dealt with. Changing rooms should be enough.

Unfortunately, European mosquitos like warm evenings just as much as their American cousins. If your hotel room's windows don't have screens, think twice before leaving your window open all day for ventilation.

Resolving Issues: If you're unhappy with something, let your hotelier know. Doing this doesn't make you an ugly American. If you state your concern to your hotelier politely, you'll likely be dealt with kindly.

If your concerns aren't being addressed, be persistent; if you aren't getting anywhere with one staff member, try approaching a more sympathetic or capable employee. Generally the hotel staff doesn't like to have complaints aired in earshot of other customers, so it can be effective to state your problems clearly and reasonably with witnesses around. The staff may accommodate you just to shut you up.

If you're in southern Europe and having trouble getting a problem solved, ask to see the complaint book, which the hotelier is legally required to show you on request. Sometimes even just asking to see the complaint book will inspire the hotelier to address your concern. If you've had a good experience, jot a friendly note in the hotel's guest book; conscientious hoteliers love to show these off to arriving guests.

Unfriendly staff, malfunctioning equipment, uncomfortable mattresses, and other hotel annoyances can be a hassle, but don't let them take the joy out of your trip. If your hotel is a disappointment, spend more time out enjoying the place you came to see.

Departure and Check Out

While it's customary to pay for your room upon departure, it can be a good idea to settle your bill the day before, when you're not in a hurry and while the manager's in. That way you'll have time to discuss and address any points of contention.

If surprise charges do pop up on your bill, ask the hotelier to explain each item you're not sure about. It's every guest's right to understand their bill.

Some unexpected charges are legitimate. For example, in many touristy areas, hotels must charge a per-day city tax that may not be included in the official rates (usually about €1-5 per person per night).

It's smart to have extra cash on hand at checkout, just in case. I've seen credit-card readers mysteriously break just as guests are checking out, requiring them to pay in cash. Even if the hotel will happily take your card, they may request that you pay the city hotel tax in cash (to simplify their bookkeeping). And it's always worth asking whether they'd give a discount for paying with cash.

If you're not heading directly to your next stop, hoteliers are almost always happy to store your bags for the day—either behind the desk or in a locked room near reception. I've never had anything stolen from a hotel's bag-storage room, but if you're worried, consider keeping your most valuable items with you for the day (and never leave your money belt behind).

SHORT-TERM RENTALS

A short-term rental—whether an apartment, house, or room in a local's home—is a popular alternative, especially if you plan to settle in one location for several nights.

Options for apartment and house rentals run the gamut, from French *gîtes* to Tuscan villas to big-city apartments. Prices vary depending on the season, size, location, and quality of the accommodation. For stays longer than a few days, you can usually find a rental that's comparable to—or even cheaper than—a hotel room with similar amenities.

Renting a room in someone's home is another alternative that can be much more affordable than a hotel, homier than a hostel, and just as comfortable as either. Depending on your host, you might also get to hang out with a local—and maybe even make a new friend.

The rental route isn't for everyone. First off, you're generally on your own. While the apartment owner or manager might offer some basic assistance, don't expect all the services of a hotel reception desk. If you like daily access to a breakfast room, fresh towels, and a sheet change, stay in a hotel. In a rental, breakfast is up to you, and your apartment or room likely won't be serviced or cleaned during a one-week stay unless you pay extra.

Some rentals, especially rooms in a local's home, are very casual affairs, without the professionalism (or privacy) you'd expect in a more formal hotel environment. Rentals often require a minimum-night stay and long lead times on cancellations. Choose a hotel instead if there's any chance your plans might change.

> ## Resources for Short-Term Rentals
>
> **Airbnb, FlipKey, Roomorama, Booking.com:** Short-term rentals of houses, apartments, and even rooms
>
> **HomeAway, VRBO, VacationRentals, RentaVilla:** Vacation rentals and short-term accommodations worldwide

Finding and Reserving Short-Term Rentals

Where to Look

Sources for rental accommodations include aggregator websites that put you in touch with the owners or managers of a range of properties (from a single room to a plush villa), and rental agencies, where a go-between facilitates your rental.

Aggregator Websites: Websites such as Airbnb, FlipKey, Roomorama, and the HomeAway family of sites (HomeAway, VRBO, and VacationRentals) let you browse properties and correspond directly with European property owners or managers. Keep in mind that, for the most part, the listings are unvetted. It's up to you to determine if a holiday house meets your particular needs in terms of location, features, and amenities.

Owners pay a fee to list their places and include photos and loads of other information (number of bedrooms and bathrooms, amenities, parking availability, nearby attractions and services, etc.) to help you make your decision. Reading reviews from previous guests can help identify trouble spots that may be glossed over in the official description.

These websites collect payment when you reserve but only release the funds to owners after you've checked in, a method of reducing fraud. A booking fee is generally built into the price. Most sites allow guests to rate hosts—and sometimes vice versa. To help renters feel safe, some sites require hosts and guests to be "verified" by providing a government-issued ID and connecting their profiles to online social networks. Hosts can gain elevated status, such as being "certified" or named a "superhost," through a track record of good service.

Rental Agencies: If you prefer to work from a curated list of accommodations, consider going through a rental agency for homes and apartments. Using an agency is convenient, the places they list have been screened, and their staff will work with you to find an appropriate accommodation. For instance, if you're traveling with a large group or aren't sure what neighborhood you want to be in, it might be easier to convey your needs to a rental agency and let them do the legwork. Agency-represented apartments typically cost more, but this method often offers more help and safeguards than booking direct.

Agencies such as InterhomeUSA.com and the more upscale RentaVilla.com list places all over Europe. Other agencies concentrate on a certain region or city. For example, Prague-stay.com focuses on apartments in Prague, while FranceHomestyle.com lists rentals throughout France.

Narrowing Your Options

Before you commit to a rental, be clear on the details, location, and amenities (for a list of questions to ask, see the sidebar on page 238).

Check out the location on a map—one person's "close to downtown" is another's "boondocks." I like to virtually explore the neighborhood using the Street View feature on Google Maps. Also consider the proximity to public transportation, and how well connected the property is with the rest of the city. Factor the cost of commuting to your sightseeing into the overall price. If you plan on driving, ask about parking.

Make sure you're aware of the property's amenities and quirks. Don't be afraid to ask questions. For example, what floor is the apartment on? Is there an elevator or is it a walk-up? Does the kitchen have a microwave, coffee maker, and so on? Is there a washer/dryer? How dependable is the Wi-Fi? If the owner or agency is anything but helpful, skip to the next place on your list.

Read reviews. If there's one complaint, you can ignore it as being from a grumpy renter. But if four or five posters comment on the same problem, pay attention. Be aware that reviewers on aggregator websites are a diverse lot, ranging from high-maintenance travelers to rugged backpackers, so expectations—and resulting opinions—may vary. A booking agency's posted reviews are almost certainly curated to weed out particularly negative ones.

Confirming and Paying

When you make a reservation, you may need to pay a deposit, which can range from 10 to 50 percent of the rental cost. Many places require you to pay the entire balance before your trip or upon arrival (possibly in cash). The easiest and safest way to pay is through the site where you found the listing; these sites can process credit-card payments and offer some degree of fraud protection. Many owners will only accept bookings through a rental site. Be wary of owners who want you to take your transaction offline to avoid fees charged by the rental site; this gives you no recourse if things go awry. Never agree to wire money—this is a key indicator of a fraudulent transaction in the making.

Since you're renting a place sight unseen, check for scams before committing. Search online for the lister's name, address, or email to see if anything suspicious pops up, and locate the physical property using Google Maps Street or Earth views. The HomeAway sites offer a rental guarantee that protects you for up to $1,000 (or more for a fee) if the owner misrepresents the property (for example, if your 200-square-foot studio facing a dumpster looks nothing like the photos of the spacious two-bedroom apartment with "lovely garden views" you thought you were renting).

Before you finalize a booking, read the rental agreement, which usually includes the house rules and the cancellation policy. Rentals can have much more rigid cancellation policies than hotels (such as 30 or 60 days, and some portion of your deposit may be nonrefundable). These policies may remain in place even in circumstances beyond your control (such as weather events that cancel flights, although it's always worth asking if the owner will let you out of your contract in an emergency).

Rental Options

Apartments and Houses

Whether in a city or the countryside, renting an apartment, house, or villa can be a fun and cost-effective way to delve into Europe. In general, if you're staying somewhere for four nights or longer, it can be worth considering an apartment or rental house (many rentals require minimum stays—typically 3-7 nights—anything less than that isn't worth the hassle of arranging key pickup, buying groceries, etc.). If it works with your itinerary, consider settling in a rental for a full week. This gives you an opportunity to really get to know a town. Renting an apartment can be a particularly good strategy if you're choosing a home-base city from which to take day trips (see the list of good home-base cities on page 56).

Apartment or house rentals can be especially cost-effective for groups. Two couples traveling together can share a two-bedroom apartment, which often ends up being less expensive than a pair of hotel rooms. Groups of backpackers find that splitting the price of a cheap apartment can cost even less than paying for several bunks at a youth hostel. Having a place to cook can further your savings. Stock your kitchen for breakfast and lunch, taking advantage of the colorful markets that pop up throughout European cities and towns, and save your money for nice dinners out.

LEFT For groups of friends, renting an apartment or house is a fun, more sociable option.

RIGHT Remember that top-floor apartments—like this one in Prague—may come with a lot of stairs.

For families, an apartment or house is a huge benefit. Kitchens make it easier and cheaper to dine in and feed picky eaters. Laundry machines are especially handy. With more than one room, parents of younger children can hang out and chat while their kids slumber (as opposed to being trapped in a hotel room with the lights out at 8 p.m.). Teenagers can stay at "home" while you go out to a restaurant: They'll feel independent, and you'll get a night on the town.

Single and Shared Rooms

Most people informally renting out rooms are in it to make a few extra bucks, not to run a full-fledged lodging business with the infrastructure and expenses that drive up costs. If you're willing to accept a very small space, a shared bathroom, or other "inconveniences," you'll be able to find remarkably affordable deals through services like Airbnb.

Renting a room in someone's home is an especially good option for those traveling alone. You're more likely to find true single rooms—with just one single bed, and a price to match. And if you're up for sharing a room with fellow guests—whether those you're traveling with or strangers—you can find a bed for a price that's lower than the going rate for hostel bunks. Some room-rental arrangements also include use of the house's kitchen and laundry facilities.

Short-Term Rental Questions

Ask these questions when booking:
- What is the cancellation policy?
- What are check-in and check-out times?
- Whom do I contact if there is a problem?
- How do I get the key? (request multiples if needed)
- What floor is the unit on? Is there an elevator?
- What amenities are available?
- Is there Wi-Fi?
- Is the kitchen fully equipped for cooking?
- Where can I park?
- Where is the closest public transportation?
- Where is the closest grocery store, pharmacy, playground?
- What is your cleaning policy/fee?

Some places allow you to book for a single night. And since you're often staying in someone's house when they're home too, you won't need to pick up a key. Just arrive at the appointed time and knock on the door. If you're staying for several nights, you can buy groceries just as you would in a rental house, or you can rely on restaurants, treating the room like a hotel room.

While you can't expect your host to also be your tour guide—or even to provide you with much info—some may be interested in getting to know the travelers who come through their home. It will likely be clear from the listing whether the hosts might be up for some socializing. (If you're interested in staying in locals' homes less as a lodger and more in the spirit of cultural exchange, see page 246.)

Rural Rentals

Having an entire farmhouse, countryside cottage, or villa to yourself is a wonderful way to immerse yourself in rural Europe. Often the owners have renovated an original rambling farmhouse or medieval estate into a series of well-constructed apartments with private kitchens, bathrooms, living areas, and individual outdoor terraces. They usually share a common pool and other amenities, and breakfast may be included.

Many of these vacation properties (*casas rurales* in Spain, *Ferienhäuser* in Germany, *gîtes* in France) are available only for a traditional Saturday-to-Saturday rental. Especially for stays in July and especially August, when much of Europe is on vacation, it may be difficult to rent a place for a shorter time. Europeans often reserve their favorite spot a year in advance, so you may have to hunt around to find an opening. (Fortunately for Americans, the British are some of the most avid seekers of weekly rental property in Europe, so there's usually plenty of English-language info.) It's wise to book several months in advance for high season (late April to mid-October).

Although a week might seem like a long time, one of the joys of staying that long in one location is *il dolce far niente* (the "sweetness of doing nothing"). Settling in one spot gives you the chance to let the days unwind without a plan. A walk at sunrise may find you in the company of the local farmer as he trims his grape vines, or the neighboring grandmother who is lovingly tending her small garden. In the evening, breathe in the fresh air as you sip your wine, and perk your ears and nostrils to the sounds and scents of the countryside. This is your chance to slow down and enjoy.

Short-Term Rental Tips

Get directions. Make sure you nail down directions to the rental prior to your arrival. Apartments, especially those in big cities, can be tricky to find. House numbers often have no obvious correlation to one another (for example, in Italy, #28 may be directly across the street from #2).

Know how to get in. Some owners will send you a combination to a keypad door lock or a lock box where they keep the key. Others will want to arrange a time to meet in person so they can give you the keys and show you around. This is your opportunity to ask for neighborhood tips. But once the owners leave, you probably won't see them again.

Read the manual. The rental property usually comes with an "instruction manual" containing information on how to operate the appliances and suggestions for local restaurants, shops, and sightseeing. The property owner's suggestions can point you to authentic local restaurants and activities you may never stumble upon otherwise. Patronize nearby mom-and-pop grocery stores, butcher shops, pastry shops, and bakeries.

Leave it like you found it. When departing, leave the place clean and in good condition—or you may lose some or all of your security deposit. Some owners may ask you to do minimal cleaning before you leave (for instance, stripping off bed linens or emptying the fridge).

HOSTELS

While Europe is no longer the budget backpacker's paradise, shoestring travelers still have their pick of several thousand hostels, each providing cheap beds where you sleep alongside strangers for $20-40 per night. Travelers of any age are welcome if they don't mind dorm-style accommodations and meeting other travelers. Most hostels offer kitchen facilities, Wi-Fi, and a self-service laundry.

If cost is your main concern, hostels are a good way to go: You're paying just for what you need, and access to kitchen facilities can seriously trim your food budget. But millions of travelers—including many older adventurers who could afford a nice hotel—love hostels just as much for the chance to connect with fellow travelers from around the world. Hosteling is a philosophy. A hosteler trades service and some privacy for a chance to stay inexpensively, simply, and communally with people from around the world.

Don't rule out "youth" hostels just because, by every standard, you're older than young. If you're alive, you're young enough to hostel just about anywhere in Europe (hostels with age cutoffs are rare). Yes, the bulk of the hosteling crowd is 18 to 26 years old—but every year there are more seniors and families hosteling. As a reader posted on my website: "My partner and I stayed in a 'youth' hostel for the first time by Lake Como and thought we'd be the oldest people there. Not so! At our table was a 60-ish couple from Sydney and a 79-year-old British woman who was backpacking alone through Europe. All three were a delight, but especially the backpacker, who said she stays in hostels for the evening company."

For students, travelers on a budget, solo travelers, groups or families who can take a whole room, and those hoping to meet other travelers, hostels can be a great option.

The Hostel Experience

Hostels vary in size, quality, and character. If a hostel is an official member of the venerable Hosteling International organization, it's probably big, institutional, and a bit rule-laden, but predictably clean, well-organized, and family-friendly (it probably also takes in lots of school groups). Although you'll still find plenty of official HI hostels (especially north of the Alps), these days they're outnumbered by independently run hostels. Independent hostels tend to be more easygoing and colorful (or chaotic and ramshackle, depending on the place).

Amenities: In general, hostels offer no-frills accommodations in clean dormitories, which typically hold four to eight bunk beds (sometimes many more), possibly along with lockers and a sink. Mixed-sex dorms are standard (except at official HI hostels), but nearly all offer some female-only rooms. If single-sex dorms are unavailable—and a dormmate is making you feel unsafe—let the staff know, and they'll do their best to accommodate you (by swapping your bunk assignment, or perhaps putting you in a private room at no extra charge). Hostels almost always provide bedding, but the towel's up to you (though you can usually rent one for a small fee).

Bathrooms are usually just down the hall and likely have a room with a few toilet stalls, and another with showers. (The most rustic, off-the-beaten-path hostels and mountain huts have no showers—but these are becoming rare.)

Private Rooms: Most hostels offer a few private rooms; beds are roughly $5-20 more per person than what you'd pay in a dorm. These are a great value for families (four-bunk rooms are common) and couples who want privacy but don't mind sleeping separately in twin beds. Private single rooms are also available (a boon for solo travelers who aren't up for the dorm experience).

One of Europe's hostels: $30 a night, your own kitchen, a million-dollar view of the Swiss Alps, and lots of friends.

Location: Big-city hostels can be overrun by young backpackers, so if a party-hearty scene sounds more annoying than fun, pay special attention to reviews about the vibe when booking. Still, you should find plenty of urban hostels offering a more subdued atmosphere.

Rural hostels, far from train lines and famous sights, are usually quiet and frequented by a more mature crowd, with relaxed backpackers striking up intergenerational friendships with outdoorsy retirees. While most hostels are conveniently located within easy access of public transportation, those traveling by car are smart to use that mobility to enjoy some of Europe's overlooked hostels.

Upscale Hostels: As Europe has grown more affluent, the average hostel experience has gotten a little cushier. Many hostels have been remodeled to provide more plumbing and smaller rooms. In recent years, a slew of "boutique" hostels has sprouted up. These "poshtels" usually come with funky, design-oriented decor, often with equally stylish on-site bars and restaurants. Most offer more private rooms and en suite bathrooms than your average hostel, but still come with affordable smaller dorms, shared kitchens, and lots of common areas. Of course, all that flair comes at a price—a bed in an upscale hostel can easily cost more than one at a budget hotel.

Finding and Booking Hostels

HostelWorld is the dominant online resource for hostel reviews and bookings (although you may pay a bit less by reserving directly with the hostel). To reserve any official HI hostel, head to HIHostels.com. Both sites collect small nonrefundable deposits at booking.

When looking for hostels, keep the following in mind.

Consider factors other than price. You might save a few bucks by choosing a bunk in a big dorm, but you've wasted your money if it costs you a decent night's sleep. Pay attention to location and atmosphere. User reviews can be helpful, but I wouldn't pay much attention to ratings for cleanliness or helpfulness of the staff (these can be negatively influenced by first-time hostelers who unfairly hold their dorm room to hotel standards).

In some hostels, there are dorms for boys...and dorms for girls.

Be prepared for peak-season competition. The most popular hostels fill up every day; don't assume you can just show up and find a bed (especially if you want a private room). If possible, book a hostel stay as soon as your schedule is set. If you want to keep your itinerary flexible, try to book at least a day or two in advance. If a

hostel shows as full online, call or email—they may be holding some beds for drop-ins. (For the best shot at nabbing a last-minute spot, arrive early in the morning, especially if the office closes at midday—otherwise you'll be just one among the scruffy gang lining up for the evening reopening, when remaining beds are doled out.)

Europe is home to all sorts of unique hostels, such as this castle overlooking the Rhine River in Bacharach, Germany.

Don't worry about HI membership. Although official HI hostels are technically for members only, nonmembers pay just a few dollars extra per night. Unless you plan to stay at a lot of HI hostels, membership probably isn't worth it, especially given the proliferation of independent hostels.

Hostel selectively. In some areas, budget hotels can make more sense than hostels. Especially if you're traveling as a couple, a cheap hotel room can beat the price of a private hostel room. This is more likely in southern Europe (Italy and Spain); the farther north you go, the bigger the price gap between hostels and the cheapest hotel rooms. (In Scandinavia, for example, locals know that hostels provide the best—and usually only—$30 beds in town...which explains all the Volvos you'll see in hostel parking lots.)

Look for unique hostel experiences. Some hostels are sightseeing destinations in themselves. For a small fraction of what you'd pay for a run-of-the-mill hotel room, you can enjoy a memorable stay in a hilltop castle (Bacharach, Germany), former stables (Nürnberg, Germany), moored ships and a converted jumbo jet (Stockholm), alpine chalets (Gimmelwald and Gryon, Switzerland), a lakefront villa (Lugano, Switzerland), former prisons (Stockholm—again—and Ljubljana, Slovenia), a medieval manor house (Shropshire, England), a 400-person tent (Munich), vintage camper trailers (Bonn, Germany), whitewashed cave houses (Santorini, Greece), artfully preserved time-warp East German apartments (Berlin), retired train cars (Scottish

Highlands), former choirboys' dorms (London), and a brothel-turned-hostel (Amsterdam, of course).

Hosteling Tips

When hosteling, it pays to pack smartly, use common sense, and take advantage of all that hostels have to offer.

Pack a few hostel extras. Bring a towel—lightweight, quick-dry towels are best—as few hostels include them with your stay (though most have towels for rent). A sleep mask and ear plugs (or headphones) help you sleep through bunkmates' late arrivals and early-morning departures. Flip-flops come in handy in bathroom stalls, and a small power strip (so lots of gear can be charged at the same time) does wonders for dormmate relations. While lockers are common in dorm rooms, they're not universal, and often don't come with a built-in lock—bring your own. Hostelers who are used to bringing a sleep sack should check ahead before packing it—concerned about bedbugs, many hostels now require you to use their linens.

Get out of your social bubble. Travelers find new friends and travel partners in every hostel. A hostel's recreation and living rooms are my favorite hangouts. People gather, play games, tell stories, share information, read, write, and team up for future travels. Even if the lights go out at 11 p.m., bunk-bed conversation can rage on. You may well find yourself propped on your elbows staring intensely into the darkness, passing around travel tales like a bucket of popcorn.

Save money by eating in. A simple breakfast is usually included in the price of your bed. Additional hearty, super-cheap meals may be served (at an extra cost but generally the cheapest hot meals in town), often in cafeteria-style settings. A typical dinner is fish sticks and mashed potatoes seasoned with conversation with new friends from Norway to New Zealand. Most hostels have a self-service kitchen, complete with utensils, pots, and pans. Larger hostels even have small grocery stores.

Hostels: Meet, drink, and be merry.

Seek sightseeing information. Most hostel lobbies are littered with brochures and bulletin boards alerting you to local tours, events, and public-transportation details; larger ones in bigger cities may also organize walking tours and pub crawls.

Alternative Budget Options

Hostels aren't the only places to find low-cost rooms in Europe. Consider these creative alternatives.

Convents: Catholic institutions, most of them in Italy, sometimes rent out rooms to travelers. The beds are twins and the decor is spartan, but it's quiet at night, and the price is right. For Italy, check Monastery Stays (www.monasterystays.com) and the Church of Santa Susanna's website, which maintains a list of such places in Rome and beyond (www.santasusanna.org, select "Resources/Convent Accommodations"). It's best to email your reservation request (most convents don't have an English website), or book through Monastery Stays for a fee.

Dorms: Student housing is often rented out between terms. In London, for example, the University of Westminster, as well as several other colleges, opens its dorm rooms to travelers from June through mid-September. Located in several high-rise buildings scattered around central London, the rooms—some with private baths—come with access to well-equipped kitchens and big lounges. Try UniversityRooms.com for leads.

Turn-Key Camping: Many of Europe's campgrounds offer sites already set up with a tent, trailer, or mobile home and outfitted with linens and kitchen gear. Two British companies are a good place to start: Eurocamp (www.eurocamp.co.uk) and Canvas Holidays (www.canvasholidays.co.uk) contract with campgrounds across continental Europe. For more on camping in Europe, see page 250.

Remember that your roommates or breakfast companions can also be great sources of advice.

Guard your valuables. Theft can be a problem in hostels. Wear your money belt (even while sleeping), and don't leave your phone—or anything else tempting—lying around. Don't worry—no one's going to steal your sneakers or journal. If the hostel doesn't offer lockers, consider securing your bag with a small combo lock, or at least clipping it to a bedpost. Any hindrance, no matter how small, makes it more likely that a thief will move on.

Note lockout hours. Institutional-feeling hostels may have midday lockout times (commonly 10 a.m. to 5 p.m.), when guests are required to vacate rooms (for cleaning and for safety's sake, if the office staff isn't around to keep an eye on things). Nighttime curfews and lockouts are even rarer—but check the hostel's policy before you go out for the evening. A curfew can be a big advantage: Hostels that don't have curfews are more likely to have drunk and rowdy hostelers returning at ungodly hours.

Exercise tolerance. The sounds you'll hear in bigger dorm halls just after everyone's turned in remind me of summer camp—giggles, burps, jokes, and strange noises in many languages. Snoring is permitted and practiced openly. School groups can turn a normally quiet HI hostel upside down, typically over school-year weekends and at any time in summer. Try to be understanding (remember, we were all noisy kids at one time).

CRASHING WITH LOCALS FOR FREE

There's no better way to get to know a new country than to stay in someone's home. There are several ways to do this for free, from swapping houses to couch-surfing to crashing on your neighbor's cousin's couch.

Staying with Europeans as a House Guest

Being a guest in a European home isn't all that different from being a guest in an American one. Before you arrange to stay with someone, though, consider the possible drawbacks of your free bed. At a hotel, B&B, hostel, or short-term rental you have no social obligations to your host, and it isn't perceived as rude to return late at night. There's also location to consider: If you're sleeping where others live, there's a decent chance you'll be in a workaday suburb, far from old-town charm or the sights you came to see. You'll probably be able to reach the city center on your own (thanks to Europe's great public transit), but that commute will cost you time and money. Nonetheless, for those aware of the trade-offs, crashing with locals can be a great option.

Volunteering and Cultural Exchanges: If you believe that travel is about community good and bringing people together, consider joining a cultural-exchange organization, which lets you stay with hosts in their home (described on page 516) or finding volunteer work abroad (see page 520). Note that while travelers do get a free bed with their hosts, the focus is much less about providing accommodation than an opportunity to connect and contribute.

Bunking with Friends (or Friends of Friends)

Staying with a friend, relative, or common acquaintance not only stretches your budget (usually along with your belly), but your cultural horizons. Try and dig up some European relatives, friends, friends of relatives, or relatives of friends. No matter how far out on the family tree they are, unless you're a real jerk, they'll be tickled to have an American visitor in their nest. I email my potential host, telling them when I'll arrive and asking if they'd be free to meet for dinner while I'm there. They answer with "Please come visit us" or "Have a good trip." It's obvious from their response (or lack of one) if I'm invited to stop by and stay awhile.

Especially if you are traveling solo and reasonably extroverted, you're likely to make new friends on the road. When people meet, they invite each other to visit. Once invited to visit, I warn my new friends that I may very well show up some day at their house, whether it's in Osaka, Auckland, Santa Fe, or Dublin. When I have, it's been a good experience.

Staying with friends or relatives (this is my Norwegian cousin) gives you a spot at a local dinner table.

Don't be afraid to follow up with indirect contacts. You'll be surprised how many friends are potential hosts on the road.

If you're afraid of being seen as a freeloader, remember that both parties benefit. A Greek family is just as curious about you as you are about them. Armed with pictures from home and a bag of goodies for the kids, make a point of giving as much from your culture as you are taking from theirs. I insist on no special treatment other than to be treated simply as part of the family. If you ask for a favor, make it easy for your host to say no. Help with the chores, don't wear out your welcome, and follow up each visit with postcards or emails to share the rest of your trip. It's easy and thoughtful to reimburse your hosts for their hospitality with a bottle of wine, a bunch of flowers, or a thank-you note, possibly with photos of all of you together.

Couch Surfing

Couchsurfing.com and a handful of similar services can put you in touch with outgoing people happy to host fellow travelers in their homes for free. Most do this out of a sincere interest in meeting interesting people, and many are in it for the good karma, having couch-surfed themselves. This service is a boon for laid-back, budget-minded extroverts who aren't too picky about where they rest their heads. Most surfers are in their

20s and traveling solo, but plenty are a decade or two older, or traveling in small groups.

Safety is a concern of any smart couch surfer. While the Couchsurfing service makes an effort toward this end (offering plenty of safety tips, listing references from travelers and hosts on member profiles, and allowing hosts to pay for name and address verification), travelers must still be on alert for creeps and scammers—they're certainly out there. My best tip for crashing with strangers: Always arrive with a backup hostel, hotel, or Couchsurfing host in mind. If you don't feel comfortable with your host, just leave (after all, it's free). Don't worry about hurting their feelings. Never let budget concerns make you put up with something that feels dangerous.

Tips for Staying with Locals

Not only are you a guest in someone's home, but you are a guest in their country. These tips can help ensure a pleasant experience.

Ask your host for guidance. People who are OK with welcoming guests in their home are usually friendly, interested in others, and eager to show off their town. You'll likely be greeted with genuine enthusiasm. Many hosts happily provide maps, sightseeing and transit information, and advice on how to make the most of your time.

Do your cultural homework. Some awkwardness is inevitable—expect to make a faux pas or two. Limit embarrassing blunders by researching, before you arrive, etiquette in the country you're visiting. Follow your host's lead—if they're not wearing shoes in the house, leave yours at the door. Be aware of what makes for touchy conversation, and do your best to get squared away on geopolitical basics— e.g., Scotland isn't in England, and Bratislava is no longer in "Czechoslovakia." To bridge a wide language gap, try to learn the elements of that country's nonverbal communication: What means "OK" in the US can mean something quite the opposite in some parts of Europe.

Communicate your plans. Clear communication and a focus on being considerate are critical when trying to bridge a linguistic or cultural divide. If you accept a bed from someone for free, it's polite to give your hosts plenty of advance warning of your arrival and not change plans at the last minute. Let your host know how long you expect to stay, whether you'll be there for dinner in the evening, and where to leave the key in the morning. If your host invites you to dinner, do your best to accept.

House Swapping and House Sitting

Many families enjoy this great budget option. They trade houses (sometimes cars, too—but most draw the line at pets) with someone at the destination of their choice. People who've tried house swapping rave about the range of places they've enjoyed for free, and about the graciousness and generosity of their swap-mates. Good places to start are HomeExchange.com, HomeLink (www.home-exchange-usa. com), Intervac Home Exchange (www.intervacus.com), and LoveHomeSwap.com.

Swapping works best for people with an appealing place to offer, and who can live with the idea of having strangers in their home, touching their stuff (of course, you can always lock up your most valuable items and precious heirlooms). Unsurprisingly, those living in swanky Manhattan apartments and beachside villas have the best pick of options in Europe, but you don't need to live in an obvious vacation spot or a mansion to find a workable exchange. Your guests may appreciate the pace of a smaller town (especially if you offer your car) and may be less interested in luxury or location than in finding a suitable place that's available when they are.

Be open to serendipitous opportunities: If you get an inquiry from someone in an unfamiliar spot, you might end up discovering a great place that you didn't know enough about to seek out. Note that your swaps don't have to be simultaneous— for example, you might stay at their place while they're off on a cruise, while they visit your place months later when you're away visiting family for the holidays.

Many swappers who could easily afford pricey trip lodgings still prefer to take the deep culture dive that a home exchange provides. As one experienced swapper told me, "When exchanging, you feel as though you are entering a neighborhood in a way a hotel cannot match. In addition to a car, you often have use of bikes, boats, toys, books, and even sometimes the exchanger's local relatives—all the comforts of home. Being stuck 'at home' on a rainy day doesn't feel like a vacation tragedy!"

With luck, you could swap for this Norwegian retreat.

Once you've found a potential host, expect to be in fairly close contact as you finalize the swap. Be very clear about your expectations, agree on how you'll handle worst-case scenarios, and get the details pinned down before you leave. Know where to find the key and how to open the door, find out beforehand how to get to the nearest grocery store, make sure your host family leaves instructions for operating the appliances, make arrangements in advance for phone and Internet charges, and ask about any peculiarities with the car you'll be driving. Veteran house swappers report that by the time these logistics are all worked out, it usually feels less like you'll be swapping with strangers, and more like you've made a new, conveniently located friend.

If you're not up for offering up your own place, look into house sitting, which offers many of the same upsides (and downsides). MindMyHouse.com has plenty of listings in Europe; the US-focused Caretaker Gazette (www.caretaker. org) also has some overseas listings.

CAMPING EUROPEAN STYLE

In Europe, camping is more of a social experience than a chance to retreat to nature. While camping can be the cheapest way to see Europe—it's the middle-class European family way to travel—relatively few Americans take advantage of Europe's thousands of campgrounds. Those who do camp in Europe give it rave reviews. A tent, pillow, and sleeping bag are all you need.

In the US, we think of campgrounds as picturesque outposts near a lake or forest. By contrast, European "campings" (the international word for campgrounds) are often located within or on the outskirts of an urban center and can range from functional (like park-and-rides) to vacation extravaganzas, with restaurants, mini water-parks, and miniature golf. Many campgrounds have small grocery stores and washing machines. In general, European campgrounds are less private than American versions, and many forbid open fires.

Aside from the biggest cities, most tourist-friendly areas have a campground within a reasonable walk

Resources for Camping

EuroCamps.net: Camping database covering all of Europe and some 15,000 campgrounds

EuroCampings.co.uk: Searchable database and user reviews on more than 9,000 campgrounds

CoolCamping.com: "Glamping" and luxury campsites in the UK and France or bus ride from the town center or train station. And if you're camping outside a major city, the money you save on parking alone will likely pay for your campsite (leave your car at the campground and take the handy bus downtown).

Campgrounds generally mirror their surroundings: If the region is overcrowded, dusty, dirty, unkempt, and chaotic, you're unlikely to find an oasis behind the campground's gates. A sleepy Austrian valley will probably offer a sleepy Austrian campground.

Some campgrounds offer bungalows with kitchenettes and four to six beds. Comfortable and cheaper than hotels, these are particularly popular in Scandinavia.

Campgrounds can fill up. But if they do, the "Full" sign usually refers to motorhomes and trailers. A small tent can almost always be squeezed in somewhere. However, "weekend campings" are rented out on a yearly basis to local urbanites, and often are full or don't allow what they call "stop-and-go" campers (you). Camping guidebooks indicate which places are the "weekend" types.

Cost: Prices at European campgrounds vary according to facilities and style, but don't be surprised if you're asked to pay by the tent, the person, and the vehicle. A camper who bicycles in might pay $5 for her tent and $3 for herself; a couple driving into the same site might pay $6 for the two of them, $5 for their tent, and $4 for their car.

Registration and Regulations: Camp registration is easy. As with most hotels, you show your passport, fill out a short form, and learn the rules. Quiet is enforced beginning at 10 or 11 p.m., and checkout time is usually noon. English is the second language of campings throughout Europe, and most managers will understand the monoglot American.

Services: Not every campground will take tents; some are RV only. Most campgrounds have laundry facilities and great showers with metered hot water—carry coins and scrub quickly. Larger campgrounds may have a grocery store and café (a likely camp hangout with an easygoing European social scene).

Equipment: You can bring your gear with you—or buy it in Europe. Tents, sleeping bags, and cooking supplies are cheaper at large European superstores than at specialty backpacking stores. European campers prefer a very

Out of Options (or Money)?

This book is not a vagabonding guide, but things happen: You run out of money, you get into town too late to find a room, or volcanic ash strands you somewhere without a place to stay. I once went 29 out of 30 nights without paying for a bed. It's not difficult...but it's not always comfortable, convenient, clean, safe—or legal.

A bench with a view

I no longer lug a sleeping bag around, but if you'll be vagabonding, bring a light bag—you'll find plenty of places to roll it out. Just keep your passport with you, attach your belongings to you so they don't get stolen, and use good judgment in your choice of a free bed. Faking it until the sun returns can become, at least in the long run, a good memory.

The Great Outdoors: Some large cities, such as Amsterdam and Athens, are flooded with tourists during peak season—and some of those tourists spend their nights dangerously in city parks. Most cities enforce their "no sleeping in parks" laws only selectively. Away from the cities, in forests or on beaches, you can pretty much sleep where you like. In my vagabonding days, I found summer nights in the Mediterranean part of Europe mild enough that I was comfortable with just my jeans, sweater, and hostel sheet.

Train Stations: Assuming the station stays open all night, it can be a free, warm, safe, and uncomfortable place to hang your hat. Most popular tourist cities in Europe have stations with concrete floors that are painted nightly with a long rainbow of sleepy vagabonds. Some stations close for a few hours in the middle of the night, and everyone is always cleared out at dawn before the normal rush of travelers converges on the station. A train ticket or rail pass entitles you to a free night in a station's waiting room: You're simply waiting for your early train. For safety, store your pack in a station locker or check it at the baggage counter.

Trains: Success hinges on getting enough room to stretch out, and that can be quite a trick. It's tempting but risky to sleep in a train car that seems to be parked for the night in a station. No awakening is ruder than having your bedroom jolt into motion and roll toward God-knows-where. If you do find a parked train car to sleep in, check to see when it's scheduled to leave. Some rail-pass holders get a free if disjointed night's sleep by riding a train out for four hours and catching a different train back for another four hours.

Airports: After a late landing, crash on an airport sofa rather than waste sleeping time looking for a place that will sell you a bed for the remainder of the night (for a guide to airport slumber, try SleepingInAirports.com). Frankfurt's airport is served conveniently by the train and is great for sleeping free—even if you aren't flying anywhere. A few large airports have sterile, womblike "rest cabins" that can be rented for as few as four hours or overnight at the price of a cheap hotel room (for example, see Yotel.com for London's Heathrow and Gatwick airports, Paris' Charles de Gaulle airport, and Amsterdam's Schiphol airport).

lightweight "three-season" sleeping bag and a closed-cell sleeping pad. I'd start without a stove, keeping meals simple by picnicking and enjoying food and fun in the campground café. If you don't want to bog down with equipment, consider a place that can set up a tent site for you (see "Turn-Key Camping" on page 245).

For a "room" with a view on a tight budget, pitch your tent in a secluded mountain valley.

Safety: Campgrounds are remarkably low-theft. Campings are full of basically honest, middle-class European families, and someone's at the gate all day. Most people just leave their gear in their vans or zipped inside their tents.

Kids: A family can sleep in a tent, van, or motorhome a lot cheaper than in a hotel. Camping offers plenty to occupy children's attention, namely playgrounds that come fully equipped with European kids. As your kids make friends, your campground social circle widens. Campgrounds are filled with Europeans in the mood to toss a Frisbee with a new American friend.

RV Camping: David Shore, co-author of *Europe by Van and Motorhome* (along with Patty Campbell), gives consults on finding and renting the right camper vehicle and offers free shipping on his book for Rick Steves readers (www.roadtripeurope.com).

Each country has companies specializing in camper van and motorhome rentals. Look for one with a pickup and drop-off location that makes sense for your itinerary. For example, Origin Campervans is centrally located in Lille, France (www.origin-campervans.com). McRent.eu has 50 rental depots across Europe. Picking up your RV or campervan in Germany could save you 19 percent, since German rental companies don't charge VAT if you rent for 31 days or longer.

Another bonus to camper-van travel: Across Europe, with a camper van or motorhome, you can sleep overnight for free in any legal parking space, including rest stops on national motorways (look for a big blue and white "P" sign).

Eating

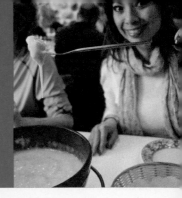

Eating in Europe is sightseeing for your taste buds. Every country has local specialties that are good, memorable, or both. Whether it's Wiener schnitzel in Vienna, salade niçoise in Nice, or wurst in Würzburg, a country's cuisine is as culturally important as its museums. But just as there are tricks for sightseeing, there are also ways to maximize your culinary journey.

Much of my experience lies in eating well cheaply. In most places, I find that I can eat well for an average of about $50 a day by mixing picnics and quick, budget eats with atmospheric restaurant meals. This budget includes a $15 lunch (cheaper if you picnic or eat fast food), a $30 dinner at a good restaurant (more with wine or dessert), and $5 for your chocolate, cappuccino, and gelato needs. This assumes that breakfast is included with your hotel room (if you have to buy breakfast, have a picnic lunch...or eat less gelato). If you splurge one day, go cheap the next; you can find a satisfying dinner for $20 or less anywhere in Europe. Galloping gluttons can thrive on $25 a day by picnicking. If you have more money, of course, it's delightful to spend it dining well.

BREAKFAST BASICS

Not long ago, I grabbed breakfast at a hotel in southern Spain. The only cereal available was a local version of frosted flakes. As there was no "mature" option, I was tickled to have a bowl. But the cereal milk was heated—apparently standard in this part of Spain—and my poor frosted flakes immediately turned to mush. Not so grrrrrrreat.

Soggy flakes or not, I find breakfast to be a fun part of my travel day, especially because the experience varies so much from one country's breakfast table to the next.

The farther north you go in Europe, the heartier the breakfasts. The heaviest is the traditional British "fry-up" or full English (or Scottish or Welsh) breakfast. This large, home-cooked meal is a fundamental part of the bed-and-breakfast experience, and generally included in your room price (for more on British breakfasts, see page 621).

A Scandinavian breakfast buffet is the perennial favorite for the "most food on the table" award. It pays to take advantage of breakfast *smörgåsbords* when you can (generally included in the cost of your room). Even at $15, it's a deal by local standards and can serve as your best big meal of the day. This all-you-can-eat extravaganza generally consists of fresh bread, cheeses, yogurt, cereal, fruit, boiled eggs, herring, cold cuts, and coffee or tea. Grab a drinkable yogurt and go local by pouring it in the bowl and sprinkling your cereal over it. Some hosts provide a roll of foil so you can pack up a lunch from the breakfast spread. If that sounds like a good idea, just ask.

Throughout the Netherlands, Belgium, Germany, Austria, Switzerland, and most points east of there, breakfast is usually included with your room. Though you can expect a more modest buffet than in Scandinavia, you'll still have plenty of options, including rolls, bread, pastries, cold cuts, cheeses, fruit, yogurt, and cereal. If a buffet has eggs, they're most likely boiled (soft or hard); scrambled or fried eggs are relatively rare.

For breakfast, Germans prefer a sandwich with cold cuts and/or a bowl of *Müsli* (an oat cereal like granola, but less sweet). Try Bircher muesli, a healthful mix of oats, nuts, yogurt, and fruit that tastes far more delicious than it looks (most commonly available in Switzerland). If breakfast is optional, take a walk to the nearest bakery—every German, Austrian, and Swiss town has at least a few bakeries offering an enticing world of bread and pastry, baked fresh that morning.

The continental breakfast: bread, jam, and coffee

As you move south and west (France, Italy, Spain, and Portugal), skimpier "continental" breakfasts are the norm. If breakfast is included with your room, it may be something basic, such as a roll with marmalade or jam, possibly a slice of ham or cheese, and coffee or tea.

Many places add items like yogurt, juice, cereal, cold cuts, cheese, fruit, sweet rolls, and eggs to the mix. If your breakfast is too sparse, supplement it with a piece of fruit and a chunk of cheese from a local market.

In many hotels in Spain and France (and some in Italy, Portugal, and elsewhere), you'll have the option of paying extra for breakfast. If that's the case, I often skip the hotel breakfast and visit the corner café, which offers more atmosphere and is less expensive.

In Italy, do as the locals do: Stop into a bar or café to drink a cappuccino and munch a *cornetto* (croissant) while standing at the bar. In France, locals often grab a warm croissant and coffee on the way to work. Queue up with the French and consider the yummy options: croissants studded with raisins, packed with crushed almonds, or filled with chocolate or cream. In Spain, start your day at a corner bar or at a colorful café near the town market hall for the *desayunos* (breakfast special, usually available until noon), which can include coffee, a roll (or sandwich), and juice. Or sample a Spanish specialty, such as *chocolate con churros* (fritters served with a thick, hot chocolate drink), *pan con tomate* (toasted baguette rubbed with garlic and tomato), or a *tortilla española* (hearty slice of potato omelet).

If you're a big coffee drinker, note that breakfast is the only cheap time to caffeinate. Some hotels will serve you a bottomless cup of a rich brew only with breakfast. After that, the cups acquire bottoms and refills will cost you. Some Europeans—especially those from big coffee-drinking countries like France and Italy—have very specific coffee etiquette (see "Know Your Joe" on page 274). Being a juice man, I keep a liter box of OJ in my room for a morning eye-opener.

Sure, you can find American-style bacon, fried eggs, and orange juice on the Continent if you look hard enough, but they're nearly always overpriced and disappointing. Instead, come to the European breakfast table with an adventurous spirit. I'm a big-breakfast traditionalist at home, but when I feel the urge for a typical American breakfast in Europe, I beat it to death with a hard roll.

RESTAURANTS

Restaurant dining can lay waste to a tight budget, but it would be criminal to pass through Europe without sampling the specialties served in good restaurants.

European restaurants are no more expensive than American ones. The cost of eating is determined not by the local standard, but by your personal standard. Many Americans can't find an edible meal for less than $30 in their hometown, but their next-door neighbors enjoy eating out for half that. If you can enjoy a $15 meal in Boston, Chicago, or Seattle, you'll eat well in London, Rome, or Helsinki for the same price. Every year I eat about 100 dinners in Europe. My budget target is $15 for a simple, fill-the-tank meal; $30 for a good restaurant dinner; and $50 for a splurge feast. Forget the scare stories. People who spend $60 per person on dinner in Dublin and then complain either enjoy complaining or are fools.

Just like at home, lunch in Europe generally costs less than dinner. If you want to stretch your budget by mixing picnics and restaurant meals, your euros will go farther if you have lunch at restaurants and picnics for dinner. Drinks (except for wine in southern Europe) and desserts can be the worst value. Skipping those, you can enjoy some surprisingly good $15 meals.

Keep in mind that restaurants and pubs don't usually serve meals continuously throughout the day. Restaurants often close in the late afternoon (about 2 p.m.) and then reopen at dinner; pubs stay open all day, but serve only drinks and snacks between lunch and dinner. For those in-between times, you'll find plenty of snack bars and cafés happy to feed you.

A fun neighborhood restaurant: no English menus, no credit cards, but good food, good prices, and a friendly staff

Finding a Restaurant

Average tourists are attracted—like moths to a light bulb—to the biggest sign on the most expensive square in town that boasts, *We speak English and accept credit cards.* This place also has an extensive printed menu with every item described in four languages. Though it might feel accessible, that's a place to avoid. It's a trap trying to snare naive, green, rich tourists.

Many European cities have a bustling, colorful "restaurant row": a street or square lined with characteristic eateries, such as Rue des Bouchers in Brussels, Rue Mouffetard in Paris, Rua das Portas de Santo

Antão in Lisbon, Leidsedwarsstraat in Amsterdam, Campo de' Fiori in Rome, Adrianou street in Athens, and Prijeko street in Dubrovnik. The restaurants on these streets usually have straightforward menus of tourist-pleasing dishes, superficial elegance, and gregarious hawkers out front trying to lure in diners. Some of these places have overpriced food and rotten service; others are frequented by natives and offer great ambience and decent value. A good guidebook, a tip from a trusted local, or simply an eye for choosing the neighborhood favorite can help you figure out which is which.

Another strategy is to leave the tourist center; there are trendy new restaurants all over European cities with innovative, affordable food. You don't need Michelin stars or a crowd-sourced review to tell you what's hot—just stroll around until you find a restaurant with a happy crowd of locals. Look for gastropubs in Great Britain, tapas bars in Spain, and *enoteca* wine bars in Italy. After a few days on the ground, you'll have no trouble telling a genuine hangout from a tourist trap.

Here are some tips for finding a good place to eat.

Look for mom-and-pop restaurants. I search out family-run places serving local specialties made with seasonal ingredients. To find these places, I look for low-rent spots a few blocks off the famous square, with a small selection of dishes featured on a handwritten menu in the native language. The menu is small because they're just going to cook up what they can sell out for the day, it's handwritten because it's shaped by whatever was fresh in the market that morning, and it's in one language because they're targeting local return customers rather than tourists.

Consult a guidebook. A reliable travel guidebook can be a good resource for finding a great place to eat. Most guidebooks list restaurants by neighborhood and locate them on a map, allowing you to peruse a selection of places near your

A small, handwritten menu in the local language is a good sign.

hotel or a major sight. Guidebook listings can help you select a restaurant based on its specialty, ambience, or cost.

Get recommendations from locals. Ask your hotel receptionist, a shop owner, or even someone on the street for a good place—not a good place for tourists, but a place they'd take a friend. If you take a food tour (described on page 285), ask your guide for recommendations.

Peruse foodie publications and apps. You'll find guidebooks, blogs, and apps dedicated to food in specific destinations. For instance, *The Good Food Guide* prints annual reviews of restaurants, pubs, and cafés around the UK based on feedback received from thousands of readers.

The *Food Lover's Guide to Paris*, from admired French-food expert Patricia Wells, has recommendations for the city's best restaurants, cafés, and bistros (book and app). David Lebovitz, formerly a pastry chef at California's Chez Panisse, now lives in Paris and shares his latest finds and favorite bakeries on his blog (www.davidlebovitz.com) and in his Paris Pastry Guide app.

Eating & Drinking in Rome, by food journalist Katie Parla, features restaurant recommendations and Roman eating customs (book, blog, and app). Elizabeth Minchilli's Eat Italy app has picks for places to eat, drink, and food-shop in Rome, Venice, Florence, and Milan.

For Europe-wide resources, try websites such as TimeOut, with articles and food guides for a number of European cities, or Spotted by Locals, which features short restaurant write-ups and insider tips from a network of bloggers.

You can also search for food and restaurant review websites specific to your destination. And many US newspapers review European restaurants in their travel sections. (The *New York Times* "36 Hours" column is a good place to start.)

Check user-review sites and apps. Websites and apps such as FourSquare, TripAdvisor, and Yelp can point you to recommendations based on reviews by other users. You can use these apps to find an eatery nearby, or to search for a place with a certain price range or type of cuisine.

Resources for Eating

SpottedByLocals.com: Recommendations from locals

TimeOut.com: Listings and reviews for restaurants, bars, and food festivals

FourSquare, TripAdvisor, Yelp: Uncurated user reviews

MealSharing.com, BonAppetour.com, EatWith.com: Social dining sites

www.ricksteves.com/travel-talks: Rick's travel skills talks, including one on eating in Europe

EatWell EU app: Healthy-eating guide to Europe

Restaurant Etiquette

Your dining experiences will go much smoother if you know what to expect at European restaurants.

Go at the right time. Super-popular restaurants sometimes have two seatings, such as one at 7 p.m. and another at 9 p.m. In general, the early seating will include more tourists, and the late seating will have more locals. I've learned that if I go to a place at 7:30 p.m., it may feel like a tourist trap; but if I go back at 10 p.m., it seems like a local favorite. One's not better than the other, but the vibe will likely be different.

These days, the Germans are splitting their bratwurst and kraut, too.

Splitting dishes is generally OK. While portions may be expensive, they're often huge and splittable. A key challenge of budget eating is ordering just enough to fill you, while leaving nothing on your plate. If a single main dish is enough for 1.5 people (as many are), split it between yourself and your travel partner, and supplement it with a bowl of soup or small first course. Waiters are generally accommodating; the prices are high for Europeans, too. But be careful in France, where splitting meals at restaurants can be frowned upon; instead, head for a café, where it's perfectly acceptable to share meals or order just a salad or sandwich, even for dinner. At any place, it's fine to split a dessert. To save more money, order a carafe of house wine instead of a bottle of fine wine.

Slow service is good service. A lot of Americans complain about how long European meals take. In America, time is money, and restaurants are all about turning tables over. In Europe, the meal is routinely the event of the night. The restaurant expects that you're there for the evening. At good restaurants, respectful, quality service will seem slow to Americans. Dishes won't always come simultaneously—it's fine to start eating when served. Many Europeans will spend at least two hours enjoying a good dinner, and, for the full experience, so should you. Fast service is considered rude service. If you need to eat and run, make your time limits very clear as you order.

Share fine things. Servers are happy to bring one dessert and as many spoons as needed.

Know each country's dining quirks. In Italy, it's common to be charged a *pane e coperto* ("bread and cover" charge) just to sit down. In Portugal, appetizers (olives, bread, etc.) that are automatically brought to your table are not free—if you touch them, you pay for them. If you see a *Stammtisch* sign hanging over a table at a German restaurant, it means that it's reserved for regulars. Spaniards eat very late—to adapt, eat lunch at 3 p.m. and dinner at 10 p.m., or go to a tapas bar, where you can get small dishes all day long.

Getting a table is a lot like at home. When entering a restaurant without reservations, talk to the host or hostess, if there is one, or catch a server's eye and signal to be sure it's OK to sit at a table that isn't marked "reserved." If the place is full and there's no official host standing by to add your name to a waiting list, ask anyone who's available. Note that since European diners take their time with a meal, it's impossible to predict how quickly the tables will turn over. You may be asked to wait, or you may be turned away.

Make reservations for higher-end places. For expensive places, it's smart to reserve a table in advance. For years as a tourist, it never occurred to me to make reservations just as I would at home. But I finally realized that it's smart to get on the phone and say, "A table for 4 people, we're coming at 8 p.m., my name is Ricardo." If you do that, you'll have a table waiting for you. Otherwise you're going to be roaming around, every place is going to be full, and you're going to be very frustrated.

Where there's smoke... No-smoking rules seem to be working in European restaurants, but watch out if you're seated outdoors, where smokers congregate to light up.

Tips for Ordering

Finding the right restaurant is only half the battle. You also need to order smartly.

Check the menu first. Most European restaurants post their menus outside. Check the price and selection before entering. If the menu's not posted, ask to see one before you commit to a place. Be aware that in parts of Europe, the word *menu* means a fixed-price meal (*menu* in French, *menù* in Italian, *Menü* in German, and *menú* in Spanish); instead, to see an à la carte menu, you want *la carte* in French, *Speisekarte* in German, *la carta* in Spanish, and so on.

Ordering in a foreign language can be fun, or it can be an ordeal. It's OK to ask for an English menu—if nothing else, you might get the waiter who speaks the most English. Many waiters can give at least a very basic translation—"cheekin, bunny, zuppa, green salat," and so on. A menu reader, phrase

Vegetarians

Vegetarians find life a little frustrating in Europe. Very often, Europeans think "vegetarian" means "no red meat" or "not much meat." If you are a strict vegetarian, you'll have to make things very clear. Write out the appropriate phrase (see below), keep it handy, and show it to each waiter before ordering.

Salad bars are abundant and great for vegetarians.

Vegetarians have no problem with continental breakfasts, which are normally meatless anyway. Meat-free picnic lunches are delicious, since bread, cheese, and yogurt are wonderful throughout Europe. Have some healthy snacks (such as nuts or fresh produce) on hand, in case you can't find a suitable meal.

It's in restaurants that your patience may be minced. For a good meal, seek out a vegetarian restaurant (most big cities have them; check online for ideas), or browse the menus at some fine-dining restaurants, many of which offer at least one good vegetarian option. In my guidebooks, whenever possible, I list good vegetarian restaurants in each city.

Cafeterias (such as the bright, cheery, affordable ones you'll find on the top floor of major department stores) are a good option for vegetarians, since you can see exactly what you're getting and select foods that suit your diet.

Each country has its own quirks: Italy seems to sprinkle a little meat in just about everything. German cooking normally keeps the meat separate from the vegetables. Hearty German salads, with beets, cheese, and eggs, are a vegetarian's delight. Vegetarians enjoy *antipasti* buffets, salad bars, and ethnic restaurants throughout Europe.

Key Vegetarian Phrases: The phrases below communicate these points: "We are (I am) vegetarian. We (I) do not eat meat, fish, or chicken. Eggs and cheese OK."

German: *Wir sind (Ich bin) Vegetarier. Wir essen (Ich esse) kein Fleisch, Fisch, oder Geflügel. Eier und Käse OK.*

French: *Nous sommes (Je suis) végétarien. Nous ne mangeons (Je ne mange) pas de viande, poisson, ou poulet. Oeufs et fromage OK.*

Italian: *Siamo vegetariani (Sono vegetariano/a). Non mangiamo (Mangio) nè carne, nè pesce, nè polli. Uova e formaggio OK.*

Spanish: *Somos vegetarianos (Soy vegetariano/a). No comemos (No como) ni carne, ni pescado, ni pollo. Los huevos y el queso OK.*

book, or translation app is helpful for those who want to avoid ordering sheep stomach instead of lamb chops.

Order regional and seasonal specials. Learn what's in season (or ask your server). In the summer, French onion soup and cheese fondue (both winter dishes) are only served at tourist traps. White asparagus and porcini mushrooms are a treat for your palate in season...but come out of the freezer the rest of the year. Truffles, at the right time, are a beautiful thing. Whenever you can, order the daily special, which usually features what's seasonal. You'll get a better value and tastier food.

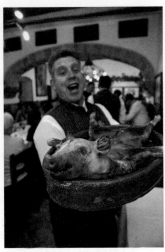

Roast suckling pig on a platter? When in Segovia...

I also make it a point to try foods that are unique to a certain region—for instance, cassoulet in the southwest of France, *cochinillo asado* (roast suckling pig) in Segovia, Spain, or *bistecca alla fiorentina* in Florence (beef from the white Chianina breed of cattle grazing throughout Tuscany). Barnacles in Portugal are very expensive, but so worth it—the best seafood I've ever eaten.

Eat family style. I love cultures that highlight family-style eating, and wherever I can, I opt for sharing. A lot of Americans think it's bad style to share plates, but believe me—the chef is more than happy for you to share so you can sample more dishes.

To max out culturally, my partner and I order and share two different meals: one high risk and one low risk. At worst, we learn what we don't like and split the chicken and fries. My tour groups cut every meal into bits, and our table becomes a lazy Susan. If anything, the waiters are impressed by our interest in their food and very often they'll run over with a special treat for all of us to sample—like squid eggs. With a gang of 10 travelers, I once ordered all 10 pizzas on the menu to come one after the other, each cut into 10 slices. We took our time, the waiters had fun, we savored a great variety, and everything was hot...it was the cheapest 10-course meal in Rome.

Order small plates rather than entrées. Sometimes, rather than getting two main courses, my travel partner and I share a memorable little buffet of appetizers—they're plenty filling, less expensive, and more typically local than entrées. These small plates go by different names throughout Europe:

Sample Fixed-Price Menu

TRATTORIA DUE TORRE 🏰🏰

STRADA FELLINI 37, ROMA

MENÙ TURISTICO €25

PRIMO PIATTO (FIRST COURSE)
- RISOTTO MILANESE
- SPAGHETTI CARBONARA
- PENNE AL PESTO
- ZUPPA MINESTRONE
- PROSCIUTTO E MELONE

SECONDO PIATTO (SECOND COURSE)
- PESCE AI FERRI
- SALTIMBOCCA ALLA ROMANA
- GRIGLIATA DI CARNE
- MELANZANE ALLA PARMIGIANA

CONTORNI (VEGETABLE SIDE DISHES)
- VERDURE DI STAGIONE
- INSALATA

DOLCI (DESSERT)
- TIRAMISU DELLA CASA
- GELATO
- FRUTTA

BEVANDE (DRINKS)
- ¼ VINO o ACQUA

BUON APPETITO!

SERVIZIO INCLUSO 10%

A fixed-price menu makes ordering easy for tourists: Choose a first course, second course, side dish, dessert, and beverage—all for a set price of €25.

tapas in Spain, *mezedes* in Greece, and *antipasti* in Italy. In Venice, *cicchetti* (small plates) are served in some bars.

Consider daily specials and fixed-price meals. Small eateries in most countries offer a fresh and economical daily special. Learn the native term (*menu del día* in Spain, *plat du jour* in France, *menù del giorno* in Italy, *dagens rett* in Norway). These are often limited to early seatings, with the time (usually before 7:30 p.m.) posted on the door and in the menu. Some classy restaurants in bigger cities in Britain and Ireland offer early-bird specials (order before 6:30 or 7 p.m.); having an early, nice dinner before attending a play or concert feels just right.

The fixed-price "tourist menu" (*menu* in France, *menù turistico* in Italy) is popular in restaurants throughout Europe's tourist zones, offering confused visitors a no-stress, three-course meal at a painless rate that usually includes service, bread, and a drink. You normally get a choice of several options for

For a good dining value, I look for a chalkboard daily special (*menu del día*).

each course. The tourist menu can be a convenient way to sample some regional flavors for a reasonable, predictable price (even thrifty locals order it).

If you have dietary restrictions, write them out on a card. Flash it while ordering and you'll get what you want.

Ask for recommendations or peek at your neighbors' plates. If you still don't know what to order, ask the server for recommendations or look for your dream meal on another table and order by pointing. People are usually helpful and understanding of the poor and hungry monoglot tourist. If they aren't, you probably picked a place that sees too many of them. Europeans with the most patience with tourists are the ones who rarely deal with them.

Travelers who agonize over each word on the menu season their whole experience with stress. If you're in a good place, the food's good. Get a basic idea of what's cooking, have some fun with your server, be loose and adventurous, and just order something.

Clarify dietary restrictions. If you have dietary concerns, such as being gluten free, vegan, or allergic to nuts, write it down and then have it translated so that you can show it to the server to avoid any communication miscues (ask a native speaker, such as your hotelier, for help, or use a translation tool). Be very explicit, such as: "I am allergic to" followed by all of the problem foods.

Drinks

Europeans, who are notorious water snobs, generally pay to drink bottled water with their meals—for taste, not health. At restaurants, your server just can't understand why you wouldn't want good bottled water to go with your good food.

Luckily, it's never expensive to order a half-liter of bottled water. It is served crisp and cold, either with or without carbonation. Some Americans don't like the bubbly stuff, but I do. Learn the local phrase for *con/avec/mit/con/*with gas or *senza/sans/ohne/sin/*without gas (in Italian, French, German, and Spanish, respectively), and you'll get the message across. Acquire a taste for *acqua con gas.* It's a lot more fun (and read on the label what it'll do for your rheumatism).

While it's possible to get tap water, to do so you may need to be polite, patient, inventive, and know the correct phrase. Availability of (and willingness to serve) tap water varies from country to country; you'll pay for it in Belgium (and in

Denmark, too, unless you order an additional beverage). It's sometimes considered a special favor, and while your glass or carafe of tap water is normally served politely, occasionally it just isn't worth the trouble.

My advice: Drink like a European. Cold milk, ice cubes, and coffee with (rather than after) your meal are American habits. Insisting on any of these in Europe will get you strange looks and a reputation as a crazy American. Order local drinks, not just to save money, but to experience the culture and get the best quality and service. The timid can always order the "American waters" (Coke, Fanta, and 7-Up), sold everywhere.

Trying regionally produced alcohol can be a great cultural experience. In Scotland, locals are passionate about finding and describing the whisky that fits their personality. Each guy in the pub has "his" whisky. And the flavors (fruity, peppery, peaty, smoky) are much easier to actually taste than their wine-snob equivalents.

In France, geography plays a big part in the country's liquid pride. *Terroir* (pronounced "tehr-wah") is a uniquely French concept. *Terroir* denotes "somewhere-ness," a combination of the macro- and microclimate, soil, geology, and culture (the accumulated experience of the people and their craft). The French don't call a wine by the grape's name. Two wines can be made of the same grape, but be of very different character because of their *terroir.* A real Chablis made from the Chardonnay grape is better than Chardonnays made elsewhere because of its *terroir.*

Drinking locally produced alcohol has another advantage: It's cheaper than your favorite import. A shot of the local hard drink in Portugal will cost a dollar, while an American drink would cost more than the American price. Drink the local stuff with local

Tap Water in Five Languages

Italian: *acqua del rubinetto*
French: *une carafe d'eau*
German: *Leitungswasser*
Spanish: *agua del grifo*
Portuguese: *água da torneira*

To get tap water in any language, do this international charade: Hold an imaginary glass in one hand, turn on the tap with the other, and make the sound of a faucet. Stop it with a click of your tongue and drink it with a smile.

German pubs don't serve minors beer—but many locals do.

people in local bars; it's a better experience than having a
Manhattan in your hotel with a guy from Los Angeles. Drink
wine in wine countries and beer in beer countries. Sample the
regional specialties. Let a local person order you her favorite.
You may hate it, but you'll never forget it.

Paying the Bill

To get the bill, you'll have to ask for it (catch the waiter's eye
and, with raised hands, scribble with an imaginary pencil on
your palm). Before it comes, make a mental tally of roughly
how much your meal should cost. The bill should vaguely
resemble the figure you expected. (It should at least have
the same number of digits.) If the total is a surprise, ask to
have it itemized and explained. Some servers make the same
"innocent" mistakes repeatedly, knowing most tourists are
so befuddled by the money and menu that they'll pay whatever number is scrawled across the bottom of the bill.

　　If you pay with a credit card, your server will likely bring
a mobile card reader to the table. These machines cut down
on fraud since your card never leaves your sight. Be aware
that you may have to enter the card's PIN rather than sign
a receipt (see the Money chapter), and there may not be an
opportunity to add a tip (see next section).

Tipping

Restaurant tips are more modest in Europe than in America.
In Europe, waiters and waitresses are paid a living wage, and
tips are considered a small bonus—to reward great service
or for simplicity in rounding the total bill to a convenient
number. In many countries, 5 percent is adequate and 10
percent is considered a big tip. Locals just leave coins on the
table, round up, or often don't tip at all.

　　Resist the urge to tip American-style in Europe. If your
bucks talk at home, muzzle them on your travels. As a matter
of principle—if not economy—the local price should prevail.
Please believe me—tipping 15 or 20 percent in Europe is
unnecessary, if not culturally ignorant. You're just raising
the bar and messing up the local balance. And it's bad style.

　　Tipping is an issue only at restaurants with waiters and
waitresses. If you order your food at a counter (in a pub, for
example), don't tip. At table-service restaurants, the tipping
etiquette and procedure vary slightly from country to country (see the "Tipping Standards by Country" sidebar).

　　In Mediterranean countries, the "service charge" (servizio in Italian, service in French, servicio in Spanish) can be

Interpreting the Bill

Examine this sample Italian restaurant bill to get used to the charges you'll see in Europe.

Check each line item. Be sure you understand what each charge was for. You don't have to speak fluent Italian to recognize *minestrone* or *spaghetti carbonara*. Even *insalata mista* isn't a stretch if you remember that you ate a mixed salad. But if it says *"4 birre"* and you don't remember drinking four beers, ask for an explanation (or an apology).

Pane e coperto ("bread and cover" charge) is a mandatory amount charged per customer just to sit down. Common in Italy, this is relatively rare in other countries–though (sadly) it's beginning to catch on at touristy restaurants in popular destinations, such as Prague.

A legitimate **servizio** (service) charge of 10 percent has been added. You don't need to leave a big tip (but if you were pleased with the service, you'd add a euro or two for each person in your party). In many cases, rather than adding the 10 percent at the end of the bill, the menu prices already include the service charge (in which case, the menu might say *"servizio incluso"*).

Note that Europeans use a comma as a decimal point–so €58,30 is the same as €58.30. For this meal, I'd hand the server €60, smile, say *grazie*, and wave my hand to suggest she should keep the change.

VIA GARIBALDI 37, ROMA

Ristorante Colosseo

DI RICARDO STEFANO

	IMPORTO
pane e coperto (x2)...	4,00
insalata caprese.....	6,00
ins. mista..........	4,00
spaghetti carbonara...	6,00
minestrone	8,00
frutta	4,00
tiramisú	5,00
vino rosso (bottiglia)...	12,00
acqua min. (litro).....	4,00
totale	53,00
servizio 10%	5,30
totale documento	**€58,30**

RICEVUTA FISCALE
COPIA PER IL CLIENTE

handled in different ways. Sometimes the menu will note that the service is included (*"servizio incluso"*), meaning that the prices listed on the menu already have this charge built in. When the service is not included (*"servizio non incluso"*), the service charge might show up as a separate line item at the end of your bill. Most fixed-price tourist deals include service.

In northern and eastern Europe, the menu or bill is less likely to address the "service charge," but you can usually assume that it's included in the prices. Lately, some restaurants—especially those in well-touristed areas in Germany and Austria—have added a "Tip is not included" line, in English, to the bottom of the bill. This is misleading, as the prices on any menu in these countries *do* include service. I wouldn't tip one cent more at a restaurant that includes this note on the bill.

Typically, it's better to hand the tip to the waiter when you're paying your bill than to leave it on the table, particularly in busy places where the wrong party might pocket the change. Servers prefer to be tipped in cash even if you pay with your credit card (otherwise the tip may never reach your server); in many cases, there isn't even a line on the credit-card receipt for a tip.

In Germanic countries, rather than leaving coins behind on the table (considered slightly rude), locals usually pay directly: When the server comes by with the bill, simply hand over paper money, stating the total you'd like to pay. For example, if paying for a €10 meal with a €20 bill, while handing your money to the server, say "Eleven, please" (or "*Elf, bitte*" if you've got your German numbers down). The server will keep a €1 tip and give you €9 in change.

Don't stress about tipping in Europe. If you're unsure what to give, ask a local (but not a waiter) about the tipping norms for that country. Virtually anywhere in Europe, you can do as the Europeans do and (if you're pleased with the service) add a euro or two for each person in your party. In very touristy areas, some servers have noticed the American obsession with overtipping—and might hope for a Yankee-size tip. But the good news is that European servers and diners are far more laid-back about all this than we are. Any tip is appreciated, the stakes are low, and it's no big deal if you choose the "wrong" amount. Don't lose sleep over walking out of a restaurant in Europe without tipping.

EUROPE'S CAFÉ SCENE

Recently, I savored a peaceful moment in Siena's great square, Il Campo, sipping a glass of *vin santo* as the early evening light bathed the red-brick stone. My five-euro drink gave me a front-row seat at the best café table on the square,

LEFT A café on Siena's main square gives you a ringside seat to all the action.

RIGHT Be a part of the lively atmosphere in a Parisian sidewalk café.

Tipping Standards by Country

Country	General Rule
Austria	Service is included, but it's common to round up (5-10 percent). Give the tip directly to your server.
Belgium	Service is included, but it's common to round up (5-10 percent).
Croatia	At some touristy restaurants, a 10-15 percent "service charge" may be added (no additional tip is necessary). Otherwise round up 5-10 percent.
Czech Republic	Service is generally included, although it's common to round up after a good meal (5-10 percent). If you speak just a few Czech words to your server, you'll get better service and won't be expected to tip more than a local; if you greet your server in English, he'll want a 15 percent tip.
Denmark	The service charge typically included in your bill may not go to the server, so for good service, add on 5-10 percent.
Estonia	Round up for good service (though never more than 10 percent).
Finland	A service charge is typically included in your bill, but the money may not go to the server, so for good service, tip 5-10 percent.
France	Prices include a 12-15 percent service charge, so most French never tip. For exceptional service, you could tip up to 5 percent—but don't feel obligated.
Germany	It's common to tip after a good meal, usually 10 percent.
Great Britain	Check the menu or bill to see if service is included (generally 10-12.5 percent); if not, tip about that much. Many London restaurants list a 12.5 percent "optional" tip on the bill, but tip only what you feel the service warrants.
Greece	Service is generally included, but it's common to round up about 10 percent. It's considered bad form to leave a single euro, though; if a bill is €10, leave a €2 tip.
Hungary	Most Budapest restaurants tack on a 10 percent service charge (possibly more in touristy areas) that should be noted on the menu and bill. No additional tip is necessary. If service isn't included, tip about 10 percent.
Ireland	Check the menu or your bill to see if service is included; if not, tip about 10 percent.

Country	General Rule
Italy	A 10 percent service charge *(servizio)* is usually built into your bill. If you wish, you can add an extra €1-2 for each person in your party (or about 5 percent). If *servizio* is not included, tip up to 10 percent.
Netherlands	Tipping is not necessary (15 percent service is usually included in the menu price), but a tip of about 5-10 percent is a nice reward for good service. Rounding up to the next euro ("keep the change") is appropriate if you get table service rather than ordering at the bar.
Norway	If there is a service charge on your bill, it may go to the owner, so you should still leave a tip (5-10 percent).
Poland	Round up 5-10 percent. At tourist-oriented restaurants, a 10-15 percent service charge may be added to your bill, in which case an additional tip is not necessary.
Portugal	Service is generally included (you'll see *serviço incluído* on menus), but for good service, it's customary to leave an additional 5 percent (10 percent for upscale restaurants or if service is not included).
Slovenia	At touristy restaurants, a 10-15 percent "service charge" may be added to your bill, in which case an additional tip is not necessary. Otherwise tip 5-10 percent.
Spain	If you order at a counter—as you often will when sampling tapas at a bar—there's no need to tip, though you can round up with a few small coins. At restaurants with table service, if a service charge is included in the bill, add about 5 percent; if it's not, leave 10 percent.
Sweden	Service is typically included, but don't assume the money goes to your server. In nicer restaurants or for great service, round up (5-10 percent).
Switzerland	Service is included with table service, but it's customary to round up the bill (no more than 5-10 percent).
Turkey	Tip about 10 percent. If you're not satisfied, tip less—or not at all. Some upscale restaurants may include a "service charge" on the bill; this goes to the owner, not the server—so still tip about 10 percent.

and for a leisurely hour I soaked up the promenading action that nightly turns Il Campo into "Il Italian Fashion Show."

Public squares like Il Campo are the physical and cultural heart of Europe's cities and towns. For Europeans, these bustling squares proclaim "community." Defined by stately architecture and ringed by shops and cafés, squares are the perfect venue for café-sitting, coffee-sipping, and people-watching. Promenaders take center stage, strolling and being seen, while onlookers perch on the periphery. To play your part, tether yourself to one of the café tables parked around any square, order a drink, and feel the pulse of the passing scene. Don't be in a hurry—spending endless hours sitting in an outdoor café is the norm. And don't worry about the price—I happily pay too much to enjoy a cup of coffee or a cocktail on the most expensive piece of real estate in a town and watch the scene go by. You're not paying for the drink. You're paying to be a part of the scene, and that is integral to a quality European experience.

Café Culture

The coffee scene is especially strong in Italy, France, Austria, Hungary, the Czech Republic, and Greece. Cafés provide a place for people to gather socially and spend hours catching up and discussing everything from politics to sports.

In Italy, cafés are commonly referred to as "bars." They serve coffee, wine, liquor, and light food such as minipizzas and sandwiches. Italians tend to stop by their favorite bar in the morning for a coffee and pastry, then throughout the day for more coffee and eventually drinks. In fact, one of my favorite bar traditions in Italy has nothing to do with coffee. Around happy hour, many bars lay out an *aperitivo* buffet, which usually includes an array of meats, cheeses, grilled vegetables, and other antipasti-type dishes. If you pay for a drink, you're welcome to nibble to your heart's content. While this spread is intended as an appetizer course before a full dinner, light eaters could discreetly turn this into a small meal (typically served around 6 p.m. or 7 p.m. until 9 p.m.).

Historically, French cafés served as a second home to the great artists, writers, and political figures of the time, like Trotsky, Stravinsky, Hemingway, and Gertrude Stein. Today, the French still flock to cafés for business meetings, encounter sessions, political discussions, and romantic inter-ludes. But many cafés also serve a practical purpose: Unlike restaurants and bistros, which are only open at meal times, cafés serve light meals throughout most of the day. You're welcome to order just a salad, a sandwich, or a bowl of soup, even for dinner, making this a lighter and less formal option for dining out.

Viennese-style coffeehouses are another institution, found not only in Austria, but also in Prague, Budapest, Kraków, and other cities of the former Austro-Hungarian empire. Though coffee boomed as an aristocratic drink in the 18th century, later, during the Industrial Age, it became a hit with the working class, who were expected to put in 12-hour shifts. Neighborhood cafés allowed urbanites to escape their tiny flats and provided warmth for those who didn't want to pay to heat their homes during the day.

Today's Viennese coffeehouses still provide a living room down the street for locals, offering newspapers, pastries, sofas, quick and light lunches, elegant ambience, and "take all the time you want" charm for the price of a cup of coffee. Rather than buy the *International New York Times* ahead of time, spend the money on a cup of coffee and read the paper for free, Vienna-style, in a café.

In European cafés, menus are two-tiered: cheaper at the bar, more expensive at a table.

Café Tips

Tourists are often stung by not understanding the rules at European cafés. In many countries, you'll pay more to sit at a table and less to stand at a bar. In general, if you're not planning to linger, it's cheaper to order and consume your drink at the bar. If you want to sit a while and absorb that last museum while checking out the two-legged art, grab a table with a view, and a server will take your order. This will cost you about double what it would at the bar. Some places also charge more for an outdoor table than for an indoor one.

If you're on a budget, always confirm the price for a sit-down drink. While it's never high profile, there's always a price list posted somewhere inside—usually by the bar or cash register—displaying either a two- or three-tiered pricing system (cheap at the bar, more at a table, possibly even more at an outside table).

If ordering from the bar, you may have to pay the cashier first, then take your receipt to the bar, where the barista will make your drink. Lingering with your bar-priced drink on a nearby public bench or across the street on the beach is usually OK—just ask first.

If you pay for a seat in a café with an expensive drink, that seat's yours for the afternoon if you like. Note that at a French café, if the table is not set, it's fine to seat yourself and just have a drink. However, if it's set with a placemat and cutlery, you should ask to be seated and plan to order a meal.

As a traveler, you naturally want to take in as many sights as you can every day. But make time in your itinerary to simply drop yourself into a café chair for a few hours. Enjoying life like the Europeans do—watching the world go by—is one of the best and most relaxing ways to go local.

Europe is brimming with atmospheric, linger-a-while cafés.

Know Your Joe

If you're a coffee lover, it pays to know the ground rules in various caffeine-loving countries.

Two of the biggest coffee cultures in Europe are Italy and France (in fact, the espresso-based style of coffee so popular in the US was born in Italy). In either place, if you ask for *"un caffè"* (Italian) or *"un café"* (French), you'll get a shot of espresso in a little cup. Most coffee drinks begin with espresso, to which they add varying amounts of hot water and/or steamed or foamed milk. Milky drinks, such as a cappuccino, *caffè latte* (Italy), *or café au lait/café crème* (France), are served to locals before noon and to tourists any time of day. To a local, cappuccino is a breakfast drink, and drinking anything with milk or cream after a meal or later in the day is thought to upset your digestion (Italians also believe having milk after eating anything with tomatoes is a travesty). If they add any milk after lunch, it's just a splash, in a *caffè macchiato* (Italy) or *noisette* (France). You're welcome to order a milkier coffee drink later in the day, but don't be surprised if you get a funny look.

If you're hankering for the closest thing to brewed coffee, ask for a *caffè americano* (Italy) or *un café allongé* (France)—an espresso diluted with hot water. Cafés in Britain, Germany, and Scandinavia are more likely to serve brewed coffee, though there are plenty of espresso places these days.

Turkish coffee refers not to a type of coffee, but to the

way the coffee is prepared: The coffee grounds float freely in the brew, leaving behind a layer of "mud" at the bottom of the cup. You'll also find this style of coffee in Greece (Greek coffee) and the Czech Republic (*turecká káva*). It's typically drunk as a digestive after dinner and sometimes after lunch. In these countries, if you take sugar, ask for it when you place your order (it's added while the coffee is being heated).

BUDGET AND ON-THE-GO OPTIONS

Europe offers a bounty of options for eating quickly and inexpensively. While cafeterias, street stands, and "to go" meals are not high cuisine, they're cheap. And sometimes what you get is just as tasty as restaurant food. Some of my favorite and most memorable meals have been consumed at a market hall or a street-corner sausage stand. For an affordable, quality lunch, line up with the local office workers: They eat out every day and they know where the good values are.

Cafeterias and Institution-Affiliated Eateries

"Self-service" is an international word. You'll find self-service restaurants in big cities everywhere, offering low-price, low-risk, low-stress, what-you-see-is-what-you-get meals. All over Europe, towering department stores offer great cafeteria lunches—often with rooftop views for no extra charge (such as at the Galeria Kaufhof in Frankfurt). These places are designed for the shopper who has a sharp eye for a good value. At a salad bar, grab the small (cheap) plate and stack it like the locals do—high. Hungry sightseers also appreciate the handy, moderately priced cafeterias they'll find in larger museums.

In Italy, a fast and cheap lunch option is a *tavola calda* ("hot table"), a point-and-shoot cafeteria with a buffet spread of meat and vegetables (it's sometimes called a *tavola fredda*, or "cold table," in the north). Don't be limited by what's displayed. If you'd like a salad with a slice of cantaloupe and a hunk of cheese, they'll whip that up for you. Belly up to the bar; with a pointing finger, you can assemble a fine meal.

If your wallet is as empty as your stomach, find a cheap, humble cafeteria that's associated with (and subsidized by)

Cafeteria leftovers: even cheaper than picnics...

a local institution—such as a university, church, hospital, charity, senior center, fire station, union of gondoliers, retired fishermen's club, and so on. Profits take a back seat to providing good food at a good price—and many of these eateries welcome the public to pull up a chair. Options range from a cafeteria in Vienna serving Austria's Supreme Court of Justice, to student canteens in university towns (such as Salzburg, Austria), to Poland's dreary-looking but cheap-and-tasty "milk bars." Don't be afraid to take advantage of these opportunities to fill yourself with a plate of dull but nourishing food for an unbeatable price in the company of locals. University cafeterias (generally closed during summer holidays) also offer a surefire way to meet educated, English-speaking young people with open and stimulating minds. They're often eager to share their views on politics and economics, as well as their English, with a foreign friend.

Bakeries and Sandwich Shops

Bakeries are a good place to pick up basic sandwiches, tiny pizzas, or something equally cheap and fast but with more of a regional flavor (such as savory pasties in England or a *croque-monsieur* sandwich in France). Britain's Pret à Manger, Norway's Deli de Luca, and Spain's Pans & Company are chains that sell good, healthful sandwiches, salads, and pastries. Local deli-like shops are popular in many parts of Europe; try a *traiteur* in France or a *rosticceria* in Italy.

Street Food and Ethnic Eats

Every country has its own equivalent of the hot-dog stand or burger joint, where you can grab a filling bite on the go for cheap—French *crêperies*, Greek souvlaki stands, Danish *pølse* (sausage) vendors, Italian *pizza rustica* takeout shops, German sausage stands, British chippies (fish-and-chips), and Dutch herring carts.

Often the cheapest hot meals in town feature cuisine

LEFT Local deli-like shops, such as this French *traiteur*, offer delicious to-go fare.

RIGHT Eat where the immigrants do, and you'll save plenty of money.

from another country. Ethnic eateries are more common in northern Europe than in southern countries like Italy or Spain. Throughout wealthy northern Europe, immigrant communities labor at subsistence wages. These people have very tasty food traditions, they have very small budgets, and they like to go out and eat. Rather than eat bland and pricey local food, they (along with savvy residents and travelers) go cheap and spicy at simple diners, delis, and takeaway stands serving Middle Eastern, Pakistani, and Asian food.

Immigrant restaurants are a godsend for tourists, especially in pricey locales like Scandinavia or Great Britain. In fact, Indian food is considered "going local" in cosmopolitan, multiethnic Britain. You'll find Indian restaurants in most British cities and even in small towns. Take the opportunity to sample food from Britain's former colony.

Of all the ethnic options in Europe, the ubiquitous kebab stand is my favorite. Kiosks selling Turkish-style *döner kebab* (rotisserie meat wrapped in pita bread), falafel (fried chickpea patties), and other Middle Eastern dishes are popular in many places, including Germany, Florence, and Paris. The best stands have a busy energy, and a single large kebab draped in wonderful pita bread can feed two hungry travelers for €5. Don't miss the *ayran*—a healthy yogurt drink popular with Turks—which goes well with your kebab.

Market Halls

Europe's old Industrial Age glass-and-steel farmers markets seem to be celebrating their hundredth birthdays by getting a new lease on life as trendy food halls. These market halls still come with the farmers' market dimension (described later, under "Markets"), but they've been spiced up with great eateries, priced for local shoppers and serving the freshest ingredients. At any stall where you see locals lining up, you know something exciting is being served.

Frankfurt's Kleinmarkthalle, a delightful, old-school

LEFT For good, affordable eats, join the locals at Frankfurt's Kleinmarkthalle.

RIGHT Market halls—such as Florence's venerable Mercato Centrale—are finding new life hosting chic eateries.

market that was saved from developers by local outcry, is now an adventure in fine eating. Torvehallerne, an upscale Copenhagen food court housed in a pair of modern, glassy buildings, is a great place to try *smørrebrød* (open-face sandwiches topped with delicious fish, cheese, cold cuts, or interesting spreads). Lisbon's Mercado de Campo de Ourique is a 19th-century iron-and-glass market that has morphed into a trendy food circus with produce stalls, fishmongers, and bakeries that sell everything from pigs' ears to designer cupcakes.

One of my favorite market halls is Florence's Mercato Centrale. It's long been enjoyable as a thriving local market selling meat, fish, produce, and other staples to a mostly local clientele. The city recently renovated the market's long-neglected upper level, which now hosts a wonderful collection of quality eateries that are as busy as the ground-level produce stalls. The food artisans at work here serve pizza and pasta, but they also dish up regional treats. The food court is a real hit with the neighborhood's office workers during the day, and provides a good insight into local eating habits. Take a peek at what's on your neighbor's plate—Florentines eat just about every bit of the cow. Stay away from the *trippa* and *lampredotto* sandwiches if you can't stomach stomach meat.

If visiting a market hall, be sure to check the hours. Some are open in the evening while others are geared toward the working crowd and close early. It's best to go at lunch. These days, in nearly any European city, I find sitting down with local shoppers at the traditional market to be a great way to enjoy lunch and feel the pulse of everyday life.

McEurope

Fast-food restaurants are everywhere. Yes, the hamburger-ization of the world is a shame, but face it—the busiest and biggest McDonald's in the world are in places like Tokyo, Rome, and Moscow. The burger has become a global thing. You'll find Big Macs in every language—it isn't exciting (and costs more than at home), but at least at McDonald's you know exactly what you're getting, and it's fast. A hamburger, fries, and shake can be fun halfway through your

You'll find Big Macs in every language.

trip. You'll also find KFC, Subway, and Starbucks almost everywhere.

American fast-food joints are kid-friendly and satisfy the need for a cheap meal and a tall orange juice. They've grabbed prime bits of real estate in every big European city. Since there's no cover charge, this is an opportunity to savor a low-class paper cup of coffee while enjoying some high-class people-watching (unless you're at Starbucks, where your paper cup will be high class, too). Many offer free Wi-Fi as well.

Each country also has its equivalent of the hamburger stand (I saw a "McCheaper" in Switzerland). Whatever their origin, they're a hit with youths and a handy place for a quick, cheap bite to eat.

PICNICS, MARKETS, AND SUPERMARKETS

The best way to feast like a European—enjoying tasty local specialties economically—is to picnic. You'll eat better while spending half as much as those who eat exclusively in restaurants. In my book, there's no better travel experience than a picnic sourced from local markets and grocers, eaten outdoors with a lively square, peaceful park, or rejuvenated harborfront as a backdrop.

I am a picnic connoisseur. While I'm the first to admit that restaurant meals are an important aspect of any culture, I picnic almost daily—and not just for budgetary reasons. It's fun to dive into a marketplace or corner grocery and interact with locals. Europe's colorful markets overflow with varied cheeses, meats, fresh fruits, vegetables, and warm-from-the-oven bread. Many of my favorite foods made their debut in a European picnic.

You can save on your food budget by visiting the corner bakery and picnicking on the grass or a bench.

To busy sightseers and budget travelers, restaurants can be time-consuming and frustrating. After waiting to be served, tangling with a menu, and consuming a pricey meal, you walk away feeling unsatisfied, knowing your money could have done much more for your stomach if you had invested it in a picnic instead.

To bolster your budget, I recommend picnic dinners every few nights. At home, we save time and money by raiding the refrigerator to assemble a pickup dinner. In Europe, the equivalent is the corner deli, bakery, produce market, or supermarket. You can also pick up a picnic from nearly anywhere willing to pack a meal to go, such as a souvlaki stand, sausage truck, *crêperie,* pizza shop, or market hall. For ideas, see the "Budget and On-the-Go Options" section (page 275). For tips on shopping at markets and grocery stores, see page 282.

Only a glutton can spend more than $15 for a picnic feast. In a park in Paris, on a Norwegian ferry, high in the Alps, at an autobahn rest stop, or on your convent rooftop, picnicking is the budget traveler's key to cheap and good eating.

Picnic Tips

Here are some tricks for picnicking like a pro:

Picnic Supplies: Buy a good knife with a can opener and corkscrew in Europe (or bring it from home in your checked luggage). In addition to being a handy plate, fan, and lousy Frisbee, a plastic lid makes an easy-to-clean cutting board. Resealable plastic baggies (large and small) are great for containing messy food and packing up leftovers. Bring a plastic cup as well as a spoon and fork for eating takeout soups and salads.

Drinks: There are plenty of cheap ways to wash down a picnic. If you're tired of filling your water bottle, you can buy drinks in supermarkets and corner grocery stores. Liter bottles of soda are inexpensive, as is wine in most countries—and local wine gives your picnic a nice touch. Neighborhood wine shops have a great selection—and most will open your bottle if you forgot your corkscrew.

Stretching Your Money: Bread has always been cheap in Europe. (Leaders have learned from history that when stomachs rumble, so do the mobs in the streets.) Cheese is a specialty nearly everywhere and is, along with milk and yogurt, one of the Continent's most affordable sources of protein. The standard low-risk option anywhere in Europe

LEFT A quick dashboard picnic halfway through a busy day of sightseeing

RIGHT Throughout France, signs direct you to the most scenic places to *"pique-nique."*

is Emmentaler cheese (the kind with holes, what we call "Swiss"). Buy fruit and veggies that are in season; see what's inexpensive and plentiful in the produce section or market. Anything American is usually pricey and rarely satisfying. Cultural chameleons eat and drink better and cheaper.

Site Selection: Proper site selection can make the difference between just another meal and *le pique-nique extraordinaire*. Since you've decided to skip the restaurant, it's up to you to create the atmosphere.

I might start the day by scouring the thriving market with my senses. Then I fill up my shopping bag and have breakfast on a riverbank. After sightseeing, I combine lunch and a siesta in a cool park to fill my stomach, rest my body, and escape the early afternoon heat. It's fun to eat dinner on a castle wall enjoying a commanding view and the setting sun. Some of my all-time best picnics have been lazy dinners accompanied by medieval fantasies in the quiet of after-hours Europe.

Punctuate a hike with a picnic. Food tastes even better on top of a mountain. Europeans are great picnickers. Many picnics become potlucks, resulting in new friends as well as full stomachs.

Picnicking in Your Hotel Room: I love taking off my shoes, stretching out, and having a simple, cheap meal while catching up on work or TV in my hotel room. I don't want an earth-shaking dinner every night. Every second or third night I just like to have a relaxing and cheap picnic in my home away from home.

When staying several nights, I cozy up my room by borrowing plates, glasses, and silverware from the breakfast room and making a pantry stocked with juice, fruits, vegetables, cheese, and other munchies. Some hoteliers dislike picnicking in rooms, as they worry about cleanliness, smells, and insects (this is especially true in France, where hoteliers uniformly detest it when guests bring food into bedrooms).

LEFT This happy gang is living simply and well on the cheap: enjoying a picnic in Assisi, the hometown of St. Francis.

RIGHT Kick back and munch a picnic dinner in your hotel room.

If you can't picnic in your room, you'll find plenty of other atmospheric places to eat. If you do picnic in your room, be tidy and considerate, and wrap up your garbage really well, or better yet, toss it out in a public waste bin.

Markets

I love the marketplaces of Europe. To me they're as important as the museums. Nearly every town, large or small, has at least one colorful outdoor or indoor marketplace. Find out when they are up and running, and make it a point to be there. You'll enjoy the local push and shove.

Assemble your picnic here; you'll probably need to hit several stalls to put together a complete meal. Make an effort to communicate with the merchants. Know what you are buying and what you are spending. Whether you understand the prices or not, act like you do (observe the weighing process closely), and you're more likely to be treated fairly. Gather your ingredients in the morning, as markets typically close in the early afternoon.

Learn the measurements. The unit of measure throughout the Continent is a kilogram, or 2.2 pounds. A kilo (kg) has 1,000 grams (g or gr). One hundred grams (a common unit of sale) of cheese or meat tucked into a chunk of French bread gives you about a quarter-pounder. If you don't know the local language, just point to the food you want and write the amount on a scrap of paper.

Check how the item is priced. Watch the scale when your food is being weighed. It'll likely show grams and kilos. If dried apples are priced at €2 per kilo, that's $2.20 for 2.2 pounds, or about $1 per pound. If the scale says 400 grams, that means 40 percent of €2 (or 80 euro cents), which is about 90 cents.

Farmers markets are a fun source for healthy picnic snacks.

Not everything is strictly priced by the kilogram. Read the little chalkboard price carefully: Particularly in the case of specialty items, you might see things priced by the ¼ kg, ½ kg, 100 g, 500 g, and so on. Or an item could be priced by the piece (*Stück* in German, *piéce* in French, *pezzo* in Italian), the bunch, the container, and so on. If the pâté seems too cheap to be true, look at the sign closely. The posted price is probably followed by "100 gr."

If no prices are posted, be wary. Travelers are routinely ripped off by market merchants in tourist centers. Find places that post the prices. Assume any stall without posted prices has a double price standard: one for locals and a more expensive one for tourists.

I'll never forget a friend of mine who bought two bananas for our London picnic. He grabbed the fruit, held out a handful of change, and said, "How much?" The merchant took the equivalent of $4. My friend turned to me and said, "Wow, London really is expensive." Anytime you hold out a handful of money to a banana salesman, you're just asking for trouble.

Point, but don't touch. Most produce stands and outdoor markets are not self-service: Tell the vendor (or point to) what you want, and let the merchant bag it and weigh it for you. It's considered rude for a customer to touch the goods.

Want only a small amount? You'll likely need only one or two pieces of fruit, and many merchants refuse to deal in such small quantities. The way to get what you want and no more is to estimate what it would cost if the merchant were to weigh it and then just hold out a coin worth about that much in one hand and point to the apple, or whatever, with the other. Have a Forrest Gump look on your face that says, "If you take this coin, I'll go away." Rarely will he refuse the deal.

Appreciate the cultural experience. Shopping for groceries is an integral part of everyday European life for good reasons: People have small refrigerators (kitchens are tiny), value fresh produce, and enjoy the social interaction.

Not up for picnicking? You'll find competitive prices and characteristic seasonal food in the little eateries that always surround these markets.

Supermarkets and Grocery Stores

I prefer local markets, but American-style supermarkets, some of which hide out in the basements of big-city department stores, are a good alternative—and some of them are very upscale. Common European chains include Aldi, Carrefour, Co-op, Despar, Dia, Konzum, Lidl, Mercadona, Migros, Monoprix, Morrisons, Sainsbury's, Spar, and Tesco. Corner grocery stores give you more color but have a smaller selection.

If it's late in the day, you may be able to score some deals. One night in Oslo I walked into an ICA supermarket just before closing to discover that they'd marked down all the deli food by 50 percent. Back in my hotel room, I ate my cheapest meal in Norway—roast chicken and fries at almost US prices.

Ready-made Food: Many supermarkets offer cheap packaged sandwiches, while others have deli counters where you can get a sandwich made to order—just point to what you want. Most supermarkets offer a good selection of freshly prepared foods, such as quiche, fried chicken, and fish, all for takeout.

At the supermarket, put your banana on the scale, push the banana button, rip off the price sticker, and stick it on your banana.

Produce: Don't be intimidated by the produce section. It's a cinch to buy a tiny amount of fruit or vegetables. Many have an easy push-button pricing system: Put the banana on the scale, push the picture of a banana (or enter the banana bin number), and a sticky price tag prints out. You could weigh and sticker a single grape. In Spain and Italy, if there is no one to serve you, the store provides plastic gloves for you to wear while picking out your produce (a bare hand is a no-no).

Drinks: Milk in the dairy section is always cheap and available in quarter, half, or whole liters. Be sure it's normal drinking milk. Strange white liquid dairy products in look-alike milk cartons abound, ruining the milk-and-cookie dreams of careless tourists. Look for local words for "whole," "half," or "light," such as *voll*, *halb*, or *lett*. Get refrigerated, fresh milk. Or look on the (unrefrigerated) shelves for the common-in-Europe but rarer-in-America "long life" milk. This milk—which requires no refrigeration until it's opened— will never go bad...or taste good.

European yogurt is delicious and can often be drunk right out of its container. Fruit juice comes in handy liter boxes (look for "100% juice" or "no sugar" to avoid Kool-Aid clones). If it's hot outside, don't expect soft drinks, beer, or wine to be chilled—most supermarkets sell these at room temperature.

Sweets: To satisfy your sweet tooth (or stock up on gifts for the folks back home), check out the dessert and candy section. European-style "biscuits" (cookies)—made by companies such as Lu, Bahlsen, or McVities—are usually a good value, as are candy bars that might cost twice as much at airport gift shops.

Supermarket Etiquette: Bring your own shopping bag, use your empty daybag, or expect to pay extra for the store's plastic bags. You may have to insert a euro to use a shopping cart—although you'll get your deposit back when you return the cart to its rack. Some stores' plastic shopping baskets have wheels and pull-out handles as a handy alternative.

It's easiest to pay cash at checkout, but if you want to use your credit card, be sure you know the PIN—the clerk may ask you to enter it (clerks may also ask for photo ID). No one will bag your groceries for you; expect to bag and pay at the same time. It's smart to start bagging immediately to avoid frustrating the shoppers behind you.

FOOD EXPERIENCES

Lately, my favorite way of becoming a temporary local is by joining a food tour or cooking class. Both are a big deal; you'll easily find many recommendations in guidebooks or online. A new trend is social dining—websites pair travelers with locals for a home-cooked meal.

Food Tours

All over Europe, guided food tours are trendy. I take many of them in hopes of finding the best ones to recommend in our guidebooks, and to learn fun new angles on the local food scene.

Typical food tours last about three or four hours, come with a mile or so of walking, and include four to eight stops. Along the way, you'll sample a variety of local flavors, all thoughtfully explained by a guide, for a bit more than the cost of a splurge dinner (typically about €50-125 per person).

Eating styles vary: Some are mobile feasts, where you stand and share a plate of little bites, while others feature sit-down dining experiences. All will fill you up, and should be considered a meal and a tour wrapped up in one (making the splurge easier to justify). During the tour, most guides are happy to recommend good restaurants and eating neighborhoods. It's smart to do food tours earlier in your trip, so you have time to try some of the recommended places or sample a favorite dish again.

I'd skip bigger tours. The best ones move at a brisk pace and max out at eight or ten people—that means you can squeeze into small shops and boutique restaurants. Some companies offer higher-end tours, which cost more, take longer, and usually include more stops where you linger and sample a greater variety of dishes. These are appreciated by foodies but may be overkill for others.

The best guides fluidly intersperse history, tradition, and

local food culture while giving you a great glimpse into daily life in a characteristic neighborhood. For instance, I recently joined a food tour of Paris's historic Marais neighborhood.

Our first stop was a bakery that had just placed in the city's annual "best baguette" contest. As we tore into our just-out-of-the-oven bread, our guide made sure we heard the telltale "crrrrriiikkk" of a perfect crust breaking. Before this tour, I never knew that the shape of a croissant could tell me if it was made with butter. (Butter produces a croissant with more or less straight sides. The curvier *croissant ordinaire* is made with lowly margarine.)

Our next stop was a *traiteur*—a gourmet deli. Locals who don't feel like cooking (worn out by their 35-hour work week) pop in here for food to go. To dress up the bread, we were given some duck *rillette* (looks like tuna salad but tastes much better) and thinly sliced ham.

Next we followed our noses to a *fromagerie*, where the cheese mongers, standing white-coated like pharmacists, welcomed us in. How to choose from the wedges, cylinders, balls, and miniature hockey pucks of cheese? Our guide coached us through a selection of goat, sheep, and cow's milk cheeses to go with our growing picnic.

Finally, we settled in at communal tables at the local wine shop to consume our pungent spread, doing our best to imitate the way French people make the most out of eating. On the best food tours, you'll come away with a happy stomach, a new favorite dish or two, and a better understanding of the way locals live and eat.

Cooking Classes

A cooking class is another fine way to roll up your sleeves and dig into the local culture. If you're an efficiency fiend like I am, these are a great use of time: You're combining a unique opportunity (learning to cook, say, pasta from scratch) with a satisfying meal, all in just a few hours.

In my experience, the best casual cooking classes are taught by trained chefs with actual restaurant backgrounds (rather than hobbyists or unemployed locals embarking on a second career), take place in a real kitchen environment (rather than a stuffy classroom or "show" kitchen), have a spirit of fun and interaction, involve small groups (allowing more personal interaction with the instructor), and—perhaps most important—are hands-on rather than demonstration-based.

You'll typically spend a couple of hours cooking, and then

sit down to a hard-earned (if not always flawlessly executed) meal. They'll send you on your way with the recipes you prepared that day. Some classes also include a shopping trip to the market.

Recently I joined one of my tour groups in Florence for a cooking class at a restaurant. Though it took a little time, it was really fun. The

With a cooking class, the kitchen is your classroom. *Bon appétit!*

group made everything from the salad to the pasta to the tiramisu. Afterwards, with the chef proudly beaming over us, we sat down to eat it—and it was as good as what you'd get in a restaurant.

Social Dining

Similar to the way the "sharing economy" has enabled travelers to stay in locals' homes via Airbnb or VRBO.com, the concept of social dining is taking off in cities around Europe. Through sites like MealSharing.com, BonAppetour.com, and EatWith.com, you can sign up to share a home-cooked meal at a local's home for a small price. Not only will you get a peek at your hosts' home and a taste of how they eat, but, they will probably be happy to share their thoughts about their city and country with you—a valuable insider perspective.

Staying Connected

One of the most common questions I hear from travelers is, "How can I stay connected in Europe?" The short answer is: more easily and cheaply than you might think.

Staying connected in Europe gets less complicated every year. The simplest solution is to bring your own phone, tablet, or laptop—and use it much as you would at home (following the tips below, such as connecting to free Wi-Fi whenever possible). Another option is to buy a European SIM card for your phone—either your US mobile or one you buy in Europe. Or you can use European landlines and computers to connect.

This chapter details what you need to know to communicate on the go easily and cost-effectively. With technology at our fingertips, going to Europe is no longer a trip to the dark side of the moon. For a very practical one-hour lecture covering tech issues for travelers, see www.ricksteves.com/mobile-travel-skills.

USING A MOBILE PHONE IN EUROPE

You'll want a mobile phone in Europe. I call museums to see if an English tour is scheduled, restaurants to check if they're open or to book a table, hotels and car-rental agencies to confirm reservations, and so on. (For tips on communicating over the phone with someone who speaks another language, see page 402.) Having a phone on hand is also useful when you're traveling with a group—you can call or text if you get separated or if there's an emergency.

Beyond voice calls and texts, smartphones put indispensable information at your fingertips—including audio tours, language translators, and transportation and mapping apps. Some people also bring a tablet or laptop for emailing or blogging, uploading or editing photos, reading, or watching movies in their downtime.

Options for Connecting

If you plan to bring a phone to Europe, start by assessing how you will use it—whether you will be making a few or a lot of phone calls, sending and receiving text messages, and how freely and frequently you'll get online to check email, look up websites, access maps, get driving directions, or use other mobile apps.

Just like at home, you'll connect through a cellular network or via Wi-Fi. A **cellular network** is available wherever your mobile provider has service. **Wi-Fi** is available wherever there's a wireless Internet hotspot. Wi-Fi is typically free (or low cost); on a cellular network you're using your monthly data allotment, and may pay extra for data roaming.

Here are your basic options. The best choice for you will depend on how you plan to use your device. More details on each option are given below.

1. Bring your own phone and sign up for an international/global plan. For most travelers, who don't visit Europe as frequently or for as long as I do, it's easiest to set up your own phone with a basic international plan from your carrier. You get to travel with your US phone number and all your contacts, making it easy to connect with folks back home anytime, anywhere.

2. Bring your own phone and do everything over Wi-Fi. More budget-conscious travelers can forego their carrier's international plan and use only Wi-Fi. You can use Wi-Fi not only to get online, but also for calling and messaging.

3. Buy a European SIM card. This option works best for those who anticipate heavy phone or data use. You buy a European SIM card to insert in your current phone—or into a cheap mobile phone that you buy for your trip.

4. Leave the devices at home. Of course, you can travel abroad without any mobile device. You can check email or browse websites using public computers and Internet cafés, and make calls from your hotel room.

Bad-Value Options: Many car-rental companies, mobile-phone companies, and even some hotels offer the option to rent a mobile phone with a European number. This is a terrible value, often with hidden fees (such as high per-minute charges).

Setting Up International Service

Using your cellular network on a pay-as-you-go basis can add up (on average, about $1.70/minute for voice calls, 50 cents to send text messages, 5 cents to receive them, and $10 to download one megabyte of data). To stay connected at a lower cost, sign up for an international service plan through your carrier. Your normal plan may already include international coverage.

Confirm that your phone will work in Europe. Nearly all newer phones work fine abroad, but check with your carrier if you're unsure.

International Rates and Plans

Rates and plan pricing varies by carrier. When researching your options, ask about the following:

Pay-As-You-Go Rates: Ask about rates for pay-as-you-go voice calling, text messaging, and data rates for the countries you're visiting. If you turn off cellular data and stick to Wi-Fi and messaging apps, it may be cheaper to forego an international plan and simply pay the standard rates if you need to use your phone in an emergency.

Bundled Voice, Text, and Data Plans: Find out the cost for an international plan for the length of your trip. Most carriers now offer a simple bundle that includes calling,

Sample International Plans

Each major mobile network has its own way of dealing with international travel. Here are the basics offerings as of this printing. Plans and rates change frequently; for the latest, check with your provider.

AT&T: AT&T's Passport option requires a one-time charge for 30 days, with three levels depending how much data you want. All tiers include unlimited text and expensive per-minute talk rates.

Sprint: All Sprint plans include unlimited text and low-speed data, and reasonable per-minute talk rates. A 1-, 7-, or 14-day supplement buys you high-speed data.

T-Mobile: All T-Mobile plans include unlimited text and lower-speed data roaming, plus reasonable per-minute talk rates.

Verizon Wireless: One-month option includes two pricing tiers, with the bottom adding on high fees for talk and text, and the upper including a moderate amount of talk and text for no extra charge; both include a basic data allowance. The pay-as-you-go TravelPass option allows you to keep all your domestic talk, text, and data allowances for a daily fee while you travel.

messaging, and data, but it's wise to ask exactly what's included, especially when it comes to data allowances.

When assessing how much data you'll need, consider that 100 megabytes lets you view about 500 websites, send/receive about 1,200 emails, stream about 30 minutes of standard-definition video, download about 150 maps (turn-by-turn directions eat up more data), or upload about 150 posts to social media (these are ballpark numbers; actual numbers vary greatly depending on which apps/websites you're using, your device, etc.). Keep in mind that if you stick to Wi-Fi you won't incur data charges.

Some plans have a 30-day duration or require you to set an end date when you sign up. If your international option is open-ended, remember upon your return to cancel any add-ons that you activated before your trip.

Wi-Fi and Data Roaming

Using Wi-Fi

Wi-Fi is easy to find, and the cheapest way to get online. Most accommodations in Europe offer free Wi-Fi, but some—especially expensive hotels—charge a fee. If Wi-Fi is important to you, ask about it when you book—and check that it'll be available in your room. As soon as I arrive at a hotel, I ask at the desk for the password and network name (in case several are in range), so I can log on right away. You'll know you're on a Wi-Fi network when you see the Wi-Fi symbol (looks like a half-rainbow) in the corner of your device's screen.

In some hotels, Wi-Fi works great; in others, the signal is less reliable or doesn't work well (or at all) beyond the lobby (many European hotels are in old buildings with thick stone walls). Often it's good enough to shoot off an email, but too slow to stream movies or make a video call. (It's smart to download media and update apps before your trip, when bandwidth isn't an issue.)

When you're out and about, cafés are usually your best bet for finding free Wi-Fi. As in North America, most McDonald's and Starbucks in Europe offer free Wi-Fi. You'll likely also find Wi-Fi at tourist offices, in city squares, within major museums, at public-transit hubs, and aboard some trains and buses. You may need to register or accept terms

Connect Cheaply

1. Use free Wi-Fi whenever possible.
2. Turn off data roaming.
3. Limit automatic updates.
4. Keep track of your data usage.
5. Use Wi-Fi calling/messaging apps.

of service to get online, and some networks limit browsing time. At cafés and restaurants, you may have to buy something to get the Wi-Fi password.

Using and Conserving Data

Using data roaming on your cellular network is handy when you can't find Wi-Fi—but it's also potentially expensive. Make sure you know your plan's data rates to avoid sticker shock later. Budgeting your data is easy if you follow these tips:

Keep track of data usage. Upon arrival in Europe, start tracking your data use. On your device's Settings menu, look for "cellular data usage" or "mobile data" and reset the counter so you can see how many megabytes you've consumed. Some carriers automatically send a text message warning if you approach or exceed your limit and will let you upgrade your package without penalty.

Save bandwidth-gobbling tasks for Wi-Fi. Even with an international data plan, I wait until I'm on Wi-Fi to Skype, stream videos, or any other megabyte-greedy tasks. If you use mapping apps such as Google Maps, there are ways to do so without using cellular data (for tips on using these apps while driving, see page 171; for details on using them to navigate around a city on foot, see page 303).

Limit automatic updates in your email and other apps. By default, many mobile apps are set to constantly check for a data connection and update information. You can cut your data use by switching off this feature, or by setting updates to occur only when you're on Wi-Fi. Start with your email: Change the settings from "auto-retrieve" to "manual," or from "push" to "fetch." This means that you'll need to manually download (or "fetch") your messages. If you receive an email with a large photo, video, or attachment, wait until you're on Wi-Fi to view it.

Tether your tablet/laptop to your phone. Rather than pay for cellular data for multiple devices, for travelers whose phone plan covers data, it can be handy to occasionally enable your phone (using data) as a mobile hotspot for your tablet or laptop. This can be a good option for downloading a map or other info while out and about—for example, use your tablet online via your phone's hotspot just long enough to download an offline-capable map or museum brochure, then get back to sightseeing with the info saved to your tablet.

Disconnect from your cellular network altogether. Because there are still ways that you can accidentally burn through data, I like the additional safeguard of manually turning off data roaming or cellular data (either works) whenever I'm not using it—check under "cellular" or "network," or ask your service provider how to do it. Then, when you need to get online but can't find Wi-Fi, simply turn it on just long enough for the task at hand. Another way to ensure you're not accidentally using data roaming is to put your device in "airplane" or "flight" mode, and then turn your Wi-Fi back on when needed (this disables phone calls and texts, as well as data).

Wi-Fi Calling and Messaging

A cheap way to stay in touch while traveling is to use a mix of calling/messaging apps. Just log on to a Wi-Fi network, then connect with any of your friends or family members who are also online and signed into the same service. (Avoid using these apps over a cellular network, which can burn through your data allowance, especially if you're making a video call.)

Voice and Video Calls: Apps such as Skype, Viber, FaceTime, and Google+ Hangouts are great for making free or low-cost voice and video calls over Wi-Fi. If you've never looked, check your phone—one or another app is often preloaded (most also work on tablets/laptops too).

In addition, many newer phones have a Wi-Fi calling feature already installed. It's especially handy when you're in an area with weak cellular coverage—but with access to a decent Wi-Fi signal, such as a countryside inn that's outside of cell range but has Wi-Fi. Just be sure to check with your carrier to know whether international Wi-Fi calling is part of your existing voice plan or subject to an extra charge.

The biggest hurdle travelers face with Wi-Fi calling is signal strength. With a solid signal, the sound quality is better than a standard phone connection; but with a weak signal, the video and audio can be choppy and freeze up. If you're struggling with your connection, try turning off the video and sticking with an audio-only call.

Internet calling makes it easy to keep in touch for free.

Skype, Viber, and Google+ Hangouts also work for making calls from your laptop to telephones worldwide. Most services charge just a few cents per minute (you'll have to prebuy some credit). For example, I use Skype to call ahead from home and reserve hotels, or while I'm traveling to confirm tomorrow's reservation without paying high fees. This is also a good, affordable way for folks back home to connect with you (if you don't have your US phone with you or don't want to be charged for receiving a call).

Text Messaging: Rather than paying per-message costs to stay in touch with family and friends back home, use an app that allows you to message over Wi-Fi to any other person using that app. Note that some of these apps, such as Apple's iMessage, will use the cellular network if Wi-Fi isn't available: To avoid this possibility, go to Settings, then Messages, and turn off the "Send as SMS" feature. See the "Resources for Wi-Fi Calling & Messaging" sidebar for options.

Resources for Wi-Fi Calling & Messaging

Facebook Messenger: Messaging for mobile devices and computers; requires Facebook account

FaceTime: Video and voice calls between iOS devices

Google+ Hangouts: Video, voice, and messaging for Android and iOS devices

iMessage: Messaging between iOS devices

Skype: Video and voice calls for most devices

Viber: Video, voice, and messaging for mobile devices

WhatsApp: Messaging and voice and video calling

Telegram: Encrypted messaging for mobile devices

Using a European SIM Card

A mobile phone with a European SIM card can be a good solution for travelers making a lot of voice calls or needing faster connection speeds than their mobile carrier provides. Fit the SIM card into a cheap phone you buy in Europe or the US (about $40 from phone shops anywhere), or use the SIM in your regular US phone (check with your carrier about unlocking it). This option gives you a European mobile number and access to cheaper rates than you'll get through your US carrier, even with an international plan.

You'll find SIM cards at mobile-phone shops, department-store electronics counters, some newsstands, and even at vending machines. Costing about $5-10, they usually include a prepaid calling/messaging credit, with no contract and no commitment. Expect to pay about $20-40 more for a SIM with a gigabyte of data. Certain SIM-card brands—including Lebara and Lycamobile, both of which operate in multiple European countries—are reliable and offer cheap international calls,

Your phone's SIM card is sometimes hiding behind the battery.

including to the US. For the best rates, buy a new SIM card every time you arrive in a new country (although the EU caps the roaming fees that local providers can charge).

I like to buy SIM cards at a phone shop where there's a clerk to help explain the options and brands. Use the European term "mobile" (pronounce it the way Brits do—rhymes with "smile") or "handy" (common in German-speaking areas). Be sure to buy the correct size SIM card for your phone (many use smaller micro or nano cards). Ask the clerk to insert and set up your SIM card. (If text or voice prompts are in another language, ask the clerk whether they can be switched to English.) In some countries you'll be required to register the SIM card with your passport as an antiterrorism measure (which may mean you can't use the phone for the first hour or two).

Find out how to check your credit balance. When you run out of credit, you can top it up at mobile-phone stores or other shops (look for your SIM card's logo in the window), or online at the manufacturer's website.

Tips: Most European SIM cards expire after a certain period of inactivity (typically 3-12 months), so use up the credit or hand it off to another traveler. Note your new phone number so you can pass it on to friends and family. Also, be sure you've saved your contacts in the phone itself, rather than on the SIM card; otherwise, you'll lose access to them when you switch SIMs. When storing phone numbers, include the plus (+) sign and the country code to ensure that your calls will go through, regardless of where you're calling from.

Mobile Movie Night

Though I prefer getting out and experiencing local nightlife while in Europe, if you enjoy decompressing with a movie or TV show after a day of sightseeing, plan ahead to use your mobile device. Download video content before your trip to avoid using data or dealing with slow Wi-Fi.

If you're accustomed to streaming content via a site such as Netflix or Hulu, don't be surprised if you're denied access from Europe; most services have geographic content restrictions (you can try using a VPN—a virtual private network, such as ExpressVPN—to get around this). Luckily Netflix now allows account holders to download content for offline use, but remember to do so before leaving home in case you can't access the service abroad.

UNTETHERED TRAVEL

If you don't want to travel with expensive devices, cords, and adapters, you can still stay connected. It's easy enough to check email or browse websites using public computers, and you can make calls from your hotel (or the increasingly rare public phone).

Most **hotels** charge a fee for placing calls—ask for the

How to Dial

Many Americans are intimidated by dialing European phone numbers. You needn't be. It's simple, once you break the code. Note that in some countries, phone numbers have varying lengths (for instance, a hotel can have a seven-digit phone number and an eight-digit mobile number).

For more dialing help, see www.howtocallabroad.com.

Dialing Internationally

If you're phoning from a US landline, your US mobile phone, a Skype account, or from a number in one European country to another (e.g., Spain to Italy), you're making an international call. Here's how to do it:

1. Dial the **international access code** (011 from a US or Canadian phone; 00 from any European phone). From a mobile phone, the "+" sign automatically selects the international access code you need (press and hold the 0 key).

2. Dial the **country code**. For example, enter 39 if you're calling Italy or 33 for France.

3. Dial the **phone number**. If the number begins with zero, drop it (except for Italian numbers).

Dialing Domestically

To make a domestic call within a European country (from a mobile phone with a local SIM card or from a landline), simply dial the phone number, including the initial 0 if there is one. Remember, if you are roaming with your US phone, you must use international dialing (above).

In some countries, much like at home, you can drop the area code if dialing within the same area code; in other countries, you must dial the full number, even if calling across the street. I keep things simple by always dialing the full phone number, including the area code or prefix.

Examples

▶ To call a Munich hotel (tel. 089/264-349) from your Berlin hotel phone, dial 089/264-349. To dial it from your hotel in Italy, dial 00, then 49 (Germany's country code), then 89/264-349 (dropping the initial 0).

▶ To call a Paris hotel (01 47 05 49 15) from your US home phone, dial 011, then 33 (France's country code), then 1 47 05 49 15 (the hotel's phone number minus its initial 0).

▶ To call a Madrid hotel (915-212-900) from a friend's house in Germany, dial 00, then 34 (Spain's country code), then 915-212-900.

▶ To call a Florence museum (055-238-8651) from your US mobile phone (whether you're in Florence or the US), dial +, then 39 (Italy's country code), then 055-238-8651 (phone number with its 0).

Calling from Europe to the US

To call the US or Canada from Europe (from a local mobile phone or landline), dial 00 (Europe's international access code), 1 (US/Canada country code), and the phone number, including area code.

So to call my office in Edmonds, Washington, from anywhere in Europe, I dial 00-1-425-771-8303; or, from any mobile phone, +1-425-771-8303.

Country Codes		Ireland & N. Ireland	353 / 44
Austria	43	Italy	39
Belgium	32	Latvia	371
Bosnia-Herzegovina	387	Montenegro	382
Croatia	385	Morocco	212
Czech Republic	420	Netherlands	31
Denmark	45	Norway	47
Estonia	372	Poland	48
Finland	358	Portugal	351
France	33	Russia	7
Germany	49	Slovakia	421
Gibraltar	350	Slovenia	386
Great Britain	44	Spain	34
Greece	30	Sweden	46
Hungary	36	Switzerland	41
Iceland	354	Turkey	90

rates before you dial. You can use a prepaid international phone card (available for $5-10 at post offices, newsstands, street kiosks, tobacco shops, and train stations) to call out from your hotel. Dial the toll-free access number, enter the PIN code from the card, then dial the number. Since you're never charged for receiving calls, it's better to have someone from the US call you in your room.

In some countries, you may still see **public pay phones,** but they're getting rarer all the time. You'll more likely to find them in post offices and train stations. Pay phones generally come with multilingual or pictograph instructions; most don't take coins but instead require an insertable phone card—get guidance from a local.

Few phone booths remain in Europe... and those that do generally take phone cards rather than coins.

Cheap **call shops,** often located in train-station neighborhoods, advertise low international rates for immigrants who want to call home cheaply, but tourists can use them, too. You'll be assigned to your own private sweatbox, make the call, and pay the bill when you're done. Before making your call, be completely clear on the rates (e.g., if there's a charge per unit, find out how long a unit is).

Most hotels have **public computers** in their lobby for guests to use; otherwise you can find them at Internet cafés and many libraries (ask your hotelier or the TI for the nearest location). On European keyboards, most letters are familiar, but a few are switched around, and the command keys are labeled differently (see sidebar).

INTERNET SECURITY ON THE ROAD

Whether you're getting online with your own device or at a public computer, using a shared network comes with the potential for increased security risks. Travelers who are too careless with their digital information can open themselves up to significant hassle and expense. Aim for a middle ground of cautiousness, and protect your computer and your personal information by heeding the following tips.

Security for Your Device

Gadget theft is an issue in Europe. Not only should you take precautions to protect your devices from thieves (see page

376 for tips), but you should also configure them so that your personal data stays private.

First, check that your device is running the latest versions of its operating system, security software, and apps. Next, consider tightening your security settings. At the very least, make sure your device is password- or passcode-protected so thieves can't easily access your information.

For an extra layer of security, set passwords for apps such as email or Facebook. It's best to use a different one for each app and log-in (a password manager can help you keep everything straight). Don't allow websites or apps—especially banking or shopping apps—to log you in automatically, and don't store passwords, PINs, account numbers, and other sensitive information on your mobile device. If the device is stolen and you use an app that accesses financial data, immediately alert your bank (as well as your mobile provider).

To stay safe on public Wi-Fi networks, customize your settings to turn off file sharing and to activate your firewall. Newer versions of Windows have a "public network" setting (choose this when you first join the network) that automatically configures your computer so it can't be "seen" by other users on the network.

Once on the road, use only secure, password-protected Wi-Fi hotspots (an open network is more vulnerable). Ask the hotel or café for the specific name of their network. Hackers sometimes create bogus hotspots with a similar or vague name (such as "Hotel Europa Free Wi-Fi") that shows up alongside a bunch of authentic networks. If you're not actively using a hotspot, turn off your device's Wi-Fi connection so it's not visible to others. Remember that even a legitimate Wi-Fi network can be hacked. Some people feel safer using a virtual private network (VPN), which encrypts your data; subscriptions start at about $5 a month.

Typing @ on European Keyboards

Keyboard layouts are a bit different in Europe, but you'll be able to find your way around. Use the "Alt Gr" key to the right of the space bar to insert the extra symbol that appears on some keys. If you can't locate a special character (such as the @ symbol), simply copy it from a Web page and paste it into your email message. Sometimes there's an option to make a foreign keyboard work like an American one (look for a box in the lower right corner of the screen where you can select your preferred keyboard).

German: Alt Gr + Q
Italian: Alt Gr + @
Spanish and Portuguese: Alt Gr + 2

Safety Tips for Using Public Computers

It's perfectly safe to check train schedules, maps, or museum hours on a public computer. The danger lies in accessing personal accounts (such as email, Facebook, or any ecommerce site) that require you to enter a login and password.

If you're traveling with your own device, make it your sole means of accessing personal accounts. But if you'll be relying on hotel-lobby computers or Internet cafés, keep in mind that you have no idea who used that computer last—or who will hop on next. Public computers may be loaded with damaging malware, such as key logger programs that keep track of what you're typing—including passwords.

If you do need to access personal accounts on a public computer, make sure that the Web browser you use doesn't store your login information. If you have the option of opening an "incognito" or "private" browser window, use it. When you sign in to any site, look for ways to ensure that the browser forgets your user name and password after you log out: For instance, click the box for "public or shared computer" or unclick any box that says "stay signed in" or "remember me." It's also a good idea to clear the Internet browser's cache, history, and cookies after you're done, so fewer artifacts of your surfing session remain—especially if you've accessed sensitive information (under the browser's "Options" or "Preferences" settings, look for a "Privacy" or "Security" category).

Finally, set up two-step verification (sometimes called two-factor authentication) for your most important accounts (such as email, social-networking, and banking). This requires you to answer a question or enter a code in addition to your password whenever you log in from an unfamiliar computer.

Accessing Financial Information Online

Financial institutions have invested heavily in security to ensure that your personal information remains secure during mobile banking—but it still pays to be careful. Before your trip, set up safeguards with your bank, such as receiving text notifications if your checking account balance drops to a certain level.

While traveling, if you want to check your banking or credit-card statements, or take care of other personal-finance chores,

Practice safe computing if visiting an internet café.

experts say it's best to use a banking app rather than sign in to your bank's website via a browser (the app is less likely to get hacked).

Refrain from logging in to any personal finance sites on a public computer. If that's not possible, a cellular network is safer than Wi-Fi, and a password-protected Wi-Fi network is safer than open Wi-Fi. Just like at home, don't click on links in unsolicited emails from your bank or respond to text messages allegedly sent by your credit-card company.

If you need to enter your credit card information online, such as for booking museum or theater tickets, make sure that the site is secure. Most browsers display a little padlock icon to indicate this; also check that the page's URL begins with "https" instead of "http." Never send a credit-card number (or any other sensitive information) over a website that doesn't begin with "https."

Be careful when emailing personal information. If there's not a secure website, it's better to relay a credit-card number by phone or fax than in an email. For extra security, a few banks, such as Citi and Bank of America, allow their customers to create virtual account numbers, which are one-time or short-term numbers linked to their regular credit card.

Getting Around in Cities

Shrink and tame big European cities by mastering subway and bus systems, hopping into the occasional taxi, and navigating smartly whether on foot or underground. By knowing where you're going and the best way to get there, you'll save time, money, and energy.

This chapter offers tips on navigation tools and on using subways, buses, taxis, and ride-booking services to get around Europe's cities. For information on using trains, long-distance buses, and ferries to link destinations, read the Trains, Buses & Boats chapter. For tips on biking, see the Outdoor Adventure chapter.

MAPS AND NAVIGATION TOOLS

In any big city, a map saves you endless time and frustration. Whether it's a detailed foldout map, the simpler map that comes in your guidebook, the map on your smartphone—or some combination—a map is essential for efficient navigation.

To orient yourself, study your map before setting out. Familiarize yourself with the city's layout. Relate the location of landmarks on your map—your hotel, major sights, the river, main streets, the train station—to each other. When you're out sightseeing, use any viewpoint (such as a church spire, tower, or hilltop) to identify landmarks, understand the lay of the land, and see where you're going next.

Using Printed Maps

The map in your guidebook is likely small and intended as an overview. You'll want to also get a decent, detailed map of your destination. You can almost always get a decent foldout map free or cheaply at the local tourist office or your hotel.

When choosing a city sightseeing map, make sure the city

center is detailed enough, as that's where you'll be spending most of your time. If you'll be relying heavily on public transit, get a map that shows not just subway stations, but also bus and tram lines and stops. For an extended stay in a sprawling city, it can be worth paying for a sturdier, more detailed map. And if rain is in the forecast, a laminated map will hold up much better.

Resources for Navigation

Google Maps app: Best route planner for walking and public transit
City Maps 2Go app: Easy-to-use maps that show your location offline

Using Maps on Your Phone

Like many smartphone owners, I've become accustomed to the convenience of having maps at my fingertips when I need to find an address or look up directions. It's amazing to pop out of a subway station, not knowing north from south, and find your location immediately on your phone.

If Using Data Roaming: If you have an international data plan, you can use data roaming on your phone to navigate. Those lucky enough to have unlimited data can roam freely, including using real-time turn-by-turn directions as you walk. Otherwise, use your data sparingly—just when you need to look up an address or get quick walking directions.

Without Data Roaming: Even though you can't look up an address on the fly or get real-time turn-by-turn directions, there's plenty you can do without using data roaming. It just takes some planning.

Thanks to its GPS function, your smartphone always knows where you are—no data connection required. Even in airplane mode, when you call up a map you've previously downloaded, you'll see a dot marking your location. And since the GPS signal doesn't use the Internet, it continues to track your location on the map as you move. You can even "pin" your destination on your map ahead of time so that you have a good idea of where you're headed.

Two apps that work well offline are Google Maps and City Maps 2Go. For either, download your city's map ahead of time, while online (using the Wi-Fi at your hotel, for example). Later, when you're on the street (and offline), just call up your map, and you're on your way.

If you want to rely on a specific walking route, look up the route on your phone while you're online at your hotel, then use it to navigate all day long. Before setting out, punch in your start and end points, and select the route you want to take. After you leave your hotel (and go offline), the map remains available on your phone. You can zoom in and out, and your location will be marked with a dot, even when you're nowhere near a Wi-Fi connection.

There are limitations: Since maps are downloaded at a fairly low resolution, you can't zoom in too far or they become unreadable. Also, you can't adjust your route unless you go back online.

PUBLIC TRANSPORTATION

Europe's public-transportation systems are so good that many urban Europeans go through life never learning to drive. Their wheels are trains, subways, trams, buses, and the occasional taxi. If you embrace these forms of transportation when visiting cities, you'll travel smarter. Nearly every European city has a fine public transportation network. Subways and trains are speedy and never get stuck in traffic jams. Buses and trams can give you a tour of the town on the way to your destination. With the proper attitude, taking public transit can be a cultural experience, plunging you into the river of workaday European life.

Tips for Riding Public Transit

Even if you've never used public transit in your hometown, these tricks can help you quickly master your transportation options in Europe's cities. You'll have the city by the tail, without having to shell out much for taxis.

Get a transit map or app. With a map, anyone can decipher the code to easy, affordable urban transportation. Paris and London have the most extensive—and the most needed—subway systems. Pick up a schematic map at the tourist office or subway ticket window, ask for one at your hotel, or print one off a website. Many city maps, even free ones, include a basic transit map.

To help you plot your travel, major transit systems offer online journey planners, and many sights list the nearest bus or subway stop on their websites and brochures. Apps for the London Tube, Paris Métro, and other subway systems work offline and save you from having to unfold an unwieldy map on a busy platform. Google Maps works as an all-around transit app in most

European cities, and its route planner has a transit option that covers both subways and buses.

Learn what's covered by a ticket. In many cities, the same tickets are good on the subway, trams, and buses, and include transfers between the systems; in other places, you'll need to buy a new ticket each time you transfer. If a ticket seems expensive, ask what it covers—$4 may seem like a lot until you learn it's good for a round-trip, two hours, or several transfers.

Consider your ticket options. Your choices, which vary per city, are individual tickets, multiticket deals, passes, and reloadable cards. You'll pay the most per ride by buying individual tickets, but this can be the way to go if you'll be taking only a few rides or prefer to get around mainly on foot.

If you're committed to using public transit, the following options will cut your per-ride costs and save you time (because you won't have to stand in a ticket line every time you travel):

- Multiticket deals offer you a set number of tickets—most notably Paris' 10-ticket *carnet*—that you can use anytime and share with companions, even on the same ride (unlike passes and cards, which can be used by only one person at a time).
- Passes allow unlimited travel on all public transport for a set number of hours or days; a 24-hour pass usually costs less than four single fares. Some passes cover sights as well or offer admission discounts. Before you buy, plan how you'll get the most use out of your pass during its period of validity.
- Reloadable cards, such as London's Oyster Card, require a deposit, subtract the cost of your rides when you use it, and can be topped off when the balance runs low.

You can buy tickets, passes, and cards at subway ticket machines or windows, and, depending on the city, on the bus

LEFT Public transit—the European treat

RIGHT With public transportation, you can zip quickly, effortlessly, and inexpensively around Europe's most congested cities.

(usually for exact change and at a slightly higher cost than the ticket-machine price), at newsstands, or in tourist offices. Ask about discounts if you're young, old, or traveling with children.

Don't try to travel for free. Many European subways, buses, and trams use the honor system. Ticket checkers (some in uniform, some incognito) patrol sporadically, and others check tickets as you exit the station—but all mean business. If you're caught without a valid ticket, even if you accidentally bought the wrong kind, you'll most likely have to pay a hefty fine, probably right on the spot.

If confused, ask for help. Europe's buses and subways are filled with people who are more than happy to help lost tourists locate themselves. Confirm with a local that you're at the right platform or bus stop before you board. If you tell them where you're going, the driver or passengers sitting around you will gladly tell you where to get off.

Expect pickpockets. While public transportation feels safe, savvy riders are constantly on guard. Per capita, there are more pickpockets on Europe's subway trains and buses than just about anywhere else. They congregate wherever there are crowds or bottlenecks: on escalators, at turnstiles, or at the doors of packed buses or subway cars as people get on and off. If there's a hubbub, assume it's a distraction for pickpockets—put a hand on your valuables. Be on the look-out, wear your money belt, and you'll do fine. (For tips on avoiding theft, see the Theft & Scams chapter.)

Subways

Most of Europe's big cities are blessed with an excellent subway system, and wise travelers know that learning this network is key to efficient sightseeing. European subways go by many names: "Metro" is the most common term on the Continent, but Germany and Austria use "U-Bahn." For Scandinavia, it's the "T-bane" in Oslo, "T-bana" in Stockholm, and "S-tog" in Copenhagen. In London, it's the "Tube" (to the British, a "subway" is a pedestrian underpass).

Subways generally operate from about 6 a.m. until midnight. Trains rarely follow a specific schedule, but just pass by at frequent but irregular intervals. Most systems have electronic signs noting when the next train will arrive.

Here are tips for smooth sailing on Europe's subways:

Study your map. Subway maps are usually included within city maps and are posted prominently at the station and usually on board. A typical subway map is a spaghetti-like tangle of intersecting colorful lines. The individual lines are color-coded, numbered, and/or lettered (and even named, in the case of London); their stations, including those at either end of the line, are also indicated. These end stations—while probably places you'll never go—are important, since they tell you which direction the train is headed and appear (usually) as the name listed on the front of the train.

As you'll constantly be reminded on London's Tube... mind the gap.

A few cities (like Rome) have just two or three subway lines, while London has more than a dozen. Some cities' subways share the tracks with express commuter trains (such as Paris' RER and Germany's S-Bahn), which make fewer stops and can usually get you across town faster.

Plan your route. Determine which line you need, the name of the end station in the direction you want to go, and (if necessary) where to transfer to another line. In the station, you'll use this information to follow signs to reach your platform. (See the sidebar on the next page for a step-by-step sample trip.) When in doubt, ask.

Validate your ticket. Once you buy a ticket, you may need to validate it in a turnstile slot (don't forget to retrieve it)—watch to see what others do. If you have an all-day or multiday ticket, you may need to validate it only the first time you use it, or not at all (ask when you buy it). Don't throw away your ticket too soon—you might need to insert it in a turnstile to exit the system (the machine might keep your ticket if it's used up). Once you're out, toss or tear used tickets to avoid confusing them with unused ones.

As you enter the subway station, insert your ticket into the slot to open the turnstile. After validating your ticket, remember to reclaim it.

Keep alert. Follow signage carefully as you navigate through the station. Confirm

Sample Subway Trip

Let's say you want to go from your hotel to the art museum on the other side of town. Your hotel is a five-minute walk from the Napoleon station on the A line. Note that the A line has two end stations: Outer Limits to the north and Suburb del Sud to the south. The art museum is on the B line, so you'll need to transfer at the

station where these two lines intersect: Java Junction.

Here's how you'll do it:

1. Entering the subway at the Napoleon station, follow signs to trains going in the direction of Outer Limits (the northern end station).
2. Ride three stops to Java Junction, get off, and follow signs to transfer to line B (in the direction of East Forest).
3. Ride the train two stops to the Michelangelo station.
4. Use the neighborhood map in the station to choose the exit closest to the museum.

Congratulations—you've survived your first European subway trip!

that you're at the right platform—heading in the right direction—before boarding. Subways can get packed during rush hour. Try to steer clear of crowds and commotion; there are usually fewer people in the first and last cars.

Stick together. If you're with a companion or group, make sure everyone knows the name of your final stop before boarding, stays close together, and agrees on a game plan in case you get separated. If a subway is about to depart as you arrive on the platform, don't rush to catch it and risk leaving behind your companions; subways run frequently, and it's far easier to wait for the next departure than to reconnect with your split-up group.

Get off at the right place. Once on the train, follow along with each stop on your map. Most cars have an electronic screen showing the next stop. Sometimes the driver or an automated voice announces the upcoming stop—but don't count on this cue, as a foreign name spoken by a native speaker over a crackly loudspeaker can be difficult to understand. Keep an eye out the window as you pull into each station; the station's name will be posted prominently on the platform or along the wall. If the train is crowded, move close to the doors one stop before you want to exit. When the train stops, the doors may open automatically, or you may need to open them yourself by pushing a button or pulling a lever. Don't panic—watch others and imitate.

If you need to transfer, follow the signs. Changing from one subway line to another can be as easy as walking a few steps to an adjacent platform—or a bewildering wander via a labyrinth of stairs and long passageways. Subway systems are clearly signed—just follow along (or ask a local for help).

Exit the station. When you arrive at your destination station, follow exit signs up toward street level, keeping an eye out for posted maps of the surrounding neighborhood to help you get your bearings. Bigger stations have multiple exits, signposted by street name or nearby landmarks. Choosing the right exit will help you avoid extra walking and unnecessary forays through busy intersections.

Subway Etiquette

- On escalators to and from platforms, stand on the right, pass on the left.
- When waiting at the platform, stand to either side of the opening doors as people exit the train. Board only after everyone who wants to leave is off.
- Talk softly on board. Listen to how quietly Europeans communicate and follow their lead.
- On a crowded train, try not to block the exit (unless your stop is next). If you're at the door of a packed train when it reaches a stop, step out of the car and to the side, let others off, then get back on.

Buses

Getting around town on city buses is a little more complicated than using the subway, but has its advantages. Since you're not underground, it's easier to stay oriented, see the landmarks, and enjoy the vibrant street life out the window. In fact, some public bus routes are downright scenic—Paris' bus #69 gives you a great sightseeing introduction for just the cost of a transit ticket. Bus stops are more closely spaced than subway stops—meaning the bus is useful even for short hops and usually gets you closer to where you need to go. And some buses go where the subway can't.

When using public transit, take full advantage of posted signs and maps. Neighborhood maps help you get oriented upon arrival.

Like subways, city buses run frequently, especially during peak hours (if a bus is packed, wait for the next one). Although night buses run less frequently and follow limited routes, they're useful for night owls who don't want to spring for a taxi. The main disadvantage of buses is that they're slowed down by traffic, so try to avoid taking them during rush hour.

To travel smartly by public bus, follow these tips:

Plan your route. You can usually get a bus map and schedule from local tourist or transit offices, print them off the bus system's website, or use a public-transit app. Many bus stops have their routes and timetables posted, and some have electronic signs noting how many minutes until the next bus arrives.

Confirm the essentials before you board. Find out if you need a ticket in advance or if you can buy it on the bus (if you buy it from the driver, you'll usually need exact change). Make sure you're getting on the right bus going in the right direction. Before you get on, mention your destination to a local or the driver. Smile and ask, for example, *"Vaticano?"*

Validate your ticket. Usually you enter at the front of the bus and show your ticket to the driver, or validate it by inserting it into an automated time-stamp box. Observe and imitate what the locals do.

Get off at the right stop. Bus stops, like subway stops, are named (usually for a cross street or nearby landmark), but their signs are often difficult to see from a moving bus. Most buses have electronic signs that announce the next stop. If they don't, it pays to stay alert. Have a sense of how long a ride should take, and know the names of the stops coming up right before yours (and the one right after yours,

LEFT If your destination is obvious—such as Florence's Duomo—choosing the right stop is easy; otherwise, ask fellow passengers for help.

RIGHT Posted bus schedules tell you when the next bus should be coming...and where it's going.

so you'll know if you've gone too far). If possible, sit near the door, so you can hop out easily. As you ride, follow along the route on your map, looking for landmarks along the way: monuments, bridges, major cross streets, and so on. If you're uncertain about your stop, get the attention of the driver or another passenger and ask, *"Prado?"* (For extra credit, preface your request with the local word for please.)

In bike-friendly cities such as Amsterdam and Copenhagen, buses often let you off directly into busy bicycle lanes. Look carefully, in both directions, as you exit.

Signal for your stop. Some buses pull over at every stop, while others only stop by request; this means you can't necessarily navigate by counting stops. If in doubt, look for a pull cord or a button with the local word for "stop," and use it to signal that you want to get off at the next stop.

TAXIS AND RIDE-BOOKING SERVICES

Taxis are scenic time savers that zip you effortlessly from one sight to the next (except during rush-hour traffic, when they're stuck like everyone else). While cabs are expensive for the lone budget traveler, a group of three or four people can often travel more cheaply by taxi than by bus or subway. Taxis are especially low-priced in Mediterranean countries and Eastern Europe. You can go anywhere by cab in downtown Lisbon or Athens for about $15.

I enjoy cab rides. Many of my favorite insider tips and most interesting conversations have come from chatting up taxi drivers. But don't trust their advice blindly; cabbies can get kickbacks for recommending (and delivering you to) a particular restaurant or attraction.

Many Americans are wired to assume that taxi drivers in other countries are up to no good. But I've found that most drivers are honest. Sure, scams happen. But with the right knowledge and a watchful eye, you'll get where you want to go without being taken for a ride.

Hiring a Taxi

In some cities, it's easy to flag down a cab; in any city, you can find cabs at a taxi stand. These stands are often listed as prominently as subway stations on city maps; look for the little Ts (or ask a local to direct

Resources for Taxis and Ride-Booking

TaxiFareFinder.com: Estimates fares and compares cabs to ride-booking costs

MyTaxi app: Taxi-finder lets you book and pay for cabs in major cities

Hailo app: Licensed cab app used mainly in Britain and Ireland

Uber: Most popular ride-booking service

you to the nearest one). When hiring a cab, make sure it has a big, prominent taxi-company logo and telephone number. Avoid using unmarked beaters with makeshift taxi lights on top.

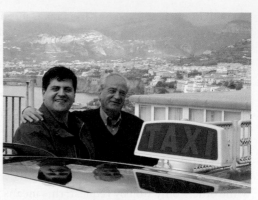

Calling for a Taxi: When you need a ride from a hotel or restaurant, you can have the staff call a taxi for you—but be aware that in many places, the meter starts ticking from the time the call is received (and there may be an additional flat fee for calling a taxi). But if you have an early morning flight to catch, it'll save you some stress (and cost nothing beyond the usual supplements) to have your hotelier book a cab for you the day before.

These Sorrento cabbies hire by the hour and would love to show you around.

Hiring Taxis at Airports and Train Stations: A taxi zipping you right to your hotel can be a relief after a long flight or train ride. But dishonest cabbies sometimes lurk at major transit points, ready to take advantage of travelers who are jet-lagged and travel-weary. To avoid problems, head for the official taxi stand and join the queue, rather than flagging a taxi down. (If you don't want to worry about getting conned the minute you arrive at a new destination—or to save money—skip the cab and link to the city center by public transportation or arrange for an airport shuttle bus.)

Ordering a Taxi on Your Mobile Phone: There are several apps that work exactly like Uber (see below) but are for booking a licensed cab. One popular European app is Hailo, which covers a limited number of cities, mostly in Great Britain and Ireland. Another is MyTaxi, which operates in Germany, Austria, Poland, Spain, and Italy.

Using Ride-Booking Services in Europe

Uber is available in many European cities, and rides can be cheaper than taxis. (As of this printing, Lyft was not active in Europe.) The service works just as conveniently in Europe as it does in the States: You request a car via the Uber app on your phone (you'll need an Internet connection or Wi-Fi), and the fare is automatically charged to your credit card.

Some countries—Germany, France, Italy, Spain, Belgium, Sweden, and the Netherlands—don't allow UberPop ride-sharing (unregulated drivers and cars), so you may find only the more expensive UberX or UberBlack (licensed cabs or limousine services).

Paying a Fair Rate (and Avoiding Scams)

It's usually best to make sure the cabbie uses the taxi meter. But for certain standard trips (such as to or from the airport), set prices are common. Learn the going rate for getting to your destination by asking your hotelier or at any tourist info point. You can check your guidebook or www.taxifarefinder.com for estimated taxi fares in larger cities. And Taxi Fare Finder's Ride Guru will compare taxi rates with services like Uber.

Sometimes tourists wrongly accuse their cabbies of taking the long way around or adding unfair extras. But what can seem like a circuitous route may still be the shortest, given pedestrianized zones and one-way streets. And many supplements are legit, based on the time of day (nights, early mornings, and weekends), amount of baggage, extra people, airport taxes, port fees, and so on.

In cities such as London, Paris, and Barcelona, meters are tamper-proof. That said, even cabbies with honest meters have ways of overcharging tourists. One common trick is for cabbies to select the pricier "night and weekend" rate on their meter during a weekday. An explanation of the different meter rates should be posted somewhere in the cab, often in English; if you're confused about the tariff, ask your cabbie to explain. If you suspect foul play, following the route on your map or conspicuously writing down the cabbie's license information can shame a cad into being honest.

At airports and train stations, look for the official taxi queue, where you'll wait in line to be assigned a taxi. Be wary of unofficial helpers who usher tourists out of line to a separate taxi area—this is often a scam that ends with your credit card number being stolen.

Paying and Tipping

Most European cab drivers will only take cash, but the times they are a-changin' thanks to Uber—which only takes credit cards. London, for example, now requires all taxis to accept credit cards. The MyTaxi and Hailo apps (described above) also take cards. But it's smart to be prepared to pay in cash.

Using small bills minimizes your chance of getting ripped off. If you only have a large bill, state the denomination out loud as you hand it to the cabbie. They can be experts at dropping your €50 note and then showing you a €20. Count your change. If, for whatever reason, I'm charged a ridiculous price for a ride, I put a reasonable sum on the seat and say good-bye. Don't be intimidated by a furious cabbie.

To tip, round up to the next euro on the fare (to pay a €13 fare, give €14); for a long ride, to the nearest 10 (for a €76 fare, give €80). If the cabbie hauls your bags and zips you to the airport to help you catch your flight, you might want to toss in a little more. But if you feel like you're being driven in circles or otherwise ripped off, skip the tip.

Taking a Taxi Between Cities

While a budget traveler would generally never dream of hiring a taxi for a trip between cities, it can actually be a fairly good value. For example, if you're next destination is a long train trip but a short drive away, a taxi can be an affordable splurge, especially if the cost is split between two or more people. Services such as Uber can be even cheaper in some places.

Consider the time you'll save over public transportation— for example, one hour of sweat-free, hotel-door-to-hotel-door service versus two sticky hours on stop-and-go public transit, including transfers to and from the train or bus station. Simply ask any cabbie what they'd charge (it could be an hourly rate or even an off-meter flat rate—they know you have a cheap public-transit alternative and could be willing to strike a deal). Or ask at your hotel if they have a line on any car or taxi services that do the trip economically. See if you can find a driver who's accustomed to taking tourists on these trips. While not technically guides, these drivers are often willing to provide some basic commentary on what you're seeing and might even suggest some interesting stops along the way.

Sightseeing

After months of planning, you're finally on the ground in Europe, and the real work—and joy— begins: sightseeing. This is when it pays to have a thoughtful plan. The pointers in this chapter will help you get oriented to your surroundings; make the most of your sightseeing time; navigate museums, churches, castles, and other sights smartly; and find your way off the beaten path.

GETTING ORIENTED

Whether tackling big cities or quaint villages, you don't want to feel like a stranger in a strange land (even though that's exactly what you are). Visitors who decide to wing it—especially in Europe's large cities—invariably waste time and miss out. Here are some other useful resources for getting acclimated to a new place.

Maps: A good map (or navigation app) and plan for getting around are essential. For details, see the previous chapter.

Guidebooks: Be sure to have a good, up-to-date guidebook. If you've arrived in Europe without one, you can find English-language guidebooks at newsstands, major sights, and bookstores. For tips on selecting a guidebook, see page 34.

Tourist Information Offices: No matter how well I know a town, my first stop is often the tourist information office. Nearly any place with a tourist industry has an information service for visitors on the main square, in the City Hall or public library, at the train station, or sometimes at airports or freeway entrances. You don't need the address— just follow the signs. A friendly and multilingual staff answers questions, hands out maps and sightseeing information, reserves hotel rooms, explains transit options, and sells sightseeing passes and concert or theater tickets.

Prepare a list of questions ahead of time. Write up a proposed sightseeing schedule. Find out if you've left out any important sights, and confirm closed days and free-admission days. Ask about special events going on during your stay. If necessary, get ideas on where to eat and sleep,

Tourist information offices are ready to help you.

although keep in mind that their advice can be biased (many tourist information offices are funded by fees and commissions from the places they recommend).

Entertainment Guides: Big European cities bubble with entertainment, festivities, and nightlife. But these events won't come to you. New in town and unable to speak the native language, travelers can be oblivious to a once-in-a-lifetime event erupting just across the bridge. A periodical entertainment guide is the key. Every big city has one, either in English (such as *What's On in Oslo* or *Time Out*, which has editions in many cities) or in the local language, but easy to decipher (such as *A Nous Paris'* "L'Agenda de la Semaine" section, a weekly review of events).

Printed guides may be available at the tourist office (where they're often free), at newsstands, English-language bookstores, or at the front desk of big, fancy hotels (look like a guest and help yourself). Many guides are also available online or as apps. Events are posted on city walls everywhere. They may be in a foreign language, but that really doesn't matter when it reads: *Weinfest, Música Folklórica, 9 Juni, 21:00, Piazza Maggiore, Entre Libre*, and so on. Figure out the signs—or miss the party.

Avoid having your hotel book your entertainment. Go to the flamenco show and get the ticket yourself. You'll learn more, save money, and be more likely to sit with locals than with a bunch of tourists. So often, tourists are herded together—by a conspiracy of hotel managers and tour organizers—at gimmicky folk evenings featuring a medley of cheesy cultural clichés kept alive only for the tourists. You can't relive your precious nights in Sevilla. Do them right—on your own.

Other Resources: Seek out firsthand advice from your hotel's staff or other travelers. Glean hints from the couple

seated next to you at breakfast, chat with the waiter who
serves you lunch, or ask a
shop owner for tips.

TOURS

Organized tours are a great
way to acclimate to a new
city and learn about its history and highlights. Tours

not only provide a city overview, they also give you an idea of
what you'll want to revisit later in your stay. Especially in big
cities, you'll find tours of all kinds, from guided walks to bus
rides that let you hop on and off at will. Audio tours are often
available for those who prefer a DIY approach.

Try a guided
walk to learn
about a town
that's prob-
ably a thousand
years older than
your hometown.

Guided Walking Tours

These are my favorite introduction to a city. Since walking
tours focus on just a small part of a larger whole (generally
the old town center), they are thorough. The tours are usually conducted in English by well-trained guides who are
sharing their town for the noble purpose of giving you an
appreciation of its history, people, and culture—not to make
a lot of money. Walking tours are personal, inexpensive, and
a valuable education. They're nearly always time and money
well spent.

In major European cities, you'll see advertisements for
"free" walking tours. While these tours are indeed free, tipping is expected; in fact, the guides don't earn money unless
you tip. On these free tours, guides—generally expat students
who have memorized a script—tend to emphasize stories
over an academic approach, and are known to take liberties
with historical events and characters. And they may take up
your valuable time with heavy promotions for their other
(paid) tours. Personally, I'd rather pay up front for hardworking guides whose goal is to make the city's history come
alive. But for travelers on a budget, these free tours provide
an affordable way to get to know a place.

Bus Orientation Tours

Many cities have fast-orientation bus tours that take you
around the city on a double-decker bus. Riding in the open
air atop a two-story bus, you get a feel for the city's layout as
the major sights roll by; most buses include live or recorded

narration. Many are structured as hop-on, hop-off tours with a circular route that connects the top sights; with an all-day pass, you can hop off to visit a sight, then catch a later bus to continue the route.

You might even go topless on some hop-on, hop-off buses.

Bus tours usually cost about $30-40. Some can be a disappointing rip-off; others are a great sightseeing tool. If you're short on time, have limited mobility, or would appreciate an overview before diving into a city, they can be worth the money. If I had only one day in a big city, I might spend half of it on one of these tours.

Before you shell out for a ticket, consider a few key factors: route, quality of narration, and for hop-on, hop-off buses, frequency. The best-value hop-on, hop-off tours leave several times an hour, visit sights I actually want to see, and feature an engaging live guide (if the guide is good, I'll stay on for the entire route). Be wary of overcrowded buses—if the top fills up, you may have no choice but to cram into the (potentially hot and stuffy) lower level. It's worth waiting for the next bus to get space on an upper level, where views come from a higher vantage point and aren't marred by smeared windows. The best scenario is enjoying the view from a topless bus on a sunny day.

Many cities also offer a public bus (such as Paris' bus #69 or Berlin's bus #100) or boat route (Amsterdam has several; Venice has the Grand Canal) that connects the city's major sightseeing attractions; you can ride these as if they were low-cost (unguided) tour buses/boats. Tourists buy the one-day pass and make the circuit at their leisure (for more on city buses, see page 309).

Local Guides

For the price of four seats on a city bus tour with forgettable recorded narration, you can often hire your own private guide for a personalized city tour. This is most cost-effective if you're traveling with a group. In my research, I rely upon these experts and find them well worth the investment.

Nearly every city in Europe has great local guides who are independent businesspeople scrambling to fill their calendars and earn a living. Private guides charge from $100 to $300 for 2-4 hours. Guides tend to cost more in big, touristy cities and in Western European countries. The farther east you travel, the cheaper they are. I strongly recommend hiring a guide in places like Prague or Poland, where per-hour costs average $35 and guides often share fascinating personal stories of life in the not-so-distant past. Sure, hiring a private guide is a splurge. But so is a nice dinner. And if you can split it with a group of people, your cost goes down.

If you're spending several days in a destination, hire a guide early in your trip. You'll get an orientation to the city, and you'll learn about time- and money-saving tips. Guides can meet you wherever you like and tailor the tour to your interests. They can also give you advice on good restaurants, shopping, transportation, and sightseeing. It's basically like renting a friend who's really smart—I always learn something. Recently, my Portuguese guide Alex took me on a little scavenger hunt through Lisbon's castle town—built back when nobles needed a safe place within the castle walls—and showed me things I hadn't noticed in 20 years of visits to Lisbon.

In addition to sightseeing, I encourage travelers to use guides for cultural experiences. For example, after a two-hour Uffizi Gallery tour in Florence, take a coffee break in a café, and follow it with a guided old-town walk featuring Roman, medieval, and modern aspects of Florence. During a visit to Amsterdam, my guide and I spent an hour enjoying a Reypenaer cheese-and-wine tasting that was just as educational (and frankly, more fun) than a tour of the Rijksmuseum. Also consider food tours, which provide wonderful insight into this very important part of each country's culture (for details, see page 285).

Although it's possible to drop by the local tourist office when you're in town and book a guide, it's better to make arrangements in advance; typically, the office will give you a guide's contact information and you'll book the guide yourself. Many tourist offices list local guides on their websites.

Local guides bring history to life.

You can also look for recommendations in guidebooks (when I meet particularly good, independent guides, I list them in my books). In some cities, you can book a local guide—as well as meetups, walking tours, and excursions—through Airbnb. Other online resources include ToursByLocals (organized tours and private guides), Vayable (food crawls, night photography tours, and other experiences), and TravelLocal (small tour operators).

Self-Guided Walks and Audio Tours

If you don't want to join an organized tour or spring for a local guide, a self-guided walk or audio tour can provide direction and meaning to your wanderings through a new city or museum.

Many tourist offices offer do-it-yourself walking-tour leaflets that provide turn-by-turn directions for an orientation walk around town (some guidebooks offer similar self-guided walks). Tourist offices often offer audio tours to accompany their self-guided walks, and most major museums offer room-by-room audioguides. Sometimes you'll borrow or rent a device preloaded with the audio content at the tourist office or museum; in other cases you'll use free Wi-Fi to download the tour to your mobile device on the spot. Increasingly, destinations and museums are offering free downloadable apps that combine tours with other digital content.

Audio tours are hard to beat: The price is right (free or low cost), the quality is reliable, and you can take the tour exactly when you like. With an audio tour, you can immerse yourself in a wonderful sight, enjoying its visual wonder while listening to information that gives it all meaning. Before you leave for Europe, it's worth looking for digital content you can download in advance to enhance your trip. For instance, the palace at Versailles offers helpful podcasts for touring its extensive palace grounds (www.chateauversailles.fr). Remember to bring earbuds.

I've produced free, self-guided audio versions of my walking and museum tours throughout Europe (download the Rick Steves Audio Europe app; see page 17). These user-friendly, easy-to-follow, fun, and informative audio tours are available for museums (for instance, Paris' Louvre and Orsay, Florence's Uffizi), churches (St. Paul's in London, St. Peter's in Rome, the Basilica of St. Francis in Assisi), ancient sites (Athens' Acropolis, Rome's Colosseum), my favorite neighborhoods (Edinburgh's Royal Mile, London's Westminster, Venice's Grand Canal), and much more.

Minivan Excursions

Some of Europe's top sights are awkward to reach by public transportation, such as the châteaux in the Loire, the *Sound of Music* sights outside Salzburg, the D-Day beaches of Normandy, the rural meadows of Cornwall, or the prehistoric cave paintings in France's Dordogne. For roughly $50-60 per half-day, an organized tour not only whisks you effortlessly from one hard-to-reach-without-a-car sight to the next, but gives you lots of information as you go. (Or, if you have a car, consider picking up the brochure for a well-thought-out tour itinerary and doing it on your own.)

Minivan tours—such as this one, to the Rock of Gibraltar—can be an ideal way for nondrivers to reach certain sights.

If you have a choice between a big, 50-seat bus (a "coach") and a minivan, I'd generally recommend the minivan. With a smaller group, you're likely to have a more engaging, entertaining guide and more camaraderie as you roll.

SIGHTSEEING STRATEGIES

Westminster Abbey, the Eiffel Tower, the Sistine Chapel—these are the reasons you go to Europe. They're also the reason millions of other tourists go. Nothing kills a sightseeing buzz like waiting in line for hours to get into a popular sight, or being crammed shoulder to shoulder in front of a masterpiece painting. But if you plan ahead, the sights you dreamed of seeing won't disappoint.

Be Strategic and Selective

Set up an itinerary that allows you to fit in your must-see sights, but be realistic about what you can accomplish in a day. As you make your plan, note the specifics of the sights on your list, especially their closed days and any evening hours (which can help extend your sightseeing day). Check the weather report a few days out and plan your indoor/outdoor time accordingly. Arrange your sightseeing to cover a larger city systematically and efficiently, one neighborhood at a time.

Save yourself for the biggies. Don't overestimate your powers of absorption. Rare is the tourist who doesn't become somewhat jaded after several weeks of travel. At the start of my trip, I'll seek out every great painting and cathedral I can. After two months, I find myself "seeing" cathedrals with a sweep of my head from the doorway, and I probably wouldn't

Medieval Sightseeing in a Modern World

Today's cities sprawl, but many, such as Florence (pictured), were once contained within medieval walls. Most of the walls were torn down long ago, to allow the cities to expand beyond their historic centers. But in Paris, Kraków, Vienna, and others, you can still see the legacy of these walls in the shape of the modern ring roads that replaced them. To pare an otherwise overwhelming city down to size, remember that nearly everything worth your sightseeing time lies within this ring.

cross the street for another Rembrandt. Don't burn out on mediocre castles, palaces, and museums. Sightsee selectively.

When possible, visit major sights in the morning (when your energy is best), and save other activities for the afternoon. Don't put off visiting a must-see sight; even if you've double-checked hours, places can close unexpectedly for a strike or restoration. On holidays, expect reduced hours or closures. In summer, some sights may stay open late. Off-season, many attractions have shorter hours.

For more spontaneous sightseeing, location-based apps such as Google Maps, Tripomatic, and Triposo point you toward sights and venues within walking distance. Tripomatic shows opening hours and user ratings and meshes with an itinerary-planning tool; Google Maps provides hours and ratings along with navigation; and Triposo sorts your options by time of day, and works well offline—including its maps.

Avoiding Lines and Crowds

Crowds are a nuisance at top European attractions, and plenty of people spend big chunks of their vacation time queueing up in long lines at popular sights. Smart tourists do whatever they can to minimize hassles and maximize their experience.

As far as I'm concerned, there are two IQs for travelers: those who queue...and those who don't. It always amazes me how the vast majority of people waste literally hours in line when, with a little advance planning, they could waltz right in. With the right information, you can avoid nearly every line that tourists suffer through. The following tricks aren't secrets. They're in any good, up-to-date guidebook. Just read ahead.

Timing Is Everything

In many cities, a number of sights tend to be closed on the same day of the week (usually Sunday, Monday, or Tuesday). It follows that, in high season, any major sight that's open when everything else is closed is guaranteed to be crowded. For example, Versailles is packed on Tuesdays, when many big museums in Paris are closed.

Many museums are free one day a month—a great deal for locals. But for visitors, it's generally worth paying the entrance fee on a different day to avoid the hordes on the free day. In Rome, the Sistine Chapel feels like the Sardine Chapel when admission is waived on the last Sunday of the month. Likewise, the Colosseum and Roman Forum are free...and a mob scene on the first Sunday of the month.

At popular sights, it can help to arrive early or go late. This is especially true at places popular with cruise excursions and big-bus tour groups. At 8 in the morning, Germany's fairy-tale Neuschwanstein Castle is cool and easy, with relaxed guides and no crowds; come an hour later without a ticket and you'll either wait a long time, find that tickets are sold out, or both. Of course, there are exceptions: On my last visit to the Acropolis in Athens, I went around noon—which was perfect timing, since cruise-ship crowds tend to flock there first thing in the morning. They were heading

It's Tuesday at Versailles, and these people now have time to read their guidebooks: "On Tuesday, many Paris museums are closed, so Versailles has very long lines."

out as I was heading in. A good guidebook will offer tips on the best times to visit a sight.

Many sights are open late one or two nights a week—another pleasant time to visit. For instance, London's Tate Modern stays open Friday and Saturday evenings, when you'll enjoy Dalí and Warhol in near solitude. Very late in the day—when most tourists are long gone, searching for dinner or lying exhausted in their rooms—I linger alone, taking artistic liberties with some of Europe's greatest works in empty galleries.

Shortcuts

Even at the most packed sights, there's often a strategy or shortcut that can break you out of the herd, whether it's a side entrance with a shorter wait, a guided tour that includes last-minute reservations, a better place in town to pick up your ticket, or a pass with line-skipping privileges.

Sometimes getting in more easily is just a matter of picking the right door. Grand as the Louvre's main entrance is, that glass pyramid stops looking impressive as you wait—and wait—to get through security. You can't bypass security checks, but you'll encounter shorter lines if you use the less crowded underground entrance.

A pricier option to skip lines at a sight is to take a guided tour. At the Vatican Museums, joining a guided tour gets you right in. In Milan, you can sign up a week ahead to take a bus tour that includes an easy stop at Leonardo's *Last Supper*, which normally books up more than a month in advance.

Self-service ticket kiosks, like those at the Louvre, Versailles, and Madrid's Prado, can provide a faster way in. On

The Eiffel Tower comes with long lines for those who don't book online in advance. With my reservation in hand, I went directly to the elevator, while this long queue of tourists waited. (None of them had my guidebook.)

a recent trip to St. Petersburg I bought my ticket to the Hermitage at a kiosk and walked right past a ticket line bulging with cruise-ship travelers—and within minutes was enjoying the czars' grand art collection. Similarly, if you buy your ticket for the Tower of London at a souvenir stand on your way to the Tower, you can skip the long line at the sight itself.

At St. Mark's Basilica in Venice, you can either snake slowly through an endless line, or go instead to a nearby church to check a large bag or backpack—then walk right to the front of the basilica's line, show your bag-claim tag, and head on in (go figure). Check your guidebook for sight-specific, insider tips.

Reservations and Advance Tickets

Certain sights are almost always jammed, all day long, most of the year (many in older edifices that weren't built to accommodate mass tourism). Fortunately, many popular sights sell advance tickets that guarantee admission at a certain time (often with a small booking fee that's well worth it). Given how precious your vacation time is, I recommend getting reservations for any must-see sight that offers them—it's worth giving up some spontaneity. While hundreds of tourists are sweating in long lines, those who've booked ahead can just show up at their reserved entry time and breeze right in. Your guidebook should have tips, or check websites for your must-see sights to see if reservations are an option.

In some cases, getting a ticket in advance simply means buying your ticket earlier on the same day. But for other sights, you may need to book weeks or even months in advance. These include places such as the Eiffel Tower, Rome's Vatican Museums, Anne Frank's House in Amsterdam, Barcelona's Picasso Museum, and Florence's famous galleries—the Accademia (Michelangelo's *David*) and the Uffizi (Italian Renaissance art). As soon as you're ready to commit to a certain date, book it.

Note that some sights require reservations, such as the Reichstag in Berlin, Leonardo's *Last Supper* in Milan, Giotto's Scrovegni Chapel in Padua, and the Borghese Gallery in Rome. For some of these, the reservations system is aimed not so much at coping with vast crowds, but toward moving people in and out efficiently.

At many great galleries, such as the Uffizi in Florence, you can wait in line for two hours... or book ahead and walk right in. Remember: Lines like this are not for the entry turnstile, but for the ticket booth.

Many museums now offer convenient mobile ticketing. Simply buy your ticket online and send it to your phone, eliminating the need to print a paper ticket.

Sightseeing Passes and Combo-Tickets

Many tourist destinations offer a citywide sightseeing pass or tourist card, which includes free or discounted entrance to many or most sights for a certain amount of time (usually

Reserving Sights in Advance

At some of Europe's most popular sights, reservations are required; at others, reservations are very smart. This list of major sights you can book ahead isn't comprehensive; check your guidebook for details on the sights you plan to visit.

Austria
Schönbrunn Palace, Vienna

France
Eiffel Tower, Paris
Orsay Museum, Paris
Picasso Museum, Paris
Versailles, near Paris
Château de Chenonceau, Loire
Cro-Magnon Caves, Dordogne
International Center for Cave Art,
   Dordogne

Germany
Reichstag, Berlin*
Neuschwanstein Castle, Bavaria
Historic Green Vault, Dresden

Great Britain
Tower of London
London Eye
Westminster Abbey, London
St. Paul's Cathedral, London
Madame Tussauds Waxworks, London
Stonehenge
Jorvik Viking Centre, York
Lennon and McCartney Homes,
   Liverpool

Hungary
Hungarian Parliament, Budapest

Italy
Vatican Museums (including Sistine
   Chapel), Rome
Borghese Gallery, Rome*
Uffizi Gallery, Florence

Accademia Gallery, Florence
Duomo Museum, Florence
Duomo's dome, Florence*
Brancacci Chapel, Florence*
Last Supper, Milan*
South Tirol Museum of Archaeology
   (Ötzi the Iceman), Bolzano
Scrovegni Chapel, Padua*

Ireland
Book of Kells, Dublin

The Netherlands
Anne Frank House, Amsterdam**
Rijksmuseum, Amsterdam
Van Gogh Museum, Amsterdam
Corrie Ten Boom House, Haarlem

Poland
Auschwitz-Birkenau Memorial*
Schindler's Factory Museum, Kraków

Spain
Sagrada Família, Barcelona
La Pedrera, Barcelona
Casa Batlló, Barcelona
Park Güell, Barcelona
Picasso Museum, Barcelona
Alhambra, Granada
Salvador Dalí House, Cadaqués*
Altamira Caves, near Santillana del
   Mar

* *Reservations required*

** *By advance reservation only
between 9 a.m. and 3:30 p.m.*

intervals of 24 hours). Such deals often include free use of public transit, a brief explanatory booklet, and a map.

In some places, passes can save you serious time and money; in others, you'd have to sightsee nonstop to barely break even. Do the math: Compare the price of the pass to the total of what you'd pay for individual admissions. But remember: Time is money. A pass is almost always worthwhile if it allows you to bypass admission lines. For instance, Paris' Museum Pass covers many top sights (the Louvre, Orsay, Notre-Dame Tower, and Versailles) and allows you to skip ticket-buying lines. The Madrid Card may not save you a lot of money, but it can help you avoid high-season lines at the Royal Palace and the Prado. Plus, with a pass, you can spontaneously visit minor sights you otherwise might not want to pay to enter.

For Rome's Colosseum, buy a combo-ticket 150 yards away at the less-crowded Forum/Palatine Hill gate—and skip directly past the not-so-smart travelers pictured here.

Combo-tickets combine admission to a larger sight with entry to a lesser sight or two that few people would pay to see. The bad news: You have to pay for multiple sights to visit one. The good news: You can bypass the line at the congested sight by buying your ticket at a less-popular sister sight. You can wait up to an hour to get into Rome's Colosseum or Venice's Doge's Palace—or buy a combo-ticket (at a participating yet less-crowded sight) and scoot inside.

Whether you have a combo-ticket or pass, never wait at the back of the line if there's any chance you can skip it. Don't be shy: March straight to the front and wave your pass or ticket. If you really do have to wait with everyone else, they'll let you know.

If You Can't Beat 'Em, Join 'Em

No matter how well-conceived your plans, it's inevitable that at some point you'll find yourself packed shoulder-to-shoulder with other visitors and their intercontinental B.O. Accept in advance that popular attractions, such as the Sistine Chapel, come with a constant and raging commotion of tourists... but that doesn't mean you should stay away.

Recently, I was unable to avoid lumbering through Versailles on one of the most crowded days of the year (a Sunday in July). It was an experience I'll never forget. A steady crush of visitors shuffled through the hot and muggy one-way route leading to the payoff: the magnificent Hall of Mirrors. Even with a mossy carpet of tourist heads, sights like these are a thrill to see—and worth every sweaty second.

Visiting Sights Smartly

Some people walk into Europe's major museums, churches, palaces, castles, and ancient sites, gawk for a few minutes, then walk out. But with a little preparation and know-how, your sightseeing will go more smoothly—and take on more significance. Here are some tips for navigating Europe's various sights.

Tickets: Before you get to the ticket window, study the list of prices. You could have a choice of individual tickets, combo-tickets, or passes. You may be eligible for discounts if you're young, old, or with children (have proof of ID, student card, etc.). Be prepared to pay cash, particularly for inexpensive sights.

Museums may have special exhibits in addition to their permanent collections. Some special exhibits are included in the entry price, while others come at an extra cost (which you may have to pay even if you don't want to see the exhibit).

Your ticket may allow in-and-out privileges (say, for a lunch break outside the museum); if this is important to you, ask.

Entry Procedure: Entering a major sight is similar to arriving in a new town—you need to get oriented. Hit the information desk for a brochure or map, find out about any special events and tours, and ask about any temporary room or wing closures.

Security Check: Many sights have a security check, where you must open your bag or send it through a metal detector. Allow extra time for these lines in your planning. A few places will confiscate the same sharp items and full water bottles that you're not allowed to carry on board a plane.

Checkroom: Most sights offer a checkroom or lockers (usually free or with a small deposit), and some require you to check daypacks and coats. They'll be kept safely. If you have something you can't bear to part with, stash it in a pocket or purse. To avoid checking a small backpack, carry it under your arm like a purse as you enter. (From a

Stroll with a chatty curator through Europe's greatest art galleries, thanks to digital audioguides.

guard's point of view, a backpack—which could bump against artwork—is generally a problem, while a purse is not.)

Touring the Sight: Many sights offer audioguides, which generally offer recorded descriptions in English. If the audioguide isn't included with admission, ask to listen to it for a couple of minutes to gauge the quality before you pay. If you bring your own earbuds, you can enjoy better sound. To save money, bring a Y-jack and share one audioguide with your travel partner. Other sights offer downloadable audio tours that you'll listen to on your own mobile device. (See "Self-Guided Walks and Audio Tours," earlier.)

Guided tours in English are most likely to be available in peak season (generally at an extra cost, but sometimes included with admission). If you're interested, confirm in advance that your visit will coincide with a tour. Or hire your own guide to take you through the museum (see "Local Guides," earlier).

Some sights run short films that are generally worth your time. I make it standard operating procedure to ask when I arrive at a sight if there is a film in English (some come with audioguides that always offer English).

Once inside, hit the highlights first, then go back to other things if you have the time and stamina. Expect changes—items can be on tour, on loan, out sick, or shifted at the whim of a curator. If the painting you crossed the Atlantic to see isn't on the wall, ask a museum staffer if it's been moved to another location.

Most sights stop selling tickets and start shutting down rooms or sections 30 to 60 minutes before closing. Guards usher people out, so don't save the best for last. Get to the far end early, see the rooms that are first to shut down, and work your way back toward the entry.

My favorite time at a major sight is the lazy last hour, when the tourists clear out. On one of my visits to the Acropolis, I showed up late and had the place to myself in the cool of early evening. Other blockbuster sights such as St. Peter's Basilica and the Palace of Versailles can be magical just before closing.

Photography: Flash photography is often prohibited in museums, but taking photos without a flash is usually allowed. Look for signs or ask. Flashes damage oil paintings and delicate artifacts, and distract others in the room. Even without a flash, a handheld camera or mobile device will take a decent picture (or buy postcards or posters at the museum bookstore). Think twice about bringing a selfie stick—they're banned at many sights.

Services: Bigger sights usually have a café or cafeteria (a good place to rejuvenate during a long visit). The WCs at sights are free and generally clean; make a point of using them whether you think you need to or not.

At the Vatican Museums it's worth fighting through the gauntlet of crowds to see the Sistine Chapel.

Museums

Europe is a treasure chest of great art and history. For some, visiting the world's greatest museums is the highlight of a European trip. For others, "museum" spells "dull." But you don't need to know how a Ferrari works to enjoy the ride. Paintings are like that. You can just stroll through a gallery and bask in the color scheme. That said, it doesn't hurt to keep in mind the following.

Learn about art and history. In my student days, I had to go to the great art galleries of Europe because my mom said it would be a crime not to. Touring places like the National Archaeological Museum in Athens, I was surrounded by people looking like they were having a good time—and I was convinced they were faking it. I thought, "How could anybody enjoy that stuff?" Two years later, after a class in classical art history, that same museum was a fascinating trip into the world of Pericles and Socrates, all because of some background knowledge. Pretrip studying makes art and artifacts more fun. When you understand the context in which things were made, who paid for it and why, what the challenges of the day were, and so on, paintings and statues become the closest thing Europe has to a time machine.

With a good guidebook, you stand a chance of finding Michelangelo's *Slaves* in the Louvre.

Don't miss the masterpieces. A common misconception is that a great museum has only great art. But only a fraction of a museum's pieces are masterpieces worthy of your time. You can't possibly cover everything—so don't try. With the help of a tour guide or guidebook, focus on just the top attractions. Most major museums provide brief pamphlets that recommend a greatest-hits plan. With this selective strategy, you'll appreciate the highlights while you're fresh. If you have any energy left afterward, you can explore other areas of specific interest to you. For me, museum going is the hardest work I do in Europe, and I'm rarely good for more than two or three hours at a time. If you're determined to cover a large museum thoroughly, try tackling it in separate visits over several days.

A victim of the Louvre

Find your favorites. On arrival, look through the museum's collection handbook or the gift shop's postcards to make sure you won't miss anything of importance to you. For instance, I love Salvador Dalí's work. One time I thought I was finished with a museum, but as I browsed through the postcards...Hello, Dalí. A museum staffer was happy to show me where this Dalí painting was hiding. I saved myself the disappointment of discovering too late that I'd missed it.

Eavesdrop. If you're especially interested in a particular piece of art, spend a half-hour studying it and listening to each passing tour guide tell his or her story about *David* or the *Mona Lisa*. They each do their own research and come up with a different angle to share. Much of it is true. There's nothing wrong with this sort of tour freeloading. Just don't stand in the front and ask a lot of questions.

Take advantage of my free audio tours. My Rick Steves Audio Europe app includes self-guided tours of the finest museums in many of Europe's greatest cities. These can make your museum going easier and more meaningful (see page 17).

Churches, Synagogues, and Mosques

European houses of worship offer some amazing art and architecture—not to mention a welcome seat and a cool respite from the heat. You may be there just to see the Caravaggio over the side altar, but others are there as worshippers. Be a respectful visitor.

A modest dress code (no bare shoulders or shorts) is encouraged at most churches, but is enforced at some larger churches and most mosques. If you are caught by surprise, you can improvise, such as using maps to cover your shoulders and tying a jacket around your hips to cover your knees. (Throughout the Mediterranean world, I wear a super-lightweight pair of long pants rather than shorts for my hot and

Boning Up on Europe's Relics

Centuries ago, relics were an important focus of worship. These holy relics, often bones, were the "ruby slippers" of the medieval age. They gave you power—got your prayers answered and helped you win wars—and ultimately helped you get back to your eternal Kansas.

The bones of monks were venerated, and sometimes even artistically arranged in crypts and chapels. In **Rome's** Capuchin Crypt, hundreds of skeletons decorate the walls to the delight—or disgust—of the always wide-eyed visitor. The crypt offers unusual ideas in home decorating, as well as a chance to pick up a few of Rome's most interesting postcards. A similar Capuchin Crypt is a highlight of many visits to **Palermo** in Sicily. In **Évora,** Portugal, osteophiles make a pilgrimage to the macabre "House of Bones" chapel at the Church of St. Francis, lined with the bones of thousands of monks.

TOP Even in death, Italians know how to look cool.
BOTTOM Head to Hallstatt's Bone Chapel.

Overcrowding in cemeteries has prompted unusual solutions. Austria's tiny town of **Hallstatt** is crammed between a mountain and a lake. Space is so limited that bones get only 12 peaceful buried years in the church cemetery before making way for the newly dead. The result is a fascinating chapel of bones in the cemetery. Hallstatt stopped this practice in the 1960s, about the same time the Catholic Church began permitting cremation.

Kutná Hora's ossuary, an hour by train from Prague, is decorated with the bones of 40,000 people, many of them plague victims. The monks who stacked these bones 400 years ago wanted viewers to remember that the earthly church is a community of both the living and the dead.

Some cities, such as Paris and Rome, have catacombs. Many cities opened up a little extra space by deboning the graveyards that used to surround medieval churches. During the French Revolution, **Paris** experienced a great church cemetery land grab. Skeletons of countless Parisians were dug up and carefully stacked along miles of tunnels beneath the city.

Seekers of the macabre can bone up on Europe's more obscure ossuaries, but any tourist will stumble onto bones and relics. Whether in a church, chapel, or underground tunnel in Europe, you might be surprised by who's looking at you, kid.

muggy big-city sightseeing.) At Turkish mosques, women must cover their heads and wear clothing that shields their legs and arms; everyone needs to remove their shoes.

At active places of worship, visitors may not be allowed inside for one or more time periods throughout the day. If you are already inside, you may be asked to leave so as not to disturb the congregation. Check your guidebook's listing to avoid showing up when a place is closed for worship (some services are open to the public). One of my favorite experiences in Great Britain is to attend evensong—a daily choral service—at a grand cathedral (see page 622).

Some churches have coin-operated audio boxes that describe the art and history; just set the dial to English, insert your coins, and listen. Coin boxes near a piece of art illuminate the work (and present a better photo opportunity). I pop in a coin whenever I can. It improves my experience, is a favor to other visitors trying to appreciate a great piece of art in the dark, and is a little contribution to that church. Whenever possible, let there be light.

Ancient Sites and Ruins

Climbing the Acropolis, communing with the druids at Stonehenge, strolling the Croatian shore in the shadow of Emperor Diocletian's palace in Split, tracing the intricate carvings on a Viking ship—the remnants of Europe's distant past bring a special thrill to those of us from the New World.

But the oldest sites are also the most likely to be initially underwhelming, especially if it's been a while since your last history class. On its own, the Roman Forum is just a cluster of crumbling columns and half-buried foundations. You've heard about it all your life, you've spent good money to get here, and your first thought upon entering is..."This is it?"

Ancient sites come to life with your imagination, aided by information. Bring a guidebook that's heavy on historical background, and consider hiring a local guide. Eager local guides tend to cluster outside major ancient sites like Delos in Greece, and Pompeii and the Colosseum in Italy, but quality varies. I prefer to book a reputable guide in advance, but if you decide to choose a guide at a sight, first talk to him or her for a bit to make sure you connect.

For some well-known places you can get books that cleverly use overlays to visually mesh the present with the past. To fire up your imagination before your trip, watch a movie or read a book set in the time and place of any site

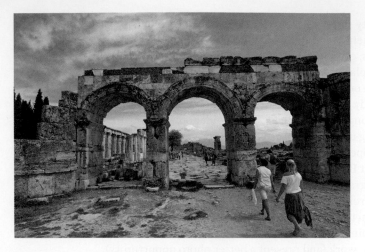

Dusty rocks or busy ancient thoroughfare? The ruins at Hierapolis, Turkey, come to life with info and imagination.

you're excited to see. Once you're there, mentally reconstruct arches and repaint facades. Clad your fellow tourists in togas. Fill a ruined cathedral with the chants of cowled monks while inhaling imaginary incense.

Many major ancient sites (especially in Greece) have both an archaeological site and a nearby museum full of artifacts unearthed there. You can choose between visiting the museum first (to mentally reconstruct the ruins before seeing them) or the site first (to get the lay of the ancient land before seeing the items found there). In most cases, I prefer to see the site first, then the museum. However, crowds and weather can also help determine your plan. If it's a blistering hot afternoon, tour the air-conditioned museum first, then hit the ruins in the cool of the early evening. Or, if rain clouds are on the horizon, do the archaeological site first, then duck into the museum when the rain hits.

Castles

Castles send the imagination soaring. Fortresses perch on hilltops from Ireland to Israel, and from Sweden to Spain, lining the Loire and guarding harbors throughout the Mediterranean.

While some of Europe's castles are fairy-tale wonderful (such as Neuschwanstein in Bavaria), others are massive, crumbling hulks (Rheinfels on the Rhine). Relatively few castles are furnished; most of their original furnishings disappeared long ago. Some castles have little more than a ticket booth, while others (like England's Warwick) have jousting competitions, catapult demonstrations, museums of medieval armor and artifacts, and well-stocked gift shops. There are even entire towns built in and around medieval castles, like Carcassonne in France.

Before visiting a castle, do your research; check to see if tours are offered. If you're visiting a ruined castle, wear good walking shoes. Bring a small flashlight if there are tunnels; claustrophobics beware. Learn the various parts of the castle; you'll appreciate your visit more if you can tell the difference between a dungeon and a donjon (a.k.a. the keep; the main tower that's the refuge of last resort if the castle is attacked).

Europe's castles generally fall into one of two categories: medieval fortresses (built to withstand sieges) and castle-palaces (residences and luxury châteaux for royalty and nobility).

With the advent of cannons, even the sturdiest medieval castles became obsolete. Many fell into ruin, used as quarries to build more practical things. You'll enjoy the best concentration of medieval ramparts and dark dungeons by touring the Rhine in Germany. To see a castle being built today with methods used in the 13th century, visit Guédelon in France (about two hours south of Paris).

From the 16th century through the 19th-century Romantic era, the rich and famous built castle-palaces as residences, culminating in Europe's most opulent palace—Versailles, just outside Paris, and its most fanciful—King Ludwig II's Neuschwanstein. Walt Disney made Ludwig's fairy-tale castle his trademark, and the rest is history.

Travelers tramping through Europe's castles will encounter a muddle of medieval bunker mentality and Romantic renovation. While confusing, this weird mix makes for great sightseeing.

Open-Air Folk Museums

Many people travel in search of traditional culture in action. But even while we're booking a ticket into the romantic past, much of Europe is squarely in the modern world. Often, the easiest way to see "traditional culture" is by exploring open-air folk museums. True, it's culture on a lazy Susan, with an often sanitized, romanticized version of an area's preindustrial lifestyle. But these museums can be simultaneously fun and enlightening—a magic carpet ride through a culture's past. In more and more places they provide your only chance for a close-up look at the "Old World."

An open-air folk museum collects traditional buildings from every corner of a country or region, then carefully

Europe's Coolest Castles

Visiting Europe can overwhelm you with too many castles to tour in too little time. To help you prioritize, here are my favorites.

Carcassonne (France): Europe's greatest Romanesque fortress-city, medieval Carcassonne is a 13th-century world of towers, turrets, and cobblestones—a walled city and Camelot's castle rolled into one.

Warwick Castle (England): The best castle in Britain, this 14th- and 15th-century fortified shell holds an 18th- and 19th-century royal residence surrounded by dandy gardens—a fairy-tale fortress that's entertaining from dungeon to lookout.

Burg Eltz (Germany): Lurking in a mysterious forest, this is my favorite European castle. Once the fortified home to three big landlord families, it retains its medieval furnishings and ambience.

Rheinfels Castle (Germany): This mightiest of Rhine castles, built in 1245, rumbles with ghosts from its hard-fought past—it withstood a siege by 28,000 French troops in 1692, but was destroyed by the French Revolutionary army a century later.

Storm Carcassonne early or late.

Warwick Castle—for kings and queens of any age

Even in ruins, Rheinfels is mighty.

Towering Eltz Castle, on Germany's Mosel River

Shimmering Château de Chillon

Reifenstein Castle, rugged inside and out

Sintra's hilltop ruins, where the winds of the past really howl

At the Ehrenberg ruins, grab a sword fern and unfetter your imagination.

Don't miss the Romantic-era interior of Hohenschwangau Castle.

Château de Chillon (Switzerland): This wonderfully preserved 13th-century castle is set romantically at the edge of Lake Geneva.

Reifenstein Castle (Italy): Situated below the Brenner Pass, Reifenstein once bottled up a strategic valley leading to the easiest way across the Alps—and features the best-preserved medieval castle interior I've ever seen.

Moorish Ruins of Sintra (Portugal): The desolate ruins of a 1,000-year-old Moorish castle is a medieval funtasia of scramble-up-and-down-the-ramparts delights and atmospheric picnic perches with vast Atlantic Ocean views.

King's Castles (Germany's Bavaria): The fairy-tale extravagance of Neuschwanstein Castle is proof that Bavaria's King Ludwig II was just "mad" about 19th-century Romanticism. Downhill, nestled near Alpsee lake, is the more stately Hohenschwangau Castle, Ludwig's boyhood home.

Ehrenberg Ruins (Austria): This ensemble of brooding ruins, connected by a valley-spanning suspension bridge, was once the largest castle complex in the Tirol region. Located near the town of Reutte, Austria, Ehrenberg offers a fascinating contrast to Ludwig's castles just across the border.

Neuschwanstein, the greatest of "Mad" King Ludwig's fairy-tale castles

reassembles them in a park, usually near the capital or a major city. Log cabins, thatched cottages, mills, old school-houses, shops, and farms come complete with original furnishings and usually a local person dressed in the traditional costume who's happy to answer any of your questions about life then and there. In the summer, these museums buzz with colorful folk dances, live music performances, and craft demonstrations by artisans doing what they can to keep the cuckoo clock from going the way of the dodo bird. Some of my favorite souvenirs are those I watched being dyed, woven, or carved by folk-museum artists. To get the most out of your visit, start by picking up a list of that day's special exhibits, events, and activities at the information center, and take advantage of any walking tours.

Folk museums teach traditional lifestyles better than any other kind of museum. As our world hurtles past 300 billion McDonald's hamburgers served, these museums will become even more important. Of course, they're as realistic as Santa's Village, but how else will you see the elves?

LEFT Traditional culture is kept alive in Europe's open-air folk museums.

RIGHT At Stockholm's Skansen folk museum, you may be entertained by this rare band of left-handed fiddlers.

BECOMING A TEMPORARY EUROPEAN

Many travelers tramp through Europe like they're visiting the cultural zoo. "Ooh, that guy in lederhosen yodeled! Excuse me, could you do that again in the sunshine so I can get a good picture?" It's important to stow your camera, roll up your sleeves, and enjoy the real thing.

By developing a knack for connecting with locals and their culture, we become temporary Europeans—approaching Europe on its level, accepting and enjoying its unique ways of life. When I'm in Europe, I strive to become a cultural chameleon—what I call a "temporary local." I consume wine in France, beer in Germany...and small breakfasts in Italy. While I never drink tea at home, after a long day of sightseeing in England, "a spot of tea" really does feel right. Find ways to really be there. Here are some ideas to consider:

Hit the back streets. Many people energetically jockey themselves into the most crowded square of the most crowded city in the most crowded month (St. Mark's Square, Venice, July)—and then complain about the crowds. If you're in Venice in July, walk six blocks behind St. Mark's Basilica, step into a café, and be greeted by Venetians who act as though they've never seen a tourist.

Play where the locals play. A city's popular fairgrounds and parks are filled with families, lovers, and old-timers enjoying a cheap afternoon or evening out. European communities provide their heavily taxed citizens with wonderful athletic facilities. In Britain, check out a public swimming pool, called a "leisure center." While tourists outnumber locals five to one at the world-famous Tivoli Gardens, Copenhagen's other amusement park, Bakken, is enjoyed purely by Danes. Disneyland Paris is great, but Paris' Parc Astérix is more French.

Take a stroll. Across southern Europe, communities relax with a *paseo*, or stroll, in the early evening. Stroll along. Join a *Volksmarch* in Bavaria to spend a day on the trails with people singing "I love to go a-wandering" in its original language. Mountain huts across Europe are filled mostly with local hikers. Most hiking centers have alpine clubs that welcome foreigners and offer organized hikes.

Go to church. Many regular churchgoers never even consider a European worship service. But any church would welcome a traveling American. And an hour in a small-town church provides an unbeatable peek into the community, especially if you join them for coffee and cookies afterward. I'll never forget going to a small church on the south coast of Portugal one Easter. A tourist stood at the door videotaping the "colorful natives" (including me) shaking hands with the priest after Mass.

Mass with the sun's rays, daily in St. Peter's

Be an early bird. Throughout Europe—on medieval ramparts, in churches, produce markets, alpine farmsteads, and Riviera villages—the local culture thrives while the tourists sleep. In Germany, walk around Rothenburg's fortified wall at breakfast time,

Europe's Best Open-Air Folk Museums

Popularized in Scandinavia, these folk museums are now found all over the world, though the best ones are still in the Nordic capitals.

Scandinavia

Skansen (Stockholm): One of the best in Europe, with more than 100 buildings from all over Sweden, craftspeople at work, feisty folk entertainment, and an Arctic camp complete with reindeer and Lapp dancing.

Funen Village (Den Fynske Landsby, near Odense): Life in 18th-century Denmark.

The Old Town (Den Gamle By, Aarhus): Danish town life in the 1700-1800s, 1920s, and 1970s.

Norwegian Folk Museum (Bygdøy, Oslo): Norway's first, with 150 old buildings and a 12th-century stave church.

Maihaugen Folk Museum (Lillehammer): Norway's best, with folk culture of the Gudbrandsdal Valley.

Seurasaari Island (near Helsinki): Reconstructed buildings from all over Finland.

The Netherlands, Germany, and Switzerland

Netherlands Open-Air Folk Museum (Arnhem): Holland's first and biggest.

Zuiderzee Museum (Enkhuizen): Lively reconstruction of Dutch traditions lost forever to land reclamation.

Museum guides in traditional dress are eager to teach at The Old Town museum in Aarhus, Denmark.

Traditional Dutch engineering at work at the Netherlands Open-Air Folk Museum

Vogtsbauernhof Black Forest Open-Air Museum (Gutach): Farms filled with exhibits on traditional German dress and lifestyles.

Ballenberg Swiss Open-Air Museum (near Interlaken): Fine collection of old Swiss buildings, arranged roughly as if in a huge map of Switzerland.

Hungary

Skanzen (Szentendre): Traditional architecture from around Hungary.

Hollókő (near Budapest): Time-capsule village that's half living hamlet, half open-air museum.

Great Britain and Ireland

Blists Hill Victorian Town (Ironbridge Gorge): Unrivaled look at the early days of the Industrial Revolution in England, with the world's first iron bridge and a glimpse at the factories that lit the fuse of our modern age.

Beamish Museum (near Durham): Life in northeast England in 1900.

St. Fagans National History Museum (near Cardiff): Traditional Welsh ways of life.

Ulster Folk and Transport Museum (near Belfast): Traditional Irish lifestyles and buildings from all over Ireland.

Muckross Traditional Farms (near Killarney): Three working farms, a schoolhouse, and other buildings from 1930s-40s Ireland.

The tiny village-museum of Hollókő is a time capsule of Hungarian tradition.

Visitors travel back to 1890s England at the Blists Hill Victorian Town.

before the tour buses pull in and turn the town into a medieval theme park. Crack-of-dawn joggers and walkers enjoy a special look at wonderfully medieval cities as they yawn and stretch and prepare for the daily onslaught of the 21st century. By waking up with the locals on the Italian Riviera in the off-season, you can catch the morning sun as it greets a sleepy village, breathe in the damp, cool air...and experience a rare Italian silence. Among travelers, the early bird gets the memories.

Root for your team. For many Europeans, the top religion is soccer. Getting caught up in a sporting event is going local. Whether enjoying soccer in small-town Italy or hurling in Ireland, you'll be surrounded by a stadium crammed with devout fans. Buy something to wear or wave with the hometown colors to help you remember whose side you're on.

Challenge a local to the national pastime. In Greece or Turkey, drop into a teahouse or *taverna* and challenge anyone to a game of backgammon. You're instantly a part (even a star) of the café or bar scene. Normally the gang will gather around, and what starts out as a simple game becomes a fun duel of international significance.

Contact an equivalent version of your club. If you're a member of an international service club, bridge club, professional association, or other organization, make a point to connect with your foreign mates.

See how the locals live. Residential neighborhoods rarely see a tourist; ride a city bus or subway into the suburbs. Browse through a department store. Buy a copy of the

Make your trip worth more by cranking up the experiences. Attending a sporting event anywhere in Europe—like this soccer match in Germany—puts you in touch with the local spirit for little money. If you're wearing a lei with colors, be sure you root for the right team. *Auf geht's Deutschland!*

Connecting with the Culture

Generally speaking, Europeans enjoy getting to know Americans—all it takes to connect is a friendly smile and genuine curiosity. Take advantage of one of the many programs and organizations set up to help bridge the cultural divide.

Meet-the-Locals Programs: Several European cities have English-speaking volunteer greeters who belong to the Global Greeter Network (www.globalgreeternetwork.com). Greeters are screened extensively, but aren't trained historical experts. Instead, they introduce visitors to their city by spending a few hours sharing their insider knowledge—their favorite hidden spots, how to navigate public transit, where to find the best bargains, etc.

A few bigger cities have more formal programs that put travelers in direct touch with locals. Dublin, the City of a Thousand Welcomes, brings volunteers and first-time visitors together for a cup of tea or a pint (free, www.littlemuseum.ie, choose "Visit"). In Paris, the group Meeting the French organizes dinners in private homes and workplace tours to match your interests or career (fee, www.meetingthefrench.com). Visitors to Copenhagen can enjoy a home-cooked meal with a family through Dine with the Danes (fee, www.facebook.com/DineWithTheDanes).

Conversation Clubs: Most large European cities, and even many small towns, have informal English-language conversation clubs, usually meeting weekly or monthly in a public space (search online or ask at the tourist information office). You may well be the only native speaker there—if so, expect an especially warm welcome. For instance, in Rothenburg, Germany, the English Conversation Club meets on Wednesdays at Mario's Altfränkische Weinstube am Klosterhof. After 9 p.m., when the beer starts to sink in, the crowd grows, and everyone seems to speak that second language a bit more easily.

Casual Meetups: While primarily designed to connect travelers with overnight hosts, Couchsurfing.com also lists "day hosts" who are happy to just meet up with like-minded visitors and swap travel stories (see page 247). For another free means of finding people with shared interests in a given city, check Meetup.com. Sponsored events include picnics, museum tours, cocktail evenings, and more.

Cooking Classes: These give you not just a taste of the culinary traditions of the area you're visiting, but also a hands-on feel for what happens in European kitchens—along with a skill you can take home. For more on cooking classes, see page 286.

local *Better Homes and Thatches* and use it to explore that particular culture. Get off the map. In Florence, most tourists stick to the small section of the city covered by the ubiquitous tourist maps. Wander beyond that, and you'll dance with the locals or play street soccer with the neighborhood gang. In Helsinki, rather than sweat with a bunch of tourists in your hotel's sterile steam room, ride the public bus into a working-class neighborhood to a rustic-and-woody $14 sauna. Surrounded by milky steam, knotty wood, stringy

LEFT Connect with people. Greeks and Turks love a game of backgammon.

RIGHT Blend into Europe: Shop at the town market.

blond hair, and naked locals, you'll have no idea which century you're in. But one thing is clear: You're in Finland.

Drop by a university. Mill around a university and check out the announcement boards. Eat at the college cafeteria. Ask at the English-language department if there's a student learning English whom you could hire to be your private guide. Be alert and even a little bit snoopy. If you stumble onto a grade-school talent show—sit down and watch it.

Join in. When you visit the town market in the morning, you're just another hungry shopper, picking up your daily produce. Traveling through the wine country of France during harvest time, you can be a tourist taking photos—or you can pitch in and become a grape picker. Get more than a photo op. Get dirty. That night at the festival, it's just grape pickers dancing—and their circle could include you.

If you're hunting cultural peacocks, remember they fan out their tails best for people...not cameras. When you take Europe out of your viewfinder, you're more likely to find it in your lap.

Outdoor Adventure

Europe's fine art and rich history are major reasons to visit. But it's also a continent filled with natural beauty—often overlooked by tourists busy sprinting from sight to sight, or searching for the perfect souvenir. A day in the great outdoors can be just as culturally fulfilling as time spent in a church or museum—and much more invigorating.

If you're an energetic person, make a point to be active in Europe. Whether walking through the city core or speeding down an alpine luge, there are plenty of ways to get your heart pumping while savoring some of Europe's outdoor attractions.

HIKING AND WALKING

From casual city strolls to pleasant day hikes to multiday alpine treks, Europe is a walker's paradise.

City Walking (and Dodging)

It's easy to get in a lot of walking time in Europe's cities and towns. Skip public transport (or save it for the end of the day, when your feet are crying for mercy), and get a literal feel for a place.

When putting together a walking itinerary, look for ways to splice in some top sights. In Rome, for example, winding up to the top of Gianicolo Hill rewards you with a lovely park and superb city views—and along the way you can knock off Bramante's Tempietto church, one of the jewels of the Italian Renaissance. In any city, a walking tour can help you get oriented (described on page 317).

Be prepared—wear good, well-broken-in walking shoes, and keep blister remedies on hand. Pace yourself—concrete and cobblestones take their toll on feet much sooner than dirt trails do.

Be on your toes: Walking in cities can be dangerous, and jaywalking can have serious consequences (scores of pedestrians are run down on the streets of Paris each year). Drivers are aggressive, and politeness has no place on the roads of Europe. Cross streets carefully, but if you wait for a break in the traffic, you may never make it to the other side. Look for a pedestrian overpass or underpass, or when all else fails, just shadow a local—one busy lane at a time—across that seemingly impassable street. Watch out for bikes as well as cars, particularly in cities with strong biking cultures, such as Amsterdam and Copenhagen.

Day Hiking

You don't need to go far into the wild to find a slice of natural Europe to explore on foot. Outstanding national parklands are scattered throughout Europe, offering wonderful ways for visitors to commune with nature. Hikers enjoy nature's very own striptease as the landscape reveals itself in an endless string of powerful poses.

Europe has good hiking for all fitness levels, sometimes aided by a variety of "lifts"—including gondolas, funiculars, cable cars, and cogwheel trains—that take less rugged explorers to the top in a sweat-free flash. Trails are generally well-kept and carefully marked (precise maps are readily available).

Hiking in the Alps

Europe's highest mountain range, the Alps extend for 750 miles and cross eight countries, each offering their own unique taste of alpine thrills. In Italy's Dolomites, for instance, a gondola whisks visitors up to Europe's largest high-alpine meadow, Alpe di Siusi, where a dramatic

Thanks to well-maintained trails, hiking in the Swiss Alps can be a walk in the park—with more spectacular scenery.

Lift Lingo

Europeans, and especially the Swiss, have come up with a variety of ways to conquer alpine peaks and reach the best viewpoints and trailheads with minimum sweat. Known generically as "lifts," each of these contraptions has its own name and definition.

Cogwheel Train: A train that climbs a steep incline using a gear system, which engages "teeth" in the middle of the tracks to provide traction. Also known as "rack-and-pinion train" or "rack railway." In German, it's a *Zahnradbahn* (*train à cremaillère* in French and *ferrovia a cremagliera* in Italian).

Funicular: A car that is pulled by a cable along tracks up a steep incline, usually counterbalanced by a similar car going in the opposite direction (meaning you'll pass the other car exactly halfway through the ride). Funiculars, like cogwheel trains, are in contact with the ground at all times. In German, it's a *Standseilbahn* (*funiculaire* in French and *funicolare* in Italian).

Cable Car: A large passenger car, suspended in the air by a cable. A cable car is generally designed for skiers and holds a large number of people (sometimes dozens at a time), who generally ride standing up. When a cable car reaches a station, it comes to a full stop to allow passengers to get on and off. In German, it's a *Seilbahn* (*téléphérique* in French and *funivia* in Italian).

Gondola: Also suspended in the air by a cable, but smaller than a cable car—generally holding fewer than 10 people, who are usually seated. Gondolas move continuously, meaning that passengers have to hop into and out of the moving cars at stations. Also, while cable-car lines usually have two big cars—one going in each direction—gondolas generally have many smaller cars strung along the same cable. In German, it's a *Gondel* (*télécabine* in French and *telecabine* in Italian).

mountainous rooftop high above the town of Bolzano serves up striking views with Italian sunshine. Within the park, buses take hikers to and from key points along the tiny road, all the way to the foot of the postcard-dramatic Sasso peaks. Meadow walks are ideal for flower lovers and strollers, while chairlifts provide springboards for more demanding hikes.

The Swiss Alps are staggeringly beautiful and unforgettable when it's sunny. On one side of you, lakes stretch all the way to Germany. On the other stands the greatest mountain panorama in Europe—the peaks of the Eiger, Mönch,

Alpine trail signs show where you are, the altitude in meters, and how long in hours and minutes it takes to hike to nearby points.

and Jungfrau. And up ahead you hear the long, legato tones of an alphorn, announcing that a helicopter-stocked mountain hut is open, it's just around the corner...and the coffee schnapps is on. That's the kind of magic that awaits anyone who makes the effort to get high in the Alps.

The Swiss Alps are great—but they're expensive. The French Alps above Chamonix—near the junction of France, Switzerland, and Italy—are a little more forgiving, and the lifts are more affordable. You can take a lift to one end, enjoy a relatively level hike known as the Grand Balcon Sud (Grand South Balcony), and then ride the lift down from the other end, for a single round-trip fare.

Throughout the Alps, trail markers are both handy and humiliating. Handy, because they show hours to hike rather than kilometers to walk to various destinations. Humiliating, because these times are clocked by local senior citizens. You'll know what I mean after your first hike.

Other Hikes in Europe

England's Cotswolds are walkers' country. The English love to walk the peaceful footpaths that shepherds walked back when "polyester" meant two girls. A two-hour trek connecting two thatched-roof towns in the Cotswolds affords intimate backyard views of farms in action: rabbits popping up in fields, ducks butt-up in millponds, and black-and-white cows jostling for space at troughs. Southern France's Cap Ferrat, near Nice, has well-maintained foot trails, perfect for short, view-struck walks above the Mediterranean.

Perhaps my favorite place to hike is in Italy's Cinque Terre. The five towns that make up the Cinque Terre are strung together by a series of trails that form a national park. Hiking these trails—a seven-mile, five-hour journey when they're all open—is one of the most exhilarating experiences in Italy. Take it slow…smell the cactus flowers and herbs, listen to birds, and enjoy spectacular vistas on all sides.

Hiking Tips

If you plan on taking day hikes, look for walking and hiking books on that region. Ask for advice from the national tourist offices of the countries you will visit. Tourist offices often have booklets of nearby self-guided hikes. You can also look into local groups that offer walks to see if one of their scheduled hikes fits with your itinerary. For example, German groups routinely plan *Volksmärsche* and welcome participation. In Great Britain, the Ramblers extend guest privileges to nonmembers who want to try one of the group walks they lead every week.

Before setting out on any hike, check locally to be sure you've made the best match between your skills, gear, and trail conditions (snow can persist on Alpine trails even into summer; Cinque Terre trails can be closed in bad weather or due to landslides). Wear sturdy shoes and carry the essentials: map, sun protection (sunscreen, hat, and/or sunglasses), extra layer, first-aid kit, water, and snacks. To leave the route cleaner than you found it, bring a plastic bag and pick up a little trail trash along the way. It would be great if American visitors—who get so much joy out of European hikes—were known for this good deed. Note that while the trails themselves are public, outside of national parks the property to either side may be private (stick to posted routes).

Hard-core hikers invest in detailed maps (1:100,000 or 1:50,000)—look for OS Ordnance Survey (Britain), Michelin (throughout Europe), IGN's Blue series (good for France), and Touring Club Italiano (Italy). Make sure the map shows general elevation gain with contour lines and/or indicates the steepness of roads.

Hut Hopping

The hikers' shelters spaced along the European trail system make walking trips a simpler proposition: There's no need to carry a tent, stove, or cooking utensils. Hundreds of huts exist to provide food and shelter for hikers. Using a smart network of trails and mountain huts spaced one convenient day's hike apart, you could walk from France to Slovenia without ever coming out of the Alps. At mountain villages, you can replenish your food supply or enjoy a hotel bed and a restaurant meal.

Most alpine huts serve hot meals and provide bunk-style

lodging. Older huts may not have showers or even hot water (you may find pay warm showers at more modern huts). It's smart to hut-hike with a travel sheet, sleeping bag liner, or hostel-style sleep sack, as many huts provide only an infrequently washed blanket. I'll never forget getting cozy in my top bunk while a German in the bottom bunk said, "You're climbing into zee germs of centuries."

Alpine huts can get booked up, especially in summer, so it's smart to reserve ahead. In the Alps, look for the word *Lager*, which means they have a co-ed loft full of $30-a-night mattresses.

BIKING

Some travelers are surprised when I tell them to consider biking in Europe. I explain that it gets you close to the ground and close to the people. Europeans love bicycles, and they are often genuinely impressed when they encounter Americans who reject the view from the tour-bus window in favor of huffing and puffing on two wheels. Your bike provides an instant conversation piece, the perfect bridge over a maze of cultural and language barriers.

City Biking

While my schedule usually won't allow a week-long pedal in the Loire Valley, I'll often do day trips in or around cities. I feel local, efficient, and even smug with my trusty and well-fitted bike. Especially during rush hour, I can get across town faster on my bike than by taxi or tram.

Europe's cities are striving to become more bike-friendly. Dozens of them have joined a European Union initiative to make bicycles on par with cars as a form of urban transport. The progress is gradual. Some cities (such as Rome and Athens) are not yet set up well for bikers, but quite a few (particularly Stockholm, Amsterdam, Copenhagen, Lucca, Salzburg, Munich, and Bruges) are a delight on two wheels, offering an extensive network of well-marked bike lanes. In these cities, rather than relying on walking or public transportation, consider making a bike your mode of transport.

Bikes cut transit times in half compared to walking, giving you more time to spend at the sights.

Rental bikes are bargains at $12-25 per day (the best deals are for multiple days); helmets aren't always available. Bike-rental shops generally provide strong locks. Always lock the frame (not the wheel) to the permanent rack. Bike thieves can be bold and brazen.

Many places (including Barcelona, Copenhagen, Dublin, London, Oslo, Paris, Stockholm, and Vienna) have citywide programs in which hundreds of free or cheap loaner bikes are locked to racks around town. While tourists can easily take advantage of these programs in cities like London and Vienna, in other places (Dublin), the systems are designed mostly for residents (some require a membership or only take European credit cards). Also, the bikes are usually very basic, sometimes in disrepair, and often plastered with ads. If you're serious about biking, rent a good one from a shop instead.

One of my favorite cities for a ride is Stockholm. Bike paths here are a city-planning priority, and they run along the entire harbor. On your bike you can join the urban paseo down Strandvägen—the harborfront of the trendiest neighborhood—to my favorite biking zone, Djurgården ("Animal Garden"), once the king's private hunting preserve. Rolling down the garden-like lane past Rosendals Slott, the summer getaway minipalace of a 19th-century king, I marvel at how, on a bike, you see things that those on tour buses never would.

If you're hesitant to take a bike out on your own in an unfamiliar place, consider a bicycle tour. Guided bike tours are popular in cities throughout Europe, as well as many bike-friendly countryside areas. You'll get a young, entertaining, often foul-mouthed, sometimes informative guide who will give you a breezy introduction to the city and a close-up look at back streets few tourists ever see. The various companies—generally started by disgruntled employees of other

LEFT Bike tours are a fun, informative, and healthy way to see great cities with an entertaining guide.

RIGHT Use your bike lock correctly. I learned this lesson the hard way...and suffered the embarrassment of returning just one wheel to my bike-rental place.

bike-tour companies—are highly competitive, and come and go all the time. Tours are typically fun, reasonable (about $30), good exercise, and an easy way to meet other travelers as well as get a new angle on an old city.

LEFT Wherever biking is fun, you'll find shops renting bikes and helmets.

RIGHT Anyone can enjoy a gentle pedal through some of Europe's flat and inviting countryside.

Countryside Biking

Biking in the boonies (using a small town as a springboard) is extremely popular in Europe. Thanks to the law of supply and demand, you can generally count on finding bike-rental shops wherever there are good bike-tripping options: along the Danube, the Rhine, and other idyllic river valleys; around Ireland's Dingle Peninsula; and in the Alps for mountain biking on service roads.

Biking is one of the most enjoyable ways to experience Austria's famous "Blue Danube." Bicyclists rule here, and you'll find all the amenities that make this river valley so popular with Austrians on two wheels. The best route starts west of Vienna in the village of Melk. From here, it's a three- to four-hour, gently downhill pedal to the riverside village of Krems. The best biking is on the south side of the river, which has a dedicated, paved bike path the whole way and plenty of vineyards and small inns (*Gasthöfe*) in the villages along the way.

In France's Loire River valley, cycling options are nearly endless since the elevation gain is generally manageable. Amboise, Chenonceaux, Azay-le-Rideau, and Chinon all make good biking bases and have places to rent cycles. The city of Blois is well-positioned as a starting point for biking forays into the countryside. You can cycle from Blois to Chambord—the monumental chateau of François I—in a level, one-hour, one-way ride along a well-marked, 10-mile route, much of it a bike-only lane that follows the river.

For the best short bike trip out of Bruges, pedal four miles each way to the nearby town of Damme—once a thriving medieval port, and then a moated garrison town, and now a tourist center. Along the way you'll enjoy a whiff of the Belgian countryside and see a working windmill while riding along a canal to a charming (if well-discovered) small market town. The route is a straight and level ride through Belgium's polder—a salt marsh that would flood each spring until it was reclaimed by industrious local farmers.

In many countries (especially France, Germany, Austria, Belgium, and the Netherlands), train stations rent bikes and sometimes have easy "pick up here and drop off there" plans. For instance, if you ride the train into Amsterdam, rent a bike at the station for a few days to get around the city...and out into the tulip fields and windmills.

Longer Bike Trips

If you're interested in long-distance biking, figure out how much of Europe you want to see. With an entire summer free, you can cover a lot of ground on a bike. But with a month or less, it's better to focus on a single country or region.

Consider bringing your bike from home, but be sure to check your airline's baggage policies for fees and restrictions. It could cost you hundreds of dollars to bring your bike, and you may need to reserve a spot for it when you book your plane ticket. But if you're planning to ride a bike for more than a week, the cost of bringing your own may beat the cost of renting one in Europe, where bikes are more expensive than in the US. And having your own bike means you'll know that it works well for you. Carry along the tools you'll need to get your bike back into riding form, so you can ride straight out of the airport.

Don't be a purist. Taking your bike on a train can greatly extend the reach of your trip, and there's nothing so sweet as taking a train away from the rain and into a sunny place. Unless you love bike camping, it makes sense to stay in hostels, hotels, or B&Bs, since it frees you from lugging around a tent and sleeping bag. If you'd rather let someone else carry your gear, try a bike tour (offered by REI, EuroVelo, and many other companies). With a guide to figure out logistics, haul supplies, and handle emergencies, all you need to do is pedal and enjoy the ride.

You can find many good books and resources on cycling in Europe, such as at the site EuropeBicycleTouring.com.

WATER FUN

Summer days are perfect for a break at the beach or on the water. Opportunities to create memorable aquatic experiences in Europe abound, whether wading beneath the Roman aqueduct of Pont du Gard in Provence, frolicking on Venice's nearby lagoon beach, the Lido, or leisurely swimming laps in your B&B pool in Tuscany. Dive in!

Beaches and Swimming

Americans are sometimes disappointed or surprised by the quality of Europe's beaches. But as long as you know what to expect, you should have a perfectly enjoyable experience.

Beach quality and ambiance vary. Some beaches are barren, pebbly or studded with spiny sea urchins, while some are equipped with fine sand, showers, and restaurants with outdoor seating. Some are family-friendly, others have a party vibe. Some have chairs and umbrellas for rent, others are BYO. Ask locals for the scoop. Throughout Europe, you'll find nude beaches, but keep in mind that any beach can be topless.

Some of Europe's best swimming might not be where you expect. Sandy beaches in Sweden's Archipelago are perfect for joining Swedes at play, while the French Riviera can be plagued with jellyfish in July and August. In Spain's South Coast, anything resembling a quaint fishing village has been bikini-strangled and Nivea-creamed (though there are still gems, such as the town of Nerja).

You'll find man-made beaches and pools in many cities, including Paris' faux beaches on the Seine's Right Bank—with pools, beach volleyball, Frisbee areas, and more; Barcelona's sandy beaches, complete with lounge chairs, volleyball, showers, WCs, bike paths, and inviting beach bars called *chiringuitos;* and Copenhagen's Harbor Baths, a former-industrial-area-turned-bathing complex.

LEFT Inviting beaches in Italy's Cinque Terre tempt you to take a vacation from your vacation.

RIGHT Punting takes practice but offers a waterside view of idyllic English towns like Cambridge.

Canoeing, Kayaking, and Punting

If you're near a lake or river, consider exploring the area by boat. Some of Europe's natural wonders and parks are best seen from the water.

In Český Krumlov, a small town in the Czech country-side, I enjoy renting a canoe or raft and paddling down to a medieval abbey (for details on this experience, see page 722). In France's unpretentious port town of Cassis, you can kayak to its exotic fjords of translucent blue water in the *calanques*—the narrow inlets created by the prickly exten-sions of cliffs that border the shore. These spiky pinnacles are located along the 13 miles of coast between Cassis and Marseille (you can get there by hiking or boat cruise, too).

When I'm in the Dordogne region of France, one of my rituals is exploring the riverside castles and villages by canoe. I can't think of a more relaxing way to enjoy great scenery while getting some exercise. Delights are revealed around each bend, and you can pop ashore whenever you like. There's always a place to stow the canoe, and plenty of welcoming villages. Two of the most picturesque are La Roque-Gageac, a strong contender for "cutest town in France," and Beynac, a perfectly preserved medieval village that winds, like a sepia-tone film set, from the shore to the castle above. You can rent plastic boats—which are hard, light, and indestructible—from many outfits in this area for a reasonable price ($15-20 for two-person canoes, $19-26 for one-person kayaks). It's OK if you're a novice—the only whitewater you'll encounter will be the rare wake of passing tour boats...and your travel partner frothing at the views.

In Madrid, head to majestic Retiro Park to rent a rowboat

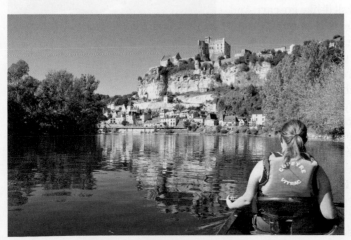

An easy paddle along the Dordogne River in France delivers excep-tional views of medieval castles.

and traverse a big lake in its center (El Estanque). At midday on Saturday and Sunday, the area around the lake becomes a street carnival, with jugglers, puppeteers, and lots of local color. Other city parks offer rental rowboats at lakes (e.g., London's Hyde Park and Paris' Bois de Vincennes). Paddle boats are popular in many cities, too.

For a different type of experience and a little levity, try punting in Britain, in which you use a pole to maneuver a long, flat-bottom boat up and down (or around and around, more likely). This is one of the best memories towns like Cambridge, Oxford, and Canterbury have to offer. Though chauffeurs are sometimes available, the do-it-yourself crowd has more fun...even if you do end up a little wet.

MORE ACTIVITIES

Adventure travel continues to be a major trend in the tourism industry. While I'm not going to suggest you drop everything to climb the Matterhorn, Europe has plenty of thrills and chills to carbonate a stodgy vacation, from screaming down a mountain luge to marveling at Cappadocia's otherworldly landscape from the basket of a hot-air balloon. And for a first-hand account of one of the greatest outdoor thrills I've ever experienced—the *via ferrata* in Switzerland—see page 699.

Riding a Luge

The *Sommerrodelbahn* ("summer toboggan run") is one of the most exhilarating alpine experiences. You take a lift up to the top of a mountain, grab a wheeled sled-like go-cart, and scream back down the mountainside on a banked course made of concrete or metal. Then you take the lift back up and start all over again.

Operating the sled is simple: Push the stick forward to go faster, pull back to apply the brake. Novices quickly find their personal speed limits. Most are cautious on their first run, speed demons on their second...and bruised and bloody on their third. A woman once showed me her travel journal illustrated with her husband's dried, five-inch-long

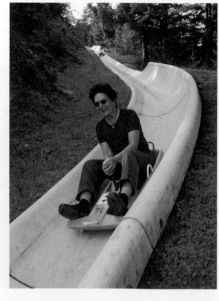

Summer luges provide thrills for any age at any speed.

luge scab. He had disobeyed the only essential rule of luging: Keep both hands on your stick. To avoid getting into a bumper-to-bumper traffic jam, let the person in front of you get way ahead before you start. You'll emerge from the course with a windblown hairdo and a smile-creased face.

You've got several luge options. In the French mountain resort of Chamonix, at the base of Mont Blanc, two concrete courses run side by side (the slow one marked by a tortoise and the fast one marked by a hare). In Austria, south of Salzburg on the road to Hallstatt, you'll pass two metal courses: one near Wolfgangsee (scenic with grand lake views) and one at Fuschlsee (half as long and cheaper).

In Germany and Austria, near "Mad" King Ludwig's Neuschwanstein Castle, you'll find two courses. One is in Austria, just beyond Biberwier (under Zugspitze, Germany's tallest mountain); the Biberwier *Sommerrodelbahn*

City Thrills

Surfing in Downtown Munich: Far from the nearest stretch of coast, surfers "hang ten" in Munich's English Garden, in the rapids of the city's little man-made river. While seeking their thrills, the surfers provide great entertainment for the ever-present crowd that gathers to watch from a bridge.

Skiing in Edinburgh: If you'd rather be skiing, the Midlothian Snowsports Centre, just outside Edinburgh, has a brush-skiing hill with a chairlift, two slopes, a jump slope, and rentable skis, boots, and poles. While you're actually skiing over what seems like a million toothbrushes, it feels like snow skiing on a slushy day. It's open nearly year-round (except, ironically, when it snows).

Zip Lining in Oslo: Outer Oslo hosts the Holmenkollen Ski Jump, with a tilted elevator that you can ride for an exciting view—and a zip line that you can rocket down for even more adrenaline. There's also a simulator (or should I say stimulator?) that lets you fly down the ski jump and ski in a virtual downhill race. My legs were exhausted after the five-minute terror.

Floating in Bern: In the summer heat, join the carp in a bracing float down Switzerland's Aare River. Hike upstream 5 to 30 minutes, then float back down to the excellent (and free) riverside baths and pools (Marzilibad) just below the Parliament building. Locals make it look easy, but the float can be dangerous—the current is swift. This is only for strong, experienced swimmers. For my first-hand account of this experience, see page 696.

A float above the surreal topography in Cappadocia, Turkey, is arguably the best hot-air balloon experience in the world.

is the longest in Austria at 4,000 feet. And just a mile from Neuschwanstein is Germany's Tegelberg course—because it's metal rather than concrete, it's often open when the other course has closed at the least sprinkle of rain.

Hot-Air Ballooning

A few years ago, I learned that even if I wasn't blessed with wings, I've got an abundance of hot air—and I can fly quite well with little more than that. I've always loved Cappadocia in central Turkey, so I took a majestic hot-air balloon ride over the fairy-chimney formations of that exotic landscape. From the moment our basket slipped from the land into the sky, I gazed in wonder, mesmerized at the erosion-shaped countryside and spectacle of colorful balloons gliding around me. As I stood in the basket of my balloon, the rhythmic bursts of flame punctuated the captain's jokes while warming my wide eyes. Illogically, the stripes on his epaulets made me feel safe as we lifted off.

You'll also find hot-air balloon companies in France's most popular regions (Burgundy, the Loire, Dordogne, and Provence are best suited for ballooning). These offer a bird's-eye view of France's sublime landscapes as you sail serenely over châteaux, canals, vineyards, Romanesque churches, and villages.

These trips aren't cheap (about $200-350), but they give lots of travelers a fine memory and stunning pictures.

Shopping

Shopping in Europe can be fun, but don't let it overwhelm your trip. Slick marketing and clever displays can shift the entire focus of your vacation toward things rather than experiences. I've seen half the members of a guided tour of the British Houses of Parliament skip out to survey an enticing array of plastic "bobby" hats, Big Ben briefs, and Union Jack panties. Focus on local experiences, and don't let your trip become a glorified shopping spree.

The thrill of where you bought something can fade long before the item's usefulness does. Even thoughtful shoppers go overboard. I have several large boxes in my attic labeled "great souvenirs." On the other hand, a few well-chosen items—a hand-painted tile from Siena, Provençal fabric from Nice, a fine old print from Athens—can help you capture the essence of a place for years to come.

WHERE TO SHOP

Avoid the souvenir carts outside of big monuments, where the goods tend to be overpriced and cheesy. Do your shopping in places that offer a fun cultural experience as well.

Outdoor Markets

The most colorful shopping in Europe—and a fun way to feel the local vibe—is at its lively open-air markets. A stroll along Portobello Road, arguably London's best street market and one of the world's biggest antiques markets, has you rubbing elbows with collectors and people who brake for garage sales. In Florence, the sprawling San Lorenzo Market has stalls of garments, accessories, and leather jackets ranging from real to vinyl. Even a place as overrun with international visitors as Istanbul's Grand Bazaar has tourist-free nooks and crannies that offer a glimpse into the real Turkey. Jump into the human rivers that flow through these venues.

Other good markets are Amsterdam's Waterlooplein, Madrid's El Rastro, and Paris' Puces St. Ouen. In London, I like the East End's Broadway Market, with foodie delights and a few arts and crafts, and south London's Ropewalk (Maltby Street Market), featuring a festival of pop-up bars and artisan food carts.

Some markets are open daily, while others erupt only on weekends or a certain day of the week—make sure to check hours locally. Remember that markets anywhere have soft prices. Bargain like mad (see "Successful Haggling," later). Pickpockets love markets—wear your money belt and watch your day bag.

Artisan Shops

Try to experience some "creative" tourism when you travel. Seek out and appreciate a local craftsperson. In Orvieto, Italy, visit the young cobbler who's passionate about preserving the art of traditional shoemaking. In Rothenburg, Germany, appreciate the printmakers selling etchings made with the same copper-plate techniques that artist Albrecht Dürer used 500 years ago. The narrow streets near Vienna's cathedral are sprinkled with old-fashioned shops that seem to belong to another era—just the place to pick out an elegant dirndl.

The artists who craft handmade guitars in Madrid, the family winemakers of Burgundy—these have all been fixtures for me in a lifetime of European travel. Before these local businesses are pushed out by the rising tide of cookie-cutter chains and synthetic conformity, seek out Europe's true artisans who are committed to doing things the old-fashioned way. You can find referrals to artisan shops through local tourist offices. In cities like Florence and Rome, tour companies offer guided excursions to private workshops. Engaging with these craftsmen is a memorable way to bring local history and culture to life (and you can return home with a memorable souvenir).

Artisans, such as this Italian cobbler, help keep traditional crafts alive.

Christmas Markets

From the beginning of Advent through Christmas (and occasionally through January 6), Europe is peppered with festive Christmas markets serving up a healthy dose of holiday spirit and plenty of handmade and traditional nutcrackers, ornaments, and sweets. Bigger markets often host carolers and other musicians, ice-skating rinks, and carousels.

In December, cities across Europe come alive with Christmas markets, such as this one in Nürnberg.

Especially in Germanic countries, Christmas markets dominate nearly every main square, from the smallest village to big cities. Nürnberg, famous for packaging its gingerbread in countless creative ways, has one of the best Christmas bazaars. In Austria, the cozy center of Innsbruck is the perfect setting for a memorable market, with the snowy Tirolean Alps hovering above medieval rooftops. Some bigger cities (Munich, Vienna, Berlin, Cologne, even smaller Salzburg) host multiple markets.

The best time to enjoy these convivial markets is in the evening, under the glow of cheerful lights. The sweet smell of *Lebkuchen* (gingerbread), *Stollen* (fruitcake-like bread), and roasting candied nuts wafts through the air. Hand-carved wooden ornaments and nativity scenes, festive wreaths, and aromatic candles line the booths. Look for nutcrackers made in the Erzgebirge region, where they originated. Seek out *Weihnachtspyriamide*—wooden structures that hold candles, often with a propeller that uses the candle's heat to spin part of the contraption.

Stroll around while sipping hot mulled wine, spiced with cinnamon, cloves, and citrus fruits. This quintessential Christmas market drink (*Gluhwein* in Germanic countries) is served in a holiday-themed ceramic mug, which itself makes a fun, affordable souvenir.

Department Stores

European department stores are generally laid out much like ours, providing an accessible and familiar-feeling place to shop. Most are accustomed to wide-eyed foreign shoppers and have some English-speaking staff. The store directories often include English. Many department stores have a souvenir section, with standard local knickknacks and postcards at far lower prices than you'll find in cute little tourist shops.

In Paris, visit Galeries Lafayette or Printemps. Harrods is London's most famous and touristy department store, but locals prefer Liberty on Regent Street. In Italy, an upscale department chain is La Rinascente, and in Spain, El Corte Inglés is everywhere. Berlin's mammoth Kaufhaus des Westens (KaDeWe) has a staff of 2,100 to help you sort through its vast selection of 380,000 items. Though lacking the charm of artisan shops and markets, department stores are a quick and easy way to check souvenirs off your list.

Boutiques and Shopping Zones

The best shopping districts not only offer interesting stores, but also let you feel the pulse of the city. In Rome, an early evening stroll down Via del Corso takes you past affordable shops—and the city's beautiful people. For top fashion—and top people-watching—stroll the streets around the Spanish Steps.

London's best and most convenient shopping streets are in the West End and West London (roughly between Soho and Hyde Park). In Vienna, Mariahilfer Strasse combines a wealth of shops with lively people-watching.

In Paris, a stroll from the Bon Marché department store to St. Sulpice allows you to sample sleek clothing boutiques and clever window displays while enjoying one of the city's more attractive neighborhoods. You don't have to buy the glitz to feel *très* French (they call window shopping *lèche-vitrines*—"window licking").

In Europe's smaller shops and classy boutiques, use your shopping etiquette. If you say "hello" when you enter, and ask before you touch an item, the salesperson will treat you like a local.

Museum Gift Shops

Gift shops at major museums (such as the Picasso Museum in Barcelona or the Van Gogh Museum in Amsterdam) are a bonanza for shoppers. Consider picking up books, postcards, unusual posters, decorative items, or clever knickknacks featuring works by your favorite artist or commemorating a historic event or sight. Museum gift shops are also a good source for books you may not see elsewhere. Before accumulating too much, keep in mind that many things (like prints and posters of universally loved art) can be ordered fairly cheaply online from home—and will save you the hassle of getting your art home.

SHOPPING TIPS

Here are some tips for shopping in Europe—from buying souvenirs and clothes to bargaining your way to the best price.

Souvenir Strategies

Shop smart, and remember that your most prized souvenirs are your memories.

Comparison shop at home. Do some research if you're looking for a particular high-end item overseas (and be aware that you can often find a similar item of better quality for a cheaper price at home). Before heading off to buy a Turkish carpet in Istanbul or leather coat in Florence, learn the going rate, types of materials, and signs of quality, if only to avoid advertising your inexperience.

Beware street vendors selling knock-offs. Streetside vendors sell counterfeit designer goods everywhere in Europe—and in many cities, it's illegal. For these vendors, it's a game of cat-and-mouse with the police. Along the busy Ramblas zone in Barcelona, vendors lay out their merchandise on a sheet with ropes attached. When police officers arrive, the vendors scatter, quickly bundling their wares as they run. In some countries (such as Italy), buying from a street vendor is illegal and can cost you a hefty fine (anywhere from €1,000 to €10,000). Be cautious and ask an informed local before going for that fake Prada bag.

Know the origin of your souvenirs. The cheapest, mass-produced souvenirs are almost always imported. If the price seems too good to be true, it probably is. Stick to reputable, family-run shops to ensure you're getting an authentic product (and supporting a local business). Even at artisan Christmas markets, be wary of cheap trinkets labeled "handmade." Evaluate as you buy. Real Italian leather, for example, should feel soft and pliable without any chemical smell. When buying glass in Venice, look closely. Genuine Venetian glass is marked with the Murano seal.

Boxloads of *Davids* await busloads of tourists.

Concentrate your shopping in countries where your dollar will stretch. You'll find the best bargains in Turkey, Morocco, Portugal, Spain, Greece, and Eastern Europe. For the price of a skimpy doily in Britain, you can get a lace tablecloth in Spain.

Be selective. Form an idea of what you want to buy in each country. I look for hand-knit sweaters in Portugal or Ireland, glass in Sweden, painted beehive panels in Slovenia, or lace in Belgium. I also like books published in Europe; these are a great value all over the Continent, with many editions that are impossible to find in the US.

Lighten your load, or wait till the end. Larger stores can arrange shipping for you, or you can ship packages home yourself (see "Shipping Things Home," later). Or simply wait for the last country you visit to go hog-wild and fly home heavy. One summer I had a 16-pound backpack and nothing more until the last week of my trip, when I hit Spain and Morocco and managed to accumulate two sets of bongos, swords, a mace, and a camelhair coat...most of which are now in boxes in my attic.

Remember the paperwork. If you intend to claim a Value-Added Tax (VAT) refund, you'll need to get the right documents from the merchant. For details on VAT as well as US customs regulations, see "VAT Refunds, Customs, and Shipping" on page 368.

Clothes Shopping

Many travelers enjoy shopping for wearable souvenirs in Europe, where the fashions can be quite different from back home. Options range from hole-in-the-wall boutiques to grand department stores to colorful street markets.

Europe-wide chains such as Mango and C&A have stylish, affordable selections. They can offer good value, especially for designer-inspired clothing. In addition, each country has its own popular chains (such as Topshop in Britain). Fashions vary by store and by country, so if you see an item you like, grab it rather than wait to pick it up at a later stop—you might never see that same style or color again. Some women like buying high-quality underwear and camisoles in Italy or France; browse for them at any large department store.

Street markets also offer clothing. Remember that prices are often soft—especially if it's near the end of the day, you're paying cash, and you're buying multiple items (such as several scarves). Don't be afraid to bargain.

Successful Haggling

In much of the Mediterranean world, the price tag is only an excuse to argue. Bargaining is the accepted and expected method of finding a compromise between the wishful thinking of the merchant and the tourist. You can generally fight prices at flea markets, touristy souvenir shops, and with

Clothes Sizing Conversion

The US, the UK, and continental Europe all use different sizing conventions. European clothes are usually cut to fit more snugly than American clothes. When shopping for clothing, use the following rules as general guidelines (but note that no conversion is perfect). Be prepared to swallow your pride and go up a size or two. If you wear a size medium sweater back home, you might need a large or extra-large in Norway.

Women: For pants and dresses, women's sizes are the same across France, Belgium, Spain, and Portugal. To figure your size, add approximately 32 to your US size (US 10 = French 42). In Italy, add 36 to your US size (US 10 = Italy 46). Sizes run slightly smaller in Germany, Austria, the Netherlands, Switzerland, and Scandinavia. In these countries, add 30 to your US size (US 10 = German 40). The UK operates on a different size system. Just add 4 to your US size (US 10 = UK 14).

For blouses and sweaters, most of Europe uses the same system. Add 8 to your US size (US 32 = European 40). In the UK, add 2 (US 32 = UK 34).

To calculate your European shoe size, add about 31 to your US size (US 7 = European 37/38); in the UK, subtract 2½ (US 7 = UK 4½).

Men: Most of Europe uses the same size system for men. For shirts, multiply your US size by 2 and add about 8 (US 15 = European 38). For jackets and suits, add 10 (US 38 = European 48). For shoes, add 32-34 (US 9 = European 41). The UK uses the same men's clothing sizes as the US. For UK shoes, subtract about ½ from your US size (US 9 = UK 8½).

Children: Most of Europe's kids' clothing is sized by height—in centimeters (although some brands are sized by age). If you plan to do much shopping for your children, convert their height to centimeters (2.54 inches = 1 cm). A US child size 8 roughly equates to 132-140 (cm). A US junior size 3 equals a European 152. For shoes up to size 13, add 16-18 (US 10 = European 26). For sizes 1 and up, add 30-32. To figure UK shoe size, subtract 1 from the US size.

street vendors, but not at modern stores or shopping malls. (Note that bargaining applies to goods, not to food sold at stands or outdoor produce markets.)

Here are a few guidelines to help you get the best bargain.

Determine if bargaining is appropriate. It's bad shopping etiquette to "make an offer" for a tweed hat in a London department store. It's foolish not to at a Greek flea market. To learn if a price is fixed, show some interest in an item but say, "It's just too much money." You've put the merchant in a position to make the first offer. If he comes down even 2 percent, there's nothing sacred about the price tag. Haggle away.

Shop around to find out what locals pay. Prices can vary drastically among vendors at the same flea market, and even at the same stall. If prices aren't posted, assume there's a double price

You can troll for quirky souvenirs at flea markets.

standard: one for locals and one for you. If only tourists buy the item you're pricing, see what an Arab, Spanish, or Italian tourist would be charged. I remember thinking I did well in Istanbul's Grand Bazaar, until I learned my Spanish friend bought the same shirt for 30 percent less. Merchants assume American tourists are rich, and they know what we pay for things at home.

Determine what the item is worth to you. Posted prices can be meaningless and serve to distort your idea of an item's true worth. The merchant is playing a psychological game. Many tourists think that if they can cut the price by 50 percent they are doing great. So the merchant quadruples his prices and the tourist happily pays double the fair value. The best way to deal with crazy price tags is to ignore them. Before you even find out the price, determine the item's value to you, considering the hassles involved in packing it or shipping it home.

Determine the merchant's lowest price. Merchants hate to lose a sale. Work the cost down, but if it doesn't match with the price you have in mind, walk away. That last amount the merchant hollers out as you turn the corner is often the best price you'll get. If *that* price is right, go back and buy. Prices often drop at the end of the day, when merchants are about to pack up.

Curb your enthusiasm. As soon as the merchant perceives the "I gotta have that!" in you, you'll never get the best price. He assumes Americans have the money to buy what they really want. Keep a poker face and don't settle for the first counter-offer.

Employ a third person. Use your friend who is worried about the ever-dwindling budget or who doesn't like the price or who is bored and wants to return to the hotel. This trick can work to bring the price down faster.

Impress the merchant with your knowledge. He'll respect you, and you'll be more likely to get good quality. Istanbul has very good leather coats for a fraction of the US cost. Before my trip I talked to some leather-coat sellers and was much better prepared to confidently pick out a good coat in Istanbul.

Ask for a deal on multiple items. See if the merchant will give you a better price if you buy in bulk (three necklaces instead of one). The more they think they can sell, the more flexible they may become.

Offer to pay cash at stalls that take credit cards. You can expect to pay cash for most things at street markets, but some merchants who sell pricier goods (nice jewelry, artwork, etc.) take credit cards, too. They're often more willing to strike a deal if you pay cash, since they don't lose any profit to credit-card fees.

Show the merchant your money. Physically hold out your money and offer him "all you have" to pay for whatever you're bickering over. He'll be tempted to just grab your money and say, "Oh, OK."

Obey the rules. Don't hurry. Bargaining is rarely rushed. Make sure you are dealing with someone who has the authority to bend a price downward. Bid respectfully. If a merchant accepts your price (or vice versa), you must buy the item.

If the price is too much, leave. Never worry about having taken too much of the merchant's time. Merchants are experienced businesspeople who know they won't close every deal.

VAT REFUNDS, CUSTOMS, AND SHIPPING

Included in the price of European products is a value-added tax (VAT)—a consumer tax on raw materials. You can't avoid paying this sales tax, but it is refundable on items that leave the country. For travelers making major purchases, the refund can be significant, so it's worth knowing how to get your refund and how to bring these items home (either in your luggage or by shipping them).

Claiming a Value-Added Tax Refund

Every year, tourists visiting Europe leave behind millions of dollars of refundable sales taxes. For some, the headache of collecting the refund is not worth the few dollars at stake. But if you do any extensive shopping, the refund is fairly easy to claim: Bring your passport along on your shopping trip, get the necessary documents from the retailer, and track down the right folks at the airport, port, or border when you leave.

The standard European Union Value-Added Tax ranges from 8 to 27 percent per country (see sidebar). Exact rates change; check online (www.uscib.org, search on "VAT") before you go.

Though you aren't entitled to refunds on the tax you spend on hotels and meals, you can get back most of the tax you paid on merchandise such as clothes, cuckoos, and crystal. You're not supposed to use your purchased goods before you leave Europe—if you show up at customs wearing your new Dutch clogs, officials might look the other way, or they might deny you a refund.

To get any refund, your purchase has to be above a certain amount—ranging from about $25 to $300, depending on the country. Typically, you must ring up the minimum at a single retailer—you can't add up your purchases from various shops to reach the required amount—so if you're doing a lot of shopping, you'll benefit from finding one spot where you can buy big. If you'll be in Europe for a long time, shop near the end of your trip. You need to collect your refund within three months of your purchase.

Only you can decide whether VAT refunds are worth the trouble. As for me, my favorite trip souvenirs are my photos, journal, and memories. These are priceless—and exempt from taxes and red tape.

VAT Rates and Minimum Purchase Amounts

Country of Purchase	VAT Standard Rate*	Minimum Purchase Amount
Austria	20%	€75.01 ($80)
Belgium	21%	€50 ($55)
Bulgaria	20%	100 BGN ($50)
Croatia	25%	740 HRK ($105)
Czech Republic	21%	2,001 CZK ($80)
Denmark	25%	300 DKK ($45)
France	20%	€175.01 ($190)
Germany	19%	€25 ($30)
Great Britain	20%	£30 ($45)
Greece	24%	€50 ($55)
Hungary	27%	54,001 HUF ($195)
Ireland	23%	€30 ($35)
Italy	22%	€155 ($170)
Netherlands	21%	€50 ($55)
Norway	25%	315 NOK ($35)
Poland	23%	200 PLN
Portugal	23%	€61.35 ($65)
Romania	20%	250 RON ($60)
Slovenia	22%	€50.01 ($55)
Spain	21%	€90.16 ($100)
Sweden	25%	200 SEK ($25)
Switzerland	8%	300 CHF ($300)

* *EU VAT standard rates are set by member countries and can fluctuate. Your refund will likely be less than the rate listed above, especially if it's subject to processing fees.*

At the Shop

The details on how to get a refund vary per country, but generally you'll need to follow the basic steps below.

Bring your passport. You'll likely be asked to present your passport when you make the purchase, in order to start the refund process.

Shop at stores that know the ropes. Retailers choose whether to participate in the VAT-refund scheme. Most tourist-oriented stores do; often you'll see a sign in the window or by the cash register (if not, ask). For any significant purchase, even at a boutique shop, it's always worth asking about a VAT refund. It'd be a shame to spend big bucks at a place and not have a chance of getting a refund.

Get the documents. When you make your purchase, have the merchant fill out the necessary refund document, often called a "tax-free form." Make sure the paperwork is done before you leave the store so there's nothing important missing. If they leave any blanks for you to fill out, be sure you understand what goes where. Attach your receipt to the form and stash it in a safe place.

The precise details of getting your money back will depend on how a particular shop organizes its refund process. Some stores may offer to handle the rest of the hassle for you (if they provide this service, they likely have some sort of "Tax Free" sticker in the window). In some cases, the merchant will reimburse your credit card on the spot. You may also be able to take your paperwork to a nearby third-party agency to get an immediate cash refund (minus a commission for the quick service; these tend to be located at money-exchange counters near touristy shopping areas—think Champs-Elysées). In either case, you may need to get the documents stamped at the border, then mail them back; if the shop or agency never received the documents, they'll charge the refund to your credit card.

If the store ships your purchase to your home, you won't be charged the value-added tax. But shipping fees and US duty can be pricey enough to wipe out most of what you'd save. Compare shipping costs to your potential VAT refund—it may be cheaper to just carry the items home with you.

At the Airport or Departure Point
Bring your paperwork and purchases, and arrive early. Assuming you left the store with your purchase, receipt, and VAT paperwork (but no refund), you'll need to get the refund processed before going home. If you've bought merchandise in a European Union country, process your documents at your last stop in the EU, regardless of where you made your purchases. So if you buy sweaters in Denmark, pants in France, and shoes in Italy, and you're flying home from Greece, get your documents stamped at the airport in Athens. (If the currencies are different in the country where you made your purchase and where you process your refund—say, pounds and euros—you may have to pay an extra conversion fee.) And don't forget—Switzerland, Norway, and Turkey are not in the EU, so if you buy in one of those countries, get your documents stamped before you cross the border.

Be careful if you leave the EU by train. Bigger train stations handling international routes will have a customs office that can stamp your documents. But depending on your route, you may have to get off the train at the last station within the EU to get your stamp; in some cases, a customs agent might board the train. Consult your rail company to learn the customs arrangement for your particular route.

Get your documents stamped at customs. At your point of departure, find the local customs office, and be prepared to stand in line. Some customs offices are positioned before airport security; confirm the customs location before going through the security check. In smaller airports, train stations, ports, and less-trafficked border crossings, finding the right customs agent can be tough—give yourself plenty of time.

At customs, an export officer will stamp your documents and may ask you to present your unused goods to verify that you are, indeed, exporting your purchase—if your purchases are inside your checked luggage, stop by customs before you check it. (Some retailers, particularly those in Scandinavia, will staple and seal the shopping bag to keep you from cheating.)

Collect the cash—sooner or later. Once you get your form stamped by customs, you have to turn it in. If your purchases were bought from a merchant who works with a refund service such as Global Blue or Premier Tax Free, find their offices inside the airport. These services take a cut of your refund (about 4 percent), but save you further fuss and delay. Present your stamped document, and they'll likely give you your refund in cash, right then and there. The refund will be in the currency of the country from which you depart; if you want to be reimbursed in a different currency, such as US dollars, you'll be subjected to their (unfavorable) exchange rates. Otherwise, they'll credit the refund to your credit card (within two billing cycles; see www.globalblue. com or www.premiertaxfree.com).

Other refund services may require you to mail the documents—either from home, or more quickly, just before leaving the country (using a postage-free, preaddressed envelope—just drop it in a mailbox after getting your customs stamp). Then you wait. It could take months. Look for a refund on your credit-card statement or for a check in the mail. If the refund check comes in a foreign currency, you may have to pay a fee ($40 or so) to get your bank to cash it.

Don't count on it. My readers have reported that, even when following all of the instructions carefully, sometimes the VAT refund just doesn't pan out. (For example, they have all the paperwork ready when they get to the airport but can't find the customs official to process it, or they turn in

Hauling Home Heavenly Wines

Wine lovers wandering through Europe face a continual dilemma: Savor the memories or haul a few favorite bottles home?

Despite the global-goods-on-demand world we live in today, your neighborhood wine shop can't always track down the wine you enjoyed at that Parisian café or Spanish tapas bar. Some wineries only sell their wine within their country, which makes it tempting to bring a few bottles home.

The downside, of course, is the schlepping—the scary prospect of a bottle breaking in your suitcase or the weight of the box dragging you down as you trudge through the airport. You might be better off seeing wine like art—something to be enjoyed, marveled at, and remembered.

Before you purchase a bottle to carry home, ask the merchant whether the wine is exported to your home state. Or take a picture of the label with your phone—you can even email it to your hometown wine shop to find out if they can have the wine waiting for you when you return.

But if you can't resist bringing wine home, keep these tips in mind.

Pack softly and carry a hard suitcase. Per TSA regulations, if you purchase liquor from an airport duty-free shop and it's able to be screened (i.e., not in an opaque, metallic, or ceramic bottle) and is in a secure, tamper-evident bag (called a STEB), you can transport it in your carry-on (a STEB can also be used for transporting foods packed in liquid or oil—if purchased at the airport duty-free shop). If not, you'll have to pack your bottles carefully in checked luggage. This works most of the time if the bottles are thickly padded with clothing in a hard-sided suitcase (though bottles can still break); they'll also have to endure the extreme cold (or heat) of the cargo hold.

Divide and conquer. If you're traveling with a partner, divide the bottles among your bags (each bottle of wine weighs about three pounds, so five bottles means 15 extra pounds). Bring a spare fold-up tote bag or duffle for your clothes that get displaced by the wine.

Know your limits. A standard bottle of wine is 750 milliliters. If you bring back more than one liter, customs regulations require you to pay duty tax based on the percent of alcohol (generally $1-2 per liter for wine). Couples can get away with three standard bottles, adding up to 2¼ liters. There's also a small federal excise tax.

Tell the truth. Be up front if you're over the limit. You may even benefit—sometimes the special customs lines move faster than the nothing-to-declare ones. If your wine is for personal use, the agents might not even tax you. It won't happen all the time, but many wine-obsessed travelers report that this can be the case.

their forms but never get paid.) These problems seem most prevalent in Italy. Your best odds are to buy from a merchant who knows how to deal with the red tape for you—but even that is not infallible.

Customs for American Shoppers
Customs regulations vary depending on whether you are bringing items home on the plane with you, or mailing them to a US address. To check US customs rules and duty rates, visit www.cbp.gov, click on "Travel," and then "Know Before You Go."

Bringing Items Home in Your Luggage
You are allowed to take home $800 worth of items per person duty-free in your luggage, once every 31 days (family members can combine their individual $800 exemptions on a joint declaration). The next $1,000 is taxed at a flat 3 percent. After that, you pay the individual item's duty rate. You can also bring in duty-free a liter of alcohol (slightly more than a standard-size bottle of wine; you must be at least 21), 200 cigarettes, and up to 100 cigars. Household effects intended for personal use, such as tableware and linens, are also duty-free.

Because food items can carry diseases or pests, they are strictly regulated. You may take home vacuum-packed cheeses; dried herbs, spices, or mushrooms; and canned fruits or vegetables, including jams and vegetable spreads. Baked goods, candy, chocolate, oil, vinegar, mustard, and honey are OK. Fresh fruits and vegetables (even that banana from your airplane breakfast) are not permitted. Meats are generally not allowed; however, canned meat is permissible if it doesn't contain beef, veal, lamb, or mutton. Just because a duty-free shop in an airport sells a food product, it doesn't mean it will automatically pass US customs. Be prepared to lose your investment.

Of course, you'll need to carefully pack any bottles of wine, jam, honey, oil, and other liquid-containing items in your checked luggage, thanks to limits on liquids in carry-ons (though there's an exception for some foods and wine purchased at a duty-free shop; see sidebar). For tips on bringing duty-free liquids onto the plane, see "What Can't I Carry On?" on page 107.

Shipping Things Home
If you buy more than you can comfortably carry, consider shipping your shopping bounty back home.

Customs regulations for items you ship amount to 10 or 15 frustrating minutes of filling out forms with the normally unhelpful postal clerk's semi-assistance. Be realistic in your service expectations. European postal clerks are every bit as friendly, speedy, and multilingual as American postal clerks.

From Europe, you can mail one package per day to yourself in the US, worth up to $200 dutyfree (mark it "personal purchases"). If you mail an item home valued at $250, you pay duty on the full $250, not $50. When you fill out the customs form, keep it simple and include the item's value (contents: clothing, books, souvenirs, poster, value $100). For alcohol, perfume containing alcohol, and tobacco valued at more than $5, you will pay a duty. You can also mail home all the "American Goods Returned" you like (e.g., clothes you packed but no longer need) with no customs concerns—but note that these goods really must be American (not Bohemian crystal or a German cuckoo clock), or you'll be charged a duty. If it's a gift for someone else, it's subject to customs fees if valued at more than $100 (mark it "unsolicited gift").

If you accumulate a box's worth of dead weight, mail it home and keep on packing light.

It's fairly painless and convenient to use regular postal services, but it can be expensive. You can usually buy boxes and tape at the post office. Post offices in some countries, such as Great Britain, France, and Germany, have limits on how big or heavy your packages can be. For heavier packages, you may need to use their postal services' affiliated package services. The fastest way to get a package home from Italy is to use the Vatican post office—or take it home in your suitcase. Every box I've ever mailed from Europe has arrived—bruised and battered but all there—within six weeks. To send precious things home fast, I use DHL; they have offices in every big city.

Theft & Scams

The odds are in your favor for enjoying a perfectly safe and incident-free trip to Europe. But anybody, whether at home or abroad, can experience unexpected problems, from inadvertently leaving a backpack on the train to getting pickpocketed in a crowd. By taking a few common-sense precautions, you'll greatly improve your chances of having a smooth trip.

PICKPOCKETING AND THEFT

While Europe has little violent crime, it does have its share of petty purse snatching, pickpocketing, phone grabbing, and general ripping off of tourists—especially in places where tourists gather. Thieves target vacationers—not because they're mean, but because they're smart. Travelers have all the good stuff in their bags and wallets. Loaded down with valuables, jetlagged, and bumbling around in a strange new environment, we stick out like jeweled thumbs. If I were a European street thief, I'd specialize in Americans—my card would say "Yanks R Us."

If you're not constantly on guard, you'll have something stolen. One summer, four out of five of my traveling companions lost cameras in one way or another. (Don't look at me.) In more than 30 summers of travel, I've been mugged once (in a part of London where only fools and thieves tread); my various rental cars have been broken into a total of six times (broken locks, shattered windows, lots of nonessential stuff taken); and one car was hot-wired (and abandoned a few blocks away after the thief found nothing to take). But not one of my hotel rooms has ever been rifled through, and never have any of my money-belt-worthy valuables been stolen.

LEFT In Spain, just say *"No, gracias"* to women trying to thrust sprigs of rosemary on you for a tip.

RIGHT Outer backpack compartments are easy pickings for thieves.

Many tourists get indignant when pickpocketed or ripped off. If it happens to you, it's best to get over it. You're rich and thieves aren't. You let your guard down and they grabbed your camera. It ruins your day and you have to buy a new one, while they sell it for a week's wages on their scale. It's wise to keep a material loss in perspective.

There probably aren't more thieves in Europe. We just notice them more because they target tourists. But remember, nearly all crimes suffered by tourists are nonviolent and avoidable. Be aware of the pitfalls of traveling, but relax and have fun. Limit your vulnerability rather than your travels.

Protecting Yourself from Theft

If you exercise adequate discretion, stay aware of your belongings, and avoid putting yourself into risky situations (such as unlit, deserted areas at night), your travels should be about as dangerous as hometown grocery shopping. Don't travel fearfully—travel carefully.

Here's some advice given to me by a thief who won the lotto.

Be prepared. Before you go, take steps to minimize your loss in case of theft. Make copies and/or take photos of key documents (see page 69 for details). Consider getting theft insurance for expensive electronics (see page 75). Leave your fancy bling at home. Luxurious luggage lures thieves. The thief chooses the most impressive suitcase in the pile—never mine.

If your smartphone disappears, you're not just out the cost of the device—but also the photos and personal data stored on it. Given the much higher risk of theft and loss

while on the road, it's smart to take
extra precautions to protect your
data before your trip: Make sure
you've got a "find my phone"-type
app, back up your data, and enable
password protection.

Wear a money belt. A money
belt is a small, zippered fabric pouch
on an elastic strap that fastens

around your waist, under your pants or skirt. I never travel
without one—it's where I put anything I really, really don't
want to lose. Wear it completely hidden from sight, tucked in
like a shirttail—over your undies and shirt, under your pants.
Most people wear the pouch over their stomach, but if you find
it more comfortable, slide it around to the small of your back.

If you need to
access your
money belt, just
reach casually
into your pants
(ignoring the
curious glances
of onlookers)
and pull it out.

Some people prefer to use a neck pouch, worn like a
necklace but under a shirt; or a hidden pocket, which loops
onto your belt, then tucks in behind it. Others use a Lycra
runners belt, tucked under their clothes.

With a money belt, all your essentials are on you as
securely and thoughtlessly as your underwear. Have you ever
thought about that? Every morning you put on your under-
pants. You don't even think about them all day long. And
every night, when you undress, sure enough, there they are,
exactly where you put them. When I travel, my valuables are
just as securely out of sight and out of mind, around my waist
in a money belt. It's luxurious peace of mind. I'm uncomfortable only when I'm not wearing it.

Those who travel with nothing worth stealing except
for what's in their money belt are virtually invulnerable. But
money belts don't work if they're anywhere but under your
clothes. I once met an American woman whose purse was
stolen, and in her purse was her money belt (that juicy little
anecdote was featured in every street-thief newsletter). If
you pull out your money belt to retrieve something, remember to tuck it back in. And don't use a fanny pack as a money
belt—thieves assume this is where you keep your goodies.

Never leave a money belt "hidden" on the beach while
you swim. Ideally, leave it locked up in your room; if that's
not an option bring a small waterproof pouch or dry bag so
your valuables can swim with you. In hostels or on overnight trains, wear your money belt when you sleep. You can
even shower with it in a hostel (hang it—maybe in a plastic
bag—from the nozzle or curtain rod). Keep your money-belt
contents dry and sweat-free by slipping them into a plastic

sheath or baggie before zipping them into the belt.

You don't need to get at your money belt for every euro. Your money belt is your deep storage—for select deposits and withdrawals. For convenience, carry a day's spending money in your pocket (a button-down flap or Velcro strip sewn into your front or back pocket slows down fast fingers). Make sure it's an amount you're prepared to lose. I don't even carry a wallet. A few bills in my shirt pocket—no keys, no wallet—I'm on vacation!

Leave valuables in your hotel room. Expensive gear, such as your laptop, is much safer in your room than with you in a day bag on the streets. While hotels often have safes in the room (or at the front desk), I've never bothered to use one, though many find them a source of great comfort. Theft happens, of course, but it's relatively rare—hoteliers are quick to squelch a pattern of theft. That said, don't tempt sticky-fingered staff by leaving a camera or tablet in plain view; tuck your enticing things well out of sight. You can also leave your room key at the front desk of many hotels while you're off exploring, so it's less likely to get lost or stolen.

Secure your bag, gadgets, and other valuables when you're out and about. Thieves want to quickly separate you from your valuables, so even a minor obstacle can be an effective deterrent. If you're sitting down to eat or rest, loop your daypack strap around your arm, leg, or chair leg. If you plan to sleep on a train (or anywhere in public), clip or fasten your pack or suitcase to the seat, luggage rack, or yourself. Most zippers are lockable, and even a twist-tie, paper clip, or key ring is helpful to keep your bag zipped up tight. The point isn't to make your bag impenetrable, but harder to get into than the next guy's.

Never set down valuable items—such as a camera, mobile device, wallet, or rail pass—on a train seat or restaurant table, where they are easy to swipe. Keep these tucked away.

Tour of a Money Belt

Packing light applies to your money belt as well as your luggage. Here's what to keep in it:

Passport: The item you least want to lose en route

Rail Pass: As valuable as cash

Driver's License: Necessary if you rent a car, and useful as collateral for rentals (bikes, audioguides, and so on)

Cards: Debit and credit cards

Cash: Larger bills

Plastic Sheath: Protective cover (a plastic baggie works) for keeping money-belt contents dry

Just-in-Case Information: Important phone numbers, email addresses, hotels, and other itinerary details

When using your phone at a café, don't place it on the bar: Put it in your front pocket (then return it to a safer place before you leave).

Some thieves can even be so bold as to snatch something right out of your hands. For instance, if you're holding up a smartphone to take a picture of the Eiffel Tower, a thief can grab it and run—and he can navigate his escape route far better than you can. Be aware of who's around you.

One way to minimize this risk is to keep valuable devices attached to you or your bag (this also reduces the chance of accidentally leaving something behind). For instance, make sure your camera strap is looped around your chest or wrist, even when snapping a photo. Or use a lanyard to attach gadgets to your daypack (if there's no interior attachment point, feed straps through zipper pulls or a sturdy safety pin hooked to the inside of your bag).

Be discreet with your hiding places. If you're keeping valuables anywhere but a money belt (I wouldn't), be as circumspect as possible. Thieves can easily identify the easiest mark—most likely the guy whose back pocket bulges out or the woman who keeps patting her bag to check that her money is still there.

Stay vigilant in crowds and steer clear of commotions. Go on instant alert anytime there's a commotion; it's likely a smokescreen for theft. Imaginative artful-dodger thief teams create a disturbance—a fight, a messy spill, or a jostle or stumble—to distract their victims. Crowds anywhere, but especially on public transit and at flea markets, provide bad guys with plenty of targets, opportunities, and easy escape routes.

Be on guard in train stations, especially upon arrival, when you may be overburdened by luggage and overwhelmed by a new location. Take turns watching the bags with your travel partner. Don't absentmindedly set down a bag while you wait in line; always be in physical contact with your stuff. If you check your luggage, keep the claim ticket or locker key in your money belt; thieves know just where to go if they snare one of these. On the train, be hyper-alert at stops, when thieves can dash on and off—with your bag.

City buses that cover tourist sights (such as Rome's notorious #64) are happy hunting grounds. Be careful on packed buses or subways; to keep from being easy pickings, some travelers wear their day bag against their chest (looping a strap around one shoulder). Some thieves lurk near subway turnstiles; as you go through, a thief might come right behind you, pick your pocket and then run off, leaving you stuck behind the turnstile and unable to follow. By mentioning these scenarios, I don't want you to be paranoid...just prepared. If you keep alert, you'll keep your valuables, too.

Establish a "don't lose it" discipline. Travelers are more likely to inadvertently lose their belongings than to have them stolen. I've known people to leave passports under pillows, bags on the overhead rack on the bus, and cameras in the taxi. Always take a look behind you before leaving any place or form of transport. At hotels, stick to an unpacking routine, and don't put things in odd places in the room. Run through a mental checklist every time you pack up again: money belt, passport, mobile phone, electronic gear, charging cords, toiletries, laundry, and so on. Before leaving a hotel room for good, conduct a quick overall search—under the bed, under the pillows and bedspread, behind the bathroom door, in a wall socket...

Leave a clue for honest finders. Accidents happen, and even the most cautious traveler can leave something behind. Maximize your chances of getting it back by taping a tiny note with your email address or travel partner's phone number to any item you really don't want to lose, making it easy for a kind soul to return it. (For phones, you could use an "If Found Please Return To" note as your lock screen.)

Theft-Proofing Your Rental Car

Thieves target tourists' cars—especially at night. More than half of the work that European automobile glass shops do is repairing windows broken by thieves.

Don't leave anything even hinting of value in view in your parked car. Put anything worth stealing in the trunk (or, better yet, in your hotel room). Leave your glove compartment open so the thief can look in without breaking in. Choose your parking place carefully. Your hotel receptionist knows what's safe and what precautions are necessary.

Make your car look as local as possible. Leave no tourist information lying around. Put a local newspaper under the rear window. Before I choose where to park my car, I check to see if the parking lot's asphalt glitters. In Rome, my favorite hotel is next to a large police station— a safe place to park.

If you rent a hatchback, leave the trunk covered during the day.

You can judge the safety of a European parking lot by how it glitters.

At night, roll back the cover so thieves can see there's nothing stored in the car. Many police advise leaving your car unlocked at night. "Worthless" but irreplaceable things (journal, memory cards full of photos, etc.) are stolen only if left in a bag. It's better to keep these things with you, or if need be, lay them loose in the trunk.

Be alert to "moving violations." In some urban areas, crude thieves reach into windows or even smash the windows of occupied cars at stoplights to grab a purse or camera.

SCAMS AND RIP-OFFS

Europe is a surprisingly creative place when it comes to travel scams. Many of the most successful gambits require a naive and trusting tourist. But don't think it can't happen to more sophisticated travelers, too. There are many subtle ways to be scammed—a cabbie pads your fare, a public Internet terminal records your password, or a waiter offers a special with a "special" increased price. Be smart: Know what you are paying for before handing over money, and always count your change. (For tips on avoiding taxi scams, see page 313.)

Scam artists come in all shapes and sizes. But if you're cautious and not overly trusting, you should have no problem. Here are some clever ways European crooks bolster their cash flow.

Such a Deal!

If a bargain seems too good to be true...it's too good to be true.

The "Found" Ring: An innocent-looking person picks up a ring on the ground in front of you and asks if you dropped it. When you say no, the person examines the ring more closely, then shows you a mark "proving" that it's pure gold. He offers to sell it to you for a good price—which is several times more than he paid for it before dropping it on the sidewalk.

The "Friendship" Bracelet: A vendor approaches you and aggressively asks if you'll help him with a "demonstration." He proceeds to make a friendship bracelet right on your arm. When finished, he asks you to pay a premium for the bracelet he created just for you. And, since you can't easily take it off on the spot,

In Berlin, the police teach the public the latest shell-game scam. On the streets of Europe, anything that seems too good to be true...is.

you feel obliged to pay up. (These sorts of distractions by "salesmen" can also function as a smokescreen for theft—an accomplice is picking your pocket as you try to wriggle away from the pushy vendor.)

Salesman in Distress: A well-spoken, well-dressed gentleman approaches you and explains that he's a leather jacket salesman, and he needs directions to drive to a nearby landmark. He chats you up ("Oh, really? My wife is from Chicago!") and soon you've made a new friend. That's when he reaches in his car and pulls out a "designer leather jacket" which he'd like to give to you as a thank you for your helpfulness. Oh, and by the way, his credit card isn't working, and could you please give him some cash to buy gas? He takes off with the cash, and you later realize that you've paid way too much for your new vinyl jacket.

Money Matters

In stores, restaurants, at ticket booths, everywhere—expect to be cheated if you're not paying attention. Be alert any time money changes hands. This includes whenever you're withdrawing money from an ATM (for more on ATM scams, see page 197). For general tips on keeping your debit and credit cards safe, see page 198. When paying for things, keep your cards in your sight, or much easier and safer, use cash. But even paying with cash can have its challenges.

Slow Count: Cashiers who deal with lots of tourists thrive on the slow count. They'll count your change back with odd pauses in hopes the rushed tourist will gather up the money early and say "*Grazie.*"

Switcheroo—You Lose: Be careful when you pay with too large a bill for a small payment. Clearly state the value of the bill as you hand it over. Some cabbies or waiters will pretend to drop a large bill and pick up a hidden small one in order to shortchange a tourist. Get familiar with the currency and check the change you're given. Be alert for Asian coins that dishonest vendors try to pass off as €2 coins.

Talkative Cashiers: The shop's cashier seems to be speaking on her phone when you hand her your credit card. But watch closely: She may surreptitiously take a picture of your card. It's enough to make you want to pay cash for most purchases, like I do.

Meeting the Locals

I want my readers to meet and get to know Europeans—but watch out for chance encounters on the street.

The Attractive Flirt: A single male traveler is approached by a gorgeous woman on the street. After chatting for a while, she seductively invites him for a drink at a nearby nightclub. But when the bill arrives, it's several hundred dollars more than he expected. Only then does he notice the burly bouncers guarding the exits. There are several variations on this scam. Sometimes, the scam artist is disguised as a lost tourist; in other cases, it's simply a gregarious local person who (seemingly) just wants to show you his city. Either way, be suspicious when invited for a drink by someone you just met; if you want to go out together, suggest a bar (or café) of your choosing instead.

Oops! You're jostled in a crowd as someone spills ketchup or fake pigeon poop on your shirt. The thief offers profuse apologies while dabbing it up—and pawing your pockets. There are similar schemes: Someone drops something, you kindly pick it up, and you lose your wallet. Or someone throws a baby into your arms as your pockets are picked. Treat any commotion (a scuffle breaking out, a beggar in your face) as fake—designed to distract unknowing victims. If an elderly woman falls down an escalator, stand back and guard your valuables, then...carefully...move in to help.

Beggars: You'll meet a lot of people with beautiful eyes, beautiful children, and sad stories. They'll step right up and say, "Euro, please give me a euro." They don't want a euro; they want your wallet. Many beggars are pickpockets. Understand that.

The "Helpful" Local: Thieves posing as concerned locals will warn you to store your wallet safely—and then steal it after they see where you stash it. If someone wants to help you use an ATM, politely refuse (they're just after your PIN code). Some thieves put out tacks and ambush

Travel smart — keep what matters in your moneybelt.
www.ricksteves.com
50 EURO EYPO

In your wallet, you've got a fake 50-euro bill (with a funny note to the thief on the back—see next page). Cut it out and take it along.

drivers with their "assistance" in changing the tire. Others hang out at subway ticket machines eager to "help" you, the bewildered tourist, buy tickets with a pile of your quickly disappearing foreign cash. If using a station locker, beware of the "Hood Samaritan" who may have his own key to a locker he'd like you to use. And skip the helping hand from official-looking railroad attendants at the Rome train station. They'll help you find your seat...then demand a "tip."

Young Thief Gangs: These are common all over urban southern Europe, especially in the touristy areas of Milan, Florence, and Rome. Groups of boys or girls with big eyes, troubled expressions, and colorful raggedy clothes politely mob the unsuspecting tourist, beggar-style. As their pleading eyes grab yours and they hold up their pathetic message scrawled on cardboard, you're fooled into thinking that they're beggars. All the while, your purse or backpack is being expertly rifled. If you're wearing a money belt and you understand what's going on here, there's nothing to fear. In fact, having a street thief's hand slip slowly into your pocket becomes just one more interesting cultural experience.

Appearances Can Be Deceiving

The sneakiest pickpockets look like well-dressed business-people, generally with something official-looking in their hand. Some pose as tourists, with daypacks, cameras, and even guidebooks. Don't be fooled by looks, impressive uniforms, femme fatales, or hard-luck stories.

Fake Charity Petition: You're at a popular sight when someone thrusts a petition at you. It's likely a woman or a teen who, often pretending to be deaf, tries to get you to sign an official-looking petition, supposedly in support of a charity (the petition is often in English, which should be a clue).

In your wallet, you've got a little cash...and this funny note to the thief (with a fake 50-euro bill on back—see previous page). Cut it out and take it along.

DEAR THIEF...

ENGLISH: Sorry this contains so little money. Consider changing your profession.

ITALIANO: Mi spiace per te che ci siano così pochi soldi. Sara' meglio che cambi lavoro.

FRANCAIS: Je suis désolé d'avoir si peu d'argent. Considérez un changement de carrière.

DEUTSCHE: Tut mir leid dass meine Geldbörse so wenig Geld enthält. Vielleicht sollten Sie sich einen neuen Beruf auswählen.

ESPAÑOL: Lamento que encuentre tan poco dinero. Vaya pensando en cambiar de trabajo.

The petitioner then demands a cash donation. At best, anyone who falls for this scam is out some euros; at worst, they're pickpocketed while distracted by the petitioner.

Beware fake charity petitioners demanding cash donations.

Phony Police: Two thieves in uniform—posing as "Tourist Police"—stop you on the street, flash bogus badges, and ask to check your wallet for counterfeit bills, "drug money," or to establish your nationality. You won't even notice some bills are missing until after they leave. Never give your wallet to anyone.

Room "Inspectors": There's a knock at your door and two men claim to be the hotel's room inspectors. One waits outside while the other comes in to take a look around. While you're distracted, the first thief slips in and takes valuables left on a dresser. Don't let people into your room if you weren't expecting them. Call the hotel desk if "inspectors" suddenly turn up.

Broken Camera: Everyone is taking pictures of a famous sight, and someone comes up with a camera or mobile phone and asks that you take his picture. But the device doesn't seem to work. When you hand it back, the "tourist" fumbles and drops it on the ground, where it breaks into pieces. He will either ask you to pay for repairs (don't do it) or lift your wallet while you are bending over to pick up the broken object.

The Stripper: You see a good-looking woman arguing with a street vendor. The vendor accuses her of shoplifting, which she vehemently denies. To prove her innocence, she starts taking off her clothes—very slowly. Once she's down to her underwear, the vendor apologizes and she leaves. Suddenly all the men in the crowd find out that their wallets have "left," too, thanks to a team of pickpockets working during the show.

LOSING IT ALL...AND BOUNCING BACK

You're winging your way across Europe, having the time of your life, when you make a simple mistake. You set your bag down next to your café chair, and before you know it...your bag is gone. Unfortunately, today's the day you tucked your passport, credit cards, and extra cash in your bag instead of in your money belt. That sinking feeling is the realization that you've lost everything but the euro or two in your pocket.

Odds are, this won't ever happen to you. But a little bit of advance preparation can make even this worst-case scenario a minor bump in your European adventure.

Don't panic. First of all, take a breath. Panic clouds your judgment. And don't beat yourself up: No matter how careful, any traveler can get ripped off or lose a bag. I once met a family in Amsterdam who managed to lose all their bags between the airport and their first hotel, but went on to have a very successful trip. A positive attitude is a great asset.

Ask for help. If you're in a country where little English is spoken, enlist the help of a local English speaker to assist you in making phone calls or explaining the situation to officials. Try your hotelier or someone at the tourist office: Even in the smallest towns, someone is likely to know at least a little English. Fellow travelers you've met and even family or friends back home can also be sources of help.

For emergency help (for any reason—police, medical, and fire), dial 112 from any phone. This toll-free number is the European Union's version of 911. In many cases, operators are able to answer in English.

File a police report. Find a police officer and report the theft or loss. Having a police report may help with replacing your passport and credit cards, and is a must if you file an insurance claim for a lost rail pass or expensive travel gear. The police may be able to direct you to a local travelers' aid office or Red Cross-like organization. And if you're lucky, someone may actually turn in your bag. That happened to me one time. My stolen bag showed up at the police station— turned in by a Good Samaritan who found it discarded after the thief rifled through its contents. Thieves don't want your

If you get ripped off, find a police officer and report the loss.

clothes or your bag. They want only what they can resell, and they discard the rest.

Gather critical information. In the best situation, you've got photocopies of your important documents on you. If you don't have your bank or embassy's contact information, look it up (if Internet access is a problem, explain the situation to your hotelier or a staffer at the tourist office, and ask to use their office computer). Your hotelier or a tourist-office staffer should be able to help you place necessary collect or toll-free calls. Retrieve information you've stored online, or solicit help from folks back home. Be careful about emailing passport and credit-card numbers. If you need important documents, have them faxed to a trusted location.

Replace your passport. This is top priority. Without a passport, you can't leave the country, and you'll find it difficult to check into a hotel or receive wired funds. You'll need to go in person to the closest embassy or consulate (in the capital and sometimes major cities, too).

You may be able to make an appointment at the embassy or consulate, or you may need to show up during open hours and wait your turn—check the embassy and consulate information at Travel.State.gov. If you can, save time by printing the required forms from the website and filling them out before you go. Having a photocopy of your passport can help; if you don't, embassy staff can look up your previous passport records, interview you and your travel partners, and even call contacts at home to verify your identity.

Every US consulate operates an American Citizen Services (ACS) office, which aids Americans traveling abroad in coping with natural disasters, receiving money, and replacing passports (if calling from Europe, dial 00-1-202/501-4444; in the US, call 888/407-4747). A replacement passport costs $140 and can generally be issued within a few

Lost It All? Follow These Steps

1. File a police report, either on the spot or later. You'll need it to file an insurance claim for a lost or stolen rail pass or travel gear, and it can help with replacing your passport or credit and debit cards.

2. Replace your passport at the nearest embassy or consulate; they're located in the country's capital and sometimes also in major cities (find locations at www.travel.state.gov for Americans, www.passportcanada.gc.ca for Canadians).

3. Cancel and replace your credit and debit cards. Toll-free numbers (listed by country) are available at the websites for Visa and MasterCard. You can also call these 24-hour US numbers collect:

   Visa: 303/967-1096
   MasterCard: 636/722-7111
   American Express: 336/393-1111

4. Contact your mobile provider to suspend service. (If you use a security app, use the "locate, lock, and wipe" feature before you cancel service altogether.)

days, or faster if you make a good case that you need it right away. If you don't have the funds, the embassy will help you contact someone at home who can wire money directly to the embassy. If no one can wire money, the embassy may waive the fee or give you a "repatriation loan"—just enough funds to cover the new passport and get you back home.

If you're Canadian, you'll need to report the loss or theft to the local police, as well as the nearest embassy or consulate. Canadian authorities will conduct an investigation into the circumstances, which may delay the processing of your request. You must complete an application form and a statutory declaration concerning the lost/stolen passport, supply two passport photos and documentary proof of Canadian citizenship, and pay the fees (for more information, see www.passportcanada.gc.ca).

Cancel debit and credit cards. Within two days, cancel your lost or stolen debit and credit cards (meeting this deadline limits your liability to $50) and order replacements. Visa, MasterCard, and American Express all have global customer-assistance centers, reachable by collect call from anywhere (see sidebar on page 387). You'll need to know the name of the bank that issued the card, card type (classic, platinum, or whatever), card number, primary and secondary cardholders' names, cardholder's name exactly as printed on the card, billing address, home phone number, circumstances of the loss or theft, and identification verification (your birth date, mother's maiden name, or Social Security number—memorize this, don't carry a copy). If you are the secondary cardholder, you'll also need to provide the primary cardholder's identification-verification details.

Your bank can generally deliver a new card to you in Europe within two to three business days. Some may even be able to wire cash to keep you going or pay for your hotel room directly. Ask about these extra services.

If necessary, arrange for a wire transfer. A friend or relative can transfer money to you via Western Union's website (or in person or over the phone at 800-225-5227). A "control number" is assigned to the transfer. If you have your passport, simply present it with the control number to a Western Union agent, who gives you cash. (Western Union has thousands of agents at banks, travel agencies, post offices, train stations, airports, currency-exchange offices, and supermarkets in Europe.) There's a hefty fee and a poor exchange rate, but the cash can be ready for pickup in a matter of hours. If you don't have your passport, Western Union lets your financial angel set up a "secret question" that only you can answer to confirm your identity. Or you can use a slower US State Department service that wires money to an embassy or consulate for pickup during business hours (see www.travel.state.gov).

It's possible to transfer money from a bank in the US to a bank in Europe, but this may take several days (you'll probably have new cards faster). If your situation is dire and you can't get anyone to wire you money, ask the consulate about a "repatriation loan." Usually this is enough money to cover a night's lodging and a plane ticket home. Your passport will be stamped "Valid for Return to US Only" until your loan is repaid. If this happens to you, don't even think about stiffing Uncle Sam—after six months the State Department forwards the paperwork to the Treasury Department and the IRS.

Replace travel documents. Point-to-point rail etickets can often be reprinted from any computer or at the station, but tickets purchased at the station and printed on special ticket paper probably can't be replaced. Unfortunately, you can't replace a rail pass—you'll need to either purchase a new pass (most likely sent from home) or new tickets to complete your trip. (If you bought Rail Europe's Rail Protection Plan, you may be able to get a partial refund when you get home.) There's no need to replace printed copies of airline, hotel, or car-rental reservations—once you have your new passport, these businesses can easily look up your reservation.

Rearrange travel plans. Depending on how long it takes to get your passport replaced—and how far you have to travel to reach an embassy or consulate—you'll probably need to rearrange your travel plans. Cancel and reschedule hotels and flights as soon as possible to avoid losing deposits or paying change fees (explaining the situation may help). If you're stuck without cash or credit cards for a few days, see if your bank or a family member back home can pay for your hotel stay.

Replace travel gear. Once you've started the process of replacing your passport and credit and debit cards, you can think about replacing travel gear such as your camera, phone, or tablet. Depending on your insurance policy, you may be able to get reimbursed for part of the replacement cost when you get home (see page 70). Decide which items are critical enough to your trip to replace immediately.

If you need to have something sent from home, have it addressed to you at a hotel you'll arrive at when it does; your hotelier will be happy to hold it for you. Allow 10 days for a letter; to speed things up, try second-day US-Europe services (such as DHL), though figure on four days for delivery to a small town. If you're not staying at a hotel (for instance, if you're camping or caravanning), you can have mail sent to any city's post office, addressed to you in care of "Poste Restante"; for convenience, pick a small town with only one post office and no crowds.

Refill prescriptions. Bring in a copy of your prescription to a pharmacy—if you don't have it, try contacting your doctor's office. They can usually fax or email a copy to you in Europe (see page 418 for more on filling prescriptions). Your optometrist can do the same for your prescription eyewear.

Replace your rental-car key. If you lose the key to your rental car, call the car-hire company with your rental agreement number and your exact location. Be prepared for considerable expense and a delay: You will be charged $200 or more for a replacement key, and you may need to wait 24 to 48 hours for delivery of new keys or even a different vehicle.

Make the best of the situation. Getting everything straightened out can take a while. Be flexible and patient. It may not help at the time, but try to remember that your loss will make for a good story when you get home. Like a friend of mine says, "When it comes... Or get... agedy + Time = Comedy."

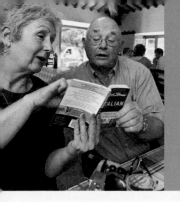

Hurdling the Language Barrier

You're probably wondering: How can you connect with the locals if you can't communicate in their language? You'll be surprised at how easy it is. Over the years, I've collected tips and tricks that help travelers who speak only English step right over that pesky language barrier. In this chapter, you'll learn how to simplify your English and communicate creatively to get your points across and your needs met.

It always helps to be able to communicate—even just a few phrases—in the local tongue. Communication also goes beyond words: It helps to know the meaning of various common gestures (and what to avoid doing).

A fear of the language barrier ~~keeps many~~ people (read: English speakers) out of Europe, but ~~the "~~barrier" is getting smaller every day. Over the last 30 years, an entire generation of Europeans has grown up speaking more English than ever. English really has arrived as Europe's second language. According to recent figures, two-thirds of all Europeans can speak English. Histori-cally, many European signs and menus were printed in four lan-guages: German, French, Eng-lish, and—depending on where you were—Italian, Spanish, or Russian. But there's been a shift. In the interest of free trade and efficiency, the European Union has established English as Europe's standard language of commerce. Now most signs are printed in just two languages:

These signs in Amsterdam's airport don't even bother with Dutch.

the native language for locals and English for everyone else. In some airports, signs are in English only.

Confessions of a Monoglot

While it's nothing to brag about, I basically speak only English. Of course, if I spoke more languages, I could enjoy a much deeper understanding of the people and cultures I visit. Still, speaking only English, I've enjoyed researching my guidebooks, leading tours, and making my TV shows, as well as navigating through wonderful vacations—getting transportation, finding rooms, eating well, and seeing the sights. However, while you can manage decently with the blunt weapon of English, you'll get along in Europe better if you learn and use a few basic phrases and polite words.

Having an interest in the native language wins the respect of those you'll meet. Language translation apps are plentiful. Pocket-size travel language dictionaries are cheap and sold throughout Europe. Buy a good phrase book before your trip, and start your practical vocabulary growing right off the bat. My phrase books are the only ones on the market designed by a guy who speaks just English (that's why they're so helpful). They are both fun and practical, with a meet-the-people and stretch-the-budget focus. Mr. Berlitz knew the languages, but he never stayed in a hotel where he had to ask, "Do you have duct tape?"

Spend bus and train rides learning. Start studying the language when you arrive—or sooner. I try to learn five new words a day. You'd be surprised how handy it is to have a

Resources for Hurdling the Language Barrier

Consider these apps:

Bravolol: Basic phrases and vocabulary with translation and transliteration; also speaks phrases in the local language and lets you save favorites

Duolingo: Great for language learning, with short lessons, multiple-choice challenges, and levels to keep you progressing

Google Translate: Translates speech, handwriting, and images containing text, such as signs; save favorite words to access offline

Microsoft Translator: Translates text, speech, and photographed text; also translates conversations when multiple devices are connected

Lonely Planet Fast Talk: Offline phrasebook that pronounces a selection of foreign phrases in the most common languages and allows you to save favorites

LEFT You don't have to speak Danish to understand these signs.

RIGHT If your taxi driver is going too fast, my phrase books will help you say, "If you don't slow down, I'll throw up."

working vocabulary of even 50 words. Take advantage of everyday conversations to learn the language. You're surrounded by expert, native-speaking tutors in every country. Let them teach you.

While Americans are notorious monoglots, many Europeans are very good with languages. Make communication easier by choosing a multilingual person to speak with. Businesspeople, urbanites, well-dressed young people, students, and anyone in the tourist trade are most likely to speak English. Many Swiss grow up trilingual, and many young Scandinavians and Eastern Europeans speak several languages. People speaking minor languages (the Dutch, Norwegians, Czechs, Hungarians, Slovenes) have more reason to learn English, German, or French since their linguistic world is so small. All Croatians begin learning English in elementary school, and—since their TV programming is subtitled—they listen to Americans talk for hours each day. Scandinavian students of our language actually decide between English and "American." My Norwegian cousin speaks with a touch of Texas and knows more slang than I do.

We English speakers are the one group that can afford to be lazy, because English is the world's linguistic common denominator. When a Greek meets a Norwegian, they speak English. (What Greek speaks Norwegian?)

Imagine if each of our states spoke its own language. That's close to the European situation, but they've done a great job of minimizing the communication problems you'd expect to find on a small continent with such a Babel of Tongues. Most information a traveler must understand

Translating Foreign Websites

Monolinguists will appreciate the fact that many European websites offer English-language versions (usually accessed by clicking on a tiny British or American flag or the abbreviation "EN"). For Web pages that are available only in the native language, a website translator is helpful.

Google's Chrome browser detects when a Web page is in a foreign language and asks if you want it to be translated to English. While less than perfect, this feature can open a whole new world of local information for travelers. Before my last trip to Copenhagen, I used Chrome's translator to read restaurant reviews written by Danish users. Even if you use Google on a different Web browser, you'll see a "Translate this Page" link in your search results next to foreign-language URLs. You can also cut and paste any text into Google Translate (translate.google.com) for an instant translation; click the speaker icon to hear the foreign words spoken aloud.

(such as road signs, menus, telephone instructions, and safety warnings) is printed either in English or as universal symbols. Europe's uniform road-sign system (see page 176) enables drivers to roll right over the language barrier. And rest assured that any place trying to separate tourists from their money will explain how to spend it in the necessary languages. English is always one of them.

Dominant as English may be, it's just good manners to know the most common polite words in the local tongue. The top 10 words in any language—mostly niceties like please, thank you, and excuse me—are more important than the next 200 words combined. You should use these top words all the time. It's bad style for you to be in a country and not to know these "nice" words.

It's also a good idea to start every conversation by politely asking, "Do you speak English?" "*Parlez-vous anglais?*" "*Sprechen Sie Englisch?*" or whatever. If they say "No," then I do the best I can in their language. Usually, after a few sentences they'll say, "Actually, I do speak some English." One thing Americans do well is put others at ease with their linguistic shortcomings.

COMMUNICATING WITH LOCALS

English may be Europe's lingua franca, but that doesn't mean everyone you encounter will be fluent. Below I've provided advice based on years of successful conversations (and amusing mishaps) while trying to talk to people for whom English is not their first language.

Use Simple English

If you have a trip coming up and don't speak French yet, be realistic, and don't expect to become fluent by the time you leave. Rather than frantically learning a few more French words, the best thing you can do at this point is to learn how to communicate in what the Voice of America calls "Special English." Your European friend is doing you a favor by speaking your language. The least we can do is make our English simple and clear.

Speak slowly, clearly, and with carefully chosen words. Assume you're dealing with someone who learned English out of a book—reading British words, not hearing American ones. They are reading your lips, wishing it were written down, hoping to see every letter as it tumbles out of your mouth. If you want to be understood, talk like

International Words

As our world shrinks, more and more words leap their linguistic boundaries and become international. Sensitive travelers develop a knack for choosing words most likely to be universally understood ("auto" instead of "car"; "kaput" rather than "broken"; "photo," not "picture"). They also internationalize their pronunciation. "University," if you play around with its sound (oo-nee-vehr-see-tay), can be understood anywhere. Be creative.

Communication by analogy is effective. Anywhere in Europe (except in Hungary), "Attila" means "crude bully." When a bulky Italian crowds in front of you, say, "*Scusi,* Ah-tee-la" and retake your place. If you like your haircut and want to compliment your Venetian barber, put your hand sensually on your hair and say "Casanova." Nickname the hairstylist "Michelangelo."

Here are a few internationally understood words. Cut out the Yankee accent and give each word a pan-European sound ("autoboooos," "Engleesh").

Hello	Camping	Europa
No	Auto	Disneyland (wonderland)
Stop	Autobus	Nuclear
Kaput	Taxi	Toilet
Ciao	Tourist	WC
Bye-bye	Beer	Police
OK	Coke, Coca-Cola	English
Mañana	Tea	Telephone
Pardon	Coffee	Photo
Bravo	Vino	Photocopy
Rock 'n' roll	Chocolate	Disco
Mamma mia	Picnic	Computer
No problem	Self-service	Sport
Super	Yankee, Americano	Internet
Sex/Sexy	Hercules (strong)	Central
Oo la la	Casanova (romantic)	Information
Moment	Attila (mean, crude)	University
Bon voyage	Fascist	Passport
Restaurant	Elephant (a big clod)	Bill Gates
McDonald's	Michelangelo (artistic)	Obama
Bank	Rambo	Holiday (vacation)
Hotel	Communist	Gratis (free)
Post (office)	Amigo	America's favorite four-letter words

a Dick-and-Jane primer. Choose easy words and clearly pronounce each syllable (po-ta-to chips.) Try not to use contractions. Be patient—when many Americans aren't easily understood, they speak louder and toss in a few extra words. (Listen to other tourists talk, and you'll hear your own shortcomings.) For several months each year, I speak with simple words, pronouncing...very...clearly. When I return home, my friends say (very deliberately), "Rick, you can relax now, we speak English fluently."

Can the slang. Our American dialect has become a super-deluxe slang pizza not found on any European menu. The sentence "Can the slang," for example, would baffle the average Euro-pean. If you learned English in a classroom for two years, how would you respond to the American who uses expressions such as "sort of like," "pretty bad," or "Howzit goin'?"

Make an educated guess and go for it. Can you read the Norwegian: "Central Sick House"? Too many Americans would bleed to death on the street corner looking for the word "hospital."

Keep your messages grunt-simple. Make single nouns work as entire sentences. When asking for something, a one-word question ("Photo?") is more effective than an attempt at something more grammatically correct ("May I take your picture, sir?"). Be a Neanderthal. Strip your message down to its most basic element. Even Neandertourists will find things go easier if they begin each request with the local "please" (e.g., *Bitte*, toilet?").

Use internationally understood words. Some Ameri-cans spend an entire trip telling people they're on *vacation*, draw only blank stares, and slowly find themselves in a soundproof, culture-resistant cell. The sensitive communica-tor notices that Europeans are more likely to understand the word *holiday*—probably because that's what the English say. Then she plugs that word into her simple English vocabulary, makes herself understood, and enjoys a much closer contact with Europe. If you say *restroom* or *bathroom*, you'll get no relief. *Toilet* is direct, simple, and understood. If my car is broken in Portugal, I don't say, "Excuse me, my car is bro-ken." I point to the vehicle and say, "Auto kaput."

Tips on Creative Communication

Even if you have no real language in common, you can have some fun communicating. Consider this profound conversa-tion I had with a cobbler in Sicily:

"Spaghetti," I said, with a very saucy Italian accent.

"Marilyn Monroe," was the old man's reply.

"Mamma mia!" I said, tossing my hands and head into the air.

"Yes, no, one, two, tree," he returned, slowly and proudly.

By now we'd grown fond of each other, and I whispered, secretively, *"Molto buono, ravioli."*

Deciphering Signs

Öffnungszeiten

VOM 4. JULI AN

Montag:	08:30 - 13:00 u.14:00 - 18:30
Dienstag:	08:30 - 13:00 u.14:00 - 18:30
Mittwoch:	08:30 - 13:00 GESCHLOSSEN
Donnerstag:	08:30 - 13:00 u.14:00 - 18:30
Freitag:	08:30 - 13:00 u.14:00 - 18:30
Samstag:	08:30 - 13:00 u.14:00 - 18:30

Hurdle the language barrier by thinking of things as multiple-choice questions and making educated guesses. This sign on a shop in Germany lists times. The top word can only mean "open times" or "closed times." I'd guess it lists hours open from (*vom* = from; if it rhymes, I go for it) the Fourth of July. Those six words on the left, most of which end in *tag*, must be days of the week (think *Guten Tag*). Things are open 8:30-13:00 *und* 14:00-18:30 (24-hour clock). On *Mittwoch* (midweek), in the afternoon...something different happens. Since it can only be open or closed, and everything else is open, you can guess that on Wednesday afternoons this shop is *geschlossen*!

He spat, "Be sexy, drink Pepsi!"

Waving good-bye, I hollered, *"No problema."*

"Ciao," he said, smiling.

Risk looking goofy. Even with no common language, rudimentary communication is easy. Butcher the language if you must, but communicate. I'll never forget the clerk in the French post office who flapped her arms and asked, "Tweet, tweet, tweet?" I understood immediately, answered with a nod, and she gave me the airmail stamps I needed. At the risk of getting birdseed, I communicated successfully. If you're hungry, clutch your stomach and growl. If you want milk, "moo" and pull two imaginary udders. If the liquor was too strong, simulate an atomic explosion starting from your

The European Babel of Tongues

Most of Europe's many languages can be arranged into one family tree. Many of them have the same grandparents and resemble each other kind of like you resemble your siblings and cousins. But occasionally, an oddball uncle sneaks in whom no one can explain.

Romance Countries (Italy, France, Spain, Portugal): The Romance family evolved from Latin, the language of the Roman Empire ("Romance" comes from "Roman"). Few of us know Latin, but being familiar with any of the modern Romance languages helps with the others. For example, your high school Spanish will help you learn some Italian.

Germanic Countries (British Isles, Germany, Netherlands, Scandinavia): The Germanic languages, though influenced by Latin, are a product of the tribes of northern Europe (including the Angles and Saxons)—people the ancient Romans called "barbarians" because they didn't speak Latin.

ITALIAN · GERMAN · ENGLISH · ROMANSH · FRENCH · DUTCH · ROMANIAN · SPANISH · DANISH · ROMANCE (LATIN) · PORTUGUESE · NORWEGIAN · CELTIC · ICELANDIC · GERMANIC · BASQUE · SWEDISH · POLISH · SLOVAK · CZECH · CROATIAN · SLOVENE · SERBIAN · (LANGUAGE OF THE GYPSIES) · SLAVIC · BULGARIAN · ROMANY · RUSSIAN · IRANIAN · BALTIC · LATVIAN · INDO-ARYAN · LITHUANIAN · GREEK · FINNISH · ESTONIAN · HUNGARIAN · INDO-EUROPEAN · FINNO-UGRIC · PIG LATIN

LANGUAGE TREE

German is spoken by all Germans and Austrians, and by most Swiss. The people of Holland and northern Belgium speak Dutch, a close relative to German. While Dutch

stomach and mushrooming to your head. If you're attracted to someone, pant.

Be melodramatic. Exaggerate the native accent. In France, you'll communicate more effectively (and have more fun) by sounding less like an American and more like Inspector Clouseau. The locals won't be insulted; they'll be impressed. Use whatever French you know. Even English spoken with a sexy French accent makes more sense to the French ear. In Italy, be melodic and exuberant, and wave those hands. Go ahead, try it: *Mamma mia!* No. Do it again. *MAMMA MIA!* You've got to be uninhibited. Self-consciousness kills communication.

Make logical leaps. Most major European languages are related, coming from (or at least being influenced by) Latin.

is not *Deutsch*, a Hamburger or Frankfurter can almost understand an Amsterdam newspaper. The Norwegians, Danes, and Swedes can read each other's magazines and enjoy their neighbors' TV shows.

Slavic Countries (Czech Republic, Poland, Slovakia, Slovenia, Croatia, etc.): Most Eastern European countries (except Hungary, Romania, and the Baltics) speak Slavic languages. While these languages are more or less mutually intelligible, spellings change as you cross borders; for example, Czech *hrad*, or castle, becomes Croatian *grad*. Farther east—in Serbia, Russia, Ukraine, Bulgaria, and elsewhere—the language sounds similar, but is written with the Cyrillic alphabet. The Baltic languages, Latvian and Lithuanian, are distantly related to Slavic tongues.

Finno-Ugric Countries (Hungary, Finland, Estonia): Hungarian, Finnish, and Estonian are more closely related to Asian languages than to European ones—likely hinting that the Hungarians, Finns, and Estonians share ancestors from Central Asia.

Multilingual Countries and Regions: Switzerland has four official languages—German, French, Italian, and Romansh (an obscure Romance tongue)—and most Swiss are at least bilingual. Because the region of Alsace, on the French-German border, has been dragged through the mud during several tugs-of-war, most residents speak both languages. Belgium waffles (linguistically), with the southern half (the Walloons) speaking French and the rest speaking Dutch.

Europe's Underdog Languages: Every year on this planet, a dozen or so languages go extinct. But thanks to Europe's determination to celebrate diversity, its underdog languages—once endangered—are thriving once more. The Basques, who live where Spain, France, and the Atlantic all touch, speak Euskara—mysteriously unrelated to any other European language. England is surrounded by a "Celtic Crescent." In Scotland, Ireland, Wales, and Brittany (northwestern France), the old Celtic language survives. Seek out these die-hard remnants in proud gift shops and bookstores, Gaelic pubs, and the Gaeltachts (districts, mostly in western Ireland, where the old culture is preserved by the government).

Knowing that, words become more meaningful. The French word for Monday (our "day of the moon") is *lundi* (lunar day). The Germans say the same thing—*Montag*. *Sonne* is sun, so *Sonntag* is Sunday. If *buon giorno* means good day, *zuppa del giorno* is soup of the day. If *Tiergarten* is zoo (literally "animal garden") in German, then *Stinktier* is a stinky animal—a skunk—and *Kindergarten* is children's garden. Think of *Vater*, *Mutter*, *trink*, *gross*, *gut*, *rapide*, *grand*, *económico*, *delicioso*, and you can *comprender mucho*.

Many letters travel predictable courses (determined by the physical way a sound is made) as related languages drift apart over the centuries. For instance, *p* often becomes *v* or *b* in the neighboring country's language. Italian menus always have a charge for *coperto*—a "cover" charge.

A Yankee-English Phrase Book

Oscar Wilde said, "The English have really everything in common with the Americans—except, of course, language." On your first trip to Britain, you'll find plenty of linguistic surprises. I'll never forget checking into a small-town bed-and-breakfast as a teenager on my first solo European adventure. The landlady cheerily asked me, "And what time would you like to be knocked up in the morning?" I looked over at her husband, who winked, "Would a fry at half-eight be suitable?" The next morn-

Hmm... Where's the "exit"?

ing I got a rap on the door at 8 a.m. and a huge British breakfast a half-hour later.

Traveling through Britain is an adventure in accents and idioms. Every day you'll see babies in prams and pushchairs, sucking dummies as mothers change wet nappies. Soon the kids can trade in their nappies for smalls and spend a penny on their own. "Spend a penny" is British for a visit to the loo (bathroom). Older British kids enjoy candy floss (cotton candy), naughts and crosses (tic-tac-toe), big dippers (roller coasters), and iced lollies (popsicles), and are constantly in need of an Elastoplast or sticking plaster (Band-Aid).

It's fun to browse through an ironmonger's (hardware store) or chemist's shop (pharmacy), noticing the many familiar items with unfamiliar names. The school-supplies section includes sticky tape or Sellotape (adhesive tape), rubbers (erasers), and scribbling blocks (scratch pads). Those with green fingers (a green thumb) might pick up some courgette (zucchini), swede (rutabaga), or aubergine (eggplant) seeds.

In Britain, fries are chips and potato chips are crisps. A beefburger, made with mince (hamburger meat), comes on a toasted bap (bun). For pudding (dessert), have some gateau or sponge (cake).

The British have a great way with names. You'll find towns with names like Upper and Lower Piddle, Once Brewed, and Itching Field. This cute coziness comes through in their language as well. Your car is built with a bonnet and a boot rather than a hood and trunk. You drive on motorways, and when the freeway divides, it becomes a dual carriageway. And never go anticlockwise (counterclockwise) in a roundabout.

Read and listen. Read time schedules, posters, multilingual signs (and graffiti) in bathrooms and newspaper headlines. Develop your ear for foreign languages by tuning in to the other languages on a multilingual tour. It's a puzzle. The more you play, the better you get.

A notepad can work wonders. Words and numbers are much easier to understand when they're written rather than spoken (especially if you mispronounce them). My back-pocket notepad is my constant travel buddy. To repeatedly communicate something difficult and important (such as medical

Gas is petrol, a truck is a lorry, and when you hit a tailback (traffic jam), don't get your knickers in a twist (make a fuss), just queue up (line up).

A two-week vacation in Britain is unheard of, but many locals holiday for a fortnight in a homely (homey) rural cottage, possibly on the Continent (continental Europe). They might pack a face flannel (washcloth), torch (flashlight), and hair grips (bobby pins) in their bum bag (never a fanny pack!) before leaving their flat (apartment). On a cold eve-

Don't take British road signs personally.

ning it's best to wear the warmest mackintosh (raincoat) you can find or an anorak (parka) with press studs (snaps). If you ring up (call) your girlfriend on your mobile (cell phone) and she witters on (gabs and gabs), tell her you're knackered (exhausted) and it's been donkey's years (ages) since you've slept. After washing up (doing the dishes) and hoovering (vacuuming), you can go up to the first floor (second floor) with a neat (straight) whisky and a plate of biscuits (cookies) and get goose pimples (goose bumps) just enjoying the view. Too much of that whisky will get you sloshed, paralytic, bevvied, wellied, popped up, ratted, or even pissed as a newt.

All across the British Isles, you'll find new words, crazy humor, and colorful accents. Pubs are colloquial treasure chests. Church services, sporting events, the Houses of Parliament, live plays, the streets of Liverpool, the docks of London, and children in parks are playgrounds for the American ear. One of the beauties of touring Great Britain is the illusion of hearing a foreign language and actually understanding it—most of the time.

Somehow, "Broken TV" just doesn't have the same ring to it.

instructions, "I'm a strict vegetarian," "boiled water," "well-done meat," "your finest ice cream," or "I am rich and single"), have it written in the local language on your notepad.

Assume you understand and go with your educated guess. My master key to communication is to treat most problems as multiple-choice questions, make an educated guess at the meaning, and proceed confidently as if I understand. At the breakfast table the waitress asks me a question. I don't understand a word she says, but I tell her my room number. Faking it like this applies to rudimentary things like instructions on customs forms, museum hours, and menus. With this approach, I find that 80 percent of the time I'm correct. Half of the time that I'm wrong, I never know it, so it doesn't really matter. And 10 percent of the time, I really blow it. My trip becomes easier—and occasionally much more interesting.

Desperate Telephone Communication

Getting a message across in a language you don't speak requires some artistry. It takes something closer to wizardry on a telephone, where you won't have any visual aids (your dynamic hand and facial expressions, for example). When attempting a phone conversation, speak slowly and clearly, pronouncing every syllable. Keep it very simple—don't clutter your message with anything more than what's essential. Many things are already understood and don't need to be said. (See? Those last six words didn't need to be written.) Use international or carefully chosen English words. When all else fails, let a local person on your end (such as a hotel receptionist) do the talking after you explain to him (with visual help, if needed) the message.

Let me illustrate with a hypothetical telephone conversation. I'm calling a hotel in Barcelona. I just arrived at the train station here, read my guidebook's list of budget accommodations, and I like Pedro's Hotel. Here's what happens:

Pedro answers, "Hotel Pedro, grabdaboodogalaysk."

I ask, "Hotel Pedro?" (Question marks are created melodically.)

He affirms, already a bit impatient, "*Sí*, Hotel Pedro."

I ask, "*Habla* Eng-leesh?"

He says, "No, dees ees Ehspain." (Actually, he probably does speak a little English or will say "*momento*" and get someone who does. But we'll make this particularly challenging. Not only does he not speak English, he doesn't want to...for patriotic reasons.)

I remember not to overcommunicate—I don't need to tell him I'm a tourist looking for a bed. (Who else calls a hotel speaking in a foreign language?) Also, I can assume he's got a room available. If his place is full, he'll say "complete" or "no hotel" and hang up. If he's still talking to me, he wants my business. Now I must communicate just a few things, like how many beds I need and who I am.

I say, "OK." (OK is international for, "Roger, prepare for the next transmission.") "Two people"—he doesn't understand. I get fancy, "*Dos* people"—he still doesn't get

Tongue-Twisters (or "Tongue-Breakers")

These are a great way to practice a language—and break the ice with the Europeans you meet. Here are some that are sure to challenge you and amuse your new friends.

GERMAN

Fischer's Fritze fischt frische Fische, frische Fische fischt Fischer's Fritze.

Fritz Fischer catches fresh fish, fresh fish Fritz Fischer catches.

Ich komme über Oberammergau, oder komme ich über Unterammergau?

I am coming via Oberammergau, or am I coming via Unterammergau?

ITALIAN

Sopra la panca la capra canta, sotto la panca la capra crepa.

On the bench the goat sings, under the bench the goat dies.

Chi fù quel barbaro barbiere che barberò così barbaramente a Piazza Barberini quel povero barbaro di Barbarossa?

Who was that barbarian barber in Barberini Square who shaved that poor barbarian Barbarossa?

FRENCH

Si ces saucissons-ci sont six sous, ces six saucissons-ci sont trop chers.

If these sausages are six cents, these six sausages are too expensive.

Ce sont seize cents jacinthes sèches dans seize cent sachets secs.

There are 1,600 dry hyacinths in 1,600 dry sachets.

SPANISH

Un tigre, dos tigres, tres tigres comían trigo en un trigal. Un tigre, dos tigres, tres tigres.

One tiger, two tigers, three tigers ate wheat in a wheatfield. One tiger, two tigers, three tigers.

Pablito clavó un clavito. ¿Qué clavito clavó Pablito?

Paul stuck in a stick. What stick did Paul stick in?

PORTUGUESE

O rato roeu a roupa do rei de Roma.

The mouse nibbled the clothes of the king of Rome.

Se cá nevasse fazia-se cá ski, mas como cá não neva não se faz cá ski.

If the snow would fall, we'd ski, but since it doesn't, we don't.

Excerpted from Rick Steves Phrase Books—full of practical phrases, spiked with humor, and designed for budget travelers who like to connect with locals.

Happy Talk

English	French	Italian	German	Spanish
Good day.	Bonjour.	Buon giorno.	Guten tag.	Buenos dias.
How are you?	Comment allez-vous?	Come sta?	Wie geht's?	¿Cómo está?
Very good.	Très bien.	Molto bene.	Sehr gut.	Muy bien.
Thank you.	Merci.	Grazie.	Danke.	Gracias.
Please.	S'il vous plaît.	Per favore.	Bitte.	Por favor.
Do you speak English?	Parlez-vous anglais?	Parla inglese?	Sprechen Sie Englisch?	¿Hablas inglés?
Yes./No.	Oui./Non.	Si./No.	Ja./Nein.	Sí./No.
My name is John.	Je m'appelle Jean.	Mi chiamo Giovanni.	Ich heisse Johann.	Me llamo Juan.
What's your name?	Quel est votre nom?	Come si chiama?	Wie heissen Sie?	¿Cómo se llamas?
See you later.	Á bientôt.	A più tardi.	Bis später.	Hasta luego.
Good-bye.	Au revoir.	Arrivederci.	Auf Wiedersehen.	Adiós.
Good luck!	Bonne chance!	Buona fortuna!	Viel Glück!	¡Buena suerte!
Have a good trip!	Bon voyage!	Buon viaggio!	Gute Reise!	¡Buen viaje!
OK.	D'accord.	Va bene.	OK.	De acuerdo.
No problem.	Pas de problème.	Non c'è problema	Kein Problem.	Sin problema.
Everything was great.	C'était super.	Tutto magnifico.	Alles war gut.	Todo estuvo muy bien.
Enjoy your meal!	Bon appétit!	Buon appetito!	Guten Appetit!	¡Qué aproveche!
Delicious!	Délicieux!	Delizioso!	Lecker!	¡Delicioso!
Magnificent!	Magnifique!	Magnifico!	Wunderbar!	¡Magnifico!
Bless you! (after sneeze)	À vos souhaits!	Salute!	Gesundheit!	¡Salud!
You are very kind.	Vous êtes très gentil.	Lei è molto gentile.	Sie sind sehr freundlich.	Eres muy amable.
Cheers!	Santé!	Salute!	Prost!	¡Salud!
I love you.	Je t'aime.	Ti amo.	Ich liebe dich.	Te quiero.

it. Internationalize, *"Dos* pehr-son"—*no comprende. "Dos hombre"*—nope. Digging deep into my bag of international linguistic tricks, I say, *"Dos* Yankees."

"OK!" He understands that I want beds for two Americans. He says, *"Sí,"* and I say, "Very good" or *"Muy bien."*

Now I need to tell him who I am. If I say, "My name is Mr. Steves, and I'll be over promptly," I'll lose him. I say, "My name Ricardo (ree-KAR-do)." In Italy I say, "My name Luigi." Your name really doesn't matter; you're communicating just a password so you can identify yourself when you walk through the door. Say anything to be understood.

He says, "OK."

You repeat slowly, "Hotel, *dos* Yankees, Ricardo, coming *pronto*, OK?"

He says, "OK."

You say, *"Gracias, adiós!"*

Twenty minutes later you walk up to the reception desk, and Pedro greets you with a robust, "Eh, Ricardo!"

EUROPEAN GESTURES

In Europe, while some gestures can help you communicate, others can contribute to the language barrier. For example, if you count with your fingers, in Europe remember to start with your thumb, not your index finger (if you hold up your index finger, you'll probably get two of something).

The "thumbs up" sign popular in the United States is used widely in most of Europe to say "OK" (it also represents the number one when counting). The "V for victory" sign is used in most of Europe as in the United States, but may get you a punch in the nose in parts of Britain, where it's an obscene gesture (if you make the "V" with your palm toward you.)

Some cultures also indicate "yes" and "no" differently: In Turkey, they shake their heads as Americans do, but someone may also signal "no" by tilting their head back. In Bulgaria and Albania, "OK" is indicated by happily shaking your head left and right—as if you were signaling "no" in the US.

Here are a few more common European gestures, their meanings, and where you're likely to see them.

Fingertips Kiss: Gently bring

the fingers and thumb of your right hand together, raise to your lips, kiss lightly, and joyfully toss your fingers and thumb into the air. This gesture is used commonly in Italy, France, Spain, Greece, and Germany as a form of praise. It can mean sexy, delicious, divine, or wonderful. Be careful—tourists look silly when they overemphasize this subtle action.

Very delicious!

Hand Purse: Straighten the fingers and thumb of one hand, bringing them all together and making an upward point about a foot in front of your face. You can hold your hand still or move it a little up and down at the wrist. This is a common and very Italian gesture for a query. It is used to say "What do you want?" or "What are you doing?" or "What is it?" or "What's new?" It can also be used as an insult to say "You fool." The hand purse can also mean "fear" (France), "a lot" (Spain), and "good" (Greece and Turkey).

Hand Shake: "Expensive" is often indicated by shaking your hand and sucking in like you just burned yourself.

Cheek Screw: Make a fist, stick out your index finger, and (without piercing the skin) screw it into your cheek. The cheek screw is used widely and almost exclusively in Italy to mean good, lovely, beautiful, or delicious. Many Italians also use it to mean clever. But be careful: In southern Spain, the cheek screw is used to call a man effeminate.

Eyelid Pull: Place your extended forefinger below the center of your eye and pull the skin downward. In France and Greece this means "I am alert. I'm looking. You can't fool me." In Italy and Spain, it's a friendlier warning, meaning "Be alert, that guy is clever."

Forearm Jerk: Clench your right fist and jerk your forearm up as you slap your right bicep with your left palm. This is a rude phallic gesture that men throughout southern Europe use the way many Americans "give someone the finger." This jumbo version of "flipping the bird" says "I'm superior" (it's an action some monkeys actually do with their penises to insult their peers). This gesture is occasionally used by rude men in Britain and Germany as more of an "I want you" gesture about (but never to) a sexy woman.

Chin Flick: Tilt your head back slightly and flick the back of your fingers forward in an arc from under your chin. In Italy and France, this means "I'm not interested; you bore me," or "You bother me." In southern Italy it can mean "No."

Health & Hygiene

Understandably, two big concerns of American travelers are staying healthy and adjusting to European plumbing. Take comfort: Doctors, hospitals, launderettes, and bathrooms aren't that different in Europe. And dealing with them is actually part of the fun of travel. This chapter provides information on staying healthy while traveling, handling jet lag, and finding medical treatment, along with tips on hygiene—from doing your laundry to mastering European bathrooms.

STAYING HEALTHY

Before You Go

When getting organized before a trip, remember to also get your medical business in order. Your health is critical to your enjoyment of your vacation.

Read up. Visit the Centers for Disease Control and Prevention's travel website (www.cdc.gov/travel) to get advice on preparing for and staying healthy during your travels.

Get a checkup. Just as you'd give your car a good checkup before a long journey, it's smart to meet with your doctor before you depart, particularly if you have any medical concerns. Ask for advice on maintaining your health on the road. Obtain recommended immunizations and discuss proper care for preexisting medical conditions. If you have health concerns, keep a copy of your records accessible, including your latest EKG or X-rays (pack these in your carry-on or store them digitally). If you have a medical device or condition that will affect airport screening, print and pack a notification card from www.tsa.gov, which allows you to discreetly describe your situation to the agent.

It's also a good idea to figure out if your health insurance covers you internationally or whether you might need to buy special medical insurance (see page 73).

Pack your prescriptions. If you take regular prescriptions—or have health problems that could flare up on your trip—bring a letter from your doctor describing the condition and any prescription medications you may need, including the generic names of the drugs. It's best to bring a big enough supply to cover your entire trip, along with a copy of your prescription in case you need more while you're abroad. Bring pharmaceuticals in their original containers (clearly labeled), and pack them in your carry-on bag (don't stow them in checked luggage, which could get lost).

Visit the dentist. Get a dental checkup well before your trip. Emergency dental care during your trip can be expensive, time consuming...and painful. I once had a tooth crowned by a German dentist who knew only one word in English, which he used in question form—"Pain?"

Take extra precautions for exotic locations. No vaccinations are required for travel in Europe. But if you're heading to more exotic destinations, such as Morocco, Russia, or Turkey, ask your doctor about any shots or medicine you might need, or consult a travel-medicine physician. Only these specialists keep entirely up-to-date on health conditions for travelers around the world.

Tell the doctor about every possible destination on your vacation itinerary, confirmed or not. Then you can have the flexibility to take that impulsive swing through Turkey or Morocco knowing that you're prepared medically and have the required shots. Ask about vaccines against hepatitis A (food- or water-borne virus) and hepatitis B (virus transmitted by bodily fluids), antidiarrheal medicines, and any additional precautions.

Countries "require" shots in order to protect their citizens from you and "recommend" shots to protect you from them. If any travel vaccines or medications are recommended, take that advice seriously. The Centers for Disease Control offers updated information on every country.

Conquering Jet Lag

Anyone who flies through multiple time zones will grapple with the biorhythmic confusion known as jet lag. Flying from the US to Europe, you switch your wristwatch six to nine hours forward. Your body says, "Hey, what's going on?" Body clocks don't reset so easily. All your life you've done things on a 24-hour cycle. Now, after crossing the Atlantic, your body wants to eat when you tell it to sleep and sleep when you tell it to enjoy a museum.

Too many people assume their first day will be made worthless by jet lag. Don't prematurely condemn yourself to zombiedom. Most people I've traveled with, of all ages, have enjoyed productive—even hyper—first days. You can't avoid jet lag, but by following these tips you can minimize the symptoms.

Leave home well rested. Flying halfway around the world is stressful. If you leave frazzled after a hectic last night and a wild bon-voyage party, there's a good chance you won't be healthy for the first part of your trip. An early trip cold was a regular part of my vacation until I learned this very important trick: Plan from the start as if you're leaving two days before you really are. Keep that last 48-hour period sacred (apart from your normal work schedule), even if it means being hectic before your false departure date. Then you have two orderly, peaceful days after you've packed so that you are physically ready to fly. Mentally, you'll be comfortable about leaving home and starting an adventure. You'll fly away well rested and 100 percent capable of enjoying the bombardment of your senses that will follow.

Use the flight to rest and reset. In-flight movies are good for one thing—nap time. With a few hours of sleep during the transatlantic flight, you'll be functional the day you land. When the pilot announces the European time, reset your mind along with your wristwatch. Don't prolong jet lag by reminding yourself what time it is back home. Be in Europe.

On arrival, stay awake until an early local bedtime. If you doze off at 4 p.m. and wake up at midnight, you've accomplished nothing. Plan a good walk and stay out until early evening. Jet lag hates fresh air, daylight, and exercise. Your body may beg for sleep, but stand firm: Refuse. Force your body's transition to the local time.

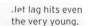
Jet lag hits even the very young.

You'll probably awaken very early on your first morning. Trying to sleep later is normally futile. Get out and enjoy a "pinch me, I'm in Europe" walk, as merchants set up in the marketplace and the town slowly comes to life. This may be the only sunrise you'll see in Europe.

Consider jet-lag cures. The last thing I want to do is promote a pharmaceutical, but I must admit that the sleep aid Ambien (generic name zolpidem) has become my friend in fighting jet lag. Managing a good seven hours of sleep a night in Europe (or after flying home) hastens my transition to local time. That way, I'm not disabled by sleepiness that first afternoon and can stay awake until a decent bedtime. Ambien can have side effects, and if misused, can be habit-forming; consult your doctor, and read and follow the directions carefully.

Other travelers rave about melatonin, a hormone that helps recalibrate your internal clock (available over the counter in the US, but illegal in some European countries).

Bottom Line: The best prescription is to leave home unfrazzled, minimize jet lag's symptoms, adopt European time, and enjoy your trip from the moment you step off the plane.

Staying Healthy While Traveling

Using discretion and common sense, I eat and drink whatever I like when I'm on the road. I've stayed healthy throughout a six-week trip traveling from Europe to India. By following these basic guidelines, I never once suffered from Tehran Tummy or Delhi Belly.

Take precautions on the flight. Long flights are dehydrating. I ask for "two orange juices with no ice" every chance I get. Eat lightly, stay hydrated, and have no coffee or alcohol and only minimal sugar until the flight's almost over.

Some people are susceptible to blood clots in their legs during long flights (factors include obesity, age, genetics, smoking, and use of oral contraceptives or hormone replacement therapy). You can reduce the risk by flexing your ankles and not crossing your legs while seated, taking short walks hourly, and staying hydrated; those at greatest risk can wear compression socks.

Eat nutritiously. The longer your trip, the more you'll be affected by an inadequate diet. Budget travelers often eat more carbohydrates and less protein to stretch their travel dollars. But protein helps you resist infection and rebuilds muscles. Supplemental super-vitamins, taken regularly, help me to at least feel healthy.

Use good judgment when eating out (and outside Europe). Avoid unhealthy-looking restaurants. Meat should be well cooked (unless, of course, you're eating sushi, carpaccio, etc.) and, in some places, avoided altogether. If you're concerned, write the local equivalent of "well done" on a

European Water

I drink European tap water and any water served in restaurants. Read signs carefully, however: Some taps, including those on trains and airplanes, are not for drinking. If there's any hint of nonpotability—a decal showing a glass with a red "X" over it, or a skull and crossbones—don't drink it. Many fountains in German-speaking countries are for drinking, but others are just for show. Look for *Trinkwasser* ("drinking water") or *Kein Trinkwasser* ("not drinking water").

The water at many European public fountains is safe to drink...unless your travel partner has dirty hands.

The water (or, just as likely, the general stress of travel on your immune system) may, sooner or later, make you sick. It's not necessarily dirty. The bacteria in European water are different from those in American water. We are capable of handling American bacteria with no problem at all, but some people can go to London and get sick. Some French people visit Boston and get sick. Some Americans travel around the world eating and drinking everything in sight and don't get sick, while others spend weeks on the toilet. It all depends on the person.

East of Bulgaria and south of the Mediterranean, do not drink untreated water. Water can be sanitized by boiling it for 10 minutes or by using purifying tablets or a filter. Bottled water, beer, wine, boiled coffee and tea, and bottled soft drinks are safe as long as you skip the ice cubes. Coca-Cola products are as safe in Egypt as they are at home.

piece of paper and use it when ordering. Preprepared foods gather germs (a common cause of diarrhea). Outside of Europe, be especially cautious. When in serious doubt, eat only thick-skinned fruit...peeled.

Keep clean. Wash your hands often, keep your nails clean, and avoid touching your eyes, nose, and mouth. Carrying hand sanitizers, such as Purell, can be helpful. However, since they target bacteria, not viruses, they should be used as an adjunct to, rather than a replacement for, hand washing with soap and warm water.

Practice safe sex. While sexually transmitted diseases are not as widespread in Europe as they are in the US, they are still common. Take precautions. Condoms are readily available at pharmacies and from restroom vending machines.

Be active. Physically, travel is great living—healthy food, lots of activity, fresh air, and all those stairs! If you're a couch potato, try to get in shape before your trip by taking long walks. People who regularly work out have plenty of options for keeping in shape while traveling. Biking is a great way to get intimate with a destination while you burn some calories. Though running is not as common in Europe as it is in the US, it's not considered weird, either. Traveling runners can enjoy Europe from a special perspective—at dawn. Swimmers will find that Europe has plenty of good, inexpensive public swimming pools.

Whatever your racket, you'll find ways to keep in practice as you travel if you really want to. Most big-city private tennis and swim clubs welcome foreign guests for a small fee, which is a good way to make friends as well as stay fit.

Get enough sleep. Know how much sleep you need to stay healthy (generally 7-8 hours per night). If I go more than two nights with fewer than six hours' sleep, I make it a priority to catch up—no matter how busy I am. Otherwise, I'm virtually guaranteed to get the sniffles.

Give yourself a break. Europe can do to certain travelers what southern France did to Vincent van Gogh. Romantics can get the sensory bends, patriots can get their flags burned, and anyone can suffer from culture shock. Europe is not particularly impressed by America or Americans, and it will challenge givens that you always assumed were above the test of reason.

On a longer trip, it can be refreshing to take a break from Europe every so often. Enjoy a long, dark, air-conditioned trip back to California in a movie theater. Visit an American embassy reading room where you can surround yourself with eagles, photos of presidents, *Time* magazines, and other Yankees. Loiter in the lobby of a world-class hotel, where the local culture is lost under a big-business bucket of intercontinental whitewash. Or simply stop at a Starbucks. A taste of home can do wonders to refresh the struggling traveler's spirit.

Women's Health Issues

For advice on women's health, I turned to Rick Steves' Europe researcher Risa Laib, who wrote the following section based on her experiences traveling solo (and pregnant) through Europe.

Feminine Products: You can find whatever medications you need in Europe, but you already know what works for you in the US. It's easiest to B.Y.O. pills, whether for cramps, yeast infections, or birth control. Some health-insurance companies issue only a month's supply of birth control pills at a time; ask for a larger supply for a longer trip. Tampons and pads are sold—for more than the US price—at

supermarkets, pharmacies, and convenience stores everywhere in Europe. But you may not see the range of brands
and sizes typical in American supermarkets, so if you prefer
a particular type, it's simpler and cheaper to bring what
you'll need from home.

Yeast and Urinary Tract Infections (UTIs): Your blad-
der can react to a sudden change in diet, especially increases
in alcohol, coffee, or juice. If you experience UTI symptoms,
drink plenty of water and use a general pain reliever. If symptoms persist, a pharmacist in Europe should be able to help.

Women prone to yeast infections should bring their own
over-the-counter medicine (or know the name and its key
ingredient to show a pharmacist in Europe). Some women get
a prescription for fluconazole (Diflucan), a powerful pill that
cures yeast infections more quickly and tidily than creams
and suppositories. If you get a yeast infection in Europe and
need medication, go to a pharmacy. If you encounter the
rare pharmacist who doesn't speak English, find an English-
speaking local woman to write out "yeast infection" for you
in the country's language to avoid an embarrassing charade.

Traveling when Pregnant: Some couples want to time
conception to occur in Europe so they can name their child
Paris, Siena, or wherever. (Be thoughtful about this, or little
Zagreb may harbor a lifelong grudge against you.) Consider
bringing a pregnancy test from home.

Generally, health care providers consider it safe for
women with healthy pregnancies to fly up until 36 weeks.
Check with your doctor and confirm the airline's policies
before booking your ticket.

Traveling in the first trimester can be rough for some
women: Morning sickness can make bus or boat rides especially unpleasant, and climbing all those stone stairs can be
exhausting. Packing light is more essential than ever. You
might find it easier to travel in the second trimester, between
weeks 14 and 28, when your body's used to being pregnant,
you're not yet too big to be uncomfortable, and you face the
lowest risks of miscarriage and preterm labor.

Wear comfortable shoes that have arch supports. If you'll
be traveling a long time, bring loose clothing (with elastic
waistbands) to accommodate your changing body. Keep your
valuables (cash, passport, etc.) in a neck pouch rather than a
constricting money belt.

Pace yourself and allow plenty of time for rest. If problems pop up, go to a clinic or hospital (for more, see "Medical
Care in Europe," later). If you'll need certain tests done (such

as an amniocentesis), find out in advance when you'll need to be home.

Seek out nutritious food (though some of it may make you nauseated, of course). Picnics are often healthier than restaurant meals. Pack baggies for carrying snacks. Bring prenatal vitamins and any other supplements you need from home.

It's actually pleasant to be pregnant in Europe. People are particularly kind. And when your child is old enough to understand, she'll enjoy knowing she's already been to Europe—especially if you promise to take her again.

Basic First Aid

It's tempting to go, go, go while you're in Europe—but if you're not careful you might push yourself to the point of getting sick. Be proactive to stay well. If you do get sick, take action to regain your health. For a list of first-aid items to pack from home, see page 91.

Headaches and Other Aches: Try requesting "paracetamol" to get acetaminophen (Tylenol) when you need to soothe headaches, sore feet, bruises, Italian traffic, and other minor problems.

Fever: A high fever merits medical attention, particularly for children. A normal temperature of 98.6° Fahrenheit equals 37° Celsius. If your thermometer reads 40°C, you're boiling at 104°F. You can use acetaminophen to bring down a fever, along with putting cold washcloths on your forehead for relief.

Colds: If you're feeling run-down, check into a good hotel, sleep well, and force fluids. (My trick during the hectic scramble of TV production is to suck on tablets of vitamin C and zinc.) Stock each place you stay with boxes of juice upon arrival. Pseudoephedrine (Sudafed) and other cold capsules are usually available, but may not come in as many varieties as you're used to at home.

Abrasions: Clean abrasions thoroughly with soap to prevent or control infection, and cover with a clean bandage. First-aid supplies are readily available at pharmacies throughout Europe.

Blisters: Moleskin, bandages, tape, or double-layer socks can prevent or retard problems with your feet. Cover any irritated area before it blisters. Many walkers swear by Body Glide Foot Anti-Blister Balm or Band-Aid Friction Block Stick (solid anti-chafing sticks sold in running shops and sporting-goods stores). Avoid problems by breaking in your shoes in advance and wearing good socks.

Fahrenheit and Celsius Conversion

For Weather   For Health

Europe takes its temperature using the Celsius scale, while we opt for Fahrenheit. For a rough conversion from Celsius to Fahrenheit, double the number and add 30. For weather, remember that 28°C is 82°F–perfect. For health, 37°C is just right.

Sprains: All those cobblestones can be tough on the ankles. If you get a sprain, try to cut back on activities that could aggravate the injury. The best advice is to ice and elevate any sprain periodically for 48 hours. A package of frozen veggies works as a cheap ice pack. If your foot or leg is swollen, soak it in cold water in a bathtub or swimming pool. When sitting around isn't an option, use an Ace bandage or air cast to immobilize, reduce swelling, and provide support. If you can't walk, consider renting a set of crutches or a wheelchair: Ask your hotel's concierge for help. Take regular doses of an anti-inflammatory drug like ibuprofen (Advil, Motrin).

Motion Sickness: To be effective, medication for motion sickness—such as dimenhydrinate (Dramamine) or cyclizine

(Marezine)—should be taken one hour before you think you'll need it. These medications can also serve as a mild sleep aid. Meclizine (Bonine) also treats motion sickness but causes less drowsiness.

Allergies: Even those immune to pollen or cat dander at home might come down with allergies when exposed to unfamiliar flora and fauna. You might not find Claritin in Europe, but you can get the generic equivalent, loratadine. For an antihistamine like Benadryl, request diphenhydramine.

Diarrhea: Get used to the fact that you might have diarrhea for a day. If you get the runs, take it in stride. It's simply not worth taking eight Pepto-Bismol tablets a day or brushing your teeth in Coca-Cola all summer long to avoid a day of the trots. I take my health seriously and, for me, traveling in India or Mexico is a bigger health concern. But I find Europe no more threatening to my stomach than the US.

I've routinely taken groups of 24 Americans through Turkey for two weeks. With adequate discretion, we eat everything in sight. At the end of the trip, my loose-stool survey typically shows that five or six travelers coped with a day of the Big D and one person was stuck with an extended weeklong bout.

To help avoid getting diarrhea, eat yogurt, which has enzymes that can ease your system into the country's cuisine.

If you get diarrhea, it will run its course. Revise your diet, don't panic, and take it easy for 24 hours. Make your diet as bland and boring as possible for a day or so (bread, rice, boiled potatoes, bananas, clear soup, toast, weak tea). Keep telling yourself that tomorrow you'll feel much better. You likely will. But if loose stools persist, drink lots of water to replenish lost liquids and minerals.

Don't take antidiarrheal medications if you have blood in your stools or a fever greater than 101°F (38°C)—you need a doctor's exam and antibiotics. A child (especially an infant) who suffers a prolonged case of diarrhea also needs prompt medical attention.

I visited the Red Cross in Athens after a miserable three-week tour of the toilets of Syria, Jordan, and Israel. My intestinal commotion was finally stilled by a recommended strict diet of boiled rice and plain tea. As a matter of fact, after five days on that dull diet, I was constipated.

Constipation: With all the bread you'll be eating, constipation, the other side of the intestinal pendulum, is (according to my surveys) as prevalent as diarrhea. Get exercise, drink water, and eat food with lots of fiber (raw fruits, leafy vegetables, prunes, or bran tablets from home). If that fails,

Good news for your health: Europe has become enthusiastic about not smoking. These days most countries prohibit smoking in enclosed public spaces. Cigarette packages make it really clear: "Smoking kills"; and Berlin's subway—like much of Europe—is now smoke-free.

try laxatives or stool softeners, and everything will come out all right in the end.

Medical Care in Europe

If you're worried about getting sick while traveling, rest assured: Most of Europe offers high-quality medical care that's as competent as what you'll find at home. The majority of Europe's doctors and pharmacists speak at least some English, so communication generally isn't an issue.

Emergencies

If an accident or life-threatening medical problem occurs on the road, get to a hospital. For serious conditions (stroke, heart attack, bad car accident), summon an ambulance. In most countries, you can call 112, the European Union's universal emergency number for ambulance, fire department, or police. Most countries also have a 911 equivalent that works as well. Or you can ask your hotelier, restaurant host, or whoever's around to call an ambulance (or a taxi for less dire situations).

Be aware that you will likely have to pay out of pocket for any medical treatment, even if your insurance company provides international health care coverage. A visit to the emergency room can be free or cost only a nominal fee, or it can be expensive, depending on where you are and what treatment you need. Make sure you get a copy of your bill so that when you return home, you can file a claim to be reimbursed. If you purchased travel insurance to serve as your primary medical coverage, call the company as soon as possible to report the injury. They can usually work directly with the hospital to get your bills paid (for information on travel insurance, see page 70).

Minor Ailments

If you get sick on your trip, don't wait it out. Find help to get on the road to recovery as soon as possible. Here are your options if you have a non-emergency situation:

Pharmacies: Throughout Europe, people with a health problem go first to the pharmacy, not to their doctor. European pharmacists can diagnose and prescribe remedies for many simple problems, such as sore throats, fevers, stomach issues, sinus problems, insomnia, blisters, rashes, urinary tract infections, or muscle, joint, and back pain. Most cities have at least a few 24-hour pharmacies.

When it comes to medication, expect some differences between the way things are done in Europe and at home. Certain drugs that you need a prescription for in the US are available over the counter in Europe. Some drugs go by different names. And some European medications can be stronger than their counterparts in the US, so follow directions and dosages carefully. Also, topical remedies are common in Europe; if you're suffering from body aches and pains, or any swelling, don't be surprised if a pharmacist prescribes a cream to apply to the problem area. If you need to fill a prescription—even one from home—a pharmacy can generally take care of it promptly. If a pharmacist can't help you, he or she will send you to a doctor or a health clinic.

Clinics: A trip to a foreign clinic is actually an interesting travel experience. Every few years I end up in a European clinic for one reason or another, and every time I'm impressed by its efficiency and effectiveness.

A clinic is useful if you need to be checked for a non-emergency medical issue, get some tests done, or if your problem is beyond a pharmacist's scope. Clinics in Europe operate just like those in the US: You'll sign in with the receptionist, answer a few questions, then take a seat and wait for a nurse or doctor.

A trip to a clinic may be free or cost a small fee. Expect to pay this fee up front, whether you're covered through your health insurance company or a special travel policy. Make sure you get a copy of the bill so you can file a claim when you return home.

Regardless of the local word for "pharmacy" (*farmacia* in Spanish), you can always look for the green cross.

House Calls: If you're holed up sick in your hotel room and would rather not go out, the hotel receptionist may be able to call a doctor who will come to your room and check you out. This option is generally more expensive than dragging yourself to a pharmacy or clinic.

Finding Medical Help

To locate a doctor, clinic, or hospital, ask around at places that are accustomed to dealing with Americans on the road—such as tourist offices and large hotels. Most embassies and consulates maintain lists of physicians and hospitals in major cities (go to www.usembassy.gov, select your location, and look under the US Citizens Services section of that embassy's website for medical services information).

If you're concerned about getting an English-speaking and Western-trained doctor, consider joining IAMAT, the International Association for Medical Assistance to Travelers. You'll get a list of English-speaking doctors in more than 90 member countries who charge affordable, standardized fees for medical visits (membership is free but donations are requested, fee pricing on website, pay provider directly at time of visit, www.iamat.org, tel. 716/754-4883).

LAUNDRY

I met a traveler in Italy who wore her T-shirt frontward, backward, inside-out frontward, and inside-out backward, all to delay the laundry day. A guy in Germany showed me his take-it-into-the-tub-with-you-and-make-waves method of washing his troublesome jeans. But you don't need to go to these extremes to have something presentable to wear. Do laundry in your hotel room, find a launderette, or splurge on full-service laundry.

Washing Clothes in Your Room

One of my domestic chores while on the road is washing my laundry in the hotel-room sink. I keep it very simple, using hotel laundry bags to store my dirty stuff, washing my clothes with hotel shampoo, and improvising places to hang things. But you can pack a self-service laundry kit: a plastic or mesh bag with a drawstring for dirty clothes, concentrated liquid detergent (either in individual travel packs or a small, sturdy squeeze bottle wrapped in a sealable baggie to contain leakage), individual spot-remover wipes, and a stretchable "travel clothesline" (a double-stranded cord that's twisted, so clothespins are unnecessary).

To make things easier, I bring a quick-dry travel wardrobe that either looks OK wrinkled or doesn't wrinkle. (I test-wash my shirts in the sink at home before I let them come to Europe with me. Some shirts dry fine; others prune up.)

Most European hotels prefer that you not do laundry in your room. Some bathrooms even have a multilingual "no washing clothes in the room" sign (which, after "eat your peas," may be the most ignored rule on earth). Interpret hoteliers' reticence as "I have lots of good furniture and fine floors in this room, and I don't want your drippy laundry ruining things." As long as you wash carefully and are respectful of the room, go right ahead.

Sometimes a hotel will remove the sink and tub stoppers to discourage washing. Bring a universal drain stopper from home, try using a wadded-up sock or a pill-bottle lid, or line the sink with a plastic bag and wash in it. Some travelers create their own washing machine with a large, two-gallon sealable baggie: soak in suds for an hour, agitate, drain, rinse.

Wring wet laundry as dry as possible to minimize dripping. Other than a clogged toilet, there's little a hotelier likes seeing less than a pool of water on their hardwood floors. Rolling laundry in a towel and twisting or stomping on it works well (if you have an extra towel—remember that many accommodations don't provide new towels every day).

Account for drying time: Cotton needs much longer to dry than the lightweight performance fabrics often used in travel clothing. Hang clothes in a low-profile, non-destructive way. Suspend them over the bathtub or in a closet. The maid hardly notices my laundry. It's hanging quietly in the bathroom or shuffled among my dry clothes in the closet. Separate the back and front of hanging clothes to speed drying. Some travelers pack inflatable hangers. Don't hang your clothes out the window or on the balcony—hoteliers find it unsightly, and you might find it has blown away when you return from dinner. Laid-back hotels will let your laundry join theirs on the lines out back or on the rooftop.

Smooth out your wet clothes, button shirts, set collars, and "hand iron" to encourage wrinkle-free

Whistler's laundry

drying. If your shirt or dress dries wrinkled, hang it in a steamy bathroom or borrow an iron and ironing board from the hotel (nearly all have loaners). A piece of tape is a good ad hoc lint-brush. In very hot climates, I wash my shirt several times a day, wring it, and put it on damp. It's clean and refreshing, and (sadly) in 15 minutes it's dry.

Using a Launderette

Go ahead and ask! There's a good chance you can share the clothesline in the B&B's backyard or on the hotel's roof.

For a thorough washing, ask your hotel to direct you to the nearest launderette. In Western Europe, nearly every neighborhood has one; in Eastern Europe, launderettes are much less common. It takes about an hour and $10-15 to wash and dry an average-size load. (Some short-term rentals have laundry facilities, and many hostels have coin-op washers and dryers or heated drying rooms.)

Better launderettes have coin-op soap dispensers, change machines, English instructions, and helpful attendants. Others are completely automated—but many of these have pictogram instructions that usually aren't too hard to parse. Look around for a sign listing the "last wash" time, and stick to it. When it's closing time, an attendant might come by to evict you, or the machines may simply stop operating.

While the exact procedure varies, it usually includes the same steps as you'd encounter at a launderette at home. If you're planning on visiting a launderette, you could pack one or two small detergent boxes, although you can typically buy some there at a dispenser. The soap compartments on most washers have three reservoirs: for prewash, the main wash cycle (normally at the top of the washer), and fabric softener. (Don't put your main soap into the prewash compartment, or it'll be washed away before its time.)

Many of Europe's launderettes are completely unstaffed—it's just you, sparse English instructions, and dirty clothes.

While you might be able to pay at the washer itself, more likely you'll have to insert your money at a central unit. Note the number of your machine, then type that number into the central unit and put in your coins (use exact change if possible—some machines don't give change). Sometimes a central unit dispenses tokens, which you then insert in the machine.

Select your cycle, either at the machine or at the central unit. Below I've listed some of the cycles you're likely to see. The first number is the temperature in Celsius for the first cycle (prewash), the second is the temperature for the second cycle (main wash), and the third is how long the whole process takes.

45° / 90° / 55 m	whites (very hot)
45° / 60° / 50 m	colors (hot)
45° / 45° / 40 m	permanent press (warm)
— / 30° / 30 m	nylon (lukewarm)
— / 20° / 25 m	delicates (cold)

Some washing machines have a built-in spin cycle, while others leave clothes totally soaked. In this case, you'll need to put your wet clothes in a special spin-dry machine (usually called a "centrifuge" or something similar) to wring out excess water before moving them to the dryer.

Some European clothes dryers are not vented to the outside, but instead collect the water from the clothes in an interior reservoir. The dryer will stop and an icon will light up when this reservoir is full and needs to be emptied. Ask an attendant if you can't figure out how.

Drying time is generally available in smaller units (5- or 10-minute increments) rather than as a full cycle. Most machines let you choose the drying temperature: low

Sample Laundry Instructions

This laundry machine hurdles the language barrier with pictographic instructions: Insert your laundry, close the door, select the program, add the soap, and insert coins to start. The buttons on the right let you select from five washing options: The first water temperature (in Celsius) is for the prewash cycle, and the second is for the wash cycle. The pictures tell you where to put the soap and softener for each selection (the last two skip the prewash—no soap needed in compartment A).

(cool and slow); medium (warmer but still slow); and high (speedy but shrinky). Because both washers and dryers at launderettes can be unpredictable, hand wash anything that you value dearly.

While waiting for your clothes, use the time to picnic, catch up on postcards and your journal, or chat with other customers. Launderettes throughout the world seem to give people the gift of gab. Many launderettes have Wi-Fi. If you ask attendants sweetly, they might be willing to transfer your clothes to the dryer, allowing you to slip out for some bonus sightseeing. (In these cases, it's appropriate to thank them by offering a small tip.)

Hiring It Out

Some launderettes offer full service, which means they'll wash, fold, and sometimes even iron your laundry. Just drop it off and come back later in the day. This service is more expensive than doing it yourself—you'll generally be charged by the kilo or by the item—but can save lots of time. Also pricey, but handiest of all: You can pay your hotel to do your laundry.

Regardless of the cost, every time I slip into a fresh pair of pants, I figure it was worth the hassle and expense.

EUROPEAN BATHROOMS

European bathrooms can be quirky by American standards. Your hotel's WC may come with luxurious heated towel racks—or a rattling fan, leaky sink, and shoebox-sized shower. My advice is to keep an open mind, wash up quickly, and get out and about in the place you came to enjoy. And remember that nothing beats a good bathroom story when you get home.

Your Hotel Bathroom

First, don't expect big spaces. Europe's hotel owners have carved out chunks of elegant bedrooms to shoehorn in pre-fab private bathrooms—and they can be very tight. Counter space is often limited, and showers can be surprisingly small, especially if you're a larger person. Be careful bending over to pick up a dropped bar of soap—you might just hit your head on the toilet or sink.

In some bathrooms, you may see a mysterious porcelain thing that looks like an oversized bedpan. That's a bidet. Tourists who aren't in the know use them as anything from

a launderette to a vomitorium to a watermelon-rind recep-
tacle to a urinal. Locals use them in lieu of a shower to clean
the parts of the body that rub together when they walk. Go
ahead and give it a try. Just remember the four S's—straddle,
squat, soap up, and swish off.

When traveling in Europe, you may need to lower your
washcloth and towel expectations. Most European hotels
don't supply washcloths. If a washcloth is part of your bath
ritual, bring a quick-drying one with you.

And, like breakfast and people, towels get smaller as you
go south. In simple places, bath towels are not replaced every
day, so hang them up to dry and reuse. This is also becoming
common practice at bigger hotels—even fancy ones—in an
effort to be eco-friendly. You may see a sign explaining that
they'll replace towels left on the floor, but not those that are
hanging to dry. In my experience, pricey hotels rarely stay
true to this promise; your towels will probably be replaced
no matter where you leave them. On the other end of the
spectrum, dorm-style accommodations don't provide towels
or soap at all, so bring your own quick-drying travel towel if
you plan on staying in hostels.

Shower Strategies

Americans are notorious (and embarrassing) energy glut-
tons—wasting hot water and leaving lights on as if electricity
were cheap. Who besides us sings in the shower? European
energy costs are shocking, so many accommodations try to
conserve where they can.

Hot-Water Hiccups: Most of the cold showers Americans take in Europe are cold only because they don't know
how to turn on the hot water. You'll find showers and baths
of all kinds. The red knob is hot and the blue one is cold—or
vice versa. Unusual showers often have clear instructions
posted. Study the system, and before you shiver, ask the
receptionist for help.

There are some very peculiar
tricks. For instance, in Italy and
Spain, "C" is for *caldo/caliente*—hot.
In Croatia, look for the switch with
an icon of a hot-water tank (usually
next to the room's light switch). The
British "dial-a-shower" features an
electronic box under the showerhead—turn the dial to select how hot
you want the water and to turn on

European
showers: Each
has its own
personality.

or shut off the flow of water (this is sometimes done with a separate dial or button). If you can't find the switch to turn on the shower, it may be just outside the bathroom.

No matter where you are in Europe, get used to taking shorter showers. Some places, especially modest accommodations, furnish their bathrooms with little-bitty water heaters that are much smaller than the one in your basement. After five minutes, you may find your hot shower turning very cold.

Handheld Showerheads: In Europe, handheld showers are common. Sometimes the showerhead is sitting loose in a caddy; other times it's mounted low on the tub. Not only do you have to master the art of lathering up with one hand while holding the showerhead in the other, but you also have to keep it aimed at your body or the wall to avoid spraying water all over the bathroom. To avoid flooding the room, you may find it easier to just sit in the tub for your shower.

Strange Drains: Speaking of flooding, in some hotels, the line between shower and bathroom is nonexistent. There may not be a shower curtain or even a shower pan to contain the water. Instead, the water simply slides into a drain in the middle of the bathroom floor.

Coin-op Showers: A few hostels and budget hotels have coin-operated showers. If you run into one of these, it's a good idea to have an extra token handy to avoid that lathered look. A "navy shower," using the water only to soap up and rinse off, is a wonderfully conservative method, and those who follow you will more likely enjoy some warm *Wasser* (although starting and stopping the water doesn't start and stop the meter).

Emergency Cords: The cord that dangles over the tub or shower in some hotels is not a clothesline; only pull it if you've fallen and can't get up. (But if the cord hangs *outside* the tub or shower, it probably controls the light—good luck with this.)

Shared Showers: The cheapest rooms sometimes feature a shared toilet and shower "down the hall." To bathoholics, this sounds terrible. But you're unlikely to find a long line for the loo: Many budget hotels have modernized by adding private bathrooms to some of their rooms, leaving fewer guests to share the remaining communal

Throughout southern Europe, even the cheapest hotel rooms come with a bidet. Europeans use them to stay clean without a daily shower.

bathrooms. You may even end up with what amounts to a private bath—down the hall.

Finding Places to Shower: If you are vagabonding or spending several nights in transit, you can buy a shower in "day hotels" at major train stations and airports, at many freeway rest stops, and in public baths or swimming pools. Most Mediterranean beaches have free, freshwater showers all the time. I have a theory that after four days without a shower, you don't get any worse, but that's another book.

Toilet Trauma

Every traveler has one or two great toilet stories. Foreign toilets can be traumatic, but they are one of those little things that can make travel so much more interesting than staying at home. If you plan to venture away from the international-style hotels in your Mediterranean travels and become a temporary resident, "going local" may take on a very real meaning.

Flummoxing Flushers: In Europe, you may or may not encounter a familiar flushing mechanism. In older bathrooms, toilets may come with a pull string instead of a handle (generally with the tank affixed to the wall rather than the toilet itself). In modern bathrooms, you may see two buttons on top of the tank—one performs a regular flush, the other (for lighter jobs) conserves water. In Great Britain, you'll likely come across the "pump toilet," with a flushing handle that doesn't kick in unless you push it just right: too hard or too soft, and it won't go. (Be decisive but not ruthless.)

Toilet Paper: Like a spoon or a fork, this is another

LEFT This high-tech public toilet offers a free, private place to do your business.

RIGHT Going local

Western "essential" that many people on our planet do not use. What they use varies. I won't get too graphic, but remember that a billion civilized people on this planet never eat with their left hand. While Europeans do use toilet paper, WCs may not always be well stocked. If you're averse to the occasional drip-dry, carry pocket-size tissue packs (easy to buy in Europe) for WCs sans TP. Some countries, such as Greece and Turkey, have very frail plumbing. If you see a wastebasket near the toilet with used toilet paper in it, that's a sign that the sewer system isn't up to snuff. Put your used TP in the wastebasket instead of flushing it. (The rule of thumb in those places: Don't put anything in the toilet unless you've eaten it first.)

Paid Toilets: Paying to use a public WC is a European custom that irks some Americans. But isn't it worth a few coins, considering the cost of water, maintenance, and cleanliness? And you're probably in no state to argue, anyway. Coin-operated toilets are the norm at highway rest areas, train stations, and even at some sights. (Many coin-op WCs have self-cleaning toilet seats; stick around after you're done to watch the show.)

Sometimes the toilet itself is free, but an attendant in the corner sells sheets of toilet paper. Most common is the tip dish by the entry—the local equivalent of about 50 cents is plenty. Caution: Many attendants leave only bills and too-big coins in the tray to bewilder the full-bladdered tourist. The keepers of Europe's public toilets have earned a reputation for crabbiness. You'd be crabby, too, if you lived under the street in a room full of public toilets. Humor them, understand them, and carry some change so you can leave them a coin or two.

Women in the Men's Room: The female attendants who seem to inhabit Europe's WCs are a popular topic of conversation among Yankee males. Sooner or later you'll be minding your own business at the urinal, and the lady will bring you your change or sweep under your feet. Yes, it is distracting, but you'll just have to get used to it—she has.

One of Europe's many unforgettable experiences is the rare squat-and-aim toilet.

Gender-Neutral Bathrooms: Some European bathrooms have shared hand-washing facilities for women and men, with adjacent but separate toilet areas. And some restrooms make no distinctions for gender at all.

Squat Toilets: The vast majority of European toilets are similar to our own. But in a few out-of-the-way places, you might find a toilet that consists simply of porcelain footprints and a squat-and-aim hole. If faced with a squat toilet, remember: Those of us who need a throne to sit on are in the minority. Throughout the world, most humans sit on their haunches and nothing more. Sometimes called "Turkish toilets," these are more commonly found in, well, Turkey.

Getting comfortable in foreign restrooms takes a little adjusting, but that's travel. When in Rome, do as the Romans do—and before you know it, you'll be Euro-peein'.

Finding a Public Restroom

I once dropped a tour group off in a town for a potty stop, and when I picked them up 20 minutes later, none had found relief. Locating a decent public toilet can be frustrating. But with a few tips, you can sniff out a biffy in a jiffy.

Coin-op Toilets on the Street: Some large cities, such as Paris, London, and Amsterdam, are dotted with coin-operated, phone booth-like WCs on street corners. Insert a coin, the door opens, and you have 15 minutes of toilet use accompanied by Sinatra Muzak. When you leave, the entire chamber disinfects itself.

Some cities have free, low-tech public urinals (called pissoirs) that offer just enough privacy for men to find relief... sometimes with a view. Munich had outdoor urinals until the 1972 Olympics and then decided to beautify the city by doing away with them. What about the people's needs? There's a law in Munich: Any place serving beer must admit the public (whether they're customers or not) to use the toilets.

Restaurants: Any place that serves food or drinks has a restroom. No restaurateur would label his WC so those on the street can see, but you can walk into nearly any restaurant or café, politely and confidently, and find a bathroom. Assume it's somewhere in the back, either upstairs or downstairs. It's easiest in large places that have outdoor seating—waiters will think you're a customer just making a quick trip inside. Some call it rude; I call it survival. If you feel like it, ask permission. Just smile, "Toilet?" I'm rarely turned down. American-type fast-food places are very common and usually have a decent and fairly accessible "public" restroom. Timid people buy a drink they don't want in order to use the bathroom, but that's generally unnecessary (although sometimes the secret bathroom door code is printed only on your receipt).

Even at American chains, be prepared for bathroom

culture shock. At a big Starbucks in Bern, Switzerland, I opened the door to find an extremely blue space. It took me a minute to realize that the blue lights made it impossible for junkies to find their veins.

Public Buildings: When nature beckons and there's no restaurant or bar handy, look in train stations, government buildings, libraries, large bookstores, and upper floors of department stores. Parks often have restrooms, sometimes of the gag-a-maggot variety. Never leave a museum without taking advantage of its restrooms—they're free, clean, and decorated with artistic graffiti. Sometimes you can access a museum's restrooms from the entry hall, without paying to go inside. Large, classy, old hotel lobbies are as impressive as many palaces you'll pay to see. You can always find a royal retreat here, and plenty of soft TP.

Photography & Sharing Your Trip

If my hotel was on fire and I could grab just one thing as I escaped, it would be my camera with its memory card filled with photos. Photographs aren't just treasured mementos that spark memories of your journey. They're also the best way to tell others about the places you've been and what you've experienced, whether you share your pictures and thoughts on the fly via social media, or collect them in scrapbooks.

TRAVEL PHOTOGRAPHY

What to Bring

These days, smartphones with high-quality built-in cameras are the handiest way for travelers to take photos—and share them immediately. Many people travel with only a phone or tablet to document their trip and are perfectly happy with the results. But I prefer a dedicated camera that takes higher-quality photos that I can enlarge and print.

Smaller point-and-shoot cameras are as compact as a smartphone but offer more settings and take better photos. Serious photographers prefer digital SLR cameras, which are bulkier but produce more professional-looking images. In between are mirrorless cameras, which offer better image quality than point-and-shoots, but aren't as large as DSLRs. When deciding what to bring, weigh your preference for portability against your desire for better image quality.

Some people prefer to capture Europe in motion. While your smartphone can shoot video, quality is much improved with a pocket-sized video camera, such as GoPro's popular "point-of-view" video cameras. Many GoPro models fit in your front pocket, and accessories make it easy to attach the camera to tripods, handlebars, helmets—you name it. Stick one to your bike helmet in Amsterdam, capture the Bavarian countryside as you glide down a hill on a luge, or create a stunning panorama video at the top of Florence's Duomo.

Besides a camera, consider bringing the following accessories. But be careful not to take so much gear that you become a slave to your gadgets.

Memory: Travel with enough digital memory to cover your entire trip. Memory is so cheap now, I'd spring for one of the bigger cards, but buy them at home; they're readily available in Europe but more expensive. You'll need higher-capacity cards if you plan to record lots of video. For more tips on saving and backing up images—especially on a long trip—see "Managing Images on the Road," later.

You can take remarkably clear low-light shots—like this serene twilight image of Moscow's Red Square—with the help of a mini-tripod.

Batteries and Chargers: Make sure to bring what you need so your camera has enough juice for the entire trip, whether it's an additional battery, a battery charger, or a charging cable. Check that the charger will work in Europe (look for the voltage numbers "110V" and "220V"), and bring a plug adapter (for details, see page 95). Be aware that you cannot pack loose lithium batteries in your checked luggage—but you can carry spare rechargeable batteries in your carry-on as long as they're sealed inside a plastic zip-lock bag or in their original packaging.

Mini-tripod: Because the flash on most cameras gives a harsh image, it's best to use existing light—which often requires a tripod. A conventional tripod is too large to lug around Europe. A mini-tripod screws into most cameras, sprouts three legs, and holds everything perfectly still for slow shutter speeds, timed exposures, and automatic shutter-release shots; some are flexible enough to wrap around posts. If you're planning to use a mini-tripod, master your delayed shutter release button.

SLR Lenses and Filters: No-frills photographers will stick with the midrange lens that comes with the camera; serious shutterbugs can look into zoom, wide-angle, or image stabilization lenses. If you invest in a zoom lens, get one that covers both ends of the visual range—close-ups to long shots. A 24-105 mm lens gives you a great medium-wide angle with adequate zoom for most shots. Make sure all your lenses have a haze or UV filter. I use a polarizer filter, which eliminates reflections, enhances color separation, and protects your lens. Don't use more than one filter at a time, and don't go cheap. Some photographers suggest using a lens shade in daylight; it keeps stray light off the front of the camera to prevent "lens flare" and enhances color saturation in your images.

Tissue, Cleaner, and Lens Cap: A lens-cleaning tissue and a small bottle of cleaning solution are wise additions. If you have an SLR, protect your lens with a cap that dangles on its string when you're shooting.

Camera Case: Stow your camera in a small, padded case inside your day bag. If you have a DSLR or extra accessories, you may need a dedicated bag. A functional and economical way to tote your gear is in a small nylon stuff bag (the type made for hikers). I steer clear of formal camera bags, which are bulky and attract thieves.

What Not to Bring: The latest unnecessary tacky tourist staple—the selfie stick—is banned in many European sights, including the Van Gogh Museum in Amsterdam, the Sistine Chapel, Notre Dame Cathedral, and the palace at Versailles. A selfie stick marks you (whether you are or not) as one of a rising flood of mindless "bucket list" travelers who photograph themselves in front of famous sights like dogs pee on fire hydrants. I don't like them.

Managing Images on the Road

Even if you have plenty of space on your camera's memory card, it's always wise to back up your images. One year, I took some of the best photos I can remember at Chartres Cathedral in France, when the setting sun brought life to the expressions on the delicately carved faces of the Gothic statues. Afterward, I celebrated with a *salade de gésiers* of bouncy lettuce and chicken innards, washed down with a life-is-good carafe of red house wine. Back at my hotel, as

Resources for Photography and Trip Sharing

Cnet.com, Steves-Digicams.com, DPReview.com: Camera reviews
PhotoSecrets.com: Tips for taking good photos
Apple, Google, Amazon, Dropbox: Cloud storage
WordPress, Blogger, Tumblr: Blogging sites
TravelPod, Tripcast, Travel Diaries, BonJournal: Online travel journals
Google Photos, Flickr, SmugMug, 500px: Sites for organizing, editing, and sharing photos
YouTube, Vimeo: Video-sharing sites
MyPublisher, Shutterfly, Snapfish: Web tools for creating high-quality photo scrapbooks
Wix, Weebly: Website builders for making digital scrapbooks
LiveTrekker app: Track and share your travel route

I sorted through my intimate moments with those statues through the viewing screen of my camera, I accidentally erased everything on my memory card. That night, I learned several important lessons: 1) Never cull photos with a wine buzz, and 2) be vigilant about backing up. You never know what might happen, from leaving your camera on a train to dropping your memory card in a puddle. Here are some tips for dealing with images while you travel.

Be selective. Cull your images ruthlessly and often, keeping only the very best shots. (The people looking at your pictures later will thank you for it.) Get in the habit of doing this periodically, even if memory-card space isn't an issue, to avoid bringing home an overwhelming number of photos.

Back up your images. Since I usually travel with a laptop, I upload my photos to my computer every so often (transfer images via a card reader, a cable, or Wi-Fi if your camera has it). For added safety, you can back up photos to a high-capacity USB flash drive or upload them to a photo-sharing service such as Google Photos or SmugMug.

Use other media. The Apple camera connection kit makes it easy to download media from your digital camera to a tablet. You can also consider a photo backup device like the HyperDrive Colorspace UDMA, a palm-sized (but pricey) gadget that has a memory-card reader, hard drive, and color screen. If you use a smartphone or tablet to take pictures or videos, a device like MediaShair Hub allows you to wirelessly transfer content to an external hard drive.

Keep it in the cloud. Apple, Google, Amazon, and Dropbox allow you to store digital content (photos, videos, documents, music, books) in their "clouds" (their networks). Most smartphones have an automatic image backup system built in. All you have to do is activate the cloud settings on your phone. Whenever you're at a Wi-Fi hotspot, your phone will automatically send your latest pictures to the cloud. You can then access this content from other cloud-enabled devices (tablet, home computer, etc.) the next time they're connected to the Internet.

Find a creative new angle.

Tricks for a Good Shot

Most people are limited by their photographic skills, not by their camera. Understand your camera. Devour the manual. Take experimental shots, make notes, and see what happens. If you don't understand f-stops or depth of field, find a photography class or book and learn (for tips on taking better pictures, visit www.photosecrets.com). Camera stores sell good books on photography in general and travel photography in particular. I shutter to think how many people are underexposed and lacking depth in this field.

The Vatican Museum staircase: Have fun with composition.

A sharp eye connected to a wild imagination will be your most valuable piece of equipment. Develop a knack for what will look good and be interesting after the trip. The skilled photographer's eye sees striking light, shade, form, lines, patterns, texture, and colors.

Look for a new slant to an old sight. Everyone knows what the Eiffel Tower looks like. Find a unique or different approach to sights that everyone has seen. Shoot the bell tower through the horse's legs, or lay your camera on the floor to shoot the Gothic ceiling.

Capture the personal and intimate details of your trip. Show how you lived, whom you met, and what made each day an adventure (a close-up of a picnic, your favorite taxi driver, or the character you befriended at the launderette).

Vary your perspective. You can shoot close, far, low, high, during the day, and at night. Don't fall into the rut of always centering a shot. Use foregrounds to add color, depth, and interest to landscapes.

Get close. Notice details. Eliminate distractions by zeroing in on your subject. Get so close that you show only one thing. Don't try to show it all in one shot. For any potentially great shot, I try several variations—then delete the ones that don't pan out. The famous war photographer Robert Capa once said, "If your pictures aren't good enough, you're not close enough." My best portraits are so close that the entire head can't fit into the frame.

People are the most interesting subjects. It takes nerve to walk up to people and take their picture. Ask for permission. (If you don't speak the language, point at your camera and ask, "Photo?") It can be difficult, but your subject will probably be delighted. Try to show action. A candid is better than a posed shot. Even a "posed candid" shot is better than a posed one. Give your subject something to do. Challenge the kid in the market to juggle oranges. Many photographers take a second shot immediately after the first portrait to capture a looser, warmer subject.

Buildings, in general, are not interesting. It does not matter if Karl Marx or Beethoven was born there—a house is as dead as its former resident. As travel photographers gain experience, they take more people shots and fewer buildings or general landscapes.

Maximize good lighting. Real photographers get single-minded at the "magic hours"—early morning and late afternoon—when the sun is very low, light is rich and diffused, and colors glow. Plan for these times. Grab bright colors. Develop an eye for great lighting; any time of day, you may luck into a perfectly lit scene. Some of my best photos are the result of great lighting, not great subjects. Take advantage of a tripod and shoot with longer exposures to create more light in an otherwise dark setting.

Even if your camera is automatic, your subject can turn out to be a silhouette. Get those faces in the sun or (even better) lit from the side. When shooting a portrait, the sun should be behind you. Have the sunlight hit the subject's face at an angle by making sure it's coming over your right or left shoulder. This creates dramatic highlights and shadows on the subject's face. Avoid shooting outdoor portraits during the lighting "dead zone," between 11 a.m. and 2 p.m. If you have to shoot then, use your camera's flash to fill the shadows that form in the eye sockets, under the nose, and under the chin. High-end cameras have an adjustable power setting on the flash. Use it to get the right ratio of sunlight to fill light.

The best people shots are up close and well lit, with a soft background.

LEFT Vary your perspective—add extra depth with a foreground.

RIGHT Fill the lens with your subject.

LEFT Capture the magic with just the right light.

RIGHT Back lighting "puts an edge" on your subject.

Don't be afraid to handhold a slow shot. Tripods enable you to take professional shots that could compete with those at the museum gift shop. But most major museums prohibit you from using a tripod or a flash (which ages paintings). Despite these restrictions, you can take good shots by holding your camera as still as possible or leaning against a wall or banister. Wait until you breathe out to take the picture (when you hold your breath, your body shakes more). Many cameras use "image stabilization" to help in these situations. (And if you still can't get that perfect shot, go to the gift store. Nearly every important museum has a good selection of top-quality cards and prints at reasonable prices.)

Bracket shots when the lighting is tricky. The best way to get good shots in difficult lighting situations is to "bracket" your shots (take several different pictures of the same scene, slightly varying the exposure and shutter speed settings for each one). You can simply delete the unsuccessful attempts.

SHARING YOUR TRIP

On my first trip to Europe at age 14, I collected and logged my journey in a file of several hundred numbered postcards, each packed with notes. Throughout the '70s and '80s, I eagerly shared my travel experiences through slideshows. But those days of slow, static, 20th-century methods are now long gone, replaced by a slew of fast, interactive advancements in social media, digital file sharing, and websites.

Social Media

While on the road and back at home, I interact with thousands of readers via my Facebook page. Each night, my favorite bedtime reading is the comments from my followers. It's become a fun way for us to experience Europe together.

With social-networking tools, you can share real-time travel stories by posting quick updates, along with photos and videos with descriptions. Facebook offers easy photo uploading and albums to organize your photos. Twitter lets you share (or "tweet") pictures and text tidbits from your mobile device as you travel. With Instagram, you can put fun filters on images and share them with friends, creating a string of pictures that document your travels. Many social media applications are compatible; for example, most allow simultaneous posting to two or more platforms, such as Facebook and Instagram.

On the LiveTrekker app, you can keep track of your travel path via GPS—even offline—and share your progress when you're connected to Wi-Fi. You can also upload photos and videos and pin them to a destination on your tracked map.

With any social media tool, be selective. You want to fascinate, not bore or annoy your friends and family. It's also important not to unwittingly share your whereabouts with strangers or advertise that your home is unguarded, especially when you're traveling. Be sure to check the privacy settings for every application and device you use. Most applications are not automatically set to "private"; you'll have to activate the privacy settings yourself.

Blogs and Online Travel Journals

While social media is optimal for quick updates, blogging is the best option for lengthy storytelling. Maintaining a blog of your travels is the perfect way to document your journey, as well as entertain family and friends with your adventures.

Popular blog hosts are WordPress, Tumblr, and Blogger. All are free and relatively easy to use, with templates and customization options. You can post text, photos, audio, video, slideshows, links, and more; set your blog to automatically publish at staggered times; and have multiple people contribute to one blog. You can also link your blog to your Facebook or Twitter account. These blogging platforms also have apps that let you post from your mobile device.

Several websites are geared specifically for trip sharing, offering features such as maps, statistics, and itineraries to document your travels. These websites, including TravelPod,

Journaling

The best way to document your trip as you travel is to pick up a pen and put your experiences to paper. Even in my days as a vagabond backpacker, I was a keen and disciplined journal writer. Journaling the old-fashioned way has no limits, word counts, or caps on creativity.

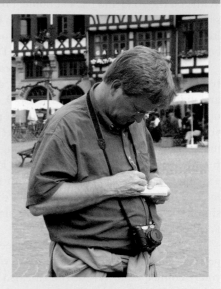

Great travel journals describe both the inner and outer journey—your physical surroundings and sensory experiences as well as your emotions and thoughts at the time. Transcribing intimate details into your journal will allow you to revisit a place time and time again, whether shared with others or kept to yourself.

Be selective in choosing a journal. I prefer a minimalist booklet with empty pages, lightweight yet stiff enough to both protect the pages and give me something solid to write on in the absence of a table. Consider a bound book; spiral notebooks tend to fall apart. I write in black ink or mechanical pencil, allowing my simple words to be the focus. Keep a pocket notebook handy to jot down brief moments or fleeting thoughts throughout the day—such as while at a bus stop or waiting for a restaurant meal. You can expand on these and add them to your actual journal when you have time.

As you write, avoid guidebook-type data and instead focus on the sentimental effects and imagery of your experiences. You don't have to give a chronological account of your journey. In fact, you probably shouldn't. Consider just sitting somewhere interesting and writing about your surroundings or focusing an entry on a specific topic: strange cultural customs or a touching moment, for instance. Throwing in creative essays will sharpen your ability to observe and understand the culture you visited.

Most importantly, don't write just to write. Ten years from now, you won't feel the need to recall the mediocre meal you grabbed at that café or the quality of the hotel's complimentary breakfast. Leave out the boring stuff. You want to include details that define the character of a place as well as your personal response. Throw in sketches, mementos, little paper souvenirs like maps and old tickets—anything that takes you back to that moment. Combining these personal touches with candid accounts and reflective musings will create a travel souvenir you'll forever cherish.

Tripcast, Travel Diaries, and BonJournal, allow you to create a travel blog or journal using a variety of tools. You can build your itinerary, chart your route on an interactive map, and add photos, videos, and stories to create a shareable overview of your journey. Mobile apps allow you to update on the go, and some sites offer the option to print your trip as a book. Certain sites are more user-friendly than others, so choose the platform that best suits your storytelling style.

Whichever host you choose, here are some guidelines for creating a memorable blog:

- When posting stories online, think about interactive elements that combine entertaining, insightful text with engaging videos and photos.
- Consider embedding slideshows or links to related websites and resources. Slideshare.net is a helpful presentation-sharing site, but you must link it to your Facebook or LinkedIn account.
- Include amusing tidbits or interesting quotes to spice up your stories.
- If struggling for inspiration, consider implementing a theme or ongoing elements like a "picture of the day."

Once Back Home...

Relive your trip by organizing, editing, improving, and sharing your digital images.

First, you'll need to download and organize your photos. You can simply create folders and subfolders on your computer, or you can use a more advanced photo-organizing program, such as the free Google Photos, which also includes editing and sharing features.

It's always smart to look at your pictures and see if you can improve them. You may already have a basic photo-editing program. More serious shutterbugs use Adobe Photoshop Elements (an easy-to-use program for novices), Adobe Lightroom, or Adobe Photoshop (for more advanced work). Editing your photos—cropping out distractions around the edges, tweaking colors, and enhancing lighting—before posting online or creating an album will improve their impact.

When it comes to sharing our images, you have many

Your friends will enjoy seeing photos of the different characters you meet.

Postcards from Europe

On my first solo trip to Europe, in 1973—just after high school graduation—I wrote postcards home nearly every day. I packed so much information onto each card it was a challenge to read them without a magnifying glass. Looking back on these exuberant little reports back to my family, I can see a travel writer in waiting.

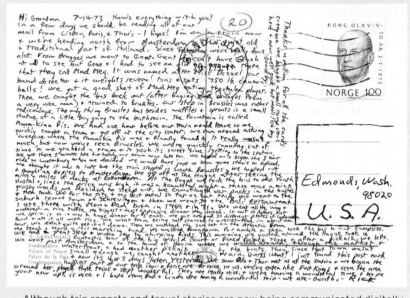

Although trip reports and travel stories are now being communicated digitally, I still find a physical picture postcard—even with a brief "Wish you were here!"-type message—a nice touch. It's fun for people back home to get a personal message that has traveled thousands of miles from another country.

If sending postcards, you may have to contend with a European post office. These can be handy and efficient or jam-packed and discouraging, depending on the country. In general, small-town post offices can be less crowded and more user-friendly. If possible, avoid the Italian male...I mean, mail. Service is best north of the Alps. Postcard stamps are often sold in machines at post offices, as well as at neighborhood newsstands, gift shops that sell cards, or your hotel's front desk. (Write your postcards before getting stamps—you may be in the next country by the time you're ready to mail them.)

To send your own photos as a postcard, try an app such as Postagram and SnapShot Postcard. For about a dollar per card (more if addressed outside the US) they will print and send custom postcards for you via snail mail. Just choose a photo from your phone along with a template, type a message, and the postcard will be on its way—all without stepping foot inside a post office.

options, from making prints of your favorite shots to designing books to creating a digital gallery or scrapbook. Multimedia-sharing sites let you unleash your images to friends and family—without holding them captive in a dark room.

Photo Sharing: Websites such as Google Photos, Flickr, SmugMug, and 500px help you organize and edit your photos. You can then share your trip pics through online albums or import them into your social-networking sites. Some even let you create videos from your photos and upload them to YouTube. SmugMug and 500px also offer the option to present your collection through your own professional-looking photography site (for a small monthly fee).

Video Sharing: The de facto video-sharing site, YouTube offers high-quality, free video hosting with detailed privacy controls. Vimeo has no limits on bandwidth or video length, so you can customize your videos and embed them into any website or blog.

Photo Books and Scrapbooks: Creating a scrapbook online is simple—a few clicks and personal touches, and you've got your own coffee-table masterpiece. Snapfish and Shutterfly are two (of many) easy-to-use sites where you can upload, view, organize, and edit photos, then order prints, photo books, cards, posters, and more. One of my favorite tools is MyPublisher, which lets you create high-quality, custom-bound, professional-looking scrapbooks. Download the site's free photo book application and customize to your heart's desire. Or make a scrapbook the old-fashioned way, with photo archival paper...and a glue stick.

Digital Scrapbooks: Using a website builder like Wix or Weebly, or one of the blogging or travel journal websites mentioned earlier, you can compile your trip notes and photos into a detailed and polished website, as a cherished tribute to your European adventure. Each year at Rick Steves' Europe, we hold a contest for our tour members to see who's created the best digital scrapbook of their recent trip with us (the top prize is a free tour). For lots of great inspiration, peruse the award-winning entries at www.ricksteves.com/tours/scrapbooks.

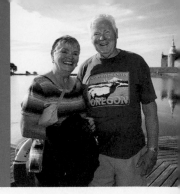

Travel Styles

Embracing new experiences is a lot easier to do if you're well prepared. This chapter addresses the special concerns and interests of solo travelers (including issues specific to women), families, seniors, and travelers with disabilities.

TRAVELING SOLO

I've talked to too many people who put off their travel dreams because they don't want to do it by themselves. If you want to go to Europe but don't have a partner, consider gathering the courage to go it alone. You'll meet plenty of people as you travel: Think of them as a montage of fun, temporary travel partners.

Traveling solo has its pros and cons—and for me, the pros far outweigh the cons. When you're on your own, you're independent and in control. You can travel at your own pace, do the things that interest you, eat where and when you like, and splurge where you want to splurge. You don't have to wait for your partner to pack up, and you never need to negotiate where to eat or when to call it a day. You go where you want, when you want, and you can get the heck out of that stuffy museum when all the Monets start to blur together. If

Traveling without a tour, you'll have the locals dancing *with* you—not for you.

ad-libbing, it's easier for one to slip between the cracks than two.

Of course, there are downsides to traveling alone: When you're on your own, you don't have a built-in dining companion. You've got no one to send ahead while you wait in line, help you figure out the bus schedule, or commiserate with when things go awry. And traveling by yourself is usually more expensive. With a partner,

Traveling alone immerses you in Europe.

hotel accommodations cost less because they're shared. Other things become cheaper too when you're splitting costs, such as groceries, guidebooks, taxis, storage lockers, and more.

But when you travel with someone else, it's natural to focus on your partner—how you're getting along, whether she meant it when she said she wasn't hungry—and tune out the symphony of sights, sounds, and smells all around you. Traveling on your own allows you to be more present and open to your surroundings. You'll meet more people—you're seen as more approachable. You're more likely to experience the kindness of strangers.

Solo travel is intensely personal. You can discover more about yourself at the same time you're discovering more about Europe. Traveling on your own is fun, challenging, vivid, and exhilarating. Realizing that you have what it takes to be your own guide is a thrill known only to solo travelers. Your trip is a gift from you to you.

Traveling Alone Without Feeling Lonely

For many people contemplating their first solo trip, loneliness is their biggest fear. Big cities can be cold and ugly when the only person to talk to is yourself. And being sick and alone in a country where no one knows you is a sad and miserable experience.

Fortunately, combating loneliness in Europe is easy. The continent is full of travelers and natural meeting places, especially in peak season. And the Internet offers ever-increasing avenues for connecting with locals eager to welcome you to their home turf.

Meeting People: You'll run across vaga-buddies every day. If you stay in hostels, you'll have a built-in family (hostels are open to all ages). Or choose small pensions and B&Bs, where the owners and fellow travelers sharing breakfast have time to talk. At most tourist sights, you'll meet more people in an hour than you would at home in a day. If you're

Traveling with a Partner

Though I love trekking through Europe by myself, there's nothing like that special lifelong bond that forms between you and the person you've dined with, slept with, and trudged around in the rain with for two weeks straight in a foreign land.

A group of travel buddies defending Caesar's empire atop Hadrian's Wall in Britain

But your choice of travel partner is critical—it can make or break a trip. Traveling with the wrong partner can be like a bad blind date that lasts for weeks. I'd rather do it alone. One summer I went to Europe to dive into as many cultures and adventures as possible. I planned to rest when I got home. My partner wanted to slow life down, get away from it all, relax, and escape the pressures of the business world. Our ideas of acceptable hotels and how much time we wanted to spend eating were quite different. The trip was a near disaster.

Traveling together greatly accelerates a relationship—especially a romantic one. You see each other constantly and make endless decisions. The niceties go out the window. Everything becomes very real; you're in an adventure, a struggle, a hot-air balloon for two. The experiences of years are jammed into weeks. If you haven't traveled with your companion before, consider a trial weekend together before merging dream trips. Any shared trip is a good test of a relationship—often revealing its ultimate course. I'd highly recommend a little premarital travel.

Many people already have their partner—for better or for worse. Couples should take particular care to minimize the stress of traveling together by recognizing each other's need for independence. Too many couples do Europe as a three-legged race, tied together from start to finish. Have an explicit understanding that there's absolutely nothing selfish, dangerous, insulting, or wrong about splitting up occasionally. This is a freedom too few travel partners allow themselves. Doing your own thing for a few hours or days breathes fresh air into your togetherness, making those shared experiences all the more memorable.

feeling shy, cameras are good icebreakers; offer to take someone's picture with his or her camera.

Take a group walking tour of a city (ask at the tourist office). You'll learn about the town and meet other travelers, too. If you're staying in a hostel, check its message board—some hostels arrange group tours.

It's easy to meet people on buses and trains. When you meet locals who speak English, find out what they think—about anything. Take your laundry and a deck of cards to a launderette and turn solitaire into gin rummy. You'll end up with a stack of clean clothes and interesting conversations.

Learn how to say "pretty baby" in the local language. If you play peek-a-boo with a baby or fold an origami bird for a kid, you'll make friends with the parents as well as the child.

Try meeting up with other solo travelers or with convivial locals through social media. Like-minded individuals can find one another on www.meetup.com, whose worldwide members welcome visitors to diverse events such as photography walks, happy hours, and weekend skiing. Interface with your social media connections to find out if anyone has friends or family in the destinations that you'll be traveling to, then drop them a note about your upcoming visit. Consider joining a hospitality-exchange network, such as Servas (see page 518), or Couchsurfing, its more low-key alternative (page 247).

Eating Out: I like the old-fashioned, face-to-face social media option of just saying to someone you meet, "Would you like to meet up for dinner?" Some countries have special meals that are more fun to experience with others. You could invite someone to join you for, say, a rijsttafel dinner in the Netherlands, a *smörgåsbord* in Scandinavia, a fondue in Switzerland, a paella feast in Spain, or a spaghetti feed in an Italian trattoria. Wondering whom to ask? People with Rick Steves guidebooks are like an extended family in Europe. My readers are on the trail of the same travel thrills, and happy to share in the adventure.

If you like company, eat in places so crowded and popular that you have to share a table, or ask other single travelers if they'd like to join you. Eat in the members' kitchen of a hostel; you'll always have companions. Make it a potluck.

If you're dining alone, consider alternatives to formal sit-down meals. Try a self-service café, a local-style fast-food restaurant, or a small ethnic eatery. Visit a supermarket deli and get a picnic to eat in the square or a park. Get a slice of pizza from a take-out shop and munch it as you walk, people-watching and window-shopping.

Phrase book + big smile = plenty of friends

If you eat alone, be busy. Use the time to learn more of the language. Practice your verbal skills with the waiter or waitress (when I asked a French waiter if he had kids, he proudly showed me a picture of his twin girls). Read a guidebook, a novel, or the *International New York Times*. Do trip planning, draw in your journal, or scrawl a few post-cards to the folks back home.

Spending an afternoon at a café is a great way to get some writing done; for the cost of a beverage and a snack, you'll be granted more peace and privacy than at a public fountain or other open space.

Evenings: Experience the magic of European cities at night. Go for a walk along well-lit streets. With gelato in hand, enjoy the parade of people, busy shops, and illumi-nated monuments. You'll invariably feel a sense of compan-ionship when lots of people are around. Take advantage of the wealth of evening entertainment: concerts, movies, and dance performances. Some cities offer tours after dark: You can see Paris by night on a river cruise.

If you like to stay in at night, get a room with a balcony overlooking a square. You'll have a front-row seat to the best show in town. Read novels set in the country you're visiting. Email travel news to your friends and family so you'll find friendly answers from another time zone in your inbox in the morning. Learn to treasure solitude. Go early to bed, be early to rise. Shop at a lively morning market for fresh rolls and join the locals for coffee.

Lodging for Solo Travelers

Solo travelers need to do some extra legwork to find hotel accommodations that offer a good value. Rarely is a single room just half the price of a double. If a double room costs $100, a single room will generally be about $80—making your stay $30 more expensive each night than if you were sharing the room and the cost. True single rooms are also relatively rare, so you may find yourself paying for a double more often than you'd like.

You can use booking websites like Booking.com or Hotels.com to find hotels that offer accommodations for solo travelers. Look in the results for true singles with one twin bed—and hopefully a price tag to match. Once you've zeroed in on the best options, book directly with the hotel of your choice.

Hostels welcome travelers of all ages and are in the busi-ness of renting out single bunks. Not only is this an afford-able option, it's an excellent way to meet others. Hostels also sometimes have private rooms, which may be cheaper than a single in a budget hotel.

Other alternatives include home-sharing services such as Airbnb, Servas, and Couchsurfing (see page 247 for more info). Here you can find affordable accommodations ranging from a young city-dweller's sofa to a guest bedroom in a farmhouse to a studio apartment all your own. Servas and Couchsurfing, in particular, are focused on bringing hosts and visitors together for cultural exchange and camaraderie.

Safety for Solo Travelers

All travelers should exercise common sense and caution when it comes to personal security abroad (see the Theft & Scams chapter). For solo travelers, this means greater self-reliance and being particularly aware of their surroundings.

Use street smarts. Be well prepared so that you don't need to depend on someone unless you want to—carry cash, a map, a guidebook, and a phrase book. Walk purposefully with your head up; look like you know where you're going. If you get lost in an unfriendly neighborhood, be savvy about whom you ask for help; seek out a police officer or a family, or go into a store or restaurant to ask for directions or to study your map.

Be proactive about public transportation. Use the same caution in taxis and on buses and subways that you would at home. Consider visiting the train or bus station the day before your departure, so you'll know where it is, how long it takes to reach it, if it feels safe, and what services it has. Reconfirm your departure time. If you're leaving late at night and the bus or train station is sketchy, hang out in your hotel's lounge or in a café until you need to head for the station.

Unless you're fluent in the language, you must accept the fact that you won't always know what's going on. Though it might seem worrisome, there's a reason why the Greek bus driver drops you off in the middle of nowhere. It's a transfer point, and another bus will come along in a few minutes. You'll often discover that the locals are looking out for you. However, a healthy dose of skepticism and an eagle eye in crowded and isolated places will help you stay safe.

Stay connected. Make it a habit to update family and friends back home about your itinerary. Talk over your plans with your hotelier before you head out, especially at night. It's smart to have someone know where you are at all times.

Trust your gut. If a situation or locale doesn't feel right, leave. It *is* better to be safe than sorry.

Tips for Solo Women Travelers

Thanks to my female staffers and their friends for assembling their top tips for women.

Every year, thousands of women, young and old, travel to Europe on their own. You can, too, by using the same good judgment you use at home. Begin with caution and figure out as you travel what feels right to you. Create conditions that are likely to turn out in your favor, and you'll have a safer, smoother, more enjoyable trip.

Theft and harassment are two big concerns for women. If you've traveled alone in America, you're more than prepared for Europe. In America, theft and harassment are especially scary because of their connection with assault. In Europe, you'll rarely, if ever, hear of violence. Theft is past tense (as in, "Where did my wallet go?"). As for experiencing harassment, you're far more likely to think, "I'm going to ditch this guy ASAP" than, "This guy is going to hurt me." Here are some tips for safe and pleasant travels.

Plan carefully for overnight train travel. If you take an overnight train, avoid sleeping in empty compartments. Rent a *couchette* for a small surcharge, which puts you with roommates in a compartment you can lock, in a car monitored by an attendant. You may be assigned to an all-female compartment as a matter of course, but if not, ask for female roommates. Certain countries, such as Spain, are better about accommodating requests than others.

Learn how to deal with European men. If you never talk to men, you could miss out on a chance to learn about the country. So, by all means, talk to men. Just choose the man and choose the setting.

In northern Europe, you won't draw any more attention from men than you do in America. In southern Europe, particularly in Italy, you'll get more attention than you're used to, but it's usually in the form of the "long look." But be aware that in the Mediterranean world, when you smile and look a man in the eyes, it's often considered an invitation. Wear dark sunglasses and you can stare all you want.

Standards of dress and modesty vary across Europe; take your cues from what local women wear. Avoid walking alone at night, particularly in unlit areas with few people

Stay in hostels to swap tales and advice with other adventurous women.

Books for the Woman Traveling Alone

Practical Advice

Gutsy Women: Stories, Advice, Inspiration (Marybeth Bond, 2012): Funny, instructive, and inspiring ideas for solo travelers

Kicking Ass on the Road: The Ultimate Guide for the Solo Woman Traveler (Sunni Dawson, 2016): Empowering guide covering everything from insurance to romance

The Solo Traveler's Handbook (Janice Leith Waugh, 2012): A how-to guide with lots of anecdotes

Women with Wanderlust: A Guide to Roaming (Melissa D. Jones, 2016): Tips and tricks gleaned from travel through 40 countries

Tales from the Road

The Best Women's Travel Writing: True Stories from Around the World (Levinia Spalding, ed., published annually): An anthology of funny and inspirational tales

Expat: Women's True Tales of Life Abroad (Christina Henry de Tessan, ed., 2002): A collection of stories about how the reality of life abroad matches up to the fantasy

Go Your Own Way: Women Travel the World Solo (Faith Conlon and others, eds., 2007): Cultural revelations mixed with advice for the female traveler

A Woman's Europe: True Stories (Marybeth Bond, ed., 2004): Europe from a totally female point of view

Humor

More Sand in My Bra: Funny Women Write from the Road, Again! (Jennifer L. Leo, ed., 2007): Travel shenanigans

The Unsavvy Traveler: Women's Comic Tales of Catastrophe (Rosemary Caperton, Anne Mathews, and Lucie Ocenas, eds., 2001): A collection of humorous and cathartic misadventures

around. Don't be overly polite if you're bothered by someone; it's important to create boundaries to protect yourself. If a man comes too close, say "no" firmly and loudly in the local language. That's usually all it takes.

If you feel like you're being followed or hassled, don't worry about overreacting or seeming foolish. Yell if the situation warrants it. Or head to the nearest hotel and chat up the person behind the desk until your would-be admirer moves on. Ask the hotelier to call a cab to take you to your own hotel, hostel, or B&B.

There's no need to tell men that you're traveling alone, or disclose whether you're married or single. Lie unhesitatingly. You're traveling with your husband. He's waiting for you at the hotel. He's a professional wrestler who retired from the sport for psychological reasons.

If you're arranging to meet a guy, choose a public place. Tell him you're staying at a hostel: You have a 10 p.m. curfew and 29 roommates. Better yet, bring a couple of your roommates along to meet him. After the introductions, let everyone know where you're going and when you'll return.

By using common sense, making good decisions, and above all else, having confidence in yourself and your ability to travel on your own, you'll be rewarded with rich experiences—and great stories to tell your friends.

FAMILY TRAVEL

When parents tell me they're going to Europe and ask me where to take their kids, I'm tempted to answer, "to Grandma and Grandpa's on your way to the airport." Europe is an expensive destination, and taking the kids along changes how you'll experience it—but in ways that may surprise you. Prioritizing neighborhood parks and public swimming pools over tourist-jammed museums and dim churches opens you up to a slower-paced, more locally grounded approach to a foreign culture.

With kids, you'll live more like a European and less like a tourist. Your children become your ambassadors, opening doors to new experiences and relationships. Your child will be your ticket to countless conversations. Some of your best travel memories may be of your son floating a wooden boat alongside Parisian *garçons* in the great pond at Luxembourg Garden, or of your daughter kicking a soccer ball with other *niñas* at a park in Madrid. Let them race their new Italian friends around Siena's main square, the Campo, while you sip your Campari.

That being said, it's easy to make the case against taking the kids along. A European vacation with kids in tow is much more about playgrounds and

Leave the Kids at Home?

If you and your partner have 20 days for a family vacation, are on a budget, and are dreaming of adult time in Europe, consider this plan: Go for 10 days without the kids and really enjoy Europe as adults rather than parents—the savings from leaving them at home will easily cover top-notch child care. Then fly home and spend the other 10 days with your kids—camping, at a water park, or just playing at home. (If your kids have an adult relative somewhere else in the US whom they'd enjoy getting to know better, offer to fly him or her to your house to kid-sit while you're gone.)

petting zoos than world-class art and evocative ruins. And traveling with kids comes at a price. Out of exhaustion and frustration, you may opt for spendy conveniences like taxis and the first restaurant you find with a kid-friendly menu. Two adults with kids spend twice as much to experience about half the magic of Europe per day than they might without.

But if you can afford it and don't mind accomplishing less as adult sightseers, traveling with your children can be great family fun, creating piles of lifelong memories. Moreover, it's great parenting, as it helps get kids comfortable with the wider world.

And lucky for you, European families enjoy traveling too. You'll find kids' menus, hotel playrooms, and kids-go-crazy zones at freeway rest stops all over Europe. Parents with a babe-in-arms will generally be offered a seat on crowded buses and sometimes allowed to go to the front of the line at museums.

The key to a successful European family vacation is to slow down and to temper expectations. Don't overdo it. Tackle one or two key sights each day, mix in a healthy dose of pure fun, and take extended breaks when needed. If you do it right, you'll take home happy memories to share for a lifetime.

Conquering peaks on your rental mountain bike (as my proud son Andy did here in Switzerland) and connecting with local families can leave your own family with the most important souvenirs—lifelong memories of times shared together.

What's the Right Age for Europe?

My children are young adults now. But after taking them to Europe every year for their first 20 years, it's fun to think back about our European trips during different stages of their childhood. When they were grade-schoolers, our trips were consumed with basic survival issues, such as eating, sleeping, and occupying their attention. By the time they entered their teens, the big challenge became making our trips educational and fun.

Some parents won't take their kids abroad until they

are old enough to truly enjoy the trip. My rule of thumb is that children should be able to stand a day of walking, be ready to eat what's in front of them, and be comfortable sleeping in strange beds. They should be able to carry their own daypacks with some clothes, a journal, and a couple of toys. I've found that children are ready for an international trip at about the same age they're ready for a long day at Disneyland.

Grade-school kids are often the easiest travelers, provided you schedule some kid-friendly activities every day. They're happiest staying in rural places with swimming pools and grassy fields to run around in, or in small towns where the crowds, chaos, and must-see sights are manageable.

High-schoolers feel that summer break is a vacation they've earned. If this European trip is not their trip, you become the enemy. Make it their trip, too, by asking for their help—give each child who's old enough a location to research. Kids can quickly get excited about a vacation if they're involved in the planning stages. Consider your teen's suggestions and make real concessions. Spending some time in cities is essential, and a day of shopping or at the beach might be more fun than another ruined abbey.

If you'd rather remove the stress of planning and still have some energy to enjoy adult company, consider taking your kids on an organized tour designed for families. For example, kids as young as eight are welcome on my Family Tours and "My Way" unguided tours. At 12, they can accompany their parents on any Rick Steves tour. Especially in summer, your kids will often find friends in the group, and you'll be able to relax with other adults.

Prepping Your Kids

Before you leave home, get your kids enthusiastic about what they'll be seeing in Europe. Encourage them to learn about the countries, cities, sights, and people they'll be visiting. Look online for articles, photos, and video clips to pique their curiosity.

Read books, both fiction and nonfiction, set in the place you're going, such as

Resources for Family Travel

Ducksters.com: Easy-to-digest info on world history, geography, and important historical figures—great preparation for visiting Europe's sights and museums

MiniTime.com: Trip-planning resources for travel with babies and kids

TravelforKids.com: Comprehensive listing of fun things to do with kids worldwide

TravelswithBaby.com: Baby and toddler travel tips from author Shelly Rivoli

Reading

Cadogan Guides' *Take the Kids* series: Child-friendly specifics for a wide variety of destinations

Fodor's *Around Paris with Kids* and *Around London with Kids:* Family-oriented guides for two of the most-visited European cities

Family on the Loose: The Art of Traveling with Kids (Bill Richards and E. Ashley Steel, 2012): Described by *Parenting* magazine as "one heck of a book" based on the authors' travels in more than 40 countries with two kids

Travels with Baby: The Ultimate Guide for Planning Travel with Your Baby, Toddler, and Preschooler (Shelly Rivoli, 2014): Award-winning manual for managing with the youngest of travelers

The Diary of Anne Frank for Amsterdam or *The Thief Lord* for Venice. For younger kids, check out M. Sasek's delightfully illustrated *This Is* series on various European destinations (*This is Venice, This is Edinburgh*, and so on). Watch movies, such as *The Sound of Music* for Salzburg, *The Red Balloon* or *Hugo* for Paris, or *The Secret of Roan Inish* for Ireland. Your hometown library can be a great resource for age-appropriate books and movies.

My website contains free access to full-length *Rick Steves' Europe* TV episodes and a variety of TV specials, which provide a fun sneak peek into the destinations you'll be visiting. Kids might also enjoy reading my blog (blog.ricksteves.com), where they can search for posts about the places and sights on your itinerary.

Get a jump on foreign phrases. Type out the top 20 or so and put them on the fridge for everyone to learn. Get the *10 Minutes a Day* language book for your destination, which comes with preprinted sticky word labels that your kids will enjoy plastering around the house. My phrasebooks are also accessible and fun to use (see page 37). Kids might especially enjoy language-learning game apps like Duolingo (see page 392).

Try to relate your children's hobbies or favorite games to the place you're visiting (draw pictures of the Eiffel Tower, play dominoes saying the numbers in Italian). Give your kids the chance to try out foreign specialties in advance by eating at ethnic restaurants, or get a cookbook and make meals together at home. Many US cities host celebrations of different cultures—look for festivals held by local communities of Greeks, Italians, Hungarians, or whatever group might be vibrant in your town or relevant to your travels.

Travel Documents for Kids

You'll need the proper documents—even babies need passports. For a child of any age, take an official copy of his or her birth certificate, along with a photocopy of his or her passport. These documents are especially important if you have a different last name than your child. For parents of adopted children, it's a good idea to bring their adoption decree as well. Keep these documents separate from your passports, as they'll be a huge help if you end up needing to get a replacement passport for your child.

If you're traveling with a child who isn't yours (say, a niece or grandkid), bring along a signed, notarized document from the parent(s) to prove to authorities that you have permission to take the child on a trip. Even a single parent traveling with children has to demonstrate that the other parent has given approval. Specifically, the letter should grant permission for the accompanying adult to travel internationally with the child. Include your name, the name of the child, the dates of your trip, destination countries, and the name, address, and phone number of the parent(s) at home.

You may want to bring extra passport photos with you. Since infants and toddlers change so quickly, carry pictures that were taken for the passport, as well as ones taken close to your departure date.

Most parents hold onto their kids' passports, but if you have older children who'll be out on their own, you could get them a money belt or neck pouch for carrying their cash and ID.

For younger kids, drape a lanyard around their necks with emergency contact information, or consider ordering custom dog tags (see www.dogtagsonline.com). Another option is an ID Inside wristband, with a hidden pocket that holds a disposable ID card (www.id-inside.com). You can easily switch out the ID card, updating your hotel name and contact info as you go. If you realize that you left your child's ID at the hotel, improvise by writing your phone number on a piece of paper to tuck into your child's pocket or inside her shoe. In a pinch, you could write your contact number—gently—on your child's arm with a pen.

What to Bring

The amount and type of gear you need depends on the age of your child. Since a baby on the road requires a lot of equipment, the key to happiness is a rental car or a long stay in one place. If you're visiting friends or family, they may be able to borrow a car seat, stroller, and travel crib so you won't have to pack it. If you have older kids, let them know they'll be hauling their own luggage through airports and down cobblestone streets. Pack as light as you can, and think hard about what you'll really need.

With little kids, I found having the best gear was more important than packing light. We would rent a car because taking everyone and everything on trains would have been miserable. Once the kids were older, however, I insisted on being mobile, and we had a family ethic whereby everyone carried their own stuff...so they'd better pack light. (This book's packing tips apply to teens just as much as to adults.)

Infants and Toddlers: It's helpful to have a stroller and a baby carrier. Bringing both will maximize sightseeing: When the bambino gets bored in one you can switch to the other, and then back. Spend a little extra on a solidly built but lightweight stroller that can easily navigate cobblestones, such as models from Peg Pérego (www.pegperegousa.com), Maclaren (www.maclarenbaby.com), or Combi (www.combiusa.com). Make sure it has a basket underneath for storing overflow items. A stroller that can recline and has a hood over which to drape a dark blanket allows you to create a good napping environment anywhere. Baby carriers are great for keeping your hands free, and are easier than a stroller on subways and buses.

Prepare to tote more than a tot. A good backpack makes an ideal combo purse/diaper bag that's hands-free and comfortable to carry all day. You can always stow it in your stroller's basket, but be on guard: Purse snatchers target parents (especially while busy, as when changing diapers).

A sturdy, lightweight stroller is essential for sightseeing with a tot in tow.

Most hotels in Europe can provide an extra crib—often called a cot—or can give you cushions or inflatable bumpers to make a safe sleeping environment on a regular bed. For years, we packed along a travel crib and it worked great—providing a safe and familiar zone for our toddler even in iffy hotel rooms. The PeaPod is a lightweight pop-up tent that fits in a small carry bag (www.kidco.com). BabyBjörn's travel crib is super lightweight and collapses down to the size of a suitcase (www.babybjorn.com). At a minimum, bring your child's sleep sack or blanket, which can be a comforting reminder of home. If all else fails, get creative: Make a kid-sized nest on the floor from pillows or couch cushions and get your young adventurer excited about indoor "camping."

In addition to being required safety equipment while driving, a car seat can be a stress-saver when traveling by plane, train, or bus. Although it makes for a bulky carry-on, your child's car seat from home is a dose of familiarity and a familiar place for a nap.

Be aware that car-seat attachment points can be different in European cars: If you bring your own seat, pack a car-seat clip in case you need to secure the seat to the shoulder-strap seat belt. You can also arrange a safety seat through your car-rental company (usually an expensive option).

If your child drinks formula, do some research—your usual formula may be available in Europe, but under a different name. Before you fly away, be sure you've packed acetaminophen (easy-dissolving tabs are best), diaper rash cream, a thermometer, and any special medications your baby may need (medically necessary liquids are exempted from the 3.4-ounce limit for carry-on liquids—but make sure they are labeled and declare them to the screener).

Older Kids: Technology can make the difference between a dream trip and a nightmare. A tablet or portable gaming device can fill long hours traveling between destinations and soak up time when dinner drags on. Load up on kid-friendly apps, ebooks, movies, and TV shows before you leave. Get a Y-jack so two kids can listen with earbuds. There's nothing like a favorite show to help calm your kids before bedtime. Consider giving each of your kids their own camera so they can take pictures and make movies from their own perspective. (Back home, encourage older kids to organize and edit photos and video clips.)

Toys: Don't pack too many toys; these take up lots of suitcase space (though it's kind to let a child choose a small toy, such as a stuffed animal, to bring from home for comfort). You can easily buy toys and sports equipment in Europe. The cheapest toy selection is often in large department stores. For the athletic child, a soccer ball guarantees hours of amusement with newfound friends on foreign turf.

A trip to the local toy store can be a fun outing. For quiet time in the hotel room, buy a set of Legos, coloring books, stickers, dolls, or other toys, which can be excitingly different from those found in the US.

Flying with Kids

Deciding whether to buy a separate plane ticket for your child under age two is a matter of what you can endure in the air: That cute gurgling baby might become the airborne hellion as soon as the seat-belt light goes off. If you elect to keep your child on your lap, you'll still pay the tax on the ticket cost for an international flight. The child doesn't get a seat, but many airlines have baby perks for moms and dads who request them in advance—roomier bulkhead seats, bassinets, and baby meals.

Kids age two and up are required to have their own seat. Some airlines offer a child's fare, which is typically 85-90 percent of the adult fare. Other airlines simply charge the full fare—a major financial owie. Children's fares may not appear when booking tickets online, so it's worth calling a travel agent to see if they can get you a discount. Generally, from age 12 on, kids pay full fare.

As soon as you buy your plane tickets, immediately grab seat assignments so your family has a better chance of being seated together. Inquire about food service on your flight; most international flights still offer a complimentary meal, but be prepared to bring snacks for your crew.

Pick flights with few connections; if your child is able to sleep on planes, a red-eye can work well. Decide if you want to sit near the aisle or window. A window seat gives your active child only one escape route, plus the added entertainment of the window. However, a toddler who needs frequent diaper changes and sits quietly may be more comfortable by the aisle. (Note that if you're using a car seat on the plane, it must be placed in a window seat so it won't block the escape path in an emergency.)

At the airport, you'll have to clear security with your brood. It's easier for you (and everyone else in line) if you're ready before entering the security line: Take off jackets, untie shoes (children under 12 can leave their

Watching the in-flight movie can help pass a few hours in the air.

shoes on), pull out liquids. All of your carry-ons, including children's bags, toys, and blankets, must go through the X-ray machine. Children who can walk without assistance will be expected to go through the metal detector separately from their parents; babies can be carried through. You may encounter a full-body scanner; you and your children can opt out of this type of screening, but you may be subjected to a thorough pat-down instead.

Some airlines and more than 150 US airports participate in the TSA Precheck program, which allows you to register to skip lines and elements of TSA screening. You get to keep your shoes on your feet and your liquids and laptops in your bags—a major help to harried parents trying to wrangle excited kids through security. Children 12 and under can accompany a prescreened parent or guardian through Precheck, but teenagers must register separately. Learn more and register at www.tsa.gov/tsa-precheck.

Some airlines have phased out early boarding for families or charge for the privilege. If your carrier doesn't offer early boarding, approach the gate agent at a quiet moment and ask if he or she can help. Tire out your tykes before boarding the plane. Some airports have play spaces—if you can't find one, take over an empty gate area. If you fly at night, consider having your child skip that afternoon's nap. While you're waiting to board, get your kids up and moving as much as possible. Finally, when you're on the plane and it's time for sleep, follow normal bedtime routines. Change your child into pajamas, tuck her in with a blanket, and read a story or two.

Be prepared. Have at least one change of clothes and plenty of diapers and wipes for your baby or toddler (Mom and Dad might want to have an extra shirt, just in case). Make sure your electronics are fully charged before boarding. Don't forget to pack earbuds for tablets and gaming devices (others on the plane will thank you). For younger kids, have lots of activities and surprises, such as books they haven't seen before, stickers, paper, washable markers, activity books, and Mad Libs.

Jet lag can be kiddie purgatory. If you can tolerate some—OK, maybe a lot of— crankiness on the first day,

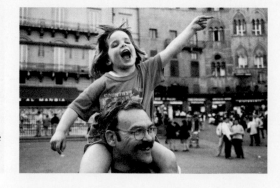

keep young children awake until a reasonable bedtime. After Junior passes out from exhaustion, hopefully the whole family will sleep through the night and wake up when the locals do. Take it easy at the beginning (maybe even starting with a rural destination), allowing a couple of low-impact days to get over jet lag (for more on dealing with jet lag, see page 408).

Family-Friendly Lodging

Instead of picking up and moving every few days, some families prefer settling down in an apartment or house, using it as their home base, then side-tripping to nearby destinations. If you're traveling with school-age kids, staying in one place for two to three nights is a good bet. Self-catering flats rented by the week, such as *gîtes* in France and villas in Italy, give a family a home on the road. To cut costs, try home-sharing services that let you swap houses with a European family. Not only is it cheaper, but you get to spend time together cooking, watching movies, and just hanging out. It's a cultural experience just to see European TV together. But be aware that European standards on televised sex and nudity are more relaxed than in the US; you might stumble on some uncensored movies, or even unbridled porn, right next to the Nickelodeon channel.

Renting or swapping a house or a flat can facilitate traveling with another family, a strategy that can make your trip easier and more fun. You'll have other adults around to help orchestrate things, and your kids will have built-in playmates.

If you're traveling with older kids, consider hostels. Families can hostel very cheaply (especially in high-priced Scandinavia). Family membership cards are inexpensive, and there's

In very tight European hotel rooms, you might have to stow your kids in the closet...or, better yet, ask for an extra bed.

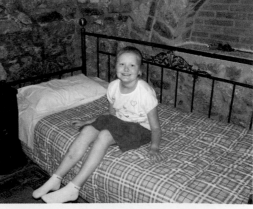

no age limit. Hostels typically have member kitchens where the family can cook and eat for the price of groceries. Some hostels offer family rooms with enough beds for all of you.

If your kids love camping, rent a camper van or small RV. Kids and campgrounds—with swings, slides, and plenty of friends—mix wonderfully. Suddenly your family and the Spanish kids over at the next tent are best amigos.

Most hotels, especially those catering to business travelers, have large family rooms. Many big, budget chain hotels allow two kids to sleep for free in their rooms. Bonus: They'll sometimes have a swimming pool. Bigger hotels are also more likely to have entertaining public spaces, such as lobbies with glass elevators or casual terraces with foosball tables. Some European chains, such as KinderHotels, appeal to families by providing playrooms, baby equipment, and professional babysitters.

In some countries, you may need to know the necessary phrases to communicate your needs. If you're a family of four and your children are young, request a triple room plus a small extra child's bed. Traveling with teenagers, you may need two rooms: a double (one big bed) and a twin (a room with two single beds). In much of Europe, a "double" bed is actually two twins put together. These can easily be separated.

Be careful about staying in small hotels or B&Bs with a baby. If your child wakes up in the middle of the night, you're going to wake up everybody else. Some B&Bs won't take children, or impose an age limit (such as no kids under 8); ask before booking.

Choosing lodging close to your daytime activities is smart if your little traveler needs to return for a nap or supplies. Having two adjoining rooms can be better for dealing with sleep issues: One jet-lagged person won't keep everyone else up, and napping will be easier. Request quiet rooms away from the street and bar. If your child is used to sleeping in his or her own space and you're all in one room, ask for one with a partition, large closet, or other area in which you can separate your child when it's bedtime (baby can even sleep in the bathroom).

If you have young children, childproof the room on arrival. A roll of duct tape makes quick work of electrical outlets. Place anything breakable out of reach. Proprietors are generally helpful to considerate and undemanding parents.

With a toddler, budget extra to get a bath in your room—a practical need and a fun diversion. If the shower has a high lip, you can at least create a kid-friendly bathing puddle.

For more information on the types of accommodations mentioned above, see the Sleeping chapter.

Feeding Kids on the Road

Start the day with a good, substantial breakfast (at hotels, kids sometimes eat free), and plan for snack breaks. Buying bread, cheese, fruit, and drinks in the morning means you can picnic anytime, anywhere. Foreign grocery stores are an adventure for kids, so bring them along to help shop.

Find the most scenic perch for your picnic.

In each country, grocery stores have different kinds of kids' treats, some of which may end up being a real hit—sparking both a country-specific passion and great memories. Another fun (and cheap) option is to get takeout food, such as bratwurst, pizza by the slice, crêpes, or sandwiches, from a street stand. You can eat your meals on a square, at a park, or on the top deck of a tour bus.

Sample gelato, croissants, or chocolate every day (gelato should be twice a day)—whatever is a "specialty" treat of the country you're in. It's a great way to get off your feet and take a break. At home, you may try to avoid bribes, but the promise of a treat can make a huge difference to everyone's cooperation when you're out and about—and don't have space for a "time out."

Seek out kid-pleasing local dishes wherever you go, including crêpes and *croque monsieurs* (grilled ham-and-cheese sandwiches) in France, *pasta bianca* (plain pasta) and *frullati* (smoothies) in Italy, *tortillas* (omelets) in Spain, and fish-and-chips in England.

Since many restaurants don't have high chairs, you might have to do a little juggling at mealtime.

Quality chain restaurants—including many local varieties you won't have seen before—provide some good go-to options that will please young pallets. An occasional Big Mac or Whopper between all the bratwurst and kraut helps keep the family happy. (And, at European fast-food joints, parents can often enjoy their own treat of a beer.)

The Steves Kids Vote on Britain's Best and Worst

Imagine being a teenager forced to spend a big part of your summer vacation with robo-tourist Rick Steves (alias Dad). Jackie and Andy did that a while ago. What were the highlights? Here are the results of the post-trip interview:

Best City: Blackpool—England's white-knuckle ride capital! The Big One (one of the world's fastest and highest roller coasters) is still the best. A tip: Avoid the old wooden-framed rides. They're too jerky for parents.

Best Nature Experience: Horseback riding through the Cotswolds with a guide who'll teach you to trot. Wear long pants. One hour is plenty.

Types of Tours: Open-deck bus tours are good for picnic lunches with a moving view. At museums, audioguide tours are nice because you can pick and choose what you want to learn about.

Worst Food: The "black pudding" that so many B&B people want you to try for breakfast...it's a gooey sausage made of curdled blood.

Best New Food: Chocolate-covered digestive biscuits and vinegar on chips (that's British for "French fries").

Most Boring Tour: The Beatles tour in Liverpool: Most kids couldn't care less about where Paul McCartney went to grade school or a place called Strawberry Fields.

Funniest Activity: The Bizarre Bath walking tour is two hours of jokes and not a bit of history. It's irreverent and dirty—but in a way that parents think is OK for kids.

Best Activities: Leisure (LEZH-ur) Centres in almost every town have good swimming pools.

Best Theater: Shakespeare's Globe in London. First tour the theater to learn about how and why it was built like the original from 1600. Then buy cheap "groundling" tickets to see the actual play right up front, with your elbows on the stage. The actors involve the audience...especially the groundlings.

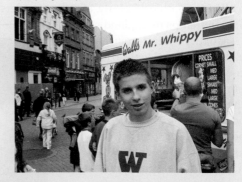

Most Interesting Demonstrations: The precision slate-splitting demonstration at the slate mines in North Wales. The medieval knight at the Tower of London who explained his armor and then demonstrated medieval sword fighting tactics—nearly killing his squire.

Eating at full-service European restaurants is a social event, but it can get stressful with small children, since service is much slower than at home. Dinner can easily take two hours, so bring something to occupy the kids while lingering. You may want to skip the white-tablecloth places and hit self-service cafeterias, relaxed cafés, or bars (kids are welcome, though sometimes restricted to the restaurant section or courtyard area). Sidewalk cafés allow parents to dine al fresco while well-behaved youngsters explore nearby. Eat by 7 p.m. to miss the adult crowd. Don't expect high chairs to be available; use your stroller in a pinch.

If your kids find certain condiments make anything palatable (I'm looking at you, ketchup), pack a small bottle of the kind they like to help make unfamiliar foods more appealing. If your kids love peanut butter, bring it from home for food emergencies—it can be hard to find or might taste different in Europe.

In restaurants (or anywhere), if your infant is making a disruptive fuss, apologetically say the local word for "teeth" (*dientes* in Spanish, *dents* in French, *denti* in Italian, *Zähne* in German), and annoyed people will become sympathetic.

If you crave a leisurely, peaceful evening out, splurge on a babysitter. Hotels often can get sitters, usually from professional agencies. The service is expensive but worth it. With older kids, we enjoyed an adult break in a nicer, romantic restaurant by giving our teenagers enough money for dinner at a diner and turning them loose for the evening. It was an adventure for them, a welcome break for all involved, and we all shared our stories back at the hotel before bedtime.

Kid-Friendly Sightseeing

Review the day's plan at breakfast with the family. Let your kids make some decisions: choosing lunch spots or deciding which stores to visit. Turn your kid into your personal tour guide and navigator. If you use my guidebooks, deputize your child to lead you on my self-guided walks and museum tours.

Since a trip is a splurge for the parents, the kids should enjoy a larger allowance, too. Provide ample money and ask your kids to buy their own treats, *gelati*, postcards, and trinkets within that daily budget. Expect older kids to carry and use the currency. If you don't want your younger child to carry

What's more fun: a museum or the Eiffel Tower?

cash, you can be the "banker" and keep a tally of expenses.

Before buying sightseeing passes for your family, consider how many of the covered attractions will be top choices for your kids. It's not worth setting an exhausting whirlwind pace to race to every attraction just to make the pass pay for itself. Instead, make a short list of the places you and your kids really want to see, and calculate whether a pass makes sense; if not, buy individual admissions. And remember that some museums are free for kids under a certain age.

Hands-on activities, such as this candlemaking demonstration, bring museums to life for kids.

Make getting somewhere as much fun as the destination. Kids love subway maps, train schedules, and plotting routes. Even the automated ticket kiosks are entertaining. Allow time for all of this, rather than just rushing onto a subway train or bus. After a teaching run, let your child lead the family on subway journeys—kids love the challenge. An added perk: Train rides are free for infants and toddlers (and sometimes even for school-age children).

Boat and bus tours can also be a hit. Your kids might not care about the Crown Jewels, but they may go nuts riding the double-decker bus getting there. Open-top, double-decker, hop-on-hop-off tour buses are great for young sightseers and provide easy transportation to the biggest sights. You can even have a picnic on top while you race through city streets. Boats are also memorable, such as a ride on a Venetian vaporetto or a glide down Amsterdam's canals.

Try a guided walking tour. Some parents are leery of group tours because they're afraid their kids will be the most disruptive members. But your kids will listen to a guide more than they will listen to you. Being in a group of adults can tone down even the wildest child.

Hands-on tours, from cheesemaking to chocolate factories, keep kids engaged. Go to sports or cultural events, but don't insist on staying for the entire event.

European parks provide a wonderland of fun, including puppet shows, pony rides, merry-go-rounds, small zoos, or playgrounds. One of my favorite places to mix kid business with pleasure is Luxembourg Garden in Paris. They have cafés and people-watching for parents, and a play area full of imaginative slides, swings, jungle gyms, and chess games for kids. You'll also find a merry-go-round, pony rides, toy rental sailboats in the main pond, and *guignols* (French marionette shows). On summer evenings, visit Paris's carnival at the Jardin des Tuileries to ride bumper cars and giant swings, try a ring toss, and eat barbe à papa ("Papa's beard," cotton candy).

Copenhagen's Tivoli Gardens is like a Hans Christian Andersen fairy tale, with games, marching bands,

shows, and rides ranging from vintage cars to a Ferris wheel that resembles a clock to roller coasters. Petzi's World, based on a popular Danish cartoon bear, offers a cuddly array of rides and activities.

European amusement parks—such as Denmark's Legoland—are fun for kids of all ages.

Many cities have public swimming pools, and bigger cities also have recreation centers or water parks (check out Paris' Aquaboulevard). For family adventures and fun memories, rent bikes, paddle boats, or rowboats. Local tourist offices can help you dig up these treats.

On days when your troop will need lots of staying power, don't wear them out with too much walking. It's worth taking a taxi to the Louvre to conserve leg strength for getting to the *Mona Lisa*. At least every other day, take an extended break. Return to your hotel or apartment after lunch for two hours for napping, reading, or listening to music. What you lose in sightseeing time, you will gain in energy levels.

Consider visiting an amusement park as an end-of-trip reward—the promise of Legoland in Denmark, Blackpool in England, or Disneyland Paris can keep your kids motoring through the more mundane attractions. Europe's open-air folk museums are a bonanza for families; it's worth a detour if your itinerary takes you near one (see page 340).

Big-Sight Survival with Kids

Europe is rich with amazing museums, churches, and art. But unlike you, kids may not appreciate the magnificence of a Michelangelo statue or the significance of an ancient temple frieze. Still, there are ways to liven up big sights. And whenever possible, go early or book ahead for big sights to avoid long lines (see my crowd-beating tips on page 323).

Ask at the information desk for activity packets designed for children; you'll find these especially at museums in Great Britain. Museum audioguides are great for older children. My kids liked them because they could choose what they wanted to learn about. Bigger sights often have audioguides tailored to the interests of school-age children. For younger children, hit the gift shop first so they can buy postcards and have a scavenger hunt to find the pictured artwork. When boredom sets in, try "I spy" games or have them count how many babies or dogs they can spot in all the paintings in the room.

Seek out kid-friendly museums. London's Natural History Museum offers a wonderful world of dinosaurs, volcanoes, meteors, and creepy-crawlies. There are no "do not touch" signs at Florence's two Leonardo da Vinci museums, where kids can use their own energy to power modern recreations of Leonardo's inventions. If you choose your destination carefully, everyone can enjoy, or at least tolerate, a museum visit.

Indulge your kids' interest in climbing and seeing the world from different angles. At Notre-Dame Cathedral, reenact hunchback Quasimodo's stunt and climb the tower. Kids love being on such a lofty perch, face-to-face with a gargoyle. A trip up Pisa's Leaning Tower or across the see-through glass walkway of London's Tower Bridge might be a much better use of time and money than another museum visit.

Precautionary Measures

Even well-behaved kids can wander off or get separated from you in a crowd. Whenever you're traveling with children in an unfamiliar place, have a go-to procedure in place in case something happens.

When visiting crowded public venues like markets or bustling museums, pause before entering to agree on a place to meet if you get separated. If you haven't established a meeting place, your kids should know to inform any nearby uniformed or official-looking person that they're lost, and to stay close to where they last saw you. In a crowded situation, having a unique family noise (a whistle or call, such as a

LEFT
Audioguides keep kids engaged and entertained on bus tours.

RIGHT
The Picasso Museum in Paris offers audio tours tailored for children.

Tips for Traveling with Teens

Watching young adults discover a wider world and engage with a new culture can be uniquely gratifying. But helping teens get excited for your trip and stay happy on the road can take some work.

The more you can let them travel on their own terms, the better. Here are some ideas for harmonious travel.

Give Them a Choice: Have your teens flip through the guidebook and point out things they want to see or do. Ask them to plan the details of a visit, such as how to get there, whether advance tickets are needed, and what everyone should know about the sight ahead of time.

Stylish Security: Teens may find travel-specific accessories and clothes, such as money belts and fast-drying fabrics, to be "lame." Send them looking for stylish alternatives, such as colorful money pouches to go under clothing, or underwear and scarves with hidden pockets. Athletic wear such as yoga or running pants often have theft-deterring zippered pockets.

Staying in Touch: Your teens can connect with friends at home and European pals they meet on their trip with Wi-Fi and apps such as WhatsApp, Snapchat, Google Talk, FaceTime, or Skype. (And messaging apps are great for keeping you and your teen in touch on the road.) Readily available Wi-Fi helps keep online habits affordable if your plan doesn't include unlimited data. Otherwise, consider buying an international data plan to avoid roaming charges (for more on using smartphones in Europe, see page 288).

Keeping a Low Profile: Reading a walking tour aloud while leading the family down the sidewalk is a major faux pas—to a teen. Download my free audio tours to let your teen listen to the narration via earbuds instead.

Cut Them Loose: Teens are usually eager to explore independently. Set a time and place to meet when you arrive at a museum or other sight so they can experience it on their own. Museum audioguides help them get the most out of it. Then compare notes when you reconvene.

When in Rome: The drinking age varies between 16 and 18 across Europe. Be ready for your kids to point this out (and decide on the family policy before they do). Ordering a glass of wine with dinner at a European restaurant may be a thrilling experience for an American teen.

A Taste of Home: When homesickness sets in, take your teenager to see a movie—American movies are commonplace (make sure your screening is subtitled). Or give in to a visit to a McDonald's or Starbucks for familiarity's sake.

"woo-woop" sound) enables you to easily get each other's attention. If the worst happens, get local authorities involved quickly.

For handy identification your kids can carry, see page 454. Before leaving the hotel for a day of sightseeing, give your kids your hotel's business card and your mobile phone number. If you're bringing phones from home, make sure your plan allows you to text each other in Europe; it's the easiest way to keep track of everyone. If your child won't have a mobile phone, make sure they know to ask to use the phone if they are lost. Consider purchasing cheap pay-as-you-go mobile phones once you arrive in Europe (explained on page 290). Show your kids how to make calls in each country you visit.

When using public transportation, make sure everyone knows the final stop, and have a backup plan for what to do if you lose each other (for example, plan to meet at your final stop or reconvene at your hotel).

Europe is not the United States of Litigation. Europeans love children, but their sense of childproofing public spaces is vastly different from ours. You may find a footbridge across a raging river has child-sized gaps between the railings. Windows in fourth-floor hotel rooms may be easy to open and unscreened. The hot water may scald you in about 30 seconds. Pay attention.

Reflecting and Connecting

Help your kids collect and process their observations. Buy a journal at your first stop, and it becomes a fun souvenir in itself. Kids like cool books—pay for a nice one. The journal is important, and it should feel that way. Encourage kids to record more than just a trip log: Collect feelings, smells, tastes, reactions to cultural differences, and so on. Grade-school kids enjoy pasting in ticket stubs or drawing pictures of things they've seen (for more on journaling, see page 438).

It can be hard for kids to hang around grown-ups all day, so help your kids connect with other children. In hot climates, kids

Journaling trip experiences is fun for kids—and lets them create a personalized souvenir.

gravitate toward the squares (in cities and villages alike) when the temperature begins to cool in the late afternoon, often staying until late in the evening. Take your children to the European nightspots to observe—if not actually make— the scene (such as the rollerbladers at the Trocadéro in Paris or the crowd at Rome's Trevi Fountain).

Just a few phrases spoken by your kids will open many doors. Make a point of teaching them "thank you," "hello," and "good-bye" in the country's language. You'll find nearly everyone speaks English, but small phrases out of the mouths of babes will melt the cool of surly museum guards or harried shop clerks.

During the trip, your kids may complain about being parted from their friends or having to visit yet another museum. But don't lose heart—sometimes the payoff comes years down the road. Your child may surprise you one day by mentioning a painting in Madrid's Prado or recalling a fact about Rome's Colosseum. Besides building memories, your investment in a trip now is a down payment on developing a true citizen of the world.

SAVVY SENIORS

More people than ever are hocking their rockers and buying plane tickets. Many senior adventurers are proclaiming, "Age matters only if you're a cheese." I've long noticed that older travelers seem younger than average in their appearance, attitudes, and energy levels. Travel is their fountain of youth.

When to Go: If you're retired and can travel whenever you want, it's smart to aim for shoulder season (April through mid-June, or September and October). This allows you to avoid the most exhausting things about European travel: crowds and the heat of summer.

Travel Insurance: Seniors pay more for travel insurance—but are also more likely to need it. Find out exactly whether and how your medical insurance works overseas. (Medicare is not valid outside the US except in very limited circumstances; check your supplemental insurance coverage for exclusions.) When considering additional travel insurance, pay close attention to evacuation insurance, which covers the substantial expense of getting you to adequate medical care in case of an emergency—especially if you are too ill to fly commercially. For more on travel-insurance options, see page 70.

Packing: Packing light is especially important for

LEFT Their fountain of youth is Europe!

RIGHT Seniors can travel as footloose and fancy-free as their teenage grandkids.

seniors—when you pack light, you're younger. To lighten your load, take fewer clothing items and do laundry more often. Fit it all in a roll-aboard suitcase—don't try to haul a big bag. Figure out ways to smoothly carry your luggage, so you're not wrestling with several bulky items. For example, if you bring a second bag, make it a small one that stacks neatly (or even attaches) on top of your wheeled bag.

Carry an extra pair of eyeglasses if you wear them, and bring along a magnifying glass if it'll help you read detailed maps and small-print schedules. A small notebook is handy for jotting down facts and reminders, such as your hotel-room number or Metro stop. Doing so will lessen your anxiety about forgetting these details, keeping your mind clear and uncluttered.

Medications and Health: It's best to take a full supply of any medications with you, and leave them in their original containers. Finding a pharmacy and filling a prescription in Europe isn't necessarily difficult, but it can be time-consuming. Plus, nonprescription medications (such as vitamins or supplements) may not be available abroad in the same form you're used to. Pharmacists overseas are often unfamiliar with American brand names, so you may have to use the generic name instead (for example, atorvastatin instead of Lipitor). Before you leave, ask your doctor for a list of the precise generic names of your medications, and the names of equivalent medications. For more on getting medical help in Europe, see page 417.

If you wear hearing aids, be sure to bring spare batteries—it can be difficult to find a specific size in Europe. If your mobility is limited, see "Travelers with Disabilities," later, for tips and resources.

Flying: If you're not flying direct, check your bag—because if you have to transfer to a connecting flight at a huge, busy airport, your carry-on bag will become a lug-around drag. If you're a slow walker, request a wheelchair or an electric cart when you book your seat so you can easily make any connecting flights. Since cramped legroom can be a concern for seniors, book early to reserve aisle seats (or splurge on roomier "economy plus," or first class). Stay hydrated during long flights, and take short walks hourly to minimize the slight chance of getting a blood clot.

Accommodations: Hotels vary widely in their amenities and layouts, so think carefully about your needs before you book. Ask about any accessibility quirks for the hotel you're considering—find out whether it's at the top of a steep hill, has an elevator or stairs to upper floors, and so on. If stairs are a problem, request a ground-floor room. Location matters too: If you stay near the train station at the edge of town, you'll minimize carrying your bag on arrival; on the other hand, staying in the city center gives you a convenient place to take a break between sights (and you can take a taxi on arrival to reduce lugging your bags).

With the advantage of a more flexible schedule, seniors can often find good alternative accommodations for longer stays. You can rent a house or apartment, or even swap houses for a week or more with someone in an area you're interested in. The swap needn't be simultaneous, and can sometimes include cars and recreational equipment like bikes and canoes (for more on rentals and house swapping, see the Sleeping chapter). Travelers' cultural exchange organizations offer you the chance to stay in locals' homes for a minimal courtesy fee and learn about your destination from those who live there (see "Educational, Exchange, and Volunteer Opportunities," later).

Getting Around: Subways involve a lot of walking and stairs (and are a pain with luggage). They also have relatively few stops; just getting to the station can be a journey on its own. Consider using city buses or taxis instead. City buses stop frequently, so you'll never have to walk far to get a ride, and with a little planning you can align your sightseeing itinerary with convenient routes. When out and about with your luggage, take a taxi. If you're renting a car, be warned that some countries and some car-rental companies have an upper age limit—to avoid unpleasant surprises, mention your age when you reserve (for details, see the Driving & Navigating chapter).

Pilgrims of all ages hike from France to Santiago de Compostela in northwest Spain.

Senior Discounts: Just showing your gray hair or passport can snag you a discount at many sights, and even some events such as concerts. (The British call discounts "concessions"; look also for "pensioner's rates.") Always ask about discounts, even if you don't see posted information about one—you may be surprised. In non-English-speaking countries, memorize the phrase for requesting a senior discount or write it down on a card to hand over at the admissions desk. Note that at some sights, senior discounts are reserved for European citizens.

Any senior can get deals on point-to-point rail tickets in Austria, Belgium, Great Britain, Finland, France, Germany, Italy, Spain, and Norway (including the Eurostar train between Britain and France/Belgium). Qualifying ages range from 60 to 67 years old. To get rail discounts in most countries—including Austria, Britain, Germany, Italy, and Spain, and a second tier of discounts in France—you must purchase a senior card at a local train station (valid for a year, but can be worthwhile even on a short trip if you take several train rides during your stay; advance-purchase discounts can be as good or better than the senior card offers). Most rail passes don't offer senior discounts, but passes for Britain (as well as the Balkans) do give seniors a break on both first- and second-class passes.

Sightseeing: Many museums have elevators, and even if these are freight elevators not open to the public, the staff might bend the rules for older travelers. Take advantage of the benches in museums; sit down frequently to enjoy the art and rest your feet. Go late in the day for fewer crowds and cooler temperatures. Many museums offer loaner wheelchairs. Take bus tours (usually two hours long) for a painless overview of the highlights. Boat tours—of the harbor, river, lake, or fjord—are a pleasure. Hire an English-speaking cabbie to take you on a tour of a city or region (if it's hot, spring for an air-conditioned taxi). Or participate in the life of local seniors, such as joining a tea dance at a senior center. If you're traveling with others but need a rest break, set up a rendezvous point. Some find that one day of active sightseeing needs to be followed by a quiet day to recharge the batteries. For easy sightseeing, grab a table at a sidewalk café for a drink and people-watching.

Educational, Exchange, and Volunteer Opportunities: For a more meaningful cross-cultural experience, consider going on an educational tour such as those run by Road Scholar (formerly Elderhostel), which offers study programs around the world for those over 50 (trips from several days to several months, www.roadscholar.org). International cultural exchange organizations like Servas offer the opportunity to meet and stay with welcoming locals—an inexpensive way to get intimate with a new place and its people (see page 516 for details). For ideas on volunteer programs, see page 518.

Long-Term Trips: Becoming a temporary part of the community can be particularly rewarding. Settle down and stay a while, doing side-trips if you choose. If you're considering retiring abroad, two good resources are the *Living Abroad* series (Moon Travel Guides), which offers a country-by-country look at the challenges and rewards of life overseas, and ExpatExchange.com, where you'll find tips and resources for expatriates.

More Tips: The AARP (American Association of Retired People) provides an extensive library of travel-related articles and advice for seniors at Travel.AARP.org, including destination guides, budget travel recommendations, and an interactive trip finder. The AARP also offers info on retiring abroad.

TRAVELERS WITH DISABILITIES

The creaky, cobblestoned Old World has long had a reputation for poor accessibility. It's the very charm of Europe—old and well-preserved—that often adds to the barriers. But Europe has made some impressive advances toward opening its doors to everyone, including travelers with limited mobility.

I'm inspired by the fact that, wherever I go in Europe, I see locals with disabilities: On the streets, in the museums, in the restaurants, and on the trains, you'll see people using wheelchairs, scooters, walkers, and canes to get around. If people with disabilities can live rich and full lives in Europe, then travelers with disabilities can certainly have an enjoyable and worthwhile vacation there, too.

Anyone with adventure in their soul can take advantage of all Europe has to offer. Levels of personal mobility vary tremendously from person to person. You need to consider your own situation very thoughtfully in choosing which attractions to visit, which hotels to sleep in, which restaurants to dine at...and which things you might want to avoid.

Trip Planning for Travelers with Disabilities

John Sage owns Sage Traveling, which plans and books accessible travel to Europe. John has taken his wheelchair to more than 90 European cities and has run into his share of challenges during his travels—but he also says that the obstacles can almost always be overcome. Here I've included excerpts, in John's own words, from his top tips for traveling in Europe.

Do your research. I hear all the time that "Venice is not wheelchair accessible" or "Paris has poor accessibility." While there are certainly some accessibility challenges, the truth is that the more research you do, the more accessible your trip will be. Avoiding bridges in Venice and hills in Paris is entirely possible. Did you know that Herculaneum's ruins are nearly identical to Pompeii's, but are wheelchair-friendly? And that cruise passengers with disabilities don't have to take the "donkey path" up the cliffs when visiting the Greek island of Santorini? Your vacation doesn't need to be a struggle—do your homework and your trip can be filled with fully accessible hotel accommodations, accessible routes between accessible tourist attractions, and wonderfully accessible travel experiences.

Book hotels far in advance. It is almost always cheaper to book your accessible hotel accommodation far in advance. Many hotels in European city centers have only one or two accessible rooms. The best ones get booked very early. For travel in the summer, make your reservations in December.

Carefully plan your route. If you know what you're getting into before you arrive in Europe, you'll have a much easier time on your trip. There'll likely be numerous ways to get to the tourist attractions you're so eager to see. Some routes will have wheelchair ramps, smooth pavement, and flat terrain; others may have steep hills, bothersome (and even dangerous) cobblestones, and flights of stairs. Research the accessibility of sidewalks, bus routes, subway stations,

Accessibility in Europe

This section was contributed by Carole Zoom, who has traveled to more than 30 countries with her scooter-style electric wheelchair and ventilator.

The concept of accessibility varies by culture. In the US, access means that an individual can use elevators, lifts, doors, entrances, and other features without any assistance. Individual autonomy is central to the American concept of access, as enshrined in the Americans with Disabilities Act (ADA).

Europe, on the other hand, subscribes to a medical rather than political model of disability. Policy tends to be focused on helping people with disabilities navigate a society built for nondisabled individuals—instead of helping society find ways to accommodate their needs. For example, in Europe an entryway with one step is considered accessible: The law assumes that disabled people will use manual wheelchairs that can be rolled up a step and/or will have family members assisting.

In the US it's illegal to discriminate based on what kind of mobility device a wheelchair user chooses. But in Europe, mobility scooter users have fewer rights than wheelchair users; scooters are seen not as a medical necessity, but as a convenience item for people who can still walk to some extent. Scooter-style wheelchairs are not allowed in some museums and other public facilities—you may be asked to walk if you can or to transfer to a manual wheelchair. If those are not options for you, be persistent in explaining your situation to museum staff.

Due to the age of many buildings in Europe, elevator access is not a given. A US citizen would assume a hotel is accessible upon hearing that it has an elevator. But many older European elevators are not large enough for American-style electric wheelchairs and scooters. Before you book a room, ask the hotel concierge for photos and exact measurements to ensure your style and size of wheelchair will fit. A hotel that hesitates to provide the info or photos you request is unlikely to be accommodating; in that case, move on and choose another.

Unlike in the US, European transit companies that operate planes, ships, trains, and buses may require advanced documentation of disability. If you need specific assistance, have your doctor fill out forms attesting to your needs before you travel, then contact the transit provider's medical desk at least 72 hours before your departure to ask how to submit them. Always confirm and reconfirm your reservations for assistance on all modes of advanced-ticketed transport.

We have an increasingly barrier-free world. But Americans going abroad need to be more aware and vigilant about accessibility than they are used to at home.

and the location of accessible building entrances before your trip. Check for accessibility information in the online visitors guides for your destinations—but be aware that not all guides will offer this type of information.

Stay in the most accessible parts of town. This is one of the hardest parts of planning your trip. You may have found a great accessible hotel, but what will you find when you walk/roll out the front door? Are there hills and stairs in all directions? Will you have to roll over cobblestones? Are there accessible restaurants nearby? It's crucial to research

Resources for Travelers with Disabilities

Tours

Accessible Journeys: Wheelchair-accessible trips, travel-planning, tips, and resources (www.disabilitytravel.com)

Accessible Tour Operators: Companies such as Rome and Italy Tourist Services (www.romeanditaly.com), Bespoke France (www.bespokefrance.com), and Christianakis Travel (Greece, www.christianakis.gr) provide accessible visits to their home turf

Disability Horizons: Online magazine with travel section covering a range of accessible tourism topics

DisabledTravelers.com: Resource site listing accessible tour operators, travel companions, van and equipment rental companies, and more

EmergingHorizons.com: Accessible travel site with tips and resources for wheelchair users and slow walkers, including the "Barrier-Free Travels" blog

FlyingWheelsTravel.com: Escorted tours and cruises, plus travel companions and ideas for independent travel

The Opening Door, Inc.: Extensive listings of disability travel organizations, access guides, tour operators, and other resources (www.travelguides.org)

SageTraveling.com: European trip-planning for people with disabilities, with guides for hire and accessibility reviews of European destinations

the hotel's neighborhood. You can use street view in Google Maps to get the lay of the land, then email the hotel with your questions.

Figure out accessible public transportation options. When choosing a hotel, don't forget to factor in the price of transportation. If you have to pay for a taxi to get to accessible restaurants, accessible shopping, and the tourist attractions, that hotel "deal" you found won't feel like such a good deal after all. In cities such as London, Paris, and Barcelona, stay near an accessible bus stop. In Berlin, Istanbul, and Venice, stay near an accessible metro, tram, or boat stop. In Florence, Cambridge, and Edinburgh, stay right in the middle of town so you can walk/roll everywhere.

Rely on the experience of other travelers with disabilities. You're certainly not the first person with disabilities to visit Europe. Find out what accessibility challenges other travelers encountered and how they got around them. Check travel forums (www.tripadvisor.com, www.cruisecritic.com, and www.ricksteves.com, for example) to find previous travelers' experiences—just be sure the information is up-to-date. Or seek out a travel agent who specializes in accessible travel. See the resources sidebar.

Have a backup plan. Even on the most perfectly

Official Help
Americans with Disabilities Act: US Department of Justice resources for those who feel they have been discriminated against due to a disability (tel. 800-514-0301 or 800-541-0383 TTY, www.ada.gov)
Aviation Consumer Protection Division (ACPD): US Department of Transportation aviation rules and how to register complaints (disability hotline: tel. 800-778-4838 or 800-455-9880 TTY, www.transportation.gov/airconsumer)

Reading
Barrier-Free Travel: A Nuts and Bolts Guide for Wheelers and Slow Walkers (Candy B. Harrington, 2009): A handy compilation of information for mobility-limited travelers, authored by the creator of the Emerging Horizons travel site
Sites Unseen: Traveling the World Without Sight (Wendy David, 2010): Tips and advice from a blind woman who globetrots without sighted companions (available in Braille and other formats from National Braille Press, www.nbp.org)
Survival Strategies for Going Abroad: A Guide for People with Disabilities (Laura Hershey, 2005): Stories and ideas from a variety of disabled travelers who have participated in international programs (free, $5 shipping, www.miusa.org)
Rick Steves' Easy Access Europe (Rick Steves, 2006): Guide for travelers with mobility challenges, with dated but still helpful information available free at www.ricksteves.com/easyaccess)

planned accessible vacation, something can go wrong. If it does, how will you deal with it? If you prepare for all the possible issues, travel with someone who can help you during your trip, and remain flexible, unexpected events won't turn into potential trip-ruining problems. What will you do if a part on your wheelchair breaks? If a train strike occurs in Italy, how will you get from Florence to Rome? With backup plans (such as packing vital spare parts for your wheelchair), you won't have to put your vacation on hold.

Consider a tour. A company that specializes in accessibility will lead you on the flattest, smoothest, shortest tour routes.

Before you take a tour or hire a guide, ask these questions:
- Is the tour guide a licensed professional? How much training has the guide received?
- What route will the guide use? Does it involve curbs, steps, steep hills, or cobblestones? Where are the accessible bathrooms located? Will the guide physically assist you if needed (i.e., push a manual wheelchair)?
- Is this a private tour, or will you be with other travelers? Are you expected to keep up with able-bodied tour members?
- How many people with disabilities have they guided in

the past year? (You want a guide who is active enough to be aware of the latest regulations or updates regarding accessibility.)

Anticipate your trip! You've done as much planning as you can. You've relied on the experience of other travelers with disabilities, and you're prepared for the unexpected. Now it's time to get excited about your trip. Majestic cities, beautiful art and architecture, fascinating history, exquisite food, and wonderful experiences await you.

Tips for Travelers with Wheelchairs

Susan Sygall is the CEO and cofounder of Mobility International USA (MIUSA), a nonprofit that links people with disabilities with work, study, teaching, volunteer, exchange, and research opportunities. It also offers a blog, resource library, and database of disability organizations. Sygall has been traveling the "Rick Steves way" since about 1973. Here, she shares some of her best tips for traveling in Europe with a wheelchair. Thanks to MIUSA's staff for help with this advice.

People who use wheelchairs, like so many of our non-disabled peers, want to get off the tourist track and experience the real France, Italy, or Portugal. Don't accept other people's notions of what is possible—I have climbed Masada in Israel and made it to the top of the Acropolis in Greece. Whether you travel alone, with friends, or with an assistant, you're in for a great adventure.

Pack light. I use a lightweight manual wheelchair with pop-off tires. I take a backpack that fits on the back of my chair and store my daypack underneath my chair in a net bag. Since I usually travel alone, if I can't carry it myself, I don't take it.

Plan for eventualities. I keep a bungee cord with me for the times I can't get my chair into a car and need to strap it in the trunk or when I need to secure it on a train. Remember that bike shops are excellent for tire repairs if you get a flat.

Susan Sygall, in Italy's Cinque Terre

Check your chair at the gate. I always insist on keeping my own wheelchair up to the airline gate, where I then check it. When I have a connecting flight, I again insist that I use my own chair.

Don't let bathroom access stop you. Bathrooms are often a hassle, so I have learned to use creative ways to transfer into narrow spaces. To be blatantly honest, when there are no accessible bathrooms in sight, I have found ways to pee discreetly just about anywhere. You gotta do what you gotta do. Bring along an extra pair of pants and a great sense of humor.

Look for freight elevators. If a museum lacks elevators for visitors, be sure to ask about freight elevators. Almost all have them somewhere, and that can be your ticket to seeing a world-class treasure.

Let wheelchairs help you. People who have difficulty walking long distances might want to bring a lightweight wheelchair or borrow or rent one when needed.

Insist on your rights. Don't confuse being flexible and having a positive attitude with settling for less than your rights. I expect equal access and constantly let people know about the possibility of providing access through ramps or other modifications. When I believe my rights have been violated, I do whatever is necessary to remedy the situation, so that the next traveler or disabled person in that country won't have the same frustrations.

Break down barriers. Try to learn some of the language of the country you're in. It cuts through the barriers when people stare at you (and they will), and also comes in handy when you need help going up a curb or a flight of steps.

Learn from locals. Remember that you are part of a global family of people with disabilities. Always get information about disability groups in the places you are going. See the resources listed on page 476 for a number of helpful organizations. They have the best access information, and many times they'll become your new traveling partners and friends.

Tips for Travelers with Impaired Vision

Carmen Papalia, who began to lose his vision in his early twenties, is a self-described "social-practice artist and nonvisual learner" who leads eyes-closed city walking tours and museum visits. For three months in 2015, he served as artist-in-residence at London's Victoria and Albert Museum.

When you travel, trust the senses that are available to you. Use them to be curious. Let them lead your exploration.

As a nonvisual traveler, I find what's interesting for me in a place. For example, I'm not a churchgoer but I went to Mass at St. Paul's in London just so I could spend time in that acoustic space. It was amazing, hearing the choir fill up the dome. In Strandhill, Ireland, I had a profound sensory experience soaking in a seaweed bath, followed by the quintessentially Irish taste of fish-and-chips for lunch. I relished pausing on a bridge over the Garavogue River in Sligo, Ireland, letting the rich waves of texture and sound consume me as the water beneath rushed out to the Atlantic.

Carmen Papalia, leading an eyes-closed city walking tour

Here are some other tips from my time traversing Europe:

Set your own terms. You can define your access and support needs and preferences, even in an unfamiliar place. Advocate for yourself; make your access considerations known, and only accept support that is consistent with your personal disability politics. Doing so gives you agency as a traveler. For example, when I am traveling alone, airline staff often ask me to sit in a wheelchair so they can push me instead of guiding me on foot to my connecting gate or to baggage claim. I always refuse. You can too; be firm about your limits.

Connect with people. The best support comes from relationships. In Europe, people are generally helpful and have a good respect for physical boundaries. Find out if the city you're visiting has a blind society or other support organization. Hostels are also great places to make friends.

Ask what museums offer. Many museums have programming such as touch tours and audioguides to help nonvisual visitors engage. I often prefer to have a friend describe the material to me. Always ask if museums offer concessions to disabled travelers and their companions. In Paris, my friend and I were able to skip the line and get free admission to many museums.

This 3-D map of Cambridge with a Braille description helps sight-impaired travelers in England's famous university town.

Accept help when necessary. Transit workers are usually approachable and willing to guide you to your platform, as well as radio ahead to your transfer point or destination to arrange for someone to meet you. In the London Tube, for example, such help is routine and friendly. Rely on hotel concierges, who can call cabs and coordinate other assistance. Menus are never accessible, but waitstaff are always happy to tell you about the food.

Learn to navigate cities. Many cities in Europe have tactile paving and various types of signals at crosswalks. For example, some intersections in the UK have a small, ridged cone underneath the signal box. The cone rotates when you can cross the street; touch it or listen for its spin. Research the places you're going so you know what to expect.

Employ all your senses. Nonvisual learners have the interesting opportunity of using other senses to initiate learning experiences. But to do this, we must actively choose to let our nonvisual senses guide our choices. It's a way of approaching the world from which even seeing travelers can benefit. I encourage all travelers to do it—your time abroad will take on much greater richness.

Bus Tours & Cruises

This book is all about mastering individual, self-directed travel. But while I advocate independent travel, I'm not against organized travel. Far from it—for more than 30 years, I've been organizing tours, taking thousands of travelers to Europe's best destinations. For many people, a bus tour or cruise is the best way to scratch their travel itch. Having someone else navigate for you, arrange where you'll sleep, and make the decisions takes the stress and work out of travel. Whether you join a bus tour or sign up for a cruise, a good organized tour can create plenty of memorable experiences.

A tour can also be the most economical way to see Europe: Large tour companies book thousands of rooms and meals year-round, and with their tremendous economic clout, they can get prices that no individual tourist can match. Similarly, the base price of mainstream cruises beats independent travel by a mile. For people looking to travel comfortably and cheaply, bus tours and cruises can be a good option, especially if you use the tips in this chapter to help you travel smartly—and through the Back Door.

TOURING EUROPE BY BUS

Taking a bus tour can be a good choice if your European vacation time is limited—but you'll want to carefully consider your options before signing up. Offerings range from luxury we-handle-everything bus tours for smaller groups to comfortable midrange tours (like mine, which are also for smaller groups) to low-end, pack-'em-in, big-bus operators for large groups. In nearly all cases, a bus tour includes a professional and multilingual guide, a comfy bus, decent hotels with mass-produced comfort, and some meals. The cheapest tours can cost less than $150 a day.

Choosing a Tour

Would you rather travel with a group of 48 or 28? Change hotels every night or enjoy two-night stays? There are plenty of variables to consider when comparing the fully-guided tours offered by travel companies.

And there are hundreds to choose from, covering a wide price range. The big names are dependable. Abercrombie & Kent, Maupintour, Tauck, and Odysseys Unlimited are high-end expensive. Cosmos and Globus are solid budget options. In between are Insight, Trafalgar, Collette—and my own tour company, Rick Steves Europe.

No matter which tour company you go with, it's important to do your research. Start by browsing your options online, asking friends, or talking to a travel agent for advice. The tour company may be very big, booking rooms by the thousands; it often even owns the hotels it uses. While these hotels fit American standards—large, not too personal, with double rooms and good plumbing, they're often on the outskirts of town. Keep in mind that the goal of most tour companies is to fill every seat on that bus. On the biggest tours, groups are treated as an entity: a mob to be fed, shown around, profited from, and moved out. If money is saved, it can be at the cost of real experience.

When considering tours, remember that some of the best

Comparing Bus Tours

When you're selecting a bus tour, the cost you're quoted isn't the only factor to consider. Investigate how many people you'll be traveling with as well as what extras you'll be expected to cover. Most tour companies include customer feedback on their websites—look around and see what previous tour members have to say. When comparing prices, remember that airfare is not included. The chart below illustrates what to expect from a range of tour companies.

	High-End	Rick Steves Tours	Low-End
Price per day	$400-950	$200-350	$175-300
Group size	20-45	24-28	40-50
Meals	50-75% included	50% included	35-50% included
Sightseeing	All included	All included	Most cost extra
Tips	All included except guide/driver	All included	None included

sellers are those that promise more sightseeing than is reasonable in a given amount of time. No tour can give you more than 24 hours in a day or seven days in a week. What a wide-ranging "blitz" tour can do is give you more hours on the bus. Choose carefully among the itineraries available.

Do you really want a series of one-night stands? Bus drivers call tours with ridiculous itineraries "pajama tours." You're in the bus from 8 a.m. until after dark, so why even get dressed?

Many who take an organized bus tour could have managed fine on their own.

The cheapest bus tours are impossibly cheap. There's literally no profit in their retail price. They can give you bus transportation and hotels for about what the tourist-off-the-street would pay for just the hotels alone. But there's a catch: These tours tend to charge extra for sightseeing, and make money by taking you to attractions and shops from which they receive kickbacks. However, savvy travelers on a tight budget can actually get the last laugh on these tours by thinking of them as a tailored bus pass with hotels tossed in. Skip out on the shopping, don't buy any of the optional tours, equip yourself with a guidebook, and do your own sightseeing every day. Just apply the skills of independent travel to the efficient, economical trip shell that these kinds of organized coach tours provide.

Having learned long ago what doesn't work when it comes to bus tours, I've made it a priority to give people taking my Rick Steves tours the best possible experience at

The standard European guide does the leading...and you do the following.

a midrange price. I keep my groups small (24-28 travelers), stay at least two nights in most locations (at centrally located hotels), and visit the important sights while also seeking out authentic cultural experiences. I offer a variety of itineraries—Europe-wide, regional, and city tours—and a variety of tour styles: fully guided tours, family-oriented tours, winter tours, and My Way tours, which let you set the sightseeing itinerary (we provide the transportation, hotels, and a tour manager).

Here's my advice for choosing a bus tour and getting the most value for your money:

Go with the smallest possible group. A small group can sightsee, dine, and sleep at places that mainstream groups can only dream of. The bigger the group, the more you're cut off from Europe's charms. When 50 tourists drop into a "cozy" pub, any coziness is trampled.

Avoid one-night stands. Frequent one-night stops can really wear you out. To help you feel settled for a good night's rest, the best tours let you sleep for two nights in the same hotel whenever possible.

Ask where your hotels are located. Hotels set in the historic heart of a city, within walking distance of major sights, make for a far more memorable trip—but some tour companies save money by parking guests in the middle of nowhere. If the tour brochure says you'll be sleeping in the "Florence area," that could be halfway to Bologna—and you'll spend half your sightseeing time on transportation to and from the city center. *Arrivederci, Firenze.* Get explicit locations before you decide.

Look for authentic eating experiences. Pick a tour that offers a generous taste of the best local dishes. A common complaint among travelers is that tour meals don't match the country's cuisine. Avoid a tour that offers too many forgettable buffets in big, impersonal hotel restaurants.

Find out about the guide. The quality of your guide can make or break your travel experience. Ask if your tour guide is salaried, or paid through tips and/or commission. Guides from most tour companies make the bulk of their income from tips and merchant kickbacks. A salaried guide can focus on creating memorable travel experiences for you—not on selling you an optional sightseeing or shopping excursion.

Take a close look at what's included—and what's not. Many budget tours expect you to shell out additional cash during your trip to cover "optional" sightseeing, charging as much as $50 or $100 extra for each excursion.

Confirm which sights you'll see. Do you at least recognize them? Don't assume that every famous museum or castle will be included in your itinerary. Some companies choose sights for their convenience rather than merit. For instance, the Lion Monument in Luzern, Switzerland is mediocre. What makes it "great" for tour companies is its easy

Some tours deliver exactly what they promise.

tour-bus parking. Meanwhile, Leonardo da Vinci's *Last Supper* in Milan may be passed over because it's expensive to visit and its mandatory reservation system is inconvenient.

Ask if the tour price is locked in once you make your deposit. Some tour outfits reserve the right to increase the price after you've signed up (depending on how many travelers sign up and/or currency fluctuations). Choose a company that guarantees the price will not change.

Read the fine print. What are the company's policies regarding cancellations, refunds, and trip interruption/cancellation insurance?

Bus Tour Self-Defense

Once you're on board with a bus tour, you'll be part of a group dynamic, but that doesn't mean you can't have any control over your trip. Here are some suggestions to help make sure the good times roll for you while you're on the road:

Be informed. A good guidebook and map are your keys to travel freedom. Get maps and tourist information from your hotel or a tourist information office. If your accommodations are located outside the city center, ask your hotelier how to catch public transportation downtown. Taxis can be affordable if you split the cost with other travelers.

Remember that it's your trip. Don't let bus tour priorities keep you from what you've traveled all the way to Europe to see. If your Amsterdam guide schedules a trip to the diamond-polishing place instead of the Van Gogh Museum (no kickbacks on Van Gogh), feel free to skip out and sightsee on your own. Your guide may warn you that you'll get lost and the bus won't wait. Keep your independence—and your hotel address in your money belt.

Questions to Ask Tour Companies

Nail down the price:
- How many nights and meals are included in the price?
- Are admission costs for sights included?
- Do singles pay a supplement? Can singles save by sharing rooms?
- Are optional excursions offered? Average cost?
- Will the guide and driver expect a tip? Approximately how much?
- Are there any other costs?
- Does a deposit lock in the advertised price?

Run a reality check on your dream trip:
- How many travelers will be on the tour?
- Roughly what is the average age and singles-to-couples ratio?
- Are children allowed? What is the minimum age?
- Which sights are on the itinerary?
- What is the driving time between destinations?
- How many nights are planned at each destination?
- Are hotels located downtown, or are they on the outskirts?
- Does each room have a private bathroom? Air-conditioning?
- How many meals are eaten at the hotel?
- What are the cancellation and refund policies?
- Can I see tour evaluations from past customers?

Discriminate among optional excursions. Some tour companies include certain activities in the price (such as half-day city sightseeing tours), then offer one or two optional special excursions or evening activities for an additional cost. While you are capable of doing plenty on your own, optional excursions can be a decent value—especially when you factor in the time and energy it requires to plan and execute logistics independently. But don't feel pressured to join. Guides may promote excursions because they get a commission. Compare prices by asking your hotelier or checking a guidebook for the going rate for a gondola ride, Seine River cruise, or whatever.

You'll find that some options are a better value through your tour than from the hotel concierge, but others aren't worth the time or money. While illuminated night tours of Rome and Paris are marvelous, I'd skip most "nights on the town." On the worst kind of big-bus-tour evening, several bus tours come together for an evening of "local color." Three hundred tourists drinking watered-down sangria and watching flamenco dancing on stage to the rhythm of their digital camera clicks is big-bus tourism at its worst.

If you shop...shop around. Many people make their European holiday one long shopping spree. This suits your guide and the local tourist industry just fine. Guides are quick to say, "If you haven't bought a Rolex, you haven't really been to Switzerland," or, "You can't say you've experienced Florence if you haven't bargained for and bought a leather coat."

Don't necessarily reject your guide's shopping tips; just keep in mind that the prices you see often include a 10-20 percent kickback. Do some comparison shopping, and don't let anyone rush you. Never swallow the line, "This is a special price available only to your tour, but you must buy now."

Keep your guide happy. Leading a tour is a demanding job with lots of responsibility, paperwork, traveler hand-holding, and miserable hours. Very often, guides are tired. They're away from home and family—often for months on end—and are surrounded by foreigners having an extended party that they're not always in the mood to join. Most guides treasure their time alone. Each traveler has personal demands,

A well-chosen tour can be a fine value, giving you a great trip and a table filled with new friends.

but don't insist on individual attention when the guide is hounded by countless others. Wait for a quiet moment to ask for advice or offer feedback.

Some guides feel threatened by independent-type tourists, but it's possible to maintain your independence without alienating your guide. Use your guide as a resource, and consider their insider advice when planning your solo sightseeing.

Seek out unjaded locals. The locals most tour groups encounter are hardened businesspeople who put up with tourists because they have to—it's their livelihood. Spending a "Bavarian evening" with 40 Americans at the most touristy beer hall in Munich, you'll meet all the wrong Germans. But if you make it a quest to find your own beer hall, it won't be long before you're clinking mugs with friendly locals. Break away. One summer night in Regensburg, Germany, I skipped out. While my tour was still piling off the bus, I enjoyed a beer—while overlooking the Danube, and under shooting stars—with the great-great-great-grandson of the astronomer Johannes Kepler.

CRUISING IN EUROPE

I once spoke to the CEO of a cruise line, who, in a previous career, sold children's snacks. As bizarre as that connection may seem, he explained to me how adults retain a natural, childlike impulse to explore, coupled with the need for a safe home to return to. While travelers love to get out of their comfort zones, doing so leads many of us to yearn all the more for a refuge or nest. Cruise ships cater to this expertly, by greeting passengers with a welcome table, cold drinks, and friendly smiles from crew members. On my first cruise, even I remember thinking, as I returned to my ship, "Whew... we're back home now."

Cruising offers a comfortable, efficient way to see Europe-if you do it smartly.

I'm not pro-cruise or anti-cruise. Taking a cruise can be a fun, affordable, time-efficient, low-hassle, and comforting way to experience Europe—provided you do it smartly. Cruise lines have no incentive to help you have a good time on your own in port—they'd rather you buy an organized excursion or stay on the ship to spend more money. So it's not only important to choose the right cruise, but also to keep your extra expenses to a minimum and equip yourself with good information to make the absolute most of your time in port. (These strategies are covered in detail by my *Mediterranean Cruise Ports* and *Northern European Cruise Ports* guidebooks, which teach cruisers how to use their precious shore time to their best advantage.)

A smart, informed cruiser can have a meaningful and culturally engaging experience while taking advantage of the economy and efficiency of cruising. Here are a few insights and suggestions for deciding whether or not to cruise—and then, if you choose to, how to pick the right one and make the best of your experience.

Is Cruising for You?

Short of sleeping on a park bench, I haven't found a more affordable way to see certain parts of Europe than cruising. On a Mediterranean cruise that includes room, board, transportation, tips, and port fees, a couple can pay as little as $100 per night—that's as much as a budget hotel room in many cities.

Cruising also works well for travelers who prefer to tiptoe into Europe, rather than dive right in. Cruising can serve as an enticing sampler of bite-sized visits, helping you decide where you'd like to return and spend more time.

It's also great for retirees (or families traveling with retirees), particularly those with limited mobility. Cruising rescues you from packing up your bags and huffing to the train station every other day. And some cruise lines offer excursions specifically designed for those who don't walk well, making it possible to access sights that might be difficult to get to on your own. A cruise aficionado who had done the math once told me that, if you know how to find the deals,

it's theoretically cheaper to cruise indefinitely than to pay for a retirement home.

Of course, independent, free-spirited travelers may not appreciate the constraints of cruising. For many, seven or eight hours in port is way too short, a tantalizing tease of a place where they'd love to linger for the evening—and the obligation to return to the ship every night is frustrating. If you're self-reliant, energetic, and want to stroll the cobbles of Europe at all hours, cruising probably isn't for you. Even so, some seasoned globetrotters find that cruising is a good way to travel comfortably on a shoestring budget.

There are different types of cruisers. Some travelers cruise because it's an efficient way to experience so many ports of call. They appreciate the convenience of traveling while they sleep, waking up in an interesting new destination each morning, and making the most out of every second they're in port. This is the "first off, last on" crowd that attacks each port like a footrace. You can practically hear their imaginary starter's pistol go off when the gangway opens.

Other cruisers come to enjoy the cruise experience itself. They enjoy basking by the pool, taking advantage of onboard activities, dropping some cash at the casino, running up a huge bar tab, and watching ESPN on their stateroom TV.

If you really want to be on vacation, aim for somewhere in the middle. Be sure to experience the ports that really tickle your wanderlust, but give yourself a "day off" every now and again in the less enticing ports to sleep in or hit the beach.

> ## Resources for Cruising
>
> **CruiseLine.com:** Consumer reviews, cruise search engine, and advice forum
> **CruiseCritic.com:** Consumer reviews of cruises and ports, cruise ship deck plans, and cruise search engine
> **CruiseCompete.com:** Comparison quotes from multiple travel agencies, including special deals
> **CruiseReport.com:** Consumer reviews and professional editorial reviews, cruise news, and special deals
> **CruiseMates.com:** Travel forums, consumer reviews, and cruise planning tips
> **AvidCruiser.com:** Informative blog, port profiles, and cruise videos
> **Ship Mate app:** Cruise and excursion planning, ship information, connect with other cruisers

How Cruises Operate

Understanding how the cruise industry makes money can help you take advantage of your cruise experience...and not the other way around. Cruising is a $40-billion-a-year business. Approximately one out of every five Americans has taken a cruise, and each year about 23 million people take one.

In order to compete for passengers and fill megaships, cruise lines offer fares that can be astonishingly low. In adjusted dollars, the price of cruises hasn't risen for several decades. Your cruise fare covers accommodations, all the meals you can eat in the ship's main dining room and buffet, and transportation from port to port. You can have an enjoyable voyage and not spend a penny more on board (though you'd still have some expenses in port). But the cruise industry is adept at enticing you with extras that add up quickly: alcohol, gambling (at onboard casinos), and cruise-company-run excursions. Other temptations include specialty restaurant surcharges, duty-free shopping, fitness classes, spa treatments, and photos.

It's very easy to get carried away—a round of drinks here, a night of blackjack there. First-timers are often astonished when they get their final onboard bill, which can easily exceed the original cost of the trip. But with a little self-control, you can limit your extra expenditures, making your supposedly cheap cruise *actually* cheap. You always have the right to say, "No, thanks" to these additional expenses.

Choosing a Cruise

Selecting a cruise that matches your travel style and philosophy is critical. Each cruise line has its own distinct personality, quirks, strengths, and weaknesses. Cruise lines fall into four basic price categories: mass-market (Royal Caribbean, Norwegian, Carnival, and Costa), premium (Celebrity, Holland America, and Princess), luxury (Azamara Club, Oceania, and Windstar), and ultra-luxury (Crystal, Regent Seven Seas, and Seabourn). River cruises offer the same range of prices and quality, but with smaller boats, fewer people, and a more intimate atmosphere (see "River Cruises," on page 493).

Here are a few factors to keep in mind:

Price: In addition to the base fare, you'll pay taxes and port fees (which can be hundreds of dollars per person), and an auto-tip of around $10-12/day for each person will be added to your bill. Also remember to budget for all the aforementioned "extras" you might wind up buying onboard.

Destinations: If you have a wish list of ports, use it as a starting point when shopping for a cruise.

Time Spent in Port: If exploring European destinations is your priority, look carefully at how much time the ship spends in each port; this can vary by hours from cruise line to cruise line. Be aware that certain cruise ports are in industrial zones miles away from the sights you want to see. You may need to take public transportation into the center of town, reducing your sightseeing time.

Ship Size: The biggest ships offer a wide

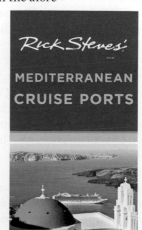

variety of restaurants, activities, entertainment, and other amenities (such as resources for kids)—but they can also foster a herd mentality and crowded shore experience for their 3,000-some passengers. Smaller ships offer fewer crowds, access to out-of-the-way ports, and less hassle when disembarking, but they also have fewer onboard amenities and generally cost much more.

Onboard Amenities: Decide which features matter to you most, including food (both quality and variety of restaurants), entertainment, athletic facilities, children's activities, and so on.

Booking a Cruise

While it's possible to book directly with the cruise line, most cruises are booked through travel agencies. There are two different types of cruise-sales agencies: a travel agency, where you can get in-person advice, or a giant cruise agency, which sells most of its inventory online or by phone. Several big cruise agencies have comparison-shopping websites, such as CruiseLine.com, CruiseCritic.com, and CruiseCompete.com.

Most cruise lines post their cruise schedules a year or more in advance. The earlier you book, the more likely you'll have your choice of sailing and of cabin type—and potentially an even better price (cruise lines typically offer discounts for booking at least 6 to 12 months before departure). While last-minute deals (usually within 90 days of departure) are fairly common on Caribbean cruises, they're relatively rare for European ones—and last-minute airfares to Europe can be that much more expensive.

Like cars or plane tickets, cruises are priced very flexibly. In general, for a mass-market cruise, you'll rarely pay the list price. (Higher-end cruises are less likely to be discounted.) It's common to see sales and other incentives, such as two-for-one pricing, free upgrades, onboard credits, or other extras.

While most cruise lines are willing to arrange your airfare to and from the cruise, you'll typically save money (and gain flexibility) by booking flights on your own. Allow plenty of time—ideally an overnight—before meeting your cruise; if your flight is delayed and you miss your ship, you're on your own to figure out how you'll meet it at the next port.

Cruising Tips

Food and Drink: Most cruise lines offer a wide range of onboard restaurants, including traditional dining rooms (with a semiformal dress code and assigned seating), casual buffet restaurants, room service whenever you want it, and

River Cruises

From the Rhine to the Danube, river cruises are a fun and relaxing way to see Europe from a different angle. Open-water sea cruises highlight many of Europe's metropolises, but they exclude the charming, smaller cities set along the Continent's historical river trade routes. River cruises fill this niche, bringing travelers closer to the true nature of a place and its people.

Budapest on the Danube is a popular river cruise destination.

The top river cruise operators—Avalon Waterways, Viking, Tauck, and AMAWaterway—offer trips that usually last one to two weeks. The most popular itineraries flow down the Danube, Rhone, Rhine, and Mosel (the Rhine's peaceful little sister), but routes are emerging along Portugal's Douro river, Italy's Po river, and more. These riverboats are notably smaller than cruise ships, which mean fewer people and a more laid-back atmosphere. Expect to share a ship with only 100 or 200 other passengers—and very few children.

You'll typically pay more per person for a river cruise than you would on a big cruise ship. Typically included in the price are some additional perks such as excursions, and beer and wine. Take advantage of included town walking tours—they are a valuable service that most sea-going cruises don't provide. Onboard activities aren't as heavily promoted as on sea cruises, but the focus on dynamic scenery and local culture is well worth the tradeoff.

Most river itineraries offer a pleasant balance of major tourist destinations and Back Door-type towns. You won't spend nights out on the open water, and you'll dock in the center of activity, with walk-off-the-ship access to everything, usually spend about three to eight hours in port before setting sail for the next destination. It's typical to visit at least one destination per day; a 10-day cruise, for example, will include stops in eight or more towns.

For major cities such as Paris or Prague, many cruise agencies offer packages that give you a few days ashore at the beginning or end of your voyage. Carefully examine the cost of such add-ons; you can likely extend your travels more economically by booking a hotel on your own.

a variety of specialty restaurants. Avoid this last kind of restaurant if you're on a budget—besides costing you a $10-30 cover charge, certain entrées incur a "supplement" ($10-20). A couple ordering specialty items and a bottle of wine can quickly run up a $100 dinner bill.

In general, water, coffee, tea, milk, iced tea, and juice are included. Other drinks cost extra: alcohol of any kind, name-brand soft drinks, fresh-squeezed fruit juices, and premium espresso drinks. (Certain luxury lines include beer and wine.)

Excursion Cheat Sheet

This simplified roundup shows which Mediterranean ports are best by organized excursion and which are doable on your own. For details, see my *Mediterranean Cruise Ports* guidebook, dedicated to helping people cruise "through the Back Door." (Baltic cruisers should look for my *Northern European Cruise Ports*.)

Destination (Port)	Excursion?
Barcelona Shuttle bus from terminal drops you right in town	No
Provence (Marseille/Toulon/La Seyne-sur-Mer) Wide range of worthwhile destinations far from the ports; an excursion can hit several of these with ease	Yes
French Riviera (Nice/Villefranche/Monaco) Entire region is easy to navigate by train or bus	No
Florence, Pisa, Lucca (Livorno) These cities are cheap and reasonably easy to reach by public transportation, but excursions offer a no-hassle connection that also includes tours of major sights	Maybe
Rome (Civitavecchia) Easy, direct train trip into town, but an excursion could help you navigate this big city	Maybe
Amalfi Coast (Naples/Sorrento) Narrow roads of the Amalfi Coast are often snarled by traffic; an excursion gives you peace of mind	Yes
Naples, Pompeii (Naples/Sorrento) Within Naples, everything is easy to reach by foot or bus; the ruins at Pompeii are a quick train ride away	No
Venice Getting downtown is easy by public transportation; even walking there is delightful in this unique city	No
Split Port is just a few steps from the easy-to-tour old town	No
Dubrovnik Very compact and easy on your own	No
Athens (Piraeus) Getting downtown is relatively easy, but sights benefit from a good guide, and an excursion offers easy connections	Maybe
Most Greek Islands Just relax and be on vacation	No
Ephesus (Kuşadası) Getting from Kuşadası to Ephesus involves considerable hassle, and a local guide is essential to understand this site	Yes
Istanbul The cruise terminals are right in the city	No

To encourage alcohol sales, many cruise lines limit how much alcohol guests can bring on board, or prohibit them from bringing any at all.

Internet Access: On-ship Wi-Fi is notoriously expensive and slow, so most cruisers find this a useless resource. While you can usually find free Wi-Fi hotspots on land, most ports have a special lounge for crew

A local guide—such as my Portuguese friend Ricardo, with his "fishy" smile—makes your shore excursion memorable and fun.

members, who make a beeline there to get online cheaply and connect with loved ones back home. Tourists are welcome to use the same cheap Wi-Fi service at these port lounges. Ask around when you dock.

Excursions vs. Independent Sightseeing: Whether it's better to sightsee on your own or with an organized excursion depends on the destination and your own level of comfort navigating Europe independently. A shore excursion efficiently takes you to a carefully selected assortment of sights, with a vetted local guide to explain everything, and is guaranteed to get you back to the ship in time (if an excursion is late, the ship will wait—but not if you're on your own). If you don't want to hassle with logistics, excursions can be a great option. But they are expensive, ranging from $40-60/person for a three-hour town walking tour to $100-150/person for an all-day bus tour.

Particularly in a place where it's easy to get into the city center on public transportation, you can have a similar experience for far less money. If you decide to go it alone, use a good guidebook or visit the local tourist information office in port. Other options are to hire a private guide to meet you at the ship and take you around or to join a scheduled walking tour of the town. As long as you keep a close eye on the time, it's easy to enjoy a very full day in port and be the last tired but happy tourist back onto the ship.

Shopping: At every stop, your cruise line will give you an information sheet highlighting local specialties and where to buy them. But be aware that cruise-recommended shops commonly give kickbacks to cruise lines and guides. This doesn't mean that the shop (or what it sells) isn't good quality; it just means you're probably paying top dollar. Many stores—not just the places working with cruise lines—jack up their rates when ships arrive, knowing they're about to get hit with a tidal wave of rushed and desperate shoppers. Before spending big money at the obvious tourist shops, be sure to check out local shopping venues, too.

Perspectives

Beyond all the practical considerations of preparing for your trip, there is one more vital task: calibrating your mind for your European experience. When you travel—whether to Europe or around the world—your best souvenir can be a global perspective. This chapter covers a range of ideas, including broadening your perspective through travel, understanding the current European political structure, recognizing the challenges and social issues facing Europe today, and learning how to travel in a socially and environmentally responsible way. Consider this a bit of food-for-thought, pretrip reading.

BROADENING YOUR PERSPECTIVE THROUGH TRAVEL

I was raised thinking the world was a pyramid with the US on top and everyone else trying to get there. I believed our role in the world was to help other people get it right... American-style. If they didn't understand that, we'd get them a government that did.

But travel changed my perspective. I met intelligent people—nowhere near as rich, free, or blessed with opportunity as I was—who wouldn't trade passports even if they could. They were thankful to be Nepali, Estonian, Turkish, Nicaraguan, or whatever. I was perplexed. I witnessed stirring struggles in lands that found other truths to be self-evident and God-given. I learned of Nathan Hales and Patrick Henrys from other nations who only wished they had more than one life to give for their country. I discovered that a "work ethic" could fall anywhere on a sliding scale of family values. I saw national pride that wasn't American. It was a challenging adjustment to my way of thinking—but it opened my mind to a whole new world of experiences I'd otherwise have ignored or derided.

Attitude Adjustment

When American tourists are unhappy, it's usually because of their stubborn desire to find the United States in Europe. Meanwhile, the happiest travelers I meet are truly taking a vacation from America—immersing themselves in different cultures and fully experiencing different people, outlooks, and lifestyles. Here are some things you can do to adjust your attitude.

What a difference perspective makes. When I bragged about how many gold medals our American Olympians were winning, my Dutch friend replied, "Yes, you have many medals, but per capita, we Dutch are doing five times as well."

Embrace the differences. Even if you believe American ways are better, your trip will go more smoothly if you don't compare. Things are different in Europe—that's why you go. And European travel is a package deal. Accept the good with the "bad." If you always require the comforts of home, then that's where you'll be happiest. On the other hand, if you're observant and tune into all the little differences, you may find great wisdom in how Europeans do things. A three-hour dinner at a French restaurant doesn't mean the service was slow or inattentive. To the French it signifies good, thoughtful service because the waiter wasn't rushing you to finish in order to turn over the table.

Don't be an "ugly American." Some Americans' trips suffer because they are treated like ugly Americans. Those who are treated like ugly Americans are treated that way because they *are* ugly Americans. They aren't bad people, just ethnocentric. These people act as though they "just got off the boat"—putting shoes on train seats, chilling grapes in the bidet, talking loudly in restaurants, snapping flash photos during Mass, hanging wet clothes out the hotel window, and consuming energy like it's cheap and theirs to waste. But you can't expect the local people to accept you warmly if you don't respect their world and their ways of doing things.

Europeans judge you as an individual, not by your nationality. If I'm treated like an ugly American, it's not because I'm an American... but because I'm acting out my ethnocentrism. If anything, my Americanness has been an asset in Europe. I've been accepted as an American friend throughout Europe, Russia, the Middle East, and North Africa. I've been hugged by Bulgarian workers on a Balkan mountaintop;

discussed the Olympics over dinner in the home of a Greek family; explained to a young, frustrated Irishman that California girls take their pants off one leg at a time, just like the rest of us; and hiked through the Alps with a Swiss schoolteacher, learning German and teaching English.

Learn about current issues. Look beyond the pretty pictures and flowery tourist brochures: A few months in advance of your trip, begin paying attention to political and economic news so you'll know what's happening in your destination (information you'll seldom find in guidebooks).

If you've studied up on an area's politics, you'll get the most out of opportunities to talk with involved locals about complex current situations. At a Paris bistro, ask your neighbors what they think of the nationalistic politics of presidential candidate Marine Le Pen. Or, at a London pub, share a pint with a few Brits and ask where they believe Britain's decision to leave the EU ("Brexit") will take them.

Wherever you go, young, well-dressed people are most likely to speak (and want to practice) English. Universities can be the perfect place to solve the world's problems with an open-minded foreigner over a cafeteria lunch. By plugging directly into the present and getting the European take on things, a traveler gets beyond traditional sightseeing and learns "today's history."

Go as a guest. Act like one, and you'll be treated like one. Tread lightly and be respectful of your surroundings. In travel, as in the rest of life, you often reap what you sow.

10 Ways to Travel as a Political Act

Lately, I've devoted a lot of time and energy to thinking about travel in a new way: as an invaluable tool for learning how to fit more thoughtfully into our ever-smaller world. For me, the great value of travel is the opportunity to pry open our hometown blinders and bring home a broader perspective. And when we implement that worldview as citizens of our great nation, we make travel a political act (which is also the title of a book I've written; see page 36). Here are my top 10 practical tips for doing just that:

The Thoughtless Traveler vs. the Thoughtful Traveler

While the thoughtless traveler slogs through a sour Europe, mired in a swamp of complaints, the thoughtful traveler fully experiences wherever he or she is.

The Thoughtless Traveler...	The Thoughtful Traveler...
...criticizes "strange" customs and cultural differences. She doesn't respect the devout Spanish Catholic's appreciation of his town's patron saint, or doesn't understand the sense of community expressed by the evening promenade in southern Europe.	...seeks out European styles of living and tries new ways of thinking and doing things. You are genuinely interested in the people and cultures you visit. You accept and try to wrap your head around differences.
...demands to find America in Europe. He throws a fit if the air-conditioning breaks down in a hotel. He insists on orange juice and eggs (sunny-side up) for breakfast, long beds, English menus, ice in drinks, punctuality in Italy, and cold beer in England. He measures Europe with an American yardstick.	...is positive and optimistic. You don't dwell on problems or compare things to "back home," and you focus on the good points of each country. As a guest in another land, you're observant and sensitive. If 60 people are dining with hushed voices in a Belgian restaurant, you know it's not the place to yuk it up.
...uses money as a shield against a genuine experience. She throws money at the locals instead of trying to engage them.	...doesn't flash signs of affluence, especially in poorer countries. You don't joke about the local money or over-tip. Your bucks don't talk.
...invades a country while making no effort to communicate with the "natives." He never bothers to learn even the basic survival phrases ("please" and "thank you"), and gets angry when the Europeans he meets "refuse to learn English." Traveling in packs, he talks at and about Europeans in a condescending manner.	...makes an effort to bridge that flimsy language barrier. You find rudimentary communication in any language to be fun. On the train to Budapest, you enter a debate with a Hungarian over the merits of a common European currency—despite only a 20-word shared vocabulary. You don't worry about making mistakes—you communicate!

1. Get out of your comfort zone. Choose Tangier over St. Tropez, or Turkey over Greece. When visiting Israel, make time to also explore the West Bank. You can enjoy far richer experiences for far less money by venturing away from the mainstream.

2. Connect with people—and try to understand them. Make itinerary decisions that put you in touch with locals who are also curious about you. Stay in people's homes (via Airbnb or Couchsurfing.com) and spend time with your hosts. Hire local guides to take you around. Seek answers for cultural riddles: Why do many Muslim women wear head coverings? Why do Americans so fiercely defend their right to own a gun? Why do Norwegians so willingly pay such high taxes?

3. Celebrate diversity and be a cultural chameleon. When encountering a cultural difference, embrace it with joy rather than with judgment...and actually join in: Eat with your fingers in Moroccan restaurants that have no silverware, dip your fries in mayonnaise in Belgium, smoke a hookah in Greece, kiss a stranger on both cheeks in France, and go to a hurling match in Ireland. Rather than gawking at the pilgrims, become one—climb Rome's Scala Santa (Holy Stairs) on your knees, feeling the pain while finding comfort in the frescoes of saints all around you.

4. Understand the contemporary context. While traveling, get caught up on local news. Go to a political rally in Scotland. Listen to expat radio on Spain's Costa del Sol. Think about how all societies are on parallel evolution-ary tracks. Imagine how the American approach to vexing societal problems might work in other places—and (more importantly) vice versa.

5. Empathize with the other 96 percent of humanity. Just like Americans have the American Dream, others have their own dreams. Make a point to put yourself in the shoes (or sandals, or bare feet) of the people you meet. Find out why Basque people are so passionate about their language... and then find a parallel in your society. As you travel, learn to celebrate the local Paul Reveres and Ethan Allens—Turkey's Atatürk, Italy's Garibaldi, and so on.

6. Identify—and understand—other societies' baggage. The US has been preoccupied with terrorism for the last generation. But other nations have their own, sometimes even heavier, baggage. Ponder societal needs even more fundamental than freedom and democracy. Why is Putin so dominant in Russia? Why would a modern and well-educated Egyptian be willing to take a bullet for the newest military dictator (as my friend in Cairo told me)? Why, in some struggling countries, does stability one up democracy?

7. Accept the legitimacy of other moralities. Be open to the possibility that controversial activities are not objec-tively "right" or "wrong." Consider Germany's approach to prostitution or the Netherlands' marijuana policy, which are both based on pragmatic harm reduction rather than moralism. Get a French farmer's take on force-feeding his geese to produce foie gras. In Istanbul, skip the touristy versions and attend an authentic two-hour Whirling Dervish ritual. Ask a Spaniard why bullfighting still thrives as the national pastime—and why it's covered not in the sports pages, but in the arts section of the local newspaper. You don't have to like the answer, but at least try to understand it.

8. Sightsee with an edge. Seek out political street art...and find out what it means. Read local culture magazines and attend arts and political events. Take alternative tours to learn about heroin maintenance clinics in Switzerland or Copenhagen's Christiania commune. Walk with a local guide through an ethnic ghetto. Meeting poor immigrants living with a spirit of abundance, ponder how so many rich people live with a mindset of scarcity.

Thank You	
Arabic	*shukran*
Bulgarian	*blagodarya*
Croatian	*hvala*
Czech	*děkuji*
Danish	*tak*
Dutch	*dank u wel*
Estonian	*tänan*
Finnish	*kiitos*
French	*merci*
German	*danke*
Greek	*efharisto*
Hebrew	*todah*
Hungarian	*köszönöm*
Italian	*grazie*
Polish	*dziękuję*
Portuguese	*obrigado*
Russian	*spasiba*
Slovak	*d'akujem*
Slovene	*hvala*
Spanish	*gracias*
Turkish	*teşekkür ederim*

9. Make your trip an investment in a better world. Our world has a lot of desperation, and travelers are the lucky few who can afford to experience what's outside their own hometowns. Travel with a goal of good stewardship—the idea that each traveler has a responsibility to be an ambassador to, and for, the entire planet. Think of yourself as a modern-day equivalent of the medieval jester: sent out by the king to learn what's going on outside the walls, and then coming home to speak truth to power... even if it is annoying.

10. Make a broader perspective your favorite souvenir. Back home, be evangelical about your newly expanded global viewpoint. Travel shapes who you are. Weave favorite strands of other cultures into the tapestry of your own life. Live your life as if it shapes the world and the future...because it does. Believe that you matter. Then make a difference.

UNDERSTANDING THE EUROPEAN UNION

Over several generations, the countries of Europe have gone from being bitter rivals to member states in one of the world's biggest economies: the European Union. Bringing together such a diverse collection of separate nations—with different languages and cultures—peacefully, is unprecedented.

Today, the European Union includes most of Western Europe (except Switzerland), a large chunk of Eastern Europe and Scandinavia, and for now, the British Isles. Britain voted in 2016 to leave the EU (the "Brexit"), but didn't instantly pull out—that will require a long negotiation, possibly lasting years.

Essentially, the EU is a free-trade zone with its own currency (the euro, used in most member countries). But it's much more than that: The EU is increasingly a political unit that looks and acts like a single nation-state. While not quite a "United States of Europe," the EU has an elected Europe-wide parliament that passes laws on economic policy and some social and foreign policy issues.

Everyone has an opinion on how well the EU works. "Eurocrats" and other optimists see it as a bold and idealistic experiment in unity, mutual understanding, and shared priorities. "Euroskeptics" view it as a bloated, overly bureaucratic monster that threatens to wring the diversity and charm out of the Old World. They especially resent the rising power (to essentially write Europe's new laws) of corporate lobbyists and that the EU has lashed economically healthy countries to troubled ones.

The EU: Past and Present

World War II left 40 million dead and a continent in ruins, and convinced Europeans that they had to work together to maintain peace. Poised between competing superpowers (the US and the USSR), they also needed to cooperate economically to survive in an increasingly globalized economy.

Just after the war ended, visionary "Eurocrats" began the task of persuading reluctant European nations to relinquish elements of their sovereignty

When I shudder at Switzerland's high taxes, my friend Olle asks, "What's it worth to live in a country with no hunger or homelessness, and where everyone—regardless of the wealth of their parents—has access to good health care and a top-quality education?"

EU Nations

The European Union: Austria, Belgium, Bulgaria, Croatia, Cyprus, Czech Republic, Denmark, Estonia, Finland, France, Germany, Greece, Hungary, Ireland, Italy, Latvia, Lithuania, Luxembourg, Malta, Netherlands, Poland, Portugal, Romania, Slovakia, Slovenia, Spain, Sweden, and (for now) the United Kingdom.

and merge into a united body. Starting in 1949, European states gradually came together to form the Common Market (also known as the European Economic Community). In 1992, with the Treaty of Maastricht, the 12 member countries of the Common Market made a leap of faith: They created a "European Union" that would eventually allow capital, goods, services, and labor to move freely across borders. The by-products would be a common currency, softened trade barriers, EU passports, and the elimination of border checks between member countries.

In 2002, most EU members adopted the euro as a single currency, and for all practical purposes, economic unity was a reality. By 2013, EU membership reached 28 nations, encompassing a vast swath of the continent. The EU is now the world's seventh largest "country" (1.7 million square miles), with the third largest population (more than 500 million people). It's also running neck-and-neck with the US for the title of world's biggest economy ($19.2 trillion GDP).

The EU is governed from Brussels and administered through a complicated network of legislative bodies, commissions, and courts that attempt to complement each country's government while minimizing encroachment on individual nation's sovereignty. The EU cannot levy taxes (that's still done through national governments), and it cannot deploy troops without each nation's approval. Unlike America's federation of 50 states, Europe's member states retain the right to opt out of some EU policies. Denmark, for example, belongs to the EU and but has yet to adopt the euro as its currency.

As Europe unites, historically subjugated peoples are enjoying more autonomy. The Scottish Parliament originated around 1235, was dissolved by England in 1707, and returned in 1999. Its extravagant and controversial Edinburgh digs *(above)* opened in 2004.

It's a delicate balance trying to develop laws and policies for all Europeans while respecting the rights of nations, regions, and individuals. An oft-quoted EU slogan is "promoting unity"—that is, economic and political—"while preserving diversity." But the European responses to the Yugoslav Wars in the early 1990s, the economic bailout of Greece, and the recent tidal wave of refugees have demonstrated that Europe isn't always prepared to speak with a single voice.

The EU is a bold experiment and, like any innovation, it's hit some snags as it's evolved (see next section). Since World War II, it has developed in a stutter—two steps forward, one step backward. On the positive side, France and Germany have woven their economies together to the degree that there likely will never again be a huge war in Europe. But

US vs. EU by the Numbers

	US	EU
Population	324 million	515 million
Land area	3.8 million square miles	1.7 million square miles
Gross domestic product (GDP)	$17.9 trillion	$19.2 trillion
Life expectancy	79.8 years	80.2 years
Infant mortality rate	5.8 deaths/1,000	4 deaths/1,000
Mobile phones	382.3 million	632.5 million
Annual military budget	$756.9 billion (4.35% of GDP)	$288 billion (1.6% of GDP)

Statistics from the CIA's World Factbook, 2016

momentum toward further integration and expansion has hit a wall. Nationalistic, isolationist movements are on the rise across Europe, and the Brexit vote will only embolden them. The potential domino effect—for Europe and beyond—is unknown.

LEFT The vast and shiny EU headquarters in Brussels welcomes visitors on guided tours to take a peek at Europe at work.

EUROPEAN CHALLENGES

Europe is grappling with a challenging economy (with resulting strikes and protests), huge numbers of refugees and immigrants, the ever-present threat of terrorism, the implications of Brexit, and "independence" movements. Here's a quick rundown on the European reality today, and how these issues could affect your trip.

RIGHT New roads are bringing the infrastructure in Europe up to speed. These EU-funded projects (such as this one in Ireland) come with a billboard and EU flag reminding drivers where the funding came from.

Economic Issues

Today Europe is paying the price—in the form of expensive bailouts and painful cutbacks—for what had been taken-for-granted services. Wealthier member countries (mostly in the north) resent being compelled to prop up the euro by rescuing their economically unsound compatriots (the so-called "PIIGS" countries, mostly in the south—Portugal, Italy, Ireland, Greece, and Spain). Meanwhile, troubled countries resent being told what to do by the richer ones, and disgruntled citizens sometimes take to the streets to protest.

Europe's economic issues are much like ours here in the US. It seems on both sides of the Atlantic we've conned ourselves into thinking we are wealthier than we really are. As societies, we've been consuming more goods than we've been producing for a long time. We import more than we export—and things are finally catching up with us. Here in the US, our priorities are warped. Many of our best young minds are going to our finest schools to become experts in finance: rearranging the furniture to skim off the top...aspiring to

Rick Steves' Europe on Public Television

My television series, *Rick Steves' Europe,* airs on more than 300 public television stations across the United States. Each half-hour show takes you to Europe's most interesting places, from great cities to off-the-beaten-path discoveries. Three shows devoted to travel skills help illustrate this book.

I've also produced multiple TV specials, including *Rick Steves' The Holy Land, Rick Steves' Andalucía, Rick Steves' Rome, Rick Steves' European Christmas* (celebrating family holiday traditions in seven different European cultures), *Rick Steves' Iran* (made in the hope of humanizing that proud if perplexing nation), *Rick Steves' Sym-*

Producer Simon Griffith, cameraman Karel Bauer, and writer/host Rick Steves—working together to bring the best of Europe home to you on public television.

phonic Journey (a visual and musical tour of European composers and countries), *Rick Steves' European Easter* (exploring the rich and fascinating mix of Easter traditions), and *Rick Steves' Luther and the Reformation* (weaving the story of Martin Luther into the historic sweep of the Protestant Reformation).

All of my TV shows are available free on demand at www.ricksteves.com/tv, where you'll also find scripts and a behind-the-scenes look at filming *Rick Steves' Europe.*

These are just some of the places covered on my TV show, *Rick Steves' Europe.*

careers where you produce little while expertly working the system in hopes of becoming unimaginably rich.

Lately, the US is reminding me of old-regime France. While surveying the extravagant châteaux outside Paris—such as Vaux-le-Vicomte—I was struck by how many of them were the homes of financiers. It's striking that about 8 percent of the US economy is tied up in the financial industry.

Whenever a society gets wealthy and well educated, its people have fewer children and live longer. (Western Europe, one of the wealthiest and best-educated parts of the world, has one of the lowest birth rates and the most geriatric populations.)

Europe's generous social entitlements were conceived in a postwar society with lots of people working, fewer living to retirement, and those living beyond retirement having a short life span. That was sustainable...no problem. Now, with its very low birth rate and aging societies, the demographic makeup of Europe has flipped upside down: relatively few people working, lots of people retiring, and those who are retired living a long time. The arithmetic just isn't there to sustain the comfortable status quo.

Politicians in Europe have the unenviable task of explaining to their citizens that they won't get the cushy golden years their parents got. People who worked diligently with the promise of retiring at 62 are now told they'll need to work an extra decade—and even then, they may not have a generous retirement waiting for them. Any politician trying to honestly explain this reality to the electorate is likely to be tossed out, since most people are not very sophisticated voters—naturally seeking a politician who tells them what they want to hear rather than the hard truth. And any austerity programs necessary to put a society back on track are also tough enough to get people marching in the streets.

I expect you'll see lots of marches and lots of strikes in Europe as they recalibrate their economy. Europeans demonstrate: It's in their blood and a healthy part of their democracy. When frustrated and needing to vent grievances, they hit the streets. I've been caught up in huge and boisterous marches all over Europe, and it's not scary; in fact, it's kind of exhilarating. *"La Manifestation!"* as they say in France. (All that marching is just too much exercise for many Americans. When dealing with similar frustrations, we find a TV station—on the left or right—that affirms our beliefs and then shake our collective fists vigorously.)

When Europe united, the poor countries (such as Ireland,

Portugal, and Greece) received lots of development aid from the rich ones (mostly Germany and France). I remember when there were no freeways in any of the poor countries. Now they are laced with German-style (and mostly German-funded) superhighways. These countries traded in their lazy currencies for the euro (which is, in a way, the mighty Deutsche mark in disguise, as the European economy is driven and dominated by Germany).

Today, it's no coincidence that the European countries that have received the most development aid are the ones who are the most debt-ridden and at risk of failing. Even with that aid, their productivity has lagged far behind the stronger economies. And, while their workforce doesn't produce as much per capita as German workers, they have a mighty currency tied to Germany. By earning wages and getting aid in euros, these nations enjoyed a false prosperity that they might not have merited—and the bursting real estate bubble made it worse. Before unity, if a nation didn't produce much and slid into crippling debt, the economy could be adjusted simply by devaluing that nation's currency. Today, there's no way to devalue the currency of a particular country on the euro, so this fix is not an option. And Europe is left wondering about the future of its euro currency.

I'm sometimes asked whether struggling economies within the EU such as Greece are safe and stable places to visit. When assessing the seriousness of any civil unrest, remember that commercial TV news has to make a profit. Producers will always grab video footage that makes a demonstration appear as exciting as possible. Unrest is generally localized—it looks frightening with a zoom lens and much less so with a wide-angle shot.

As a traveler, I don't worry about it. True, I wouldn't want to be a Greek worker counting on a retirement that may not come. But as a visitor, you'll scarcely be aware of these problems. I was recently in Greece and enjoyed a warm welcome, great food, and wonderful beaches. Expect a few demonstrations and a few strikes. But you can also expect rich travel experiences and a society thankful that you decided to spend a slice of your vacation time and money in their country.

And also remember that, even when we in the US and Europe consider ourselves in an "economic crisis," the vast majority of people on this planet would love to have our economic problems. By any fair measure, as societies, both the US and Europe are filthy rich. These economic woes are no

Gay and Lesbian Rights in Europe

In keeping with its generally progressive politics, much of Europe tends to be supportive of rights for its gay and lesbian citizens. The European Union specifically includes gay and lesbian citizens in its antidiscrimination laws. The Netherlands–and Amsterdam in particular–has offered equal rights to gays and lesbians for decades. The world's first legal marriage for a gay couple occurred in Amsterdam in 2001.

In general, northern Europe and larger cities are more progressive when it comes to gay rights. In other places, the record is mixed, with fewer legal rights but pockets of tolerance. Same-sex marriage is legal in many European countries, including the Netherlands, Norway, Sweden, Denmark, Belgium, France, Spain, England, Scotland, Wales, and Ireland. Austria has a vibrant gay scene in its cities and Paris has a gay neighborhood (the Marais), but many rural French communities adhere to an unspoken "don't ask, don't tell" ideology of not flaunting one's sexuality. Italy is a similar story of general acceptance but raised eyebrows in rural areas and in the south. Some of Greece's islands are well-known gay destinations.

In progressive Amsterdam, this "Homomonument"–shaped like a giant pink triangle–honors all gays and lesbians who have been persecuted for their sexual orientation.

Eastern European capitals such as Prague and Budapest have liberal attitudes on par with what you'll find in big Western European cities, and same-sex unions are recognized in the Czech Republic, Hungary, and Slovenia. But the farther east and south you venture in the former Soviet Bloc, the less progressive things become. Particularly in rural areas of far Eastern Europe, responses range from reasonably accepting to outright hostility. And Russia's intolerance toward gays and lesbians nearly overshadowed the 2014 Winter Olympics. (For a country-by-country checklist, search Wikipedia for "LGBT rights in Europe.")

more a sign of the total failure of European "socialism" than the 2008 economic crisis in the US indicated the final collapse of American capitalism.

Refugees and Immigration

Europe is grappling with an influx of immigrants from the developing world, including a recent surge of refugees from war-torn countries in the Middle East, Asia, and Africa. Racial diversity is more common in the melting-pot United States (where more than one-third of the population is non-white), but the majority of people living in Europe are Caucasian. A few places (such as former colonial powers Great

Refugees and Safety of Travelers in Europe

I can understand a traveler mixing up fear and risk and reconsidering a trip to Europe after a terrorist event. But I've also heard from Americans nervous about traveling to Europe due to the refugee crisis there.

Fortunately, the surge of refugees making their way from Turkey, Greece, Syria, and north Africa to Germany or northern countries has little to do with our safety as we travel. In 2016 more than 900 Rick Steves bus tours traveled throughout Europe, and our guides reported that the refugee situation never put their groups in any kind of risk. A couple of groups were inconvenienced at border crossings clogged with immigrants—but I would consider those small delays a positive opportunity to gain a little insight into the refugees' plight.

Apart from the perception of risk, some travelers think it's inconsiderate or somehow wrong to vacation in the proximity of so much desperation. Logically and morally, vacationing on a Greek isle during the refugee crisis is no more right or wrong than enjoying a beach in Hawaii or Florida. In fact, avoiding a country because of the refugee situation only exacerbates the economic fallout, taking needed income from locals caught in the middle. React to terrorism how you need to, but don't let the refugee crisis impact your travel planning.

Britain and the Netherlands) have absorbed transplants from their overseas holdings for many centuries, but most of Europe was largely homogenous well into the 20th century. In the decades since World War II—as Europe has built a new prosperity, and immigrants have arrived seeking a better life—Europe has slowly become more ethnically diverse.

Tolerance and celebrating diversity are major tenets of the EU. But for some Europeans, that's easier said than done. As immigrants from every corner of the world (mostly Africa, the Middle East, the Caribbean, South Asia, and South America) come to Europe, many white Europeans struggle to adapt. Some are frustrated by large numbers of immigrants—and their European-born children—who, the critics claim, stick together in tight communities, cling to the culture of their homeland, and are slow to adopt European culture. The immigrants would likely counter that they've found few opportunities to integrate with their European neighbors.

And just as in the US, immigrants are sometimes perceived as challenging lifelong residents for jobs, or as taking advantage of the welfare system. (Struggling whites don't see themselves as "racist"; they see immigrants as undeserving newcomers "cutting in line" for social programs that they've waited legally and patiently for and are now not receiving.)

Another thorny issue is the friction between European Christianity and the Islamic faith of many immigrants.

Recent large-scale migration from Syria, Iraq, Afghanistan, and other countries has caused a crisis across Europe, with the EU struggling to respond in a cohesive way. But this increased flow of refugees, while certainly newsworthy, needs to be kept in historical and practical perspective.

If you're wondering how this may affect your travels in Europe, I'd say not at all. While this is the biggest such migration since World War II, European history is a long and steady story of difficult refugee movements. (In the late 1940s, people were forcibly relocated from entire regions, causing great suffering.) There are refugee crises around the planet today that equal this event in pain and misery, but go unnoticed because they don't affect the rich world. The big difference with the current story: The refugees are heading to Europe rather than to some other poor, war-torn, and dysfunctional region. Crisis-hungry commercial news is looking for something sensational to talk about 24/7. And desperate people in boats and on foot create dramatic images that catch our attention.

What's the impact on Europe? Europe consists of roughly a half-billion people. The refugee influx totals one or two million people. Europe can certainly absorb these struggling people into its societies and workforces. Europe needs immigrant labor as much as the US does. Who else will pick our crops, tend our gardens, hang our drywall, and look after our children and aging parents? While that's the clichéd image of an immigrant laborer, both Europe and the US can attribute their economic success to smart, innovative, and industrious newcomers who contribute mightily to their adopted societies.

These refugees are leaving miserable and dangerous worlds, taking huge risks in the process. Thousands have died trying to cross the Mediterranean to Europe. And terrible hardships are being experienced at Europe's borders.

Is opening the doors of the rich world even wider—enough to allow in the tens of millions of people who'd like to swap worlds—the right answer? I don't think so. Personally, I don't want to see tiny countries such as Finland or Iceland overwhelmed by hundreds of thousands of refugees, which would fundamentally change their societies.

I think the most compassionate and practical approach is to deal with the existing stream of refugees generously and help these immigrants (so eager to join the workforce) assimilate into First World economies. But we must also focus on making the world they fled more stable and prosperous by changing our approach to the developing world. This can happen both from a trade policy point of view and from a military point of view (because, if we're honest, most wars take place in the poor world and are fueled by rich countries with an eye on more fuel).

And, to a great extent, countries that are in danger of "failing" (such as Libya and Iraq) are those whose borders were drawn by Western powers a century ago with no regard to ethnic realities. Those countries, at this point, can only be ruled by an authoritarian government; the imposition of democracy would lead only to chaos.

In the name of compassion and decency (as well as our own security and well-being, for those motivated purely by such things), it's time for the rich world to get serious about making life more stable and comfortable in the places so many refugees are risking everything to leave. Any "hardships" we might incur are hardships we should not shirk, considering the colonial roots of much of the developing world's instability.

Terrorism

Times change. But, it seems, terrorism is always with us—whether in the US (9/11, the 2015 San Bernardino killings, the 2016 Orlando nightclub shootings) or in Europe (Norway's 2011 Utøya Island massacre and more recent attacks attributed to the Islamic State in Paris, Brussels, Nice, and Berlin). Every superpower is seen by angry people beyond its borders as an evil empire. All have had insurgents nipping at them. Romans had what they called "barbarians." Habsburgs had "anarchists." And today, Americans and Europeans have terrorists.

Most of the time, travelers can be blissfully oblivious of terrorism. But there's always a chance that terrorists will strike just before, or during, your trip.

If that happens, take a deep breath. Survey the situation. And don't let fear and worry overwhelm the facts. Numbers don't lie: The odds against being killed by terrorists are astronomical (about one in 20 million). You're twice as likely to be struck by lightning. If you want to worry about something, worry about

Armed guards at major sights—such as Paris' Notre-Dame-are Europe's new reality.

this: Each year, more than 30,000 Americans are shot to death in the US (8 times the per-capita gun-caused deaths in Europe).

According to the Centers for Disease Control and Prevention, from 2001 to 2014, a total of 440,095 people were killed by guns on US soil. Compare that to 3,412: the number of Americans who died worldwide during that same time as victims of terrorism (most of them at home, during 9/11). Since 9/11, the number of Americans killed by Muslim extremists on our shores was 123. Considering that statistic and the danger of gun violence on the streets of America, if you really care about your loved ones...you'll take them to Europe tomorrow.

Paris' see-through garbage cans give terrorists one less place to hide a bomb.

The US State Department issues travel advisories for foreign countries (www.travel.state.gov). Consider these, but don't follow them blindly. Certain warnings (for example, about civil unrest in a country that's falling apart) could be grounds to scrub my mission. But I travel right through most advisories (which can seem politically motivated). A threat against the embassy in Rome doesn't affect my sightseeing at the Pantheon. For other perspectives, check the British (www.fco.gov.uk) and Canadian (www.travel.gc.ca) government travel warnings.

Sure, terrorist threats can have a tangible impact on your travels, usually in the form of increased security lines, disrupted flight plans, and other inconveniences. For instance, to get on a train or into a great museum, you may have to go through extra security. It's harder to find a place to check your bags because of concern about bombs (and it might cost you $8, as you're paying for the machine that scans your bag). If something unusual is happening in the world, carefully confirm flight schedules and local information, and allow plenty of time to get where you're going and through security. Remember that Europe is on guard: They have a lot of challenges, and a lot of soft targets. If I get stuck in a long security line, I use the extra time to meditate on the fundamental causes of terrorism, aggressive American trade policies, and the fact that half of humanity is struggling to survive on $2 a day.

Having been in Europe during some high-profile terrorist events, I've been impressed by the local response. Europeans have a knack for bouncing back and refusing to give in to the attackers' desire to incite terror. They don't surrender their emotions and politics to sensational news coverage. Europeans keep the risk and tragedy of terrorism in perspective. As a matter of principle, it seems, they refuse to be terrorized by terrorists, and so should we. Europeans know that if they overreact to a terrorist event, they make a small bomb much bigger in its impact.

Security on Europe's premium trains can be tight. At this London train station, the police keep a close eye on who boards the Eurostar for Paris.

In response to terrorism, I believe we owe it to the victims not to let the terrorists win by feeling threatened, curtailing liberties, or changing our lifestyles. That's exactly the response they are hoping for. Sure, it's natural for our emotions to get the best of us. But, especially given the impact of sensational media coverage and opportunistic fearmongers, we need to respond intelligently and rationally. It's important that we not confuse fear with risk, that we not overreact, and that we strive to build commonality between people.

After an attention-grabbing attack, some Americans choose to put their travel dreams on hold and stay home. But the most powerful thing we can do as Americans to fight terrorism is to get out there and better understand the rest of the world. When we travel it makes it tougher for their propaganda to dehumanize us, and it makes it tougher for our propaganda to dehumanize them. It helps us all connect, gain empathy for each other, and celebrate the diversity on this planet. We find ourselves more inclined to build bridges and less inclined to build walls. Travel is a powerful force for peace and a powerful way to fight terrorism.

Two weeks after 9/11, I was in Padua, the town where Copernicus studied and Galileo taught. The square was filled with college students sharing drinks and discussing America's response to "our new reality." As we talked, I kept dipping little strips of bread into a puddle of olive oil on my plate, tiptoe-style. Watching me do this, my new friend said, "You make the *scarpette*...little shoes."

My Italian wasn't good enough to tell him my thoughts: Travel is a celebration of life and freedom. Terrorists will not take that away from me. My mission in life is to inspire Americans to travel, one by one—"making the little shoes"—to absorb and savor the wonders of Europe.

In a world of easy access to explosives and vivid media, terrorism is likely here to stay. And our challenge to maintain a free and open society is here to stay, as well. Europe is strong. It will pursue both safety and the bad guys. And, as a matter of principle, its people will continue to embrace freedom. As a matter of principle, I will keep on traveling. If we refuse to be terrorized, the terrorists lose—and we win.

Union or Divorce?

When I first traveled to Europe, it was a hodgepodge of border crossings and currencies. Today I can seamlessly travel from Madrid to Munich with one currency and virtually no passport control.

But between the economic crisis of the mid-2000s, the recent flood of refugees from war-torn countries, a few high-profile terrorist attacks, the UK's Brexit vote, and the populist and nationalist emotions that brought the US its new president in 2017, the ties that bind the EU are feeling frayed. Nations that have long had open borders are building fences with razor wire and high-tech cameras. Right-wing parties in France and the Netherlands are making EU secession a top priority—and their growing vote totals indicate these are no longer fringe groups.

In certain regions, forces want to break apart nations that have been united for centuries. In Belgium in 2010-2011, tension between the country's Dutch- and French-speaking halves led to a caretaker government for a world-record 541 days. Although Scottish voters rejected an independence referendum in 2014, a year later the Scottish National Party became a significant kingmaker in British national elections. In the wake of Brexit, Scottish nationalists predict that they would win the next independence vote. And in Spain, leaders in the Catalunya region want to leave the country even as the national government and constitutional courts say it's illegal.

I remain a staunch supporter of the European Union. But with Britain's decision to leave the EU, my idealism took a serious blow. I used to say that the EU, despite its cumbersome political correctness and almost comically excessive regulations, has taken root and become an entrenched part of Europe's fabric. After all, it has created a free trade zone big enough to compete with the US and the emerging economies of China and India, and it has helped keep Europe at peace. But with Brexit, suddenly the future is murky. The EU will shrink from 28 to 27 member nations and lose 17 percent

Travelers of Color in Europe

People who are not of European descent may worry about how they'll be treated abroad. In short, does it matter that you look different from most Europeans? I've collected the following advice from a wide range of people of color who have lived or traveled extensively in Europe.

First off, your Americanness will probably be more notable to the Europeans you meet than the color of your skin. Most Europeans can spot Americans a mile away. And, because American culture is pervasive worldwide, any stereotypes Europeans might have about your race are likely formed by our own popular culture—our actors, musicians, and athletes. For example, the former Obama presidency informed the way Europeans think about black Americans.

Travelers of color and mixed-race couples tell me that their most common source of discomfort in Europe is being stared at. While this might seem to indicate disapproval, it's more likely a combination of curiosity and impoliteness. Put simply, for some Europeans, you're just not who they're used to seeing. Their response to a person of color likely isn't hostility, but naiveté. (One traveler suggested that this isn't racism so much as "rarism"—Europeans reacting to the novelty of an unusual-to-them ethnicity.)

of its economic clout. Britain and Europe must deal with the reality and uncertainty of an acrimonious divorce.

I don't want to be glib or naive about the challenges facing the EU and Britain. Extricating the British Isles from the EU is going to be a long and difficult process. But I've chosen to look on the bright side of life: For American travelers, Europe just got even more interesting. And, if fear is part of the problem, the value of international travel is even greater now.

SOCIALLY RESPONSIBLE AND EDUCATIONAL TRAVEL

My travels—whether in Egypt, El Salvador, Turkey, India, the Holy Land, Cuba, or the Netherlands—have taught me about my own country as well as the rest of our world. Travel has sharpened both my love of what America stands for and my connection with our world. I've learned to treasure—rather than fear—the world's rich diversity. And I believe that America—with all its power, wisdom, and

By our standards, many Europeans—at least outside of Britain—tend to be opinionated and blunt. What's considered polite conversation in Europe can be shockingly different from our own unwritten rules, and that often includes discussing race. Of course, this can be not only jarring but also hurtful—and yet some travelers also tell me they find it weirdly refreshing ("at least it's out in the open").

Travelers of color report being frustrated by racial profiling, particularly at border crossings or airport security. (In many places, this is a somewhat socially acceptable means of targeting undocumented immigrants.) It's quite possible you'll be closely scrutinized—more closely than most travelers of European ancestry—before being allowed to continue on your way.

If you're concerned about how you'll be treated in a specific destination, ask fellow travelers of your ethnicity about their experiences. An excellent resource for African Americans, including destination-specific reports from several travelers, is the website I'm Black and I Travel (www.imblacknitravel.com).

Will you encounter unfriendliness in your travels? Definitely. But be careful not to over-attribute grumpiness to racism. In the words of one American traveler of color: "I think we're more likely to interpret bad behavior from non-Americans as being racist because of our history with white Americans. Often their impatience is just because we're American, and we're clueless about other people's cultures and practices."

No matter your ethnicity, the best advice for any traveler is to have a positive attitude. If you feel uncomfortable or mistreated, head somewhere else. And remember that most Europeans are as interested in learning about you as you are in learning about them.

goodness—can do a better job of making our world a better place. By connecting me with so many people, travel has heightened my concern for people issues: a well-educated electorate, a healthy environment, civil liberties, quality housing, nutrition, health care, and education.

As we learn more about the problems that confront the earth and humankind, more and more people are recognizing the need for the world's industries—including tourism—to function as tools for peace. According to the World Travel and Tourism Council, tourism is a $7.2 trillion-a-year industry and directly or indirectly employs more than 284 million people. As travelers become more sophisticated and gain a global perspective, the demand for socially, environmentally, and economically responsible means of travel will grow. Peace is more than the absence of war, and if we are to continue enjoying the good things in life—such as travel—the serious issues that confront humankind must be addressed now. Although the most obvious problems relate specifically to travel in the developing world, European travel also offers some exciting socially responsible opportunities.

"Voluntourism" and Cultural Exchanges

For some travelers, making the world a better place becomes the driving focus of their trip. Combining a cause you really care about with a place you've always wanted to see can make your trip especially rewarding. Various organizations sponsor "volunteer vacations," work camps, and other service projects in needy countries, including Global Volunteers (www.globalvolunteers.org), Volunteers for Peace (www.vfp.org), and Service Civil International (www.sciint.org). If you're wondering whether a charitable organization is reputable, a good place to start is Charity Navigator (www.charitynavigator.org), a nonprofit organization that rates US-based charities on their accountability and transparency.

Or, consider taking an educational tour. While not explicitly service-oriented, these can do a brilliant job of broadening horizons. I've gone on three trips to Central and South America with the Center for Global Education and Experience (at Augsburg College in Minneapolis)—some of the most vivid and perspective-stretching travel experiences I've ever enjoyed (www.augsburg.edu/global; for trip journals of my CFGE experiences in El Salvador and Nicaragua, see www.ricksteves.com/centam). For more resources, see the suggestions in the sidebar on page 520, or try searching online for "volunteer vacation" or "volunteer travel."

If you've got more time and stamina than money, consider Workaway.info, which connects you with families or small organizations offering room and board in exchange for volunteer work, usually manual labor (gardening, carpentry, painting).

Culturally curious travelers can sign up with one of several hospitality exchange organizations. These groups connect travelers with host families with the noble goal of building world peace through international understanding. Guests sightsee less but engage more in everyday life with their hosts—talking, sharing, and learning. You'll arrive as a stranger at new destinations, but leave as a friend.

Although no money changes hands, these exchanges aren't for people simply out to travel cheap—the logistics involved aren't worth it. Most organizations screen members (with varying degrees of stringency) and set ground rules about length of stay. Opening your own home to visitors is encouraged, but not required. Servas is the oldest and largest of these organizations ($98 to join, www.usservas.org). London-based Globetrotters Club runs a similar network of hosts and travelers ($20 annual membership, www.globe-trotters.co.uk), as do several groups that are free to join, such as the Hospitality Club (www.hospitalityclub.org). Other organizations serve specialized audiences (women, Jewish travelers, touring cyclists, gay travelers). Friendship Force International organizes homestay tours for small groups, also with a goal of fostering international goodwill (www.thefriendshipforce.org). Many travelers swear by these exchanges as the only way to really travel, and they treasure their global list of friends.

Student Travel

I feel strongly about the value of students incorporating a little world travel into their university experience. Ninety-six percent of humanity lives outside our borders—and we risk being left in the dust if our next generation of leaders and innovators doesn't know how to effectively engage the world. Sending our students overseas is not a luxury. It's a necessity. Urge the young people in your lives to get a passport and see the world as a classroom.

Good universities all encourage students to take a semester abroad. Interested students can get the details at their campus foreign-study office.

Here's my personal take—from a parent's perspective—on what's to be gained by spending a semester or two overseas. When my son, Andy, was a college student, he enjoyed a fabulous semester abroad in Rome. The fundamental decision for students like Andy—along with whether they should miss fall football season or the fun of spring on campus—is choosing between Europe and the developing world. A semester in Africa or Latin America gives a real-life experience in the rough-and-tumble reality of poverty and powerfully humanizes the often-quoted statistic that "half of humanity is trying to live on $2 a day." Time spent in China or India (whose economies are growing at a much faster pace than their conventional Western European counterparts) introduces a student to emerging economic powerhouses that will compete with our country throughout that student's work life. And a semester in Europe offers (for many) an opportunity to connect with our roots; follow up on language, art, and history courses already taken; and enjoy that traditional Grand Tour of the Old World.

The real education of a semester abroad takes place outside the classroom. It's hard for students to really focus on lectures and homework with so many cultural experiences

Resources for Studying, Volunteering, or Working Abroad

BUNAC.org: Group coordinating student work and volunteer experiences
CIEE.org: Organization offering for-credit study abroad programs
HelpX.net: Directory of short-term work in exchange for food and housing
InterExchange.org: Opportunities for both working and volunteering abroad
TransitionsAbroad.com: Resource for working or studying abroad
USServas.org: Service organization for international hosts and travelers
WorldTeach.org: Organizes volunteer teaching in developing countries
Workaway.info: Connects travelers with short-term work in exchange for housing
WSAEurope.com: Weekend tours for students studying in Europe

so close (and parents so far). Each week the buzz is about who's going where on the weekend (weekends last three days, as foreign study programs don't hold class on Friday). From his base in Rome, Andy would gather a small gang for each three-day weekend: skiing in the Swiss Alps, hiking in the Cinque Terre, biking the Amalfi Coast, or sharing an apartment in Cefalù, Sicily. It came so naturally to him (I wonder why?) that he's even formed a tour company for students abroad (Weekend Student Adventures—WSAEurope. com), and he's published a guidebook, *Andy Steves' Europe: City-Hopping on a Budget.*

Learning the language, making new friends from around the world, flirting with foreigners, getting comfortable with a bustling new city, and mastering the late-night scene while going through the motions in classes all add up to a life-changing and unforgettable semester. And it's a bonding experience with fellow students who will be friends for life.

Global Warming and Going "Green"

During a heat wave several years ago in Italy, I switched hotels because it was too hot to sleep without air-conditioning. It was the first time I had done that, and it was a kind of personal defeat—since I've always prided myself on not needing air-conditioning.

There's no doubt in Europe (and among Europeans) that things are warming up. Nearly everywhere in the Alps, summer skiing is just a memory, and—even in the winter— ski resorts are in desperate straits for lack of snow. (These days, new ski lifts in Europe routinely come with plumbing for snowmaking equipment.) Eating outdoors in formerly cool-climate Munich or Amsterdam now feels like a tradition. Dutch boys wait years for a frozen canal to skate on.

Scandinavia is seeing a spike in summertime visitors from Spain and Italy seeking a break from the heat.

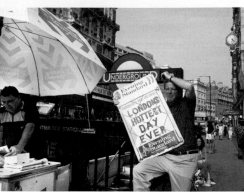

As they've sweltered through summer after summer, Europeans (and their visitors) have long embraced the "inconvenient truth" that things are heating up.

A theme that keeps crashing into my reporting on Europe is how real climate change is, and how tragic it is that some people deny it just for their own economic convenience. Everywhere I go in Europe, I see the results of literally billions of dollars being invested in infrastructure changes that will allow Europe to live in the future that we are creating. Europeans (with a fatalistic acceptance of the momentum created by reliance on fossil fuels and the values of many international corporations) have taken a pragmatic view: Climate change is a reality, and there's not much we can do to change it—but we can prepare for it. For instance, the German city of Hamburg—situated just up a big river from the sea, and therefore in danger of storm surges—has raised 60 miles of embankments...and artfully designed the ones in the city center to be inviting people zones.

Still, Europeans are doing their part to try to be environmentally responsible. In particularly "green" Denmark, residents must pay for the disposal of a car when they first buy it, while entire towns are competing to see which will be the first to become entirely wind-powered. London levies an $18 "congestion charge" on drivers entering the city center during peak hours. This cuts down on both pollution and traffic, and the money generated helps fund the city's energy-efficient bus system.

In an effort to reduce reliance on cars, many European cities have become aggressively bike-friendly, with well-groomed bike lanes and even free or very cheap loaner bikes for quick rides within town. Next to Amsterdam's Centraal station stands a high-rise garage—not for cars, but for bicycles. While these ideas sound laughably idealistic to some oil-addicted American cynics, Europeans are making them a reality, and environmentally conscious travelers can take advantage of them, too.

When it comes to global climate change, we travelers—who burn fossil fuels with every intercontinental flight and bus tour—are contributing to the problem. A day of reckoning is coming, when honest travelers will agree that flying to Europe pumps more carbon into the atmosphere than our earth can handle to sustain the climate we all find comfortable. Europeans are starting to see "carbon taxes" that force consumers to pay for zeroing out the negative impact their purchases have on the environment. I have friends who, despite cheap airfares, ride the train to minimize the environmental cost of their intra-European travel.

As a business that promotes travel, my company (Rick Steves' Europe, Inc.) has been exploring the ethics of our work and what we can do to offset our carbon footprint. We're making our office as energy-efficient as possible, and we've made extensive use of 100 percent recycled fabric in the travel bags we manufacture. I am determined to grapple with the consequences of climate change by finding a way to help those who travel go carbon-neutral...or better.

Meanwhile, do your part to conserve energy. If your hotel overstocks your room with towels, use just one. Carry your own soap and shampoo rather than rip open all those little soaps and shampoo packets. Bring a water bottle instead of using and tossing a plastic bottle at every hotel. Turn off the light when you leave your room. Limit showers to five minutes. And be open to European standards of green and sustainable living.

Of course, there's plenty more that can be done to counterbalance the environmental costs of international travel. But even in small ways, we can make a difference.

Consuming Responsibly

Understand your power to shape the marketplace by what you decide to buy, whether in the grocery store or in your choice of hotels. In my travels (and in my writing), whenever possible, I patronize and support small, family-run businesses (hotels, restaurants, shops, tour guides). I choose people who invest their creativity and resources in giving me simple, friendly, sustainable, and honest travel experiences—people with ideals. Back Door places don't rely on slick advertising and marketing gimmicks, and they don't target the created needs of people whose values are shaped by capitalism gone wild. Consuming responsibly means buying as if your choice is a vote for the kind of world we could have. This not only makes for happier travels now, it will help assure happy travels for future generations.

Back Doors

Europe is your playground...and it's time for recess.

Traveling Through the Back Door

The travel skills covered in the first half of this book enable you to open doors most travelers don't even know exist. Now I'd like to introduce you to some of my top European destinations, where you'll have a chance to put those skills to work. I'm the matchmaker, and you and the travel bug are about to get intimate. By traveling vicariously with me through this selection of places and sights, you'll get a peek at my favorite parts of Europe. And, just as important, by internalizing this lifetime of magical travel moments, you'll develop a knack for finding your own.

Europe's Top Destinations

Europe Through the Back Door is the first book I ever wrote. In the early days, Back Doors to me were Europe's undiscovered nooks and undeveloped crannies: all-day walks on an alpine ridge, sword-fern fantasies in a ruined castle, and untrampled towns that had, for various reasons, missed the modern parade (like Gimmelwald, Dingle, Salema, and the Cinque Terre). But with ever more sophisticated travelers armed with ever-better guidebooks, places I "discovered" 25 or 30 years ago are now undeveloped and noncommercial only in a relative sense. And certain places that I really raved about now suffer from Back Door congestion.

Europe's Top Destinations

So now, rather than isolate a few locations and call them "Back Doors," I'm giving you a country-by-country rundown of my favorite destinations throughout Europe and sharing some of my most unforgettable experiences...in the hope that they will inspire you to travel and fill your own journal with

Ratings & Map Legend

I use the following symbols to rate destinations in this book:

▲▲▲   Don't miss
 ▲▲   Try hard to see
  ▲   Worthwhile if you can make it

I've written these chapters to give you the flavor of each country, not for you to navigate by. My various guidebooks provide all the details necessary to splice your chosen Back Doors into a smooth trip (see page 35).
Bon voyage!

■ Castle	········ Ferry/Boat Route
▪ Point of Interest	----- Trails & Paths
▲ Mountain Peak	⊛ Capital City
)(Mtn. Pass	♠ National Park

your own memories. This approach is less about finding the undiscovered places and more about demonstrating how thoughtful Back Door travel—anywhere you go—can get you beyond tourist traps, broaden your perspective, and enrich your travel experience. This is my niche—teaching people how to be travelers (as opposed to tourists).

Each corner of Europe has a unique and genuine charm. A destination is worthy simply because it exists, with people who proudly call it home. With a Back Door angle, you can slip your fingers under the staged culture of any destination and actually find a pulse. It's clear to me that the more you understand a region, the more you appreciate and enjoy it.

Italy

When travel dreams take people to Europe, Italy is often their first stop. There's something seductively charming about this country, its people, and *la dolce vita*. I always feel at home in Italy, whether struggling onto a crowded bus in Rome, navigating the fun chaos of Naples, sipping a cocktail in a Venetian bar, or sitting on the banister of Florence's Ponte Vecchio for a midnight street-music concert.

Italy is the cradle of European civilization. As you explore, you'll stand face-to-face with iconic images from its 2,000-year history: the Colosseum of ancient Rome, the medieval Leaning Tower of Pisa, a cornucopia of Renaissance achievement (Michelangelo's *David* and the Sistine Chapel, for example), and the playful exuberance of the Baroque, perhaps best seen in the Bernini-designed fountains and squares of Rome.

Italy has it all—encompassing German-flavored Alps, romantic hill towns, peaceful lakes lined with 19th-century villas, sun-baked Sicily, the business center of Milan, Mediterranean beaches (like the Cinque Terre), and the art-drenched cities of Venice, Florence, and Rome. The country is reasonably small and laced with freeways and train lines, so you're never more than a day's journey from any of these places. And everywhere you can enjoy Italy's famous cuisine and wine.

I love Italy for its idiosyncrasies—the fun, the unpredictability, and the serendipity. And that comes with frustrations and complications. Precision in Italy seems limited to the pasta (which is exactly and reliably *al dente*). The country bubbles with emotion, traffic jams, strikes, and irate Italians shaking their fists at each other one minute and walking arm in arm the next. Have a talk with yourself before you cross the border. Promise yourself to relax, and remember it's a package deal.

Accept Italy as Italy. Savor your cappuccino, dangle your feet over a canal, and imagine what it was like centuries ago. Ramble through the rabble and rubble, and mentally resurrect those ancient stones. Get chummy with the winds of the past—and connect with the pleasures of the moment. Travel memories here are low-hanging fruit: They're yours to harvest.

From fragments of once grandiose Roman statues to bobbing gondolas ready for romance, Italy has sightseeing treats for everyone.

FAVORITE SIGHTS AND MEMORABLE EXPERIENCES IN ITALY

Swept Away in Rome

Not long ago in Rome, I spent an entire sunny afternoon in my hotel room, tinkering with changes to the next edition of my guidebook. I had time for just a quick break, but stepping outside was dangerous. There's a strong current of distractions in this city. Just by turning the corner from my hotel, I was swept out into a Roman sea, teeming with colorful and fragrant entertainments. I didn't make it back for hours.

I flowed downhill to the Pantheon, the influential domed temple that served as the model for Michelangelo's dome of St. Peter's and many others. I stopped at the portico—nicknamed "Rome's umbrella," a fun, local gathering spot in a rainstorm—from where I saw a symphony of images: designer shades and flowing hair backlit in the magic-hour sun; a flute section of ice-cream lickers sitting on a marble bench in the spritz of a fountain; strolling Romanian accordion players who refused to follow their conductor; and the stains of a golden arch on a wall marking where a McDonald's once sold fast food. The entire scene was corralled by pastel walls, providing the visual equivalent of good acoustics.

As I let go of the Pantheon's columns, the current swept me past siren cafés and out onto Via del Corso, which since ancient times has been the main north-south drag through town. On my swim through the city, this was the deep end. The rough crowd from the suburbs comes here for some cityscape elegance. Today they'd gooped on a little extra grease and were wearing their best leggings, heels, and T-shirts.

Veering away from the busy pedestrian boulevard, I came upon Fausto, a mad artist standing proudly amid his installation of absurdities. While eccentric, he seemed strangely sane in this crazy world. He's the only street artist I've met who personally greets viewers. After surveying his tiny gallery of hand-scrawled and thought-provoking tidbits, I asked for a card. He gave me a handmade piece of wallet-sized art, reminding me that his "secretary" was at the end of the curb: a plastic piggy bank for tips.

Next came the market square Campo de' Fiori, which usually creates its own current in the hours after the fruit and vegetable vendors have packed up. But today the square felt like a punished child. After a Roman teenager drank herself into a coma, police banned the consumption of alcohol in outdoor public spaces. It's like someone turned on the lights at a party before midnight.

I passed a homeless man, tattered but respectfully dressed, leaning against a wall. He was savoring a cigar and a bottle of wine while studying Rome's flow as if it held a secret. Next, I chatted with twins from Kentucky, giddy about their Roman days as they celebrated their 40th birthday together. Their Doublemint smiles and high energy made a great case for embracing the good life.

Moving on to Piazza del Popolo, the vast oval square known for its symmetrical design and art-filled churches, I ducked into the Church of Santa Maria del Popolo just as the ushers closed the doors for Mass. Inside, the white noise of Roman streets became the incense-scented hum

Fast Facts

Biggest cities: Rome (capital, 2.7 million), Milan (1.3 million), Naples (1 million)
Size: 116,000 square miles (similar to Arizona), population 61 million
Locals call it: Italia
Currency: Euro
Key dates: 5th century A.D., the fall of the Roman Empire; 15th century, the birth of the Renaissance
Biggest festivals: Carnevale (usually February, especially big in Venice), Palio horse races (July 2 and August 16, Siena)
Handy Italian phrases: *Buon giorno* (good day; bwohn **jor**-noh), *Per favore* (please; pehr fah-**voh**-ray), *Grazie* (thank you; **graht**-see-ay), *Mi fanno male i piedi!* (My feet hurt!; mee **fah**-noh **mah**-lay ee pee-**eh**-dee)
Tourist Info: Italia.it

The charms of Rome have a current like a river, and being swept away—from the Pantheon to the Spanish Steps—is part of the experience.

of a big church with a determined priest—and not enough people. With my hands folded as if here to worship, I slipped down the side aisle to catch a glimpse of a Caravaggio, that late-16th-century thriller of Italian painting.

Stepping back outside, I found myself at the north entrance of the ancient city. Determined to swim back to my hotel and my work, I passed the same well-dressed bum with the cigar and the buzz, still intently caught up in the city. I imagined being in his pickled head for just a moment.

Near him, guys from Somalia launched their plastic fluorescent whirlybirds high into the twilight sky. These street trinkets keep African immigrants from starving. They make me wish I had made a museum from all the goofy things people have sold on the streets of Rome over the years—from flaming *Manneken-Pis* lighters to five-foot-tall inflatable bouncing cigars to twin magnets that jitter like crickets when you play with them just so.

Finally, with a struggling stroke, I made it back to the safety of my hotel, where none of that Roman current is allowed in. The problem: While taking a break from writing, I came home with even more to write about. In Rome, one thing leads to another, and if you're trying to get on top of your notes, it can be perilous to go out.

Tuning in to Tasty Italy

Tuscany is a region fiercely proud of its Chianina beef, from white cows. Recently, while in the town of Montepulciano, I sank my teeth into a carnivore's dream come true. In a stony cellar, under one long, tough vault, I joined a local crowd for dinner. The scene was powered by an open fire in the far back of the vault. Flickering in front of the flames was a huge hunk of red beef, lying on the counter like a corpse on a gurney. Like a blacksmith in hell, Giulio—a lanky man in a

T-shirt—hacked at the beef with a cleaver, lopping off a steak every few minutes.

In a kind of mouth-watering tango, he pranced past the boisterous tables of customers, holding a raw slab of beef on butcher's paper as if handling a tray of drinks. Giulio presented the slabs to each table of diners, telling them the weight and price (the minimum was about $40) and getting their OK to cook it. He'd then dance back to the inferno and grill the slab: seven minutes on one side, seven on the other. There was no asking how you wanted it done; *this* was the way it was done.

Eating a steak at Giulio's place—Osteria dell'Acquacheta— is just one of my many memorable Italian dining experiences. And over the years, I've come up with some observations about food and Italy.

If America's specialty is fast food, Italy's is slow food: locally grown ingredients, in season, bought daily, prepared with love, and enjoyed in social circumstances with friends and family. While American food often has to look good, travel well, and be available all year, Italian food does none of that—it just has to taste good.

A perfect example is *vignarola*, a holy trinity of artichoke, peas, and fava beans. It's only available during a brief perfect storm of seasonality in spring, when everything is bursting with flavor. Italian chefs and home cooks religiously prep the vegetables—trimming the artichokes, cleaning the peas, and shelling the fava beans—to create this traditional dish that signals spring at its fullest.

While I've never liked putting up with TV noise when grabbing a simple meal in Italy, I now see that when an eatery has the TV playing, it's often because it's where the local workers drop by to eat—and that indicates a low price and a good value.

LEFT In Tuscany, enthusiastic carnivores can have the meal of a lifetime at a rustic steakhouse.

RIGHT For many Italians, "a good marriage" is the relationship between their favorite wine and what's on the plate.

Italy's Top Destinations

Rome ▲▲▲　　　　　　　　　　　　allow 3-5 days

Italy's capital, studded with ancient architectural remnants, floodlit fountain squares, and Vatican opulence

Top Sights

Colosseum Huge stadium where gladiators squared off
Pantheon Antiquity's best-preserved domed temple
Roman Forum Ancient Rome's main square, with ruins and grand arches
St. Peter's Basilica World's most influential church, with Michelangelo's *Pietà* and dome
Vatican Museums Western civilization's finest art, including the Sistine Chapel
Borghese Gallery Bernini sculptures plus paintings by Caravaggio, Raphael, and Titian

Florence ▲▲▲　　　　　　　　　　　　2-3 days

Walkable Renaissance wonderland and Tuscan capital with iconic Duomo (and other grand churches), palaces, museums, and Italy's best gelato

Top Sights

Accademia Michelangelo's *David* and powerful (unfinished) *Prisoners*
Uffizi Gallery Greatest collection of Renaissance paintings anywhere
Bargello Sculpture museum of Renaissance greats
Duomo Museum Original sculptured masterpieces from Florence's cathedral
Duomo Imposing Gothic cathedral with bell tower, baptistery, and Renaissance dome

Nearby

Pisa Leaning Tower and surrounding Field of Miracles
Lucca Charming city with walled old center
Volterra and San Gimignano Stony, characteristic hill towns

Venice ▲▲▲　　　　　　　　　　　　1-3 days

Romantic island-city famous for St. Mark's Square and Basilica, the Grand Canal, and singing gondoliers

Milan ▲▲　　　　　　　　　　　　1 day

Powerhouse city of commerce and fashion, with spiny Duomo, prestigious opera house, and Leonardo's *Last Supper*

Lake District ▲　　　　　　　　　　　　1-2 days

Low-key resort towns with majestic alpine vistas and aristocratic Old World romance on **Lake Como** and **Lake Maggiore**

Cinque Terre ▲▲▲　　　　　　　　　　　　1-3 days

Picture-perfect Riviera hamlets strung along a rugged coastline laced with hiking trails

Hill Towns of Central Italy ▲▲　　　　　　　　　　　　1-3 days

Postcard villages of the Italian heartland: cathedral-capped **Orvieto,** minuscule **Civita,** wine-soaked **Montalcino** and **Montepulciano,** Renaissance-perfect **Pienza,** and classically Tuscan **Cortona**

Assisi ▲▲　　　　　　　　　　　　1 day

St. Francis' hillside hometown, with a divine basilica decorated by Giotto

Siena ▲▲▲　　　　　　　　　　　　1 day

Italy's ultimate hill town, with grand square and strikingly striped cathedral

Naples ▲▲   1-2 days

Gritty port city featuring vibrant street life and a top archaeological museum

Nearby

Pompeii Famous ruins of the ancient town buried by Mount Vesuvius' eruption

Sorrento and Capri Seaside resort port and jet-set island getaway

Amalfi Coast String of seafront villages tied together by scenic mountain road

With more time, consider visiting

Dolomites Italy's rugged rooftop, with alpine meadows and a Germanic flair

Padua University town with Giotto's gloriously frescoed Scrovegni Chapel

Verona Town with Roman amphitheater plus Romeo and Juliet sights

Ravenna Coastal town known for its top Byzantine mosaics

To go gourmet and not go broke, I go to a small, classy *enoteca* (wine bar). The bars are owned and operated by food evangelists who thoughtfully design the food menu to complement the wine list. A great wine costs about $10 a glass. Rather than bog down on an expensive entrée, I order top-end on the *antipasti* (starter) and *primi piatti* (first course) list. By doing that, I usually end up with the freshest meats and cheeses and the chef's favorite pasta dish of the day.

I've realized I should stay away from restaurants famous for inventing a pasta dish. Alfredo (of fettuccini fame) and Carbonara (of penne fame) are both Roman restaurants—and they're both much more famous than they are good.

One of my favorite Italian specialties isn't even on the menu: good conversation. In Rome, I talked about dessert with a man at a nearby table. He told me how his grandfather always said, in the local dialect, "The mouth cannot be finished until it smells of cows." In other words, you must finish the meal with cheese.

Another time, I shared a delightful dinner with a local guide, Giuseppe, and his wife, Anna. She greeted each plate with unbridled enthusiasm. Suddenly Giuseppe looked at me and said, "My wife's a good fork." Misunderstanding him, I blushed. My face said, "Come again?" And Giuseppe clarified, saying *un buona forchetta*...a good fork—that's what we call someone who loves to eat."

To me, Italian cuisine is a symphony—the ingredients are the instruments. The quality is important, and the marriage of ingredients is what provides the tonality. When things are in tune, you taste it.

The Long Italian Meal

For many Italians, dinner is the evening's entertainment. Italians eat in courses, lingering over each one; a three-hour meal is common. A typical meal might start with *antipasti* (such as *bruschetta* or a plate of cold cuts and veggies). Next comes the *primo piatto* (first dish—such as a pasta, risotto, or soup), then the *secondo piatto* (usually meat or seafood), and finally, *dolce* (dessert). For most travelers, the full multi-course meal is simply too much food. A good rule of thumb is for each person to order any two courses, such as an *antipasto* and *primo piatto* (sharing is perfectly acceptable). When you want the bill, you'll have to ask for it (possibly more than once). For Italians, the meal is an end in itself, and only rude waiters rush you. To "eat and run" is seen as a lost opportunity.

Florence: The Cultural Capital of Europe

Geographically small but culturally rich, Florence is home to some of the greatest art and architecture in the world. It was in Florence, in about 1400, that the Renaissance began. After wallowing for centuries in relative darkness, Western civilization was suddenly perky, making up for lost centuries with huge gains in economics, science, and art. And Florence was at the center of it all.

Wealthy merchant and banking families—like the Medici, who ruled Florence for generations—demonstrated their civic pride (and showed off) by commissioning great art. Because of them, in a single day I can look Michelangelo's *David* in the eyes, fall under the seductive sway of Botticelli's *La Primavera*, and climb the modern world's first dome, which caps the cathedral and still dominates the skyline.

In Florence, great art is everywhere—even my hotel. I enjoy staying at Loggiato dei Serviti—a former monastery, crisp with elegance and history. The hotel's entrance is on a quintessentially Florentine square, with a beautifully arcaded building—the first designed by Brunelleschi (the man who engineered the cathedral's famed dome). The building, once an orphanage, now shelters the local down-and-outs on its elegant porch. While these well-worn people used to get me down, now I realize that for 500 years, vagabonds and street people who couldn't afford a bedroom like the one I call home in Florence could still enjoy the architecture (or at least the shade). Since the days of the Renaissance greats, they have set up camp for free, under the loggia eave of my fancy front door.

From my room, I can look across the way to the Accademia Gallery and its art school. The courtyard in between is gravelly with broken columns and stones set up for students to carve. All day long I hear the happy pecking and chirping of chisels

Ticket Tricks

Italy's most popular museums and churches can have long lines and lots of crowds. Here are some tips for avoiding lines at the most congested sights.

- Book tickets ahead of time if visiting the Uffizi Gallery or the Accademia Gallery in Florence, or the Vatican Museums (including the Sistine Chapel) in Rome.
- Consider getting a museum pass, such as the Firenze Card or the Roma Pass, which puts you in the fast lane at sights like Florence's Uffizi Gallery or Rome's Colosseum. Buy these passes at a tourist information office or at lesser-visited sights (such as the Church of Santa Maria Novella in Florence or Palatine Hill in Rome) to avoid standing in line. In Venice, a combo-ticket covers the popular Doge's Palace (with long lines) and the less-visited Correr Museum—guess where you should buy the ticket?
- Some sights require a reservation, including the Scrovegni Chapel in Padua, the Borghese Gallery in Rome, Leonardo's *Last Supper* in Milan, and the Brancacci Chapel and the Duomo's dome in Florence.

gaining confidence as they cut through the stone. If they need inspiration, students only need to dip into the Accademia's exhibition space.

Entering that gallery is like walking into a temple of humanism. At the high altar stands Michelangelo's colossal statue of *David*, the slingshot-toting giant slayer. This perfect man represents humankind finally stepping out of medieval darkness. Clothed only in confidence, his toes gripping the pedestal, *David* sizes up his foe, as if to say, "I can take this guy." The statue was an apt symbol for the city, inspiring Florentines to tackle their Goliaths.

Until 1873, *David* lived not in the Accademia, but in the city's great square, Piazza della Signoria. A replica *David* marks the spot where the original once stood. With goony eyes and a pigeon-dropping wig, the fake *David* seems a bit dumbfounded, as tourists picnic at his feet and policewomen clip-clop by on horseback.

One edge of Piazza della Signoria opens into the long arcaded courtyard of the Uffizi Gallery, the museum that once housed the offices of the Medici. A permanent line of tourists waits patiently in the shade to see this best-any-where collection of Italian paintings. Lounging between the columns, enterprising artists sketch the tourists and display their work. And filling the niches all around are life-size statues of Leonardo, Dante, Lorenzo de' Medici, and a dozen other Renaissance greats—Florentines, every one of them.

My favorite Florentine painter—Botticelli—has a few special paintings inside the Uffizi. His *Primavera* shows the personification of Spring—and the Renaissance in full bloom.

Botticelli's *Primavera*, a highlight of the Uffizi Gallery

In Florence, Brunelleschi's dome towers above much of the finest art in Europe. Yet cross the Arno River, and you're in a rustic zone of traditional artisans.

Botticelli painted a splendid innocence, where a maiden can walk barefoot through a garden scattering flower petals from a fold in her dress and call it a good day's work—and where the Three Graces can dance naked with no more fanfare than the happy do-si-do of butterflies. To me, the delicate face of Botticelli's Spring is the purest expression of Renaissance beauty in Florence.

Today, Florence's artistic legacy lives on across the Arno River, in the Oltrarno neighborhood—home to small shops featuring handmade furniture, enameled jewelry, marbled papers, and finely glazed pottery. One artisan drew me into his shop as if inviting me on a journey. Under a single dangling light bulb, he hammered gold leaf into a dingy halo, breathing life back into a faded statue that had originally been crafted by a neighbor of his—five centuries ago. Hundreds of years after the Renaissance, the spirit of creation remains alive and well in Florence.

The Cinque Terre: Italy's Riviera

"A sleepy, romantic, and inexpensive town on the Riviera without a tourist in sight." That's the mirage travelers chase around busy Nice and Cannes. Pssst! Although hardly free of tourists, the most dream-worthy stretch of the Riviera rests in Italy just across the border, between Genoa and Pisa. It's Italy's Cinque Terre.

Leaving the nearest big city, La Spezia, your train takes you into a mountain. Ten minutes later, you burst into the sunlight. Your train nips in and out of the hills, teasing you with a series of Mediterranean views. Each scene is grander than the last: azure blue tinseled in sunbeams, carbonated waves hitting desolate rocks, and the occasional topless sunbather camped out like a lone limpet.

The Cinque Terre (pronounced **chink**-weh **tay**-reh), which means "five lands," is a quintet of villages clinging to this most inaccessible bit of Riviera coastline. Each is a variation on the same theme: a well-whittled pastel jumble of homes filling a gully like crusty sea creatures in a tide pool. Like a gangly clump of oysters, the houses grow on each other. Residents are the barnacles—hungry, but patient. And we travelers are like algae, coming in with the tide.

The rugged villages of the Cinque Terre, founded by Dark Age locals hiding out from marauding pirates, were long cut off from the modern world. Only with the coming of the train was access made easy. Today, the villages draw hordes of hikers, and the castles protect only glorious views. To preserve this land, the government has declared the Cinque Terre a national park. Visitors hiking between the towns now pay a small entrance fee (about $8 for a one-day pass), which stokes a fund designed to protect the flora and fauna and keep the trails clean and well-maintained.

The government, recognizing how wonderfully pre-served these towns are, has long prohibited anyone from constructing any modern buildings. For that reason, today there are no big, comfortable hotels in the area—great news for Back Door travelers because it keeps away the most obnoxious slice of the traveling public: those who need big, comfortable hotels. But rugged travelers, content to rent a room in a private home or simple *pensione,* enjoy a land where the villagers go about their business as if the sur-rounding vineyards are the very edges of the earth.

Overseen by a ruined castle, with the closest thing to a natural harbor, Vernazza is my Cinque Terre home base. Only the occasional noisy slurping up of the train by the mountain reminds you there's a modern world out there somewhere.

From Vernazza's harbor, wander through the jumble of a tough community living off the sea...or living off travelers who love the sea. The church bells dictate a relaxed tempo. Yellow webs of fishing nets, tables bedecked with umbrellas, kids with plastic shovels, and a flotilla of gritty little boats tethered to buoys provide splashes of color. And accompany-ing the scene is the soundtrack of a dream...a celebrate-the-moment white noise of children, dogs, and waves.

Vernazza's one street connects the harbor with the train station before melting into the vineyards. Like veins on a grape leaf, paths and stairways reach from Main Street into this watercolor huddle of houses. All of life is summer reruns in this hive of lazy human activity. A rainbow of laundry flaps as if to keep the flies off the fat grandmothers who clog ancient doorways.

Residents spend early evenings doing their *vasche* (laps), strolling between the station and the breakwater. Sit on a bench and study this slow-motion parade.

Today, at the top end of town, Vernazza's cruel little road hits a post. No cars enter this village of 600 people. Like the breakwater keeps out the waves at the bottom of the town, the post keeps out the modern storm at the top. But Vernazza's ruined castle no longer says "stay away." And its breakwater—a broad, inviting sidewalk edged with seaside boulders—sticks into the sea like a finger beckoning the distant excursion boats.

The five pastel ports of Italy's Cinque Terre were established as hideouts from pirates in the Middle Ages. Today, villagers will eagerly rent you a room and drizzle pesto on your pasta.

Barefoot in Venice

When you know where to look, there's so much to see in Venice. Stepping ashore after a boat ride from the airport, I noticed everything seemed particularly vivid in this beautifully decrepit cityscape: the pilings rotten at the water line; a funeral boat with an iron casket-rack lashed to the center of the hull; chandeliers lighting a mansion's ceiling frescoes; white marble inlay lining the edges of the stairs over a bridge. In Venice, always look both ways when you pass over a bridge, as lovely views can hit you from any direction.

But there are times when the magic suddenly stops. I needed to check out the parking situation at the edge of the city, and the traffic appalled me. As I dodged the crazy Italian drivers, the contrast between mainland and island was clear. What a charming world the Venetians enjoy—it's free of traffic noise and, as pedestrians, they completely own their byways.

A boat ride took me to the nearby island of Burano, which is famous for humble fishermen's houses and squinting lacemakers. I noticed how the pastel colors of the homes are getting more and more vibrant. The place is just darling (an adjective I've never used to describe a town before).

But the rising sea has forced Burano to raise its canal-side pavement. I could see a strip of fresh bricks above the water line. Houses that could be made higher have had their ground floors raised, leaving them with shorter ceilings.

Venice has been battling rising water levels since the fifth century. Venice now floods about 100 times a year—usually from October until late winter—a phenomenon called *acqua alta*. During these floods, some high-end hotels lend wading boots to their customers. Wooden benches are placed end-to-end in St. Mark's Square to create elevated sidewalks. But these turn into total gridlock, as the square-sized crowds jostle for space on the narrow wooden walkways.

On this trip, St. Mark's Square was as dry as ever. At Caffè Florian, the most venerable café on the square, the manager lamented how, in the last decade, the café's elegance has been trampled by poorly dressed tourists (not unlike me, I must admit). Still, I love this place, with its smoke-stained mirrors, white-tuxedoed waiters, and finicky piano and string quartet, which somehow gets called an "orchestra."

While you can enjoy a romantic drink here with live music and all the tourists, I opted for a quiet cup of coffee in the morning, when the square was empty. Surrounded by the patina of faded elegance, I marveled at how the history popped with the architecture and without the modern tourism. The Gothic was so lacy, and the Renaissance so

Venice is awash with wonders—from the cultural grounding that comes with going barefoot on the flooring *"alla veneziana"* to the surge of the gondolier's oar as you glide under the Bridge of Sighs.

capable. It looked like a pure, computer-generated Venetian cityscape—only it was real. In so many ways, when you get up early and stay out late, you enjoy a different, and it seems, more authentic Venice.

Likewise, on the vaporetto water buses, there's a stark contrast between the midday/rush-hour mobs and the easy-going joy of riding at quiet times. Venice is two cities: one garishly touristic and the other so romantic and tranquil that it makes you go *fortissimo* in describing it.

In Venice, I spend my evenings visiting restaurants to consider for my guidebooks, then return to my favorite for dinner. This dining derby is my nightly ritual in Italy. Tonight, when the waiter asked me how I liked my wine, I said, *"Complicato"*—and he served up his house Amarone, a local red. I drank it like a monkey climbs a tree. Just when the branches were getting pretty bendy, he capped the meal with a glass of Sgroppino, a Venetian after-dinner slushy of lemon juice, lemon gelato, Prosecco, and vodka. It's my new favorite taste treat.

Done with dinner, I retreated to my hotel room. The speckled "Venetian pavement"—the city's characteristic floor made of a broken hodgepodge of marble fragments and then polished—greeted my bare feet. While some might mistake it for cheap linoleum, it's far from that—it's treasured here and quite expensive. It flexes with the settling of the buildings and is costly to maintain, but it's so characteristic. My feet connected with that floor in a way my feet have never before connected with flooring—happily grounding me in Venice.

Bella Tuscany

After checking in to my Tuscan *agriturismo*, my host, Signora Gori, takes me on a welcome stroll. Our first stop is a sty dominated by a giant pig. "We call him Pastanetto—'the little pastry.'" While the scene through my camera's viewfinder is pristine and tranquil, the soundtrack is not. As a horrendous chorus of squeals comes from a rustic slaughterhouse on the horizon, she says, "This is our little Beirut." I stow my camera, deciding to simply absorb the attention I'm enjoying from a host who is both old-money elegant and farmhouse-tough. The Gori family estate is Tuscany in the rough.

The Italian landscape is dotted with *agriturismi* like this one—traditional family farms renting out spare rooms to make ends meet. To qualify officially as an *agriturismo*, the farm must still generate more money from its farm activities—whether growing olives, making wine, or producing prosciutto—and most sell or serve the food they produce to guests. Don't confuse these with farmhouse B&Bs, which aren't actual farms, though they can be fine places to stay. If you want the real thing, make sure the owners call their place an *agriturismo*.

Hiking to the slaughterhouse, we enter a room dominated by a stainless-steel table piled with red sides of pork. Signora Gori says, "Here begins prosciutto." Burly men in aprons squeeze the blood out of hunks of meat the size of dance partners. Then they cake the ham hocks in salt to begin a curing process that takes months. While the salt helps cure the meat, a coating of pepper seals it. In spooky but great-smelling rooms, towering racks of ham hocks age. A man, dressed and acting like a veterinarian, tests each ham by sticking it with a horse-bone needle and giving it a sniff.

Back outside, Signora Gori takes me into the next barn, where fluffy white lambs jump to attention in their hay, kicking up a sweet-smelling golden dust. Backlit by stray sunbeams, it's a dreamy, almost biblical scene. Picking up a baby lamb, she gives it an Eskimo kiss—nose to nose. She explains, "I must really know my sheep." Their milk is turned into Pecorino cheese.

Strolling down another lane, we observe the family's team of vintners just as Signora Gori's brother empties a bucketful of purple grapes into a dump truck. The load tumbles from the truck into a grinder, which munches through the bunches, spitting stems one way and juice with mangled grapes the other. As the juice flows through pipes into a cellar, the brother explains that wine-making is labor-intensive, "but right now the grapes are doing all the work."

And as the new grapes ferment, we taste the finished product. A key word for your Tuscan travels is *corposo*—full-bodied. Lifting the elegant glass to my lips, I sip the wine while enjoying the pride in the eyes of those who made it. Satisfied, I say, "*Corposo.*" They say, "*Si, bello.*"

That night at dinner, we're joined by the rest of the Gori family. The two sons dress and act like princes home on break from some Italian Oxford. Sitting down to a classic Tuscan table—where things are simple, harmonious, and unhurried—with a glass of good red wine, I nod to my hosts, knowing I've found the art of Tuscany.

After dinner, full and content, we sip port and enjoy a backgammon board that has provided evening fun for 200 years in this very room. Surrounded by musty portraits putting faces on this family's long lineage, I realize that this—a special moment for me—is just another night on the farm here in the Gori home.

Naples: Just Do It

All my life, Naples has been the symbol of chaos, stress, and culture shock for European travel. I remember my first visit as a wide-eyed 18-year-old. I stepped off the train into the same vast Piazza Garibaldi that many years later still strikes everyone who visits it as a big paved hellhole. On that first visit, a man in a white surgeon's gown approached me and said, "Please, we need blood for a dying baby." I made a U-turn, stepped back into the station, and made a beeline for Greece.

The city is calmer now, but Naples remains uniquely thrilling. One of my favorite sightseeing experiences anywhere in Italy is simply wandering Spaccanapoli, the long, straight, narrow street that runs through the historic center and bisects the city. Living in the streets is quintessentially Neapolitan—people here seem perfectly adept at enjoying life with their domestic worlds tumbling right out onto the gritty pavement. Naples may be an urban jungle, but it's a warm and welcoming place. Like Cairo or Bombay, it's appalling and appealing at the same time, the closest thing to "reality travel" you'll find in Western Europe. But this tangled mess

Lurking deep in old Naples, you know you can't be a local...but you can imagine.

still somehow manages to breathe, laugh, and sing—with a captivating Italian accent.

An essential stop on any Naples visit is the Archaeological Museum, which offers the closest possible peek into the artistic jewelry boxes of Pompeii and Herculaneum. The actual archaeological sites, while impressive, are barren—the best frescoes and mosaics ended up here. The Secret Room displays R-rated Roman "bedroom" art. A highlight is the Farnese Collection—a giant hall of huge, bright, and wonderfully restored statues excavated from Rome's Baths of Caracalla. You can almost hear the *Toro Farnese* snorting. This largest intact statue from antiquity (a third-century copy of a Hellenistic original, showing a tangled group of people with a raging bull) was carved out of one piece of marble and later restored by Michelangelo.

Take time to explore Naples. This living medieval city is its own best sight. Couples artfully make love on Vespas, while surrounded by more fights and smiles per cobblestone than anywhere else in Italy.

Paint a picture with these thoughts: Naples has the most intact ancient Roman street plan anywhere. Imagine life here in the days of Caesar, with streetside shop fronts that close up to form private homes after dark. Today is just one more page in a 2,000-year-old story of city activity: all kinds of meetings, beatings, and cheatings; kisses, near misses, and little-boy pisses.

For a peek behind the scenes in the shade of wet laundry, venture down a few narrow streets lined by tall apartment buildings. Black-and-white death announcements add to the clutter on the walls. Widows sell cigarettes from plastic buckets. Buy two carrots as a gift for the woman on the fifth floor if she'll lower her bucket down to pick them up.

In search of cheap eats (near major sights) that I can

recommend to my guidebook readers, I walk behind the
Archaeological Museum and meet exuberant Pasquale,
the owner of a tiny deli. Rather than do the cheapskate
"how much?" question, I just let fun-loving and flamboyant
Pasquale surprise me.

He turns making a sandwich into a show, and I watch,
enthralled. After demonstrating the freshness of his rolls as if
squeezing the Charmin, he lays a careful pavement of salami,
brings over the fluffy mozzarella ball as if performing a kidney
transplant, slices a tomato with rapid-fire machine precision,
lovingly pits the olives by hand before hanging them like little
green paintings on a tasty wall, and then finishes it all off with
a celebratory drizzle of the best olive oil. Five euros and a smile
later, I have my cheap lunch and a new guidebook listing.

After saying goodbye to Pasquale, I step outside to look
for a bench upon which to enjoy my lunch and watch the
spirit of Naples roll by.

Civita: A World Apart

The hill towns of central Italy hold their crumbling heads
proudly above the noisy flood of the 21st century and offer
a peaceful taste of what eludes so many tourists. Sitting on
a timeless rampart high above the traffic and trains, hearing only children in the market as the rustling wind ages
the weary red-tile patchwork that surrounds me, I find the
essence of Italy.

Of all the hill towns, Civita di Bagnoregio is my favorite.
People who've been here say "Civita" (chee-**vee**-tah) with
warmth and love. This precious chip of Italy is a traffic-free
community with a grow-it-in-the-valley economy.

Civita teeters atop a pinnacle in a vast canyon ruled by
wind and erosion. Over the years its population has dropped,
but the town survives to serve a steady stream of tourists.
The saddle that once connected Civita to its bigger and
busier sister town, Bagnoregio, eroded away. Today a bridge
connects the two towns. A man with a Vespa does the same
work his father did with a donkey—ferrying the town's goods
up and down the umbilical bridge that connects Civita with a
small, distant parking lot and the rest of Italy. Rome, just 60
miles to the south, is a world away.

Entering the town through a cut in the rock made by
Etruscans 2,500 years ago, and heading under a 12th-century
Romanesque arch, you feel history in the huge, smooth
cobblestones. This was once the main Etruscan road leading
to the Tiber Valley and Rome. Inside the gate, the charms

of Civita are subtle. Those searching for arcade tourism wouldn't know where to look. There are no lists of attractions, orientation tours, or museum hours. It's just Italy. Civita is an artist's dream, a town in the nude. Each lane and footpath holds a surprise. The warm stone walls glow, and each stairway is dessert to a sketch pad or camera.

Smile and nod at each passerby. It's a social jigsaw puzzle, and each person fits. The old woman hanging out in the window monitors gossip. A tiny hunchback lady is everyone's daughter. And cats, the fastest-growing segment of the population, scratch their itches on ancient pillars.

Explore the village. The basic grid street plan of the ancient town survives—but its centerpiece, a holy place of worship, rotates with the cultures: first an Etruscan temple, then a Roman temple, and today a church. The pillars that stand like bar stools in the square once decorated the pre-Christian temple. The heartbeat and pride of the village, this is where festivals and processions start, visitors are escorted, and the town's past is honored.

Just around the corner from the church, on the main street, is La Cantina de Arianna, a family-run wine cellar, trattoria, and bruschetteria. Pull up a stump and let the family serve you *panini* (sandwiches), wine, and a cake called *ciambella*. The white wine has a taste reminiscent of dirty socks. But it's made right here. After eating, ask to see the cellar with its traditional winemaking gear and provisions for rolling huge kegs up the stairs. Grab the stick and tap on the kegs to measure their fullness.

Somehow keeping its head above the flood of the 21st century, the hill town of Civita di Bagnoregio survives and welcomes the adventurous traveler.

Explore further through town. At Antico Frantoio Bruschetteria, venture into their back room to see an interesting collection of old olive presses. This local equivalent of a lemonade stand sells bruschetta to visitors. Bread toasted on an open fire, drizzled with the finest oil, rubbed with pungent garlic, and topped with chopped tomatoes—these edible souvenirs stay on your breath for hours and in your memory forever.

At the end of town, the main drag shrivels into a trail that leads past a chapel (once a jail) and down to a tunnel—now barred to entry—that was cut through the hill under the town in Etruscan times. Tall enough for a woman with a jug on her head to pass through, it may have served as a shortcut to the river below. It was widened in the 1930s so farmers could get between their scattered fields more easily.

Civita has only a few restaurants, which cluster near the piazza. At Trattoria Antico Forno ("Antique Oven"), you eat what's cooking. Owner Franco slices and dices happily through the day. Spaghetti, salad, and wine on the Antico Forno patio, cuddled by Civita—I wouldn't trade it for all-you-can-eat at Maxim's.

Spend the evening. After dinner, sit on the church steps and observe the scene. They say that in a big city you can see a lot, but in a small town like this you can feel a lot. The generous bench is built into the long side of the square, reminding me of how, when I first discovered Civita back in the 1970s and 1980s, the town's old folks would gather here every night. Children play on the piazza until midnight. As you walk back to your car—that scourge of the modern world that enabled you to get here—stop under a lamp on the donkey path, listen to the canyon...distant voices...a clicking chorus of crickets.

More Italian Experiences

In Assisi with St. Francis: I have a personal ritual of enjoying a quiet picnic on the rampart of a ruined castle high above Assisi, the town of St. Francis. I look down at the basilica dedicated to the saint, then into the valley, where a church stands strong in the hazy Italian plain. It marks the place where Francis and his friars started the Franciscan order, bringing the word of God to people in terms all could embrace. Hearing the same birdsong that inspired Francis, and tasting the same simple bread, cheese, and wine of Umbria that sustained him, I calm my 21st-century soul and ponder Francis' message of love, simplicity, and sensitivity to the environment.

A Dove on a Zipline: One spring day, I couldn't resist joining a multitude that had gathered in front of Orvieto's cathedral. For generations, citizens of this small Umbrian town have celebrated the Pentecost—the descent of the Holy Ghost upon the Apostles—in this spot. The anticipation built and built, and then, suddenly, it happened: A dove in a little plastic tube rocketed down a zipline and into a nest of fireworks at the front of the church, setting it all ablaze. After the fireworks exploded, a fireman climbed up to see if the dove was OK. It was. And that was great news, as it brings good luck to the town and fertility to the last couple married in Orvieto.

The Allure of Lake Como: Sleepy Lake Como is a good place to take a break from the obligatory turnstile culture of central Italy. It seems that half the travelers I meet here have tossed their itineraries into the lake and are actually relaxing. The town of Varenna offers the best of all lake worlds. On the quieter side of the lake, with a tiny harbor, narrow lanes, and its own villa, Varenna is the right place to munch a peach and ponder the place where Italy is welded to the Alps. Other than watch the visitors wash ashore with the landing of each ferry, there's wonderfully little to do here. Varenna's volume goes down with the sun. At night, it whispers *luna di miele*—honeymoon. And a good place to enjoy that romance is on its lakefront promenade, the *passerella*. After dark, it's adorned with caryatid lovers pressing silently against each other in the shadows.

Siena Soul: Unlike its rival, Florence, Siena is a city to be seen as a whole rather than as a collection of sights. While memories of Florence consist of dodging Vespas and pickpockets between museums, Siena has an easy-to-enjoy Gothic soul: Courtyards sport flower-decked wells, churches modestly hoard their art, and alleys dead-end into red-tiled rooftop panoramas. Climb to the dizzy top of the 100-yard-tall bell tower and reign over urban harmony at its best. At twilight, first-time poets savor that magic moment when the sky is a rich blue dome no brighter than the medieval towers that seem to hold it high.

Siena is famous for hosting the frantic Palio horse race, held every year on July 2 and August 16. Dirt is brought in and packed down over the pavers of Il Campo, the town's main square, to create the track's surface, and mattresses are strapped onto the sharp corners of surrounding buildings. On the big day, the horses are taken into church to be blessed (it's considered a sign of luck if a horse leaves droppings in the church). The snorting horses and their nervous riders—each representing a Sienese neighborhood—line up to await the starting signal. Then they race like crazy, while spectators, hungry for victory, wave the scarves of their district. After the winning horse crosses the line (with or without its rider), the prevailing neighborhood goes berserk with joy. If you go, you won't see much—but you'll feel it. It's a real medieval moment.

On My Knees in Rome: All of my Protestant life I've watched hardscrabble pilgrims and frail nuns climb Rome's Scala Santa on their knees. These are the "Holy Stairs" of Pontius Pilate's palace that Christ climbed the day he was condemned. This year, a voice inside me said "Do it!" So I picked up the little pilgrim's primer explaining what holy thoughts to ponder on each step, knelt down, and—one by one—began climbing. Knees screaming, weathered faithful struggling up the staircase with me, I climbed the 28 wooden steps. In my pain, the frescoed art surrounding the staircase snapped into action, goading me on. And, while my knees would never agree, the experience was beautiful.

Whether pondering wisteria villas on Lake Como *(left),* screaming for your favorite rider in Siena's Palio *(center),* or struggling on your knees up the steps Jesus climbed on the day he was condemned *(right),* sightseeing in Italy has an impact on the traveler.

CULTURE AND TRADITIONS: EVERYTHING'S SO...ITALIAN

Style Matters

For Italians, it's very important to exhibit a positive public persona—a concept called *la bella figura.* While some Americans don't think twice about going to the supermarket in sweats, Italians dress well anytime they leave the house—and they'd rather miss their bus than get all sweaty and mussed-up rushing to catch it. An elderly woman will do her hair and carefully put on makeup for her monthly doctor's appointment, and no matter how hot it gets, Italian men wear long pants—never shorts (except at the beach).

Communicating with Italians

Because they're so outgoing and their language is so fun, Italians are a pleasure to communicate with. They are animated and even dramatic. You may think two people are arguing when in reality they're agreeing enthusiastically. Body language is an important part of communicating, especially hand gestures. For instance, the "cheek screw" (pressing a forefinger into their cheek and rotating it) is used to mean good, lovely, or beautiful. A chin flick with the fingers bunched up means "I'm not interested; you bore me." Italians have an endearing habit of speaking Italian to foreigners, even if they know you don't speak their language—and yet, thanks to gestures and thoughtfully simplified words, it somehow works.

Social Time

Italian families and communities are more close-knit than many others in the modern world. Many Italians, especially in rural regions and small towns, still follow the traditional siesta schedule (called *reposo* in Italy). At about 1 p.m., shops close and people go home for a three-hour break to have lunch, socialize with friends and family, and run errands.

Early evening is the time for the ritual promenade called the *passeggiata*, when shoppers, people watchers, families, and young flirts on the prowl all join the scene to stroll arm in arm and spread their wings like peacocks. In a more genteel small town, the *passeggiata* comes with sweet

In Italy, the temptations are on parade—in the streets and in the gelato shops. Any town... any evening... *la vita è bella.*

whispers of *"bella"* (pretty) and *"bello"* (handsome). In Rome, the *passeggiata* is actually a cruder, big-city version called the *struscio* (meaning "to rub"), and people utter the words *"buona"* and *"buono"*—meaning, roughly, "tasty."

Gelato

Gelato is an edible art form. While American ice cream is made with cream and has a high butterfat content, Italian gelato is made with milk. It's also churned more slowly, making it denser. With less air and less fat than American-style ice cream, gelato is more flavorful. To find the best *gelateria*, look for the words *artiginale, nostra produzione*, and *produzione propia*, meaning it's made on the premises. Seasonal flavors and pastel hues (not garish colors) are also good signs. Gelato displayed in covered metal tins (rather than white plastic) is more likely to be homemade. To avoid having your request for a cone turn into a €10 "tourist special," survey the size options and be very clear in your order. My advice is to get plenty of vitamin G. Italy is best explored with long, meandering walks, and nothing refuels the body and spirit like cones of gelato.

Is the Pope Catholic?

Italy, home of the Vatican, is still mostly Catholic. Although Italians will crowd into St. Peter's Square with rock-concert energy to catch a glimpse of "il Papa," they're not particularly devout. And while most people would never think of renouncing their faith, they don't attend church regularly. They baptize their kids at the local church (there's one every few blocks), but they hold modern opinions on social issues, often in conflict with strict Catholic dogma. Italy is now the land of legalized abortion, a low birth rate, nudity on TV, socialist politics, and a society whose common language is decidedly secular. The true dominant religion is life: motor scooters, soccer, fashion, girl-watching, boy-watching, good coffee, good wine, and *il dolce far niente* (the sweetness of doing nothing).

Coffee, Italian-Style

Italians are religious about their coffee. Every coffee drinker has a certain style and a favorite place to buy it. If that place is closed, many would rather skip their coffee altogether. According to Italians, you can tell if coffee is good just by looking at it. When the beans are ground correctly, it comes out of the machine first a creamy brown color, then darker.

Italians tend to drink their coffee with less water than Americans (as one friend put it, "If we are so thirsty, we have a Coke"). In fact, the espresso-based style of coffee that's popular in the US was born in Italy. Most Italian drinks begin with espresso, to which the barista adds varying amounts of hot water and/or steamed or foamed milk. *Un caffè* is just a shot of espresso in a little cup; the closest thing to American-style drip coffee is a *caffè americano*—espresso diluted with hot water. Milky drinks, like *cappuccino* or *caffè latte*, are served to locals before noon...and to tourists any time of day. (Italians believe that milk can be properly digested only in the morning.) If Italians add any milk after lunch, it's just a splash, in a *caffè macchiato*—coffee "marked" or "stained" with milk.

Italy Travel Resources from Rick Steves

Guidebooks
Check out Rick's guidebooks covering all of Italy; Rome; Venice; Florence & Tuscany; Naples & the Amalfi Coast; the Cinque Terre; Milan & the Italian Lakes District; and Central Italy's hill towns; plus his Italian phrase book

Audio Europe
Download Rick's free Audio Europe app, with self-guided audio tours of sights and neighborhoods in Rome (Vatican Museums, Pantheon, St. Peter's Basilica, Forum, Colosseum, Sistine Chapel, Trastevere, Jewish Ghetto, Heart of Rome Walk), Florence (Accademia Gallery, Uffizi Gallery, Bargello Museum, Museum of San Marco, Renaissance Walk), Venice (Frari Church, St. Mark's Basilica, St. Mark's Square, Grand Canal), Siena (City Walk), Assisi (Basilica of St. Francis, Town Walk), and the ancient sites of Ostia Antica and Pompeii

TV Shows
The quintessence of Italy with Rick as your host, viewable on public television and at RickSteves.com. Episodes cover Rome, Florence, Venice, Venice day trips (Verona, Padua, and Ravenna), Assisi, Siena, Tuscany, Italian Alps, Cinque Terre, Amalfi Coast, Naples and Pompeii, Italy's hill towns, Milan, Lake Como, and Sicily

Organized Tours
Small group tours, with itineraries planned by Rick: Italy in 17 Days; Village Italy in 14 Days; South Italy in 13 Days; Best of Sicily in 11 Days; Heart of Italy in 9 Days; Venice, Florence & Rome in 10 Days; Rome in 7 Days; My Way: Italy in 13 Days; Best of Europe in 14 or 21 Days (including stops in Italy)

For more on all of these resources, visit RickSteves.com. For Italy trip-planning tips, see www.ricksteves.com/europe/italy.

France

France is Europe's most diverse, tasty, and, in many ways, most exciting country to explore. With luxuriant forests, forever coastlines, grand canyons, and Europe's highest mountain ranges, France has cover-girl looks. You'll also discover a dizzying array of artistic and architectural wonders—soaring cathedrals, chandeliered châteaux, and museums filled with the cultural icons of the Western world.

Moving from region to region, you feel as if you're crossing into different countries. Paris is in the heart of France. To the west is Normandy, with the historic D-Day beaches and the ethereal island-abbey of Mont St-Michel. To the south is the Loire river valley, filled with luxurious châteaux, and the Dordogne region, with prehistoric caves, medieval castles, and hill-capping villages. Near Spain is Languedoc, crowned by castles, from the fortress town of Carcassonne to remote Cathar ruins. Closer to Italy, sunbaked and windswept Provence nurtures Roman ruins and rustic charm, while the Riviera celebrates sunny beaches and yacht-filled harbors. And to the east, travelers encounter the villages of Germanic Alsace, the vineyards of Burgundy, and Europe's highest snow-capped Alps.

In France, *l'art de vivre*—the art of living—is not just a pleasing expression; it's a building block for a sound life. With five weeks of paid vacation, plus every Catholic holiday ever invented, the French have become experts at living well. It's no accident that France is home to

In France, *l'art de vivre* is something every traveler can aspire to learn.

linger-longer pastimes like café lounging, fine dining, and barge cruising. The French insist on the best-quality croissants, cheese, mustard, and sparkling water; they don't rush lunch; and an evening's entertainment is usually no more than a lovingly prepared meal with friends. France demands that the traveler savor the finer things.

As you travel through this splendid country, slo-o-o-ow down. Spend hours in cafés dawdling over *un café,* make a habit of unplanned stops, and surrender willingly to *l'art de vivre.*

FAVORITE SIGHTS AND MEMORABLE EXPERIENCES IN FRANCE

Circling in on the Arc de Triomphe in Paris

I have a funny ritual I follow whenever I'm in Paris. I ask my taxi driver to take me around the Arc de Triomphe—two times. My cabbie plunges into the grand roundabout where a dozen boulevards converge on this mightiest of triumphal arches. Like referees at gladiator camp, traffic cops are stationed at each entrance to this traffic circus, letting in bursts of eager cars. As marble Lady Liberties scramble up Napoleon's arch, heroically thrusting their swords and shrieking at the traffic, all of Paris seems drawn into this whirlpool. Each time, being immersed in the crazy traffic with my cabbie so in control makes me laugh out loud.

In the mid-19th century, Baron Haussmann set out to make Paris the grandest city in Europe. The 12 arterials that radiate from the Arc de Triomphe were part of his master plan for a series of major boulevards that would intersect at diagonals. At the crisscross points, he had monuments (such as the Arc de Triomphe) erected as centerpieces. As we zip around the circle, it's obvious that Haussmann's plan did not anticipate the automobile.

My cabbie explains to me, "If there is an accident here, each driver is considered equally at fault. This is the only place in Paris where the accidents are not judged. No matter what the circumstances, insurance companies split the costs fifty-fifty. In Paris, a good driver gets only scratches, not dents."

Fast Facts

Biggest cities: Paris (capital, 2.2 million), Marseille (1.5 million), Lyon (1.5 million)

Size: 215,000 square miles (roughly twice the size of Colorado), population 65 million

Currency: Euro

Key date and biggest festival: July 14, Bastille Day, the start of the French Revolution in 1789

Per-capita snail consumption: 500 per year

Handy French phrases: *Bonjour* (good day; bohn-zhoor), *S'il vous plait* (please; see voo play), *Merci* (thank you; mehr-see), *J'aime le fromage* (I like cheese; zhehm luh froh-mahzh)

Tourist info: US.France.fr

The commotion of cars fights to get to the arch at the center as if to pay homage to the national spirit of France. Cars entering the circle have the right-of-way; those in the circle must yield. Parisian drivers navigate the circle like a comet circling the sun—making a parabola. It's a game of fender-bender chicken. This circle is the great equalizer. Tippy little Citroëns, their rooftops cranked open like sardine lids, bring lumbering buses to a sudden, cussing halt.

While we're momentarily stalled on the inside lane, I pay and hop out. As the cabbie drives away, I'm left feeling small under Europe's ultimate arch. Here the flame of France's unknown soldier—flickering silently in the eye of this urban storm—seems to invite me to savor this grandiose monument to French nationalism.

The Arc de Triomphe affords a great Paris view, but only to those who earn it—there are 284 steps to the top. At the top, I look down along the huge axis that shoots like an arrow all the way from the Louvre, up the Champs-Elysées, through the arch, then straight down the Avenue de la Grande-Armée to a forest of distant skyscrapers around an even bigger modern arch in suburban La Défense. I love the contrast between the skyscrapers in the suburbs and the more uniform heights of buildings closer to the arch. The beauty of Paris—basically a flat basin with a river running through it—is man-made. There's a harmonious relationship between the width of its grand boulevards and the standard height and design of the buildings. This elegant skyline is broken only by venerable historic domes and spires—and the lonely-looking Montparnasse Tower, which stands like the box the Eiffel Tower came in. The appearance of this tower served as a wake-up call in the early 1970s to preserve the historic skyline of downtown Paris.

Paris is a capital of grand monuments and grand boulevards.

France's Top Destinations

Paris ▲▲▲   allow 3-5 days

World capital of art, fashion, food, literature, and ideas, offering
historic monuments, grand boulevards, and corner cafés

Top Sights
Notre-Dame Cathedral Paris' most beloved church
Sainte-Chapelle Gothic cathedral with peerless stained glass
Louvre Europe's oldest and greatest museum, starring *Mona Lisa* and *Venus de Milo*
Orsay Museum Nineteenth-century art, including Europe's best Impressionist collection
Eiffel Tower Paris' soaring exclamation point
Arc de Triomphe Triumphal arch with viewpoint marking start of Champs-Elysées

Nearby
Versailles The ultimate royal palace
Chartres Cathedral Best example of Gothic architecture, statues, and stained glass
Giverny Monet's flowery gardens, which inspired many of his paintings

Normandy ▲▲   2-3 days

Pastoral mix of sweeping coastlines, half-timbered towns, and intriguing cities,
including **Rouen** (Joan of Arc sights and soaring Gothic cathedral), artistic
seaside **Honfleur,** historic **Bayeux** (famous tapestry), stirring D-Day beaches and
museums, and pretty-as-a-mirage island abbey of Mont St-Michel

Brittany ▲   1 day

Windswept and rugged peninsula, with a gorgeous coast, Celtic ties, and two
notable towns: medieval **Dinan** and the beach resort of **St-Malo**

Loire Valley ▲▲   1-2 days

Lushly romantic area of picturesque towns (**Amboise** and **Chinon**) and hundreds
of castles and palaces

Dordogne ▲▲   2 days

Region of prehistoric cave paintings (including Lascaux), lazy canoe rides past
medieval castles, market towns **(Sarlat),** and, for wine lovers, nearby **St-Emilion**

Languedoc-Roussillon ▲   1-2 days

Sunny southern region, highlighted by **Albi**'s Toulouse-Lautrec museum,
Carcassonne's perfectly preserved city walls, and the seaside village of **Collioure**

Provence ▲▲▲   2-3 days

Home to Van Gogh sights in **Arles,** the famed medieval bridge and Palace of the
Popes in **Avignon,** Roman history (including a pair of amphitheaters and the Pont
du Gard aqueduct), rock-top villages (including **Les Baux**), the **Côtes du Rhone**
wine road, and the quintessentially Provençal hill towns of the **Luberon**

French Riviera ▲▲▲   2-3 days

A string of coastal resorts, including cosmopolitan and art-crazy **Nice,** beachy
Villefranche-sur-Mer, glitzy **Monaco,** easygoing **Antibes** (with a Picasso
museum), and hill-capping **Eze-le-Village**

French Alps ▲   2 days

Spectacular mountain scenery featuring the scenic, lakeside city of **Annecy**; Europe's highest peak, Mont Blanc; and the world-famous **Chamonix** ski resort (with lift to Italy)

Burgundy ▲▲   1-2 days

Region of bountiful vineyards, rustic cuisine, and age-old spirituality, with the compact wine capital of **Beaune** (and nearby wine roads), France's best-preserved medieval abbey **(Fontenay),** and a magnificent Romanesque church **(Vézelay)**

With more time, consider visiting

Reims and Verdun Historic cathedral, champagne cellars, and WWI battle sites
Alsace Franco-Germanic region dotted with wine-road villages
Lyon Metropolitan city with Roman ruins and delicious cuisine

The grandest of boulevards emanating from the arch, the Champs-Elysées, used to be even grander. From the 1920s through the 1960s, it was lined with top-end hotels, cafés, and residences—pure elegance. Parisians actually dressed up to come here. Then, in 1963, the government pumped up the neighborhood's commercial metabolism by bringing in the RER (commuter train). Suburbanites had easy access, McDonald's moved in, and *pfft*—there went the neighborhood. Still, the Champs-Elysées remains the country's ultimate parade ground, where major events all unfold: the Tour de France finale, Bastille Day parades, and New Year's festivities. With its monumental sidewalks, stylish shops, venerable cafés, and glimmering showrooms, this is Paris at its most Parisian.

Joyride in a Loire Valley Restaurant

French cuisine is sightseeing for your taste buds. You're not just paying for the food. A meal can be a three-hour joyride for the senses—as rich as visiting an art gallery and as stimulating as a good massage.

Not long ago, I dined at a fine restaurant in Amboise, in the midst of France's château-rich Loire Valley, with Steve Smith, the co-author of my France guidebook. Aurore, our waitress, was enchanting. She smiled as I ordered escargot for my first course. Getting a full dozen escargot rather than the typical six snails doubles the joy. Eating six, you're aware that the supply is very limited, but with twelve, there's no end to your snail fun. Add a good white wine, and you've got a full orchestral accompaniment.

My crust of bread lapped up the homemade garlic-and-herb sauce. I asked Aurore how it could be so good. With a sassy chuckle she said, "Other restaurateurs come here to figure that out, too." Then she added, "It's done with love." While I've heard that line many times, here it seemed believable.

In France, slow service is good service. After a pleasant pause, my main course arrived: tender beef with beans wrapped in bacon. Slicing through a pack of beans in their quiver of bacon, I let the fat do its dirty deed. A sip of wine, after a bite of beef, seemed like an incoming tide washing the flavor farther ashore.

My crust of bread, a veteran from the escargot course, was called into action for a swipe of sauce. Italians brag about all the ingredients they use. But France is proudly the land of sauces. If the sauce is the medicine, the bread is the syringe. Thanks to the bread, I enjoyed one last encore of the meat and vegetables I'd just savored.

In France, luxuriate over a dinner, as if taking your palate out to a spa. And, when it comes to the cheese course, don't hold back.

Shifting my chair to stretch out my legs, I prepared for the next course—a selection of fine cheeses. It sounds like a lot of food, but portions are smaller in France, and what we cram onto one large plate they spread out over several courses.

Aurore brought out her cheese platter on a rustic board, the vibrant-yet-mellow colors promising a tantalizing array of tastes. As cheese needs wine, I checked my wine bottle like I would my gas tank before driving home. Noticing the restaurant crowd thinning, I reminded myself that there was no rush. I liked hearing the quiet murmur of other diners, as eating among appreciative patrons is part of the sensory experience.

Finished with the cheeses, I leaned back to stifle a burp, just as Steve announced, "And here comes dessert." Mine was a tender crêpe papoose of cinnamon-flavored baked apple with butterscotch ice cream, garnished with a tender slice of kiwi. That didn't keep me from reaching over for a snip of Steve's lemon tart with raspberry sauce.

Our entire meal cost about $60 each. You could call it $20 for nourishment and $40 for three hours of bliss. Even if you're not a foodie, I can't imagine a richer sightseeing experience, one that brings together an unforgettable ensemble of local ingredients, culture, pride, and people.

Well-Fed Geese in the Dordogne

With elbows resting on a rustic windowsill on a farm in France's Dordogne region, I'm watching Denis grab one

In France, the geese run free on the farm and are force-fed to fatten their livers for foie gras. Being high on the food chain is always nice, but never so nice as when eating in France.

goose at a time from an endless line of geese. In a kind of peaceful, mesmerizing trance, he fills each one's gullet with corn. Like his father and his father and his father before him, Denis spends five hours a day, every day, all year long, sitting in a barn surrounded by geese.

Denis rhythmically grabs a goose by the neck, pulls him under his leg and stretches him up, and slides the tube down to the belly. He pulls the trigger to squirt the corn in, slowly slides the tube up the neck and out, holds the beak shut for a few seconds, lets that goose go, and grabs the next.

Many of my friends express disgust when I tell them I've witnessed geese being force-fed—the traditional way farmers fatten the livers to make foie gras, a prized delicacy in the Dordogne. Some people want to boycott French foie gras for what they consider inhumane treatment of the geese. That's why I was on the goose farm—to learn more about *la gavage*, the force-feeding process.

Elevage du Bouyssou, a big homey goose farm a short drive from the market town of Sarlat, is run by Denis and Nathalie Mazet. Their geese are filled with corn three times a day for the last months of their lives. They have expandable stomachs and no gag reflex, so the corn stays there, gradually settling as it is digested and making room for the next feeding. Watching Denis work, I wonder what it must be like to spend so much time with an endless cycle of geese. Do geese populate his dreams?

While Denis takes care of the geese, Nathalie meets tourists—mostly French families—who show up each evening at 6 p.m. to see how their beloved foie gras is made. The groups stroll the idyllic farm as Nathalie explains that they raise a thousand geese a year. She stresses that the key to top-quality foie gras is happy geese raised on quality food in an unstressed environment. They need quality corn and the same feeder.

The Mazets sell everything but the head and feet of their geese. The down feathers only net about 30 cents a goose. The serious money is in the livers. A normal liver weighs a quarter-pound. When done with the force-feeding process, the liver weighs about two pounds. (With a thousand geese, they produce a ton of foie gras annually—Nathalie says, "Barely enough to support one family.")

Like other French supporters of *la gavage*, Nathalie points out that their free-range animals are in no pain and live six months. By contrast, most American chickens live less than two months in little boxes and are plumped with hormones. Who's to say which system is better or worse?

In the Dordogne, farmers in the markets pass out petite goose-liver sandwiches as they evangelize about their foie gras, and every meal seems to start with a foie-gras course. After a few days of this rich eating, I leave with a strong need for a foie gras detox and a plate of vegetables.

On Top of Provence's Pont du Gard

The south of France offers many sightseeing treats. And when it comes to something stony and ancient, it's hard to beat the Roman aqueduct called the Pont du Gard.

This region is named Provence because it was the first "foreign" conquest as ancient Rome set about building its vast empire. Since it wasn't Rome proper, they called it "Provincia Romana" (province of Rome)—and the name stuck.

The Romans left behind some impressive examples of engineering in their first province, including the Pont du

The Pont du Gard is the most famous and scenic stretch of a 30-mile-long Roman aqueduct.

Gard, one of the most striking—and most visited—sights in all of France. This impressively preserved Roman aqueduct was built in about 19 B.C. Throughout the ancient world, aqueducts were like flags of stone that heralded the greatness of Rome.

Although most of the aqueduct runs on or below ground, at Pont du Gard it spans a canyon on a massive bridge—one of the most remarkable surviving Roman ruins anywhere. Even after many visits, I'm forever in awe of the ability of the ancient Roman engineers. This structure, built with perfectly cut stones fitted together without mortar, was designed to slope ever so slightly—less than an inch every hundred yards—as part of a 30-mile canal system that let water flow effortlessly into the city of Nîmes, supplying nine million gallons of water per day (about 100 gallons per second) to one of ancient Europe's largest cities.

The classic view of the aqueduct, from the river, is something every visitor sees. But recently, I joined a tour that took me through the water channel at the top of the Pont du Gard. Following a guide, I actually walked the length of this ancient bridge—a much more memorable experience.

I love to cap my Pont du Gard visit in Nîmes, where you can see what is considered the best-preserved arena of the Roman world and a stunning temple that rivals Rome's Pantheon as the most complete and splendid building that survives from the Roman Empire.

And at a small excavation site, sitting next to the street, is the castellum: a modest-looking water distribution tank that was the grand finale of the 30-mile-long aqueduct. Looking at the spout marking the end of that amazing structure, I imagine the jubilation locals felt when water gushed freely (with nobody having to carry it) into their city. And then, looking down into the castellum's collection tank, I marvel at a bit of social compassion those ancient

In summer, you can actually hike through the water channel at the top of the Pont du Gard.

Romans engineered into their water system: The lowest water pipes powered the public wells that graced neighborhood squares. The higher pipes—which got water only when the supply was plentiful—routed water to the homes of the wealthy, to public baths, and to decorative but nonessential

fountains. I guess losing to the Roman Empire wasn't all bad—even if you lived in the provinces.

Contemplating the Toll of World War II in Normandy

On a small square in a Normandy town, an elderly French-man approaches me, singing "The Star-Spangled Banner." In 1944, British, Canadian, and American troops invaded this area, beginning the end of World War II—and the French apparently haven't forgotten. But of course, reminders are still abundant. Seventy-five miles of France's north coast are littered with WWII museums, monuments, cemeteries, and battle remains left in tribute to the courage of the armies that successfully carried out the largest amphibious military operation in history: D-Day.

Wandering the beach of Arromanches—ground zero for the D-Day invasion—I take in the remnants of the Allied-built man-made harbor, Port Winston, which gave the Allies a foothold in Normandy, allowing them to begin their victorious push to Berlin and the end of the war. Several rusted floats—once supports for hastily built pontoon roads—are mired on the sand. I can just make out what's left of an anti-aircraft gun on a concrete block in the sea. I'm thankful that, instead of the sound of artillery, all I hear are birds and surf.

Later, I visit Omaha Beach, the eye of the D-Day storm. In the cemetery, a striking memorial with a soaring statue represents the spirit of American youth. Around the statue, giant reliefs of the Battle of Normandy and the Battle of

To remember the heroes of Normandy, visit the American Cemetery above Omaha Beach.

Europe are etched on the walls. Behind is the semicircular Garden of the Missing, with the names of 1,557 soldiers who were never found.

Nearly 10,000 brilliant white marble tombstones glow in memory of the Americans who gave their lives to free Europe. Wandering among the peaceful, poignant sea of headstones, I read the names, home states, and dates of death inscribed on each, and think of the friends and families affected by each lost life. It's a struggle to reconcile the quiet beauty of the setting with the horrible toll of that battle.

Not just in Normandy, but all over France, I'm reminded of the gratitude the French feel for what American troops did for their country. I remember filming one of my public-television shows at a charming little mom-and-pop château. When I'm filming, I'm on a mission—the sun's going down, and we've got work to do. But the aristocratic couple whose family had called that castle home for centuries insisted, "We must stop and have a ceremony because we have an American film crew here working in our castle." They cracked open a fine bottle of wine and brought out—with great ceremony, as if it were a precious relic—the beautiful 48-star American flag they had hoisted over their château on that great day in 1944 when they were freed by American troops. They implored us, "Please go home and tell your friends that we will never forget what America did for us."

Medieval Carcassonne

Before me lies Carcassonne, the perfect medieval city. Like a fish that everyone thought was extinct, Europe's greatest Romanesque fortress-city somehow survives.

Located in southeastern France, medieval Carcassonne is a 13th-century world of towers, turrets, and cobblestones. It's a walled city and Camelot's castle rolled into one, frosted with too many day-tripping tourists. At 10 a.m., the sales-people stand at the doors of their main-street shops, their gauntlet of tacky temptations poised and ready for their daily ration of customers. But an empty Carcassonne rattles in the early morning or late-afternoon breeze. Enjoy the town early or late, or off-season. Spend the night.

I was supposed to be gone yesterday, but it's sundown and here I sit—imprisoned by choice—curled in a cranny on top of the wall. The moat is one foot over and 100 feet down. Happy little weeds and moss upholster my throne. The wind blows away many of the sounds of today, and my imagination "medievals" me.

Twelve hundred years ago, Charlemagne stood below with his troops, besieging this fortress-town for several years. As the legend goes, just as food was running out, a cunning townswoman had a great idea. She fed the town's last bits of grain to the last pig and tossed him over the wall. Splat. Charlemagne's restless forces, amazed that the town still had enough food to throw fat party pigs over the wall, decided they'd never succeed in starving the people out. They ended the siege, and the city was saved. Today, the walls that stopped Charlemagne open wide for visitors.

Carcassonne, in the south of France, is Europe's greatest fortress city.

Paris' Ultimate Market Street

I grew up thinking that cheese was no big deal. It was orange, and the shape of bread was square: slap, fwomp... sandwich. Even though I'm still far from a gourmet eater, my time in Paris—specifically in the Rue Cler street market—has substantially bumped up my appreciation of good cuisine (as well as the French knack for good living). Rue Cler, lined with shops spilling out into the street, feels like village Paris—in the skinny shadow of the Eiffel Tower.

Parisians shop almost daily for three good reasons: Refrigerators are small (tiny kitchens), produce must be fresh, and shopping is an important social event. Strolling down Rue Cler, I soon spot a friend, Marie-Alice. She beckons me to the strawberry display. "You must shop with your nose," she says, burying hers in a basket of lush fruit.

We follow our noses to a long, narrow, canopied cheese table. Marie-Alice bounces her finger over a long line of cheeses: wedges, cylinders, balls, and miniature hockey pucks all powdered white, gray, and burnt marshmallow—it's a festival of mold. *Oh là là* means you're impressed. If you like a cheese, show greater excitement with more *las*. *Oh là là là là*. She holds the stinkiest glob close to her nose, takes a deep, orgasmic breath, and exhales, "Yes, this smells like zee feet of angels."

Inside the shop, we browse through some of the several hundred types of French cheese. A cheese shop

Visiting the Eiffel Tower

A stroll along Rue Cler works well with a visit to the nearby Eiffel Tower. There are two ways to get up the tower: smart or stupid. Get a reservation—those who just show up waste lots of time waiting in line. Book an entrance time in advance (www.toureiffel.paris) and scoot right in. Just be sure to reserve well ahead in peak times such as summer; tickets go on sale three months in advance and can sell out within hours.

(known as BOF, for *beurre, oeuf, fromage*) is the place where people go for butter, egg, and cheese products. In the back room are *les meules*, the big, 170-pound wheels of cheese. The "hard" cheeses are cut from these. Don't eat the skin of these big ones—they roll them on the floor. But the skin on most smaller cheeses—like Brie or Camembert—is part of the taste. As Marie-Alice says, "It completes the package."

Across the street we pause at a table of duck, pigeon, quail, and rabbit. Marie-Alice sorts through the dead. With none of the tenderness shown in the cheese shop, she hoists a duck. Rubbing a thumb toughly on its rough and calloused feet, she tells me that well-used feet indicate that the birds ran wild on a farm instead of being confined in an industrial kennel.

The ruddy-faced butcher, wearing a tiny plaid beret and dressed in a white apron over a fine shirt, is busy chopping. He's the best-dressed butcher I've ever seen. A battalion of meat hooks hang in orderly lines from the ceiling. The white walls bring out the red in the different cuts of meat.

At the nearby bakery, French women, thick and crusty after a lifetime of baguette munching, debate the merits of the street's rival boulangeries. It's said that when bakers do good bread, they have no time to do good pastry. If the baker specializes in pastry, the bread suffers. But this shop bucks the trend—the women and Marie-Alice agree that this baker does both equally well.

A man with working-class hands steps out the door, cradling a bouquet and a baguette in his arms—and heads off to gather the rest of his daily meal. If you want to learn the fine art of living, Parisian-style, Rue Cler is an excellent classroom.

More French Experiences

Inside the Lascaux Caves: In France's Dordogne region, proud guides compare the prehistoric paintings in the Lascaux caves to Michelangelo's frescoes in the Sistine Chapel. Hyperbole, I thought—until I saw Lascaux IV. It's a painstakingly created copy of the actual cave, which the public is no longer allowed to visit. Swept away by its grandeur, I soon forget it's a replica.

The vast cave looks amazingly like my (healthy) colonoscopy scan. Main difference: The cave is covered with paintings made 17,000 years ago, when mammoths and saber-toothed cats roamed the earth. This was a sophisticated project executed by artists from the impressive Magdalenian culture. In the museum, filled with original Magdalenian artifacts, I begin to feel a connection with these people. Looking at the oil lamps, I can imagine the wonder of wandering under flickering flames that lit the Sistine Chapel of the prehistoric world.

Magnificence on a Mudflat: I love to scamper far from shore at low tide, shoes in my hands, across the mud flat in the vast Bay of Mont St-Michel in northwestern France. Splashing across black sand and through little puddles, I head for a dramatic abbey reaching to heaven from a rock surrounded by a vast and muddy solitude, where hermit monks sought seclusion since the sixth century. The silhouette of the Gothic Mont St-Michel sends my spirits soaring today, just as it did the spirits of weary pilgrims in centuries past. Though a dreamscape from a distance, Mont St-Michel can be a human traffic jam until late afternoon. It's some consolation to remember that, even in the Middle Ages, the abbey-town was a commercial gauntlet, with stalls selling souvenir medallions, candles, and fast food. I prefer to ramble on the ramparts after dark, when the tourists are gone and the island is magically floodlit. At night, it's easy to

The sights and experiences of France range from caves painted 17,000 years ago, to medieval island abbeys, to cable cars zipping you to thin-air alpine summits.

ponder the promise of desolation and the simple life of solitude that attracted monks to this striking spot so long ago.

Getting High in Chamonix: Europe's ultimate mountain lift
towers high above the tourist-choked French resort town of
Chamonix. Ride the Aiguille du Midi *téléphérique* (gondola)
to the dizzy 12,600-foot-high tip of a rock needle. Chamonix
shrinks as trees fly by, soon replaced by whizzing rocks, ice,
and snow, until you reach the top. Up there, even sunshine is
cold. The air is thin. People are giddy (those prone to altitude
sickness are less giddy). Fun things can happen if you're not
too winded to join locals in the halfway-to-heaven tango.

The Alps spread out before you. In the distance is the
bent little Matterhorn. You can almost reach out and pat the
head of Mont Blanc, the Alps' highest point.

Next, for Europe's most exciting border crossing, get into
the tiny red gondola and head south to Italy. Dangle silently
for 40 minutes as you glide over glaciers and a forest of peaks
to Italy. Hang your head out the window; explore every corner of your view. You're sailing a new sea.

At Helbronner Point, you'll descend into Valle d'Aosta in
Italy, the land of cappuccino, gelato, and *la dolce vita*.

Chamonix, the Aiguille du Midi, and the Valle d'Aosta—
surely a high point in anyone's European vacation.

CULTURE AND TRADITIONS: EVERYTHING'S SO...FRENCH

Play the Markets

Market days have been a central feature of life in rural
France since the Middle Ages. No single event better symbol-
izes the French preoccupation with fresh products and their
strong ties to the soil than the weekly market. Many locals
mark their calendars with the arrival of prized seasonal produce, such as truffles in November.

Most markets take place once a week in the town's main
square and, if large enough, spill onto nearby streets. Markets combine fresh produce; samples of wine and locally produced brandies or ciders; and a smattering of nonfood items,
like knives, berets, kitchen goods, and cheap clothing. The
bigger the market, the greater the overall selection—particularly for nonperishable goods.

Market day is as important socially as it is commercially—it's a weekly chance to resume friendships and get
the current gossip. Neighbors catch up on the butcher's barn

renovation, see photos of the florist's new grandchild, and relax over *un café*. Dogs sit beneath café tables while friends exchange kisses. Tether yourself to a bench and observe: Three cheek-kisses are for good friends (left-right-left); a fourth kiss is added for friends you haven't seen in a while.

Wine Talk

The French sum up the unique natural conditions where a wine is produced in one word: *terroir* (pronounced "tehr-wah"). It means "somewhere-ness," a particular combination of macro- and microclimate, soil, geology, and the accumulated experience of the winemakers. Two wines can be made from the same grape but be of very different character because of their *terroir*. The best vintners don't force their style on the grape. They play to the wine's strength, respecting the natural character of the sun, soil, and vine—the *terroir*.

Grapevines are creepers, with roots going through the topsoil and into the geology deep down. The roots are commonly 150 feet long and deep. While topsoil can be influenced by the vintner, the deep geology cannot, and this gives the wine a distinct character. The French do not allow irrigation, thus forcing the grapes to search deep for water. A good grape, in the French view, must suffer.

Dealing with the French in French and English

French people value politeness, and take pride in their culture, tradition, and language. You'll get better treatment if you learn and use the simplest of French pleasantries. Begin every encounter with "*Bonjour* (or *S'il vous plaît*), *madame* (or *monsieur*)," and end it with "*Au revoir* (or *Merci*), *madame* (or *monsieur*)."

The French are language perfectionists—they take their language (and other languages) seriously. Often they speak more English than they let on. This isn't a tourist-baiting tactic, but timidity on their part about speaking another language less than fluently. If you want them to speak English, say, "*Bonjour, madame (or monsieur). Parlez-vous anglais?*" They may say "*non,*" but if you continue talking and butchering their language, they'll soon say, "Well, actually, I do speak some English."

Bowling *Boules*

In small squares in every Provençal village and city, you're likely to find the local gang playing *boules,* the horseshoes of southern France. Every French boy grows up playing *boules* with Papa and *Ton-Ton* (Uncle) Jean. It's a social-yet-serious sport, and endlessly entertaining to watch—even more so if you understand the rules.

Boules (also known as *pétanque*) is played with heavy metal balls (*boules*, about the size of oranges) and a small wooden target ball (*le cochonnet*—"piglet," about the size of a ping-pong ball). Whoever gets his *boule* closest to the *cochonnet* scores.

I like to pause and watch old-timers while away the afternoon tossing shiny silver balls on gravelly courts—and if I feel like creating a memory, I give it a try myself.

Persnickety Perceptions

The good life in France—music, culture, an appreciation of fine wine and food—is seductive but intimidating to Americans. No one wants to make a "mistake" when picking a wine, croissant, or cheese. For a long time, I thought there was something affected and pseudo-sophisticated about all this finicky Frenchness. I once asked a wine merchant in Paris to suggest a good bottle to go with snails, and he wanted to know how I planned to cook them. I had envisioned a good Chardonnay, but *mais non*—not "flinty" enough—only a Chablis would do.

I felt inept for making the wrong pairing and annoyed by the wine seller's hair-splitting choosiness. But then I thought of the way I catalogue the nuances of baseball—it's taken me a lifetime of slowly absorbing the game's rules and situations to simply "know" the game the way the Frenchman "knows" wine. All the stuff that matters to me—how far the runner is leading off first base, who's on deck, how a batter does against left-handed pitchers, when to put in a pinch runner—would be nonsense to a French person. The next time I mortify my French friend by putting a little ketchup on my meat, I'll just remember that with two outs and a full count, he'll have no idea why I know the runner's off with the pitch.

France Travel Resources from Rick Steves

Guidebooks
Check out Rick's guidebooks covering all of France; Paris; Provence & the French Riviera; the Loire Valley; Normandy; and Basque Country Spain & France; plus his French phrase book

Audio Europe
Download Rick's free Audio Europe app, with self-guided audio tours, including a walk through historic Paris and tours of the Louvre, Musée d'Orsay, and Versailles Palace

TV Shows
The quintessence of France with Rick as your host, viewable on public television and at RickSteves.com. Episodes cover Paris, Paris side trips, the Loire Valley, the French Alps, Burgundy, Alsace, Dordogne, Normandy, Provence, and the Riviera

Organized Tours
Small group tours, with itineraries planned by Rick: Paris & the Heart of France in 11 Days; Loire to the South of France in 13 Days; Paris in 7 Days; Eastern France in 14 Days; Basque Country of France & Spain in 9 Days; My Way: France in 13 Days; Best of Europe in 14 or 21 Days (including stops in France)

For more on all of these resources, visit RickSteves.com. For France trip-planning tips, see www.ricksteves.com/europe/france.

Spain

For the tourist, Spain means many things: bullfights, massive cathedrals, world-class art, Muslim palaces, vibrant folk life, whitewashed villages, bright sunshine. You'll find all of this, but the country's charm really lies in its people and their unique lifestyle. From the stirring communal *sardana* dance in Barcelona to the sizzling rat-a-tat-tat of flamenco in Sevilla, this country creates its own beat amid the heat.

Spain is in Europe, but not *of* Europe, thanks largely to the Pyrenees Mountains that physically isolate it from the rest of the Continent. For more than 700 years (711-1492), Spain's dominant culture was Muslim, not Christian. And after a brief Golden Age in the 16th century (financed by New World gold), Spain retreated into three centuries of isolation. Spain's seclusion contributed to the creation of its distinctive customs—bullfights, flamenco dancing, and a national obsession with ham. Even as other countries opened up to one another in the 20th century, the fascist dictator Francisco Franco virtually sealed off Spain from the rest of Europe's democracies. But since Franco's death in 1975, Spaniards have swung almost to the opposite extreme, becoming wide open to new ideas and technologies.

Spain's spread-out geography makes it less a centralized nation than a collection of distinct regions. In the central plain sits the lively urban island of Madrid. Just south is holy Toledo, a medieval showpiece and melting-pot city with Christian, Muslim, and Jewish roots. Farther south is Andalucía, home to sleepy, whitewashed hill towns and three great cities: Granada (topped with the Alhambra palace), Córdoba (with a massive mosque and pretty patios), and Sevilla (where Holy Week is celebrated as if God were watching). Spain's south coast offers a palm-tree jungle of beach resorts along the Costa del Sol, a taste of British fish-and-chips in Gibraltar, and a laid-back launch pad to Morocco (from Tarifa).

To Spain's far north is San Sebastián and the Basque Country, which combine sparkling beaches, cutting-edge architecture, and the *pintxo* (a local—and often gourmet—take on tapas). Nearby is Pamplona, where bulls and tourists run for their lives. Gregarious pilgrims hike through the town on their long journey across northern Spain to the cathedral town of Santiago de Compostela. Along the Mediterranean coast (to the east), Spain has an almost Italian vibe. Trendy Barcelona, where Antoni Gaudí's architecture makes waves, keeps one eye cocked toward trends sailing in from the rest of the Continent.

The Alhambra in Granada, the last Moorish stronghold on the Iberian Peninsula, is a vivid reminder of the splendor of the Muslim society that ruled Spain for centuries.

FAVORITE SIGHTS AND MEMORABLE EXPERIENCES IN SPAIN

Good Morning in Santiago

I'm tucked away in Santiago de Compostela, in the northwest corner of Spain. I have a three-part agenda: to see pilgrims reach their goal in front of the cathedral, to explore the outdoor market, and to buy some barnacles in the seafood section—then have them cooked for me, on the spot, in a café.

Whenever I'm here, I make a point to be on the big square at the foot of the towering Cathedral of St. James around 10 in the morning. That's when scores of well-worn pilgrims march in triumphantly from their last overnight on the Camino de Santiago (Way of St. James)—a 30-day, 500-mile hike from the French border.

Humble hikers have trod these miles since the Middle Ages to pay homage to the remains of St. James in his namesake city. (I love the idea that the first guidebook ever written talked up "going local, packing light, and watching out for pickpockets" for pilgrims traveling the Camino a thousand years ago.) Arriving in the church square, they step on a scallop shell symbol embedded in the pavement in front of the cathedral. I witness joy and jubilation sweep over those who finish this journey.

Pilgrims often ask me to take a photo for them. Then

they say, "I've got to go meet with St. James," and—as has been the routine for a thousand years—they head into the cathedral.

Two blocks away, the market is thriving, oblivious to the personal triumphs going on over at St. James' tomb. There's something fundamental about wandering through a farmers market early in the morning anywhere in the world: Salt-of-the-earth people pull food out of the ground, cart it to the city, and sell what they've harvested to people who don't have gardens.

Dried-apple grandmothers line up like a babushka cancan. Each sits on a stool so small it disappears under her work dress. At the women's feet are brown woven baskets filled like cornucopias—still-dirty eggs in one; in the next, greens clearly pulled this morning, soil clinging to their roots. One woman hopes to earn a few extra euros selling potent homebrews, her golden bottles stoppered with ramshackle corks.

Fast Facts

Biggest cities: Madrid (capital, 3.3 million), Barcelona (1.6 million)
Size: 195,000 square miles (roughly twice the size of Oregon), population 48 million
Locals call it: España
Currency: Euro
Key date: November 20, 1975, Prime Minister Francisco Franco dies, ending nearly four decades of dictator rule
Languages: You'll find four—Castilian (what we call Spanish, spoken country-wide), Catalan (NE Spain), Galego (NW Spain), Euskara (Basque region)
Biggest festivals: Semana Santa (Holy Week, before Easter, best in Sevilla), Running of the Bulls (July, Pamplona)
Handy Spanish phrases: Hola (hello; **oh**-lah), Por favor (please; por fah-**bor**), Gracias (thank you; **grah**-thee-ahs), Soy rico y soltero (I'm rich and single; soy **ree**-koh ee sohl-**teh**-roh)
Tourist info: Spain.info

Babushkas sit behind rickety card tables filled with yellow cheeses shaped like giant Hershey's Kisses...or, to locals, breasts. This local cheese is called *tetilla*—that's "tit"—to revenge a prudish priest who, seven centuries ago, told a sculptor at the cathedral to redo a statue that he considered too buxom. Ever since, the townsfolk have shaped their cheese exactly like what the priest didn't want them to see carved in stone. You can't go anywhere in Santiago without seeing creamy, mild *tetilla*.

In vendors' stalls, spicy red chorizo hangs in sausage chains, framing merchants' faces. Chickens, plucked and looking as rubber-like as can be, fill glass cases. A selection of pigs' ears, mixed with hooves going nowhere, fills a shoebox. The ears, translucent in the low rays of the morning sun, resemble neatly flattened conch shells. At the best stalls, short ladies with dusty, blue-plaid roller carts jostle for deals.

The sound of cascading clams and castanet shrimp—red, doomed, and flipping mad—greet me as I enter the seafood hall. Fisherwomen in rubber aprons and matching gloves sort through folding money. From one vendor I buy my barnacles *(percebes)*—at about $16 a pound, they're one-third the price I'd pay in a bar. I get a little less than a half-pound and hustle my full bag over to the market café called Churro Mania. There, Ramon and Julia boil them up for a few dollars. Feeling quite like a local—sipping my beer so early in the morning—I wait for my barnacles to cook.

Then comes the climax of my morning: Julia brings my barnacles, stacked steaming on a stainless steel plate, as well as bread and another beer. I'm set. Twist, rip, bite. It's the bounty of the sea condensed into every little morsel: edible jubilation in Santiago.

Gaudí's Barcelona Dreaming

Barcelona's most famous architect, Antoni Gaudí, speckled the city with his Art Nouveau fantasies at the beginning of the 20th century. His buildings bloom with flowery shapes, race with galloping gables, and bend with organic curves. A prime example, the apartment building called La Pedrera, has walls of wavy stone and an undulating rooftop, where 30 chimneys play volleyball with the clouds. At Casa Batlló, a green-blue ceramic facade, tibia-esque pillars, and shell-like balconies are inspired by nature, while the humpback roofline suggests a cresting dragon's back.

But Gaudí's best-known and most persistent work is the Sagrada Família church. I've long said that if there's one building I'd like to see in Europe, it's the Sagrada Família... finished. The church, an epic work-in-progress for more than a hundred years, promises to be the most exciting church built in our lifetimes. If there is a miracle anywhere in the world of architecture, it is this church. Climb up stairs between the melting ice-cream-cone spires for a

If there's one building I'd like to see completed, it's Gaudí's wondrous Sagrada Família church in Barcelona. And it's well on its way.

gargoyle's-eye perspective of a living, growing, bigger-than-life building. Local craftsmen often finish up their careers by putting in a couple of years working on the project. The hope: to finish it by 2026—the 100th anniversary of Gaudí's death. By then, it's my bet that Gaudí will be sainted.

Gaudí fans also enjoy the artist's magic in the colorful, freewheeling Park Güell, a 30-acre hilltop garden once intended to be a high-end housing project. Carpeted with fanciful mosaics, dotted with sculptures (including a famous tiled lizard), and offering grand views of the city and the glittering Mediterranean beyond, this park is a great place to cap a day of Barcelona dreaming.

Strolling Córdoba's Back Streets

The Andalusian town of Córdoba has a glorious Moorish past. The town's centerpiece is its massive Mezquita. Magical in its grandeur, this huge mosque dominates the higgledy-piggledy old town around it. A wonder of the medieval world, the Mezquita is remarkably well-preserved, giving visitors a chance to appreciate the glory days of Muslim rule. But like most big sights, the Mezquita is surrounded by a touristy zone of shops and tour-group-friendly restaurants.

To separate from the crush of tourists, I wander the back streets. Exploring the residential lanes of old Córdoba, I'm quickly all alone with the town. Away from modern-day tourism, it's easy to catch an evocative whiff of the old.

I keep an eye out for colorful patios, framed by decorative ironwork gates. A common feature of houses throughout Andalucía, patios are taken very seriously here. The Romans used them to cool off, and the Moors added lush, ornate

Córdoba, in the south of Spain, comes with exquisite patios *(left)* and the biggest mosque Europe ever saw *(right)*.

touches. The patio functioned as a quiet outdoor living room, an oasis from the heat. Inside the see-through gates, roses, geraniums, and jasmine spill down whitewashed walls, while fountains play and caged birds sing.

I continue wandering after dinner. It's almost midnight—everyone's out, savoring a cool evening. I'm drawn to a commotion on a square. Short men with raspy tobacco voices and big bellies—called *curvas de felicidad* (happiness curves)—jostle and bark as a dozen little school girls rattle a makeshift stage with flamenco flair, working on their sultry.

Well after midnight, the city finally seems quiet. I return to my hotel and climb into my bed. Just as I doze off, a noisy and multigenerational parade rumbles down the cobbled lane. Standing in my underwear and wrapped in the drapes, I peer secretively out my window. Below, a band of guitars and castanets funnels down my narrow alley. Grandmothers—guardians of a persistent culture—make sure the children pick up their Andalusian customs. Finally, one woman looks up at me, catches my eye, and seems to nod, as if satisfied that I am witnessing the unwavering richness of their traditional way of life.

Feeling the Heat in Madrid

Changing cultures is always fun. I love to feel disoriented, as I am when I first arrive in a new place. Recently, following a stint in Austria, I switched to Madrid. I felt myself going from crisp rationality to casual disorganization.

When I'm in Madrid, I try to book a room with a balcony overlooking the Times Square of Spain, Puerta del Sol.

Spain's Top Destinations

Barcelona ▲▲▲ allow 3 days

Catalan capital with atmospheric Gothic old town, elegant new town, and striking art and architecture by resident artists Antoni Gaudí, Pablo Picasso, and Joan Miró

Top Sights
Picasso Museum Works from the artist's early years
Ramblas Colorful, touristy pedestrian zone with thriving market
Barri Gòtic Old town maze of streets with towering cathedral
Gaudí's Architecture Sagrada Família Church, La Pedrera, and Park Güell
Catalan Art Museum World-class showcase of this region's art

Nearby
Figueres and Cadaqués Salvador Dalí sights
Montserrat Dramatic mountaintop monastery
Sitges Beach resort

Madrid ▲▲▲ 3 days

Spirited Spanish capital, boasting top-notch art treasures, stately squares, a lively tapas scene, and urban Spain at its best

Top Sights
Royal Palace Sumptuous national palace
Prado Museum Masterpieces by Velázquez, Goya, and El Greco
Centro de Arte Reina Sofía Modern art, including Picasso's epic *Guernica*
Thyssen-Bornemisza Museum Especially good Impressionist collection

Nearby
El Escorial Palace and mausoleum of Spanish royalty
Segovia Storybook town with a towering Roman aqueduct

Toledo ▲▲ 1 day

Hill-capping former capital, with a colorfully complex history, a magnificent cathedral, and works by hometown boy El Greco

Salamanca ▲ 1 day

Spain's quintessential university town, with the country's finest main square

Sevilla ▲▲▲ 2 days

Soulful cultural capital of Andalucía, with a spectacular cathedral (the world's largest Gothic church), the Alcázar (labyrinthine Moorish palace), tangled former Jewish Quarter, teeming evening paseo, and fantastic flamenco

Andalucía ▲▲ 2-3 days

Classic heartland of southern Spain, home to **Córdoba** (with Spain's top surviving Moorish mosque, the Mezquita) and whitewashed hill towns (including **Arcos de la Frontera** and **Ronda**)

Granada ▲▲▲ 1 day

Grand Moorish capital with the magnificent Alhambra palace and Spain's best old Moorish quarter

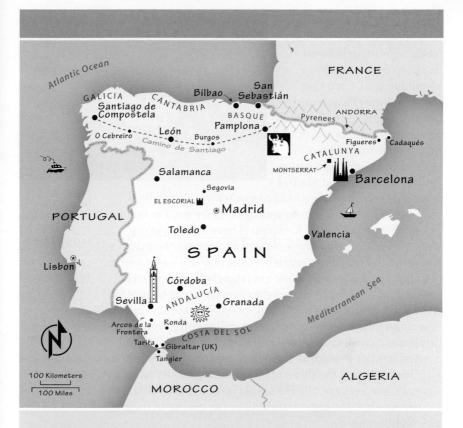

Basque Country ▲▲   3-4 days

Anchored by the culinary capital of **San Sebastián** and the more workaday **Bilbao** (home to the dazzling Guggenheim Museum), with sleepy seaside retreats and colorful villages scattered through the green countryside

Camino de Santiago ▲   4-5 days

Centuries-old pilgrimage route running across the top of Spain from France to **Santiago de Compostela** in green Galicia, with stops along the way at big cities **(Pamplona, Burgos, León)** and charming villages **(Puente la Reina, O Cebreiro)**

With more time, consider visiting

Cantabria Rustic northern coast with high-mountain scenery and prehistoric cave art

Tarifa Charming beach-resort town and handy base for day trip to Morocco

Gibraltar A slice of Britain on a giant rock

This square, like so many in Europe, has gone from a traffic nightmare to a park-like people zone. Within a 10-minute walk I can visit the great Royal Palace; my favorite paintings in the Prado Museum; and Plaza Mayor, the ultimate town square.

To get acclimated, I get up early. Walking around Madrid at 8 a.m., people seem in a kind of fog. It's not clear who is starting their day and who is ending it. As for me, I'm intent on crossing off my rituals for Spain (I have a list for every place I travel): digging into a plate of *pimientos de Padrón* (these lightly fried, little green peppers play Russian roulette with my taste buds...only a few are jalapeño-spicy); savoring a slice of *jamón ibérico*—the most expensive cured ham, made from acorn-fed, black-hooved pigs; people-watching while downing a tall glass of *horchata*, that milky, nutty, refreshing drink; eating really really late; and being really, really hot.

And it is hot in Madrid. Even in the evening, things are so hot, they've moved the times of bullfights two hours later—to 9 p.m. People here say, "Be thankful you're not in Sevilla." I catch myself assessing restaurants by the quality of their air-conditioning.

But despite the heat, Madrid is vibrant. Even the living-statue street performers have a twinkle in their eyes. As always, Spain is a festival of life.

Anywhere in southern Europe, enjoy the relative cool of summer evenings by joining the festival of locals out and about. Each summer evening, Madrid's plazas become community gathering places.

Queen of the White Hill Towns

Arcos de la Frontera smothers its hilltop, tumbling down all sides like the train of a wedding dress. While larger than most other Andalusian hill towns, it's equally atmospheric. The labyrinthine old center is a photographer's feast. Viewpoint-hop through town. Feel the wind funnel through the narrow streets as drivers pull in car mirrors to fit around tight corners.

Residents brag that only they see the backs of the birds as they fly. To see why, climb to the viewpoint at the main square high in the old town. Belly up to the railing—the town's suicide jumping-off point—and look down. Ponder the fancy cliffside hotel's erosion concerns, orderly orange groves, flower-filled greenhouses, and the fine views toward Morocco.

The thoughtful traveler's challenge is to find meaning in the generally overlooked tiny details of historic towns such as Arcos. On one visit, I discovered that a short walk from Arcos' church of Santa María to the church of St. Peter is littered with fun glimpses into the town's past.

The church of Santa María faces the main square. After Arcos was reconquered from the Moors in the 13th century, this church was built—atop a mosque. In the pavement is a 15th-century magic circle: 12 red and 12 white stones—the white ones marked with various constellations. When a child came to the church to be baptized, the parents would stop here first for a good Christian exorcism. The exorcist would stand inside the protective circle and cleanse the baby of any evil spirits.

Small towns like Arcos come with lively markets. On my last visit, I was encouraged by the pickle woman to try a *banderilla,* named for the bangled spear that a matador sticks into a bull. As I gingerly slid an onion off the tiny skewer of pickled olives, onions, and carrots, she told me to eat it all at once. Explosive!

Near the market is a convent. The spiky security grill over the window protects cloistered nuns. Tiny peepholes allow the sisters to look out unseen. I stepped into the lobby to find a one-way mirror and a blind, spinning, lazy Susan-type cupboard. I pushed the buzzer, and a sister spun out some boxes of freshly baked cookies for sale. When I spun back the cookies with a *"No, gracias,"* a Monty Python-esque

Arcos de la Frontera perches on its cliff.

voice countered, "We have cupcakes as well." I bought a bag of these *magdalenas*, both to support their church work and to give to kids on my walk. Feeling like a religious Peeping Tom, I actually saw—through the not-quite one-way mirror—the sister in her flowing robe and habit momentarily appear and disappear.

Walking on, I passed street corners plastered with recycled Roman columns—protection from reckless donkey carts. The walls are scooped out on either side of the windows, a reminder of the days when women stayed inside but wanted the best possible view of any people-action in the streets.

Arcos' second church, St. Peter's, really is the second church. It lost an extended battle with Santa María for papal recognition as the leading church in Arcos. When the pope finally recognized Santa María, pouting parishioners from St. Peter's even changed their prayers. Rather than say, "María, mother of God," they prayed, "St. Peter, mother of God."

The tiny square in front of the church—about the only flat piece of pavement around—serves as the old-town soccer field for neighborhood kids. I joined the game and shared my cupcakes, savoring this idyllic slice of village Spain.

Holy Week in Sevilla

Holy Week (Semana Santa)—the week between Palm Sunday and Easter—is celebrated with intense fervor in Spain. All over the country, Semana Santa processions clog the streets. But nobody does Holy Week better than Sevilla.

Even if all you care about on Easter is chocolate, it's inspiring to witness the intense devotion of Sevillians during Holy Week. The scene is a holy spectacle. Paraders in purple-

The bell tower of Sevilla's cathedral

and-white cone hats shuffle past me, carrying crusader swords and four-foot candles. Like American kids scrambling for candies at a parade, Spanish kids collect dripping wax from religious coneheads, attempting to amass the biggest ball on a stick for their Easter souvenir. In bars, all eyes are fixed on the TVs, watching not soccer or bullfighting...but live coverage of their town's Holy Week procession.

When you meet Spaniards, it's common to ask which football team they support. But in Sevilla, you also ask which Virgin Mary they favor. The top two in town are La Virgen de la Macarena and La Esperanza de Triana (same Mary, different churches). On Thursday during Holy Week, it's a battle royale of the Madonnas, as Sevilla's two favorite virgins are paraded through the streets simultaneously.

The procession squeezes down narrow alleys. Legions of drums crack eardrums in the confined space. Kids sit wide-eyed on parents' shoulders. A gilded, candlelit float rumbles by, edging bystanders against rustic ancient walls. I look up, and high in the sky I see what Good Friday is all about: An extremely Baroque Jesus lurches forward under the weight of that cruel cross, symbolically climbing to his crucifixion. Later, it occurs to me that he floated not on wheels, but on boys. Unseen and unheralded, bent under all that tradition, a team of boys had been trudging for hours through the throngs.

Gilded and glittering floats are parked in churches until they are paraded through the streets on holy days.

The Running of the Bulls in Pamplona

Like a cowboy at a rodeo, I sit atop my spot on the fence. A loudspeaker says, "Do not touch the wounded. That's the responsibility of health personnel." A line of green-fluorescent-vested police sweeps down the street, clearing away drunks and anyone not fit to run. Cameras are everywhere—on robotic arms with remote controls vise-gripped to windowsills, hovering overhead on cranes, and in the hands of nearly every spectator that makes up the wall of bodies pressed against the thick timber fence behind me.

I'm at the Festival of San Fermín in Pamplona. Each July, a million revelers come to this proud town in the Pyrenees foothills for music, fireworks, and merrymaking. But most of all, they come for the Running of the Bulls, when fearless (or foolish) adventurers thrust themselves into the path of six furious bulls each day for a week.

The street fills with runners. Nearly everyone is wearing the standard white pants, white shirt, and red bandana. San Fermín, patron of this festival, was beheaded by the Romans 2,000 years ago, martyred for his faith. The red bandanas evoke his bloody end.

The energy surges as 8 a.m. approaches. The street is so full, if everyone suddenly ran, you'd think they'd simply trip over each other and all stack up, waiting to be minced by angry bulls. Then it's eight, and the sound of a rocket

During Pamplona's famed Running of the Bulls, the mark of a good run is to feel the breath of the bull on the back of your legs.

indicates that the bulls are running. The entire half-mile-long scramble takes about two and a half minutes. The adrenaline surges in the crowded street. The sea of people spontaneously begins jumping up and down like hundreds of red-and-white human pogo sticks—trying to see the rampaging bulls to time their flight.

For serious runners, this is like surfing—you hope to catch a good wave and ride it. A good run lasts only 15 or 20 seconds. You know you're really running with a bull when you feel his breath on your pants.

Like a freak wave pummeling a marina, the bulls rush through. It's a red-and-white cauldron of desperation. Big eyes, scrambling bodies, the ground quaking, someone oozing under the bottom rail. Then, suddenly, the bulls are gone, people pick themselves up, and it's over. Boarded-up shops open up. The timber fences are taken down and stacked. The nine-day cycle of the festival, built around the Running of the Bulls, is both smooth and relentless.

Soaking Up San Sebastián Sunshine

Jostling with enthusiastic eaters at the bar, I munch on my last spider crab open-face sandwich. A tiny plate of toothpicks is all that's left of my meal. I keep them because the bartender will count them to tally the bill.

I'm in the beach resort of San Sebastián, just over the French border in Spain. This is the Basque Country, where bright white chalet-style homes with patriotic red-and-green shutters dot lush, rolling hills. The Pyrenees Mountains soar high above the Atlantic. And surfers and sardines share the waves. Insulated from mainstream Europe for centuries, this plucky region has maintained its spirit while split between Spain and France.

Shimmering above the breathtaking bay of La Concha,

The Basque resort of San Sebastián is a hit for its crescent-shaped beach and its gourmet tapas.

elegant and prosperous San Sebastián has a favored location, with golden beaches bookended by twin peaks and a cute little island just offshore. With a romantic setting, a soaring statue of Christ gazing over the city, and a late-night lively old town, San Sebastián has a Rio de Janeiro aura.

The highlight of the old town is its incredibly busy and colorful tapas bars—though here, these appetizers are called *pintxos*. Local competition drives bars to lay out the most appealing array of petite gourmet snacks. The selection is amazing. Just wander the streets (Calle Fermín Calbetón is best) and belly up to the bar in the liveliest spot.

The bartender insists I drink one more glass of *txakolí*—the local sparkling white wine. It's on the house...and nearly from the ceiling, as he theatrically pours from as high as he can reach to aerate the drink. No one but me marvels as the house wine high-dives expertly into my glass.

More Spanish Experiences

Toledo's grand cathedral

Toledo's Magnificent Cathedral: Just 30 minutes by train from Madrid, Spain's former capital crowds 2,500 years of tangled history onto a high, rocky perch protected on three sides by a natural moat, the Tajo River. Toledo's highlight is its Gothic cathedral, which is shoehorned into the old center, with an exterior that rises brilliantly above the town's medieval clutter. The cathedral's spectacular altar—real gold on wood—is one of the country's best pieces of Gothic art. The sacristy is a mini Prado Museum, with masterpieces by the likes of Francisco de Goya, Titian, Peter Paul Rubens, Diego Velázquez, Caravaggio, and

Giovanni Bellini, not to mention 18 El Grecos. The interior is so lofty, rich, and vast that visitors wander around like Pez dispensers stuck open, whispering "Wow."

Granada at Sunset: Granada's magnificent Alhambra was the last stronghold of the Moorish kingdom in Spain. At the end of the day, I head to my favorite viewpoint in the city—the San Nicolás terrace—and enjoy the breathtaking vista over the palace. It comes with great Roma (Gypsy) music nearly all day long. Pop a few euros into the musicians' hat, sit down with a nice picnic, and enjoy an open-air concert as good as any you might pay for. And the view can't be beat, as the setting sun makes the Alhambra glow red.

A Taste of Britain in Spain: I can't resist popping into the British colony of Gibraltar whenever I'm in southern Spain. Gibraltar is hardly signposted in Spain, as if Spain wishes the British colony didn't exist. But when you see that famous "Rock of Prudential" standing boldly above the sea, you know it's here to stay. The place is quirkily and happily British: They have big three-pronged English plugs, their own Gibraltar pound currency, and an Anglican church headquarters. The food is a throwback to the days when English food really was as bad as its reputation. Hotels are twice as expensive as those across the border in Spain (and not as comfortable). The imported macaque monkeys might try to steal your bananas. Nevertheless, tourism is booming. Midday, the pedestrian-friendly main street is a human traffic jam. Twice as many planes are landing in the colony every day. When you walk across the airstrip that marks the border between Spain and what's left of the British Empire, it's more important than ever to look left, right—and up.

LEFT The Alhambra glows at sunset.

RIGHT Gibraltar's famous rock

CULTURE AND TRADITIONS: EVERYTHING'S SO...SPANISH

Bullfighting

The Spanish bullfight is as much a ritual as it is a sport. Originally a form of military training, with refined knights fighting the noble beast from horseback, bullfighting today consists of a series of six bulls facing off against a matador and his team of fighters. Each ritual killing lasts 20 minutes. Then another bull romps into the arena.

While controversial to many for its brutality, aficionados insist that bullfighting is an art form. The Catalunya region banned the practice in 2012, but it remains popular in places such as Sevilla, Madrid, and Ronda, the birthplace of modern bullfighting. Personally, I find the spectacle rather pathetic and cruel, and prefer to get my bullfight "culture" by popping into a bull bar. My favorite is La Torre del Oro, right on Madrid's Plaza Mayor. Its interior is a temple to bullfighting, festooned with gory decor. For many people, a quick sangria or beer in a bar like this is more than enough nasty for their Spanish vacation.

Flamenco

Although flamenco is performed throughout Spain, this music-and-dance art form has its roots in the Roma (Gypsy) and Moorish cultures of Andalucía. And even if flamenco concerts in Sevilla, Granada, and other Andalusian towns are designed for tourists, they are still real and riveting. For a more local-feeling experience, be at a bar (such as La Carbonería in Sevilla) after midnight, when spirited flamenco singing erupts spontaneously.

At any flamenco performance, sparks fly. The men do most of the flamboyant machine-gun footwork. The women often concentrate on the graceful turns and smooth, shuffling step of the *soléa* version of the dance. I always watch the musicians. Flamenco guitarists, with their lightning-fast finger-roll strums, are among the best in the world. The intricate rhythms are set by castanets or the hand-clapping (called *palmas*) of those who aren't dancing at the moment. In the raspy-voiced wails of the singers, you'll hear echoes of the Muslim call to prayer.

Tapas

Tapas bars are everywhere in Spain. Serving small portions of seafood, salad, meat-filled pastries, and deep-fried tasties, they offer a casual, cheap, and very local way of eating.

Chasing down a particular bar nearly defeats the purpose and spirit of tapas—they are impromptu. Just drop in at any lively place. I look for noisy bars with piles of napkins on the floor (go native and toss your trash, too), lots of locals, and the TV blaring.

You'll generally eat standing up in tapas bars. Standing makes sense if you're on a budget because food and drinks are usually cheapest served at the *barra* (counter). To get started with a basic glass of red wine, you can ask for *un tinto*. But by asking for *un crianza*, you'll get a better aged wine for only a little extra money.

When you're ready to order your food, be assertive or you'll never be served. *Por favor* (please) grabs the guy's attention. Then quickly rattle off what you'd like (pointing to other people's food if necessary). Don't worry about paying until you're ready to leave (your server is keeping track of your tab).

The Spanish Eating Schedule

Spaniards eat late. Lunch is anywhere between 1 and 4 p.m., and dinner doesn't even cross their minds until at least 9 p.m. To get by in Spain, you'll either have to adapt to the Spanish schedule and cuisine, or scramble to get food in between. You can have an early, light lunch at a tapas bar. Or do as many Spaniards do and have a *bocadillo* (baguette sandwich) at about 11 a.m. to bridge the gap between their coffee-and-roll breakfast and late lunch (hence the popularity of fast-food *bocadillo* chains). Then, either have your main meal at a restaurant around 3 p.m. followed by light tapas for dinner; or reverse it, having a tapas meal in the afternoon, followed by a late restaurant dinner.

Night Owls

Spain comes to life in the cool of the evening, when it's prime time. Whole families pour out of their apartments to stroll through the streets and greet their neighbors—a custom called the paseo. Even the biggest city feels like a rural village. The whole town strolls—it's like "cruising" without cars. Streets are polished nightly by the feet of families licking ice cream; buy an ice-cream sandwich and join the parade. Some people duck into bars for a drink or to watch a big soccer match on TV. They might order a bite to eat, grazing on tapas. Around 10 p.m. in the heat of summer, it's finally time for a light dinner. Afterward, even families with young children might continue their paseo or attend a concert. Spaniards are notorious night owls. Many clubs and restaurants don't even open until after midnight. Dance clubs routinely stay open until the sun rises, and young people stumble out bleary-eyed and head for work. The antidote for late nights? The next day's siesta.

Spain Travel Resources from Rick Steves

Guidebooks
Check out Rick's guidebooks covering all of Spain; Barcelona; Madrid & Toledo; and Sevilla, Granada & Southern Spain; plus his Spanish phrase book

Audio Europe
Download Rick's free Audio Europe app, with self-guided audio tours, including walks through Barcelona and Madrid

TV Shows
The quintessence of Spain with Rick as your host, viewable on public television and at RickSteves.com. Episodes cover Madrid, Barcelona and Catalunya, northern Spain and the Camino de Santiago, Andalucía, Sevilla, the Basque Country, Toledo and Salamanca, Granada, Córdoba, and the Costa del Sol

Organized Tours
Small group tours, with itineraries planned by Rick: Best of Spain in 14 Days; My Way: Spain in 11 Days; Best of Barcelona & Madrid in 8 Days; Best of Basque Country of Spain & France in 9 Days

For more on all of these resources, visit RickSteves.com. For Spain trip-planning tips, see www.ricksteves.com/europe/spain.

Portugal

Portugal has an appealing mix of hardscrabble cities, sweet port wine, wistful blue tiles, heartfelt ballads, and weather-beaten faces. Tucked into a corner of the Iberian Peninsula, Portugal seems somewhere just beyond Europe—prices are a bit cheaper, and the pace of life is noticeably slower. The traditional economy is still based on fishing, cork, wine, and textiles.

Portugal isn't showy—even its coastal towns lack glitzy attractions. The beach and the sea are enough, as they have been for centuries. They were the source of Portugal's seafaring wealth long ago, and are the draw for tourists today. The country's long coastline has some tucked-away gems that feel authentic—the beach towns of Salema (on the south coast) and Nazaré (on the west).

Portugal is more diverse than its neighbor Spain, as it's inhabited by many people from its former colonies in Brazil, Africa, and Asia. Especially in Lisbon, Portugal's Old World capital, you are as likely to hear lively African music as wistful Portuguese fado. The town of Fátima attracts devout pilgrims, while the university towns of Coimbra and Èvora have a youthful vibe.

The birthplace of port wine, Portugal's Douro Valley is famed for its vineyards.

With a rich culture, affordable prices, and a salty setting on the edge of Europe, Portugal understandably remains a popular destination. If your idea of travel includes friendly locals, exotic architecture, windswept castles, and fresh seafood with chilled wine on a beach at sunset, you'll love this rewarding corner of Europe.

FAVORITE SIGHTS AND MEMORABLE EXPERIENCES IN PORTUGAL

Lisbon Gold

When I first came to Lisbon in the 1970s, the colorful Alfama neighborhood—then the shiver-me-timbers home of Lisbon's fisherfolk—was one of the places that charmed me into becoming a travel writer. On my last trip here— 30-something years later—I noticed that much of the area's grittiness has been cleaned up. Old fishermen's families have been replaced by immigrant laborers. Widows no longer wear black after their husbands die. Once-characteristic fish stalls have moved off the streets and into more "hygienic" covered shops.

But the Alfama, which tumbles down from the castle to the river, remains one of the most photogenic neighborhoods in all of Europe. Wandering deep into this cobbled cornucopia of Old World color, I always get lost. Little streets squeeze into tangled stairways and confused alleys. Bent houses comfort each other in their romantic shabbiness, and the air drips with laundry and the smell of fresh clams and raw fish.

Like its salty sailors' quarter, Lisbon is a ramshackle but charming mix of now and then. Its glory days were the 15th and 16th centuries, when Vasco da Gama and other explorers opened new trade routes, making Lisbon the queen of Europe. Later, the riches of colonial Brazil boosted Lisbon even higher. Then, in 1755, an earthquake (estimated at 9.0)

LEFT A typical Alfama street and resident

RIGHT Lisbon's vintage trolleys are perfect for a joyride.

leveled two-thirds of the city. Within a month, a new city was designed, and downtown Lisbon was quickly rebuilt on a progressive grid plan, with broad boulevards and square squares.

Following the quake, Portugal's rattled royalty chose to live out in suburban Belém, in wooden rather than stone buildings. Five miles from downtown, this district is now a stately pincushion of important Golden Age sights such as the Monastery of Jerónimos, with Vasco da Gama's tomb. The area is guarded by the ornate Belém Tower, which has kept an eye on Lisbon's harbor since 1520. It was the last sight sailors saw as they left, and the first thing they'd see when they returned—loaded down with gold, diamonds, and venereal diseases.

The more modern-feeling Baixa is the rebuilt center of Lisbon. This flat shopping area features grid-patterned streets and utilitarian architecture (buildings are uniform, with the same number of floors and similar facades). The Baixa's pedestrian streets, inviting cafés, bustling shops, and elegant old storefronts give the district a certain magnetism. I find myself doing laps up and down the pedestrians-only main boulevard in a people-watching stupor.

On my must-do list in Lisbon is stopping at a bar to have *pastel de bacalhau*, a fried potato-and-cod croquet. Bacalhau (salted cod) is Portugal's national dish. Imported from Norway, it's never fresh, and kids think it's a triangular fish because of the way it's sold. I think that Portugal must have the only national dish that's imported from far away—strange, and yet befitting of a nation known for seafaring explorers.

Another quintessential Lisbon experience is to take a trolley ride. The city's trolleys—many of which are vintage models from the 1920s—shake and shiver through the old parts of town, somehow safely weaving within inches of

Fast Facts

Biggest cities: Lisbon (capital, 564,000), Porto (238,000), Coimbra (102,000)

Size: 35,000 square miles (slightly smaller than Indiana), population 10.5 million

Currency: Euro

Key dates: November 1, 1755, a severe earthquake and tsunami nearly destroy Lisbon and coastal communities; April 25, 1974, the Carnation Revolution marks the last gasp of the Salazar dictatorship and the beginning of Portuguese democracy

Biggest festivals: Fátima Pilgrimage (May 13 and October 13), Semana Santa (Easter Holy Week)

Major export: Half the world's cork comes from Portugal

Handy Portuguese phrases: *Olá* (hello; oh-**lah**), *Por favor* (please; poor fah-**vor**), *Obrigado/Obrigada* (thank you—said by male/female; oh-bree-**gah**-doo/dah), *Fala inglês?* (Do you speak English?; **fah**-lah een-**glaysh**)

Tourist info: VisitPortugal.com

parked cars, climbing steep hills, and offering breezy views of the city (rubberneck out the window and you will die). They're perfect for a Rice-A-Roni-style Lisbon joyride. I enjoy hopping off the trolley for the hilltop viewpoint near São Jorge Castle—a good starting point for touring the Alfama district since you'll stroll down rather than hike up.

To complement all your Lisbon sightseeing, be sure to get out and be with the locals. One summer evening I found myself at a fairground watching Portuguese families at play. I ate dinner surrounded by chattering locals ignoring the ever-present TVs, while great platters of fish, meat, fries, salad, and lots of wine paraded frantically in every direction. A seven-year-old boy stood on a chair and sang hauntingly emotional folk songs. With his own dogged clapping, he dragged applause out of the less-than-interested crowd and then passed his shabby hat. All the while, fried ducks dripped, barbecues spat, dogs squirted the legs of chairs, and somehow local lovers ignored everything but each other's eyes.

Sunny Salema

The Algarve, in southern Portugal, is my favorite stretch of Iberian coastline. I fantasize about being here on a real vacation—nursing a drink in a still-wet bathing suit, hauling in octopus pots, hiking to the beach, and exposing skin that's never seen the sun.

Warm and dry, the Algarve was once known as Europe's last undiscovered tourist frontier. But it's well discovered now, and if you go to the places featured in most tour brochures, you'll find it paved, packed, and pretty stressful. Still, there are a few great beach towns left along the coast, perfect for soaking up rays in the summer.

My favorite hideaway is the little fishing town of Salema. It's at the end of a small road just off the main drag between the big city of Lagos and the rugged southwest tip of Europe,

Portugal's Top Destinations

Lisbon ▲▲▲   allow 2-3 days

Lively, hilly port and capital, with historic trolleys, grand squares, fado clubs, fine art, and distinctive neighborhoods

Top Sights

Bairro Alto and Alfama Golden Age and medieval districts
Belém Waterfront district with Monastery of Jerónimos
Gulbenkian Museum Fine art from Ancient Egypt to Art Nouveau

Nearby

Sintra Fairy-tale castles set in verdant hills

Algarve ▲▲▲   2-3 days

Sunny southern coast, with fishing village **Salema,** end-of-the-road **Cape Sagres,** and beach-party town **Lagos**

Nazaré ▲▲   1-3 days

Traditional fishing village turned surfing capital, and a springboard for nearby sights: **Batalha** (grand monastery), **Fátima** (famous pilgrimage site), **Alcobaça** (huge Gothic church), and **Óbidos** (walled hill town)

Porto and the Douro Valley ▲▲   1-2 days

Gritty hillside port city with charming old town, near the scenic Douro Valley, birthplace of port wine

Évora ▲▲   1 day

Whitewashed little college town with big Roman, Moorish, and Portuguese history encircled by its medieval wall

Coimbra ▲▲   1 day

Portugal's Oxford, home to an Arab-influenced old town and bustling with students from its prestigious university

Cape Sagres. Here the tourists and fishermen sport the same stubble. It's just you, a beach full of garishly painted boats, your wrinkled landlady, and a few other globetrotting experts in lethargy.

When I first came here, in the late 1970s, the road into town wasn't paved. I turned up in the early evening, driving a group of eight tour members in a minivan and with no reservations. I parked at one end of the town, flagged down some locals, and asked for rooms: *"Quartos?"* Eyes perked, heads nodded, and I got nine beds in three homes for 20 bucks each.

While the main street looks pretty much the same today, the character of the town is changing. Nowadays, beach towns like Salema are becoming the playgrounds of an international crowd of retirees and vacationers, who stay in newly built gated communities and golf clubs on the inland hilltops. Many of the ladies who once rented out rooms have disappeared, chastened by stricter government regulations (necessary, as southern Europe learns to pay its taxes). There are fewer shoestring-budget backpackers to keep them in business anyway.

Salema is still a fishing village—but just barely. It has a split personality: The whitewashed old town is for locals, and the other half was built for tourists—both groups pursue a policy of peaceful coexistence on the beach. Tourists laze in the sun, while locals grab the shade.

In Portugal, restaurateurs are allowed to build a temporary, summer-only beachside eatery if they provide a lifeguard for swimmers and run a green/yellow/red warning-flag system. The Atlântico restaurant, which dominates

In Salema, on Portugal's south coast, two worlds merge as fishermen share the beach with travelers.

Salema's beach, takes its responsibility seriously—providing lifeguards and flags through the summer...and fresh seafood by candlelight all year long.

Salema's sleepy beauty always kidnaps my momentum. My typical day begins and ends with the sound of waves. In the morning, I amble over to one of the hidden beaches within walking distance of town. I grab a late lunch overlooking the water, spend the afternoon relaxing on the beach, catch the sunset with a drink in my hand, have a nice beachside dinner of grilled sardines, and then fall asleep to the strumming beat of the surf. The next day I do it all over again.

Exploring Colorful Coimbra

A couple of hours north of Lisbon, Coimbra is the Oxford or Cambridge of Portugal—the home of its most venerable university. It's also the country's easiest-to-enjoy city—a mini-Lisbon, with everything good about urban Portugal without the intensity of a big metropolis. I couldn't design a more delightful city for a visit.

At Coimbra's colorful market, the character of the vibrant town shines through.

Any stroll through Coimbra comes with lots of color. I love wandering the inviting, Arab-flavored old town—a maze of narrow streets, timeworn shops, and tiny *tascas* (budget eateries). A pedestrian street divides the old town into the lower part (Baixa) and the upper (Alta). Historically, only the rich could afford to live within the protective city walls of the Alta. Even today, the Baixa remains a poorer section, with haggard women rolling wheeled shopping carts, children running barefoot, and men lounging on squares as if wasting time is their life's calling.

A favorite old-town stop of mine is the Mercado Municipal. Though nearly every city in Europe has a vibrant farmers market, in many cases, the character has been lost thanks to the EU asserting itself and raising hygiene standards. But in Coimbra, the color and twinkle survive. I appreciate that I can still feel the wrinkled and fragrant pulse of the town and see the "salt of the earth" in the faces of the women selling produce while their men are off in the fields—or in their beloved "little chapels" (a.k.a. bars).

Coimbra's university is the city's leading attraction, highlighted by one of Europe's best surviving Baroque libraries, which displays 55,000 books in 18th-century splendor. The zealous doorkeeper locks the door at every opportunity to keep out humidity, so you need to buzz to get into this 300-year-old temple of books.

The interior is all wood. Even the "marble" on the arches is painted wood, since real marble would add to the humidity. The resident bats—who live in the building, but not the library itself—are well cared for and appreciated. They eat insects, providing a chemical-free way of protecting the books, and alert the guard to changing weather with their "eee-eee" cry.

Whenever I'm visiting a university, I try to eat at its on-campus cafeteria if open to tourists. Generally, that's where I find the cheapest meals and the most interesting crowd of fellow diners in town (and usually the locals most likely to speak English well). During busy times here in

Coimbra gives travelers a taste of urban Portugal without the big-city intensity.

Coimbra, all seats are taken, and you're very likely to find yourself munching with law students and their professors.

At the end of the day, it's worth seeking out fado. Though this folk music is generally performed by Portuguese women, in Coimbra, men sing the fado. Rather than the songs about love, loss, and hopelessness that are common in Lisbon's fado, songs here tend to be literary translations or follow themes students can relate to. Singers are accompanied by the Coimbra-style Portuguese guitar. A modern statue of a guitar, which morphs into the slinky and nubile body of an inviting woman, graces an old town lane. It's a reminder of the local belief that a good musician plays his guitar with art and passion, as if loving a woman.

You can watch fado at various clubs, though my favorite performances are by the roving bands of students, dressed in their signature black capes and serenading around town for tips—and the hearts of their admirers. For me, listening to this unique, mournful music, performed in its unique Coimbra style, feels like just the right way to end a day in this distinctive city.

More Portuguese Experiences

Our Lady of Fátima: In 1917, three kids encountered the Virgin Mary near the central Portugal village of Fátima and were asked to return on the 13th of each month for six months. The final apparition was witnessed by thousands of locals. Ever since, Fátima has been on the pilgrimage trail—mobbed on the 13th of each month through the spring and summer.

Wandering around today's modern town, I'm impressed by how it mirrors my image of a medieval pilgrim gathering place: oodles of picnic benches, endless parking, and desolate toilets for the masses. On my last visit, the vast esplanade leading to the site of the mystical appearance was quiet, as only a few solitary pilgrims slowly shuffled on their knees down the long, smooth approach. In the basilica, a forest of candles dripped into a fiery trench that funneled all the melted wax into a bin—to be resurrected as new candles. Just beyond the basilica, 30 stalls lining a horseshoe-shaped mall awaited the 13th. Even without any business, old ladies still manned their booths, surrounded by pilgrim trinkets—including gaudy wax body parts and rosaries that would be blessed after Mass and taken home to remember Our Lady of Fátima.

Nazaré Dreaming: I got hooked on the Atlantic village of Nazaré back when colorful fishing boats littered its beach. Now the boats moor comfortably in a modern harbor outside town, and the beach is packed with sunbathers and surfers. But I still like the place. This fishing town turned resort is both black-shawl traditional and beach-friendly. The back streets are good for a wander and a fine look at Portuguese family-in-the-street life. Older ladies wear skirts made bulky by traditional petticoats, and men stow cigarettes and fish hooks in their stocking caps. Laundry flaps in the wind, kids play soccer, and fish sizzle over tiny curbside hibachis. Squadrons of salted fish are crucified on nets pulled tightly around wooden frames and left to dry under the midday sun. Locals claim they are delightfully tasty—but I'll take their word for it. Off-season Nazaré is almost empty of tourists— inexpensive, colorful, and relaxed, with enough salty fishing- village atmosphere to make you pucker.

The Alentejo Plain: Deep in the heart of Portugal, sur- rounded by cork trees and the vast, bleak beauty of the Alen- tejo region, I drive toward the walled city of Évora. It sits on lots of history. Outside of town stand 92 stones—2,000 years older than Stonehenge—erected by long-ago locals to make a celestial calendar. Évora's old center is crowned by the gran- ite Corinthian columns of a stately, ruined Roman temple. Tourists wander wide-eyed through the town's macabre 16th-century chapel, decorated with human bones meant to remind worshippers of their mortality.

The people of the Alentejo are uniformly short, look at tourists suspiciously, and are the butt of jokes in this corner of Europe. Libanio, my Évora guide, said it was the mark of a people's character to laugh at themselves. He asked me, "How can you tell a worker is done for the day in Alentejo?" I didn't know. He said, "When he takes his hands out of his pockets." My guide continued more philosophically: "In your land, time

Portugal's top experiences include witness- ing pilgrims at Fátima *(left),* savoring the beach at Nazaré *(center),* and hanging out with locals in Évora *(right).*

is money. Here in Alentejo, time is time. We take things slow and enjoy ourselves." I'm impressed when a region that others are inclined to insult has a strong local pride.

CULTURE AND TRADITIONS: EVERYTHING'S SO...PORTUGUESE

Fado

The songs of fado, the folk music of Portugal, reflect the country's bittersweet relationship with the sea. Fado, which means "fate," originated in the mid-1800s in Lisbon's rustic neighborhoods. These mournfully beautiful and haunting ballads are usually about lost sailors, broken hearts, romance gone wrong, and the yearning for what might have been if fate had not intervened. Fado, like a musical oyster, is sexy and full of the sea.

The singer (*fadista*) is accompanied by a 12-string *guitarra portuguesa* (with a round body like a mandolin) or other stringed instruments unique to Portugal. Fado singers typically crescendo into the first word of the verse, like a moan emerging from deep inside. The singers rarely over-act—they plant themselves firmly and sing stoically in the face of fate.

One of my favorite fado bars is A Baiuca, in Lisbon's Alfama district. Here mustachioed mandolin pluckers hunch over their instruments, lost in their music, while the kitchen staff peers from a steaming hole in the wall, backlit by their flaming grill. There's not a complete set of teeth in the house. The waiter delivers plates of fish and pitchers of cheap cask wine to tables. Then, doubling as a Portuguese

At Portugal's fado bars, patrons sip wine while tuning in to the mournful melodies.

Ed Sullivan, he stops to introduce the star, who wears blood-red lipstick, big hair, and a black mourning shawl over her black dress—with a revealing neckline that promises that there is life after death.

Convent Sweets and Monks' Treats

Many of Portugal's pastries are called "convent sweets." During its days as a trading powerhouse, Portugal had access to more sugar than any other European country. Even so, sugar was so expensive that only the upper classes could afford it routinely. Historically, the daughters of aristocrats who didn't marry into suitably noble families ended up in high-class convents, bringing precious sugar with them. Over time, the convents became famous as keepers of wondrous secret recipes for exquisite pastries, generally made from sugar and egg yolks (the whites were used to starch the nuns' habits). *Barriga de freira* ("nuns' belly") and *papo de anjo* ("angel's double chin") are two such traditional fancies that you'll see in sweets shops.

While nuns baked sweets, the monks took care of quenching thirsts with *ginjinha,* a sweet liquor made from the sour cherry-like ginja berry, sugar, and brandy. Try it with or without berries (*com elas* or *sem elas*) and *gelada* (if you want it poured from a chilled bottle). The oldest *ginjinha* joint in Lisbon is a colorful hole-in-the-wall in the Baixa district, which sells shots for about a buck. In Portugal, when people are impressed by the taste of something, they say, *"Sabe que nem ginjas"* (It tastes like ginja).

Beware of Appetizers

In Portugal's restaurants, there's no such thing as a free munch. If the server puts appetizers on your table before you order, they'll appear on your bill. If you don't want them, push them to the side—you won't be charged if you don't touch the food (which ranges from olives, bread, and pâtés to a veritable mini-buffet of tasty temptations). Simple appetizers usually cost about €1 each, so even if you eat a couple of olives, it won't break the budget.

In Portugal you can discover a new favorite pastry *(left),* or make a pilgrimage to Porto's harbor—where port wine ages *(right).*

Barnacles!

Gooseneck barnacles (*percebes*) are a salty delicacy. These little taste treats are expensive because they're so dangerous to harvest—they grow on rocky promontories in narrow inlets where the waves and currents are fierce. (Connoisseurs know that they are fresh only from April through September—otherwise they're frozen.) Merchants in coastal towns sell the crustaceans on the street as munchies. They'll happily demonstrate how to eat them and give you a sample, figuring if you try just one briny morsel, you'll buy a kilo. Local bars serve *percebes* with beer, like corn nuts.

Port Party

Much of the world's port wine comes of age in Porto, in northern Portugal. The grapes are grown about 60 miles upstream in the Douro River Valley. A young port is produced, which sits for a winter in silos before being shipped downstream to Porto's Vila Nova de Gaia district. There it ages for years in wooden barrels stored in "lodges" on the cool, north-facing bank of the Douro. For wine connoisseurs, touring a port-wine lodge (*cave do vinho do porto*) and sampling the product is a must-see attraction.

For most people, "port" means a tawny port, which is aged for 10 to 40 years. But there are multiple varieties of port. Wood ports are aged in wooden vats or barrels, and vintage ports are aged in bottles. *Reserva* on the label means it's the best-quality port (and the most expensive). As for me, I'm not choosy. As I always say, "Any port in a storm..."

Portugal Travel Resources from Rick Steves

Guidebooks
Check out Rick's guidebooks covering all of Portugal; Lisbon; plus his Portuguese phrase book

Audio Europe
Download Rick's free Audio Europe app, with self-guided audio tours, including a walk through Lisbon

TV Shows
The quintessence of Portugal with Rick as your host, viewable on public television and at RickSteves.com. Episodes cover Lisbon, the Algarve, and Portugal's heartland (Nazaré, Fátima, and Coimbra)

Organized Tours
Small group tours, with itineraries planned by Rick: Heart of Portugal in 12 Days

For more on all of these resources, visit RickSteves.com. For Portugal trip-planning tips, see www.ricksteves.com/europe/portugal.

Great Britain

From the grandeur and bustle of London, to a rich and royal history that inspired Shakespeare, to some of the quaintest towns you'll ever experience, Great Britain is a delight. Stand in a desolate field and ponder a prehistoric stone circle. Do the Beatles blitz in Liverpool, and walk in the Lake District footsteps of Wordsworth. Discover your favorite pub and have a pint of beer with the neighborhood gang. Tackle some Welsh words, relax in a bath in Bath, and shake paws with a Highland sheepdog. There's something unparalleled yet familiar about traveling in Great Britain.

Three very different countries—England, Wales, and Scotland—make up Great Britain (add in Northern Ireland, and you've got the United Kingdom). England is the center in every way: the seat of government, the economic power-house, the bastion of higher learning, and the cultural heart. Anchored by thriving London, England has everything from castles to cathedrals and sheep-speckled hillsides to dark-wooded pubs.

Humble, charming little Wales is a land of stout castles, salty harbors, slate-roofed villages, stunning mountains, and lusty men's choirs. Traditional and beautiful, Wales sometimes feels trapped in another century. But soon you'll awaken to the distinctive, poetic vitality of this small country.

And then there's rugged, feisty, colorful Scotland—the yin to England's yang. Whether it's the laid-back, less-organized nature of the people, the stony architecture, the unmanicured landscape, or simply the haggis, go-its-own-way Scotland stands apart. Its sights are subtle, but the misty glens, brooding castles, hardy bagpipers, and warm culture are engaging.

I love traveling in Great Britain. It hosts the heritage of the greatest empire the world has ever lived under, yet bears the humiliation of a struggling economy, with remnants of its former empire owning much of its capital city. Its pomp, which seems to serve as a quaint reminder of former grandness, feels almost designed for tourists. Still, a visit here connects you with people, nature, heritage, and culture, all of which combine to make Great Britain such a rewarding destination.

FAVORITE SIGHTS AND MEMORABLE EXPERIENCES IN GREAT BRITAIN

Edinburgh's Royal Mile

There's no better introduction to Edinburgh—the historical, cultural, and political capital of Scotland—than a walk straight down the spine of the old town. Stretching from a hill-topping castle to a queen's palace, this ramble is appropriately called the Royal Mile. Despite being crammed with tourists, it's one of Europe's best sightseeing walks.

I begin my stroll on the bluff where Edinburgh was born and where a castle now stands. Over the centuries, this mighty fortress was home to many of Scotland's kings and queens. Today it's well worth touring to see the old buildings, stunning views, and crown jewels.

As Edinburgh grew, it spilled downhill along the tight, sloping ridge that became the Royal Mile. Back in the vibrant 1600s, this was the city's main street, bustling with breweries, printing presses, and banks. With tens of thousands of citizens squeezed into the narrow confines of the old town,

Edinburgh's Royal Mile entertains from top to bottom, from connoisseur's whisky at Cadenhead's shop to St. Giles Cathedral, where John Knox preached the Reformation.

there was nowhere to go but up. So builders lined the street with multi-story residences (called tenements)—some 10 stories and higher.

Truth be told, these days much of the Royal Mile is a touristic mall—all tartans, sightseers, and shortbread. But it remains packed with history, and intrepid visitors can still find a few surviving rough edges of Auld Reekie, as the old town was once called (for the smell of smoke and sewage that wafted across the city). Exploring back alleys and side lanes, it's easy to imagine Edinburgh in the 17th and 18th centuries, when out-of-towners came here to marvel at its "skyscrapers," and thousands of people scurried through these alleyways, buying and selling goods and popping into taverns.

Scotland is a proud nation, and everywhere I turn, the Royal Mile is littered with symbols of that pride—from a statue of philosopher David Hume, one of the towering figures of the Scottish Enlightenment of the mid-1700s, to its very own Church of Scotland, embodied by St. Giles Cathedral. Filled with monuments, statues, plaques, and stained-glass windows dedicated to great Scots and moments in history, St. Giles serves as a kind of Scottish Westminster Abbey.

St. Giles is also the home church of the great reformer John Knox, whose fiery sermons helped turn once-Catholic Edinburgh into a bastion of Protestantism. Knox's influence was huge. His insistence that every person should be able to read the word of God firsthand helped give Scotland an educational system 300 years ahead of the rest of Europe. Just down the road from St. Giles is the John Knox House, featuring atmospheric rooms, period furniture, and a fun little dress-up corner that lets me play out my Great Reformer fantasy.

But I'm eager to get to one of my favorite stops along the Mile: Cadenhead's Whisky Shop. Founded in 1842,

Fast Facts

Biggest cities: London (capital, 7.8 million), Birmingham (1 million), Glasgow (600,000), Liverpool (450,000)

Size: 95,000 square miles (about the size of Michigan), population 61.5 million

Currency: British pound

Key date: 1533, King Henry VIII breaks with the Catholic Church and establishes himself as the head of the Church of England, setting the English Reformation in motion

Biggest festivals: Chelsea Flower Show (May, London), Edinburgh International Festival (August, music, dance, and theater)

Language: Predominantly English, but also Scottish Gaelic and Welsh Cymraeg

Handy British phrases: *I'm bloody knackered* (I'm so exhausted), *Don't get your knickers in a twist* (Don't get all upset), *Bob's your uncle* (obviously), *Sod off* (Screw off), *That's a load of bollocks* (That's a bunch of nonsense)

Tourist info: VisitBritain.com

Great Britain's Top Destinations

ENGLAND

London ▲▲▲   allow 3-5 days

Thriving metropolis packed with world-class museums, monuments, churches, parks, palaces, theaters, pubs, Beefeaters,
double-decker buses, and all things British

Top Sights
Westminster Abbey Britain's most important church
British Museum World's greatest chronicle of Western civilization
National Gallery European paintings from Leonardo, Botticelli, Van Gogh, and more
British Library Top literary treasures of the Western world
Tower of London Castle, palace, and prison housing the crown jewels
St. Paul's Cathedral Christopher Wren's domed masterpiece

Nearby
Greenwich Maritime center with famous observatory
Windsor Queen's primary residence
Cambridge England's classic university town

Bath ▲▲▲   2 days

Genteel Georgian city, built around the remains of an ancient Roman bath

Nearby
Glastonbury New Age mysticism, abbey ruins, and a holy hill
Stonehenge and Avebury Prehistoric stone circles
Wells and Salisbury Serene Gothic cathedrals

Cotswolds ▲▲   1-2 days

Quaint villages—cozy market town **Chipping Campden,** popular hamlet **Stow-
on-the-Wold,** and handy transit hub **Moreton-in-Marsh**—scattered over a hilly
countryside and near one of England's top palaces, Blenheim

Lake District ▲▲   1-2 days

Idyllic lakes-and-hills landscape, with enjoyable hikes and joyrides, time-passed
valleys, William Wordsworth and Beatrix Potter sights, and the charming home-
base town of **Keswick**

Durham and Hadrian's Wall ▲   1-2 days

Youthful working-class university town with magnificent cathedral, within an easy
drive of the Roman ruins of Hadrian's Wall

York ▲▲▲   1-2 days

Walled medieval town with grand Gothic cathedral, excellent museums (Viking,
Victorian, railway), and atmospheric old center

WALES

North Wales ▲▲   1-2 days

Scenically rugged land filled with evocative castles, the natural beauty of Snowdonia National Park, and the tourable slate mines at **Blaenau Ffestiniog,** all
accessible from the cute castle town of **Conwy**

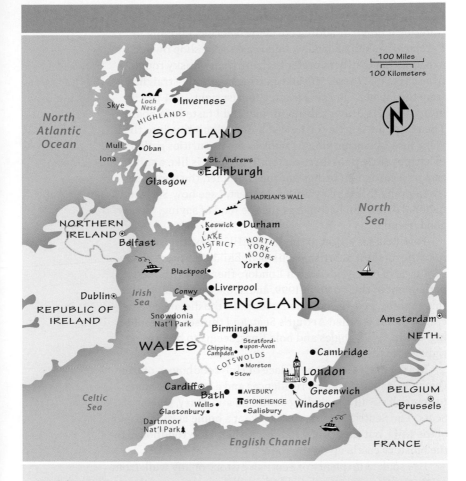

SCOTLAND

Edinburgh ▲▲▲   2 days
Proud Scottish capital, with an imposing castle on a bluff, attraction-studded
Royal Mile, and Georgian New Town with trendy shops and eateries

Nearby
St. Andrews Famous golf town and Scotland's top university

Highlands ▲▲   1-2 days
Traditionally Scottish mountainous region, with the handy hub of **Inverness** (near
Loch Ness and Culloden Battlefield) in the north, and the home-base town of
Oban in the south, with boat trips to the historic isles of **Mull** and **Iona**

With more time, consider visiting
Liverpool Gentrified English port city and the Beatles' hometown
Stratford-upon-Avon Shakespeare's home and fine theater
Glasgow Workaday but revitalized city with fun nighttime scene

Cadenhead's prides itself on bottling good whisky without watering it down or adding cosmetic coloring. Popping in, I'm shown a shelf of aged wooden casks. The shop owner explains that distillers prefer to drink their whisky rough, from casks like these: "It's like getting your milk straight from the farmer." But this is not a tourist sight—so I pay for my whisky. He draws a dram for me, and I taste it. Whoa! Then he pours a little spring water on it. Squinting into the glass, he coaches me along: "Look at the impurities gathering in a happy little pool there on top. The water is like a spring rain on a garden—it brings out the character, the personality." Sipping this whisky with an expert, I see how Scotland's national drink can become, as they're fond of saying, "a very good friend."

Fortified, I walk on to the Royal Mile's next attraction: the modern Scottish parliament building. After three centuries of being ruled from London, the Scots regained a parliament of their own in 1999, and a few years later built this striking, eco-friendly home for it. In the distance is the craggy summit called Arthur's Seat, and this soaring building, mixing wild angles and bold lines, seems to be surging right out of the rock.

My very last stop is the Palace of Holyroodhouse, one of Queen Elizabeth's official residences and a long-time home to Scottish royalty, including James IV and Mary, Queen of Scots. The Scottish monarchs also kept a home at the top end of the Mile, but they preferred the cushier Holyroodhouse to the blustery castle up on the rock.

I've soaked up plenty of Scottish history on my walk from castle to palace. But no Royal Mile walk is complete without popping into a pub—and there's no shortage of them—where a bit of live music and whisky await.

History Comes Alive at Westminster Abbey

Eddie the Verger is posted in his red robe with a warm smile at the exit of London's Westminster Abbey. His responsibility: to sort through those visitors who want to enter the abbey to worship, and those who are masquerading as worshippers in order to sidestep the high entrance fee.

Westminster Abbey is the most famous English church in Christendom, where royalty has been wedded, crowned, and buried since the 11th century. A thousand years of English history—3,000 tombs, the remains of 29 kings and queens, and hundreds of memorials to poets, politicians, scientists, and warriors—lie within its stained-glass splendor, making it a must-see on any London trip. Dropping by, I tell Eddie I'm working on the Rick Steves book, and he says, "I'd like a word with that Rick Steves. He implies in his guidebook that you can pop in to worship in order to get a free visit."

I tell him who I am, and we sort it out. Really charmed by Eddie, I agree that I'll encourage visitors to attend the free worship service for the experience of it, not to dodge the admission fee. (I highly recommend a sung evensong, which takes place six days a week.)

Eddie deposits me in the abbey, and I visit like any other tourist—enjoying the great audio tour narrated by Jeremy Irons. Listening to the actor's soothing voice, I have some private time with great history: the marble effigy of Queen Elizabeth I, modeled after her death mask in 1603—considered the most realistic likeness of her; the coronation chair that centuries of kings and queens sat upon right here on their big day; the literary greats of England gathered as if conducting a posthumous storytelling session around the tomb of Geoffrey Chaucer (Mr. *Canterbury Tales*); the poppies lining the Grave of the Unknown Warrior, an ordinary soldier who lost his life in World War I; the statue of Martin Luther King Jr., added above the west entrance in 1998 as an honorary member of this now heavenly English host; and so much more.

Then Eddie takes me into a place that no tourist goes—the Jerusalem Chamber, where long-ago monks set up shop to translate the Bible from ancient Greek into English, creating the King James Version (finished in 1611). These reformers faced real danger in getting the word of God into the people's language, and knowing the importance of their heroic steps back then, I got shivers and chills (much as I

London on the Cheap

London is one of Europe's most expensive cities. Here are some tips for stretching your pennies and pounds:

- Gorge on London's many free museums: the British Museum, British Library, National Gallery, National Portrait Gallery, Tate Britain, Tate Modern, and Victoria and Albert Museum.
- Go to a free evensong service at (the otherwise expensive) Westminster Abbey or St. Paul's.
- Look for free performances such as lunch concerts at St. Martin-in-the-Fields Church, the Changing of the Guard at Buckingham Palace, rants at Speakers' Corner in Hyde Park, and the legislature at work in the Houses of Parliament.
- Join an inexpensive London Walks tour. Or, cheaper yet, take advantage of the free guided London walks in the Rick Steves Audio Europe app.
- Get discounted same-day tickets at theater box offices or from the official TKTS booth at Leicester Square.
- Consider hosteling (www.yha.org.uk) or staying in dorms (late June to mid-September; the University of Westminster is one option with doubles, www.westminster.ac.uk/summeraccommodation).

With Eddie the Verger *(left)* at Westminster Abbey *(right)*

did at Germany's Wartburg Castle, where I saw the room in which Martin Luther did essentially the same thing for the German-speaking world).

I thank Eddie on my way out; we part as friends. He's glad that tourists will be less likely to try to sneak into the abbey for free. And for me, it's been worth the visit to look back in time, remembering the writers, reformers, royalty, and soldiers who put the "great" in Great Britain.

The Quaint and Quirky Cotswolds

For three decades, I've said it's a temptation for a travel writer to overuse the word "quaint." I reserve my use of it for describing England's Cotswold villages, in the gentle, hilly region northwest of London. By quaint, I don't mean just thatched cottages and charming teahouses. There's a quirkiness here—a sort of impoverished nobility and provincial naiveté that has something to do with being time-passed. Whatever it is, it charms me to no end.

I like the north Cotswolds best. Two of the region's coziest towns are Chipping Campden, featuring what the great British historian G. M. Trevelyan and I call the finest High Street in England; and Stow-on-the-Wold, with good pubs, antique stores, and cute shops draped seductively around a big town square. Both are close to Moreton-in-Marsh, which has good public transportation connections and lacks the touristic sugar of the other towns. Any of these villages makes a fine home base for your exploration of the thatch-happiest of Cotswold towns and countryside.

Between Stow and Chipping Campden, the tiny hamlets of Snowshill, Stanton, and Stanway get my nomination for the cutest Cotswold destinations. Sweet as marshmallows in hot chocolate, they nestle side by side, each spiced with eccentric characters and odd bits of history.

Snowshill, a little bundle of delight, has a photogenic triangular square. On one corner stands Snowshill Manor. This dark, mysterious old palace is filled with the lifetime collection of the long-gone Charles Paget Wade. It is one big, musty celebration of craftsmanship, from finely carved spinning wheels to frightening samurai armor to tiny elaborate figurines carved by long-forgotten prisoners from the bones of meat served at dinner. It's clear that Wade dedicated his life and fortune to fulfilling his family motto: "Let Nothing Perish."

The sister villages of Stanton and Stanway are separated by a great oak forest and grazing land, with parallel waves in the fields echoing the furrows plowed by medieval farmers. It's my selfish tradition here to let someone else drive so I can hang out the window, enjoying a windy flurry of stone walls and sheep, all under a canopy of ancient oaks.

In Stanton, flowers trumpet, door knockers shine, and slate shingles clap. It's as if a rooting section is cheering me up the town's main street. The church, however, betrays a pagan past. Stanton is at the intersection of two ley lines (which some new-age types consider a source of special power) connecting prehistoric sights. Many churches such as Stanton's were built on pagan holy ground and are generally dedicated to St. Michael—the Christian antidote to pagan mischief. Michael's well-worn figure, looking down at me from above the door, seems to say, "It's all clear now—good Christians may enter." Sitting in the back pew, fingering grooves worn into the wooden posts by sheepdog leashes (at a time when a man's sheepdog accompanied him everywhere), I'm reminded that it was wool money that built this church.

Stanway, while not much of a village, is notable for its venerable manor house. The Earl of Wemyss (pronounced "Weemz"), whose family tree charts relatives back to 1202, occasionally opens his melancholy home to visitors. Musty

England's Cotswold villages are made to order for the word "quaint."

and threadbare, it feels like a trip back in time. You'll often find his lordship roaming about. The manor dogs have their own cutely painted "family tree," but the earl admits that his last dog, C.J., was "all character and no breeding." Once, while I was marveling at the 1780 Chippendale exercise chair in the great hall, the earl surprised me. Jumping up onto the tall leather-encased spring, and with the help of the high armrests, he began bouncing. A bit out of breath, he explained, "In grandmama's time, half an hour of bouncing on this was considered good for the liver."

The earl's house has a story to tell. And so do the docents—modern-day peasants who, even without family trees, probably have relatives in this village going back just as far as their earl's. If you probe cleverly, talking to these people gives a rare insight into this quirky, authentic slice of England.

A Day in Regal Bath

Shaking off my umbrella, I walked up to my B&B and climbed the stairs to my room, exhausted after a long day exploring Bath. When I blew my nose, I noticed a spray of red dirt on the Kleenex—and I remembered the snuff.

At the Star Inn, the most characteristic pub in town, the manager Paul keeps a tin of complimentary snuff tobacco on a ledge for customers. Earlier that evening I tried some, questioning Paul about it while a drunk guy from Wales tried to squeeze by me holding two big pints of local brew over my head. Paul said that English coal miners have long used it because cigarettes were too dangerous in the mines, and they needed their tobacco fix. He wanted me to take the tin. I put it back on the ledge and said I'd try it again the next time I stopped by.

From the hospitality of its people to its architectural beauty and aristocratic charm, Bath is one of those places that seems made for tourists. Just 90 minutes west of London by train, the city is known for its grand abbey (the last great medieval church erected in England), stately Georgian-era buildings, and restorative thermal baths (said to have cured Queen Mary of infertility and Queen Anne of gout). Despite its

In Bath, you'll enjoy a lazy picnic surrounded by Georgian elegance.

flood of sightseers, I still find Bath to be one of the most enjoyable cities in Britain.

I started my day joining a gang of curious visitors in front of the abbey, where volunteer guides divide up the tourists for a free walk around town. My guide, a retired school-teacher, explained that the volunteer-touring tradition started in 1930, when the mayor—proud of the charms of his historic town—took the first group gathered here on a walk. The mayor's honorary guide corps has been leading free walks daily ever since.

The musical highlight of my day was a worship service at Bath Abbey. The service was crisp, eloquent, and traditional. I was struck by the strong affirmation of the worshippers' Catholic heritage, the calls for sobriety, and the stress on repentance (including repeated references to how we are such wretched sinners).

For 2,000 years, Bath's mineral spa has been attracting those in need of a cure.

The Anglican worship ritual is carefully shuttled from one generation to the next. That continuity seemed to be underlined by the countless tombs and memorials lining walls and floors—worn smooth and shiny by the feet of worshippers over the centuries. With the living and the dead all present together, the congregation seemed to raise their heads in praise as sunlight streamed through windows. This bright church is nicknamed the "Lantern of the West" for its open, airy lightness and huge windows.

The church was packed with townsfolk—proper and still. As I sat among them at offering time, the pastor caught me off-guard with his gentility. He said, "If you're a visitor, please don't be embarrassed to let the plate pass. It's a way for our regular members to support our work."

Later that night, heading home from the Star Inn, I was surrounded by young kids partying. English girls out clubbing wiggled down the street like the fanciest of fish lures—each shaking their tassels and shimmying in a way sure to catch a big one.

The rock star Meatloaf was playing a big concert in the park, and during his performance, much of Bath rocked with him. Although the concert was sold out, I gathered with a hundred freeloaders, craning our necks from across the river for a great view of the stage action.

Bath's an expensive town in an expensive country. The young couple hired to manage the elegant Georgian guest-house I was staying in told me they took the gig just to live in Bath. As they put it, "Workaday English can't really afford to live here." They have an apartment in the basement, but they go through the grand front door just to marvel at the elegant building they live in. I don't blame them. The grandeur of Bath—wonderfully accessible to a tourist—is simply unmatched.

Highlands Magic

Years ago, I met a dear man on a deserted roadside in the Scottish Highlands. I was scrambling to make a TV show about the area, and as if placed there by heaven's Central Casting, this tender giant of a man was bagpiping to the birds, the passing clouds, and the occasional motorist. He had picked a spot that seemed intentionally miles from nowhere. We stopped, and he graciously demonstrated his pipes, giving us a tour of that fascinating symbol of Scottish culture. I've never forgotten that wonderful chance meeting.

The Scottish Highlands are filled with magic and mystery. In the northernmost reaches of Scotland, the Highlands feature a wild, severely undulating terrain that's punctuated by lochs (lakes) and fringed by sea lochs (inlets) and islands. Whenever I want a taste of traditional Scotland, this is where I come.

About two hours north of Edinburgh, the tiny village of Kenmore—little more than the fancy domain of its castle, a church set in a bouquet of tombstones, and a line of humble houses—offers a fine dose of small-town Scottish flavor. One day a year, it hosts its Highland Games festival—and one year I was lucky enough to be there, mixing it up with the locals. The open field was filled with families having a fun day out

PIOB MHOR of SCOTLAND
KILTMAKERS &
HIGHLAND OUTFITTERS

watching tug-of-wars, little kids' sprints, gunnysack races, bands of marching pipers, and Highland dancing. While the girls impatiently and anxiously awaited their time with the bagpiper on stage, the big boys took turns tossing big things: Stones, hammers, and the caber (a log the size of a small telephone pole) were sent end-over-end to the delight of those gathered.

Loch Tay, near Kenmore, is a fascinating place. All across Scotland, archaeologists know that little round islands on the lochs are evidence of crannogs—circular lakefront houses built by big shots about 2,500 years ago. In the age before roads, people traveled by boat, so building houses on waterways made sense. There are 18 such crannogs on Loch Tay, and one is now the Crannog Centre, a museum dedicated to demonstrating the skills every crannog homeowner needed, such as making fire by rubbing sticks.

There can be very few Scots whose ancestors were not connected to working the land. And sheepdogs have a long rural lineage, too. The dogs herding sheep today are the direct descendants of a long-ago breed domesticated in the British Isles. In the Highlands, the best way to get a taste of this aspect of farm culture is at a good sheepdog show.

Recently, on a remote Highlands farm, I drove up a long rutted drive with one of my tour groups. As we stepped onto the grass, a dozen eager border collies scampered to greet us. Then came the shepherd, whom the dogs clearly loved and followed like a messiah. He proceeded to sit us down in a natural little amphitheater in the turf and explain all about his work. With shouts and whistles, each dog followed individual commands and showed an impressive mastery over the sheep. Then, with good, old-fashioned shears, we each got our chance to shear a sheep—who took it calmly, as if at a beauty salon.

The Highlands' past is written all over its landscape. Perhaps no other place is as evocative as the memorial battlefield of Culloden, near Inverness. In 1746, Jacobite troops (most of them Highlanders) gave it their all to put the Catholic Bonnie Prince Charlie on the English throne... and failed. While only about 50 English soldiers died, the Highlanders lost about 1,500 men. Bonnie Prince Charlie declared, "Every man for himself!" as he galloped away. The Highlanders were routed.

The victorious English pushed an aggressive campaign of cultural assimilation. After Culloden, they banned the wearing of kilts, the playing of bagpipes, and even the Gaelic language—effectively spelling the end of the clan system.

Near Culloden is another fascinating sight—the Clava Cairns. I always knew about England's famous stone circles, but I hadn't realized that Scotland had fancy-pants, over-achieving knuckle draggers, too. At Clava Cairns, set in a peaceful grove of trees, are the remains of three stone burial mounds, each cleverly constructed 4,000 years ago with a passageway that the sun illuminates, as if by magic, with each winter solstice. Wandering through these thought-provoking cairns, knowing they're as old as the pyramids, is a highlight of a Highlands visit.

When in Britain, Take a Hike

After decades of visits to Britain, I finally took some time to slow down and do some real hiking. One thing I learned: Even if you only have two or three hours, taking a hike is about the best time you can invest in places of outstanding natural beauty. Every day has a few hours to spare. What else is so important between 4 o'clock and dinnertime? Because of these walks, I took home vivid memories.

In the Lake District, I struggled up and over Catbells, a 1,480-foot hill above the lake called Derwentwater. The weather had almost kept me in, but I was glad I ventured out. I welcomed the comedic baaing of sheep, and the wind "blowing the cobwebs out" (as my B&B host warned). On previous visits, when I'd stayed down by the lake, I'd look up to see hikers silhouetted like stick figures on this ridge. Now I was one of those sky-high figures myself. With the weather storming overhead like a dark army, the wind buffeting in

Hiking in England's Lake District, you can find your own majestic perch overlooking a scenic valley *(left)* or stumble upon a surprise view of Derwentwater *(right)*.

my ears, and 360-degree views commanding my attention—I wanted to turn cartwheels.

Anywhere in Britain, blustery weather is just a part of the scene. Most "bad weather" comes with broken spells of brightness, and it doesn't pay to get greedy for more (like outright sunshine). You wish for and are thankful for brightness. As they say here, there's no bad weather, just inappropriate clothing.

And, oh, the joy of a pub after a good hike. Studying the light on ruddy faces while munching hearty pub grub has always been part of the magic of travel in Britain. When your skin is weather-stung and your legs ache happily with accomplishment, the pub ambience takes on an even more inviting glow.

Dartmoor Calling

A fine way to mix Neolithic wonders and nature is to explore one of England's many turnstile-free moors. You can get lost in these stark and sparsely populated time-passed commons, which have changed over the centuries about as much as the longhaired sheep that seem to gnaw on moss in their sleep. Directions are difficult to keep. It's cold and gloomy, as nature rises like a slow tide against human constructions. A crumpled castle loses itself in lush overgrowth. A church grows shorter as tall weeds eat at the stone crosses and tilted tombstones.

Windswept and desolate, Dartmoor National Park in southwest England is one of the few truly wild places you'll find in this densely populated country. With more Bronze Age stone circles and huts than any other chunk of England,

The stone circles at Dartmoor National Park are as old as the pyramids.

Dartmoor is perfect for those who dream of experiencing their own private Stonehenge sans barbed wire, police officers, parking lots, tourists, and port-a-loos.

On one visit, I trekked from the hamlet of Gidleigh through a foggy world of scrub brush and scraggy-haired goats on a mission to find a 4,000-year-old circle of stone. Venturing in the pristine vastness of Dartmoor, I sank into the powerful, mystical moorland—a world of greenery, eerie wind, white rocks, and birds singing but unseen. Climbing over a hill, surrounded by sleeping towers of ragged, moss-fringed granite, I was swallowed up. Hills followed hills followed hills—green growing gray in the murk.

Then the stones appeared, frozen in a forever game of statue maker. For endless centuries they waited patiently, still and silent, as if for me to come. I sat on a fallen stone, observing blackbirds and wild horses. My imagination ran wild, pondering the people who roamed England so long before written history, feeling the echoes of druids worshipping and then reveling right here.

More British Experiences

My Favorite Welsh Town: In North Wales, miles of green fields are dotted with grazing sheep. My preferred home base for exploring this region is the town of Conwy. Built in the 1280s to give the English king Edward I a toehold in Wales, it also served as a busy port, back when much of Europe was roofed with Welsh slate. Today it boasts the best medieval walls in Britain, a protective castle dramatically situated on a rock overlooking the sea, and a charming harbor that locals treat like a town square. Facing the harbor is the Liverpool Arms pub, a salty and characteristic hangout built by a captain who ran a ferry service to Liverpool in the 19th century. On summer evenings, the action is on the quay. It's a small town, and everyone comes out to enjoy the local cuisine—chips, ice cream, and beer—and to savor that great British pastime: tormenting little crabs. If you want to do more than photograph the action, rent gear from the nearby lifeboat house. Mooch some bacon from others for bait, and join in. It's catch-and-release. The scene is mellow, multigenerational, and perfectly Welsh.

Hunting Ghosts in York: Just two hours north of London by express train, York has a rich history—from its Roman origins to its role as a Viking trading center. It's got the largest Gothic church in Britain, and, as locals love to add, "a giant bell." Just as a Boy Scout counts the rings in a tree, you can count the ages of York by the different bricks in the city wall: Roman on the bottom, then Danish, Norman, and the "new" addition"—from the 14th century. With all this history, joining a walking tour makes for a wonderful introduction to the city. Charming old Yorkers volunteer their time to give energetic, entertaining, and free two-hour walking tours every day of the year. Or, for a little more gore, you can pay to join one of the many ghost walks advertised all over town. While generally I find ghost walks to be little more than goofy entertainment, if any city can claim to be legitimately haunted, it would be York. At night, the old town center is crawling with creepy, black-clad characters leading wide-eyed groups of tourists around on various ghost walks. On my last trip, I spent an evening sampling several different walks—and woke up screaming at 2 a.m.

Scotland's Second City: Lately, I've been appreciating what I consider to be the "second cities" of Europe. These places— from Marseille to Porto, Antwerp to Belfast, Hamburg to Bilbao—often have a rough, Industrial Age heritage and a rust-belt vibe that keeps them honest, unvarnished, and nonconformist. Take Glasgow: Even though it is Scotland's largest city, it takes second place to Edinburgh (which wins out for its impressive sights and capital status). Nonetheless, Glasgow has a wonderful energy and plenty of sights, including Art Nouveau architecture from Charles Rennie Mackintosh and fine museums. But the highlight is the city's street scene, which percolates in places like the Golden Zed, a Z-shaped pedestrian shopping zone that zigzags through town. Just strolling up its lanes—listening to buskers, enjoying the people-watching, and remembering to look up at the architecture above the modern storefronts—is a treat. And rather than letting graffiti artists mess up the place with random or angry tagging, the top street artists are given

Britain offers a fine set of experiences: from English garrison towns like Conwy, built seven centuries ago to keep down the Welsh (left), to ghost tours that really grab you in York (center), to fun and spirited public art on the streets of Glasgow (right).

entire walls to paint. These murals are almost sightseeing destinations in themselves.

Walking Hadrian's Wall: For years I've visited Hadrian's Wall, the remains of the 73-mile fortification the Romans built nearly 2,000 years ago. It marked the northern end of their empire, where Britannia stopped and where the barbarian land that would someday be Scotland began. The Romans got all the way up here, and then they said, "OK, this is good enough; let's call it an empire. We don't want to mess with the Picts. We'll just build a big wall right here." But until recently, I never ventured beyond the National Trust properties, the museums, and the various parking lot viewpoints.

This time, cameraman in tow, I grabbed a sunny late afternoon to actually hike the wall. When you're scrambling along Roman ruins, accompanied by the sound of the wind, surveying vast expanses of Britain from rocky crags that seem to rip across the island—like a snapshot that has frozen some horrific geological violence in mid-action—you need to take a moment and simply absorb your setting. As my cameraman did his work, I did just that. I imagined I was a legionnaire on patrol in dangerous and distant Britannia, at the empire's northernmost frontier...with nothing but this wall protecting me from the terrifying, bloodthirsty Picts just to the north. It was a goose-pimple experience, as the Brits would say.

CULTURE AND TRADITIONS: EVERYTHING'S SO...BRITISH

Pubs and Beer

Pubs are a basic part of the British social scene, and whether you're a teetotaler or a beer guzzler, they should be a part of your travel here. A pub is where the whole neighborhood goes to meet people. If you sit at a table you might get some privacy; if you sit at a stool at the bar, you'll have all sorts of friends.

Whenever I'm in London, I make it a point to savor a pint at the Anglesea Arms in South Kensington. In my mind, this place is everything a British pub should be: filled with musty paintings and old-timers, beautiful people backlit, dogs wearing Union Jack vests, a long line of tempting tap handles advertising the beers and ales available, and flower boxes spilling color around picnic tables—perfect for a warm summer evening.

Britain's pubs still provide the best places to hang out with the locals.

Brits take great pride in their beer, and many think that drinking beer cold and carbonated, as Americans do, ruins the taste. At pubs, long-handled pulls are used to literally pull the traditional, rich-flavored "real ales" up from the cellar. These are the connoisseur's favorites: fermented naturally, varying from sweet to bitter, often with a hoppy or nutty flavor. Short-handled pulls at the bar mean colder, fizzier, mass-produced, and less interesting (at least to Brits)—keg beers. Pubs are also a fine (and economical) place to sample traditional dishes, like fish-and-chips, roast beef, bangers and mash (sausages and mashed potatoes), and meat pies—though increasingly, "gastropubs" are raising the culinary bar, with menus that mingle updated English and international fare. For me, eating in a fine pub under ancient timbers is the best and most atmospheric way to dine in Britain.

B&Bs and the British Breakfast

No one does bed-and-breakfasts better than the Brits. You'll find these small, quaint, family-run accommodations everywhere in Great Britain. Besides the company of charming hosts, the best part of staying at a B&B is the huge, home-cooked breakfast, called a "fry-up," a "full English/ Scottish/Welsh breakfast," or a "heart attack on a plate." Most B&B owners take pride in their breakfasts. Each morning, you sit down at an elegant and very British table setting in an intimate dining room. You can order whatever parts of the fry-up you desire: Canadian-style bacon, sausage, eggs, broiled tomatoes, mushrooms, greasy pan-fried toast, sometimes potatoes, and coffee or tea. Or, rather than a big plate of cardiac arrest, you can go to the buffet table and help yourself to cereal, juice, yogurt, and fruit.

B&Bs are not without drawbacks. Because they're often housed in older buildings, rooms are commonly smaller and more cramped than hotels. They can have thinner walls and creaky floorboards, so you might hear other guests creeping around at night. And while most rooms have an "en suite" (attached) bathroom, some rooms come with a "private bathroom" instead, which can mean that the bathroom is all yours, but it's across the hall. Yet I happily make the trade-off for the personal touches that B&Bs do offer—whether it's joining my hosts for tea in the afternoon or relaxing by a communal fireplace at the end of the day. Compared to hotels, B&Bs give you double the cultural intimacy for half the price.

Evensong

One of my top experiences in Britain is to attend evensong at a great church. During this evening worship, a singing or chanting priest leads the service, and a choir—usually made up of both men's and boys' voices—sings the responses. The most impressive places for evensong include Westminster Abbey and St. Paul's Cathedral in London, King's College Chapel in Cambridge, Canterbury Cathedral, Wells Cathedral, York Minster, and Durham Cathedral.

Wherever you attend, arrive early and ask to be seated in the choir. You're in the middle of a spiritual Oz as 40 boys sing psalms—a red-and-white-robed pillow of praise, raised up by the powerful pipe organ. You feel as if you have elephant-size ears, as the beautifully carved choir stalls—functioning as giant sound scoops—magnify the thunderous, trumpeting pipes. If you're lucky, the organist will run a

In Britain, some things never change: The breakfasts are as traditional and hearty as ever *(left),* and the Brits love their afternoon tea *(right).*

spiritual musical victory lap as the congregation breaks up. Thank God for evensong. Amen.

Afternoon Tea

The best way to experience this most British of traditions is to attend an afternoon tea. This ritual generally takes place around 3 p.m. and is something to be savored over a couple of hours. Menus include several options. "Cream tea" is simply a pot of tea and a homemade scone or two with jam and thick clotted cream. "Afternoon tea" usually comes with a three-tiered platter of dainty sandwiches, scones, and small pastries. Don't confuse afternoon tea with "high tea," which to Brits generally means a more substantial late-afternoon or early-evening meal, often served with meat or eggs.

Depending on where you go, afternoon tea can get pricey, especially in London (it's nearly $70 per person at the Ritz). You can save money by tucking in at a department store or bookstore café. Still, for maximum opulence and ambience, it can be worth raising a pinky in one of Britain's grand tea rooms, such as the Wolseley or Fortnum & Mason in London, Bettys Café Tea Rooms in York, or my favorite—the Pump Room in Bath, a classy Georgian hall just above the Roman baths.

Great Britain Travel Resources from Rick Steves

Guidebooks
Check out Rick's guidebooks covering London; England; Scotland; and all of Great Britain (including England, Scotland, and Wales)

Audio Europe
Download Rick's free Audio Europe app, with self-guided audio tours, including walks through Westminster and the City of London; tours of the British Museum, British Library, and St. Paul's Cathedral; and a walk down Edinburgh's Royal Mile

TV Shows
The quintessence of Great Britain with Rick as your host, viewable on public television and at RickSteves.com. Episodes cover England (London, Bath, York, Lake District, Cornwall, Southeast England, West England), Wales, and Scotland (Edinburgh, Highlands, Islands)

Organized Tours
Small group tours, with itineraries planned by Rick: England in 14 Days; London in 7 Days; South England in 13 Days; Scotland in 10 Days

For more on all of these resources, visit RickSteves.com. For Great Britain trip-planning tips, see www.ricksteves.com/europe and click on "England," "Scotland," or "Wales."

Ireland

One of the many reasons I love traveling in Ireland is that it gives me the sensation I'm understanding a foreign language. The Irish have that amazing gift of gab—a passion for conversation. And they're experts at it. Ireland is a sparsely populated island of hardscrabble communities. And along with lush, unforgettable vistas and an endearing heritage, it's the people that make the Emerald Isle such a delight to visit.

This 300-mile-long island, ringed with some of Europe's most scenic coastal cliffs, is only 150 miles across at its widest point—no matter where you go in Ireland, you're never more than 75 miles from the sea. Ireland is dusted with prehistoric stone circles, cliffside fortresses, burial mounds, and standing stones—some older than the pyramids.

Given its small size and geographic isolation, Ireland has had an oversized impact on the world. It was Ireland's Christian monks who tended the flickering flame of literacy through the Dark Ages, and Ireland later turned out some of modern literature's greatest authors (from Jonathan Swift and W. B. Yeats to James Joyce and Oscar Wilde). In the 1800s, great waves of Irish emigrants sought new opportunities abroad, making their mark in the US, Canada, New Zealand, and Australia.

Politics and religion divide Ireland. The Republic of Ireland, to the south, encompasses 80 percent of the island and is an independent nation of 4.6 million predominantly Catholic people. Northern Ireland, with 1.8 million people (roughly half Protestant and half Catholic), remains a part of the United Kingdom—like Scotland or Wales—and pledges allegiance to the Queen.

I'd say no visit to Ireland is complete without a visit to both the North and the Republic. Wherever you venture—from Dublin to Dingle, from bogs to Belfast—you'll find an engaging culture and plenty of locals ready and eager to help you experience and enjoy it firsthand.

FAVORITE SIGHTS AND MEMORABLE EXPERIENCES IN IRELAND

Dublin Spirit

A while back, I spent a week in Dublin vacationing with my then-teenaged kids. I had a hunch that Dublin would deliver on family fun... and it was grand.

The city is safe, lively, easy, and extremely accessible. Each night we enjoyed spirited and affordable entertainment. Both kids connected with their Irish heritage. We were all pretty wide-eyed at the thriving late-night scene in Temple Bar, Dublin's beer-drinking hotspot. While run-down through most of the 20th century, this now-trendy center feels like the social heart of booming Dublin and is great for people-watching. The girls are wrapped up like party favors, and the guys look like they're on their way home from a rough-and-tumble hurling match.

Nowadays, except for baked beans at breakfast, forget "eating Irish" in Dublin. Going local here is going ethnic. A multinational food court we visited took diversity to extremes: Chinese were cooking Mexican, Poles were running the Old Time American diner, a Spaniard was serving sushi, and Irish were running

Fast Facts

Biggest cities: Dublin (capital of Republic, 1.3 million), Belfast (capital of Northern Ireland, 300,000), Cork (119,000)

Size (entire island): 32,595 square miles (about the size of Indiana), population 6.6 million

Locals call it: Éire

Currency: Euro (Republic of Ireland), British pound (Northern Ireland)

Key date: December 6, 1921, Ireland wins independence from Britain before plunging into a year-long civil war that ends up dividing the country

Biggest festival: St. Patrick's Day (March 17)—although it's a bigger deal for Irish Americans than for people who still live in Ireland

Leprechauns per square mile: 1.7

Handy Irish phrases: *Dia duit* (hello; **jee**-ah gwitch), *Conas atá tú?* (How are you?; Cun-us ah-**taw** too), *Go raibh maith agat* (thank you; guh rov mah **ug**-ut), *Pionta Guinness, le do thoil* (A pint of Guinness, please; pyun-**tah** Guinness leh duh hull), *Slainte!* (Cheers!; **slawn-**chuh)

Tourist info: Ireland.com

In Ireland, make a point to connect with the Irish—whether on the streets, at the stadiums, or in the nightlife zones.

the Thai concession. Save your craving for pub grub for the small towns.

We went to Croke Park, the longtime stadium for Gaelic sports, joining 50,000 screaming Irish football fans. (Irish football is a kicking, tackling, running game.) Tickets were $40. I got to talking with a man seated next to us, telling him we went to the Abbey Theater the night before to see a play by Oscar Wilde. He asked me the cost, and I said $40 per person. He said to his wife, "Imagine paying $40 just to see a play." She said that, to a theatergoer, spending $40 to see a football game would be just as strange.

We'd spent another $40 outside the stadium so that my kids and I would each have a scarf or hat with the correct team colors (gold and green—we were rooting for Donegal). I thought back to a game I'd attended here 20 years earlier, when the "colors" were cheaply dyed crepe-paper hats that sold for a buck. In the rain, my colors ran from my paper hat down onto my face, gold and green...I was for Donegal even back then. During both games I recall being careful—for my own safety—to sit with Donegal fans and cheer at the right times. I'll never forget the creative cursing. My vocabulary grew like never before.

Pouring out of the stadium with what seemed like half of Dublin, it occurred to me that we were the only tourists in sight.

Belfast: The Troubles and the *Titanic*

Wandering through energetic downtown Belfast, it's hard to believe that the bright and bustling pedestrian center was once a subdued security zone. That precaution was necessitated by the Troubles (1968 to 1998), the long and violent struggle to settle Northern Ireland's national identity. The Unionist majority (mostly Protestant) wanted to remain part of the United Kingdom, and the Nationalist minority (mostly Catholic) wanted to become part of the Republic of Ireland.

As a young tour guide back in the 1970s, I had a passion for getting my travelers beyond their comfort zones. In those days, a trip to Ireland was made meaningful by seeing towering stacks of wood in Belfast destined to be anti-Catholic bonfires and talking with locals about sectarian hatred. Now, after a 1998 power-sharing agreement brought an end to on-the-streets fighting, security checks are a thing of the past.

But evidence of the old challenges remains. In downtown Belfast, I hired a cabbie to take me on a guided tour of the original home bases of the Troubles—the Catholic working-class neighborhood of Falls Road, and the Protestant ones of Shankill Road and Sandy Row.

Our first stop was a sad structure called a "peace wall," which separated the Catholics from the Protestants in the former no-man's-land between the Shankill and Falls roads. It's one of a number of walls erected in Belfast when the Troubles started. Now 40 feet high, the wall started as 20 feet of concrete, was extended with 10 feet of corrugated metal, and finally topped with 10 feet of wire mesh—all with the intent of stopping projectiles from sailing over it. Although meant to be temporary, barriers like this stay up because of lingering fears among the communities on both sides.

My cabbie also brought me past Belfast's Felons' Club— where membership is limited to those who've spent at least a year and a day in a British prison for political crimes. At the Milltown Cemetery, I hopped out of my guide's old black cab to see a memorial to Bobby Sands and nine other hunger strikers, who starved themselves to death for the cause of Irish independence.

To get an up-close dose of the Unionist perspective, I walked along Sandy Row—a working-class-Protestant street.

Sightseeing in Northern Ireland ranges from political murals remembering a titanic political struggle to exhibits describing the birthplace of a *Titanic* disaster.

Ireland's Top Destinations

REPUBLIC OF IRELAND

Dublin ▲▲▲   allow 2 days

Bustling Irish capital, with fine museums, fascinating walking tours (history, pubs, literature, music), a passionate rebel history along with the trappings of now long-gone British rule, and a rambunctious pub district

Top Sights

National Museum: Archaeology Interesting collection of ancient Irish treasures
Kilmainham Gaol Historic political prison-turned-museum
Trinity College Home of illuminated Book of Kells manuscript from the Dark Ages

Nearby

Brú na Bóinne Boyne Valley's ancient pre-Celtic burial mounds
Battle of the Boyne Site Location of the pivotal battle that established Protestant rule
Trim Castle Biggest Norman castle in Ireland
Glendalough Evocative Dark Ages monastic ruins set in the Wicklow Mountains

Kilkenny ▲▲   1 day

Inland medieval town, just an hour from the hilltop church ruins known as the Rock of Cashel

Waterford ▲   1 day

Historic port town with famous Waterford Crystal Visitor Centre

County Cork ▲▲   1-2 days

Two quaint harbor towns: gourmet capital **Kinsale** and emigration hub **Cobh**—the *Titanic's* last stop

Ring of Kerry ▲▲   1-2 days

Mountainous, lake-splattered region with famous loop drive, prehistoric ring forts, and sweet home-base town of **Kenmare**

Dingle Town and Peninsula ▲▲▲   2 days

Fishing village, traditional Irish-music pub paradise, and launch pad for gorgeous peninsula loop drive with plenty of mysterious stone forts and a possible trip to the desolate yet evocative Blasket Islands

County Clare ▲▲   1 day

Rugged western fringe, with the stunning Cliffs of Moher, stone landscape of the Burren, and trad music crossroads of **Doolin**

Galway ▲   1 day

University city with thriving pedestrian street scene and great pubs

Aran Islands ▲▲▲   1 day

Three windswept islands (**Inishmore** is best) laced with rock walls, crowned by Iron Age ring forts, and inhabited by hardy fisherfolk

Connemara and County Mayo ▲▲   1 day

Green, hilly outback of cottages, lakes, and peaks

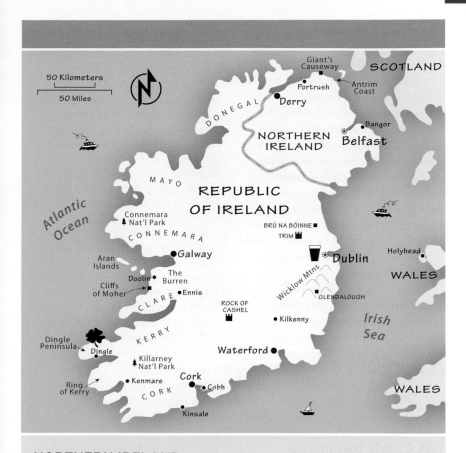

NORTHERN IRELAND

Belfast ▲▲   1-2 days
Industrial Revolution metropolis with stirring political murals and *Titanic* museum, near the charming Victorian seaside town of **Bangor**

Antrim Coast ▲▲   1 day
Scenic area embracing the beach resort of **Portrush,** geologic wonderland of the Giant's Causeway, and cliff-edge ruins of Dunluce Castle

Derry ▲   1 day
Walled city that ignited Ireland's "Troubles"—with an insightful city history museum and access to the rugged beauty of County Donegal

Along the way I passed murals filled with Unionist symbolism, such as a depiction of William of Orange's victory over the Catholic King James II in the Battle of the Boyne.

With more peaceful times, the character of these murals is slowly changing. Paramilitary themes are gradually being covered over with images of pride in each neighborhood's culture. A recurring motif is the *Titanic* ocean liner, built by a predominantly Protestant workforce in Belfast's shipyard. (A typical souvenir T-shirt reads, "Titanic—it was OK when it left here.")

In fact, Belfast has turned its ties to the ill-fated ship into a $155-million touristic landmark. Titanic Belfast, a high-tech, six-story museum, rises adjacent to the dry dock where the *Titanic* took shape. It's part of the quiet optimism that's taken hold in Belfast. Perhaps one day visitors will associate the city more with its proud shipbuilding industry than with political and religious conflict.

Money Matters

The Republic of Ireland uses the euro currency. Northern Ireland, part of the United Kingdom, uses the pound sterling, the same currency in circulation in England, Scotland, and Wales. The pound notes issued by banks in Northern Ireland look slightly different from the British pound sterling, but they are worth the same and are technically interchangeable. Nonetheless, if you're also traveling to Great Britain, note that "Ulster" pounds are considered "undesirable" in England. Banks in either region can exchange them for English pounds at no charge. Don't worry about the coins, which are accepted throughout Great Britain and Northern Ireland.

The Dingle Peninsula

Be forewarned: Ireland is seductive. I fell in love with the friendliest land this side of Sicily. It all happened in a Gaeltacht—an area of traditional culture where the government protects the old Irish ways and Irish is spoken. But Irish culture is more than just the ancient language. You'll find it tilling the rocky fields, singing in the pubs, and lingering in the pride of the small-town preschool that brags "all Irish." Signposts are in Irish only, with many in the old Irish lettering. If your map is in English...good luck.

Green, rugged, and untouched, the Dingle Peninsula is my favorite Gaeltacht. For more than 30 years, my Irish dreams have been set here, on this sparse but lush peninsula where residents are fond of saying, "The next parish is Boston."

Of the peninsula's 10,000 residents, 1,500 live in Dingle town (An Daingean). Its few streets, lined with ramshackle but gaily painted shops and pubs, run up from a rain-stung harbor. During the day, teenagers—already working on ruddy

On Ireland's Dingle Peninsula, humble farms feel haunted with memories of the Great Potato Famine *(left)* and villages seem built to weather great storms *(right)*.

beer-glow cheeks—roll kegs up the streets and into the pubs in preparation for another tin-whistle night.

Fishing once dominated Dingle, and the town's only visitors were students of old Irish ways. Then, in 1970, the movie *Ryan's Daughter* introduced the world to Dingle, followed in 1992 by *Far and Away*. The trickle of fans grew to a flood, as word spread of Dingle's musical, historical, gastronomical, and scenic charms—not to mention Fungie the friendly dolphin, who hangs out in the harbor.

Dingle town sits on the Dingle Peninsula, which makes a perfect 30-mile loop for a bike ride (or drive). While only tiny villages lie west of Dingle town, the peninsula is home to half a million sheep. Cycling around the peninsula feels like a trip through an open-air museum. The landscape is littered with monuments left behind by Bronze Age settlers, Dark Age monks, English landlords, and Hollywood directors.

Talk with the chatty Irish you'll encounter along the roadside. I once met an elfish, black-clad old man in the little town of Ventry (Ceann Tra'). When I asked if he was born here, he breathed deeply and said, "No, 'twas about six miles down the road." I asked if he'd lived there all his life. He said, "Not yet." When I told him where I was from, a faraway smile filled his eyes as he looked out to sea and sighed, "Aye, the shores of Americay."

The wet sod of Dingle is soaked with medieval history. In the darkest depths of the Dark Ages, peace-loving, bookwormish monks fled the chaos of the Continent and its barbarian raids. They sailed to this drizzly fringe of the known world and lived their monastic lives in lonely stone igloos or "beehive huts," which you'll see dotting the landscape.

Parts of the peninsula are bleak and godforsaken. Study the highest fields, untouched since the planting of 1845, when the potatoes never matured and rotted in the ground. You can still see the vertical ridges of the potato beds—a reminder of that year's Great Potato Famine, which eventually, through starvation and emigration, cut Ireland's population by one-quarter.

Rounding Slea Head, the point in Europe closest to America, the rugged coastline offers smashing views of deadly black-rock cliffs and the distant Blasket Islands (Na Blascaodai). The crashing surf races in like white horses, while long-haired sheep—bored with the weather, distant boats, and the lush countryside—couldn't care less.

The tip of the peninsula is marked by a chalky statue of a crucifix. It faces the sea, but about half the time, it seems it's actually facing an impenetrable cloud and being whipped by sheets of rain. It rains with gusto here. I imagine that Dingle cows have thicker eyelids, evolved over the centuries to survive sideways rain. The Gallarus Oratory, a 1,300-year-old church made only of stone, is famously watertight—unless the rain is hosing in sideways. I've been splattered inside. I've driven over Conor Pass with the visibility at zero, ragamuffin sheep nonchalantly appearing like ghosts in the milky cloud. I've huddled, awaiting a chance to step out, in farmhouses abandoned in the Great Famine. Yes, the weather is a force on the peninsula. But when the sun does come out, everything rejoices.

More Irish Experiences

Slog on the Bog: One of the simple pleasures of Ireland's landscape is bouncing on a springy peat bog. Walk a few yards onto the spongy green carpet. (On wet days, you might squish into a couple of inches of water.) Find a dry spot, and jump up and down to get a feel for it. Have your companion jump; you'll feel the vibrations 30 feet away.

These bogs once covered almost 20 percent of Ireland. As the climate got warmer at the end of the last Ice Age, plants began growing along the sides of the many shallow lakes and ponds. When the plants died in these waterlogged areas, there wasn't enough oxygen for them to fully decompose. Over the centuries, the moss built up, layer after dead layer, helping to slowly fill in the lakes and eventually becoming peat. Peat was Ireland's standard heating fuel for centuries—sliced out of bogs, stacked to dry, and then burned like presto logs in fireplaces and stoves. In the old days, four or five good men could cut enough peat in a day to keep a family warm through the cold Irish winter. Today, a few locals—nostalgic for the smell of a good turf fire—still come to desolate bogs to cut their own fuel.

Bleak and Beautiful Inishmore: Strewn like limestone chips hammered off the jagged west coast, the three Aran Islands confront the wild Atlantic with stubborn grit. The largest, Inishmore, is nine miles of rock with one sleepy town, a few fishing hamlets, and a weather-beaten charm. The landscape is harsh, with steep, rugged cliffs and wind-swept rocky fields stitched together by stone walls. So barren is this landscape that fishermen had to collect seaweed, sand, and manure to create tiny patches of soil for growing vegetables. This blustery island's stark beauty alone is worth a visit, but the blockbuster sight is Dún Aenghus, an Iron Age stone fortress that hangs spectacularly and precariously on the edge of a sheer cliff 200 feet above the ocean. You'll feel like the westernmost person in Europe, lying down on the rock—your head hanging over the cliff-edge—high above the crashing Atlantic.

LEFT On the far west coast of Ireland, mighty cliffs plunge into the sea while locals gaze out and say, "Ah, the next parish over...is Boston."

RIGHT On the northern coast, the hexagonal basalt pillars of the Giant's Causeway offer a stony playground for visitors.

Giant's Causeway: With camera handy, explore this stretch of Northern Ireland's coastline, famous for its bizarre basalt columns. The shore is covered with largely hexagonal pillars, sticking up at various heights. It's as if the earth were offering God his choice of 37,000 six-sided cigarettes.

Geologists claim the Giant's Causeway was formed by volcanic eruptions more than 60 million years ago. As the surface of the lava flow quickly cooled, it contracted and crystallized into columns (resembling the caked mud at the bottom of a dried-up lakebed, but with deeper cracks). As the rock later settled and eroded, the columns broke off into the many stair-like steps that now honeycomb the Antrim Coast.

Of course, in actuality, the Giant's Causeway was made by a giant Ulster warrior named Finn MacCool, who knew of a rival giant living on the Scottish island of Staffa. Finn built a stone bridge over to Staffa to spy on his rival and found out that the Scottish giant was much bigger. Finn retreated back to Ireland and had his wife dress him as a sleeping infant, just in time for the rival giant to come across the causeway to spy on Finn. The rival, shocked at the infant's size, fled back to Scotland in terror of whomever had sired this giant baby. Breathing a sigh of relief, Finn knocked down the bridge. Today, proof of this encounter exists in the geologic formation that still extends undersea and surfaces at Staffa. For cute variations on the Finn story, as well as details on the ridiculous theories of modern geologists, drop by the Giant's Causeway Visitors Centre.

In Ireland I enjoy the feeling of understanding a foreign language. And the people you meet love to talk. Whether on a harborside stroll or in a pub between sets of traditional music, try striking up a conversation.

CULTURE AND TRADITIONS: EVERYTHING'S SO...IRISH

Gaelic and the Gift of Gab

Want to really get to know the Irish? Ask for directions to your next destination. It's almost always a rich experience and a fast way to connect with locals. Nearby friends often chime in with additional tidbits that may or may not be useful, and soon it's a communal chitchat session.

That legendary Irish "gift of gab" has its roots in the ancient Celtic culture. With no written language (until the arrival of Christianity), the ancient Celts passed their history, laws, and folklore verbally from generation to generation. Even today, most transactions come with an ample side-helping of friendly banter (called *craic* in Irish). As a local once joked, "How can I know what I think until I hear what I say?"

Traditional Irish Music

The Irish seem born with a love of music. At social gatherings, everyone's ready to sing his or her "party piece." Performances are judged less by skill than by uninhibited sincerity or showmanship. Nearly every Irish household has some kind of musical instrument on a shelf or in a closet.

Live traditional music is a weekly (if not nightly) draw at any town pub worth its salt. There's generally a fiddle, flute or tin whistle, guitar, bodhrán (goat-skin drum), and maybe an accordion. Occasionally the fast-paced music stops, the band puts down their instruments, and one person sings a heartfelt lament—a sad story of lost love or emigration to a faraway land. This is the one time when the entire pub will stop to listen. Spend a lament studying the faces in the crowd.

A session can be magic, or it can be lifeless. If the chemistry is right, it's one of the great Irish experiences. The tunes churn intensely while the drummer dodges the fiddler's playful bow. Sipping their pints, they skillfully maintain a faint but steady buzz. The floor on the musicians' platform is stomped paint-free, and barmaids scurry artfully through the commotion, gathering towers of empty, cream-crusted glasses. Make yourself right at home, "playing the boot" (tapping your foot) under the table in time with the music.

Eating and Drinking in an Irish Pub

Pub is short for "public house"—an extended living room where, if you don't mind the stickiness, you can feel the pulse of Ireland. Today the most traditional, atmospheric pubs are in Ireland's countryside and smaller towns.

In much of Ireland, when you say "beer, please" at a pub, you'll get a pint of "the tall blonde in the black dress"—Guinness, Ireland's king of beers. If you want a small beer, ask for a "glass" (a half-pint). Never rush your bartender when he's pouring a Guinness. It takes time—almost sacred time. If you don't normally like Guinness, try it in Ireland; it doesn't travel well and is better in its homeland.

Pub grub is Ireland's best eating value, but don't expect high cuisine. This is comfort food: Irish stew (mutton with mashed potatoes, onions, carrots, and herbs), soups and chowders, coddle (stewed layers of bacon, pork sausages, potatoes, and onions), fish-and-chips, boxty (potato pancakes filled with fish, meat, or veggies), and champ (potato mashed with milk and onion). In coastal areas, mackerel, mussels, and Atlantic salmon join the menu. Irish soda bread nicely rounds out a meal.

Ireland Travel Resources from Rick Steves

Guidebooks
Check out Rick's guidebooks covering all of Ireland (including the Republic of Ireland and Northern Ireland); Dublin; and Northern Ireland

TV Shows
The quintessence of Ireland with Rick as your host, viewable on public television or at RickSteves.com. Episodes cover the best of Northern Ireland (including Belfast) and the Republic of Ireland, including Dublin, Waterford, the Ring of Kerry, Dingle, Galway, and the Aran Islands

Organized Tours
Small group tours, with itineraries planned by Rick: Ireland in 14 Days; Heart of Ireland in 8 Days

For more on all of these resources, visit RickSteves.com. For Ireland trip-planning tips, see www.ricksteves.com/europe/ireland.

Scandinavia

Scandinavia is Western Europe's most prosperous, pristine, and progressive corner. For the tourist, it is the land of Viking ships, brooding castles, fishy harbors, deep green fjords, medieval stave churches, and quaint farmhouses—juxtaposed with the sleek modernism of the region's cities. A visit here connects you with immigrant roots, contemporary European values, and the great outdoors like nowhere else.

Denmark is by far the smallest of the Scandinavian countries (although it once ruled Norway and part of Sweden). Danes are proud of their mighty history, and yet they're easygoing with a delightfully wry sense of humor. Denmark's capital, Copenhagen, is freewheeling and modern, while the country's cozy islands seem set in a century gone by.

Norway is stacked with superlatives—it's the most mountainous, most scenic, and, thanks to its offshore oil fields, most wealthy of the Scandinavian countries. Perhaps above all, Norway is a land of epic natural beauty, its steep mountains and deep fjords carved out and shaped by an ancient ice age. The country's capital, Oslo, is wonderfully walkable, its museums reflect its seafaring heritage, and its parks are unforgettable.

Sweden, far bigger than Denmark and far flatter than Norway, is graced with vast forests, countless lakes, and picturesque islands. Its sleek capital, Stockholm, is as appealing as its archipelago, perfect for cruising. This family-friendly land is home to Ikea, Volvo, WikiLeaks, ABBA, and summer vacations at red-painted, white-trimmed cottages.

Residents of the Scandinavian countries are, for the most part, confident, happy, and healthy. They speak their minds frankly, even about subjects others might find taboo, like sex. They're well-educated and well-traveled. Though reserved and super-polite at first, they're quick to laugh and don't take life—or themselves—too seriously.

FAVORITE SIGHTS AND MEMORABLE EXPERIENCES IN SCANDINAVIA

Cozying Up to Ærø

The Danish word for "cozy," *hyggelig*, perfectly describes the little island of Ærø. Few visitors to Scandinavia even notice this sleepy, 6-by-22-mile isle on Denmark's southern edge. But Ærø has a salty charm. It's a peaceful and homey place, where baskets of strawberries sit for sale on the honor system in front of farmhouses. Its tombstones are carved with sea-inspired sentiments such as: "Here lies Christian Hansen at anchor with his wife. He'll not weigh until he stands before God."

Ærø's main town, Ærøskøbing, is a village-in-a-bottle kind of place. I wander down cobbled lanes right out of the 1680s, when the town was the wealthy home port to more than 100 windjammers (today the harbor caters to German and Danish holiday yachts). Stubby little porthole-type houses, with their birth dates displayed in proud decorative rebar, lean on each other like drunken sailors. It's OK to peek through the windows into living rooms. (If people want privacy, they shut their drapes.) I notice, mounted to several old houses, angled "snooping mirrors" that afford someone seated inside a wide view of the entire street. Antique locals are following my every move—a thought that fills me with comfort rather than paranoia.

On the Danish isle of Ærø, the town of Ærøskøbing is a ship-in-a-bottle place.

The post office dates to 1749, and cast-iron gaslights still shine in the night. On summer evenings, you can hang out with the locals in the town's one pub or, even better, join the night watchman, who takes anyone who is interested on a historic stroll through town. That's the only action going on after dark. During midnight low tides it can be so quiet, you can almost hear the crabs playing cards.

A strong social ethic permeates Danish society, and I really feel that on Ærø. Here, you're welcome to pick berries and nuts, but historically the limit has been "no more than would fit in your hat." For years I recommended Mrs. Hansen's bike-rental depot next to the gas station at the edge of town. One day, a big hotel in town (with far more economic clout) decided to rent bikes, too. I saw Danish communalism in the reaction of a local friend: "They don't need to do that—that's Mrs. Hansen's livelihood." In Denmark, looking out for Mrs. Hansen's little bike-rental business is a matter of neighborly decency.

And Ærø's subtle, breezy charms are best enjoyed on a bike. Pedaling into the idyllic countryside, I find myself saying "cute" more than I should as I roll past sweet little hamlets and traditional U-shaped farms (designed to block the wind and protect cows, hay, and people). After struggling uphill to the island's 2,700-inch-high summit—a "peak" aptly named Synnes Hoej ("Seems High")—I wind past a fine 12th-century church, a cliffside viewpoint, a 6,000-year-old burial place, and a little brewery.

Then, as I coast back into Ærøskøbing as the sun is setting, I roll right on through to Urehoved beach—where a row of tiny huts lines the strand, and Danes gather to barbecue

Fast Facts

Biggest cities: Copenhagen (capital of Denmark, 1.2 million), Stockholm (capital of Sweden, 910,000), Oslo (capital of Norway, 658,000)

Size: Denmark—16,600 square miles (twice the size of Massachusetts), population 5.5 million; Norway—148,900 square miles (slightly larger than Montana), population 5 million; Sweden—174,000 square miles (a little bigger than California), population 9.6 million

Locals call it: Danmark (Denmark), Norge (Norway), Sverige (Sweden)

Currency: Danish crown (*krone*, officially DKK), Norwegian crown (*krone*, NOK), Swedish crown (*krona*, SEK)

Key date: A.D. 793, the Viking Age begins

Biggest festival: Midsummer Eve (summer solstice celebrations—with feasting, music, and dancing around the maypole in Sweden, and with bonfires, picnics, and processions in Norway and Denmark)

Handy Danish phrases: *Goddag* (hello; goh-**day**), *Tak* (thank you; tack), *Ingen ko på isen* (no worries, no problem; literally, "No cow on the ice"; ing koh paw **ees**-ehn)

Handy Norwegian phrases: *God dag* (hello; goo dah), *Takk* (thank you; tahk), *Det regner trollkjerringer!* (It's raining cats and dogs!; literally, "It's raining troll hags!"; deh **ray**-nehr **trohl**-shehr-ring-ehr)

Handy Swedish phrases: *Goddag* (hello; goh-**dah**), *Tack* (thank you; tack), *Fartkontroll* (speed trap; **fahrt**-kohn-trohl)

Tourist info: GoScandinavia.com

shrimp and sing songs. The huts are little more than a picnic table with walls and a roof—each carefully painted and carved—stained with generations of family fun, sunsets, and memories of pickled herring on rye bread. It's a perfect Danish scene where a favorite word, *hyggelig*, takes cozy to enjoyable extremes.

Cool, Calm Copenhagen

Copenhagen has always impressed me. Its improbable aspects just work so tidily together. Where else would Hans Christian Andersen, a mermaid statue, Europe's first great amusement park, and lovingly decorated open-face sandwiches be the icons of a major capital?

For the tourist, Copenhagen is compact, with its key sights radiating out from the Rådhuspladsen (City Hall Square), the bustling heart of the city. This used to be the fortified west end of town. In 1843, the king cleverly quelled a revolutionary-type thirst for democracy by giving his people a place to gather in Tivoli Gardens—just beyond the walls.

Tivoli, the granddaddy of amusement parks, is still going strong, but the walls and moats of medieval Copenhagen are long gone. They've been replaced by a ring of lush parks and tranquil lakes that are appreciated by the nearly naked sunbathers who savor the short Danish summer—oblivious to the history all around them.

From Rådhuspladsen, a series of lively pedestrianized streets and inviting squares called Strøget bunny-hops through the old town. Established in 1962, Strøget was Europe's first major pedestrian boulevard, and it's become the model for people zones throughout the world.

A leisurely stroll down Strøget leads to Nyhavn harbor, which lounges comfortably around its canal. Here in the old sailor's quarter, a few lonely tattoo parlors and smoky

Copenhagen's Nyhavn (New Harbor) is no longer a rollicking quarter of prostitutes and sailors' bars. But it does come with good-looking Danes showing off their tattoos.

taverns stubbornly defend their salty turf against a rising tide of expensive cafés. Glamorous sailboats fill the canal, where any historic all-wood sloop is welcome to moor.

While tattoos were once the mark of crusty old seadogs, today they are Danish chic. Young bodybuilders, showing off muscles, tans, and tattoos, clog the harborside promenade as they down bottles of local beer. While all this public beer-drinking is off-putting to some, it's perfectly legal. Many young Danes can't afford the highly taxed alcohol sold in bars, so instead they buy their beers at a convenience store and "picnic drink" in squares and along canals. The outdoor beer drinking in Denmark is pretty much the same as consuming a brew in a British pub...just without the building.

For a quick meal, locals grab a *pølse*—a local hot dog—and wash it down with chocolate milk. Sold from sausage wagons (*pølsevogne*) throughout the city, the Danish *pølse* has resisted the onslaught of our global, Styrofoam-packaged, fast-food culture. What the locals call the "dead man's finger" is fast, cheap, tasty, and, like its American cousin, almost worthless nutritionally.

Another option is Denmark's tasty open-face sandwich (*smørrebrød*), overflowing with a variety of toppings and sold wrapped and ready to go in many corner shops. There's no more Danish way to picnic; a favorite spot is the waterfront park where the *Little Mermaid*—of Hans Christian Andersen fame—sits demurely on her rock. The tradition calls for three sandwich courses: herring first, then meat, then cheese, washed down with a local beer. *Skål!*

For the Danes, small really is beautiful.

Delightful, Surprising Oslo

When I was a 14-year-old kid, I traveled through Europe with my parents. One of my best memories from this trip is of sleeping on a ship from Copenhagen to Oslo, and waking up to the pristine Oslofjord. Sitting on the deck and for the first time enjoying the Norwegian scenery—the land of my grandparents—was a thrill. Years later, sailing down the same fjord to Oslo—this time on a giant cruise ship—was a wonderful travel déjà vu.

I love Norway—probably because I'm Norwegian. Three of my grandparents grew up in Norway. (Two homesteaded in Edmonton. One was a relatively famous and often-drunk ski jumper in Leavenworth, Washington.) On a previous TV shoot in Oslo, I told my producer, "Everyone here looks like my brother." He was shocked (having traveled with me for

Scandinavia's Top Destinations

DENMARK

Copenhagen ▲▲▲   allow 2-3 days
Canal-laced, fun-loving Danish capital city with fine museums, well-presented palaces, hordes of bikes, and a flourishing culinary scene

Top Sights
  Tivoli Gardens Classic Danish amusement park
  National Museum History of Danish civilization
  Rosenborg Castle and Treasury Renaissance castle of "warrior king" Christian IV
  Christiania Colorful counterculture squatters' colony

Nearby
  Roskilde Noteworthy Viking ship museum, plus cathedral packed with royal tombs

Central Denmark ▲▲   2 days
Peaceful, bike-perfect isle of **Ærø,** with Denmark's best-preserved 18th-century village, and the busy town of **Odense,** with Hans Christian Andersen museum

Jutland ▲   1 day
Family-friendly region with Legoland park and Denmark's second-largest city, **Aarhus,** with traffic-free core, modern art museum, and open-air folk museum

NORWAY

Oslo ▲▲   2-3 days
Norway's businesslike capital city, with stately fjordside setting, innovative architecture, grand palaces and museums, and enjoyable parks

Top Sights
  City Hall Palace of good government, slathered with symbolic murals
  National Gallery Norway's cultural and natural essence, captured on canvas
  Vigeland Park Sprawling park strewn with nudes by sculptor Gustav Vigeland
  Bygdøy Neighborhood of excellent museums about seafaring, Vikings, and folk culture

Sognefjord ▲▲▲   1-2 days
Norway in a Nutshell, a trip through fjord country—by train, bus, and boat— passing waterfalls, forests, and spectacular vistas, with functional towns **Flåm** and **Aurland** along the way

Gudbrandsdal and Jotunheimen Mountains ▲   1-2 days
Lush green valley with touristy **Lillehammer** and access to a rugged mountain range with fine hikes and drives

Bergen ▲▲   2 days
Salty port city and medieval capital of Norway, with bustling fish market, colorful Hanseatic quarter (Bryggen), and a funicular to great views over town

South Norway ▲   1-2 days
Harborside **Stavanger** (with its Norwegian Emigration Center, Petroleum Museum, and nearby Pulpit Rock), time-passed and remote Setesdal Valley, and resort town of **Kristiansand**

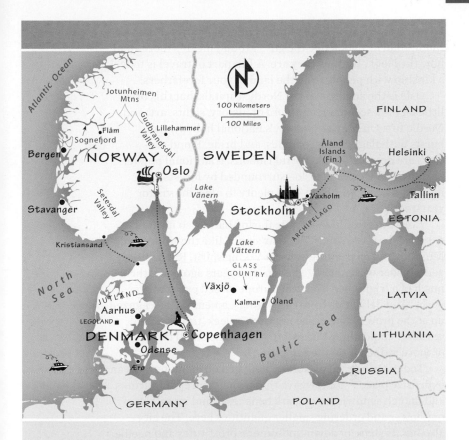

SWEDEN

Stockholm ▲▲▲   2-3 days

Sweden's stunning capital, scattered over 14 islands and bubbling with energy and history

Top Sights

Skansen Europe's first and best open-air folk museum
***Vasa* Museum** Marvelous showcase for a once-sunken 17th-century warship
Nordic Museum Fascinating peek at 500 years of traditional Swedish lifestyles
Gamla Stan Picturesque, cobbled old-town island
Royal Palace Grand collections and pomp-filled changing of the guard

Nearby

Stockholm Archipelago Scenic island chain stretching into the Baltic Sea

Southeast Sweden ▲   1-2 days

Densely forested region punctuated by worthwhile emigration and glass museums in **Växjö**; a 12th-century castle in **Kalmar;** the holiday island of **Öland;** and "Glass Country," famous for its glassworks

12 years) and said, "I didn't know you had a brother." I don't. But if I did, he'd look like the guys around me. It's more than how they look. It's how they are. A fun part of travel is to feel a kinship with people from the land of your forefathers.

Oslo is the smallest of the Nordic capitals, but this brisk little city is a scenic *smörgåsbord* of history, sights, art, and Nordic fun. On May 17, Norway's national holiday, Oslo bursts with flags, bands, parades, and pride. Blond toddlers are dressed up in colorful ribbons, traditional pewter buckles, and wool. But Oslo—surrounded by forests, near mountains, and on a fjord—has plenty to offer the visitor year-round.

Norway is traditionally a seafaring nation, so it's no surprise that Oslo's most popular sights, like the Viking Ship Museum, tell an exciting story of Viking spirit. Rape, pillage, and plunder were the rage a thousand years ago. Back then much of a frightened Western Europe closed every prayer with, "And deliver us from the Vikings, amen." When I gazed up at the prow of one of the museum's sleek, time-stained vessels, I could almost hear the shrieks and smell the armpits of those redheads on the rampage.

Today, Oslo is full of Norwegians rich on oil money. It's an expensive place—so expensive that people share their drinks and munch sandwiches on park benches. I find myself chewing slower and ordering smaller quantities here. The city also has its share of down-and-outers: prostitutes and needle junkies. While wasted people seem to rot on Oslo's curbs, the lack of violent crime here is impressive by any standard.

Overall, I am always struck by how peaceful Oslo feels. A congestion fee keeps most cars out of the town center, while

The rooftop of Oslo's gleaming marble opera house slopes into the harbor and is a popular venue for outdoor concerts.

tunnels take nearly all the rest under the city. The waterfront, once traffic-choked and slummy, has undergone a huge change. With vehicles sent underground, upscale condos and restaurants are taking over.

When the sun's out, Oslo's parks are packed. A common ailment here is *solstikk*, or sunstroke—literally, "sun sting." Wandering through a sunny Vigeland Park, where sculptor Gustav Vigeland's 192 bronze and granite nudes strut their stuff, I can't miss the real-life nudity. All of Scandinavia has a casual approach to nakedness (I'm not talking just mixed saunas—many Americans are amazed at what's on prime-time TV here). Women unabashedly sunbathe topless, and parents let their kids run naked in city parks and fountains. It's really no big deal.

Oslo's Vigeland Park is a showcase for the work of Gustav Vigeland. Its centerpiece is a towering monolith of life.

For years, I've told the story about my Eureka moment when I was that 14-year-old kid in Vigeland Park. I knew my parents loved me very much, and I looked around and saw a vast park speckled with other families—parents loving their children just as much. Right then it occurred to me how our world is filled with equally lovable children of God. I've traveled with this wonderful truth ever since.

As much as I love Norway, goat cheese, and my blond cousins, sometimes I need to inject some color into my days here. Oslo, too, seems to relish the fact that there's more to life than white food and fair hair. The city's rough-and-tumble immigrant zone—a stretch of street called Grønland—is where Turks, Indians, Pakistanis, and the rest of Oslo's growing immigrant community congregates. Colorful greengrocers' carts spill onto sidewalks and ethnic restaurants literally add spice to the otherwise pretty tame cuisine. The area's a hit with locals and tourists, and I love dining streetside here. It's relatively cheap—and seeing a rainbow of people and a few rough edges makes the city feel less Wonder Bready.

And that's the beauty of Oslo. Just when you think you have it figured out, it gives you a taste of something different.

Norway's Fjordland Beauty

If you go to Norway and don't get out to the fjords, you should have your passport revoked. The country's greatest claim to scenic fame is its deep and lush fjords. Sognefjord,

Norway's longest (120 miles) and deepest (more than a mile), is the ultimate natural thrill Norway has to offer.

For the best one-day look at Sognefjord, I like to do "Norway in a Nutshell." This package of well-organized train, ferry, and bus connections lays this beautiful natural feast before you on a scenic platter. Ambitious travelers can see the whole shebang in one very full day, but slowing down and spending the night is more relaxing.

Every morning, northern Europe's most spectacular train ride leaves from Oslo toward fjord country. Cameras smoke as this train roars over Norway's mountainous spine. The barren, windswept heaths, glaciers, deep forests, countless lakes, and a few rugged ski resorts create a harsh beauty. The railroad is an amazing engineering feat. Completed in 1909, it's 300 miles long and peaks at 4,266 feet—which, at this Alaskan latitude, is far above the tree line. You'll go under 18 miles of snow sheds, over 300 bridges, and through 200 tunnels along the way.

When the train reaches the mountain plateau station of Myrdal, a 12-mile spur line drops you 2,800 breathtaking feet to the village of Flåm, on an arm of the Sognefjord. This is a party train. The engineer even stops it for a photo op at a particularly picturesque waterfall along the way.

From Flåm, ardent "Nutshellers" zip immediately from the train to catch the most scenic of fjord cruises. The boat takes you up one narrow arm of the Sognefjord—the Aurlandsfjord—and down the next—the even narrower

On the Sognefjord, Norway shows off its scenic beauty.

Nærøyfjord. For 90 minutes, camera-clicking tourists scurry on the drool-stained deck like nervous roosters, scratching fitfully for a photo to catch the magic. Waterfalls turn the black-rock cliffs into a bridal fair. You can nearly reach out and touch the sheer, towering walls. The ride is one of those fine times when a warm camaraderie spontaneously combusts among strangers, all of whom traveled from the farthest reaches of the globe to share this experience.

At the end of Nærøyfjord, the boat docks at the nothing-to-stop-for town of Gudvangen, where waiting buses shuttle passengers back to the main train line and the overnight train to Oslo. You'll sleep through all the scenery you saw on the way out.

While the "Nutshell" trip is fast-paced bliss, if you want to dig deeper into the Sognefjord—just like the glaciers did during the last ice age—spend the night. There's something poetic about summer evenings on a fjord. The mellow, steady, no-shadow light hardly changes from 8 p.m. until 11 p.m.

When settled in a village in a Victorian-era fjordside hotel, I spend lots of time sitting on the porch, mesmerized by Norwegian mountains. Rather than jagged, they're bald and splotchy, with snow fields on top and characteristic cliffs plunging into inky fjords.

After dinner, I stroll through the village enjoying the blond cherubs running barefoot through the stalled twilight. Cobbled lanes lead past shiplap houses to rock cliffs—their gullies and cracks green with trees.

I sit on a lonely pier and look up. Half the sky is taken up by the black rock face of the mountain. The steady call of gulls and the lazy gulping of small boats taking on little waves provide a relaxing soundtrack. As I feel my pulse slow, I am thankful to be in Norway.

Stockholm's Island Getaways

One-third water, one-third parks, one-third city, Stockholm is built on an archipelago of 14 islands woven together by 50 bridges. And the islands don't stop at the city limits—they keep going for 80 miles into the Baltic Sea.

The local name for this archipelago is "Skärgården"—literally "garden of skerries." The skerries—meaning rocks—are leftover granite, carved out and deposited by glaciers. The area closer to Stockholm has bigger islands and more trees. Farther out, the glaciers lingered longer, slowly grinding the granite into sand and creating smaller islands.

For years I've simply flown over this famed archipelago,

or glided by it on a big cruise ship heading for Helsinki. Finally, I filmed one of my TV shows in Stockholm, diving into the scenic daisy chain stretching out from its downtown. Locals love to brag that there are 34,000 islands (but they must be counting every mossy little rock). A hundred are served by ferries. Even if an island isn't an official stop, ferries will dock on request...or to plop down the day's mail.

With so many islands to choose from, every Swede seems to have his or her favorite. Don't struggle too hard with the "Which island?" decision. Get a quick look on a half- or full-day package excursion from Stockholm's harbor. Or, do it on your own by ferry and overnight on an island.

Vaxholm, the nearest island, is practically a suburb, as it's connected by bridge to Stockholm. Skip past it to the more appealing (and traffic-free) Grinda. It's a rustic isle—half-retreat and half-resort—made to order for strolling through the woods, paddling a kayak, savoring an oh-so-Swedish meal in the rustic-chic lodge, or just chilling out in the floating sauna that bobs in the harbor.

Svartsö ("Black Island"), a short hop beyond Grinda, is the "Back Door" option of these isles. Unlike Grinda, Svartsö is home to a real community of just 80 year-round residents. Leafy and green Svartsö is less trampled than other islands (just one B&B and a top-notch steak house run by Stockholm foodies), but it is reasonably well-served by ferries. There's little to do—walk, bike, eat steak.

Out on the distant fringe of the archipelago—the last stop before Finland—sits the proud village of Sandhamn, on the island of Sandön. Literally "Sand Harbor," the town has a long history as a posh center for boating life—it's Sweden's answer to Nantucket. The headquarters of the Royal Swedish Yacht Club is here, making Sandhamn an extremely popular

The archipelago that stretches from Stockholm to the Baltic Sea is an idyllic and watery wonderland for nature-loving Swedes.

stop for boaters—from wealthy yachties to sailboat racers. A long sandy beach, perfect for families, stretches out on one side of the island.

But honestly, I wouldn't mind if I never get off the ferry. For me, the real highlight of an archipelago trip is the ride itself. Perched on the breezy rooftop sundeck with the Swedes, I position my lounge chair to catch just the right view and sun. It's a pleasure to key in to the steady rhythm of the ferries lacing this beautiful world together. Seeing the contentment of people savoring nature and quality time together, I'm convinced that the journey truly is the destination.

More Scandinavian Experiences

Copenhagen's Alternative Village: In the middle of Copenhagen, you'll find an unlikely hippie commune called Christiania. Surrounded by all that Danish perfection and orderliness, it's a funky enclave of squatters and rebels who operate their own little idealistic society. While hard drugs are emphatically forbidden (that's one of Christiania's rules), marijuana is sold as openly as the current political climate will tolerate—and sellers routinely press whatever boundaries are in place. Somehow, despite the best efforts of developers and the city government, Christiania has survived for more than 40 years. On my last visit, as I entered Christiania, I saw a huge mural that pretty much sums up the spirit of the place: "Only dead fish drift with the current."

Remarkably, Christiania has become the third-most-visited sight among tourists in Copenhagen. Move over, *Little Mermaid*. Some visitors see dogs, dirt, and dazed people. Others see a haven of peace, freedom, and no taboos. But watching parents raise their children with Christiania values of peace and freedom, I've come to believe more strongly than ever in this do-your-own-thing haven.

Hobnobbing in Norway: Not long ago, I was at a cousin's dinner party with a dozen people in Oslo. Because I was there, everyone simply spoke English. I felt like it was an inconvenience, but it fazed no one. Topics were fascinating. One man, an author who had just completed a book on FDR, talked with me about the intricacies of American post-WWII politics like no one I've ever met. Someone else suggested that the international phone prefix system must have originated in America, as the US is no. 1—and Norway is a lowly 47. Another guest observed that Midwest Americans speak louder than other Americans, and wondered if it was for the same reason that West Coast Norwegians talk louder than people from Oslo: They are always trying to be heard above the constant wind. Two new parents gently debated the various ways to split their paid maternal and paternal leave. People seemed very content—these Norwegians were just loving their salmon, shrimp, and goat cheese.

Revealing National Galleries: In the space of a week, I visited national galleries in Oslo, Stockholm, and Copenhagen. Each museum was a little palace of culture, showing off the nature of the land and the psyche of its people. In Scandinavia, paintings don't celebrate kings and popes. Instead, artists focus on the tumultuous symphonies of nature, exaggerating its power and awesomeness. When country folk do appear, they're the piccolo section—tiny but in sharp focus, barely surviving, but with grace. Many Scandinavian paintings are people's art—featuring bridal voyages (with traditional jewelry and formal wear), low church devotion (featuring renegade Lutherans who would not follow state dictates, until they ran out of patience and moved to Wisconsin), and solid families at work and play. The slice-of-life scenes seem to just as often be slice-of-death scenes: In one canvas, a stoic family fills their rowboat, carrying the coffin of a dead daughter, her sister clutching the funeral flowers through the bitter ride. And there's evidence of struggles with a puritanical 19th-century Protestant society and the psychological problems that resulted—leading artist Edvard Munch to let out a silent, bloodcurdling *Scream*.

All Aboard the *Smörgåsbord*: Nobody visits Scandinavia for the cuisine, but there's one culinary tradition I never miss: the Swedish *smörgåsbord* (known in Denmark and Norway as the *store koldt bord*). With so much wholesome Nordic food spread out in front of me, I must pace myself.

LEFT In Copenhagen's Christiania, a banner proclaims, "Live life artistically. Only dead fish drift with the current."

CENTER Edvard Munch's *Scream* at Oslo's National Gallery

RIGHT The traditional *smörgåsbord* is a grand buffet and your chance to feast on many Scandinavian specialties in one sitting.

Thinking of the *smörgåsbord* as a five- or six-course meal, I take small portions, making several trips to the buffet. I start with the herring dishes, boiled potatoes, and *knäckebröd* (Swedish crisp bread); then, I sample the other fish dishes (warm and cold) and more potatoes; next, it's on to salads, egg dishes, and various cold cuts; and after that, the meat dishes—it's meatball time! I pour on some gravy and plop on a spoonful of lingonberry sauce, and have more potatoes—while other roast meats (hey, is that reindeer?) and poultry tempt me. With a few empty pockets still to fill in my stomach, I sample the Nordic cheeses, delicious seasonal fruits, and bread, and then raid the racks of traditional desserts, cakes, and custards. Stuffed, I cap the meal with coffee to keep from passing out.

CULTURE AND TRADITIONS: EVERYTHING'S SO...SCANDINAVIAN

Mamma Mia!

Sweden spent years trying to find a place for a museum to honor its national treasure, the disco group ABBA. And now there is one—ABBA: The Museum, in Stockholm. For a time, ABBA was a bigger business than Volvo. And even though the group disbanded in 1982, its songs are still on plenty of playlists. They've sold more than 380 million records, and the musical *Mamma Mia!* (based on their many hits) has been enjoyed on screen and in theaters by millions of people. The museum, like everything about ABBA, is slickly promoted and aggressively commercial, with pricey tickets (about $30). But if you like ABBA, it's lots of fun. The museum has plenty of actual ABBA artifacts, re-creations of the rooms where the group did its composing and recording, lots of high-energy video screens, and plenty of interactive stations. The

LEFT At Stockholm's popular ABBA museum, any tourist can hang out with the band.

RIGHT Medieval stave churches are a reminder that Christian Vikings employed their ship-building skills for the Church.

best part is the "digital key" included with admission: You get to record a music video, karaoke-style, as a fifth member of the group, then pick up the production from the museum website.

Stave Churches

Stave churches are the finest architecture to come out of medieval Norway. These medieval houses of worship—tall, skinny, wooden pagodas with dragon's-head gargoyles—are distinctly Norwegian and palpably historic, transporting you right back to the Viking days. Wood was plentiful and cheap, and locals had an expertise with woodworking (from all that boat-building). In 1300, there were as many as 1,000 stave churches in Norway. Today, 28 remain. See two or three, and they start to look the same—but exploring at least one of them is a must. The fairest stave church in Norway? Two near the Sognefjord are tops: Hopperstad (overlooking a fjord) and Borgund (in a valley with an adjacent excellent museum). These time-machine churches take you back to early Christian days, when there were no pews and worshippers stood through the service. The churches are extremely vertical: The beams inside and the roofline outside lead your eyes up, up, up to the heavens.

Coffee Breaks

When sightseeing your way through Stockholm, be sure to join in the local tradition of the *fika*—Sweden's ritual coffee break. People in Sweden must drink more coffee per capita than in just about any other country. The *fika* is to Swedes what the *siesta* is to Spaniards. While typically a morning or afternoon break in the workday, it can happen any time, any day.

Cheap-ish Eats

There are ways to take a bite out of Scandinavia's high cost of dining. First, take full advantage of your hotel's bountiful breakfast buffet. When out sightseeing, grab lunch from a street vendor or a food market, or at a restaurant offering a daily special.

In Copenhagen, get a *pølse* (hot dog) from the sausage wagon. In Oslo, hit a *gatekjøkken* (fast-food joint), such as Deli de Luca, for a sandwich, salad, or a classic *pølse med brød* (hot dog in a bun). You'll save 12 percent in Norway by getting takeaway food from a restaurant rather than eating inside; even McDonald's has a two-tiered price list. In Stockholm, dine at a restaurant advertising *dagens rett*, a cheap lunch special.

Anywhere in Scandinavia you can save money by going to a grocery store and shopping for a picnic. In Norway, I've even cooked up my own dinner using an *engangsgrill* ("one-time grill"), a disposable foil barbecue that costs just a few bucks at a supermarket. On balmy evenings, Oslo is perfumed with the smoky fragrance of one-time grills as the parks fill up with Norwegians eating out on the cheap.

Fika fare includes coffee along with a snack or pastry—
usually a cinnamon bun. You can get your *fika* fix at just
about any café or *konditori* (bakery) in Stockholm. The coffee
(drip-style, usually with a refill) and a cinnamon bun cost
about what you'd pay at a Starbucks back home.

Dane Mellow

Danes (not to mention Swedes and Norwegians) like to joke
about the flat Danish landscape, saying that you can stand
on a case of beer and see from one end of the country to the
other. Denmark's highest point, in Jutland, is only 560 feet
above sea level. But I find Denmark to be simply cute, cute,
cute. The place feels like a pitch 'n' putt course sparsely
inhabited by blond Vulcans. Poll after poll lists Danes as the
most content and happy people on the planet.

Legoland, a wildly popular amusement park built from
millions of Lego bricks, crawls with adorable little ice-
cream-licking, blond children. Even fueled by piles of sugar,
the place is so mellow. Kids hold their mothers' hands and
learn about the Lego buildings, or smile contentedly as they
whip around on the carousel.

Throughout the countryside, newly paved roads are
lined by perfectly smooth bike lanes—one for each direction.
Even in the country, there are more bikes than cars. No one's
uptight. When there's a little traffic jam, everyone takes it in
stride. Damn those Danes.

Scandinavia Travel Resources from Rick Steves

Guidebooks
Check out Rick's guidebooks covering Scandinavia (including Denmark, Norway,
and Sweden); Stockholm; Copenhagen & Denmark; and Norway

TV Shows
The quintessence of Scandinavia with Rick as your host, viewable on public televi-
sion and at RickSteves.com. Episodes cover Denmark (Copenhagen, Ærø Island,
Jutland), Norway (fjords, Bergen, Oslo), and Sweden (Stockholm)

Organized Tours
Small group tours, with itineraries planned by Rick: Scandinavia in 14 Days

*For more on all of these resources, visit RickSteves.com. For Scandinavia trip-
planning tips, see www.ricksteves.com/europe and click on "Denmark," "Norway,"
or "Sweden."*

The Netherlands

Windmills, wooden shoes, cheese, tulips, and lots of bicycles: These images conjure up the traditional view of the Netherlands, a.k.a. Holland. (While North and South Holland are just two of the country's 12 provinces, they're so dominant that people use the names Holland and the Netherlands interchangeably.) But dig deeper and you will discover that the country also has high-tech culture, far-out architecture, and no-nonsense people with a global perspective.

For many Americans, this is a great place to start your first European vacation. The Dutch generally speak English, pride themselves on their frankness, and like to split the bill. As connoisseurs of world culture, they appreciate Rembrandt paintings, Indonesian cuisine, and the latest French films, but with a nonsnooty, blue-jeans attitude.

The capital, Amsterdam, is a laboratory of progressive living, bottled inside Europe's most 17th-century city. Like Venice, this city is a patchwork quilt of canal-bordered islands, anchored upon millions of wooden pilings. But unlike its dwelling-in-the-past cousin, Amsterdam sees itself as a city of the future, built on good living, cozy cafés, great art, street-corner jazz, and a spirit of live-and-let-live.

Because the Netherlands is compact and flat, it's easy to do day trips from Amsterdam (or nearby Haarlem, which also makes a good home base). The slick, efficient train system gets you anywhere in just hours. Choose from an array of activities and sights: the market in cozy Haarlem, the open-air folk museum in Arnhem, cheese in Edam, porcelain in Delft, or a trip through polder country out to the sea.

Approach the Netherlands as an ethnologist observing a fascinating and unique culture. A stroll through any neighborhood is rewarded with things that are commonplace here but rarely found elsewhere. Carillons chime quaintly in neighborhoods selling sex, as young professionals smoke pot with impunity next to old ladies in bonnets selling flowers.

FAVORITE SIGHTS AND MEMORABLE EXPERIENCES IN THE NETHERLANDS

Amsterdam Street Scenes

Unlike any city in Europe, Amsterdam opens like a fan out of its central train station. It just seems right for a trading center to open up from that lifeline to the world.

Stepping from the train station, I look down Damrak, the main drag, which flushes visitors past cheers of commercial neon into the old center. It's always been this way. After all, long before there was a station, this was a mighty port with a waterway cutting through the center of town, following the route of today's Damrak.

Outside the station, trams glide and canal-boat hustlers hawk their offerings. Street people wearing stocking hats over matted hair, black boots, and heavy coats in the sun choose the most public places in town to snooze. Children pedal to school as if in a small town, and pairs of policemen add no stress to the laid-back scene. Tourists pop out of the station, eager to explore.

First-time sightseers leaving the station carry a predictable checklist of sights. The Anne Frank House is on the right, the Red Light District is on the left, and Damrak leads right through the middle toward two great museums—the Rijksmuseum (filled with works by Rembrandt and Vermeer) and the Van Gogh Museum—standing like cultural bulldogs on the opposite side of town.

Fast Facts

Biggest cities: Amsterdam (capital, 820,000), Rotterdam (615,000), The Hague (500,000)

Size: 16,000 square miles (about twice the size of New Jersey), population 16.8 million

Locals call it: Nederland

Currency: Euro

Key date: July 26, 1581, the Dutch declare their independence from Habsburg Spain

Biggest festival: King's Day (April 27)

Bikes per Dutch citizen: 1.3

Handy Dutch phrases: *Hallo* (hello; hol-**loh**), *Alstublieft* (please; **ahl**-stoo-bleeft), *Dank u wel* (thank you; dahnk yoo vehl), *Nou breekt mijn klomp!* (Well, I'll be damned!; literally, "That breaks my wooden shoe"; now brayk men kloomp)

Tourist info: Holland.com

LEFT In Amsterdam, a fast-food stall shows God giving Adam the cone of fries.

RIGHT The best way to get around Amsterdam is by bike or by trolley.

But to me, Amsterdam's unpredictable street scenes—crude one moment, then charming the next—are at least as rewarding as the city's fine museums. Walking down Damrak, I find it a crass perversion of traditional Dutch culture. Wooden shoes hang forlornly on a wall between a bank and a McDonalds. Nearby, a sex museum known as the temple of Venus promises a look at "sex through the ages," including the Sado Club, the Torture Tower, and the oldest sex shop in Amsterdam. Visitors are stopped first by the poster of Marilyn Monroe fighting a randy gale, then lured in by a sultry mannequin wearing a provocative dress and a huge smile as she rides a bicycle with a single, hardworking piston.

But slices of Holland survive. Just past a gimmicky torture museum, the sound of an old-time barrel organ revives traditional Amsterdam and cheers me up. It's a two-man affair. While grandpa works the crowd, the boss is in the back spinning the wheel and feeding tunes punched into a scroll, as if feeding bullets into a musical machine gun.

The street organ is a mini carnival, painted in candy-colored pastels and peopled with busy figurines. Whittled ballerinas twitch to ring bells while Cracker Jack boys crash silver dollar-sized cymbals. Playing his coin-tin maracas and wearing a carved-on smile, the old man looks like an ornamental statue that has just leapt to life. While shoppers trudge by, two tourists break into a merry waltz. Another hugs a day bag between her knees and winks into her camera's viewfinder.

Nearby, the Vlaamse Frites kiosk is painted with take-offs on great art. This art has a purpose: to make you hungry for Flemish-style French fries. On one side of the kiosk, God gives Adam the cone of fries (a variation on this decorates the Sistine Chapel). On the opposite side is Van Gogh's famous "French Fried Potato Eaters." The peasants, for whom Vincent always had an affinity, are shown solemnly sitting down to a bountiful platter of bright yellow fries. All they need is mayonnaise, the Dutch choice over ketchup.

Warming my hands around my cone of salty fries, I wander down a back street to a charming canal lined with tipsy houses. As their foundations of pilings rot or settle, they lean on each other, looking as if someone has stolen their crutches. Suddenly, away from the tourists and street-scene bustle, I'm in 17th-century Amsterdam, seeing the Dutch Golden Age reflected in the quiet canal.

Seeing Red in Amsterdam

With just a slight swing off Dam Square, I start walking down Warmoesstraat, one of Amsterdam's oldest streets. Lining the street are sex shops, a condom shop with a vast inventory, men-only leather bars, and a smartshop selling "100 percent natural products that play with the human senses." There's no doubt I've entered into Amsterdam's famous Red Light District.

The Red Light District is located in the old sailors' quarter. In fact, the city seems to have taken everything sailors did, put it in a jar, and let it germinate for 200 years. Today that jar is open, and browsers are welcome.

The Dutch have a similarly practical approach to prostitution as they do to the recreational use of marijuana. Rather than criminalize it, they control it with a policy they call "pragmatic harm reduction." Generally, prostitutes (or "sex workers") pay rent for their space and run an independent business with no need for pimps. They are unionized and get their business license only if they are periodically checked by a doctor and are not spreading diseases. If a prostitute has a

Red lights reflect on the canals in Amsterdam, where, as in much of Europe, prostitution is legal.

The Netherlands' Top Destinations

Amsterdam ▲▲▲   allow 2-3 days
Canal-laced city filled with cozy cafés, great art, Golden Age history, and progressive people

Top Sights
Rijksmuseum Premier collection of Dutch Masters art
Van Gogh Museum 200 paintings by the angst-ridden artist
Canal Boat Tours Best cruise through city's fabled waterways
Anne Frank House Young Anne's hideaway during the Nazi occupation
Dutch Resistance Museum Powerful and insightful look at years under Nazi occupation

Haarlem ▲▲   1 day
Classic Dutch town (and handy home base) highlighted by a landmark market square, towering church, Corrie ten Boom House, and the Frans Hals Museum

Delft ▲▲   1 day
Charming, canal-lined hometown of Vermeer and the Delftware pottery factory

Edam ▲▲   1 day
Adorable cheese-making village with peaceful canals

Arnhem ▲▲   1 day
Unremarkable city but for Holland's top open-air folk museum and a first-rate modern-art museum

The Hague ▲   1 day
Big-city seat of Dutch government offering the excellent Mauritshuis Gallery and Golden Age art

With more time, consider visiting
Rotterdam Europe's busiest port, with soaring architecture and 21st-century buzz
Alkmaar Friday-morning cheese market, near Zaanse Schans Open-Air Museum
Utrecht Bustling student city with charming central zone and top rail museum

---

dangerous client and needs help, she pushes a button to summon not a pimp, but the police.

By the time I reach the area around De Oude Kerk, the oldest church in Amsterdam, I've hit the neighborhood's most dense concentration of prostitution. The church is the holy needle around which the unholy Red Light District spins. Rooms with big windows under red neon lights line the narrow alleys. In window after window, I see women in panties and bras winking at horny men, rapping on the window to attract attention, or looking disdainfully at sightseers. As the steeple chimes, women from Jamaica holler, "Come on, dahling."

Rubbing shoulders with a hungry gaggle of Dutch boy regulars, I rubberneck my way to the most popular window on the street. There, framed in smoky red velvet, stands a sultry blonde. Her ability to flex and shake her backside brings the slow, gawking pedestrian flow to a stuttering stop. And it makes me just one of the faceless, rutting masses. Next up: an exotic woman wearing a black lace power-suit and enough lipstick to keep a third grader in crayons. Just making eye contact leaves me weak—and ready to rejoin the cute and quaint Holland back in the sunshine.

The Dutch remind me that a society has to make a choice: Tolerate alternative lifestyles or build more prisons. And they always follow that up by reminding me that Americans—so inclined to legislate morality—lock up seven times as many people per capita as Western Europeans do. Either Americans are inherently more criminal people, or we need to reconsider some of our laws.

By the end of my walk, I've seen a lot—from prostitutes to the ghosts of pioneer lesbians to politically active druggies with green thumbs. This is Amsterdam's hardcore, nonstop, live-couples, first-floor-straight, second-floor-gay paseo. The kid in me delights in the spectacle. The tour guide in me jumps at this opportunity to give readers such a unique memory as this red light ramble. But the father in me cringes at the sight of a 10-year-old schoolgirl, book bag on her back, studying a window full of vibrators, whips, and sex toys.

In truth, the Red Light District seems to have something to offend everyone. Whether it's in-your-face images of graphic sex, exploited immigrant women, whips and chains, passed-out drug addicts, the pungent smells of pot smoke and urine, or just the shameless commercialism of it all, it's not everyone's cup of tea. Amsterdam is a bold experiment in 21st-century freedom: It may box your Puritan ears. And, although I encourage people to expand their horizons, it's perfectly OK to say, "No, thank you."

Now, it's time to go back to my hotel and take a shower.

Haarlem with Herring Breath

A Dutch Masters kind of town, Haarlem is an easy place to start a European trip. While mighty Amsterdam is just a 20-minute train ride away, cute Haarlem provides a comfy base and a more genteel experience.

The centerpiece of Haarlem is its delightful Grote Markt (main square), where 10 streets converge. A noisy traffic circle in the 1960s, the now-car-free area has become the town's social and psychological hub—Haarlem's civic living room.

Today I'm standing on the square under the towering church spire, tempted to eat a pickled herring. The sign atop the mobile van reads: "Jos Haring—Gezond en Lekkerrr" (healthy and deeeeeelicious).

I order by pointing and ask, *"Gezond?"*

Jos hands me what looks more like bait than lunch, and says, *"En lekkerrr."*

I stand there—not sure what to do with my bait—apparently looking lost. Jos, a huge man who towers over his white fishy counter, mimes swallowing a sword and says, "I give you the herring Rotterdam style. You eat it like this. If I chop it up and give you these"—he points to the toothpicks—"this is Amsterdam style."

As I take a bite he asks, "You like it?"

Even with three "r"s on the delicious, "It's salty" is the only polite response I can muster.

"Yes. This is not raw. It is pickled in salt. Great in the hot weather. You sweat. You need salt. You eat my herring."

It's Saturday—market day, when Haarlem's main square bustles like a Brueghel painting. The scene cheers me with a festival of flowers, bright bolts of cloth, evangelical cheese pushers, and warm, gooey syrup waffles. Gazing at the church, I'm appreciating essentially the same scene that Dutch artists captured centuries ago in oil paintings that now hang in museums. The carillon clangs with an out-of-tune sweetness only a medieval church tower can possess.

Savoring the merry dissonance, and taking tiny Amsterdam-style bites of my Rotterdam herring, I wander deeper into the market, happy that Jos is piling chopped onion on herring, contributing to the amazing ambience of this scene. Dodging flower-laden one-speed bikes, I feel like part of the family here. I'm immersed in Holland—with herring breath.

Haarlem's main square is a community gathering point. And there, like in nearly every Dutch town, you'll find a stand selling pickled herring. Locals declare the fish to be *gezond en lekker* (healthy and delicious).

The Dutch Made Holland

Today my long-time Dutch friends, Hans and Marjet, are driving me to polder country—the vast fields reclaimed from the sea where cows graze, tiny canals function as fences, and only church spires and windmills interrupt the horizon.

Hans is behind the wheel. He injects personality-plus in all he does, whether running a B&B or leading tours for Americans. And bouncy Marjet, with a head of wispy strawberry-blonde hair, red tennis shoes, and a knack for assembling a Salvation Army-chic outfit for under $20, is the sentimental half of this team.

On each of my visits, they show me a new slice of Holland, renewing my belief that the more you know about Europe, the more you'll uncover what's worth exploring.

It's early summer, and the landscape is streaked with yellow and orange tulip fields. Hans points out a quaint windmill along a dreamy canal.

"Every time I take a tour group through Holland's

countryside," I say, "someone in the back of the bus marvels, 'Everything's so Dutch.'"

The windmills were used to pump the polders dry. An area that was once a merciless sea is now dotted with tranquil towns. Many of the residents here are older than the land they live on, which was reclaimed in the 1960s. All this technological tinkering with nature has prompted a popular local saying: "God made the Earth, but the Dutch made Holland."

We motor past sprawling flower mogul mansions, then through desolate dunes. The tiny road dwindles to a trailhead. Hans parks the car, and we hike to a peaceful stretch of North Sea beach. Pointing a stick of driftwood at a huge seagoing tanker, Hans says, "That ship's going to the big port at Rotterdam. We're clever at trade. We have to be. We're a small country."

Holland welcomes the world's business, but Holland is not designed for big-shots. Hans explains, "Being ordinary is being prudent. If you grow above the grains, you'll get your head cut off. Even our former queen prefers to do her own shopping."

While Hans and I talk, Marjet collects shells with the wide-eyed wonder of a 10-year-old. "Cheap souvenirs," Hans teases. One cliché the Dutch don't dispute is their frugality. Hans quizzes me: "Who invented copper wire? Two Dutch boys fighting over a penny."

Marjet scuffs through the sand, her pockets full of

Charming Dutch villages sit on land reclaimed from the sea by pumping excess water into canals.

seashells, her scarf flapping in the wind like a jump rope. Under big, romping white clouds, we're surrounded by Holland.

More Dutch Experiences

Wartime Hideaways: Through the ages, the Dutch have given refuge to the persecuted. But they couldn't protect their citizens from the Nazis—more than 100,000 Dutch Jews died in the Holocaust. In Amsterdam, Anne Frank's House gives the cold, mind-boggling statistics of Nazi cruelty some much-needed intimacy. Even bah-humbug types who are dragged in because it's raining and their partners read the diary find themselves caught up in Anne's story. And the small town of Haarlem has Corrie ten Boom's "Hiding Place," which gives the other half of the Anne Frank story—the point of view of those who risked their lives to hide Dutch Jews during the Nazi occupation. During the war, Corrie and her family hid Jews and resistance fighters in their apartment above a clock shop. One night, with six people hiding behind a wall in Corrie's bedroom, the Nazis raided the house. Though they didn't find the hiding place, they did come across a suspiciously large number of ration coupons and sent the ten Boom family to a concentration camp. Only Corrie survived and later wrote her inspirational book, *The Hiding Place*.

Cannabis and Coffeeshops: Having been decriminalized decades ago, marijuana causes about as much excitement in the Netherlands as a bottle of beer. People can grow their own—cannabis seed sets are even sold in garden centers. Or they simply drop by a coffeeshop—a café that sells marijuana. For tourists, the open use of marijuana can feel either somewhat disturbing or exhilaratingly liberating.

Coffeeshops sell marijuana and hashish both in prerolled joints and in little baggies. They loan out bongs and inhalers, and dispense rolling papers like toothpicks. Pot, while sold openly in coffeeshops, is tightly regulated here. It's not sold to minors, and you can only buy a little at a time. Because they're not allowed to advertise marijuana, you may have to ask to see the cannabis menu. In some coffeeshops, you actually have to push and hold down a button to see an illuminated menu—the contents of which look like the inventory of a drug bust. Coffeeshop baristas warn Americans (who aren't used to the strength of the local stuff) to try a lighter leaf. If you do overdo it, the key is to eat or drink something sweet to avoid getting sick. Cola is a good fast fix, and coffeeshops keep sugar tablets handy.

Charming Delft: Delft is a typically Dutch, "I could live here" town. An hour southwest of Amsterdam, it boasts an intelligent exhibit on hometown boy Johannes Vermeer, two grand churches squirreling away royal tombs, and the factory that produces Delft Blue earthenware. But despite some fine sights, Delft is best enjoyed by simply wandering around, watching people, munching local syrup waffles, and daydreaming on canal bridges. Looking out, you'll see reflections in canals that would inspire Monet to set up his easel. On a summer day, the entire town twinkles and ripples like water lilies.

Netherlands in Bloom: The Dutch love plants. And the granddaddy of the European flower festivals is Keukenhof, the greatest bulb-flower garden on earth. Open only for two months in spring, Keukenhof blossoms with seven million tulips, hyacinths, and daffodils that conspire to thrill even the most horticulturally challenged visitor. Located near the city of Leiden, this place is packed with tour groups daily—go in the late afternoon for the fewest crowds and the best light on all those happy flowers. If you can't get out to Keukenhof, try Amsterdam's De Hortus Botanical Garden, with 4,000 varieties of plants spread throughout several greenhouses and a tropical palm house. One of the oldest botanical gardens in the world, it dates from 1638, when medicinal herbs were grown here. Even today, no mobile phones are allowed in its café or terrace because "our collection of plants is a precious community—treat it with respect."

LEFT In Haarlem, tour the Corrie ten Boom house and see the "Hiding Place."

CENTER Cannabis starter kits are sold next to tulip bulbs in the Netherlands, but you're smart not to import them.

RIGHT Each spring the Super Bowl of tulips is held at Keukenhof, an hour south of Amsterdam.

CULTURE AND TRADITIONS: EVERYTHING'S SO...DUTCH

Dutch Cheese

Cheese is a staple of the Dutch culture and economy. Cows have always proven to be more reliable than crops in this marshy landscape. And because cheese offered similar nutritional value to milk, but lasted much longer without refrigeration, it was taken on long sea voyages. Holland was the first country to export cheese, and today this small country remains one of the world's biggest cheese exporters.

The Netherlands' most famous cheeses are Edam (covered with red wax) and Gouda. Gouda can be young or old—*jong* is mellow while *oude* is salty, crumbly, and strong, sometimes seasoned with cumin or cloves. To sample Dutch cheese in Amsterdam, try the Reypenaer Tasting Rooms, whose delightful shop offers an hour-long cheese tasting (smart to reserve ahead). Or, for the real deal, head to the town of Alkmaar, Holland's cheese capital, with its bustling Friday-morning cheese market in spring and summer. Early in the morning, cheesemakers line up their giant orange wheels in neat rows on the square. Prospective buyers (mostly wholesalers) examine and sample the cheeses and make their selections. Then the cheese is sold off with much fanfare, as an emcee narrates the action (in Dutch and English). To close the deal, costumed cheese carriers run the giant wheels on something resembling a wooden stretcher back and forth to the Weigh House, just as they have for centuries.

Netherlands Clichés

What do windmills, canals, wooden shoes, and tulips have in common? Where did all of these Dutch icons come from?

Dutch clichés abound in the Netherlands, where cheese shops dot every corner and classic windmills still churn in the breeze.

It's all about the land. After diking off large tracts of land below sea level (*Netherlands* means "low lands"), the Dutch used windmills to harness wind energy to pump the excess water into canals. This drained the land, creating pockets of dry ground upon which to build. Wooden shoes (*klompen*) allowed farmers to walk across soggy fields, and since they could float, the shoes were easy to find if they came off in high water. Then in the mid-1500s, the Holy Roman Emperor's ambassador to Constantinople sent some tulip bulbs westward. The people here found that these hardy flowers grew well in the sandy soil near dunes, and tulips have become synonymous with Dutch culture ever since.

Ethnic Eats

The tastiest "Dutch" food isn't actually Dutch—it's Indonesian. As a former Dutch colony, Indonesia has had a mighty influence on the Dutch cuisine scene. Find any *Indisch* restaurant and experience a rijsttafel (literally, "rice table"). A rijsttafel features an assortment of dishes that shows off the varied cuisines of the different Indonesian islands. You'll get as many as 30 spicy dishes ranging from small sides to entrée-sized plates and a big bowl of rice or noodles. These feasts can be split and easily fill two people.

Surinamese cuisine is also popular in the Netherlands. This mix of Caribbean and Indonesian influences features dishes like *roti* (spiced chicken wrapped in flatbread) and rice (white or fried) served with meats in sauces (curry and spices). Why Surinamese food in Amsterdam? In 1667, Holland traded New York City ("New Amsterdam") to Britain in exchange for the small South American country of Suriname. When Suriname gained independence in 1975, 100,000 Surinamese immigrated to Amsterdam, sparking a rash of Surinamese fast-food outlets.

Going Dutch on a Bike

If you rent a bike in the Netherlands, you'll need to learn the rules of the road. Use arm signals, follow the bike-only traffic signals, stay in the obvious and omnipresent bike lanes, and yield to traffic on the right. Fear oncoming trams and tram tracks. Carefully cross tracks at a perpendicular angle to avoid catching your tire in the rut. Obey all traffic signals, and walk your bike through pedestrian zones. Use the bell to warn other bikers and pedestrians, and be sure to lock your bike.

If you are a pedestrian, look carefully both ways before crossing the brick-colored pavement on the side of the road—this is for bikes. As the Dutch believe in fashion over safety, no one here wears a helmet.

Biking

The Netherlands' flat land makes it a biker's dream. And in Amsterdam, bikes are by far the smartest way to travel. Everyone—bank managers, students, pizza delivery boys, and police—use bikes to get around town, and much of my own Amsterdam experience is framed by my black bike handlebars: the shiny wet cobbles, powering up a bridge to coast down it and halfway to the next bridge, getting pinged by passing bikes and pinging my bell to pass others.

The Dutch average four bikes per family. Many people own two: a long-distance racing bike and an in-city bike, often deliberately kept in poor maintenance so it's less enticing to the many bike thieves. The Dutch appreciate the efficiency of a self-propelled machine that travels five times faster than walking, without pollution, noise, parking problems, or high fuel costs. A speedy bicyclist can traverse Amsterdam's historic center in 10 minutes. Meanwhile, pedestrians enjoy the quiet of a people-friendly town where bikes outnumber cars.

Netherlands Travel Resources from Rick Steves

Guidebooks
Check out Rick's guidebooks covering Amsterdam & the Netherlands

Audio Europe
Download Rick's free Audio Europe app, with self-guided audio tours, including walks through the old center of Amsterdam, the Red Light District, and the Jordaan neighborhood

TV Shows
The quintessence of the Netherlands with Rick as your host, viewable on public television and at RickSteves.com. Episodes cover Amsterdam and Dutch side-trips

Organized Tours
Small group tours, with itineraries planned by Rick: Heart of Belgium & Holland in 11 Days; Best of Europe in 21 Days (including stops in the Netherlands)

For more on all these resources, visit RickSteves.com. For Netherlands trip-planning tips, see www.ricksteves.com/europe/netherlands.

Belgium

Belgium falls through the cracks. Nestled between Germany, France, and the Netherlands, it's famous for waffles, sprouts, and a statue of a little boy peeing. But visitors find Belgium to be one of Europe's best-kept secrets. After all, Belgium produces some of Europe's best beer, creamiest chocolates, and tastiest French fries. From funky urban neighborhoods to tranquil convent courtyards, from old-fashioned lace to high-powered European politics, from cows mooing in a pastoral countryside to gentrified medieval cityscapes bristling with spires...little Belgium entertains.

It's here in Belgium that Europe comes together: where Romance languages meet Germanic languages; Catholics meet Protestants; and nations meet in Brussels—the capital of the European Union. Its crossroads location has made Belgium strong: Belgians are savvy businesspeople, excellent linguists, and savvy chefs who've learned how to blend delicious culinary influences from various cultures.

When I asked a local, "What is a Belgian?" he answered, "We are a melting pot. We're a mix culturally: one-third English for our sense of humor, one-third French for our love of culture and good living, and one-third German for our work ethic."

Bruges, a wonderfully preserved medieval gem, and Brussels, one of Europe's great cities, are the best two first bites of Belgium. Historic, well-preserved Ghent and big, bustling Antwerp are also worth a visit. To round out your Belgian experience, spend a few hours in the Flemish countryside around the town of Ypres—both for the pastoral scenery and to visit World War I's Flanders Fields.

While not "undiscovered" (especially popular Bruges), Belgium is certainly underrated. Those who squeeze in a day or two for Belgium wish they had more time. Like sampling a flavorful praline in a chocolate shop, that first enticing taste just leaves you wanting more. Go ahead, it's OK—buy a whole box of Belgium.

FAVORITE SIGHTS AND MEMORABLE EXPERIENCES IN BELGIUM

Bewitched by Bells in Bruges

With Renoir canals, pointy gilded architecture, vivid time-tunnel art, and stay-awhile cafés, Bruges is a joy. Where else can you bike along a canal, quench your thirst with gloriously good beer, savor heavenly chocolate, and see a Michelangelo statue, all within 300 yards of a bell tower that rings out "Don't worry, be happy" jingles?

Whenever I'm in Bruges, I visit the tall bell tower that has shaded the city's Market Square since 1300. With its medieval crenellations, pointed Gothic arches, round Roman arches, flamboyant spires, and even a few small flying buttresses, the tower is a sight in itself. Carillon concerts are played on its bells a few evenings each week. You can hear the tunes ringing out from anywhere in the town center, but to catch the performance while sitting in the tower courtyard is a ritual for me.

One evening I arrived early for the concert, so I had time to climb the tower's 366 steps. Just before the top is the carillon room. On each quarter hour, its 47 bells—tuned to 47 different notes—ring mechanically.

Fast Facts

Biggest cities: Brussels (capital, 1.1 million), Antwerp (508,000), Ghent (249,000)

Size: 12,000 square miles (slightly smaller than Maryland), population 10.4 million

Locals call it: België (Dutch), Belgique (French)

Currency: Euro

Key date: 1830, Belgium declares independence from the Netherlands

Languages: Dutch (to the north; Flemish is the local Dutch dialect), French (to the south)

Biggest festivals: Carnival (Mardi Gras celebrations), Ommegang Pageant (July, Brussels, medieval festival)

Handy Dutch phrases: *Hallo* (hello; **hal**-loh), *Alstublieft* (please; **ahl**-stoo-bleeft), *Dank u wel* (thank you; dahnk oo vehl)

Handy French phrases: *Bonjour* (good day; bohn-zhoor), *S'il vous plaît* (please; see voo play), *Merci* (thank you; mehr-see)

Tourist info: VisitFlanders.com, VisitBelgium.com

It's *bellissimo* at the top of the hour. During concerts, the bells are played by a *carillonneur* on a manual keyboard.

After my carillon close-up, I took a seat in the courtyard and gazed up at the lofty brick tower. The *carillonneur* popped his head out a window, and like a kid who checks in with a parent before going down a playground slide, he gave his audience a wave. Then he disappeared and began hammering—literally hammering. A carillon keyboard looks like the foot pedals of a big organ, but it is played by the little-finger sides of bare, clenched fists.

After the concert, the gathered audience clapped, and the *carillonneur* appeared again—his tiny head jutting out the little window to happily catch our applause. The crowd dissipated, but I waited at the tower base to personally thank him. A few minutes later, he was at street level, in his overcoat, looking like any passerby. I shook his hand and found myself gripping a freakishly wide little finger. A lifetime of pounding the carillon had left him with a callus that had more than doubled the width of his pinky.

In a town with a knack for excellence, I'd met just one more artist perfecting his craft.

Carillon concerts are played on the bells of the tower overlooking the Market Square in Bruges.

Bruges Brews

In Bruges, pubs are not just pubs, they're destinations. Belgians appreciate a pub that's not owned by a single brewery, freeing them up to sample from the hundreds of microbrews made in their country. Pubs in the old center—places you'd think would be overrun by tourists—are the proud domain of locals. The fact that monasteries have historically brewed the finest Belgian beers aligns perfectly with their personal theology.

On a recent visit, I plunked myself down on a stool at a local pub with an Old Masters ambience. Wanting to check the material I had in my guidebook on Belgian beers, I planned to pick the bartender's brain, but I found myself surrounded by beer experts—all happy to clue me in on the 300 available choices. They advised me to forego my standard procedure of ordering what's on tap. Because the selection of specialty beers is so vast, no single brew can be consumed quickly enough to keep kegs from going old and stale. Those in the know prefer their beer from the bottle.

Different beers, depending on their taste temperament, are served cold, cool, or at room temperature. A critical part of the beer culture here is that the glass must fit the beer (to best bring out the beer's character). The better pubs have shelves lined with dozens of slightly different glasses, each marked with a beer's insignia. If the pub runs out of the right glass, the bartender will check to see if you'd like to change your order. Many Belgian connoisseurs will switch beers rather than use the wrong glass.

Soon I had a chemistry lab of four different beers in front of me. My selection included Brugse Zot, or "the fool"—the top beer brewed in Bruges and considered one of Belgium's best. Kriek beer is made bitter with cherry. I was told that raspberry-flavored Lambic is what you order if you "don't like beer." My favorite was a complex and creamy Chimay, brewed by Trappist monks. Licking my lips, I thought that Chimay would almost make celibacy livable.

Brussels' Grand Place

There's no better place to take in Brussels' ambience than its spectacular main square, the Grand Place. This colorful cobbled courtyard, encircled by fanciful facades, is the heart

Brussels has perhaps the grandest square in Europe—La Grand Place—and perhaps the silliest tourist attraction in the world—the *Manneken-Pis*. With each visit, you'll see the little guy peeing through a different outfit.

Belgium's Top Destinations

Bruges ▲▲▲   allow 1-2 days

Perfectly pickled Gothic city with charming cobbles, cozy squares, dreamy canals, divine chocolate, and unbeatable beer

Top Sights

Market Square 14th-century landmark square and bell tower
Groeninge Museum Top-notch 15th-century paintings
Sint-Janshospitaal Memling Collection Glowing Flemish Primitives masterpieces housed in medieval hospital

Nearby

Damme Charming market town a bike-ride away through the countryside
Flanders Fields Infamous WWI battlefields

Brussels ▲▲   1-2 days

Urbane capital of Belgium, the European Union, and NATO, with one of Europe's grandest squares, colorful urban zones, and a beloved statue of a little boy peeing

Top Sights

Grand Place Cobbled main square lined with medieval guild halls and chocolate shops
Royal Museums of Fine Arts Old Masters, huge Art Nouveau collection, and three floors of Magritte

Antwerp ▲▲   1 day

Gentrified port city with excellent museums, Belgium's best fashion, and an engaging mix of urban grittiness and youthful trendiness

Ghent ▲   1 day

Pleasant, lively university city with historic quarter and breathtaking Van Eyck altarpiece in its massive cathedral

---

of heart-shaped Brussels. The site where farmers and merchants once sold their wares in open-air stalls today hosts shops and cafés selling chocolates, waffles, beer, mussels, fries, and lace. It's the perfect backdrop for concerts, flower markets, and sound-and-light-shows—and there's always good people-watching.

The Town Hall's 300-foot-tall tower dominates the square, topped by a golden statue of St. Michael slaying a devil. Fancy smaller buildings—former guild halls—give the Grand Place its majestic medieval character.

Just three short blocks away is Brussels' most famous attraction and the most obvious example of Bruxellois irreverence: the *Manneken-Pis*, a 17th-century statue depicting a little boy urinating. Visiting VIPs have a tradition of bringing an outfit for the statue; he can be costumed as anything from a Beefeater to Elvis as his steady stream carries on.

There are several different stories behind this little

squirt: He was a naughty boy who peed inside a witch's house so she froze him. Or the little tyke loved his beer, which came in handy when a fire threatened the wooden city—he bravely put it out. Want the truth? The city commissioned the statue to show the freedom and joie de vivre of living in Brussels, where happy people eat, drink...and drink...and then pee.

More Belgian Experiences

Antwerp's Ode to Industrialism: I can't think of a more visit-worthy train station than the Industrial Age-meets-Art Nouveau marvel in Antwerp, giddy with steel and glass. Built at the turn of the 20th century, the station is a work of art and a loud-and-clear comment on a confident new age. Its main facade is like a triumphal arch on a temple of time, crowned by a grand clock. Imagine the station's debut: Just a generation earlier, people thought you might die if you traveled at more than 30 miles per hour. Timetables didn't need to be exact. Now, journeys that previously took days could be done in hours—and things ran according to the clock.

Life and Death in Flanders Fields: In far western Belgium, in the desolate WWI battlefield known as Flanders Fields, poppies were the first flowers to bloom once the dust (and mustard gas) cleared. Hundreds of thousands of soldiers took their last breaths here. Today, the poppy, representing sacrifice and renewal, is the symbol of Flanders Fields.

When touring in this area, I have to remind myself that everything I see—every building, every tree—dates from after the war's end in 1918. The devastation was monumental. You can't drive through this part of Flanders without passing countless artillery craters, monuments and memorials, stones marking this advance or that conquest, and war cemeteries standing stoically between the cow-speckled pastures. Local farmers routinely pull rustic relics of World War I from the earth when they till their fields. Every local has his own garage collection of "Great War" debris fished out of the troubled earth.

European Union Headquarters in Brussels: This sprawling complex of glass skyscrapers is a cacophony of black-suited politicians speaking 23 different Euro-languages. It's exciting just to be here—a fly on the wall of a place that charts the future of Europe. The high-tech Parlamentarium, a fun and informative exhibit, is designed to let you meet the EU and understand how it works. And you can get inside the European Parliament itself by joining a free tour. The grand finale is the vast Hemicycle, where the parliament members sit. It's the largest multilingual operation on the planet. Yes, there are now some Euroskeptics sitting in this hall, but somehow things get done "with respect for all political thinking...consolidating democracy in the spirit of peace and solidarity."

Tiny Belgium's attractions range from a mighty Industrial-Age train station in Antwerp *(left)*, to the vast and evocative WWI cemeteries of Flanders Fields *(center)*, to the glassy headquarters of the European Union in Brussels *(right)*.

CULTURE AND TRADITIONS: EVERYTHING'S SO...BELGIAN

World Capital of Chocolate

With a smile, the shop owner handed me a pharaoh's head and two hedgehogs and said that her husband was busy downstairs finishing off another batch of chocolates. Happily sucking on a hedgehog, I walked out of the small chocolate shop with a 100-gram assortment of Bruges' best pralines.

Belgium—home to Godiva, Neuhaus, and Leonidas—is one of the world's largest exporters of chocolate, and produces some of Europe's creamiest confections. The two basic types are pralines (what we generally think of as "chocolates"—a hard chocolate shell with various fillings) and truffles (a softer, crumblier shell, often spherical, and also filled). Which is better? It takes a lot of sampling to judge. Locals swear by their personal chocolatier and buy with a concern for freshness—yesterday's chocolate just won't do. This can be disastrous for chocoholics during heat waves: If the weather's too hot, the chocolate makers close down.

Belgian Waffles

Waffles are a famous Belgian treat. There are two kinds: Liège-style (warm, dense, and very sweet—with a sugary crust), and Brussels-style (light and fluffy, dusted with powdered sugar). Although Americans think of Belgian waffles for breakfast, Belgians generally have them as a late-afternoon snack—though the delicious Liège-style waffles are sold 'round the clock to tourists as an extremely tempting treat. You'll see little windows, shops, and trucks selling these *wafels*, either plain (for Belgians and purists) or topped with fruit, jam, chocolate sauce, ice cream, or whipped cream (for tourists).

A Belgian waffle just tastes better in Belgium. And if you're one to gild the lily, there is a world of toppings from which to choose.

Just Say No...to Ketchup

Belgium has some of the tastiest "French" fries in Europe. Get a paper cone of warm fries at a *frituur* (fry shop) or a *frietkot* (fry wagon). One time a local chef took me into his kitchen to witness the double frying that makes the fries taste so good. (The first pass is to cook the potatoes; the second is to brown them.) My friend picked up a single fat fry, gave it a waggle, and then dipped it into its second hot-oil bath. Something about his nervous giggle reminded me of the kid who showed me my first dirty magazine. Belgians dip their fries in mayonnaise or other flavored sauces, not ketchup. But don't worry; most places provide ketchup for Americans.

No Tap Water at Restaurants

I'd rather drink free tap water than pricey bottled water in a European restaurant. But forget about it in Belgium—it can't be had. Belgian restaurateurs are emphatic about that. Tap water may come with a smile in the Netherlands, France, and Germany, but that's not the case in Belgium, where you'll either pay for water, enjoy the beer, or go thirsty.

Belgium Travel Resources from Rick Steves

Guidebooks
Check out Rick's guidebooks covering Bruges, Brussels, Antwerp & Ghent

TV Shows
The quintessence of Belgium with Rick as your host, viewable on public television and RickSteves.com. Episodes cover Bruges and Brussels

Organized Tours
Small group tours, with itineraries planned by Rick: Heart of Belgium and Holland in 11 Days

For more on all of these resources, visit RickSteves.com. For Belgium trip-planning tips, see www.ricksteves.com/europe/belgium.

Germany

Germany is a young nation (united in 1871) with a long history. It's as modern as it is traditional. You can experience all the cultural clichés you want, from enjoying strudel at the bakery, to shopping for a cuckoo clock, to chugging a stein of beer while men in lederhosen play oompah music. The countryside is dotted with half-timbered villages like Rothenburg, looking as medieval as ever. But despite its respect for traditions, Germany truly is a 21st-century country. Laced together by bullet trains, its cities gleam with futuristic architecture, world-class museums, rejuvenated waterfronts, and people-friendly parks.

The country is blessed with spectacular scenery, and the nature-loving Germans know how to enjoy it: taking lifts to jagged peaks, hiking through the Black Forest, and cruising on rivers such as the moseying Mosel and the raging, castle-lined Rhine. The country boasts hundreds of castles, some ruined and mysterious, and others right out of a Disney fairy tale.

In contrast to its beautiful image, the country has a troubled 20th-century past. In the capital of Berlin and throughout Germany, you'll see respectful acknowledgment of this tumultuous era, with thought-provoking documentation centers, somber monuments, and haunting concentration camps.

Traditionally—and in some ways even today—German culture divides at a sort of North-South Mason-Dixon Line. Northern Germany was barbarian, is predominantly Protestant (thanks to Martin Luther), and tackles life aggressively, while southern Germany (Bavaria) was Roman, is largely Catholic, and enjoys a more relaxed tempo (think of soaking in spas). Americans' nostalgic image of Germany is beer-and-pretzel Bavaria, probably because that was "our" sector after the war.

Germany is a country of paradoxes. From modern sky-scrapers to medieval castles, speedy autobahns to meander-ing back roads, Nouveau German cuisine to old-fashioned *Wurst*, Germany truly offers something for everyone.

Germany ranges from half-tim-bered medieval cuteness (Rothenburg) to towering skyscraper zones (Berlin).

FAVORITE SIGHTS AND MEMORABLE EXPERIENCES IN GERMANY

Cruising the Rhine River

Jostling through crowds of Germans and tourists in the Rhine River village of Bacharach, I climb to the sun deck of the ferry and grab a chair. With the last passenger barely aboard, the gangplank is dragged in and the river pulls us away.

On the romantic Rhine River gorge, cafés at castles offer grand views of busy river traffic.

I'm captivated by the Rhine. There's a rhythm to the mighty river that merges with its environment: black slate cut from plains above, terraced vineyards zigzagging up hills, husks of crumbling cas-tles, and stoic spires of stone churches slicing vertically through townscapes. While the Rhine is more than 800 miles long, the 36 miles from Mainz to Koblenz are by far the most interesting. This is the Romantic Rhine, a power-ful stretch of the river slash-ing a deep and scenic gorge. And the best way to see it is to cruise it.

Passengers' parkas flap in the cool wind as the rugged hillscape gradually reveals castles both ruined and restored. All along the Rhine, it seems each castle and every rock comes with a story. Many of the castles were "robber-baron" fortresses built by petty princes and two-bit rulers back when there were several hundred independent little states in what is today's Germany. The castle owners raised heavy chains across the river when boats came—and lowered them only when the merchants had paid their duty. We sail close by one of the many scenic fortresses—Pfalz Castle—which was built on an island in the middle of the river.

As the cliffs get steeper, the rocks darker, and the river faster, the scenery becomes more dramatic. With the boat's sun deck filled mostly with beer-sipping, ice-cream-licking Germans, our collective pulse quickens as we approach the mythological climax of this cruise. Over the ship's blow horns comes the story of the Loreley—a rocky bluff where a maiden seduced sailors into shipwrecks—followed by a lusty rendition of the Loreley song. Parents point to the bluff, featured in the fairy-tale memory of every German schoolkid.

According to legend, a thousand years of skippers have dreaded the Loreley. Because of the reefs just upstream, many ships never made it beyond the bluff. Sailors (after days on the river) blamed their misfortune on the legendary siren, with her long blonde hair almost covering her body, who'd lured boatloads of drooling sailors to her river bed.

Our boat survives the Loreley and docks in St. Goar, a classic Rhine tourist town. Its massive ruined castle overlooks a half-timbered shopping street and leafy riverside park, busy with sightseeing boats and contented strollers. Sitting like a dead pit bull above St. Goar,

Fast Facts

Biggest cities: Berlin (capital, 3.4 million), Hamburg (1.8 million), Munich (1.5 million)

Size: 138,000 square miles (about half the size of Texas), population 81 million

Locals call it: Deutschland

Currency: Euro

Key date: October 3, 1990, two Germanys become one after the fall of the Berlin Wall (November 1989)

Biggest festivals: Oktoberfest (early autumn, Munich), Christmas markets (late November through Christmas Eve, Nürnberg and elsewhere)

Handy German phrases: *Guten Tag* (hello; **goo**-tehn tahg), *Bitte* (please; **bit**-teh), *Danke* (thank you; **dahn**-keh), *Noch ein Bier!* (Another beer!; nohkh īn beer)

Tourist info: Germany.travel

Of all the Rhine castle ruins to tour, Rheinfels is the mightiest.

Rheinfels Castle—the single best Rhineland ruin to explore—rumbles with ghosts from its hard-fought past.

The Rhine Valley is storybook Germany, a world of legends and medieval castles. Through it all, the quiet, deep-gray power of the river flows as steadily as time itself, a dance floor where ferries, barges, and sightseeing boats do their lumbering do-si-do past fabled and treacherous rocks.

Celebrating Democracy at Berlin's Reichstag

In Berlin, a must-see for any traveler is the Reichstag, the country's parliament building. Topped with a glass cupola that visitors can climb, this building is more than just the meeting place for parliament—it's also a symbol of German democracy.

From 1933 to 1999, this historic building—upon whose rooftop some of the last fighting of World War II occurred—sat a bombed-out and blackened hulk, overlooking the no-man's-land between East and West Berlin. After unification, Germany's government returned from Bonn to Berlin. And, recognizing this building's cultural roots, they renovated it—incorporating modern architectural design and capping it with a glorious glass dome.

This old-meets-new building comes with powerful architectural symbolism. The glass dome is designed for German citizens to climb its long spiral ramp to the very top and literally look down (through a glass ceiling) over the shoulders of their legislators to see what's on their desks. The Germans, who feel they've been manipulated by too many self-serving politicians over the last century, are determined to keep a closer eye on their leaders from now on.

The glassy dome of Berlin's Reichstag welcomes German citizens as well as tourists.

I was in Berlin in 1999 during the week that the renovated Reichstag reopened to the public. That day, I climbed to the top of the dome and found myself surrounded by teary-eyed Germans. Anytime you're surrounded by teary-eyed Germans, something exceptional is going on. It occurred to me that most of these people were old enough to remember the difficult times (either during or after World War II), when their city lay in rubble. For them, the opening of this grand building was the symbolic closing of a terrible chapter in the history of a great nation. No more division. No more communism. No more fascism. They had a united government and were entering a new century with a new capitol filled with hope and optimism.

Castle Day in Bavaria and Tirol

Three of my favorite castles—two famous, one unknown—can be seen in one busy day. If you tackle "Castle Day," you'll visit Germany's Disney-like Neuschwanstein Castle, the more stately Hohenschwangau Castle at its foot, and the much older Ehrenberg Ruins, across the Austrian border in Reutte.

Reutte makes a fine home base. From here, catch the early bus across the border to touristy Füssen, the German town nearest Neuschwanstein. From Füssen, you can walk, pedal a rented bike, or ride a bus a couple of miles to Neuschwanstein.

Neuschwanstein is the greatest of King Ludwig II's fairytale castles. It's one of Europe's most popular attractions, so reserve ahead online (otherwise, arrive by 8 a.m. to buy a ticket). If you choose a combo-ticket, you'll first visit Ludwig's boyhood home, Hohenschwangau Castle, and then the neighboring Neuschwanstein on the hill. If you arrive late, you'll spend a couple of hours in the ticket line and may find all tours booked.

Ludwig's extravagance and Romanticism earned this Bavarian king the title "Mad" King Ludwig...and an early death. After Bavarians complained about the money Ludwig spent on castles, the 40-year-old king was found dead in a lake under suspicious circumstances.

Hohenschwangau Castle, where Ludwig grew up, offers a good look at his life. Like its more famous neighbor, it takes about an hour to tour. Afterward, head up the hill to Ludwig's castle in the air.

Neuschwanstein Castle, which is about as old as the Eiffel Tower, is a textbook example of 19th-century Romanticism. After the Middle Ages ended, people disparagingly named that era "Gothic," or barbarian. Then, all of a sudden, in the 1800s it was hip to be square, and Neo-Gothic became the rage. Throughout Europe, old castles were restored and new ones built—wallpapered with chivalry. King Ludwig II put his medieval fantasy on the hilltop not for defensive reasons, but simply because he liked the view.

The lavish interior, covered with damsels in distress,

Germany's Top Destinations

Berlin ▲▲▲

allow 3-5 days

Vibrant and reunified capital, featuring state-of-the-
art museums, cutting-edge architecture, and trendy
neighborhoods, along with evocative monuments of the Wall
that once divided the city and country

Top Sights

Reichstag Historic parliament building with a modern glass dome
Brandenburg Gate Gateway at the former border of East and West
Memorial to the Murdered Jews of Europe Compelling monument
German History Museum Narrative of the country's tumultuous past
Berlin Wall Memorial Exhibits at the lone surviving stretch of intact Wall
Pergamon and Neues Museums Classical and Egyptian antiquities
Gemäldegalerie Top collection of Old Master European paintings

Nearby

Potsdam Frederick the Great's palace playground
Sachsenhausen Concentration camp museum and memorial

Munich ▲▲▲

2 days

Lively, livable city with a traffic-free center, good museums, Baroque palaces,
stately churches, rollicking beer halls, and sprawling parks

Top Sights

Marienplatz Main square with glockenspiel show
Hofbräuhaus Famous beer hall
Residenz Opulent palace and treasury of Bavarian royalty
Art Museums Alte Pinakothek, Neue Pinakothek, and Pinakothek der Moderne

Nearby

Dachau First Nazi concentration camp, now a museum
Andechs Monastery Monk-brewed beer in bucolic setting

Bavaria ▲▲▲

2-3 days

Alps-straddling region boasting the fairy-tale castles of Neuschwanstein,
Hohenschwangau, and Linderhof (with Ehrenberg across the Austrian
border); inviting villages such as the handy home base **Füssen** and adorable
Oberammergau; and the towering Zugspitze and its high-altitude lifts

Rothenburg and the Romantic Road ▲▲

1-2 days

Well-preserved medieval city with half-timbered buildings, cobbled lanes, and
walkable walls; a popular stop on the Romantic Road scenic route through lovely
countryside and time-passed towns

Rhine Valley ▲▲

2 days

Mighty river steeped in legend, where storybook villages (including charming
home-base towns **Bacharach** and **St. Goar**) cluster under imposing castles, such
as Rheinfels and Marksburg

Mosel Valley ▲▲

1-2 days

Peaceful meandering river lined with tiny wine-loving cobbled towns, such as
handy **Cochem** and quaint **Beilstein,** plus my favorite European castle, Burg Eltz

Baden-Baden and the Black Forest ▲   1-2 days

High-class resort/spa town of **Baden-Baden,** with pampered bath experiences and a grand casino; lively university city of **Freiburg** and cozy village of **Staufen;** and forested countryside rife with healthy hikes, folk museums, and cuckoo clocks

Nürnberg ▲▲   1 day

Old town core and great museums, along with thoughtful reminders of Nazi past and a huge Christmas market

With more time, consider visiting

Dresden Baroque palaces, WWII history, and delightful riverside scene

Erfurt and Wittenberg Martin Luther's stomping grounds

Frankfurt Skyscrapers and modern-day urban Germany

Cologne Riverside city highlighted by spectacular Gothic cathedral

Hamburg Rejuvenated port city with infamous nightlife

Leipzig Bach and Cold War sights in the former East Germany

Trier Roman monuments, including the Porta Nigra gate

dragons, and knights in gleaming armor, is enchanting. (A little knowledge of Wagner's operas goes a long way in bringing these stories to life.) Ludwig had great taste for a mad king. Read up on this political misfit—a poetic hippie king in the realpolitik age of Bismarck. After the tour, climb farther up the hill to Mary's Bridge for the best view of this crazy yet picturesque castle.

This is a busy day. By lunchtime, catch the bus to Reutte and get ready for a completely different castle experience. With picnic and directions in hand, walk 30 minutes (or take a taxi) out of town to the Ehrenberg Castle Ensemble, the brooding ruins of four castles. If Neuschwanstein was the medieval castle dream, Ehrenburg is the medieval castle reality. The 13th-century rock pile provides a super opportunity to let your imagination off its leash.

The impressive castle ensemble (once consisting of four buildings) was built to defend against the Bavarians and to bottle up the strategic Via Claudia trade route, which cut through the Alps as it connected Italy and Germany. For centuries, the castle was the seat of government, which ruled an area called the "judgment of Ehrenberg" (roughly the same as today's district of Reutte). When the emperor came by, he stayed here. In 1604, the ruler moved downtown into more comfortable quarters, and the castle was no longer a palace. After several battles, the castle eventually fell into disrepair, leaving only this evocative shell and a whiff of history.

You can see Ehrenberg's castles reconstructed on Reutte's restaurant walls. Ask at your hotel where you can find a folk evening full of slap-dancing and yodel foolery. A hot, hearty dinner and an evening of Tirolean entertainment

Fanciful castles decorate the foothills of the Alps along the German-Austrian border. King Ludwig's Neuschwanstein is less than a century older than the castle it inspired at Disneyland.

is a fitting way to raise the drawbridge on your memorable "Castle Day."

Getting Naked in Baden-Baden

Since the Roman emperor bathed in the mineral waters of Baden-Baden, this Black Forest town has welcomed those in need of a good soak. In the 19th century, it was Germany's ultimate spa resort, and even today the name Baden-Baden is synonymous with relaxation in a land where the government still pays its overworked citizens to take a little spa time.

It's long been a frustration for me that Americans won't go to a European spa because they're too self-conscious to get naked with a bunch of strangers. For me, enjoying the baths at Friedrichsbad in Baden-Baden is one of Europe's most elegant experiences. If you come here, don't miss out.

My experience kicked off with a weight check—92 kilos. The attendant led me under the industrial-strength shower—a torrential kickoff, pounding my head and shoulders and obliterating the rest of the world. He then gave me slippers and a towel, ushering me into a dry-heat room with fine wooden lounges—slats too hot to sit on without the towel.

Finally, it was time for my massage. I climbed gingerly onto the marble slab and lay belly-up. The masseur held up two mitts and asked, "Hard or soft?" In the spirit of wild abandon, I said "hard," not even certain what that would mean to my skin. I got the coarse, Brillo-Pad scrub-down, but it was still extremely relaxing. Finished with a Teutonic spank, I was sent off into the pools.

Nude, without my glasses, and not speaking the language, I was gawky. On a sliding scale between Mr. Magoo and Woody Allen, I was everywhere, careening between steam rooms and cold plunges.

In the end, it all led to the mixed section. This is where Americans get uptight. The parallel spa facilities intersect, bringing men and women together to share the finest three pools. Here, all are welcome to glide under exquisite domes in perfect silence, like aristocratic swans. Germans are nonchalant, tuned into their bodies and focused on solitary relaxation. Tourists are tentative, trying to be cool, but more aware of their nudity. Really, there's nothing sexy about it. Just vivid life in full flower.

The climax is the cold plunge. I'm not good with cold water—yet I absolutely loved this. You must not wimp out on the cold plunge.

Finally, the attendant escorted me into the quiet room

and asked when I'd like to be awoken. I told him closing time. He swaddled me in hot sheets and a brown blanket and laid me down warm, flat on my back, among 20 hospital-type beds. Only one other bed was occupied; he seemed dead. I stared up at the ceiling and some time later was jolted awake by my own snore.

Leaving, I weighed myself again: 91 kilos. I had shed 2.2 pounds of sweat. Stepping into the cool evening air, I was thankful my hotel was a level two-block stroll away. In my room, I fell in slow motion onto my down comforter, the big pillow puffing around my head like the Flying Nun. Wonderfully naked under my clothes, I could only think, "Ahhhh. Baden-Baden."

Standing at the Top of the World

One of my favorite places to be in Europe is atop the Zugspitze—the highest point in Germany. Standing on this 9,700-foot peak, you can't help but marvel at the thought that you are above everyone else in the entire country—number one out of 82 million. From here, facing south, I feel like a maestro conducting a symphony of snow-capped peaks, as the mighty Alps stretch seemingly forever to the right and left.

The Zugspitze also marks the border between Germany and Austria. There are two separate terraces—Bavarian and Tirolean—connected by a narrow walk that once served as the border station. Before Europe united, you had to show your passport just to walk across the mountaintop. Crossing was a big deal—you'd get your passport stamped at a little blue house and shift your currency from shillings to marks.

Lifts from both countries meet at the top. As if waging an epic battle of alpine engineering, just a few years after the Austrians built a cable car to their Zugspitze station, the Germans drilled through the mountain (in 1931) so that a cogwheel train could deposit nature lovers on a glacier just below their side of the summit.

The Zugspitze marks the border of Germany and Austria. Although Germany's highest peak, it's just a wannabe among Austria's mightier Alps.

Today, whether you ascend from the Austrian or German side, this is one of the few opportunities to straddle the border between two great nations while enjoying an incredible view. Once you're done admiring the mountains, you can head to the restaurant that claims—irrefutably—to be the "highest *Bier-garten* in Deutschland."

Medieval Rothenburg

Thirty years ago, I fell in love with Rothenburg in the rough. At that time, the town still fed a few farm animals within its medieval walls. Today its barns are hotels, its livestock are tourists, and Rothenburg has turned into a medieval theme park.

But Rothenburg is still the best-preserved medieval town in Germany—and possibly all of Europe. Many also consider it a horrible tourist trap. The place is stampeded midday with visiting tour groups, eager to buy faux traditional Christmas ornaments. The town even created its own traditional pastry—the *Schneeball* (a powdered-doughnut-like "snowball"). Yet when I pass through its medieval gates, I feel like a kid who just got a three-day pass for all the rides at Disneyland. I simply love Rothenburg.

In Rothenburg, medieval life comes alive in its cobbled alleys. The ramparts are intact, still walkable, and come complete with arrow slits for notching an imaginary crossbow. The fish tanks next to the water fountains continue to evoke the days when marauding armies would besiege the town, and the townspeople would survive on the grain in its lofts and the trout in its tanks. The monastery garden still has its medicinal herbs. And the Medieval Crime and Punishment Museum shows graphically how people were disciplined back when life was nasty, brutish, and short. Some travelers react with horror; others wish for a gift shop.

But beyond the medieval ambience, it's the local residents who bring the town to life. Hans-Georg, the night watchman, stokes his lamp and walks wide-eyed tourists through the back lanes telling stories of hot oil and great plagues.

In Rothenburg, Germany's best-preserved medieval walled town, you can skip the "snowballs" (*Schneeballen*, a "tradition" kept alive for tourists), but don't miss spending a delightful hour touring with the night watchman.

Spry Klaus, who runs a B&B above his grocery store, takes travelers jogging with him each evening at 7:30. Another B&B owner, Norry, plays in a Dixieland band, loves to jam, and has invented a fascinating hybrid saxophone/trombone called the Norryphone.

At the English Conversation Club, held every Wednesday night at a town pub, locals enjoy a weekly excuse to get together, drink, and practice their fanciest English on each other and on visiting tourists. Once Anneliese, who runs the Friese shop (my favorite souvenir store in town), invited me to join her. So I meandered into the pub through candlelit clouds of smoke and squeezed a three-legged stool up to a table already crowded with family and friends.

Anneliese poured me a glass of wine, then pulled a *Schneeball* from a bag. Raising a cloud of powdered sugar as she poked at the name on the now empty bag, she said, "Friedel is the bakery I explained you about. They make the best *Schneeball*. I like it better than your American doughnut. Every day I eat one. But only at this bakery."

For years, Anneliese has playfully tried to get me to write good things about *Schneeballen*. I put *Schneeballen* (which originated in a hungrier age as a way to get more mileage out of leftover dough) in that category of penitential foods—like lutefisk—whose only purpose is to help younger people remember the suffering of their parents. Nowadays these historic pastries are pitched to the tourists in caramel, chocolate, and other flavors unknown in feudal times.

Shoving a big doughy ball my way, Anneliese said, "You like to eat this?"

I broke off a little chunk, saying, "Only a teeny-weeny *bisschen*."

After I left the pub for the night, I passed Hans-Georg, the night watchman dressed in medieval garb, finishing up his spiel in the town square with his group: "Now I must call the 'all's well.' You, my friends, should hurry home. Bed is the best place for good people at this hour."

Heading toward my hotel, I heard him calling, "All's well!"

More German Experiences

My Favorite Castle: Nestled in an enchanted forest just above the Mosel River, Burg Eltz is my favorite castle in all of Europe. The castle avoided wars and was never destroyed, remaining in the Eltz family for more than eight centuries. The current owner, an elderly countess who enjoys flowers, always has grand arrangements adorning the public rooms.

The castle is furnished throughout basically as it was 500 years ago. That's unusual in castles. For your best approach, start from the Moselkern train station on foot. After hiking for more than an hour through an ancient forest where you'd expect Friar Tuck or Martin Luther to be hiding out, the castle of your fantasies suddenly appears.

Paying Homage in Berlin: Germany's capital city is speckled with touching memorials that honor victims of past sins. The Memorial to the Murdered Jews of Europe, consisting of 2,711 gravestone-like pillars, was the first formal, government-sponsored Holocaust memorial. Using the word "murdered" in the title was intentional, a sign that Germany, as a nation, was officially admitting to a crime. The Monument to the Murdered Sinti and Roma of Europe remembers the roughly 500,000 Sinti and Roma (Gypsy) victims of the Holocaust. The Memorial to Politicians Who Opposed Hitler is a simple row of slate slabs dedicated to the 96 members of the Reichstag who were persecuted and murdered because they didn't agree with Chancellor Hitler. One place with little to see is the site of the bunker where Hitler committed suicide in 1945. It's just a rough parking lot with an information plaque.

Simple, Unspoiled Erfurt: Long ago I gave up looking for an untouristy, half-timbered medieval German town. But recently, I stumbled upon it in the sleepy town of Erfurt. The capital of the German region of Thuringia, Erfurt has history swinging from its eaves. It's the rare city in the center of Germany that emerged relatively unscathed from World War II, after which it became stuck in the strange cocoon of East German communism for half a century. Erfurt is most notable as the place where Martin Luther studied and became a monk, essentially planting the seeds from which grew the Protestant Reformation in 1517. Without the pivotal accomplishments

LEFT Burg Eltz, on the Mosel River, is my favorite castle to tour in Germany.

CENTER The Memorial to Politicians Who Opposed Hitler in Berlin is a reminder of the hell Germany lived through in the 1930s and 1940s.

RIGHT For Luther fans, Erfurt is a must-see.

of the Reformation, the Bible would still be read in Latin and interpreted for us by priests. For me, as a Lutheran, coming to Erfurt is a bit like a Catholic going to Rome.

CULTURE AND TRADITIONS: EVERYTHING'S SO...GERMAN

Beer and *Biergartens*

One of the most satisfying sounds you'll hear in Germany is a big *whop!* as they tap a classic old wooden keg of beer. Hearing this, every German knows they're in for a good, fresh mug.

Germans are serious about their beer. It's regulated by the Reinheitsgebot (Purity Decree) of 1516—the oldest food and beverage law in the world—which dictates that only four ingredients may be used: malt, yeast, hops, and water. There are four main types of Germanic beers: pale lager (*helles Bier*), dark beer (*dunkles Bier*), white/wheat beer (*Weissbier or Weizenbier*), and pilsner.

The best place to sample Germanic beer culture is at a *Biergarten*, where long skinny tables stretch beneath shady chestnut trees. This is where Germans meet up with friends and family, relax, and maybe grab a bite to eat. Picnickers can bring their own food or buy it from a self-service stand, then sit at any table without a tablecloth. Covered tables are reserved for people who are being served.

My favorite *Biergarten* (and German beer) is an hour's drive outside Munich at the Andechs Monastery. The stately church stands as it has for centuries, topping a hill at the foot of the Alps. Its Baroque interior—and its beer hall—both stirs the soul and stokes the appetite. The hearty meals come in medieval proportions. Whenever I come here, I get a knuckle of pork, spiral-cut radishes, sauerkraut, a huge pretzel, and a liter of beer (called *eine Mass*, though I'd call it "ein pitcher"). What's more Bavar-ian than that? Once I asked my Ger-man friend if they sell half-liters of beer, to which he replied, "This is a *Biergarten*, not a kindergarten!"

Sausage, Sausage Everywhere

Unless you're a vegetarian, it's hard to leave Germany without sampling sausage (*Wurst*). Options go far beyond the hometown hot dog. There are literally hundreds of regional variations, including *Nürnberger* (short, spicy, the size of your little finger, and served three in a bun); *Currywurst* (grilled, sliced up, and drenched with a curry-infused tomato sauce); and *Weisswurst* ("white" veal sausage that's boiled, peeled, and eaten with sweet mustard and a fresh soft pretzel).

Most fast-food restaurants (*Schnell Imbiss*) offer sausage on the menu, but I like to go local at a sausage stand (*Würstchenbude*). In Berlin, I look for human hot dog stands. These hot-dog hawkers don an ingenious harness that hangs off the body, allowing them to cook and serve *Wurst* on the fly.

Munich's Oktoberfest

The 1810 marriage reception of King Ludwig I (the grandfather of "Mad" King Ludwig II) was such a success that it turned into an annual bash. These days, Munich's Oktoberfest lasts just over two weeks—from late September into early October. Every night, eight huge beer tents fill with thousands of people eager to show off their stein-hoisting skills. A million gallons of beer later, they roast the last ox. If you plan to come, reserve a room early (Oktoberfest.de).

Christmas Markets

German towns big and small have been lighting up with Christmas markets (*Christkindlesmarkt*) each December for centuries. One of the biggest is Nürnberg's market, with 200 wooden stalls selling handicrafts from local artisans. A traditional center for toy-making in Germany, Nürnberg offers up market ambience that's classier than your average crafts fair, with no canned music, fake greenery, or plastic kitsch. As far back as 1610, a proclamation warned that "indecent joke articles would be confiscated."

Christmas markets are more than a shopping spree; they're places to enjoy a genuinely homey atmosphere. You'll wrap your mittens around a mug of hot-spiced wine while carolers sing in the background. Because a throwaway cup would ruin the experience, you'll pay a deposit for a nicely decorated ceramic mug. You can either return the mug or keep it as a collectible, as each year there's a different model.

Fast, Dependable Trains

At 12:14, I settle into my seat on the luxurious German bullet train, and at 12:16, we glide out of the station. In no time, I'm rocketing toward my next destination. German trains are as slick as can be—clean, modern, comfortable, and on time. ICE trains are the country's fastest, zipping from city to city up to 200 miles per hour. IC and EC trains are slower, only relatively—up to 125 miles per hour. Inexpensive regional trains are substantially slower, but can help stretch a budget.

Fast trains allow you to maximize sightseeing. For instance, on an ICE train, you can get from Munich to Nürnberg in just one hour or from Frankfurt to Cologne in less than 90 minutes. German trains are so quiet and efficient that I almost miss the old clackity-clackity rhythm

of the rails. It's been replaced by a nearly silent swoosh, as futuristic trains cut like bullets through the green and tidy countryside.

Germany Travel Resources from Rick Steves

Guidebooks
Check out Rick's guidebooks covering all of Germany; Berlin; and Munich & Salzburg; plus his German phrase book

Audio Europe
Download Rick's free Audio Europe app, with self-guided audio tours, including walks through Berlin, Munich, Rothenburg, and a best of the Rhine tour

TV Shows
The quintessence of Germany with Rick as your host, viewable on public television and at RickSteves.com. Episodes cover Berlin, Munich and the Alps, Dresden and Leipzig, Frankfurt and Nürnberg, Hamburg and the Luther Trail, Cologne and the Black Forest, and Rothenburg and the Rhine River; plus look for the TV special, *Luther and the Reformation*

Organized Tours
Small group tours, with itineraries planned by Rick: Best of Germany in 12 Days; Germany, Austria & Switzerland in 14 Days; Berlin, Prague & Vienna in 12 Days; Munich, Salzburg & Vienna in 8 Days; My Way: Alpine Europe in 12 Days; Best of Europe in 14 or 21 Days (including stops in Germany)

For more on all of these resources, visit RickSteves.com. For Germany trip-planning tips, see www.ricksteves.com/europe/germany.

Switzerland

Mountainous, efficient Switzerland is one of Europe's most appealing destinations. Wedged neatly between Germany, Austria, France, and Italy, Switzerland borrows what's best from its neighbors—and adds a healthy dose of chocolate, cowbells, and cable cars. Fiercely independent and decidedly high-tech, the Swiss stubbornly hold on to their quaint traditions, too.

Despite the country's small size, Switzerland's regions maintain their distinct cultural differences, partly because historically the wild geography has kept people apart. Switzerland has four official languages: German, French, Italian, and Romansh. And yet, regardless of which language is spoken, the entire country is unmistakably Swiss. Everywhere you go, you'll notice a dedication to order and organization, right down to the precision stacking of a woodpile.

Switzerland has more than its share of cosmopolitan cities (Zürich, Luzern, Bern, Lausanne, Lugano), but let's face it—travelers don't flock to Switzerland for its cities. The Alps are the premier destination. Alpine villages (such as Gimmelwald) give you a taste of rural Switzerland, and are the perfect base for riding lifts to dramatic alpine panoramas and taking unforgettably scenic hikes.

FAVORITE SIGHTS AND MEMORABLE EXPERIENCES IN SWITZERLAND

The Swiss Alps in Your Lap

When I say I'm planning to go to Gimmelwald, Swiss people assume I mean Grindelwald, the famous resort in the next valley. When assured that Gimmelwald is my target, they lean forward, widen their eyes, and—with their singsongy Swiss-German accent—ask, "Und how do you know about Gimmelvald?"

This traffic-free village, hanging nonchalantly on the edge of a cliff high above the Lauterbrunnen Valley, has more cow troughs than mailboxes. Here, white-bearded old men smoke hand-carved pipes, and blond-braided children play "barn" instead of "house." Big stones sit like heavy checkers on old rooftops, awaiting nature's next move. While these stones protect the shingles from violent winter winds, in summer it's so quiet you can hear the cows ripping tufts of grass. There's nothing but air between Gimmelwald and the rock face of the nearby Jungfrau Mountain. Small avalanches across the valley look and sound like distant waterfalls. Kick a soccer ball wrong and it ends up a mile below, on the valley floor.

Gimmelwald was never developed like neighboring towns because its residents made sure it got rated an "avalanche zone," and developers couldn't get building permits. Consequently, while neighboring villages are dominated by

High in the Swiss Alps, farmer Peter cuts hay to feed his cows, gathers it on a tarp *(left)*, and rides his bovine salad down the steep slopes, as if on a barge, to his barn in the humble village of Gimmelwald *(right)*.

condos owned by big-city folks who come by only for vacations, Gimmelwald is still inhabited by locals—about 120 in all—and its traditions survive.

Gimmelwald is a poor town whose traditional economy depends on government subsidies for survival. Each year, its citizens systematically harvest the steep hillside outside their windows. Entire families cut and gather every inch of hay. After harvesting what the scythe can reach, they pull hay from nooks and crannies by hand. Half a day is spent harvesting what a machine could cut in two minutes on a flat field. But this is how the farmers of Gimmelwald have made their living forever—lovingly cutting the hay, to feed the cows, to make the cheese, to feed us people.

From Gimmelwald, a modern gondola goes up the nearly 10,000-foot-high peak of the Schilthorn. For the most memorable breakfast around, I ride the early-morning gondola up to the summit and its solar-powered revolving restaurant. There, I sip my coffee slowly to enjoy an entire panoramic rotation of the Eiger, Mönch, and Jungfrau mountains.

Outside, I watch hang gliders methodically set up and jump into airborne ecstasy. It's possible to hike straight down from the summit, but the first gondola station below the peak, Birg, is the best starting point for high-country hikes. Two minutes from the Birg station and I'm completely alone, surrounded by a harsh and unforgiving alpine world. A black ballet of rocks is accompanied by cowbells and a distant river. Wisps of clouds are exclamation points. After a steep descent, I step out of the forest at the top end of the village I call home. Walking over a pastel carpet of gold clover, bellflowers, and daisies, I'm surrounded butterflies and cheered on by a rant chorus of grasshoppers, bees, crickets.

Fast Facts

Biggest cities: Zürich (377,000), Geneva (188,000), Basel (165,000), Bern (capital, 126,000)

Size: 16,000 square miles (almost twice the size of New Jersey), population 8 million

Locals call it: Officially it's the Confoederatio Helvetica (Latin for Swiss Confederation); also known as Die Schweiz (German), Suisse (French), Svizzera (Italian), and Svizra (Romansh)

Currency: Swiss franc

Languages: Swiss German (most of Switzerland), French (to the west), Italian (to the south), Romansh (southeastern mountains)

Key date: 1815, Switzerland's borders (and its neutrality) are established at the Congress of Vienna

Biggest festival: Fasnacht pre-Lenten carnival (February/March, countrywide but biggest in Basel, Bern, and Luzern)

Mountain peaks exceeding 10,000 feet: 437

Handy Swiss-German phrases: *Grüezi* (hello; **grit**-see), *Merci* (thank you; **mehr**-see), *Uf Widerluege* (goodbye; oof **vee**-dehr-loo-eh-geh), *Meh schoggi, bitte* (More chocolate, please; meh **shoh**-chih **bit**-teh)

Tourist info: MySwitzerland.com

Switzerland's Top Destinations

Berner Oberland ▲▲▲   allow 2-3 days

High-mountain region popular for its characteristic villages and scenic hikes, lifts, and train rides, in the shadow of the Eiger, Mönch, and Jungfrau peaks

Top Sights

Gimmelwald Time-warp village overlooking Lauterbrunnen Valley
Schilthornbahn Cable car soaring to 9,748-foot Schilthorn peak
Jungfraubahn Train to 11,333-foot Jungfraujoch saddle, with snow activities
Männlichen to Kleine Scheidegg Hike Easy, mostly downhill hike with Eiger views

Bern ▲▲▲   1 day

Cozy Swiss capital, lassoed by a meandering river and embedded with shopping arcades, fine museums, and a Gothic cathedral

Appenzell ▲▲   1 day

Traditional region known for pastoral scenery, appealing folk museums, remarkably fragrant cheese, and the cliffs of Ebenalp

Lake Geneva and French Switzerland ▲▲   1-2 days

Switzerland's best castle, lakeside Château de Chillon; the cute cheese-making village of **Gruyères;** and the steeply situated, urbane, *très* French-speaking city of **Lausanne**

Luzern ▲▲   1 day

Thriving city on a mountain-ringed lake, with historic wooden bridges and well-presented museums; Golden Pass scenic rail journey to Montreux starts here

Zürich ▲▲   1 day

Another tidy city on a pretty lake, bustling with Swiss commerce, upscale shops, and an atmospheric old town

The finish line is a bench that sits at the high end of Gimmelwald—one of my "savor Europe" depots. From my perch, I survey the village. Chocolate log cabins are buttressed by a winter's supply of firewood lovingly stacked all the way to the eaves. Grassy fields radiate a vibrant green, as if plugged into the sun. In the Alps, nature and civilization mix it up comfortably, as if man and mountain shared the same crib.

River Swimming in Bern

It's a hot August day, and the waterfront park along the Aare River, in Switzerland's capital city of Bern, is packed with wet and happy people. They're hiking upstream in swimsuits just to float back into town. I join them—marveling at how

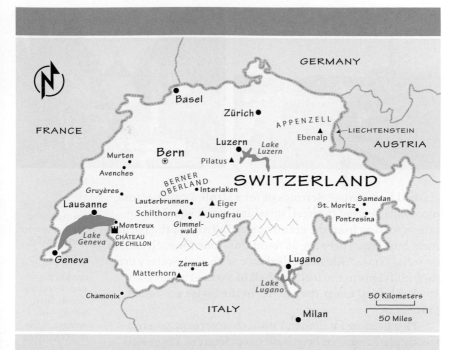

Lugano ▲   1 day

Leading city of Italian-speaking Switzerland, with Mediterranean feel; starting point for Bernina Express bus-and-train journey through the Swiss Alps and Italy, passing jaw-dropping mountains, glaciers, and waterfalls

With more time, consider visiting

Murten Walled village, with nearby Roman ruins and museum in **Avenches**
Zermatt Glitzy ski resort with old-fashioned core at the foot of the Matterhorn
Pontresina, Samedan, and St. Moritz Romansh-speaking mountain resort area

this exercise brings out the silly in a people who are generally anything but.

Every hundred yards, concrete steps lead into the swift-flowing river, which looks glacial blue, but is surprisingly warm. Leaping in, I'm immediately caught up in the racing current and propelled toward the grand city center, along with other carefree swimmers and a flotilla of rubber rafts.

Nearing downtown, I stroke over to snare a metal stair railing—I'm nervous that I'll miss the last one and rush toward the city's scary weir and, it seems, oblivion. Hanging onto the railing with me is a tanned and wiry grandmother and several giddy children, clearly enjoying an afternoon going up and down the river.

I crawl out, dry off, and put on the clothes that I'd

stashed here earlier. Setting out for a stroll, I come across more kids beating the heat, splashing in the squirt fountains spurting from the granite plaza in front of the parliament building. There are 26 fountains—one for each canton, or Swiss "state." Kids happily dance with each watery eruption, oblivious to the fact that half of Switzerland's gold stock is buried under the square, in the Swiss version of Fort Knox.

That evening for dinner, I walk downstream, where a trendy restaurant has been built over the river. I'm seated over see-through floorboards that expose the water where my tasty local trout might have been caught. The noisy roar of the rushing river masks the conversations of patrons sipping beer on open-air sofas.

Bern's old town, packed into a tight bend in the river, is a joy to explore on foot. After dinner, I amble through the lanes lined with miles of shopping arcades. This is my kind of shopping town: Prices are so high, there's no danger of buying. The local slang for the corridor under these arcades is *"Rohr"* (German for pipe). To stroll through the town is to go *"rohren"* (piping).

As the city grew over the centuries, its successive walls and moats were torn down, providing vast, people-friendly swaths of land. Today these elongated "squares" are popular for markets and outdoor cafés—the top places to be seen in the evening. I come upon an open-air performance by a jazz band whose lead instrument is a long alphorn, an improbable meeting of tradition and modernity.

Although I've said it's almost criminal to spend a sunny Swiss day anywhere but high in the Alps, the cities of Switzerland can be a delight, and I'd make an exception for urban but easygoing Bern.

Most people come to Switzerland for the mountains, but its cities are worth visiting, too. Located within a tight bend in the Aare River, the capital, Bern, with its fine arcades, is the most charming.

The most I can handle in alpine thrills is a *via ferrata*. Hitched to the cable with carabiners, I worked my way along the cliff high above the Lauterbrunnen Valley floor.

Scared Silly on the *Via Ferrata*

I'm careful not to list activities in my guidebooks that may encourage a traveler to take a risk on something that's dangerous. So when friends in the Lauterbrunnen Valley started talking about a great new outdoor experience called a *via ferrata*—a mountain route with fixed cables—I had to check it out myself.

I enlisted my B&B host, Olle, to join me. We put on helmets and mountaineering harnesses, clipped our carabiners into the first stretch of the 1.5-mile-long cable, and set off with a local guide. My hike on the "iron way" from Mürren to Gimmelwald proved to be the highlight of my entire trip.

The route took us along the very side of the cliff, like tiny window washers on a geologic skyscraper. About half of the route is easily walked, and I was lulled into wondering, what's the big deal? But for several hundred yards, the path literally hangs out over...nothing. The "trail" ahead of me was a series of steel rebar spikes jutting out from the side of the mountain. The cable, carabiner, and harness were there in case I passed out. For me, physically, this was the max. I was almost numb with fear.

At some points, ladders drilled vertically into the cliff made it easier (in my case, possible) to scramble up or down. There were three thrilling canyon crossings—by zipline, on a single high wire (with steadying wires for each hand), and he "iron way," finished with a terrifying hanging bridge.

After one particularly harrowing crossing—gingerly taking one rebar step after another—I said to the guide, "OK, now it gets easier?" And he said, "No. Now comes *die Hammer Ecke* (Hammer Corner)!" For about 500 feet, we crept across a perfectly vertical cliff face—feet gingerly gripping rebar loops, cold and raw hands on the cable, tiny cows and a rushing river 2,000 feet below me, a rock face rocketing directly above me—as my follow-the-cable path bent out of sight.

Three hours after we had clipped in, we finally reached the end. Olle and I beamed, exhilarated that we had survived our little personal test. We hugged our guide like a full-body high-five, knowing this was the thrill of a lifetime. For the next several nights, though, I awoke in the wee hours, clutching my mattress.

More Swiss Experiences

Switzerland's Best Castle: I like to imagine myself as a member of the aristocracy that inhabited Château de Chillon in the Middle Ages. The castle is set wistfully at the edge of Lake Geneva on the outskirts of Montreux. Remarkably well preserved, it has never been damaged or destroyed—it's always been inhabited and maintained. Because it's built on a rocky island, Château de Chillon has a uniquely higgledy-piggledy shape that combines a stout fortress and dank prison (on the land side) with a visually splendid residence (on the lake side). Over the centuries, the romantic castle has inspired a multitude of writers—Lord Byron, Victor Hugo, Charles Dickens, Goethe, Ernest Hemingway. (You can still see where Byron scratched his name into a column.) All the sumptuous detail indoors can't compare with what's outside, though. At the end of my visit, I curl up on a windowsill to enjoy lake views fit for a king.

Riding High: Switzerland's best attraction might just be hiding between the cities and the villages. In this land of rugged mountains and picture-perfect farms—perhaps more

LEFT Château de Chillon

RIGHT Scenic train riding in Switzerland

than anywhere else in Europe—the journey is the destination. Several trains, many with special panoramic cars, run picturesque routes through the country's prettiest places. The Glacier Express, which traverses southern Switzerland, gets my vote for the most scenic of these rides. Designed to maximize sightseeing thrills, the route is a masterpiece of railway engineering, with the train running through 91 tunnels and crossing 291 bridges. A toothed rack between the tracks helps the hardworking train drag itself up steep gradients, and these same teeth help slow the train on downhill sections. Using powerful snowplow engines to keep the track open through the snowy winter, the Glacier Express runs year-round.

CULTURE AND TRADITIONS: EVERYTHING'S SO...SWISS

Cheese Cuisine

The Swiss eat about 150,000 tons of cheese per year. After a few days of cheese plates for breakfast, cheese sandwiches for lunch, and cheese specialties for dinner, even the biggest cheese lovers might find they need a dairy detox.

There are two kinds of Swiss restaurants—with and without cooked cheese. The Swiss eat out at a "cooked cheese" restaurant because they don't want to perfume their houses with the smell. Some cheese dishes are meant for sharing, like raclette and fondue. For raclette, cheese is slowly melted on a special grill; as the cheese softens, diners scrape a chunk off and eat it with potatoes, pickled onions, and gherkins. Fondue is Switzerland's best-known cheese dish, made with Emmentaler or Gruyère melted with white wine, garlic, nutmeg, and cherry schnapps. Eating it is a

From a steamy fondue treat *(left)* to cheering the cows along on the day they head up to the high meadows *(right)*, Switzerland's traditions are alive, well, and accessible for travelers.

communal affair, with everyone dipping cubes of bread into the melted cheese with a long fork. A Swiss friend told me: "When we Swiss plan a cozy party we add '*FIGUGEGL*' to the invitation. It's pronounced like a word: fee-**goo**-geck-ul. This stands for '*Fondu isch guet und git e gueti Luune*' (Fondue is good and gives a good mood). When you read this, you know a good time is planned."

More Cowbells

Swiss dairy farming in the mountains isn't lucrative, but a lifestyle chosen to keep tradition alive. Rather than lose their children to the cities, Swiss farmers have the opposite problem: Kids argue about who gets to take over the family herd.

In summer, farmers strap elaborate ceremonial bells on their cows and take them up to huts at high elevations, where they stay for about 100 days. When the cows arrive at their summer home, the bells are hung under the eaves.

Hired hands get up at dawn to milk the cows, take them to pasture, and then milk the cows again in the evening. It's too difficult to transport the milk down to the village, so it is made into treasured "Alp cheese" right on the mountain. The character of each wheel of cheese is shaped by the herbs and flowers munched by the cows, and locals claim they can tell which valley the cows grazed in by the taste.

Meanwhile, the farmer follows the seasons up into the mountains, making hay while the sun shines and storing it above the huts. In late summer, the cows start down from the high pastures, moving from hut to hut, eating the hay prepared for them. The day the cows return to their home village is an impromptu festival, with the farmers parading their animals through town to their winter barn.

Money, Money, Money

A graffito in Zürich jokes: "Zürich = *zu reich, zu ruhig*" (too rich, too quiet). In a country with a reputation for being one of Europe's most expensive, Zürich is the major hub of

Dining on a Budget

Grocery stores and cafeterias are a godsend for thrifty travelers in pricey Switzerland. Larger grocery stores often have a great selection of prepared foods and picnic fixings—perfect for al fresco dining. In most big cities, major department stores have a self-service eatery with lush salad bars, tasty entrées, and fresh-squeezed juices. Swiss hostels usually offer a fine four-course dinner that's often open to nonguests—just call first to reserve a spot.

Quench your thirst at Switzerland's free drinking fountains—with fresh, mountain-chilled water—in squares and other central points around cities and towns. Fill your bottle from the spout of any well-maintained public fountain unless you see a *kein Trinkwasser* ("not drinking water") sign.

international banking and finance. A huge part of the Swiss economy is based on providing a safe and secret place for wealthy people from around the world to stash their money. (When bank fees are figured in, tax cheats and white-collar crooks actually get negative interest to keep their money anonymously in Switzerland.) Switzerland sticks to its own Swiss franc, partly because adopting the euro currency would require complying with European Union regulations, putting an end to the country's lucrative secrecy.

Switzerland Travel Resources from Rick Steves

Guidebooks
Check out Rick's guidebook covering all of Switzerland; plus his 3-in-1 French, Italian & German phrase book

TV Shows
The quintessence of Switzerland with Rick as your host, viewable on public television and at RickSteves.com. Episodes cover the Alps, Luzern, Lausanne, Bern, and Zürich

Organized Tours
Small group tours, with itineraries planned by Rick: Best of Switzerland in 12 Days; Germany, Austria & Switzerland in 14 Days; My Way: Alpine Europe in 12 Days; Best of Europe in 14 or 21 Days (including a stop in Switzerland)

For more on all of these resources, visit RickSteves.com. For Switzerland trip-planning tips, see www.ricksteves.com/europe/switzerland.

Austria

Austria offers gorgeous alpine scenery, great museums, cobbled quaintness, and decadent pastry. Once the dynastic home of the Habsburg Empire (one of Europe's grandest), Austria is content to bask in good living and its opulent past. The Habsburgs built a vast kingdom of more than 50 million people by making love, not war—having lots of children and strategically marrying them into the other royal houses of Europe.

Today, this small, landlocked country clings to its storied past more than any other nation in Europe. The waltz is still the rage. Music has long been a key part of Austria's heritage. The giants of classical music—Haydn, Mozart, Beethoven—were born here or moved here to write and perform their masterpieces. Music lovers flock to Salzburg every summer to attend its popular festival. Vienna has the much-loved

The gardens of Schönbrunn Palace, just outside Vienna, are made for endless wandering.

Opera House and Boys' Choir. But traditional folk music is also part of the Austrian soul. The world's best-loved Christmas carol, "Silent Night," was written by two Austrians with just a guitar for accompaniment. And don't be surprised if you hear yodeling for someone's birthday.

The country is much more than its famous cities of Vienna and Salzburg. Awash with mountains and waterfalls, Austria is sprinkled with small towns (such as Hallstatt), ruined castles (Ehrenberg), and tucked-away farms (everywhere).

Austrians are relaxed, gregarious people who love hiking in the outdoors as much as enjoying a good cup of coffee in a café. With one of Europe's longest life spans and shortest work weeks, they specialize in *Gemütlichkeit*—meaning a warm, cozy, focus-on-the-moment feeling.

It must be nice to be past your prime—no longer troubled by being powerful, able to kick back and celebrate life, whether engulfed in mountain beauty or bathed in lavish high culture.

Fast Facts

Biggest cities: Vienna (capital, 1.8 million), Graz (275,000), Linz (200,000), Salzburg (148,000)

Size: 32,400 square miles (about the size of South Carolina), population 8.2 million

Locals call it: Österreich ("Eastern Realm")

Currency: Euro

Key date: June 28, 1914, Archduke Franz Ferdinand of Austria is assassinated, setting off World War I

Language: German, with many words (especially for food) exclusive to Austria

Biggest festival: Salzburg Festival (late July and August, classical music)

Handy German phrases: *Grüss Gott* (Austrian version of hello, "May God greet you"; grews goht), *Bitte* (please; **bit**-teh), *Danke* (thank you; **dahn**-keh)

Tourist info: Austria.info

FAVORITE SIGHTS AND MEMORABLE EXPERIENCES IN AUSTRIA

Lovely, Lovable Hallstatt

When I think of my favorite towns in Europe, I'll take the offbeat places, where creaky locals walk gingerly on creaky floorboards, and where each balcony sports a one-of-a-kind flowerbox. The tiny town of Hallstatt, positioned picture-perfectly on the shore of Lake Hallstatt, is just such a place.

Hallstatt, a two-hour train ride east of Salzburg, is the pride and joy of the Salzkammergut Lake District. It's a gentle land—idyllic and majestic—where lakes and mountains are shuffled sloppily together...the perfect place to commune with nature, Austrian-style. Even just arriving at Hallstatt is fun—from the train station, people take a shuttle boat across a lake to get to town. It's rare that a place's charm will get me out of bed early, but there's something about the glassy waters of Lake Hallstatt viewed from the high end of town: The church spire is mirrored in the tranquil water, and then the shuttle boat slices through the reflection—like a knife putting a swirl in the icing on a big cake.

Bullied onto its lakeside ledge by a selfish mountain, Hallstatt seems tinier than it is. Its pint-size square is surrounded by ivy-covered guesthouses and cobbled lanes. It's a toy town, tourable on foot in about 10 minutes. But the ledge couldn't hold Hallstatt forever, and many of its buildings climb the mountainside. Still, land is limited—so limited that there's not enough room for the dead. Remains evicted from the cemetery are stacked neatly in an eerie chapel of decorated bones. Each skull has been carefully named, dated, and decorated. The men's skulls are painted with ivy, and the women's with roses.

Nearly three thousand years ago, this area was the major salt producer of Europe, when salt—a natural preservative for food—was in great demand. The economic and cultural boom put Hallstatt on the map back in Flintstone times. A humble museum next to the tourist office shows off Hallstatt's salty past. For a better look, I took a guided tour of what's said to be the world's oldest salt mine, located a thrilling funicular ride above downtown Hallstatt. Dressed up in an old miner's outfit, I walked through a tunnel dug in 1719 and into the mountain where the salt was mined, explored several caverns, and screamed down a long wooden chute while praying for no splinters.

These days, it can be a challenge to find vivid cultural traditions that survive in well-discovered places like Hallstatt. But on a recent visit, as the sun rose late over the towering Alps, my friend, who runs a restaurant in town, took me for a spin in his classic boat. It's a *Fuhr*, a centuries-old

Austria's Top Destinations

Vienna ▲▲▲   allow 2-4 days

Genteel and worldly capital city, brimming with a rich
Habsburg heritage (spectacular palaces and top-notch art
museums), grand classical music, a refined café tradition, and
convivial wine gardens

Top Sights

St. Stephen's Cathedral Enormous, historic Gothic cathedral
Hofburg Former winter palace of Habsburg emperors, with a treasury of crown jewels
Schönbrunn Palace Spectacular summer residence, with manicured gardens
Kunsthistorisches Museum Exhibit of Habsburgs' collection of European masters
Vienna Opera Internationally renowned opera house

Salzburg ▲▲▲   2 days

Musical mecca huddled under a dramatic castle, with an old town full of winding
lanes, Baroque churches, Mozart landmarks, and *Sound of Music* kitsch

Salzkammergut ▲▲   1-2 days

Scenic land of lakes and forested mountains, starring the dramatically situated,
picturesque village of **Hallstatt**

Danube Valley ▲   1-2 days

Romantic, bikeable valley dotted with ruined castles, offset by the glorious Melk
Abbey and poignant Mauthausen concentration camp memorial

Tirol ▲   1-2 days

Austria's mountain-sports region encompasses view-rich **Innsbruck** and quaint
Hall; farther west, **Reutte** is a good castle home-base

boat design, which was made wide and flat for shipping heavy bushels of locally mined salt across shallow waters. Lunging rhythmically on the single oar, he said, "An hour on the lake is for me like a day of vacation." I asked about the oarlock, which looked like a skinny dog-chew doughnut, and he told me, "It's made from the gut of a bull—not of a cow, but a bull."

Returning to the weathered timber boathouse, we passed a teenage boy with a wooden club systematically grabbing trout from the fishermen's pen and killing them one by one with a stern whack to the noggin. Another man carried them to the tiny fishery to be gutted by a guy who, 40 years ago, did the stern whacking. A cat waited outside the door, confident his breakfast would be a good one. And restaurateurs and homemakers alike—their dining rooms decorated with trophies of big ones that didn't get away—lined up to buy fresh trout to feed the hungry tourists, or a good fish to cook for a special friend.

Traditions are embattled everywhere by the modern world, yet they manage to survive. Despite tourism—and sometimes thanks to tourism—traditional Europe hangs in there. So when I want to cloak myself in *Gemütlichkeit*, flowers, and cobblestones, I visit Hallstatt—where, when friends invite you to visit, they say, "Please come by. I'll cook you a good fish."

Toasting Vienna's Love of Life

If any European capital knows how to enjoy life, it's Vienna. Compared to most modern urban centers, the pace of life here is leisurely. Chatting with friends at a wine garden is not a special event but a regular, frequent occurrence.

For many Viennese, the living room is down the street at the neighborhood coffeehouse, which offers fresh pastries,

From rich chocolate cakes to cozy wine gardens, it's hard not to get caught up in the good life when visiting Austria.

light lunches, a wide selection of newspapers, and a "take all the time you want" ambience (in spite of famously grumpy waiters). One of my ritual stops is at Café Hawelka. Draped in its circa-1900 decor, this smoke-and-coffee-stained café seems frozen in time, with paintings by struggling artists (who couldn't pay for coffee), velvet couches, and a phone that rings for regulars. I could be sitting in a chair that had once been occupied by Trotsky, Hitler, Stalin, Freud, or any number of historical figures who rattled around Vienna 100 years ago. Savoring a

Fast Food, Austrian-Style

In Austria, you're never far from a *Würstelstand* (sausage stand). Most bakeries sell small, cheap sandwiches; look for *Leberkäsesemmel* (roll filled with Austrian meatloaf) as well as *Schnitzelsemmel* (schnitzel sandwich). *Stehcafés* (food counters) usually offer open-face finger sandwiches (*belegte Brote*) with a wide array of toppings. For a quick bite, have a deli make you a *Wurstsemmel*—a basic sausage sandwich.

Buchtel (a marmalade-filled doughnut), I ponder how Vienna was a place of intellectual tumult at the end of World War I, as Europe's family-run empires crumbled.

Another one of my Vienna rituals is to pop into Demel, the ultimate Viennese chocolate shop and bakery. It's filled with Art Nouveau boxes of choco-dreams come true: *Kandierte Veilchen* (candied violet petals), *Katzenzungen* (chocolate shaped like "cats' tongues"), and an impressive cancan of cakes—including the Sacher torte, a local specialty. Apart from its apricot filling, the Sacher-torte recipe seems pretty simple...chocolate on chocolate. Fancy shops like Demel boast "K.u.K." on their signs, meaning good enough for the "König und Kaiser"—king and emperor (same guy). Easily the saddest thing I witnessed one summer was when, promptly at closing time, all the unsold cakes and pies on Demel's luxurious shelves were unceremoniously dumped into big plastic garbage bags.

For another royally good experience, I head to Vienna's wine gardens—the *Heurigen*. Clustered in foothills at the city's doorstep, mostly in the legendary Vienna Woods, wine-garden restaurants feature cold-cut buffets paired with fine Austrian wines in an old-village atmosphere with strolling musicians. If I'm in town during fall, I try the *Sturm*, the semifermented new wine made in the fall from the season's first grape harvest. Of the many wine-garden suburbs, I like untouristy Nussdorf.

No matter where I turn in this pleasant city, it's clear that culture is king, and locals are experts at celebrating the art of good living. Here's to Vienna: *Prost!* Cheers!

Alpine Escapes

Even those who know a Rocky Mountain high find something special about the Alps. It's exhilarating to hike on the hilly, wooded trails, passing happy yodelers, sturdy grannies, and dirndled moms with apple-cheeked kids.

In western Austria, the same mountains that put Innsbruck on the vacation map surround nearby Hall. For a lazy look at life in the high Alps around these towns, drive up to 5,000-foot Hinterhornalm and walk to a remote working farm.

Begin your ascent in Gnadenwald, a chalet-filled village sandwiched between Hall and its Alps. Pay at the toll hut, then wind your way upward, marveling at the crazy amount of energy put into this road, to the rustic Hinterhornalm restaurant. This place serves hearty food with a cliff-hanger of a view. Hinterhornalm is a hang-gliding springboard. On sunny days, it's a butterfly nest of thrill seekers ready to fly.

From there, it's a level 20-minute walk to Walderalm, a cluster of three dairy farms with 70 cows that share their meadow with the clouds. The cows ramble along ridgetop lanes surrounded by cut-glass peaks. The ladies of the farms serve soup, sandwiches, and drinks (very fresh milk in the afternoon) on rough plank tables. Below you spreads the Inn River Valley and, in the distance, tourist-filled Innsbruck.

Another alpine escape is Fallerschein, west of Innsbruck. Barely accessible by car, this isolated log-cabin village is smothered with mountain goodness, set in a flower-speckled world of serene slopes, sleepy cows, and musical breezes. Here thunderstorms roll down its valley as if it were God's bowling alley. But the blissfully simple pint-size church on the high ground seems to promise that this huddle of houses will remain standing. The people sitting on benches are Austrian vacationers or clandestine lovers who've rented cabins. Fallerschein is notorious as a hideaway for those having affairs.

More Austrian Experiences

Savoring Salzburg: Salzburg, a musical mecca, is forever smiling to the tunes of Mozart and the *Sound of Music*. The city puts on a huge annual festival as well as constant concerts. With eight million sightseers prowling its cobbled lanes each year, the city can feel pretty touristy. You don't go to Salzburg to avoid the sightseers. You go to experience a town that, in spite of the crowds, is thoroughly entertaining.

After rambling through the old town and past the glorious cathedral, I like to take the funicular up to the towering Hohensalzburg Fortress. One of Europe's mightiest castles, it dominates Salzburg's skyline and offers commanding views of city and countryside.

Another way to take in town and country is on a *Sound of Music* bus tour, sampling Salzburg sights, movie locations, and lovely stretches of the surrounding Salzkammergut Lake District. I took this tour skeptically and actually liked it, even though rolling through the Austrian countryside with 30 Americans singing "Doe, a deer..." is pretty cheesy. But, no matter. With its musical legacies, magnificent scenery, and rich history, Salzburg is a symphony—and you don't have to climb every mountain to enjoy it.

Evocative Castles: Outside the sleepy town of Reutte, not far from the German border, are the ruins of four buildings that once made up the largest fort in Tirol—Ehrenberg. There's the fortified Klause toll booth on the valley floor, which levied duties along the Via Claudia in Roman times; Ehrenberg, the oldest castle on the first hill (from 1296); Fort Claudia, a smaller castle across the valley; and Schlosskopf, the mighty and more modern castle high above. For the best overview of the site, wobble over the 1,200-foot-long pedestrian bridge suspended 300 feet above the valley floor, connecting Ehrenberg with Fort Claudia. (To combine a visit to Ehrenberg with "Mad" Kind Ludwig's castles just across the border, see "Castle Day in Bavaria and Tirol," page 681.)

When I first visited Ehrenberg, one castle crowned its mountain like an ornery barnacle; the others were lost in a thick forest. Inspired, I hiked up into the misty mountain of meaningless chunks of castle wall pinned down by trees,

LEFT Salzburg has a main street lined with traditional business signs.

CENTER One of Europe's biggest castles keeps watch over Salzburg.

RIGHT The stark and evocative Ehrenberg ruins above Reutte moss, and sword ferns. But now the hungry forest has been cut away to reveal the castle ensemble, and children and adults with medieval fantasies can leap from rampart to rampart...sword ferns swinging.

CULTURE AND TRADITIONS: EVERYTHING'S SO...AUSTRIAN

Musical Notes

Vienna has a long history as Europe's music capital, and music lovers make a pilgrimage of sorts to see the houses of the composers who lived and worked here. The homes of Schubert, Brahms, Haydn, Beethoven, and Mozart all host museums—but they are mostly small and forgettable. For the best music history experience, I like the Haus der Musik, a museum that honors the great Viennese composers with fine artifacts and fun interactive exhibits. You can try your hand at virtually conducting the Vienna Philharmonic—if you mess up, the "musicians" will refuse to play.

Classical music performances are everywhere in town, booking up to 10,000 seats a night. The Vienna State Opera alone belts out 300 glittering shows a year. Fans of toe-tapping waltzes head to the Kursalon, an elegant hall in the main city park, where Johann Strauss directed concerts 100 years ago. The Vienna Boys' Choir performs in the Hofburg's Imperial Music Chapel. Mozart lovers choose the intimate Theater an der Wien, designed in 1801 especially for Wolfie's operas. This gilded high culture can be surprisingly affordable—a standing-room ticket for the opera is about the same price as a cinema ticket. Major events can be sold out for weeks—although there are plenty of live music options available without advance booking.

In Vienna's Haus der Musik, you can virtually conduct the city's famed orchestra.

During the summer, a thriving people scene erupts each evening in the park in front of Vienna's City Hall, where filmed opera and classical music performances are shown for free. Comfy benches with room for about 2,000 viewers face the 60-foot-wide screen. Scores of food stands and picnic tables are set up. There are no plastic cups, thank you, just real plates and glasses—Vienna wants the quality of the dining experience to be as good as the music. And the people-watching? It's *con brio.*

Mountains

Much of Austria's character is found in its mountains. Austrians excel in mountain climbing and winter sports such as downhill skiing, which was born in Tirol. When watching ski races, you'll often see fans celebrating with red-and-white flags at the finish line: Austria has won more Olympic medals in alpine skiing than any other country. Innsbruck alone—twice the host of the Winter Olympics—is surrounded by 150 mountain lifts, 1,250 miles of trails, and 250 hikers' and skiers' huts. Ski lifts are busy both winter and summer, taking nature lovers to dizzying heights, where the views are big, and the hiking possibilities are endless.

Enjoy some *Germknödel* goodness at high altitude.

Taking a break at a cozy, hospitable hut is a traditional part of Austrian mountain fun. High-altitude huts serve fortifying treats such as *Germknödel* (a sweet dumpling topped with poppy seeds and laced with plum jam), *Kaiserschmarrn* (a cut-up and sugared pancake), and *Glühwein* (red wine mulled with cinnamon and oranges).

Coffee

The story of coffee in Austria is steeped in legend. In the late 17th century, the Ottoman Turks were laying siege to Vienna. A spy working for the Austrians infiltrated the Ottoman ranks and got to know the Turkish lifestyle...including their passion for a drug called coffee. After the Austrians persevered, the ecstatic Habsburg emperor offered the spy anything he wanted. The spy asked for the Ottomans' spilled coffee beans, which he gathered up to start the first coffee shop in town. (It's a nice story. But actually, there was already an Armenian in town running a coffeehouse.)

In the 18th century, coffee boomed as an aristocratic

Take your pick of one of Vienna's many elegant and venerable coffeehouses.

drink. In the 19th-century Industrial Age, people were expected to work 12-hour shifts, and coffee became a hit with the working class, too. By the 20th century, the Vienna coffee scene became so refined that old-timers remember when waiters brought a sheet with various shades of brown (like paint samples) so customers could make clear exactly how milky they wanted their coffee.

Austria Travel Resources from Rick Steves

Guidebooks
Check out Rick's guidebooks covering Vienna, Salzburg & the Tirol; plus his German phrase book

Audio Europe
Download Rick's free Audio Europe app, with self-guided audio tours, including a Salzburg town walk, Vienna city walk, and tours of Vienna's St. Stephen's Cathedral and Ringstrasse

TV Shows
The quintessence of Austria with Rick as your host, viewable on public television and RickSteves.com. Episodes cover Vienna and the Danube, the Austrian Alps, and Salzburg

Organized Tours
Small group tours, with itineraries planned by Rick: Germany, Austria & Switzerland in 14 Days; My Way: Alpine Europe in 12 Days; Munich, Salzburg & Vienna in 8 Days; Berlin, Prague & Vienna in 12 Days; Best of Europe in 21 Days (including a stop in Austria)

For more on all of these resources, visit RickSteves.com. For Austria trip-planning tips, see www.ricksteves.com/europe/austria.

Czech Republic

Despite being wedged between Germany and Austria, and battered by 20th-century wars and communist domination, the Czechs have managed to forge one of the most comfortable and easy-to-explore countries of Eastern Europe. Today, the Czech Republic is enjoying an unprecedented prosperity.

The country is composed of two main regions—Bohemia to the west and Moravia to the east, with a tiny slice of Silesia in the upper-right corner. As the longtime home of the Czechs, Bohemia is circled by a naturally fortifying ring of mountains and cut down the middle by the Vltava River. It's best known for its capital city of Prague and its rollicking beer halls. By contrast, the wine-growing region of Moravia is more Slavic and colorful, and more focused on farming.

Prague's Old Town Square

Ninety percent of the tourists who visit the Czech Republic see only Prague...and for good reason. Prague is one of Europe's best-preserved cities. It's an architectural time warp, filled with sumptuous Art Nouveau facades, high art, grand buildings, and back lanes out of the 18th century. You'll feel like royalty strolling down the "King's Walk" from the cathedral into the old town. And the city offers a wide-ranging menu of classical concerts and arguably the best beer in Europe.

Outside the capital, you'll enjoy great prices, few tourists, traditional towns, and surprising experiences—whether canoeing through Bohemia, touring the bone chapel in Kutná Hora, or soaking in hot peat soup in Třeboň.

As you travel, talk with Czech people—they bring recent history to life in a way that books can't. And wherever you go, you'll feel the Czech spirit: in the vibrant energy of Prague, the charm of quaint villages like Český Krumlov, and the gentle beauty of the countryside, dotted by wild poppies.

Fast Facts

Biggest cities: Prague (capital, 1.2 million), Brno (380,000), Ostrava (336,000)

Size: 31,000 square miles (similar to South Carolina), population 10.6 million

Locals call it: Česká Republika; Prague is "Praha"

Currency: Czech crown (*koruna*, Kč, officially CZK)

Key date: January 1, 1993, Czechoslovakia peaceably splits into the Czech Republic and Slovakia

Biggest festival: Prague Spring (May-June, international music)

Handy Czech phrases: *Dobrý den* (hello; **doh**-bree dehn), *Prosim* (please; **proh**-zeem), *Děkuji* (thank you; **dyack**-khuyi), *Na zdraví!* (Cheers!; nah zdrah-**vee**)

Tourist info: CzechTourism.com

FAVORITE SIGHTS AND MEMORABLE EXPERIENCES IN THE CZECH REPUBLIC

A Historical Walk Through Prague

Prague is a traveler's dream city: exotic but easy, affordable, and with plenty of great sightseeing. My favorite way to soak up the magic is by connecting Prague's major sights with a stroll through its relatively compact core. You'll get an up-close look at charming cobbled streets and extravagant facades while feeling the sweep of Prague's history, starting at the ninth-century castle from which Czech leaders have ruled for more than 1,000 years, and ending at the square where Czechs gained their freedom from communism just a few decades ago.

Perched on a hill overlooking the city, Prague Castle is hailed as being the biggest anywhere, with a 1,500-foot-long series of courtyards, churches, and palaces. If exhausting

Prague's beloved Charles Bridge, straddling the Vltava River, offers one of the most delightful strolls in Europe.

is a measure of big, I'll buy that claim. Whenever I visit the castle, I feel as if I'm in a pinball machine—rolling downhill, bouncing from sight to sight before funneling out the lower gate. The highlight is St. Vitus Cathedral, where locals go to remember Saint Wenceslas, patron saint of the Czechs. This "good king" of Christmas-carol fame was not a king at all, but a wise, benevolent duke of Bohemia. After being assassinated in 935, Wenceslas became a symbol of Czech nationalism. His tomb sits in an extremely fancy chapel.

From the castle, I follow the "King's Walk" into town. This was the ancient route of coronation processions. After being crowned in St. Vitus Cathedral, the new king would walk through the historic town, cross the Charles Bridge, and finish at the Old Town Square. If he hurried, he'd be done in 20 minutes.

The much-loved Charles Bridge gets my vote for Europe's most pleasant quarter-mile stroll. Built in the 1350s, it now features a chorus line of time-blackened Baroque statues towering above a fun string of street vendors and musicians. I love to be on the bridge when the sun is low for the best light, people-watching, and photo opportunities.

After crossing the bridge, I follow the shop-lined street to the Old

Avoiding Rip-Offs in Prague

Con artists and pickpockets are definitely an issue in Prague. The city's taxis are notorious for hyperactive meters. At restaurants, tourists are routinely served cheaper meals than what they ordered, given a menu with a "personalized" price list, charged extra for things they didn't get, or shortchanged. Pickpockets—from little children to adults dressed as professionals—target Western tourists. Heed these tips:

- When paying with cash, always count your change.
- In taxis, ask for an estimate up front and insist on using the meter.
- Never let your credit card out of your sight.
- In restaurants, closely examine your bill. Tax is always included in the price, so it shouldn't be tacked on later.

Town Square. One of the city's top sights, the colorful square is bordered by pastel buildings in diverse architectural styles: Gothic, Renaissance, Baroque, Rococo, and Art Nouveau. This has been a market square since the 11th century, though today, many of the old-time market stalls have been replaced by cafés, touristy horse buggies, and souvenir hawkers. The square's centerpiece is a memorial to Jan Hus, a local preacher who complained about church corruption. Tried for heresy and burned in 1415, Hus has long symbolized the fight for Czech freedom.

Memorial to Czech martyr Jan Palach on Prague's Wenceslas Square

Going beyond the "King's Walk," I head to Wenceslas Square, the heart of urban, modern Prague. Whenever I'm here, I'm reminded of the struggles of the Czech people. As my friend Honza explains it, this is where the most dramatic moments in modern Czech history have played out. The Czechoslovak state was proclaimed here in 1918. In 1969, Jan Palach set himself on fire here to protest the puppet Soviet government. And 20 years after his death, massive demonstrations on the square led to the overthrow of the communist government.

"Night after night we assembled here, pulled out our key chains, and jingled them at the president's window, saying, 'It's time to go home now,'" explains Honza. "Then one night we gathered...and he was gone. We had won our freedom." Just being on Wenceslas Square, envisioning the events of November 1989, is compelling. But being here with one of the demonstrators drilled into me the jubilation of a small country winning its freedom from a big one.

Making It Personal with a Local Guide

Prague is one city where, more than just about anywhere else, I recommend hiring a local guide. For about $30 an hour, you get a guide and companion who is expert at giving meaning to your wandering. And if, like me, you are forever fascinated by slice-of-life stories from people who had to live through the Cold War in the Warsaw Pact, it's even more engaging.

On one tour, my guide reminisced about 1989 and how, with the arrival of freedom and the fall of the Iron Curtain,

Russian-language teachers suddenly had to teach English. There were no textbooks, and Russian teachers took cram courses in English so they could teach their students sentences like "Deez eez my bruder" ("This is my brother"). The fun thing for school kids those first few years was that they knew more English from watching Rambo movies than their teachers did from taking the cram courses.

Another guide talked of how, in her youth, she could only dream of drinking a nice cold Coca-Cola. She said, "We couldn't drink Coke, but we could collect the cans tourists threw away. I had five cans. My friend had ten."

Throughout Eastern Europe, guides artfully weave personal memories like these into their time with you.

Boning Up on Kutná Hora

The refreshingly authentic town of Kutná Hora sits upon what once was Europe's largest silver mine. In its heyday, much of the Continent's coinage was minted right here. If you're not claustrophobic, you can don a miner's helmet and climb down to explore the medieval mining shafts. Centuries of mining in the narrow wet shafts have made the ground beneath town resemble a giant honeycomb.

But I'm more fascinated by the Sedlec Church, just outside town. On the outside, the little church looks normal. But inside, the bones of 40,000 people decorate the walls and ceilings. Plagues and wars in the 14th and 15th centuries provided all the raw material necessary for these creepily creative designs. The display was created 400 years ago by monks. Their mission: to remind you (mid-vacation) that before long, you'll be in the same state—so give some thought to how you might be spending eternity. Later bone stackers at Kutná Hora were more interested in design than theology, as evidenced by an illuminating chandelier that includes every bone in the human body.

Czech Republic's Top Destinations

Prague ▲▲▲ · allow 2-3 days

One of Europe's most romantic cities, with a remarkably well-preserved old town, a thriving new town packed with Art Nouveau, and fascinating 20th-century history

Top Sights

Old Town Square Beautiful main square with Astronomical Clock
Prague Castle Sprawling hilltop complex of museums, churches, and parks
Charles Bridge Atmospheric, statue-lined bridge enlivened by street music
Jewish Quarter Powerful collection of Jewish sights

Nearby

Kutná Hora Workaday Czech town with offbeat bone church
Terezín Concentration camp memorial
Konopiště, Karlštejn, and Křivoklát Trio of impressive castles

Český Krumlov ▲▲ · 1 day

Charming Bohemian hill town huddled under a castle and hugging a river bend

Southern Bohemian Towns ▲ · 1-2 days

Třeboň, home to a famous peat spa; **Telč,** with a spectacular main square; **Třebíč,** with echoes of Jewish history; and sleepy Renaissance gem **Slavonice**

Olomouc ▲ · 1 day

Moravian cultural capital, vibrant university city, and home of stinky cheese

With more time, consider visiting

Wallachia Time-passed, mountainous region
Mikulov Wine region, highlighted by the cellars of Pavlov

Spas and Fishy Cuisine in Třeboň

Třeboň, an inviting medieval town in South Bohemia, sits near a biosphere of artificial lakes that date back to the 14th century. Rather than unprofitable wet fields, the nobles wanted ponds that swarmed with fish. Over the years, what was marshland was transformed into a clever combination of lakes, oak-lined dikes, wild meadows, Baroque villages, peat bogs, and pine woods.

These days, people come from near and far to soak in peat, the dark, smelly sludge that's thought to cure aching joints and spines. So I decided to check it out. Immersed in a *One Flew Over the Cuckoo's Nest* ambience, I was ushered to a changing cubicle. The attendant mimed I should take everything off. I climbed into a stainless-steel tub, she pulled a plug, and I quickly disappeared under a rising sea of dark-brown sawdust broth. When finished, I showered off the sludge, then laid face down in what felt like a nurse's office while my attendant gave me a vigorous massage. I walked out with my shirt stuck to my skin by a mucky massage cream...and without a clue what soaking in that peat soup was supposed to accomplish.

Třeboň is also the fish-raising capital of the country. So if you visit Třeboň, you have to eat fish. Like the Italians do with pasta, the Czechs of Třeboň cook fish with both passion and variety. One time, I went to a local eatery and ordered all the fishy appetizers on the menu. The result was a tapas-style meal of "soused" (pickled) herring, fried loach, "stuffed carp sailor-fashion," cod liver, pike caviar, and something my Czech friends translated as "fried carp sperm." I said, "You can't fry sperm." And everyone at my table insisted that, while female fish have a whole trough full of eggs (caviar), the males have a trough full of the male counterpart—and it's cookable. Fried carp sperm tasted like fried oyster, and it had the same texture, too.

While the Czech town of Třeboň sees few American travelers, it's famous locally for its trout.

As we ate, I noticed that the writing on my beer glass said, "Bohemia Regent anno 1379." It occurred to me that I was drinking and eating the same thing that people here have been consuming for over 600 years: local brew and fish from the reservoir just outside the town gate.

More Czech Experiences

Canoeing in Český Krumlov: With its simple beauty and wonderfully medieval feel, Český Krumlov is the quaint, small-town Europe that many people dream of experiencing. An especially pleasant way to connect with this fairy-tale town is from the waters of the Vltava River. It's easy to rent a canoe or rubber raft from the outfitters in town. Floating down the lazy river, you'll pass through Bohemian forests and other villages, drifting past cafés and pubs happy to welcome you for a break. You'll eventually end up at a 13th-century abbey. From here, hop on the outfitter's shuttle back to town or borrow a bike from them and pedal back along the path.

Prague's Lennon Wall: After John Lennon's death in 1980, Prague's Lennon Wall spontaneously appeared. This was back in Cold War times, when Lennon's visionary ideas inspired many locals. They'd paint "All You Need Is Love," "Imagine," and other graffiti borrowed from Lennon on the wall. Night after night, the police would paint over the graffiti. And day after day, it would reappear. Until independence came in 1989, travelers, freedom lovers, and hippies gathered here. Silly as it might seem, this wall is remembered as a place that gave hope to locals craving freedom. Although the tension and danger associated with this wall are long gone, it remains a colorful, nostalgic, and poignant place to visit.

In the Czech Republic, you can canoe into the wonderfully medieval town of Český Krumlov *(left)* and exercise your freedom of thought at Prague's Lennon Wall *(right).*

The Stinky Cheese of Olomouc: Try the sour, foul-smelling, yet beloved specialty of the Haná region, Olomouc cheese sticks (*olomoucké tvarůžky*). The milk goes through a process of natural maturation under chunks of meat. Czechs figure there are two types of people in the world: *tvarůžky* lovers and sane people. The *tvarůžky* are so much a part of the Haná and Czech identity that when the European Union tried to forbid the product, the Czech government negotiated for special permission to continue to rot their milk. Zip a few of these stinkers in a baggie, and you can count on getting a train compartment to yourself.

Intrepid travelers can sample the infamous "stinky cheese" of Olomouc.

CULTURE AND TRADITIONS: EVERYTHING'S SO...CZECH

Classical Music

From Antonín Dvořák to Gustav Mahler, the Czech Republic has a rich heritage in classical music. You'll find it everywhere in Prague, which has museums dedicated to the lives and work of Dvořák, Bedřich Smetana (the father of Czech classical music), and Mozart, who hailed from Austria but spent a lot of time here.

Each day, classical concerts designed for tourists fill delightful Old World halls and churches, including the Art Nouveau Municipal House (where the Prague Symphony Orchestra plays), the classical Neo-Renaissance Rudolfinum (home of the Czech Philharmonic), and the National Theater (great for opera and ballet). Or you can simply drop by Castle Square and see Josef and his Prague Castle Orchestra playing for free on the street. A highlight is hearing them play Smetana's masterwork, *Die Moldau* (the unofficial anthem of the Czech Republic). If I were the mayor of Prague, I'd book this trio for the rest of their musical days to bring joy to the city's many tourists at the gateway to its most visited sight and the orchestra's namesake, Prague Castle.

Czech Beer

Czechs are among the world's most enthusiastic beer drinkers—adults drink an average of 80 gallons a year. Whether you're in a restaurant or traditional beer hall, beer (*pivo*) hits your

The Czech Republic is a land where classical music bursts out in the streets and the cuisine sticks to your ribs.

table like a glass of water does in the States. A new serving will automatically appear when the old glass is almost empty. (You must tell the waiter not to bring more.) On my early trips, I used to have a big beer at lunch and spend the rest of the day wobbly...sightseeing on what I called "Czech knees." Now I resist a momentum-killing beer at lunch and finish each day with a fresh draft beer.

The Czechs invented Pilsner-style lager in Plzeň, and the result, Pilsner Urquell, is on tap in many pubs. Other good beers include Krušovice, Gambrinus, Staropramen, and Kozel. Each establishment serves only one brand of beer on tap (to find out which, look for its sign outside). Unlike many other Europeans, Czechs don't mix beers, and they don't bar-hop. They say, "In one night, you must stay loyal to one woman and to one beer."

Stick-to-Your-Ribs Cuisine

The Czechs have one of Europe's most filling cuisines. Heavy on meat, potatoes, and cabbage, it's hearty and tasty—designed to keep peasants or sightseers fueled through a day of hard work. Expect thick soups, rustic bread, and meaty main dishes such as beef goulash or wild boar. Czech dumplings (*knedlíky*) are a staple. These aren't round, puffy dough balls—they resemble slices of steamed white bread and are meant to be drowned in gravy. There are also sweet dumplings loaded with fresh strawberries, blueberries, apricots, or plums, and garnished with custard and melted butter.

Czech Republic Travel Resources from Rick Steves

Guidebooks
Check out Rick's guidebooks covering Prague & the Czech Republic and Eastern Europe

Audio Europe
Download Rick's free Audio Europe app, with self-guided audio tours, including a walk through Prague

TV Shows
The quintessence of the Czech Republic with Rick as your host, viewable on public television and RickSteves.com. Episodes cover Prague, Olomouc, Třeboň, and Český Krumlov

Organized Tours
Small group tours, with itineraries planned by Rick: Prague & Budapest in 8 Days; Berlin, Prague & Vienna in 12 Days; and Eastern Europe in 14 Days

For more on all of these resources, visit RickSteves.com. For Czech Republic trip-planning tips, see www.ricksteves.com/europe/czech-republic.

Poland

Poland may not appear at the top of many travelers' wish lists, and that's just one reason you may want to visit. With gorgeous towns, evocative sights, an epic history, and low prices, Poland is a diamond in the rough. While parts of the country are still cleaning up the industrial mess left by the Soviets, visitors today are speechless when they set foot on the country's vibrant main squares, in-love-with-life pedestrian drags, and sophisticated shopping boulevards.

Poland is as big as Italy and nearly as populous as Spain. It's also quite flat, with rolling fields. This lack of natural barriers—and Poland's proximity to powerful neighbors (Germany, Russia, Austria, Sweden)—have left the country with a troubled history that's often meant being part of someone else's empire.

This dynamic past has inspired a powerful patriotism among Poles. They are a kind-hearted people: noble, soft-spoken, and quite shy. Occasionally they strike first-time visitors as brusque. But extroverts quickly learn that all it takes is a smile and a friendly hello (*Dzień dobry!*) to break through the tough exterior that helped these people survive Poland's difficult times.

The 10 million Americans who trace their roots to Poland find something enticingly familiar here, from the comfort food their Busia cooked them to the kindness of distant cousins they encounter. Many return home with a renewed appreciation for their mother country.

Poland's best attractions are its

big cities: the cultural capital and university burg of Kraków; the picture-perfect old merchant town of Gdańsk; and the cosmopolitan business hub of Warsaw. Leaving these population centers, you're immersed in a gently beautiful countryside, where humble farmers work the same plots and live the same uncomplicated, agrarian lifestyle of their great-grandparents.

The resilience of Poland's culture and the warmth of its people inspire me. Thankfully, these are good times in Poland, a nation with a rich past and an exciting future.

FAVORITE SIGHTS AND MEMORABLE EXPERIENCES IN POLAND

Charismatic Kraków

Kraków is easily Poland's best destination: a beautiful, old-fashioned city buzzing with history, enjoyable sights, tourists, and college students. Although the country's capital moved from here to Warsaw 400 years ago, Kraków remains Poland's cultural and intellectual center. Of all the Eastern European cities claiming to be "the next Prague," Kraków is for real.

The old town, within Kraków's medieval walls, converges on one of the most charismatic squares in Europe: the Main Market Square. I choose a café, sink deep into my chair, and absorb the gorgeously intact buildings around me.

Vast as it is, the square has a folksy intimacy. It bustles with street musicians, cotton-candy vendors, gawking tourists, local teens practicing break-dancing moves for tips, and the lusty coos of pigeons. A folk band—swaggering in their colorful peasant costumes—gives me a private little concert. Feeling flush, I tip them royally. (Perhaps too royally. Be warned: A big tip gets you "The Star-Spangled Banner.")

I suddenly hear a bugle call. Glancing around, I eventually pan up to see its source: a trumpet poking out the window of the tallest tower of

Fast Facts

Biggest cities: Warsaw (capital, 1.7 million), Kraków (757,000), Łódź (747,000)

Size: 121,000 square miles (similar to New Mexico), population 38.5 million

Locals call it: Polska

Currency: Polish złoty

Key date: August 14, 1980, Lech Wałęsa leads the first successful workers' strike in Soviet territory

Biggest festivals: Jewish Cultural Festival (late June-early July, Kraków), St. Dominic's Fair (late July-mid-August, Gdańsk, market stalls, musical performances, and general revelry)

Handy Polish phrases: *Dzień dobry* (hello; jehn **doh**-brih), *Proszę* (please; **proh**-sheh), *Dziękuję* (thank you; jehn-**koo**-yeh), *Na zdrowie!* (Cheers!; nah **zdroh**-vyeh)

Tourist info: Poland.travel

the hulking, red-brick St. Mary's Church. Just as I spot the sun glinting off of the trumpet's bell, the song stops abruptly, causing the crowd below to chuckle and applaud appreciatively. This tune—performed every hour on the hour—comes with a legend: During the 1241 Tatar invasion, a watchman saw the enemy approaching and sounded the alarm. Before he could finish, an arrow pierced his throat—which is why today, the music still stops *subito*, partway through.

Ready to move on from my perch, I toss a few złotys on the table to cover my tab—and head underground into the Rynek Underground Museum. The Main Market Square sits on top of 500 years of history. When it was renovated recently, workers found so many coins, tools, and artifacts of archaeological value that the city opened this excellent museum. Here, at 12 feet below street level, I get an intimate look at medieval Kraków life.

Back on the streets of modern Kraków, I find that this city, more than any other in Europe, is made for aimless strolling. As I linger my way through town, I'm lucky enough to stumble into Staropolskie Trunki ("Old Polish Drinks"), a friendly little place with a long bar and countless local vodkas and liquors—each one open and ready to be sampled. For about $3, I get a complete vodka education with a cheery local bartender who talks me through five different tastes.

Happy after my private vodka tour, I keep walking to clear my head. Eventually I wind up in Kazimierz, the city's historic Jewish Quarter. Once upon a time, the majority of Europe's Jewish people lived in Poland. And Kraków was their social and political base. Few Jews still live in the neighborhood, but the spirit of their traditions survives in a handful of synagogues and cemeteries.

Kazimierz is one of the many places where the big events of World War II intersected with ordinary, everyday lives.

Kraków, with its vast yet people-friendly main square and its countless cafés and pubs, manages to be both trendy and convivial at the same time.

The businessman Oskar Schindler ran his factory here, saving the lives of more than a thousand of his Jewish workers. Now, one of Europe's best museums about the Nazi occupation fills the building where Schindler and his employees worked. While the museum tells the story of Schindler and his workers, it also broadens its perspective to take in the full experience of all of Kraków during the era of Nazi rule.

While tourists come to see Kazimierz's historic sights during the day, this isn't a "preserved" neighborhood. It's lively and fun. Throngs of young clubbers clog the streets after dark. The Kazimierz market square retains the gritty flavor of the town before tourism and gentrification. And countless bohemian-chic restaurants make Kazimierz a destination for dinner. On a balmy summer night, it's the perfect spot to end a day in Poland's "second" city.

Historic, Heroic Gdańsk

A port city on the Baltic Coast of Poland, Gdańsk is truly amazing— and amazingly historic. You may associate it with dreary images of striking shipyard workers from the nightly news in the 1980s—but this is one of northern Europe's most historic and picturesque places.

Milk Bars

All over Poland, you'll find "milk bars" *(bar mleczne)*—cafeterias that combine good, affordable meals with a fun cultural experience. These are leftovers from communist times, when the government subsidized low-cost eateries for its workers. Despite the misleading name, milk bars serve not just milk, but all sorts of traditional Polish dishes.

The idea of a cheap and hearty meal survived communism, and, decades later, you'll still find a wide variety of these budget cafeterias. Some are slick and modern, with excellent food and slightly higher prices. Others are holdovers from the old days (with a certain Soviet *je ne sais quoi*), where you can snare a fast and forgettable meal for about $5. Just head to the counter and point to what you want.

Gdańsk's appealing old town boasts block after block of red-brick churches and narrow, colorful, ornately decorated burghers' mansions. The riverfront embankment, with its trademark medieval crane, oozes salty maritime charm. When the Polish kings came to visit this well-to-do city, they'd gawk along the same route trod by tourists today— which is still called the "Royal Way." Entering through the old town's ornamental gateway, I overheard a fellow traveler gasping, "It's like stepping into a Fabergé egg!"

North of the town center, the charms of the old core fade

Poland's Top Destinations

Kraków ▲▲▲   allow 2-3 days

Poland's cultural, intellectual, and historical capital, with an easy-to-enjoy old town, thought-provoking Jewish quarter, important castle, many churches, and one of Europe's finest town squares

Top Sights

Main Market Square Stunning core of Kraków and a people magnet any time of day
Wawel Castle and Cathedral Poland's historical and spiritual heart
Churches St. Mary's (Gothic altarpiece) and St. Francis Basilica (Art Nouveau)
Kazimierz Jewish quarter with synagogues, cemeteries, and Oskar Schindler's factory

Nearby

Auschwitz-Birkenau Notorious concentration camp, now a compelling memorial
Wieliczka Salt Mine Sprawling underground caverns with sculptures hewn from salt
Nowa Huta Planned workers' suburb, offering an evocative taste of communist times

Warsaw ▲▲   1-3 days

Poland's modern capital, with an appealing urban tempo, stately and sophisticated boulevards, a reconstructed old town, and cutting-edge museums (covering WWII history, Fryderyk Chopin, Jewish culture, Polish art, and more)

Gdańsk ▲▲   2 days

Historic trading city, featuring a showpiece old town lined with marvelous facades, a salty maritime charm, and the shipyard where Lech Wałęsa's Solidarity trade union challenged the communists

as you approach the Gdańsk shipyard. For me, the hike to the shipyard isn't about sightseeing; it's a pilgrimage. This is where the Polish Solidarity union was born, kicking off the beginning of the end of Soviet domination in Eastern Europe. It's remarkable to think that it all came down to the gumption of just a motley collection of workers, led by electrician-turned-labor-organizer Lech Wałęsa.

My guide, Agnus, told the story vividly as we stood at

Gdańsk, a rugged port town on Poland's Baltic coast (left), remembers its shipyard workers who heroically helped bring down the Soviet Union (right).

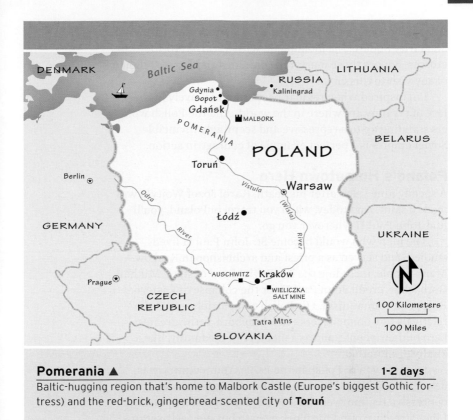

Pomerania ▲   1-2 days

Baltic-hugging region that's home to Malbork Castle (Europe's biggest Gothic fortress) and the red-brick, gingerbread-scented city of **Toruń**

the gate under a "Solidarity" banner—draped where a big "LENIN" sign once hung. For 18 days in 1980, protestors huddled behind the shipyard's main gate, refusing to leave until they had won unprecedented concessions from the communists—including the right to strike. A crude yellow board lists the workers' original demands. Their action sparked a wave of strikes and sit-ins that spread along the industrialized north coast of Poland.

When Solidarity negotiated its way to victory in 1980, one of their conditions was that the Soviets let Poland erect a monument to workers killed a decade earlier while demonstrating for the same workers' rights. The government agreed, marking the first time a communist regime ever allowed a monument to be built to honor victims of communist oppression. Lech Wałęsa likened it to a harpoon in the heart of the communists.

The towering monument, with three crucified anchors on top, was designed, engineered, and built by shipyard workers. Just four months after the historic agreement was signed, the monument was finished. Today on Gdańsk's Solidarity Square, the monument, with a trio of 140-foot-tall crosses, honors those martyred comrades and is a highlight of any visit to this city.

I'm inspired when regular people stand bravely in the face of tyranny anywhere in the world. And the Polish workers standing up to a repressive and seemingly invincible Soviet empire is a perfect example of courage in action.

Poland's Hometown Hero

A speedy nine years after his death, Karol Józef Wojtyła was made a saint. And today, when you travel in Poland, you'll find John Paul II wherever you go.

The man who would become St. John Paul II lived, studied, and served as a priest and archbishop in Kraków. Many people, including the last Soviet head of state, Mikhail Gorbachev, credit John Paul II for the collapse of Eastern European communism. His Polish compatriots—even the relatively few nonbelievers—saw him both as the greatest hero of their people, and as a member of the family, like a kindly grandfather.

Imagine you're Polish in the 1970s. Your country was devastated by World War II, and has struggled under an oppressive regime ever since. Food shortages are epidemic. Lines stretch around the block even to buy a measly scrap of bread. Life is bleak, oppressive, and seems hopeless. Then someone who speaks your language—someone you've admired your entire life, and one of the few people to successfully stand up to the regime—becomes one of the world's most influential leaders. A Pole like you is the spiritual guide of a billion Catholics. He makes you believe that the impossible can happen. He says to you again and again: "Have no fear." And you begin to believe it. It's not hard to see why many consider John Paul II to be the greatest Pole in history.

Saint John Paul II is remembered as a favorite son by Poles.

Since his sainthood, the entire country has been ramping up celebrations. At the edge of Kraków, the new John Paul II Center is an impressive place to visit. Consecrated in 2013, the church is big and dazzling, with art in the lower sanctuary highlighting the pope's illustrious ministry. A museum displays his personal effects and gifts given to him from admirers around the world.

About an hour outside Kraków, in the town of Wadowice, the John Paul II Family Home and Museum fills four floors of the tenement building where his family lived through his adolescence. Visitors can see the actual rooms where he grew up and a collection of his belongings.

But for me, one of the best John Paul II experiences is seeing all of the smaller churches throughout Poland, each of which seems to have a chapel dedicated to their saint. Seeing a man of our own time up on the wall, glorified with the apostles and other saints, is powerful. You can almost feel the charismatic presence of this historic figure, who will be honored for ages to come.

More Polish Experiences

Warsaw Reborn: Warsaw is Poland's capital and biggest city. It's huge, famous, and important, but not particularly romantic. (If you're looking for Old World quaintness, head for Kraków.) The fun of Warsaw is to walk through the city's parks, enjoy a little Chopin in the composer's hometown, marvel at its fast-growing skyline, and just connect with big-city people who are as warm and charming as small-town folk.

Warsaw is also an inspiration to visit. To think it was literally bombed flat and rebuilt since 1945 is amazing. When I'm there, I can't help but fixate on the cost of war. I know how lovingly I collect and organize my physical world in my house. But virtually every house in Warsaw was destroyed in 1945...so many cultural and personal treasures simply gone forever.

Warsaw has been rebuilt from the rubble of World War II.

And, now, just two generations later, Germans and Russians stroll through the city on vacation—joking, enjoying ice cream cones, and snapping photos. Of course, we need to forgive and move on. I'm just amazed at how good Poland is at it. Perhaps some other countries—victims of similar horrors—can learn from the Poles.

Look, but Don't Lick: Just outside Kraków is the remarkable Wieliczka Salt Mine, which has been producing salt since at least the 13th century. A tour of the complex, which spreads over nine levels and 100 miles of tunnels, shows how generations of Wieliczka miners spent their days underground, rarely seeing the sun. Some of these miners carved statues from the salt: legendary figures from the days of King Kazimierz, the famous astronomer Copernicus, and even the region's favorite son, Pope John Paul II. Your jaw will drop as you enter the enormous underground chapel, carved in the early 20th century. Everything, from the altar to the grand chandelier, was chiseled from the rock salt. The remarkable relief carving of the Last Supper looks good enough to lick.

LEFT Outside Kraków, a vast salt mine comes with a cavern carved to be a church.

RIGHT At Auschwitz-Birkenau, death was mass-produced with diabolical efficiency.

Lessons of Auschwitz-Birkenau: A trip to once-upon-a-time Europe can be a fairy tale. It can also help tell the story of Europe's 20th-century fascist nightmare. While few travelers go to Europe to dwell on the horrors of Nazism, most people value visiting the memorials of fascism's reign of terror and honoring the wish of its survivors—"Forgive, but never forget."

No such sight in all of Europe is as powerful as Auschwitz-Birkenau. This Nazi concentration camp—strategically located in the heart of Jewish Europe, in occupied Poland—was the site of the systematic murder of more than a million innocent people.

Today, visitors make the pilgrimage west of Kraków to tour the grounds, with its vast field of chimneys stretching to the horizon. A visit begins by crossing under the notorious gate with the cruelly mocking message *Arbeit Macht Frei* ("Work sets you free"). The broken-down crematoria and the train tracks that delivered their victims are silent remnants of unspeakable horrors.

Why is this somber place worth a bit of our vacations? Because we can learn from it. Auschwitz-Birkenau is committed to making the point that intolerance lives on—genocide is as recent as conflicts in Rwanda, Sudan, and Syria.

Even today, Machiavellian politicians can hijack great nations, artfully manipulating fear, patriotism, and mass media to accomplish their destructive agendas.

CULTURE AND TRADITIONS: EVERYTHING'S SO...POLISH

Churchgoing Catholics

Poland is arguably Europe's most devoutly Catholic country. Nearly all Polish children are baptized as Roman Catholics, and almost everyone who gets married has a church wedding. In small Polish towns, there's a strong contemporary tradition of building huge, architecturally daring churches as a sign of civic pride and deep respect for the Catholic faith. The architecture of these modern houses of worship sometimes feels more slapdash and done-on-the-cheap than the great churches of an earlier age (which were often built over centuries). But the spirit that fills them is powerful.

When you travel around Europe, you rarely see new churches. And the old churches you see often feel more dead than alive...kept going more for tourists than for worshippers. But in Poland, churches are alive with the faithful.

Polish Food

Polish food is hearty and tasty, with lots of "cold-weather" ingredients: potatoes, dill, berries, beets, and rye. Polish soups are a highlight, especially *barszcz* (borscht, the savory beet soup) and *żurek* (a hearty sourdough soup with a hard-boiled egg and pieces of *kiełbasa* sausage). Another familiar Polish dish is pierogi, ravioli-like dumplings with various

LEFT During communist times, Poles built bold new churches as a statement.

RIGHT A plate of Polish food fills the stomach and warms the body.

fillings: minced meat, sauerkraut, mushroom, cheese, or even blueberry.

And, of course, there's *wódka* (vodka). The most famous brand, Żubrówka, comes with a blade of grass from the bison reserves in eastern Poland. The bison "flavor" the grass... then the grass flavors the vodka. It's strong—but if you down your vodka quickly, it only hurts once. Poles often mix Żubrówka with apple juice, creating a cocktail called *szarlotka* ("apple cake"). *Na zdrowie!*

Poland Travel Resources from Rick Steves

Guidebooks
Check out Rick's guidebooks covering Kraków, Warsaw & Gdansk, and Eastern Europe

TV Shows
The quintessence of Poland with Rick as your host, viewable on public television and at RickSteves.com. Episodes cover Kraków, Auschwitz, and Warsaw

Organized Tours
Small group tours, with itineraries planned by Rick: Best of Eastern Europe in 14 Days

For more on all of these resources, visit RickSteves.com. For Poland trip-planning tips, see www.ricksteves.com/europe/poland.

Hungary

A proud oddball planted firmly in the center of Europe, Hungary mixes a refined elegance (from its days as Vienna's powerful sidecar of the Austro-Hungarian Empire), post-communist rejuvenation, cultural artifacts of a unique Asian heritage, spicy food, exotic thermal baths, endearingly eccentric locals, and Europe's single most underrated capital city. The more you know Hungary, the more you grow to love it.

Throughout history, various cultures from the mysterious East have stampeded to Europe, terrorized the Continent, and eventually retreated home. But only one group stuck around. The original Hungarians—called the Magyars—arrived here in A.D. 896, after a long migration from the steppes of Central Asia. After a few generations of running roughshod over Europe, they decided to convert to Christianity, adopt European ways, and integrate with their neighbors. And even though modern-day Hungarians are fully European, there's still something about the place that's distinctly Magyar.

The grand spas of Hungary recall the glory days of the Austro-Hungarian Empire.

Budapest—the sprawling Hungarian capital on the banks of the Danube—is a city of nuance and paradox. But those who grapple with it are rewarded with great sights, excellent restaurants, and vivid memories.

While one in five Hungarians lives in Budapest, the countryside plays an important role in Hungary's economy—this has always been a heavily agricultural region. The country's large towns and small cities—including my favorites, Eger and Pécs—offer the visitor a refreshing contrast to the congested metropolis at the country's heart.

FAVORITE SIGHTS AND MEMORABLE EXPERIENCES IN HUNGARY

Budapest Remembers the Cold War

Traveling in Europe in the 1980s, I got in touch with my Czech friend, Lída, and told her I was coming to Prague for a visit. "If you don't mind," she said, "maybe we can meet in Budapest instead? I have been dying to try a Big Mac!"

If communism was a religion during the Cold War, Budapest was sin city. Offering tourists from communist countries a taste of the decadent West, Budapest had a famously progressive economic system dubbed "goulash communism." Meeting up with Lída in Budapest, we strolled down the shopping street called Váci utca. An excited mob gathered in front of a shop that was selling Adidas shoes. Lída explained that this was the only place in all of Eastern Europe where wannabe capitalists could drool over window displays featuring fancy sportswear that cost two months' wages. Up ahead, Ronald McDonald stood on the street corner like a heretic prophet cheering on the downtrodden proletariat. I'll never forget waiting an hour—in a line that stretched around the block—for American "fast" food. But as Lída finally bit into that long-awaited Big Mac, a deeply satisfied smile spread across her face. That evening, we went to hear Bruce Springsteen at the local stadium. With 50,000 rock fans, you could feel freedom ready to combust all around.

Today, that time feels like ancient history, and Hungarians under age 30 have no living memory of communism. But Budapest still has one of Eastern Europe's best sights for those fascinated by the Red old days: Memento Park.

When regimes come crashing to

Fast Facts

Biggest cities: Budapest (capital, nearly 2 million), Debrecen (205,000), Miskolc (165,000)

Size: 36,000 square miles (similar to Maine), population 10 million

Locals call it: Magyarország

Currency: Hungarian forints (Ft or HUF)

Key date: A.D. 896, seven original Magyar tribes arrive in the Carpathian Basin after a long migration from Central Asia, creating what would become Hungary

Biggest festivals: Formula 1 races (July, Budapest), Sziget Festival (August, Budapest, one of Europe's biggest rock and pop music events)

Handy Hungarian phrases: *Jó napot kívánok* (hello; yoh **nah**-pot **kee**-vah-nohk), *Kérem* (please; **kay**-rehm), *Köszönöm* (thank you; **kur**-sur-nurm), *Egészségedre* (cheers; **eh**-gehs-shay-geh-dreh)

Tourist info: GotoHungary.com

In Budapest's Memento Park, the sculpted figures that once glorified the communist goals of the state are now gathered together in a nostalgic game of statue maker.

the ground, so do their monuments. And, while most Eastern Europeans quickly disposed of any statues of Stalin, Lenin, and their local counterparts, some clever entrepreneur collected Budapest's into an open-air museum. The result is Memento Park, located in the countryside several miles outside the city center, boasting an entertaining jumble of once fearsome, now almost comical statues, gesturing frantically in an otherwise empty field, as if preaching their ideology to each other for eternity.

A visit to Memento Park is a lesson in Socialist Realism, the art of communist Europe. They took censorship to new extremes: Under the communists, art was acceptable *only* if it furthered the goals of the state. Aside from a few important figureheads, individuals didn't matter. Everyone was a cog in the machine, a strong and stoic automaton, an unquestioning servant of the nation.

The gift shop hawks a fun parade of communist kitsch. On my last visit, I picked up a CD featuring 20 patriotic songs—*The Greatest Hits of Communism*—and a Stalin vodka flask. Observing the capitalist bustle of today's Budapest, it occurs to me that Stalin, whose estate gets no royalties for all the postcards and tacky souvenirs featuring his mug, must be spinning in his communist grave.

Heat Wave in a Budapest Ruin Pub

Budapest's trendiest clubs are called "ruin pubs." Inhabiting ramshackle old buildings in the city center, they feel like a gang of squatters made a trip to the dump yesterday and grabbed whatever was usable, moved in today, and are open for business tonight.

This fast-combusting nightlife scene fills the city's long-derelict, now-gentrifying Jewish Quarter. On hot nights, the pubs spill out into shoddy courtyards, creating the feeling

Hungary's Top Destinations

Budapest ▲▲▲   allow 2-3 days

Grand, Danube-spanning cityscape peppered with opulent buildings, fine restaurants and cafés, rejuvenated streets and squares, and avant-garde "ruin pub" nightlife

Top Sights
Thermal Baths Fun Széchenyi, genteel Gellért, and classic Rudas
Hungarian Parliament Riverside behemoth with over-the-top interior
Hungarian State Opera House Neo-Renaissance splendor and affordable opera
House of Terror Remembrance of Nazi and Soviet crimes
Buda Castle Historic hilltop ensemble of palaces, churches, and museums

Nearby
Memento Park Open-air museum of communist statues
Szentendre Colorful, Balkan-feeling riverside artist colony
Esztergom Unassuming town with Hungary's biggest and most important church
Gödöllő Palace Summer palace of Habsburg monarchs

Eger ▲▲   1 day

Strollable town with inviting main square, gorgeous Baroque buildings, invigorating thermal baths, and fine wines

Pécs ▲▲   1 day

City featuring a unique mosque-turned-church, good museums, and colorfully tiled facades

With more time, consider visiting
Sopron Charmingly well-preserved old town
Hollókő Intriguing open-air folk museum, still inhabited by villagers

of a cozy living room missing its roof...under the stars. Enjoying a drink here, I'm reminded of creatures that inhabit discarded shells in a tide pool. The formula really works. With the come-as-you-are atmosphere, these clubs attract people who make a point not to be fashion slaves. And, for adventurous travelers of any age, it's easy to meet people.

Budapest's ruin pubs provide a great chance for travelers to connect with locals (and the local hard liquor).

I end up sitting with Peter (who designs ruin pubs), Laura (who works at a hotel), and Sandra (whose father's company introduced pornography to Hungary after freedom in the 1990s). I say how much I like the shabby lounge atmosphere of a ruin pub, and Laura declares that this one, Szimpla Kert (which means "Simple Garden"), is the mecca of ruin pubs.

Ruin pubs come with a bit of communist kitsch. Many of the regulars who love these lounges were toddlers during the last years of communism. Never having experienced its downside, they have fond memories of those "good old days," when the pace of life was slower and families were tighter-knit. Ruin pubs sell nostalgic commie soft drinks along with cocktails.

Peter buys everyone a round of spritzes (rosé with soda water). He's excited about the new ruin pub he just designed across town, and wants us to go there. I comment on how well the design works. He explains how these clubs are the soul of underground culture here. It's the anti-club: flea market furniture, no matching chairs, a mishmash of colors. It's eclectic—"designed to be undesigned."

More Hungarian Experiences

Enchanting Eger: The small city of Eger, in northern Hungary, remains refreshingly off the tourist trail. Egerites socialize in their inviting main square, watched over by one of Hungary's most important castles, and go about their daily routines in a people-friendly, traffic-free core amidst lovely Baroque buildings.

The town is also at the heart of one of Hungary's best-known wine regions. A good place to sample local wines is Sirens' Valley, a series of atmospheric wine caves burrowed into the hillsides just outside of town. A wine-tasting must is Eger's famous Bull's Blood blend of reds. When asked to

Eger, with striking architecture *(left)*, and Pécs, with decorative tilework *(right)*, are the two most interesting towns in Hungary outside of Budapest.

explain the name, one vintner told me: "In 1552, when the Ottomans laid siege to Eger, they were astonished by the ferocity of the town defenders. Local wine sellers knew that the Muslim invaders wouldn't drink alcohol, so they told them it was bull's blood." Of course, since locals only started making this wine in the 1850s, the story is bunk. But as the vintner says, "If it convinces visitors to buy a bottle, where's the harm?"

Colorful Pécs: It takes a lot to get me excited about decorative tiles. But the small Hungarian city of Pécs—at the southern tip of the country—somehow manages. This is the hometown of the Zsolnay family, who innovated the "pyrogranite" method for creating architectural tiles that are as delicate-looking and vibrantly colorful as a fine vase, but frost-proof and as hard as stone. During Hungary's late-19th-century heyday, buildings all over the country were slathered with vibrant ornamentation. Today, Pécs retains the highest concentration of this distinctively Hungarian form of art, the old tile factory has been turned into a crisp and colorful cultural center, and local museums and shops explain the story of the Zsolnay clan and their finest creations. My favorite tiles are glazed with eosin, another Zsolnay invention that shimmers with a

The Tricky Hungarian Tongue

The Hungarian language is of Asian origin—unrelated to any other tongue in Europe (except distant cousins Finnish and Estonian). The language befuddles their neighbors and tourists alike. For example, the letter *s* by itself sounds like "sh," while the combination *sz* is "s." That's why the capital is called "boo-daw-pesht," while "Liszt" sounds like "list." Like other Eastern cultures, Hungarians list a person's family name first, and the given name last. So the composer Franz Liszt is called "Liszt Ferenc" in his homeland.

Hungarians tend to be traditional and formal in the way they speak—a waiter greets diners with *Tessék parancsolni* (Please command, sir) while a polite young man greeting an older woman might say, *Kezét csókolom* (I kiss your hand). On the other hand, Hungarians use two different words as a *ciao*-like informal "hi" and "bye": the local word *szia* (which sounds like "see ya") and the English word "hello." So you may hear a Hungarian begin a conversation with "See ya!" and end it with "Hello!"

unique range of subtly shifting colors—like the gossamer wing of a butterfly.

CULTURE AND TRADITIONS: EVERYTHING'S SO...HUNGARIAN

Taking the Plunge

I don't feel like I'm *really* in Hungary until I take a dip in one of the country's many thermal baths. While it may sound intimidating, enjoying a hot-water soak is very accessible, even to tourists. Thermal baths are basically like your hometown swimming pool...except the water is superheated, there are plenty of jets to massage away your stress, and you're surrounded by Speedo- and bikini-clad Hungarians. It's sightseeing, a cultural experience, and relaxation, all rolled into one.

Locals brag that if you poke a hole in the ground anywhere in Hungary, you'll find a hot-water spring. Budapest alone has 123 natural springs and some two-dozen thermal baths (which are actually part of the health-care system—doctors might prescribe a soak and a massage instead of medicine). At most baths, men and women are usually together, and you can keep your swimsuit on the entire time. But there are also a few gender-segregated, clothing-optional areas.

A typical bath complex has multiple pools: Big pools with warm water are for serious swimming, while the smaller, hotter thermal baths are for relaxing and soaking. You'll also usually find a dry sauna, a wet steam room, a cold plunge pool, and sunbathing areas. Many baths have fun flourishes: bubbles, whirlpools, massage jets, wave pools, and so on.

One of my favorites is Budapest's Széchenyi Baths—a big, yellow, copper-domed complex in the middle of City Park. Stepping into the lobby, I survey the long price list. I then try to explain what I want to the cashier: a bath ticket with a private changing cabin (for just a few dollars more). Once inside, I'm immediately lost in a labyrinth of hallways, until a white-smocked attendant directs me to my cabin. After I rent a towel and slip into my swimsuit, I'm finally ready for some hot-water fun.

Immersed in 100-degree water under glorious Baroque

ceilings, I enjoy some of Europe's most memorable people-watching. Hungarians of all shapes and sizes stuff themselves into tiny swimsuits and strut their stuff. Housewives float blissfully in warm water. Potbellied elder statesmen stand in chest-high water around chessboards and ponder their next moves. Easing my way into the steaming water, I submerge myself nostril-deep—and feel the accumulated impact of a day of busy sightseeing ebb away.

Budapest's Cafés

In the late 19th century, a vibrant café culture boomed in Budapest, just as it did in Vienna and Paris. The *kávéház* (coffeehouse) was a

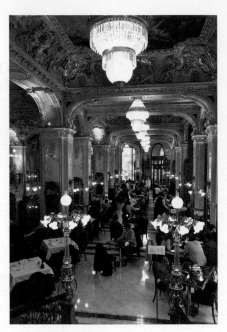

local institution, allowing workers to get a jolt of caffeine to power them through a 12-hour workday and giving city dwellers a place to escape their tiny flats (and avoid having to pay for heat at home). For the price of a cup of coffee, they could come to a café to enjoy warmth, companionship, and loaner newspapers.

Realizing that these neighborhood living rooms were breeding grounds for dissidents, the communists closed the cafés or converted them into *eszpresszós* (with uncomfortable stools instead of easy chairs) or *bisztrós* (stand-up fast-food joints with no chairs at all). Today, nostalgia is bringing back the *kávéház* culture. A favorite activity is whiling away the afternoon at a genteel coffeehouse, sipping a drink or nibbling a delicate layer cake. Budapest has many impressive cafés, but the undisputed champ is the palatial New York Café—which makes other fancy coffeehouses feel like a strip-mall Starbucks.

Hungarian Cuisine

Hungarian cuisine features meat, tomatoes, and peppers (*paprika*) of every shape, size, color, and flavor. Peppers can be stewed, stuffed, sautéed, baked, grilled, or pickled. For seasoning, red shakers of dried paprika join the salt on tables. There are two main types of paprika spice: sweet (*édes*), used for cooking, and hot (*csípős* or *erős*), used to adjust your own plate to your preferred amount of heat.

On menus, chicken or veal *paprikás* comes smothered in a spicy, creamy red stew, and is served with dumpling-like boiled egg noodles. Hungarian *gulyás leves* (shepherd's soup) is a clear, spicy broth with chunks of meat, potatoes, and other vegetables—not the thick "goulash" stew you may be expecting. Cold fruit soup (*hideg gyümölcs leves*) is a sweet, cream-based treat—generally eaten before a meal, even though it tastes more like a dessert.

Wine and Spirits

Hungary boasts 22 designated wine-growing regions, scattered across the country. In addition to the standard international grapes (such as Riesling and Chardonnay), Hungary corks up some interesting alternatives. Tokaji—which French King Louis XV called "the wine of kings, and the king of wines"—is a sweet, late-harvest, honey-colored dessert wine made from noble-rot grapes, which burst and wither on the vine before being harvested.

Hungary is also proud of its fruit-flavored firewater (*pálinka*) and—most of all—Unicum, a bitter liquor made of 40 different herbs and aged in oak casks. Featured in a series of whimsical, vintage, Guinness-like ads, Unicum is a point of national pride and has a history as complicated as its flavor. To sample this local answer to Jägermeister, look for the round bottle with the red-and-white cross.

Hungary Travel Resources from Rick Steves

Guidebooks
Check out Rick's guidebooks covering Budapest and Eastern Europe

TV Shows
The quintessence of Hungary with Rick as your host, viewable on public television and at RickSteves.com. Episodes cover Budapest

Organized Tours
Small group tours, with itineraries planned by Rick: Best of Eastern Europe in 14 Days; Prague & Budapest in 8 Days

For more on all these resources, visit RickSteves.com. For Hungary trip-planning tips, see www.ricksteves.com/europe/hungary.

Slovenia

Tiny Slovenia is one of Europe's most unexpectedly rewarding destinations. At the intersection of the Slavic, German, and Italian worlds, Slovenia blends the best of each culture. And though it's just a quick trip away from the tourist throngs in Venice, Munich, Salzburg, and Vienna, Slovenia has stayed off the tourist track—making it a more authentic Back Door destination.

Though only half as big as Switzerland, Slovenia will surprise you with all it has to offer. You can hike on alpine trails in the Julian Alps, go spelunking in some of the world's best caves in the Karst, get your urban fix in the vibrant capital of Ljubljana, and ride a romantic *pletna* boat across beautiful Lake Bled. And be sure to make time to relax with a glass of local wine and a seafood dinner while watching the sun dip into the Adriatic.

Today, it seems strange to think that Slovenia was ever part of Yugoslavia. In fact, Slovenia feels more like Austria, both in its landscape and in the personality of its people. Slovenes are more industrious, organized, and punctual than their fellow former Yugoslavs...yet still friendly, relaxed, and Mediterranean. They won't win any big wars (they're too well-adjusted to even try), but they're exactly the type of people you'd love to chat with over a cup of coffee. And the Slovenian language is as mellow as the people. The worst they can say in their native tongue is, "May you be kicked by a horse." Rather than say "Damn it!" they'll exclaim, "Three hundred hairy bears!"

Slovenia is an endearing, undiscovered gem. Just make sure when planning a trip to Slovenia that you allow enough time to explore this delightful land.

FAVORITE SIGHTS AND MEMORABLE EXPERIENCES IN SLOVENIA

Bells and Bridegrooms in Lake Bled

With its sweeping mountain panoramas and Romantic Age aura, Lake Bled is Slovenia's top alpine resort. Since the Habsburg days, this is where Slovenes have taken their guests—from kings to cousins—to show off the country's natural wonders.

The focal point of any Lake Bled visit is to ride a *pletna* boat to the fairy-tale island in the middle of the lake. Boarding my *pletna*, I strike up a conversation with the oarsman, Robert. With close-cropped blonde hair and piercing blue eyes, he's younger than I'd expect for such a traditional profession. He explains that he built his boat by hand, following a design passed down from father to son for centuries. There's no keel, so Robert must work hard to steer the flat-bottomed boat with each stroke. Leaning back, I appreciate his rhythmic rowing, which sends us gliding smoothly across the lake's mirrored surface—neatly bisecting a perfect reflection of the cliff-capping castle overhead.

From the boat dock where Robert drops me off, I look up a long, stony staircase. Lake Bled is a popular wedding location, and after the ceremony, it's traditional for grooms to carry—or *try* to carry—their brides up all 99 of these steps to prove themselves "fit for marriage." On summer Saturdays, you'll see a steady procession of brides and grooms here. Trudging up the stairs carrying only my camera—and getting winded near the top—I'm glad not to be hauling a spouse.

Summiting the island, I'm face-to-face with the pretty Baroque Church of the Assumption. Inside, a long rope hangs down in front of the altar. Visitors take turns grabbing hold, pulling hard, and being lifted momentarily off their feet to the sound of a clanging bell in the adjacent campanile. Supposedly, ringing the bell three times with one pull will make your fondest wish come true. I can't resist giving the rope a tug.

Fast Facts

Biggest cities: Ljubljana (capital, 270,000), Maribor (158,000)

Size: 7,800 square miles (size of New Jersey), population 2 million

Locals call it: Slovenija

Currency: Euro

Key date: June 25, 1991, Slovenia declares independence from Yugoslavia

Language: Slovene

Biggest festivals: Ljubljana Festival (summer-long music fest), Kurentovanje (spring Mardi Gras celebration, town of Ptuj)

Handy Slovene phrases: *Dobar dan* (hello; **doh**-behr dahn), *Prosim* (please; **proh**-seem), *Hvala* (thank you; **hvah**-lah), *šnopc* (schnapps; "schnapps")

Tourist info: Slovenia.info

The Slovenian mountain resort of Lake Bled has an enchanting church on its island and hardworking boatmen to get you there.

After Robert gives me a lift back to shore, I stroll the promenade around Lake Bled. Handsome villas line the lake, including what was once the vacation getaway of the Yugoslav president-for-life Tito, who huddled here with foreign dignitaries like Indira Gandhi and Nikita Khrushchev. After Tito died in 1980, his villa was converted into a classy hotel with a James Bond ambience. In one suite, you can actually sleep in the dictator's bed.

Completing my circle around the lake, I settle in at a waterfront café and dig into a Lake Bled specialty: a delicate layer cake of vanilla custard, whipped cream, and crispy wafers. Slovenes are proud of their local pastries—and the beauty of their land. Eating my delicious cream cake, surrounded by the majesty and serenity of Lake Bled, it's easy to see why.

Laid-Back Ljubljana

As a tour guide, I enjoy introducing my American travelers to Slovenia's capital, Ljubljana. Although Slovenia is known as the most industrious of the Balkan countries, this vest-pocket capital's mellow ambience and lively riverfront café scene are revelations. The leafy riverside promenade crawls with stylishly dressed students sipping *kava* and polishing their near-perfect English. Surveying this scene, invariably one of my tour members wonders aloud, "Doesn't anybody here have a job?"

Ljubljana's residents work hard. But, with the country's main university campus right downtown, the city also knows how to play hard. Socializing and people-watching seem to be the national pastimes.

While Ljubljana has slick new museums opening each year, ultimately this town is all about ambience. The cobbled

Slovenia's Top Destinations

Ljubljana ▲▲   allow 1-2 days
Vibrant capital oozing with cobbled ambience, trendy
boutiques and eateries, unique architecture by Jože Plečnik,
and inviting riverside promenade

Lake Bled ▲▲▲   1-2 days
Alpine lake resort with a church-topped island, cliff-hanging castle, famous
desserts, and proximity to mountain thrills

Julian Alps ▲▲   1 day
Cut-glass peaks, tranquil Soča River Valley, adventure-sports capital Bovec, and
fine WWI museum in Kobarid, all connected by a twisty mountain road

Karst Region ▲   1 day
Arid plateau with world-class caves (Škocjan and Postojna), Lipizzaner stallion
stud farm at Lipica, scenically situated Predjama Castle, great wines, and "slow
food"

With more time, consider visiting
Logarska Dolina Remote mountain valley with traditional lifestyles
Piran Atmospheric seaside resort town
Ptuj Charming-if-sleepy historic town topped by a castle

core of Ljubljana is an idyllic place that sometimes feels too good to be true. The spunky mayor is on an eternal crusade to pedestrianize the entire city, block by block. Fashion boutiques and al fresco cafés jockey for control of the old town, and people enjoy a Sunday stroll any day of the week. Easygoing Ljubljana is the kind of place where graffiti and crumbling buildings seem elegantly atmospheric instead of shoddy.

Ljubljana, the trickiest capital in Europe to pronounce, is shaped by the artistic genius of Jože Plečnik, the greatest Slovenian architect of the 20th century.

The Ljubljanica River, lined with cafés, restaurants, and a buzzing market hall, bisects the city. The outdoor farmers market is a hive of activity, where big-city Slovenes buy directly from the producers. Some farmers still use wooden carts to hand-truck veggies in from their garden patches in the suburbs.

After being damaged by an earthquake in 1895, Ljubljana was rebuilt in the Art Nouveau and Art Deco styles that were so popular at the time. A generation later, the homegrown architect Jože Plečnik bathed the city in his distinctive classical-meets-modern style: sleek and eye-pleasing, artfully ornamented with columns and geometrical flourishes.

Like Gaudí shaped Barcelona and Bernini shaped Rome, Plečnik made Ljubljana what it is today. Because he walked to work each day and had to live with what he designed, Plečnik was particularly thoughtful about incorporating aesthetics, nature, and human needs into his projects. The result is like feng shui on an urban scale. Enjoy his picturesque market colonnade, Triple Bridge, and Cobbler's Bridge.

For a more personal look at the architect, I enjoy visiting his home, decorated exactly as it was the day Plečnik died in 1957. On my first visit, this nondescript house underwhelmed me. But as the docent, Ana, proudly walked me from room to room—revealing the quirky but beautiful furniture and artful bric-a-brac Plečnik designed, as well as souvenirs from around the world that inspired him—I found myself seduced by his genius.

Standing in Plečnik's bedroom, Ana explained with emotion how important this great man was to her tiny nation. Inspecting a table strewn with his drawings, equipment, and personal items (including his glasses and the hat he was famous for wearing), I began to feel as though Plečnik himself had invited me over for dinner.

That's a feeling I get again and again throughout Slovenia. This cozy land and its welcoming people just have a way of making visitors fall in love with them.

High in the Slovenian Alps

The Julian Alps, crowning the northwestern corner of Slovenia, are laced with hiking paths, blanketed with deep forests, and speckled with ski resorts and vacation chalets. Beyond every ridge is a peaceful alpine village nestled around a quaint Baroque steeple.

The single best day in the Julian Alps is spent driving up and over the breathtaking Vršič Pass and back down via the Soča River Valley. Navigating the pass takes 50 hairpin turns—24 on the way up, 26 on the way back down—each one numbered and labeled with the altitude in meters. Curling on twisty roads between the peaks, I am treated to stunning high-mountain scenery and charming hamlets.

But as beautiful as this area is, it has a dark side. During World War I, 10,000 Russian prisoners of war labored here, building the pass road. At switchback #8, I leave my car by a rushing mini waterfall and hike up through the woods to a humble little Orthodox chapel. In 1916, an avalanche thundered down here, killing more than a hundred workers. The surviving prisoners erected the rustic chapel where the final victim was found.

Just after switchback #24, I reach the summit at just over 5,000 feet, where a mountain hut offers amazing alpine views. Twisting back down the other side of the mountains—and getting dizzy on the serpentine roads—I get my first view of the Soča River Valley. The Soča—with water somehow both crystal clear and spectacularly turquoise—is a mecca for kayakers and other whitewater adventurers, who call it "Adrenaline Valley."

Though peaceful now, this area saw some of the fiercest

Don't Skip the Sticker

Slovenia's sleek network of expressways is one of Europe's best—but these aren't "free"-ways. Drivers on expressways must display a toll sticker, called a *vinjeta*. If renting a car in Slovenia, it probably comes with a sticker (ask just to be sure). If you're driving in from elsewhere, buy one at a gas station near the border. Be warned: This rule is taken very seriously. Police check frequently, and drivers without stickers are given a large fine on the spot.

Slovenia's beautiful Julian Alps *(left)* were the scene of fierce and bloody fighting during World War I, as the mausoleum at Kobarid *(right)* attests.

fighting of World War I. Known as the Soča Front—or the Isonzo Front in Italian—the million casualties here gave it the nickname "Valley of the Cemeteries." The fighting between the Italian and Austro-Hungarian armies was waged not in the valleys, but at the tops of the mountains.

Finally, I reach the humble village of Kobarid, with the valley's best collection of World War I sights. The town was immortalized by Ernest Hemingway, who drove a Red Cross ambulance nearby (and later wrote about Kobarid in *A Farewell to Arms*).

I stop at Kobarid's excellent museum, which tells the story of the Soča Front and humanizes the suffering of this horrific but almost forgotten corner of World War I. The exhibits focus not on guns and heroes, but on the stories of the common people who fought and died here. I gaze into the eyes of a generation of young men—imported from the farthest reaches of the Habsburg Empire to fight a hopeless battle on a frigid mountaintop. Graphic images of war injuries are juxtaposed with a display of medals earned—suggesting the question, was it worth it?

Next, I head up to the hilltop mausoleum just above town. The octagonal pyramid holds the remains of 7,014 Italian soldiers—victims of just one battle. Standing on the broad terrace at the top of the gigantic monument, I'm surrounded by a 360-degree panorama of cut-glass peaks. Visually tracing the twinkling Soča River back the way I've come, I think: Only Slovenia combines epic scenery and poignant history, all in one dizzying corkscrew drive.

More Slovenian Experiences

Spectacular Spelunking: About an hour south of Ljubljana, Slovenia's Karst region is honeycombed with a vast network of caves and underground rivers. Spelunkers agree that this region has some of the most remarkable caves on the planet, including my favorite, the Škocjan Caves. Visitors begin by seeing a multitude of formations in a series of large caverns. Guides tell the story as, drip by drip, stalactites grow from spaghetti-thin strands to mighty sequoia-like stone pillars. The experience builds and builds as you go into ever-more-impressive grottoes, and you think you've seen the best. But then you reach the truly colossal final cavern, where the sound of a mighty river crashes through the mist. It's a world where a thousand evil Wizard of Oz monkeys could comfortably fly in formation. Crossing a breathtaking footbridge 150 feet above the torrent gives you faith in Slovenian engineering. Finally, the cave widens, sunlight pours in, and you emerge—like lost creatures seeking daylight—into a lush canyon.

World-Class Horses: Lipizzaner stallions—known for their noble gait and Baroque shape—were made famous by Vienna's Spanish Riding School. The Lipica Stud Farm, near the Škocjan Caves, was founded in 1580 to provide Lipizzaners for the Habsburg court in Vienna. While the stuffy Viennese cousins of Slovenia's Lipizzaners still perform under chandeliers, at Lipica visitors can get nose to nose with the stallions. You'll learn how they're raised and trained, and—on most days—get to watch them train or perform. The Lipizzaners' clever routine—stutter-stepping sideways to the classical beat and hopping in the air on their hind legs—thrills horse lovers and casual viewers alike.

CULTURE AND TRADITIONS: EVERYTHING'S SO...SLOVENIAN

Hayracks and Beehives

Coming from such a small country, locals are proud of the few things that are distinctly Slovenian. Two such icons of Slovenian culture are roofed hayracks and beehive panels.

Because of the frequent rainfall in Slovenia, hayracks are protected by a roof that allows the hay to dry. You'll see these distinctive roofed hayracks scattered across the hillsides, especially in the northwest. Souvenir shops sell postcards and miniature wooden models of this unlikely national symbol.

Slovenia also has a strong beekeeping tradition. Slovenian beekeepers believe that painting the fronts of the hives makes it easier for bees to find their way home, so for centuries, they have illustrated their hives with vivid, whimsical scenes of folk life, bible stories, historical events, and so on. A lovable beekeeping museum in the village of Radovljica (near Lake Bled) explains the history of beekeeping. But if you can't make it there, replica beehive panels—a favorite form of folk art—are sold everywhere as souvenirs.

Slovenian Food

Traditional Slovenian food has a distinctly Germanic vibe—including the "four S's": sausage, schnitzel, strudel, and sauerkraut. One local dish to look for is *štruklji*, a dumpling-like savory layer cake, which can be stuffed with cheese, meat, or vegetables. But cosmopolitan Slovenia—at an intersection of cultures—isn't too hung up on traditional grub. Locals favor a wide range of cuisines: Mediterranean, French, Asian, Mexican, and so on. Ljubljana has some of the best—and most varied—restaurants in the former Yugoslavia.

Drinking in Slovenia

Slovenia is proud of its good wines, its many varieties of flavored brandies, and the local lager with a warm-and-fuzzy name that suits the culture: Smile. But its most unusual beverage is Cockta, a cola with an unusual flavor (which supposedly is made from berry, lemon, orange, and 11 herbs).

Slovenia's charms are subtle—like its trademark hayracks and its passion for the berry-flavored cola, Cockta.

Originally called Cockta-Cockta, the drink was introduced during the communist period as an alternative to the difficult-to-get Coca-Cola. These days, even though Coke is widely available, nostalgic Slovenes still have a taste for the Cockta they grew up on. Be adventurous, buy a bottle to drink, and ponder the power of an acquired taste.

Slovenia Travel Resources from Rick Steves

Guidebooks
Check out Rick's guidebooks covering Croatia & Slovenia and Eastern Europe

TV Shows
The quintessence of Slovenia with Rick as your host, viewable on public television and at RickSteves.com. Episodes cover Ljubljana, Lake Bled, Soča Pass, Škocjan Caves, Predjama Castle, and Lipica Stud Farm

Organized Tours
Small group tours, with itineraries planned by Rick: Best of Eastern Europe in 14 Days; Best of the Adriatic in 14 Days

For more on all these resources, visit RickSteves.com. For Slovenia trip-planning tips, see www.ricksteves.com/europe/slovenia.

Croatia

Sunny beaches, succulent seafood, and a taste of
la dolce vita...in Eastern Europe?

Croatia, with thousands of miles of coastline,
is Eastern Europe's Riviera. Holiday makers love
its pebbly beaches, predictably balmy summer
weather, and dramatic mountains. Croatia is also
historic. With ruined Roman palaces, Byzantine
mosaics, Venetian bell towers, medieval walls,
Habsburg villas, and even communist concrete,
past rulers have left their mark.

One tragic exception to Croatia's mellow history came
in the early 1990s, when the country declared independence
from Yugoslavia, sparking an ugly war. Today the bloodshed
is in the past. While a trip to Croatia offers thoughtful travelers the opportunity to understand a complicated chapter
of recent history, most visitors focus instead on the appealing towns and natural wonders the country has long been
known for.

Dubrovnik is still the "Pearl of the Adriatic," with its
old town encircled by a medieval wall. The town of Split is—
astonishingly—built in, on, and around a Roman palace. The
stunning Plitvice Lakes National Park, sparkling with waterfalls, attracts hikers and photographers. And, for a coastal
getaway, it's easy to fall in love
with the village of Rovinj, on
the Istrian Peninsula.

Dubrovnik,
with its mighty
walls and
inviting beach

Over the last several years,
Croatia has reclaimed its
status as a tourist hotspot. In
the summer, its long coastline
is crawling with a Babel of
international guests. And yet,

despite the tourists, this place remains distinctly and stubbornly Croatian.

FAVORITE SIGHTS AND MEMORABLE EXPERIENCES IN CROATIA

Romantic Rovinj

Idyllic Istria, a wedge-shaped peninsula at Croatia's northwest corner, is an engaging mix of Croatia and Italy. While most of the Croatian coast was Italian-dominated for centuries, Istria remained part of Italy for even longer. Today, bilingual street signs remind visitors that both languages are still official.

My favorite little town on the Istrian coast is Rovinj. Surrounded by the Adriatic on three sides, this town is like a little hunk of Venice draped over a hill. A visit here produces a collage of vivid travel memories: Boats laden with kitschy shells for sale bob giddily in the harbor, while the bell tower's rickety staircase tests climbers' faith. From the top, on a clear day, you can see Venice. And capping the tower, a patron-saint weathervane valiantly faces each menacing cloud front that blows in from the sea. She swivels with the breeze to provide locals with a primitive, but eerily accurate, weather report.

Walking through the market puts me in a good mood. I feel like Marilyn Monroe singing to a bunch of sex-starved GIs. Babushkas push grappa and homemade fruit brandies on me. Istria is one of Europe's top truffle regions, and small, pricey bottles of pungently flavored oils invite me to bring that taste home with me. The merchants' sample walnuts are curiously flavorful. I'll buy a bag on my way out of town.

Strolling the cobbled back lanes, I wander into a time-warp bar that takes "untouristy" to almost scary extremes. The town fishermen and alcoholics (generally, it seems, one and the same) are smoking, bantering loudly, and getting too

LEFT Rovinj, on the tip of the Istrian Peninsula, is my favorite stop between Venice and Dubrovnik.

RIGHT Croatians are clever at turning their rocky shores into romantic cocktail bars.

drunk on cheap homemade beer to notice the nude pinups plastering the walls. Suddenly, all eyes are on me... and I feel like a rabbit at the nocturnal house at the zoo. But they quickly go back to their chattering, laughing, and drinking. My friend explains that they're speaking the local Istrian vernacular—a Croatian-Italian hybrid.

That evening, walking along "restaurant row"—the seafront promenade where interchangeable fish joints desperately vie for diners' attention—I stumble on Valentino Cocktail Bar, where travelers nurse drinks on the rocks...literally. Patricia, the elegantly coiffed and exactingly made-up owner, hands out pillows and invites you to plunk down in your own seaside niche. Fish, attracted by the bar's underwater lights, swim by from all over the bay. The sun sets on a gorgeous Istrian evening, classy candelabras twinkle in the twilight, and couples cozy up to each other and the view. Sipping my white Croatian wine, I keep thinking, simply, "romantic."

> ## Fast Facts
>
> **Biggest cities:** Zagreb (capital, 790,000), Split (178,000), Rijeka (129,000)
>
> **Size:** 22,000 square miles (similar to West Virginia), population 4.5 million
>
> **Locals call it:** Hrvatska
>
> **Currency:** Croatian kunas (kn)
>
> **Key date:** October 8, 1991, Croatia declares its independence from Yugoslavia
>
> **Biggest festivals:** Dubrovnik Summer Festival (July-August, music), Moreška sword dance (twice a week in summer, on the island of Korčula)
>
> **Handy Croatian phrases:** *Dobar dan* (hello; **doh**-bar dahn), *Molim* (please; **moh**-leem), *Hvala* (thank you; **hvah**-lah), *plaža* (beach; **plah**-zhah)
>
> **Tourist info:** US.Croatia.hr

Wandering Dubrovnik's City Walls

Jockeying my way between cruise-excursion groups, I climb the steep steps to the top of the still-stout medieval walls that surround Dubrovnik. As I begin a slow, circular, hour-and-a-half walk around the fortified perimeter of one of Europe's best-preserved medieval towns, I snap photos like crazy of the ever-changing views. On one side is a sea of red rooftops; on the other side, the actual sea.

My B&B host holds a mortar shell—a souvenir of the 1991 shelling of Dubrovnik *(left)*. Houses that were hit are the ones with newer, brighter red tiles *(right)*.

Near the Pile Gate, I pause to enjoy a full frontal view of the Stradun, the 300-yard-long promenade that runs through the heart of Dubrovnik's old town. In the Middle Ages, merchants lined this drag; before that, it was a canal. Today this is the main artery of the city: an Old World shopping mall by day and sprawling cocktail party after dark.

Farther along, I look down and see a peaceful stone terrace perched above the sea, clinging to the outside of the city walls. Generously shaded by white umbrellas, this is my favorite Dubrovnik escape, a rustic outdoor tavern called Buža. The name means "hole in the wall"—and that's exactly what you'll have to climb through to get there. Filled with mellow tourists and bartenders pouring wine into plastic cups from tiny screw-top bottles, Buža comes with castaway views and Frank Sinatra ambience.

Looking inland from my ramparts perch, my eyes fall on a random arrangement of bright- and dark-toned red roof tiles. In this complex and often-troubled corner of Europe, even a tranquil stroll around the walls comes with a poignant history lesson. After Croatia declared independence in 1991, the Yugoslav National Army laid siege to this town and lobbed mortars over the hill. Today, the new, brighter-colored tiles mark houses that were hit and have been rebuilt. At a glance, it's clear that more than two-thirds of the old town's buildings suffered bomb damage.

Surveying the rooftops, my thoughts turn to Pero, my B&B host, who spent years after the war turning the bombed-out remains of his old-town home into a fine guesthouse. Upon my arrival last night, Pero uncorked a bottle of *orahovica* (the local grappa-like firewater). Hoping to write that evening with a clear head, I tried to refuse the drink. But this is a Slavic land. Remembering times when I was force-fed vodka in Russia by new friends, I knew it was hopeless. Pero made this hooch himself, with green walnuts. As he slugged down a shot, he handed me a glass, wheezing, "Walnut grappa—it recovers your energy."

Pero reached under the counter and held up the mangled tail of a

Croatian Beaches

Croatia is known for its glimmering beaches. However, most are pebbly or rocky rather than sandy—and spiny sea urchins are not uncommon. In addition to your swimsuit, pack a pair of water shoes for wading, as well as a beach towel. Good sunscreen, a hat, bug spray, and sturdy shoes (for hiking to some of the more secluded beaches) can also be handy.

Many of Croatia's beaches are nude. If you want to work on an all-around tan, seek out a beach marked *FKK* (from the German *Freikörper Kultur*, or "free body culture"). But don't get too excited—these beaches seem to be most beloved by people you'd rather see with their clothes on.

Croatia's Top Destinations

Dubrovnik ▲▲▲
allow 1-3 days

The "Pearl of the Adriatic," highlighted by walkable medieval walls; great beaches; and Mount Srđ, a Napoleonic fortress with spectacular views

Nearby

Mljet National Park Undeveloped island retreat

Cavtat Art-packed resort village

Pelješac Peninsula Dramatic coastal scenery and Croatia's best vineyards

Ston Small town with giant fortifications

Dalmatian Islands ▲▲
1-2 days

Low-key **Korčula,** with walled old town and fjord-like backdrop, and ritzy **Hvar,** with seductive beaches

Split ▲▲
1 day

Bustling city with extensive Roman palace ruins and busy seaside promenade

Istria ▲▲
2-3 days

Italian-feeling region with Croatia's prettiest town **(Rovinj)**, Roman ruins **(Pula)**, and picturesque wine-and-truffles hill towns **(Motovun)**

Plitvice Lakes National Park ▲▲▲
1 day

Forested canyon filled with crystal-clear lakes, stunning waterfalls, and easy trails

Zagreb ▲▲
1-2 days

Capital city boasting quirky museums, lush parks, and a colorful urban bustle

mortar shell, describing how the gorgeous stone and knotty-wood building he grew up in suffered a direct hit in the siege. He put the mortar in my hands. Just as I don't enjoy holding a gun, I didn't enjoy touching the twisted remains of that mortar. Pero explained that he gets a monthly retirement check for being wounded in the war, but he got bored and didn't want to live on the tiny government stipend—so he went to work rebuilding his guesthouse.

I took Pero's photograph. He held up the mortar and smiled. I didn't want him to hold up the mortar and smile, but that's what he did. He seemed determined to smile—as if it signified a personal victory over the destruction the mortar had wrought.

It's impressive how people can weather tragedy, rebuild, and move on. Despite the terrors of war just a couple of decades ago, life here is once again very good, and, from my perch here atop the city walls, filled with promise.

Magical Motovun

Croatia is more than the sea, and diverse Istria offers some of the country's most compelling reasons to head inland. In the Istrian interior, between humble concrete towns crying out for a paint job, you'll find vintners painstakingly reviving a delicate winemaking tradition, farmers pressing that last drop of oil out of their olives, trained dogs sniffing out truffles in primeval forests, and a smattering of fortified medieval hill towns offering sweeping views over the surrounding terrain. The best of these hill towns is Motovun, featuring a colorful old church and a rampart walk with the best spine-tingling vistas in the Istrian interior.

On my first visit to this region, I drove halfway across Croatia and arrived late at night. Through a driving rainstorm, I wound and wound up through the dark to Motovun's summit. The road got narrower and narrower. When I ran out of road, I parked, got out, and walked to my hotel, with no sense of what the town even looked like. The next

Croatia's Istrian Peninsula is famed for its hill towns like Motovun *(left)* and its a cappella singing groups *(right)*.

morning, I awoke before my alarm rang and pushed open my lumbering shutters. The heavy rainstorm had cleaned the air, and an early-morning light invigorated the colors of the glistening red-tile roofs, the rustic stone rampart, and a lush landscape of rolling hills and simple farms.

The next year, I returned to Motovun with my film crew. During a break, while strolling the town's cobbles and marveling at how dead it was, I heard a men's a cappella group practicing. I snooped around to find out where they were. Around the corner, I went up a short flight of stairs and stared at a closed door separating me from their heavenly singing. I gently pushed the door open just a crack to see the singers. It was a traditional *klapa* group of a dozen men, sitting in a half-circle with their backs to me. Standing before them was the group's director, a woman with springy hair who looked like a mad, young, female Beethoven. She saw me, ran to the door, and invited me in. I pulled out a chair and savored the chorus.

A short time later, I ran to get my film crew. We unanimously agreed it was a magic moment, and we filmed it. The group ended up kicking off our Croatia episode with a wonderful bit of serendipity. Not only did it make for good television, but it was also a reminder to me of an important travel lesson: When out wandering, be bold. Remember, it's worth running the risk of having a door shut in your face—in order to risk being welcomed in.

More Croatian Experiences

Quirky Zagreb: In addition to its cosmopolitan bustle, generous parks, and in-love-with-life café-and-restaurant scene, Croatia's capital is home to some of Europe's most delightfully offbeat museums. The Museum of Naive Art showcases a uniquely Croatian art form: paintings by untrained peasant artists. (In the early 20th century, art-world highbrows embraced this sort of unschooled art as evidence that artistic ability is inborn rather than taught.) The movement's founder, Ivan Generalić, typically painted wintry scenes on glass (in winter, he wasn't busy working the fields, and glass was the cheapest material available).

Just across the street is the equally endearing Museum of Broken Relationships, featuring true stories of failed couples from around the world, told in their own words. Displayed alongside their story is an actual item that embodies the relationship (from angry gnomes to sex toys to discarded wedding albums), in addition to the predictable "he cheated on me so I broke his favorite fill-in-the-blank" items. The collection has struck such a chord, they've taken it on the road, garnering fans in cities worldwide.

Hiking in a Waterfall Wonderland: Plitvice Lakes National Park, two hours south of Zagreb, is one of Europe's most spectacular natural wonders. Imagine Niagara Falls diced and sprinkled over a heavily forested Grand Canyon. There's nothing like this lush valley of 16 terraced lakes, laced together by waterfalls, boat rides, and miles of pleasant plank walks. Countless cascades and water that's both strangely clear and full of vibrant colors make this park a misty natural wonderland. Before I came here, I thought I really knew Europe. Then I discovered Plitvice and realized you can never exhaust Europe's surprises.

Layers of History in Split: Croatia's "second city," Split, has an atmospheric old town core that's built amid the foundations of a fourth-century Roman palace. When the Emperor Diocletian retired, he built a vast residence for his golden years here in his native Dalmatia. After Rome fell and the palace was abandoned, a medieval town sprouted from its shell. The hallways of the palace became streets, the rooms morphed into squares, and to this day, residents are actually living inside the walls of Diocletian's palace. Squeezed

Croatia's charms range from the Museum of Naive Art in Zagreb *(left),* to Plitvice, a dramatic natural wonderland *(center),* to the town of Split, whose nucleus was the fourth-century palace of Roman emperor Diocletian *(right).*

between the old town and the harborfront is a nicely land-scaped pedestrian promenade called the Riva, where the sea of Croatian humanity laps at the walls of the palace. Strolling locals finish their days in good style here—just enjoying life's simple pleasures in a city that so seamlessly weaves its past and present into one.

CULTURE AND TRADITIONS: EVERYTHING'S SO...CROATIAN

Staying with Locals

Private accommodations throughout Croatia (and especially along the coast) offer travelers a characteristic alternative to big, overpriced resort hotels. There are *sobe*—individual rooms for rent—or *apartmani*, which are a bit larger and have a kitchen. The simplest *sobe* allow you to experience Croatia on the cheap, at nearly youth-hostel prices, while giving you a great opportunity to connect with a local family. The fanci-est *sobe* are still affordable and can be downright swanky, with hotelesque amenities (private bathroom, air-condition-ing, satellite TV, and so on) and as much or as little contact with your host family as you like.

Succulent Seafood

While Italian-style pastas and pizzas are common through-out Croatia, it's more memorable to splurge on a seafood dish, especially when vacationing on the coast. Croatians say that a fish should swim three times: first in the sea, then in olive oil (as you cook it), and finally in wine (when you eat it). But be careful when ordering: Most fish dishes are priced by weight rather than by the portion (a one-kilogram portion feeds two hungry people).

Be open and adventurous. Seafood items that may sound unappetizing can be a delicious surprise. For instance, a good, fresh anchovy, done right, has a pleasant flavor and a melt-in-your-mouth texture. The menu item called "small fried fish" is generally a plate of deep-fried minnows. Another specialty is octopus salad, a flavorful mix of octopus, tomatoes, onions, capers, and spices.

Harmonious Croatian Voices

Traditionally found in Dalmatia, *klapa* music features the hauntingly beautiful sound of men's voices harmonizing a cappella, like a barbershop quartet with a soothing Adriatic flavor. Typically the leader begins the song, and the rest of the group follows behind him with a slight delay. Mariachi-style *klapa* groups perform in touristy areas, including what was once the entry vestibule of the Emperor Diocletian's palace in Split. Just listening to a few glorious tunes in this grand space with grand acoustics provides an unforgettable soundtrack for your trip.

Croatia Travel Resources from Rick Steves

Guidebooks
Check out Rick's guidebooks covering Croatia & Slovenia; Dubrovnik; and Eastern Europe

TV Shows
The quintessence of Croatia with Rick as your host, viewable on public television and at RickSteves.com. Episodes cover Split, Plitvice Lakes National Park, Zagreb, Rovinj, Dubrovnik, and the Dalmatian Coast

Organized Tours
Small group tours, with itineraries planned by Rick: Best of Eastern Europe in 14 Days; Best of the Adriatic in 14 Days

For more on all of these resources, visit RickSteves.com. For Croatia trip-planning tips, see www.ricksteves.com/europe/croatia.

Greece

With its classical past and hang-loose present, Greece offers something for every traveler. As the cradle of Western civilization, Greece boasts some of the world's greatest ancient monuments. But it also has plenty more to offer, including succulent seafood, inviting islands, whitewashed houses with bright-blue shutters, and a mellow, Zorba-the-Greek ambience.

Most tourists come here for a quick visit to Athens to bask in the greatness of the Acropolis and then head to an island to bask in the sun. But for a true Back Door experience, consider some of my favorite destinations on the mainland, such as the home of the ancient oracle at Delphi, the birthplace of the Olympics in Olympia, the Gibraltar-style fortress at Monemvasia, the stark Mani Peninsula, or the elegant-but-cozy port town of Nafplio, near two of Greece's greatest ancient sites—Mycenae and Epidavros.

Greece is easy on travelers. The people are welcoming

and accommodating. Greeks pride themselves on a concept called *filotimo*—literally "love of honor," but roughly translated as openness, friendliness, and hospitality. Social faux pas by unwary foreigners are easily overlooked by Greeks.

The country is going through some tough economic times, but the pace of life remains relaxed. People work in the mornings, then take a midafternoon siesta, when they gather with their families to eat the main meal of the day. On warm summer nights, they stay up very late, even kids. Families spill into the streets to greet their neighbors on the evening stroll. For entertainment, they go out to eat, ordering large amounts and sharing it family-style.

It's a joy to surrender to the Greek way of living. All the things you're looking for—deep-blue water, mouth-watering food, striking scenery, and the thrill of connecting with ancient history—are here waiting for you. With its long history and simple lifestyle, Greece has a timeless appeal.

> ## Fast Facts
>
> **Biggest cities:** Athens (capital, 800,000), Thessaloniki (375,000), Piraeus (172,000)
> **Size:** 51,485 square miles (roughly the size of Alabama), population 10.8 million
> **Locals call it:** Hellas
> **Currency:** Euro
> **Key date:** 776 B.C., the first Olympic Games are held
> **Biggest festivals:** Athens & Epidavros Festival (June and July in Athens and Epidavros on the Peloponnese), Carnival Season, a.k.a. Apokreo (weeks prior to Orthodox Lent)
> **Annual per-capita cheese consumption:** 55 pounds (mostly feta, highest in the world)
> **Handy Greek phrases:** *Gia sas* (hello; yah sahs), *Parakalo* (please; pah-rah-kah-**loh**), *Efharisto* (thank you; ehf-hah-ree-**stoh**), *Ne* (yes; neh), *Ohi* (no; **oh**-hee)
> **Tourist info:** VisitGreece.gr

FAVORITE SIGHTS AND MEMORABLE EXPERIENCES IN GREECE

Cockcrow on Hydra

Hydra—less than two hours south of Athens by ferry—offers the ideal Greek island experience, without a long journey across the Aegean.

Hydra has one real town, no real roads, no cars, and not even any bikes. Zippy water taxis whisk you from the quaint little harbor to isolated beaches and tavernas. Donkeys are the main way to transport things here. These surefooted beasts of burden, laden with everything from sandbags and bathtubs to bottled water, climb stepped lanes. Behind each mule-train toils a human pooper-scooper; I imagine picking up after your beast is required. On Hydra, a traffic jam is three donkeys and a fisherman.

On Greece's idyllic isle of Hydra, the only traffic is donkeys.

While the island is generally quiet, dawn here taught me the exact meaning of "cockcrow." On Hydra, the end of night is marked with much more than a distant cock-a-doodle-doo: It's a dissonant chorus of cat fights, burro honks, and what sounds like roll call at an asylum for crazed roosters. After the animal population gets that out of its system, it's like one of the old gods hits "snooze" and the island slumbers a little longer.

Tourists wash ashore with the many private and public boats that come and go, but few venture beyond the harborfront. Today, after my barnyard awakening, I decided to head uphill, and my small detour became a delightful little odyssey. While I had no intention of anything more than a lazy stroll, one inviting lane after another drew me up, up, up to the top of the town. Here, shabby homes enjoyed grand views, tired burros ambled along untethered, and island life trudged on, oblivious to tourism.

Over the crest, I followed a paved riverbed down to the remote harbor hamlet of Kaminia, where 20 tough little fishing boats jostled within a tiny breakwater. Children jumped fearlessly from rock to rock to the end of the jetty, ignoring an old man rhythmically casting his line.

As I trudged into town, a rickety woven-straw chair and a tipsy little table at Kodylenia's Taverna were positioned just right, overlooking the harbor. The heavy, reddening sun commanded, "Sit." I did, sipping ouzo and observing a sea busy with taxi boats, ferries connecting this oasis with Athens, freighters—like castles of rust—lumbering slowly along the horizon, and a silhouetted cruise ship anchored like it hadn't moved in weeks. Ouzo, my anise-flavored drink of choice on this trip, and my plastic baggie of pistachios purchased back in town were the perfect complements to the setting sun. Blue and white fishing boats jived with the chop. I'd swear the cats—small, numerous as the human residents of this island, and oh so feminine—were watching the setting sun with me. An old man flipped his worry beads, backlit by the golden glitter on the harbor. Three men walked by, each reminding me of Spiro Agnew.

As darkness settled, my waiter—who returned here to his family's homeland after spending 20 years in New Jersey, where he "never took a nap"—brought a candle for my table. My second glass of ouzo came with a smudge of someone's big fat Greek lipstick. Wiping it off before sipping seemed to connect me with the scene even more. The soft Greek lounge music tumbling out of the kitchen mixed everything like an audio swizzle stick. I glanced over my shoulder to the coastal lane home. Thankfully, it was lamplit.

Walking home, under a ridge lined with derelict windmills, I tried to envision Hydra before electricity, when spring water flowed and the community was powered by both wind and burros. At the edge of town I passed a bar filled with noisy cruise-ship tourists, and was thankful I'd taken the uphill lane when I left my hotel that morning. Locals, proud of the extravagant yachts moored for the night, like to tell of movie stars who make regular visits. But the island is so quiet that, by midnight, all the high rollers seem to be back on board watching movies. Sitting on a ferry cleat the size of a stool, I scanned the harbor—big flat-screen TVs flickered from every other yacht.

Back in Hydra town, I observed the pleasant evening routine of strolling and socializing. Dice clattered on dozens of backgammon boards, entrepreneurial cats seemed busy, children chased soccer balls, and a tethered goat chewed on something inedible in its low-profile corner. From the other end of town came the happy music of a christening party. Dancing women filled the building, while their children mimicked them in the street. Farther down, two elderly, black-clad women sat like tired dogs on the curb.

Succumbing to the lure of a pastry shop, I sat down for some honey-soaked baklava. I told the baker I was American. "Oh," he said, shaking his head with sadness and pity, "you work too hard."

I answered, "Right. But not today."

Communing with Athens' Ancients

For decades, I recommended that travelers to Athens—long infamous for its sprawl, noise, and pollution—see the big sights, then get out. But visiting it recently, I saw a dramatic change. New driving laws, along with a marvelous subway system, have made the city less congested. While it used

Greece's Top Destinations

Athens ▲▲▲   allow 2-3 days
Greece's sprawling, congested capital, featuring first-class
ancient ruins, atmospheric old Plaka quarter, and thriving
ramshackle nightlife

Top Sights
   Acropolis Hilltop capped by architectural jewel, the Parthenon
   Acropolis Museum Glassy modern temple for ancient art
   Ancient Agora Marketplace and meeting point of ancient Athens
   National Archaeological Museum World's best collection of ancient Greek sculpture

Nafplio ▲▲▲   1-2 days
Tidy midsized town with a cozy port, elegant old town, hilltop fortress, and easy
day trips to two amazing ancient sites

Nearby
   Mycenae Ancient fortress city with iconic Lion Gate and beehive tomb
   Epidavros Best-preserved theater of the ancient world, with astonishing acoustics

Hydra ▲▲▲   1-2 days
Idyllic car-free island with picturesque harbor, casual beaches, and enticing
coastal hikes

Santorini ▲▲   1-2 days
Black-sand beaches and postcard-perfect towns clinging to the rim of a caldera
(flooded volcano crater)

Mykonos ▲▲   1-2 days
Quintessential Greek isle with whitewashed village and pulsating nightlife

---

to turn my hanky black in a day, the air now seems much
cleaner. And the city is much more people-friendly, with
welcoming pedestrian boulevards and squares filled with
benches, shade-giving trees, and inviting cafés rather than
parked cars. But the big draw still remains its ancient sites.
Nowhere else in the world will you feel like you've journeyed
back in time to the birthplace of Western civilization itself.

Crowned by the mighty Parthenon, the Acropolis rises
ethereally above the sprawl of modern Athens. I consider
the Parthenon the finest temple from the ancient world:
Simple, balanced, and orderly, it sums up the Greek Golden
Age. Unlike most ancient sites, the Acropolis we see today
was started and finished within two generations—a snapshot
of the Golden Age set in stone. I visit late in the day, as the
sun goes down, when the white Parthenon stone gleams a

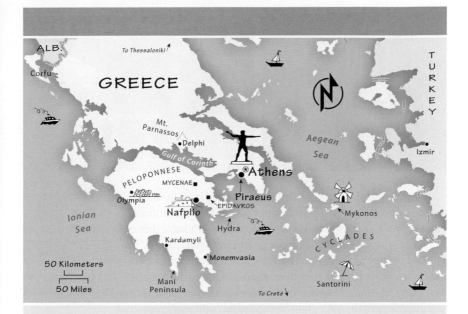

Kardamyli and the Mani Peninsula ▲   1-2 days
Unspoiled beach town of Kardamyli and jumping-off point for the Mani
Peninsula's dramatic hill towns and jagged coastlines

With more time, consider visiting
Olympia Stunning temple and stadium ruins at birthplace of the ancient games
Monemvasia Gibraltar-like rock peninsula with million-dollar views
Delphi Where ancients came to consult the oracle

creamy golden brown, and what had been a tourist war zone
is suddenly peaceful.

While the Acropolis was the city's ceremonial showpiece,
the ancient Agora, at its foot, was the real heart of classical
Athens. For some 800 years, this marketplace was the hub of
all commercial, political, and social life, as well as home to
many of the city's religious rites.

Little remains of the Agora, other than one very well-preserved temple and a rebuilt portico. But wandering this field
of humble ruins with an Athenian guide reminds me of the
value of connecting with great local guides. Fay ("like Faye
Dunaway," she explained) was a wealth of insights mixed
with attitude: "We Greeks smoke, hate breakfast, and just
can't get along with each other. But give us a common enemy
and we become tight as a fist."

Still stately after all these centuries, the Parthenon tops Athens' majestic Acropolis. And at the base of the hill is the state-of-the-art Acropolis Museum.

She also explained that Greeks designed on a human scale—appropriate for their democracy. When the Romans came, they added gigantism. As Romans didn't have democracy, their leaders had a taste for grandeur—putting an "un-Greek" veneer of power on the Agora with pompous staircases, fancy pavement, and oversized temples and statues. You can tell Roman statues from Greek ones because Roman ones are larger than life, not freestanding (always propped on something), with "too much robe" and interchangeable heads. Masters of both imperial ego and efficiency, they reused stone bodies, economically replacing just the head with each new emperor. That's why lots of Roman statues are headless, with scooped-out necks.

From the Agora, it's on to Athens' best modern attraction, the Acropolis Museum. Housed in a striking, glassy building that gives a postmodern jolt to the otherwise staid, concrete cityscape, the museum houses various artifacts from the Acropolis. It's well worth a visit, although for me, the main attraction will always be the Parthenon itself.

At the end of the day, a ritual for me is to wander the old town under the floodlit Parthenon, munching a souvlaki rolled in greasy pita bread and pretending that Athens is the same small, charming village at the foot of the Acropolis that it was many centuries ago.

Greece Goes Wild

The Mani Peninsula—the southern tip of mainland Greece—feels like the end of the road. It's stark and sparse. If Greece had an O.K. Corral, this is where it would be. And the town of Kardamyli would be the saloon where everyone goes for a drink.

Today the Mani is a peaceful region of rustic villages and untrampled beaches. Only goats thrive here. While mountains edged with abandoned terraces hint that farming was once more extensive, olives have been the sole major Mani export for the last two centuries. Many Mani towns feature sumptuous, old, fresco-slathered churches—pockets of brightness in this otherwise parched land.

Sealed off from the rest of the country by a ridge of mountains, the peninsula has—over the centuries—harbored refugees, fleeing whatever crises were gripping the rest of Greece. People would hide out in the mountains, far from the coast and marauding pirate ships. And when they weren't fighting foreign invaders, they would fight each other.

Clambering up ridges are empty, ghostly villages fortified with towers. The most characteristic is Vathia. Built on a rocky spur, Vathia was an extreme example of what can happen when neighbors don't get along. In this vendetta-ville, 80-some houses were split north/south into two rival camps, which existed in a state of near-permanent hostility.

After spending a day driving around the Mani, exploring its rugged landscape and contentious history, I enjoy unwinding in Kardamyli, a humble beach town with a "Bali in a dust storm" charm. This handy base for exploring the Mani Peninsula works like a stun gun on my momentum. On my last trip, I felt as if I could have stayed for days, just eating well and hanging out. It's the kind of place where travelers plan their day around the sunset.

Having dinner at my favorite beach taverna under a leafy canopy brings back memories of my first meal here 20-some years ago: I had settled my chair into the sand under a bare and dangling lamp, and felt a faint but refreshing

Travel Through Greece's Economic Woes

Don't expect your visit to museums and ancient sites to go like clockwork. Virtually all of the big sights are run by the troubled Greek government, so opening and closing times can change on short notice. It's smart to arrive well in advance of listed closing times and to hit your must-see attractions in the morning, especially if traveling outside of summer. While museum websites may claim they list the latest hours, you'll get more reliable, up-to-date information by asking your hotelier or checking with a tourist information office. Watch out for the switch between high-season and low-season schedules.

While Greece's economic troubles are real for its workers (and I wouldn't want to be a local counting on my retirement), it's no big deal for travelers. If you're a tourist looking for a place in Athens' countless trendy eateries and watering holes, you'll be impressed not by an economic slowdown but what feels like boom time. Don't let news of turbulent demonstrations scare you away. Sure, there are some angry marches that come with the imposition of austerity programs. They're designed to make it on the evening news. And there may be a few closures and strikes. But this is the reality: Traveling in Greece is safe, your vacation dollar is needed, you'll enjoy a particularly warm welcome, and you'll likely return home with a better sense of how sensational media coverage can wrongly shape our perceptions.

Greece's rugged Mani Peninsula is dotted with ghost towns, souvenirs of a tough environment and a hard-fought past.

spritzing. Looking around for the source of the mist, I saw a tough Greek teenager in a swimsuit the size of a rat's hammock tenderizing a poor octopus to death by whipping it like a wet rag, over and over, on a big flat rock. The octopus would be featured that night on someone's dinner plate—but not mine.

These days, light bulbs still swing in the breeze—but, no longer naked, they're dressed in gourd lampshades. I sit under an eave enjoying the view. I love gazing into the misty Mediterranean, knowing the next land is Africa. The inky waves churn as the red sun sets.

More Greek Experiences

The Allure of Nafplio: My vote for the most charming town in Greece is Nafplio, on the Peloponnesian Peninsula. Nestled under cliffs at the apex of a vast bay, Nafplio has a unique pride. Its role as the first capital of independent Greece once made it a prestigious port town. And although its glory days have faded, the town retains a certain genteel panache, with palm-tree waterfronts, and narrow and atmospheric back streets that are lined with stately Venetian houses and inviting shops. Owing to its prestigious past, Nafplio's harbor is guarded by three castles (all wonderfully floodlit at night): one on a small island, another just above the old town, and a third capping a tall cliff above the city. With its harborfront setting and pleasant present-day vibe, Nafplio doesn't even need tourists—and doesn't disappoint them.

Nafplio also serves as a handy home base for touring the historic ruins of Mycenae and Epidavros. Mycenae, as ancient to Golden Age Greeks as Socrates and Plato are to us, has an archaeological mystique to it. And Epidavros entices visitors to actually try out the famed acoustics of the best-preserved theater in the ancient world.

Olympic Original: For more than a thousand years, the Olympic Games were held in their birthplace—Olympia, a sacred village in the Peloponnese. Besides the stadium, Olympia's Temple of Zeus was one of the great tourist destinations of the ancient world, boasting a then-world-famous 40-foot statue of Zeus by the great sculptor Pheidias. Today, Olympia is one of the best opportunities for a hands-on antiquity experience. Despite the crowds that pour through here, Olympia is a magical place, with ruins nestled among lush, shady groves of pine trees. Its once-majestic temple columns—toppled like a tower of checkers by an earthquake— are as evocative (with the help of the excellent museum) as anything from ancient times. And you just have to play "On your mark, get set...go!" on that original starting block from the first Olympic Games. As you line up, crank up your imagination, light a torch, and refill the stadium with 40,000 fans. Olympia can still knock you on your discus.

Magnificent Monemvasia: This gigantic rock juts up improbably from the blue-green deep, just a few hundred yards offshore from the Peloponnese peninsula. Often referred to as the "Gibraltar of Greece," it is a fascinating showcase of Byzantine, Turkish, and Venetian history dating back to the 13th century. Its remarkably romantic walled Lower Town hides on the sheltered side of the burly rock, tethered to the mainland by only a skinny spit of land (Monemvasia means "single entry"). A steep, zigzag path leads up to the even bigger Upper Town, whose fortress, in its day, was considered the mightiest in Byzantine Greece. Today its scant ruins sprawl evocatively across the broad summit. Climbing Monemvasia takes only about half an hour, but on top, spend as long as you want, getting lost in the Middle Ages.

CULTURE AND TRADITIONS: EVERYTHING'S SO...GREEK

Greek Cuisine

The food in Greece is simple...and simply delicious. The Greeks have an easy formula, and they stick with it. The four Greek food groups are olives (and olive oil), salty feta cheese, ripe tomatoes, and crispy phyllo dough. Virtually every dish you'll have here is built on a foundation of these tasty building blocks.

My favorite way to eat in Greece is to order a main dish and a medley of *mezedes* (appetizers) to share with my companions. The selection, while predictable and routine after 10 dinners, never gets old for me: *tzatziki* dip, garlic dip, fava bean dip, or a mix of all three on a single serving platter; fried eggplant or zucchini; Greek salad; and big grilled peppers—red or green—stuffed with feta cheese. Usually there's also something from the sea, such as grilled calamari, sardines, or a plate of fried small fish (three inch), very small fish (two inch), or very, very small fish (one inch). With three-inch fish, leave the head and tail on the plate (and try not to wonder about the once inky, now dry black guts). With the smaller fish, you'll leave nothing but a line of greasy fingerprints on the fringe of your paper tablecloth.

My go-to fast-food meal in Greece is souvlaki—meat grilled on a skewer and served on a plate or wrapped in pita bread to make a sandwich. When you get it "to go," the meat (often pork or lamb) is tucked into a wonderful greasy pita pocket with lettuce, tomato, onions, and *tzatziki*. It's often bulked up with doughy French fries and wrapped in wax paper that you peel back as you eat. As international fast-food places move in, the traditional souvlaki stand is harder to find...but more worthwhile than ever to seek out and enjoy.

Religion

The Greek Orthodox Church remains a strong part of everyday life here. Ninety-five percent of all Greeks consider themselves Orthodox, even if they rarely go to church. Their faith was a rallying point during centuries of foreign occupation, and today the Greek constitution recognizes Orthodox Christianity as the prevailing religion of Greece. Greek lives are marked by the age-old rituals of baptism, marriage, and funeral.

Orthodox elements appear everywhere. Icon shrines dot the highways. Orthodox priests—with their Old Testament beards, black robes, necklaces, cake-shaped hats, and families in tow—mingle with parishioners on street corners. During the course of the day, Greeks routinely pop into churches to light a candle, asking for favors. Greek lotharios in track suits reverently bend at the waist to kiss an icon, which is already slathered with lipstick from a steady stream of devout visitors. Even local teens who seem far from religious make the sign of the cross when passing a church.

Orthodox Easter, which is often later than the Catholic/Protestant Easter, is celebrated with gusto and tradition. For instance, on Good Friday in Kardamyli, a processional passes through town and the priest blesses each house. At midnight on Holy Saturday, townspeople turn off their lights and come to the main square. The priest emerges from the church with a candle and spreads light through the candle-carrying crowd, who then take the light home with them. Gradually the entire town is illuminated...and the fireworks begin.

Drinking in Greece

Greece is a rough land with simple wines. A local vintner told me there's no such thing as a $50 bottle of fine Greek wine. I asked him, "What if I want to spend $30?" He said, "You can buy three $10 bottles." With dinner, I like to order *retsina* wine, a post-WWII rotgut with a notorious resin flavor that's long been famous as the working man's Greek wine. It makes you want to sling a patch over one eye and say, "Arghh." The first glass is like drinking wood. The third glass is dangerous: It starts to taste good. If you drink any more, you'll smell like it the entire next day.

With a new generation of winemakers (many of them trained abroad), Greece is receiving more recognition for its wines. More than 300 native varietals are now grown in Greece's wine regions. But like many locals, I often skip the wine and go for a cold beer, or the cloudy, anise-flavored ouzo, supposedly invented by monks on Mount Athos.

Greek Dance

In Greece, dancing is a part of everyday life. If you go to a special occasion such as a wedding or baptism, you can see all ages dancing together. With arms outstretched or thrown across one another's shoulders, Greeks form a circle to perform their traditional dances. (In the old days, mixed couples were linked by handkerchiefs instead.) Often they dance to folk songs accompanied by a *bouzouki*, a long-necked mandolin. These days the music is usually amplified, fleshed out with a synthesizer, and tinged with pop influences.

Some of the dances you might see are the graceful *kalamatianos* circle dance, the *syrtaki* (famously immortalized by Anthony Quinn in *Zorba the Greek*), and the dramatic solo *zimbetikos*. A few dancers might get carried away, "applaud" by throwing plates or flowers, and then dance on the tables into the wee hours. Wherever you are in Greece, ask locals where you might enjoy some live music and dancing with dinner or after. It can be a smashing time.

Greece Travel Resources from Rick Steves

Guidebooks
Choose from Rick's regional and city guides on Greece and Athens

Audio
Download Rick's free Audio Europe app, with self-guided audio tours, including a walk through Athens and tours of the Acropolis, Ancient Agora, and National Archaeological Museum

TV Shows
The quintessence of Greece with Rick as your host, viewable on public television and at RickSteves.com. Episodes cover Athens, the Peloponnese Peninsula, and the islands of Hydra, Santorini, Samos, and Lipsi

Organized Tours
Small group tours, with itineraries planned by Rick: Athens and the Heart of Greece in 14 Days

For more on all these resources, visit RickSteves.com. For Greece trip-planning tips, see www.ricksteves.com/europe/greece.

Index

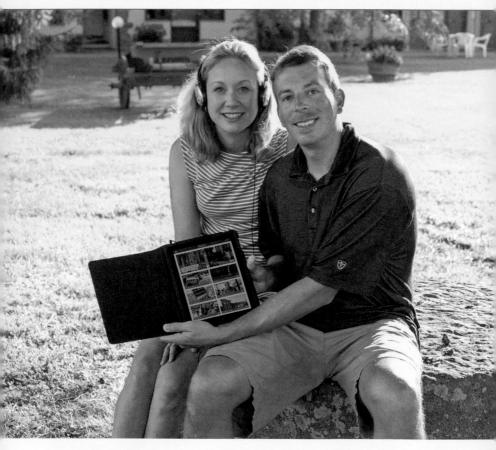

Explore Europe

At ricksteves.com you can browse through thousands of articles, videos, photos and radio interviews, plus find a wealth of money-saving travel tips for planning your dream trip. And with our mobile-friendly website, you can easily access all this great travel information anywhere you go.

TV Shows

Preview the places you'll visit by watching entire half-hour episodes of Rick Steves' Europe (choose from all 100 shows) on-demand, for free.

ricksteves.com

your travel dreams into affordable reality

Radio Interviews

Enjoy ready access to Rick's vast library of radio interviews

covering travel tips and cultural insights that relate specifically to your Europe travel plans.

Travel Forums

Learn, ask, share! Our online community of savvy travelers is a great resource for first-time travelers to Europe, as well as seasoned pros. You'll find forums on each country, plus travel tips and restaurant/hotel reviews. You can even ask one of our well-traveled staff to chime in with an opinion.

Travel News

Subscribe to our free Travel News e-newsletter, and get monthly updates from Rick on what's happening in Europe.

Audio Europe™

Pack Light and Right

Gear up for your next adventure at ricksteves.com

Light Luggage

Pack light and right with Rick Steves' affordable, custom-designed rolling carry-on bags, backpacks, day packs and shoulder bags.

Accessories

From packing cubes to moneybelts and beyond, Rick has personally selected the travel goodies that will help your trip go smoother.

Shop at ricksteves.com

Rick Steves has

Experience maximum Europe

Save time and energy

This guidebook is your independent-travel toolkit. But for all it delivers, it's still up to you to devote the time and energy it takes to manage the preparation and logistics that are essential for a happy trip. If that's a hassle, there's a solution.

Rick Steves Tours

A Rick Steves tour takes you to Europe's most interesting places with great guides and

great tours, too!

with minimum stress

small groups of 28 or less. We follow Rick's favorite itineraries, ride in comfy buses, stay in family-run hotels, and bring you intimately close to the Europe you've traveled so far to see. Most importantly, we take away the logistical headaches so you can focus on the fun.

Join the fun

This year we'll take thousands of free-spirited travelers— nearly half of them repeat customers—along with us on four dozen different itineraries, from Ireland to Italy to Athens. Is a Rick Steves tour the right fit for your travel dreams? Find out at ricksteves.com, where you can also request Rick's latest tour catalog. Europe is best experienced with happy travel partners. We hope you can join us.

See our itineraries at rlcksteves.com

A Guide for Every Trip

BEST OF GUIDES

Full color easy-to-scan format, focusing on Europe's most popular destinations and sights.

Best of France
Best of Germany
Best of England
Best of Europe
Best of Ireland
Best of Italy
Best of Spain

COMPREHENSIVE GUIDES

City, country, and regional guides with detailed coverage for a multi-week trip exploring the most iconic sights and venturing off-the-beaten-track.

Amsterdam & the Netherlands
Barcelona
Belgium: Bruges, Brussels,
  Antwerp & Ghent
Berlin
Budapest
Croatia & Slovenia
Eastern Europe
England
Florence & Tuscany
France
Germany
Great Britain
Greece: Athens & the Peloponnese
Iceland
Ireland
Istanbul
Italy
London
Paris
Portugal
Prague & the Czech Republic
Provence & the French Riviera
Rome
Scandinavia
Scotland
Spain
Switzerland
Venice
Vienna, Salzburg & Tirol

THE BEST OF ROME

Rome, Italy's capital, is studded with
Roman remnants and floodlit-fountain
squares. From the Vatican to the Colosseum, with crazy traffic in between, Rome
is wonderful, huge, and exhausting. The
crowds, the heat, and the weighty history

of the Eternal City where Caesars walked
can make tourists wilt. Recharge by taking siestas, gelato breaks, and after-dark
walks, strolling from one atmospheric
square to another in the refreshing evening air.

Rick Steves guidebooks are published by Avalon Travel,
an imprint of Perseus Books, a Hachette Book Group company.

POCKET GUIDES

Compact, full color city guides with the essentials for shorter trips.

Amsterdam
Athens
Barcelona
Florence
Italy's Cinque Terre
London
Munich & Salzburg
Paris
Prague
Rome
Venice
Vienna

SNAPSHOT GUIDES

Focused single-destination coverage.

Basque Country: Spain & France
Copenhagen & the Best of Denmark
Dublin
Dubrovnik
Edinburgh
Hill Towns of Central Italy
Krakow, Warsaw & Gdansk
Lisbon
Loire Valley
Madrid & Toledo
Milan & the Italian Lakes District
Naples & the Amalfi Coast
Northern Ireland
Normandy
Norway
Reykjavik
Sevilla, Granada & Southern Spain
St. Petersburg, Helsinki & Tallinn
Stockholm

CRUISE PORTS GUIDES

Reference for cruise ports of call.

Mediterranean Cruise Ports
Northern European Cruise Ports

Complete your library with...

TRAVEL SKILLS & CULTURE

Study up on travel skills before visiting "Europe through the back door" or gain insight on European history and culture.

Europe 101
European Christmas
European Easter
European Festivals
Europe Through the Back Door
Postcards from Europe
Travel as a Political Act

PHRASE BOOKS & DICTIONARIES

French
French, Italian & German
German
Italian
Portuguese
Spanish

PLANNING MAPS

Britain, Ireland & London
Europe
France & Paris
Germany, Austria & Switzerland
Ireland
Italy
Spain & Portugal

Rick Steves books are available from your favorite bookseller.
Many guides are available as ebooks.

HOW WAS YOUR TRIP?

If you enjoyed a successful trip with the help of this book and would like to share your discoveries, please fill out the survey at www.ricksteves.com/feedback. Thanks in advance for your feedback. We're all in the same traveler's school of hard knocks...and it's OK to compare notes. Your feedback helps us improve this book for future travelers!

For our latest travel tips, tap into our information-packed website: RickSteves.com. To check out fellow readers' hotel and restaurant reviews—or leave one yourself—visit my travel forum at www.ricksteves.com/travel-forum. For updates to this book, check www.ricksteves.com/update.

Rick Steves' Europe is more than Rick Steves. All 100 of us are pooling our travel experience and working hard to help you enjoy the trip of a lifetime!

ACKNOWLEDGMENTS

Grazie to the following for sharing their knowledge: Cameron Hewitt and Risa Laib (travel savvy, vision, and original writing for this book); Dave Hoerlein (artful maps, public-transit tips); Wide World Books & Maps (guidebooks, www.wideworldtravelstore.com); Tim Tattan (radio); Joan Robinson and Margaret Cassady (women's packing tips); Todd and Carla Hoover (cruising); Elizabeth Holmes (travel agents, overseas flights); Laura Terrenzio (train travel); Gretchen Strauch (train travel and accommodations); Alfred Celentano at Europe by Car and our colleagues at Auto Europe/Kemwel (car rental and leasing); Chris Rae (driving and navigating); Cory Mead (technology); Ruth Arista (wine transport); Alan Spira, M.D., and Craig Karpilow, M.D. (health for travelers); Lisa Friend (travel apps, family travel, and health); Amy Lysen (Couchsurfing); Marcy Lay (home swaps and cultural exchange); France Freeman (home exchange); Kevin Williams (technology for travelers); Rick Garman (accommodations); Tara Swenson (health advice); Arlan Blodgett, Stewart Hopkins, Chris Luczyk, and Sabine Schrader (photography); Heidi Van Sewell and Michelle Kono (tours); Yumiko Sato (bus tours and cruises); John Sage, Susan Sygall, Carole Zoom, and Carmen Papalia (travelers with disabilities); Jennifer Hauseman (gay travelers); Audrey Edwards and Leiane Cooke (travelers of color); Andy Steves (study abroad); and Aaron Harting (green travel).

Dank u wel for the travel expertise, editing, and many contributions to this book from the Book Department at Rick Steves' Europe. *Merci* for support from my entire well-traveled staff at Rick Steves' Europe, including Gene Openshaw, Steve Smith, Rich Sorensen, and Craig Davidson. *Muchas gracias* to Simon Griffith for directing and producing our *Rick Steves' Europe* television series with such passion and artistry.

Finally, *tusen takk* to my parents for dragging me to Europe when I didn't want to go.

Photo Credits

Avalon Travel
An imprint of Perseus Books
A Hachette Book Group company
1700 Fourth Street
Berkeley, CA 94710

For a complete list of Rick Steves guidebooks, see page 36.

Printed in China by RRD Shenzen.
First printing September 2017.

For the latest on Rick's lectures, guidebooks, tours, public television series,
and public radio show, contact Rick Steves' Europe, 130 Fourth Avenue North,
Edmonds, WA 98020, tel. 425/771-8303, fax 425/771-0833, www.ricksteves.
com, rick@ricksteves.com.

ISBN 978-1-63121-625-1
37th Edition

Rick Steves' Europe
Managing Editor: Jennifer Madison Davis
Special Publications Manager: Risa Laib
Assistant Managing Editor: Cathy Lu
Editors and Researchers: Glenn Eriksen, Tom Griffin, Katherine Gustafson,
Suzanne Kotz, Carrie Shepherd
Editorial & Production Assistant: Jessica Shaw
Editorial Interns: Leslie Fisher, Meesha Sundarum
Graphic Content Manager: Sandra Hundacker
Maps & Graphics: David C. Hoerlein, Lauren Mills, Mary Rostad

Avalon Travel
Senior Editor and Series Manager: Madhu Prasher
Editor: Jamie Andrade
Associate Editor: Sierra Machado
Editorial Intern: Rachael Sablik
Copy Editor: Kelly Lydick
Proofreader: Patrick Collins
Indexer: Stephen Callahan
Interior Design: McGuire Barber Design
Typesetting: Tabitha Lahr
Maps & Graphics: Kat Bennett
Cover Design: Kimberly Glyder Design